# Going Global

UNU World Institute for Development Economics Research (UNU/WIDER) was established by the United Nations University as its first research and training center and started work in Helsinki, Finland, in 1985. The purpose of the Institute is to undertake applied research and policy analysis on structural changes affecting the developing and transitional economies, to provide a forum for the advocacy of policies leading to robust, equitable, and environmentally sustainable growth, and to promote capacity strengthening and training in the field of economic and social policy making. Its work is carried out by staff researchers and visiting scholars in Helsinki and through networks of collaborating scholars and institutions around the world.

# Going Global

Transition from Plan to
Market in the World
Economy

edited by Padma Desai

The MIT Press
Cambridge, Massachusetts
London, England

This book was set in Palatino on the Monotype "Prism Plus" PostScript Imagesetter by Asco Trade Typesetting Ltd., Hong Kong.

Printed and bound in the United States of America.

Library of Congress Cataloging-in-Publication Data

Going global : transition from plan to market in the world economy /
    edited by Padma Desai.
        p.   cm.
    "Papers were discussed at a conference in Helsinki in the early
    summer of 1995"—Pref.
    Includes bibliographical references and index.
    ISBN 0-262-04161-8 (alk. paper)
    1. International economic integration. 2. Central planning.
3. Privatization. 4. Commercial policy. 5. Investments, Foreign.
I. Desai, Padma.
HF1418.5.G64   1997
337.1—dc21                                                    97-14607
                                                                  CIP

For
Manmohan Singh,
friend and reformer

*yogah karmasu kauśalam*

# Contents

# Contributors

Manmohan Agarwal
Department of Economics
Jawaharlal Nehru University

András Blahó
Department of Economic and
Social Information and Policy
Analysis
United Nations

Josef C. Brada
Department of Economics
Arizona State University

Michael Connolly
Department of Economics
University of Miami

Padma Desai
Department of Economics
Columbia University

David Dollar
Policy Research Department
World Bank

Richard S. Eckaus
Department of Economics
Massachusetts Institute of
Technology

Heiner Flassbeck
Deutsches Institut für
Wirtschaftsforschung

Péter Gál
Department of World Economy
Budapest University of Economics

Jürgen von Hagen
Zentrum für Europäische
Integrationsforschung
University of Bonn and
School of Business
Indiana University

Lutz Hoffmann
Deutsches Institut für
Wirtschaftsforschung

Urpo Kivikari
Turku School of Economics and
Business Administration

Kalev Kukk
Member of Estonian Parliament
Member of Board of the Bank of
Estonia

Ali M. Kutan
Department of Economics
Southern Illinois University
Edwardsville

Ludger Lindlar
Faculty of Economics
University of Groningen

Börje Ljunggren
Ambassador of Sweden to Vietnam

Stanislaw Wellisz
Department of Economics
Columbia University

# Foreword

During the early 1990s, UNU/WIDER had three important research projects dealing with the former socialist countries, focusing on the *internal* problems of the transition process. Subsequently, UNU/WIDER shifted attention to the *external* aspects, dealing with the interactions of these countries with the rest of the world. The present volume is the result of a major project entitled The Integration of the New Market Economies of Europe and Asia into the World Economy: The Changing Internal and External Factors and Global Implications. The project was designed to make up for the insufficient attention given in the earlier efforts to the impact of the external factors on the transition process. The concept of integration used in the project implied the reentry of the former socialist countries and the entry of China and Vietnam into global markets via various means of cooperation under new political, institutional, and economic conditions.

The participation of a country in the global system has various dimensions. Among them is the historical development of the economy, which influences the country's place in the global division of labor. There are also geographical, economic, political, institutional, and cultural dimensions in the reintegration process. These are interrelated, and shaped by various internal and external factors including location, size, natural endowments, human resources, development level, economic structure, political and institutional patterns, and competitiveness. The external factors include the global or regional regulatory framework influencing the relations of participants in exchange, the international trading regime, patterns of competition in the principal foreign markets, the role and interests of transnational corporations in integrating a country into their global production and marketing systems, and the degree and type of the fusion or linkage of markets for goods, capital, services, and labor. These factors are not constant. The changes reflect, on the one hand, the constantly fluctuating market system, and on the other, the shifting positions of countries as price-takers or price-makers in the global markets. The impact of the external political and economic environment on a country may be positive or negative. The global markets are also in the process of major structural and spatial changes.

The project will lead to two volumes. The present volume focuses on the international implications of domestic changes in the former socialist countries. Issues such as exchange rate management and policies concerning foreign trade and capital flows, insofar as they affect integration into the world economy, are analyzed at length. The papers in the forthcoming second volume will complement the analysis here.

The countries were selected on the basis of the specific features of their integration into the global markets. The chapters cover the Czech Republic, Hungary, the former German Democratic Republic, Poland; Estonia, Latvia, Lithuania, Russia, Kazakhstan, and Uzbekistan; and China and Vietnam. Finland and India were also included because of their special relations with the ex-socialist countries requiring adjustments. The republics of former Yugoslavia were omitted due to the unsettled political problems in the region and the absence of dominating trends there.

Diverse issues relating to the global implications of the institutional and policy changes in Central and East Europe, the post-Soviet states, China, Vietnam, and India are analyzed in the volume. The Director of UNU/WIDER, Giovanni Andrea Cornia, joins me in thanking Padma Desai of Columbia University, who coordinated the first part of the project, and her colleagues, who contributed the country chapters. We consider the volume an important addition to an understanding of the complex problems of the transition process and of the interaction between domestic and external factors in shaping it.

Mihály Simai,
Research Professor,
Institute for World Economics,
Hungarian Academy of Sciences,
and
Former Director, UNU/WIDER

# Preface

The research project underlying this volume of essays was financed by the United Nations University/World Institute for Development Economics Research (UNU/WIDER), Helsinki. The project design was developed at a Helsinki conference in the late spring of 1994, and the papers were discussed at a conference in the early summer of 1995.

Many friends and colleagues have helped me steer a vastly ambitious project to its successful completion. I would like to thank Mihály Simai, former director of UNU/WIDER, for asking me to direct it; Lorraine Taivainen of UNU/WIDER, for lightening my task in organizing the conferences in Helsinki; Manmohan Agarwal, Shailendra Anjaria, Josef Brada, Michael Connolly, David Dollar, K. C. Fung, Michael Gavin, Brigitte Granville, Vijay Joshi, Deena Khatkhate, Jean-Maurice Léger, Carol Leonard, Ian Little, Costas Michalopoulos, Prabhakar Narvekar, Mario Nuti, Richard Portes, Nicholas Stern, and Alan Winters for helpful suggestions regarding data sources, frequent conversations, and insightful comments; Eugene Beaulieu for excellent research assistance; and Karen Halliburton and Gordon Wong for helping me edit successive drafts of the volume.

The book is dedicated to Manmohan Singh, former Finance Minister of India, a bold reformer and skillful policy maker, who initiated India's transition to an open market economy in the summer of 1991.

# Introduction

Padma Desai

These essays analyze the continuing integration of several transition economies of Europe, the former Soviet Union (FSU), and Asia into the world trading and financial system. The authors of the essays on the countries studied in this volume discuss the market-oriented adjustment policies of each with regard to the trade and exchange rate regimes. They also assess the economy's progress in diversifying its trade structure and orienting it toward hard currency markets and in attracting foreign direct investment (FDI). Their analyses span the period 1990–95.

The authors consider the issues of macroeconomic stabilization and price liberalization insofar as they influence the management of foreign trade and foreign exchange arrangements. Similarly, privatization is introduced into the discussion to the extent that it helps cut back budgetary support of state-owned enterprises (thereby easing the fiscal stress), stimulates foreign trade (by dismantling state trading organizations, for example), and attracts FDI in privatized companies.

Suitable norms need to be adopted, however, for assessing the comparative performances of these transition economies in the initial years of their opening up into the world economy. I develop them in this chapter and thus am able to compare and rank the integration record of these countries and to address the critical issue of the transition debate, that is, whether speedier reform in these economies has facilitated their faster entry into the world economy.[1]

The answer to this question raises analytical issues concerning the assessment of reform speed and the choice of the outcome indicators that might be associated with it. For example, should GDP growth rate be adopted as the sole index of a successful reform strategy? Should a rising unemployment rate, which raises formidable challenges for policy makers en route to economic stabilization, be included in the assessment? Since the objective is to assess the globalization of these transitional economies, what indices on the external front should we look for in order to make such an assessment? And how does the presence or absence of successful general reform relate to the success or failure of globalization?

In seeking answers to these and related questions, I rely on the authors' in-depth analyses of the transition strategies adopted by policy makers in the selected countries. The detailed record (which I enlarge and update through mid-1996 in the Appendix) helps me discuss and develop meaningful criteria for assessing the successes and failures of the transition process; for ranking the countries according to these criteria; and, finally, for emphasizing the analytical issues that arise when reform speed is correlated with these rankings.

Given the small sample, my conclusions are tentative but nevertheless interesting. Reform speed, as defined below, appears to be significantly correlated with the GDP growth rate, with the emergence of a liberalized foreign exchange and foreign trade regime by the end of the period studied, and with positive globalization outcomes such as increased FDI flows (measured as their contribution to gross fixed investment at the end of the period examined). It also correlates well with declining inflation rate over the period, though somewhat poorly with the decline of inflation from its peak to the next year in the "shock therapy" mode.

Speedy reform thus seems desirable, for its general economic results as for globalization. However, this conclusion must be tempered by the fact that speedy reform seems to be associated negatively with the unemployment rate, so that we may well be facing a short-run trade-off between growth and globalization, on the one hand, and unemployment, on the other. In practice, these short-run trade-offs could mean that speedy reform may not be politically sustainable: The electorate may not be willing to put up with the short-term increase in unemployment even though, in the long run, the faster growth would create more jobs. The reformers may then have to choose, for political viability, slower reform strategies. They may well decide that a slower output recovery or expansion in the short run might yield a higher growth rate later by keeping the transition on track, whereas a rapid turnaround, which results in unsustainable unemployment (or income disparities or real wage decline), might be politically destabilizing.[2]

## The Criteria of Country Selection

A few words on the selection of the countries studied in this volume are in order. A qualifying country had to be centrally planned in the past and undergoing a market transition in the present. Thus, the volume includes the Czech Republic, Hungary, the former German Democratic Republic (East Germany hereafter), and Poland in Central and East Europe; Estonia, Latvia, and Lithuania in Northern Europe; Russia, Kazakhstan, and Uzbekistan among the post-Soviet states; and China and Vietnam in Asia. In contrast with the usual focus on the European transition economies or the post-Soviet states or both, it adopts a more variegated sample by including the Asian reforming economies.[3]

Finland, the host country of the research project leading to this volume, was included simply because it constitutes the flip side of the transition economics of socialist countries. While the latter countries have been moving away from socialism, in varying ways and with various results that are examined in this volume, that very transition has had a severe impact on some countries, especially Finland, a market economy, because of the sudden termination of significant socialist-style trade arrangements with the former Soviet Union. Finland has had to cope with this fallout from the dissolution of the Soviet Union in December 1991, an adjustment examined carefully in Chapter 6. Obviously, however, Finland does not qualify for inclusion in the extensive cross-national transition experiences examined in the present chapter and is therefore excluded from that analysis below.[4]

On the other hand, India, though formally not a centrally planned economy (CPE), does qualify. The Indian economy has long been marked by public ownership of much industry and a Kafkaesque network of regulatory controls on private decisions relating to investment, production, and trade. Also, the Indian rupee was not convertible on current or capital account. The economy had, in effect, many of the regime features that the socialist transition economies have wanted to shed. And, like these economies, India began serious reforms in the early 1990s.

A principal objective of reforms in these economies has been to move into the world trading and financial system. In order to accomplish this goal, their policy makers have needed to control inflation under a regime of market prices and private ownership of assets, liberalize their foreign trade arrangements, unify and stabilize their exchange rates, manage them so as to maintain trade competitiveness, and offer attractive incentives to foreign investors.

The country authors analyze in depth the interaction between these objectives aimed at globalization, and the policies adopted to achieve them in the context of the general reform effort and the specific constraints and advantages obtaining in their respective countries. These country policies are summarized in some detail, for ready reference, in tabular form in the Appendix.

Analysis requires, however, that I proceed first with a functional classification of the chosen countries into groups based on the nature and speed of their reforms, so that this in turn can be related to the globalization outcomes, among other things.

### Defining "High-," "Medium-," and "Low-Speed" Reformers

The countries fall into three groups: the high-, medium-, and low-speed reformers. Speed reflects several dimensions. An early start is one element. Rate of (effective) implementation of initiated reforms is another. Comprehensiveness of the reforms is yet another. The last element is perhaps the most important in practice: A reform package usually includes several components, among them price decontrol, fiscal and monetary tightening to slash inflation, the unification and convertibility (on current account) of the currency, trade liberalization, and the undertaking of privatization.

Given the different dimensions that can be combined in several ways, I have chosen to classify countries into three groups below by using qualifying characteristics that draw on the country experiences (that have been analyzed in the volume) and thus make the comparative analysis more meaningful.

First, it therefore makes sense to characterize as high-speed reformers those countries that opt for a comprehensive policy package, introduce it early, and maintain it in place. However, it is sometimes difficult to decide whether a country belongs to the high-speed category if the different elements of the reform package are pursued at strikingly different speeds. For example, Vietnam has moved swiftly and effectively on price decontrol, currency unification, and stabilization but has seriously lagged behind on trade liberalization and privatization. Should it be included in the high-speed category? I believe so, in view of the seriousness of the problems where it did implement swift and decisive reforms. This amounts, then, to exercising one's best judgment on the reform process observed, which is inevitable when many dimensions are involved.[5]

Second, the medium-speed reformers, commonly known as gradualists, often start policy reform packages on time but are typically slow to implement key elements. I need to emphasize here that the debates in the literature on Russian reform between "shock therapists" such as Jeffrey Sachs and "gradualists" such as myself have been about the speed of reform on one critical dimension: the speed at which stabilization should be undertaken. In early 1992, when Prime Minister Yegor Gaidar announced, and tried to implement shock therapy in the form of a drastic and immediate reduction of the Russian budget deficit from an estimated high, 17 to 21 percent of GDP in 1991, to zero by the first quarter of 1992, he failed because the Supreme Soviet (the parliament) rejected such a drastic program, exactly as gradualists feared.[6] The view of the shock therapists—that gradualism in attacking high inflation would not work at all and would spell continuing inflationary chaos—has been belied not just by academic analysis such as mine in Desai (1994a, 1994b, 1994c, 1995a, 1995b) but also by the undeniable fact that gradual and firm application of macroeconomic discipline, with the aid of International Monetary Fund (IMF) monitoring, indeed reduced inflation significantly during the Yeltsin–Chernomyrdin–Chubais government of 1994–96.[7]

Thus, given the political constraints faced by a transition economy, it may well be prudent to go easy on certain critical components of a policy package, even though this places the country in the "medium-speed," gradualist category. The Russian case, with the quick reversal of shock therapy upon stabilization, makes an appropriate illustration. But this slowing of speed on stabilization, while other feasible elements such as privatization, exchange rate unification, and price decontrol were being pushed ahead, is then to be regarded as sensible and "efficient."

These approving words, however, do not apply to the "gradualism" that simply reflects intellectual confusion or bureaucratic inertia or ideological obscurantism, clearly identifiable as such in the early episodes of the "market socialism" reforms in the transition economies. In these cases, there were limited nods toward the market mechanism without a true grasp of the market principles. Thus, the limited reforms in Russia under Mikhail Gorbachev suffered from the incoherence that attempts at converting communism to some form of "market socialism," more user-friendly to the old ways of central planning, inevitably implied.[8]

The third category of "low-speed" reformers could have been countries that embraced "market socialism." However, this approach had been generally discredited, and rightly so, fairly early on, and the countries making the transition have generally abandoned the illusion that such an approach makes any sense. Thus, the category of "low-speed" reformers here applies to those countries that have generally delayed starting on their reforms still later in the the period 1990–95 and also happen to be moving slowly on most fronts.

The countries in this volume are assigned immediately below to these three groups, with the reasons for the category choice set forth briefly.

## Assigning Countries to the Three Groups

Poland obviously belongs to the high-speed reformers. Its transition package of January 1990 had the ideal program: The budget deficit was to be reduced sharply, with a view to slashing inflation; almost all prices were freed; the zloty was unified, devalued, and fixed against the dollar; trade restrictions were abolished; and tariffs were either removed or drastically lowered. The Czech Republic, the Baltic states, and Vietnam adopted similar transition packages. Speed also was the essence of East Germany's transition from a socialist to an open market economy: The full economic, monetary, and social union of East Germany with West Germany on July 1, 1990, implied that a slow transformation during which East Germany might have rebuilt itself economically (while retaining its political autonomy and its monetary and fiscal system) was ruled out. The East German case was unique, however, because speed involved reunification rather than macroeconomic stabilization per se.

By contrast, post-1990 Hungary and post-Mao China in the medium-speed group adopted a slow agenda. The Hungarian policy makers failed to get a decisive grip on macroeconomic stabilization and on the devaluationary expectations of insiders and outsiders with regard to the Hungarian forint until mid-1995. China's reforms under Deng Xiaoping were deliberately slow. Foreign trade was tightly controlled, import restrictions were in place, dual prices and multiple exchange rates prevailed, and inflation control was shaky.

India also belongs to this group of medium-speed reformers. In July 1991, it was hard put to break away from the legacy of a misdirected, import-substituting, and overregulated economy that had existed for almost four decades. The planners had assigned a dominating role to the state in industry and infrastructure, imposed licensing requirements on private investment, controlled the foreign trade and foreign exchange systems, and practically banned foreign investment. As a result, the growth rate was far below the economy's potential, and a bloated government administration, unviable public sector enterprises, and recurring subsidy schemes to benefit the poor had bred financial indiscipline.

The Indian reforms proceeded on all fronts in July 1991 but in a gradualist mode. Cutting of the budget deficit, although on track, was slow-paced: The domestic debt-servicing burden constrained the reforming government's ability to lower the budget deficit, which remained at an annual average high of 6.2 percent of GDP from April 1, 1992, to March 31, 1996. Again, prices of important items (such as fertilizers and energy) continued to be administered. Consumer goods imports were gradually being freed from licensing requirements despite the introduction of current account convertibility. Tariff rates, though reduced, remained unduly high by 1996. Privatization was barely begun. Labor market flexibility in hiring and firing was still a goal toward which no effective start had been made. But there was no doubt that the reforms were in place and would continue to expand in old and new areas over time.

The post-Soviet states belong to the group of low-speed reformers. Kazakhstan and Uzbekistan, both members of the ruble zone until the end of 1993, faced four-digit inflation at the start of the 1990s because macroeconomic stabilization policies were delayed under Gorbachev (1985–91) in Russia, which dominated the zone. Stabilization floundered in 1992 under acting Prime Minister Gaidar, in the end forcing Russian policy makers to employ a sustained regimen of fiscal discipline (which remained somewhat off target) and monetary control (which was increasingly on track).

Severe stabilization measures eventually became necessary in Kazakhstan and Uzbekistan, which began their transition in 1994 by adopting their own currencies. Kazakhstan's inflation control under IMF monitoring was in the end one of the sharpest among the transition economies. Its late start, with little done to reform the economy before 1994, qualifies it as a member of the low-speed category. Among the sample countries, the pace of trade liberalization was the slowest in Uzbekistan, which was also a late starter with respect to inflation control.

Finally, it is not enough for the analysis I undertake below to assign countries to these three groups. I need to rank order them within the groups, a task that raises some judgment calls, for instance, when I have to address two countries with similar transition agendas. For example, does Poland rank ahead of the Czech Republic within the high-speed group?

Recall that I assess reform speed according to the announcement and pursuit of the comprehensive, ideal reform package as well as the timing thereof such that earlier is better. Of the six high-speed candidates, four—Poland, Estonia, Latvia, and Lithuania—starting with triple- or quadruple-digit inflation rates, adopted rigorous programs of orthodox stabilization consisting of the five key components I have outlined. The Baltic lands also broke away from the ruble zone, introduced their currencies, and, like Poland, unified their exchange rates and liberalized their trade regimes, led by Estonia and followed by Latvia and Lithuania, in that order, in the rigor and timing of the necessary measures. The highly comprehensive Czech reform program was, however, less demanding, being called upon to tame a much lower inflation rate of 56 percent in 1990. I therefore rank it after Poland, Estonia, Latvia, and Lithuania. Finally, if timing and speedy inflation control were the only criteria, Vietnam could have been at the top. It was, however, placed in the last position in the group because its policy package, announced in 1989, lacked full dimensionality by failing to pursue trade liberalization and privatization with any determination or success.[9]

The medium-speed countries—Hungary, India, and China—which avoided the swift, simultaneous reform strategy, are rank-ordered on the basis of the market orientation of their transition in 1991. The Indian reform package of the summer of 1991, consisting of a unified and (current account) convertible currency, removal of restrictions on private investment, abolition of quantitative trade restrictions (except licenses for consumer goods imports), and reduced import tariffs was more liberal than comparable 1991 measures in China. Hungary's reform momentum in 1991 was ahead of the pace in both the Asian economies.

Finally, Russia, Kazakhstan, and Uzbekistan belong indisputably to the group of low-speed reformers, with Russia at the top and Uzbekistan at the bottom: Russia has moved more quickly than the other two, and more decisively on privatization, for instance; Uzbekistan has lagged seriously in starting reforms and has mainly opted for stabilization rather than a wider range of reforms.

Having allocated the countries to the three categories, and ranked them as well, I now proceed with the substantive analysis. In particular, I do the following:

• Note several commonalities of experience that cut across nearly all countries and the three groups

• Examine the differing levels of global integration achieved by the various countries at the end of the period by developing four different indicators[10]

• Rank-order countries by their speed of reform (just accomplished above) and by their performance on these indicators of global integration (to be done below), and examine whether greater speed leads to greater globalization

• Undertake similar correlations between rank ordering in terms of speed and in terms of indices of unemployment, inflation, and growth rates, to determine whether greater speed is associated with better within-period economic performance, thereby promising better future performance

• Reach broad judgments on the general question of the relationship between transition strategies and globalization

## Common Features of the Transition by the End of 1995

As 1995 closed, nearly all economies were marked by a few common achievements and failures in regard to the management of inflation, freeing of prices, reform of the exchange rate and trade regimes, growth performance, and unemployment rates. I review these before turning in the next sections to an analysis of the significant differences.

### Prices and Inflation Control

Almost all prices (except those of household utilities) had been freed everywhere except in the Asian and the three post–Soviet economies. The exceptions in the latter group related mostly to prices of important raw materials: of energy in India, Russia, and Kazakhstan; of fertilizers in India; and of cotton and grain in Uzbekistan, which continued to diverge from world prices toward the end of 1995.

In China and India, inflation had always been modest, though India had begun its reforms under a cloud in this regard and would bring inflation firmly back under control, to under 5 percent annually, by fiscal 1995/96 (from April 1 to March 31). Everywhere else, extreme inflation and even hyperinflation had been the inherited state. And everywhere, it was in turn brought down from these extreme levels. Nonetheless, high inflation persisted in 1995, with double-digit inflation rates afflicting the European and Asian economies while triple-digit ranges persisted in the post-Soviet states (in contrast to the earlier four-digit levels).

Real interest rates were positive in all the economies, and the policy makers had moved away from direct methods of credit control. However, except in the Czech Republic, they struggled with high fiscal deficits (as a proportion of GDP). Budgetary expenditures ran ahead of government revenues.[11]

The inflow of foreign funds in varying amounts, especially of short-term capital, aggravated inflationary pressures in most economies. The gradual emergence of relatively high real interest rates attracted capital inflows, occasionally requiring authorities to switch to a new mode of foreign exchange management (as in the Czech Republic) or undertake capital control measures (as in India toward the end of 1995 and stretching into early 1996).[12] At the same time, some (the Baltic states, in particular) encountered difficulties in neutralizing the extra money supply (generated by the inflow of foreign funds) because their financial institutions could not undertake effective sterilization.

### Exchange Rate Management

All exchange rates had been unified and made convertible for current account transactions. However, the requirement that export earnings be surrendered at the prevailing market rate, fully or partly, sooner or later, to a state agency or a commercial bank had continued except in the Czech Republic, the Baltic states, and Kazakhstan, in which it was abolished in 1995. Policy makers in the remaining countries had announced plans to remove the surrender requirement and advance toward complete current account convertibility in 1996 or later.

The nominal exchange rates had declined everywhere, whereas the real exchange rates had been appreciating for most of the period under consideration.[13] (Monthly rates of real exchange rate movements are stated in Table I.1.) The only exceptions were Uzbekistan (where the sum had depreciated in terms of the ruble) and Vietnam (where the dong had decreased slightly in terms of the dollar). This reflected the fact that the inflation rate differential at home and abroad had kept ahead of the rate of depreciation in the nominal exchange rate.

The monthly rate of currency appreciation moved closely with the country inflation rate. In other words, low inflation economies generally experienced lower rates of real exchange appreciation (Table 1). The appreciating real exchange rate, however, had negative implications for the competitiveness of exports and import substitutes, in turn creating problems for those involved in trade policy management.

### Foreign Trade

At the end of 1995, tariff barriers were still high everywhere, having been reduced and then raised again or not reduced significantly to begin with. Thus, except in the Czech Republic and Estonia, tariffs were being raised in the European countries. The Asian economies had high tariffs with only a lowering of the initial extreme rates (with continuing quantitative restrictions in China and bureaucratic impediments in Vietnam despite the current account convertibility). The post–Soviet states maintained high import tariffs (in Russia), some export quotas and taxes (despite progress in removing them in Russia and Kazakhstan), and state orders of tradables at distorted prices (in Uzbekistan).

Almost all countries had formed "spaghetti bowls" of crisscrossing bilateral trade agreements as they sought regional trading advantages.

### Growth Rates

The growth rates of GDP had improved in all countries, having turned around from negative rates, or plateaued at negative levels, or increased from high or low positive levels.

Thus, growth rates had bounced back to positive values after sharp drops in the European economies and had bottomed out, still in the negative range, in the post-Soviet subset. China and Vietnam, both high growth performers, did not experience a recession, but the Indian growth rate had dipped to 0.9 percent in fiscal 1991/92.

### Unemployment Rates

Unemployment rates had risen everywhere in the European countries except the Czech Republic. Policy makers in the Asian economies (which traditionally have high disguised unemployment in their massive rural sectors) were strongly pressed to continue financial support of state-owned industry in order to maintain employment of the organized "labor aristocracy" in the urban sector.

### Reformers at Risk

Halfway through the transition period in some of the European economies (Poland, Hungary, and the Baltic states) and by mid-1996 in the others (the Czech Republic and Russia, despite Yeltsin's reelection as president), reformers were either out or in a minority in coalition governments or legislatures. As a result, progress in market reform had to be balanced with concern for societal welfare. The "window of opportunity" for reform had narrowed, and the days of "extraordinary politics" had receded into the past.

Similar pressures for moderating the social costs of the transition were of concern to the authoritarian leaderships of post-Soviet Kazakhstan and Uzbekistan, and also of Communist China and Vietnam, which opened the reform "window of opportunity" selectively.[14] The Indian reformers were

**Table I.1**
Foreign exchange regime, internal and external performance indicators in transition economies: 1990–96

| | | Start of reform | Inflation rate (%) | Real GDP growth rate (%) | Unemployment rate (%) | Current account balance (% of GDP) | Debt servicing ratio | Monthly real exchange rate appreciation (average %) | Exchange rate regime | Currency convertibility | Foreign exchange regime ranking in 1995 |
|---|---|---|---|---|---|---|---|---|---|---|---|
| Czech Republic | 1991 | January 1991 | 56.1 | −14.2 | 2.8 | 4.5 | 7.3 | 1.9 (December 1990–March 1994) | Pegged to DM (0.65) and U.S.$ (0.35) | Full current account. Almost full capital account | 1 |
| | 1992 | | 11.1 | −6.6 | 3.1 | 0.3 | 11.4 | | | | |
| | 1993 | | 20.8 | −0.3 | 3 | 1.9 | 9.1 | | | | |
| | 1994 | | 10 | 2.6 | 3.2 | 0.3 | — | | | | |
| | 1995 | | 9.1 | 5.2 | 2.9 | −4.2 | — | | | | |
| | 1996 | | 8 | 5.5 | — | — | — | | | | |
| Hungary | 1991 | Mid-1990 | 34.2 | −11.9 | 7.5 | 0.9 | 35 | 2.7 (July 1990–December 1994) | Preannounced crawling peg | Surrender requirement. No capital account | 9 |
| | 1992 | | 22.9 | −4.3 | 12.3 | 0.9 | 38.6 | | | | |
| | 1993 | | 22.5 | −2.3 | 12.1 | −9.6 | 47.4 | | | | |
| | 1994 | | 18.9 | 2 | 12.1 | −9.5 | 60.8 | | | | |
| | 1995 | | 28.2 | 2 | 10.4 | −5.3 | 45 | | | | |
| | 1996 | | 24 | 2 | — | — | — | | | | |
| Poland | 1990 | January 1990 | 585.8 | −11.6 | 6.1 | 1.1 | 5.2 | 4.7 (January 1990–September 1993) | Preannounced crawling peg | Surrender requirement. No capital account | 7 |
| | 1991 | | 70.3 | −7.6 | 11.8 | −2.8 | 6.6 | | | | |
| | 1992 | | 43 | 1.5 | 13.6 | −0.3 | 9.3 | | | | |
| | 1993 | | 35.3 | 4 | 15.7 | −2.7 | 10.6 | | | | |
| | 1994 | | 33.3 | 5 | 16 | — | — | | | | |
| | 1995 | | 27.8 | 7 | — | — | — | | | | |
| | 1996 | | 20 | 5.5 | — | — | — | | | | |

| Country | Year | | | | | | | | | | |
|---|---|---|---|---|---|---|---|---|---|---|---|
| Estonia | 1990 | Early 1990 | 23.1 | −8.1 | — | — | — | 10.1 (June 1992–November 1994) | Pegged to DM. Currency board | Full convertibility | 2 |
| | 1991 | | 210 | −8 | — | — | — | | | | |
| | 1992 | | 1069 | −22 | 4.8 | 9.2 | 3.2 | | | | |
| | 1993 | | 89 | −7 | 8.9 | 0.7 | 1.7 | | | | |
| | 1994 | | 48 | 6 | 8.1 | −6.4 | 0.5 | | | | |
| | 1995 | | 25 | 6 | — | — | — | | | | |
| | 1996 | | — | — | — | — | — | | | | |
| Latvia | 1991 | 1992 | 124.4 | −8.3 | — | — | — | 5.6 (January 1993–June 1995) | De facto currency board up to April 1995. Currently pegged to SDR | Full convertibility | 3 |
| | 1992 | | 951.2 | −35 | — | 1.8 | — | | | | |
| | 1993 | | 109.1 | −15 | 4.9 | 6.8 | 2 | | | | |
| | 1994 | | 35.7 | 2 | 6.4 | −2.5 | 5 | | | | |
| | 1995 | | 25 | 1 | 6.4 (1st half) | — | — | | | | |
| | 1996 | | — | | | — | | | | | |
| Lithuania | 1991 | February 1991 | 224.7 | −13.4 | 0.3 | — | — | 9.6 (January 1993–March 1995) | Pegged to $. Currency board | Full convertibility | 4 |
| | 1992 | | 1020.5 | −37.7 | 1 | 11 | 0.2 | | | | |
| | 1993 | | 410.4 | −24.2 | 2.5 | −5.7 | 0.6 | | | | |
| | 1994 | | 72.1 | 1.7 | 4.2 | −3.7 | 0.9 | | | | |
| | 1995 | | 35 | 3 | 6.6 | — | — | | | | |
| | 1996 | | — | 3 | — | — | — | | | | |
| Russia | 1991 | January 1992 | 92.7 | −13 | — | — | — | 7.9 (July 1992–December 1994) | Managed float until mid-95. Adjustable band thereafter | Surrender requirement. No capital account | 11 |
| | 1992 | | 1353 | −19 | 4.8 (Oct) | — | 27.2 | | | | |
| | 1993 | | 896 | −12 | 5.5 | −0.5 / 2.1 | 29.7 | | | | |
| | 1994 | | 302 | −15 | 7.1 | −0.9 / 0.5 | 27.4 | | | | |
| | 1995 | | 190 | −4 | 7.4 (Jan) | −0.4 / 0.6 | 24.4 | | | | |
| | 1996 | | — | 3 | — | — / — | — | | | | |

**Table I.1** (continued)

| | | Start of reform | Inflation rate (%) | Real GDP growth rate (%) | Unemployment rate (%) | Current account balance (% of GDP) | Debt servicing ratio | Monthly real exchange rate appreciation (average %) | Exchange rate regime | Currency convertibility | Foreign exchange regime ranking in 1995 |
|---|---|---|---|---|---|---|---|---|---|---|---|
| Kazakhstan | 1991 | November 1993 | 90.9 | -13 | — | -1.9 \| -1.7 | — | 22.4 (May 1994–September 1994) | Managed float | Surrender requirement abolished in 1995. No capital account | 10 |
| | 1992 | | 1381 | -14 | 0.5 | -2.8　0.3 | — | | | | |
| | 1993 | | 1662 | -12 | 9.3 | 2.2　-15.2 | 0.4 | | | | |
| | 1994 | | 1880 | -25 | 11 | -4.1　-2.8 | 2.9 | | | | |
| | 1995 | | 180 | -12 | — | — | 6.6 | | | | |
| | 1996 | | — | — | — | — | — | | | | |
| Uzbekistan | 1991 | Early 1994 | 82.2 | -0.9 | 4.5% in 1994 plus 37% workforce underemployment in agriculture | -2 \| 22.5 | — | 40 (depreciation) January 1992–February 1994 | Managed float | Surrender requirement. No capital account | 12 |
| | 1992 | | 644.9 | -11.1 | | -3.1　-8.7 | — | | | | |
| | 1993 | | 534.2 | -2.3 | | 4.1　-10.3 | — | | | | |
| | 1994 | | 785.1 | -3.5 | | -2.4　-8.9 | 10.5 | | | | |
| | 1995 | | 325 | -4 | | — | 18.3 | | | | |
| | 1996 | | — | — | | — | — | | | | |
| China | 1991 | Agrarian: 1978; Price: 1985; Trade & foreign exchange: major reform in 1991 | 5.1 | 8 | 27% of rural workforce estimated to be in surplus. 2.9% of urban workforce officially unemployed | 4.3 | 11.8 | 2 (depreciation) May 1993–March 1994; 3.3 (appreciation) March 1994–August 1994 | Managed float | Surrender requirement. No capital account | 5 |
| | 1992 | | 8.6 | 13.2 | | 1.3 | 10.2 | | | | |
| | 1993 | | 17 | 13.8 | | -2.9 | 10.7 | | | | |
| | 1994 | | 21 | 11.9 | | — | 9 | | | | |
| | 1995 | | 14.8 | 10.2 | | 2.2 | 9.7 | | | | |
| | 1996 | | 10 | 8.9 | | 0.8 | 9.9 | | | | |
| Vietnam | 1991 | 1989 | 72.5 | 6.3 | Substantial disguised unemployment in the rural workforce, which is estimated at 73% of total | -1.9 | 19.9 | 0.5 (Depreciation) January 1991–August 1995) | Managed float | Surrender requirement. No capital account | 6 |
| | 1992 | | 32.6 | 8.6 | | -0.7 | 22.1 | | | | |
| | 1993 | | 14.4 | 8.1 | | -8.3 | 26.5 | | | | |
| | 1994 | | 14.5 | 8.8 | | -7.6 | 20.2 | | | | |
| | 1995 | | 19.8 | 9.5 | | -8 | 8.4 | | | | |
| | 1996 | | — | — | | — | — | | | | |

| | | | | | | | | | |
|---|---|---|---|---|---|---|---|---|---|
| Apr 1 '91/Mar 31 '92 | Mid-1991 | 13.5 | 0.9 | Substantial disguised unemployment in the rural workforce, which is estimated at 70% of total | 31.6 | −0.7 | Alternating low levels of appreciation followed by depreciation | Managed float | Surrender requirement. No capital account | 8 |
| India | 1992/93 | 9.6 | 4.3 | | 30.4 | −1.6 | | | | |
| | 1993/94 | 7.5 | 4.3 | | 25.4 | −0.3 | | | | |
| | 1994/95 | 10.3 | 5.3 | | 27.3 | −0.4 | | | | |
| | 1995/96 | 4.5–4.7 | 5.5–6 | | 24.7 | −0.9 | | | | |
| | 1996/97 | — | — | | | | | | | |

*Sources:* The table is put together from information in IMF sources and EBRD, *Transition Report 1995* (1995) and *Transition Report Update 1996* (1996) figures are forecasts.

*Notes:* Inflation rate is based on consumer price index or retail price index. The percentages are average annual changes.

Unemployment rate (unofficial and therefore higher than official estimates) refers to unemployed workers as percentage of workforce. There are serious conceptual issues of defining unemployment and practical problems in tracking down the necessary information for the sample countries.

Unemployment is a structural phenomenon in the three Asian economies, which have not faced the labor layoff associated with macroeconomic stabilization measures during the period. Nor have their policy makers risked releasing urban workers from state-owned factories by pursuing active privatization policies.

Details on exchange rate regime and currency convertibility for each economy are in the Appendix. "Surrender requirement" requires that exporters surrender their export earnings, in part or fully, to a government agency or to commercial banks, increasingly to the latter.

"Current account balance" includes trade balance and balances of nonfactor services (such as transport and tourism), of factor services (such as interest receipts and payment), and of transfers (such as technical assistance). For Russia, Kazakhstan, and Uzbekistan, the percentages of current account balance/GDP in the first column refer to the balance with non-FSU trading partners and in the second column with FSU trading partners. Consolidated balances are available in IMF reports.

Export earnings in the (denominator of the) debt service ratio include merchandise export and nonfactor service earnings.

Real exchange rate movements are calculated from information in IMF sources. Details of monthly real exchange rate movements of the Indian rupee are as follows: Appreciation of 1% during July 1991–September 1992; depreciation of 2.6% during September 1992–January 1993; appreciation of 3.1% during January 1993–April 1993; depreciation of 1% during April 1993–May 1994; appreciation of 0.6% during May 1994–April 1995.

The information in each category depends on the source from which it is taken and, therefore, differs from country data reported by authors in their chapters. Inflation rates in the table, which are average annual changes, differ from end-year changes reported in some country chapters.

turned out in 1996; however, the reasons are complex and the new Indian government cannot be interpreted as being "antireform."

An analysis of the interaction between the politics and the economics of the transition is beyond the scope of this essay. However, the rebound of the positive, and the bottoming out of the negative, real GDP growth rates during the attempted transition must be weighed against the unemployment record (as I do later)[15] for an objective assessment of the performance of the real economy, as well as for distinguishing between desirable and feasible reform speeds (a distinction the *World Development Report 1996* overlooks).

These common features notwithstanding, the sample countries have undoubtedly integrated into the world economy at varying speeds, this integration or globalization being the central concern of the present volume. I now turn to selecting the indicators of globalization before anything more can be said about the factors contributing to it in the transition economies' actual experience.

**Going Global: The Indicators**

A fully open economy can be defined as having a convertible currency (on current and capital accounts) and a trade regime without tariffs and nontariff barriers. At the other end of the spectrum, an economy may have an exchange rate that is neither unified nor convertible on the current and the capital accounts. The tariff barriers may also be high, though quantitative restrictions (QRs) effectively constrain imports. Export taxes and restrictions also may obtain. For nonmarket economies, state trading organizations may constitute effective trade-restrictive devices.

The economies under consideration here fall somewhere in between. The question is: How does one assess their relative openness or global integration? Short of building computable general equilibrium (CGE) models within which the counterfactual of free trade may be compared with the reality, a procedure that is itself subject to massive errors and conceptual fudges in implementation, we have to go by satisficing but not altogether satisfactory proxies. I propose here to adopt five indicators.

First, I pick three indicators that reflect the implementation of appropriate policies. They are fairly obvious and plausible: convertibility of the currency, liberalization of the foreign trade arrangements, and the creation of a positive climate for attracting foreign direct investment (FDI). A country with a fully convertible currency, which in turn requires decisive inflation control, gets the top billing.[16] Next, a country with a liberal trade

regime marked by low import tariffs and minimal export taxes or subsidies also acquires a top policy ranking. Finally, a positive environment
to attract FDI that is characterized by suitable tax incentives, adequate
financial and physical infrastructure, and continuing restructuring of industry puts a country ahead in the ranking. I rank all countries according
to their policy regimes in these three areas in 1995.

The next two indicators relate to performance reflecting, ceteris paribus,
these policy frameworks. Thus, greater integration may be defined in
terms of an economy's greater trade participation—more precisely, in
terms of the familiar ratio of exports plus imports to GDP. Given the fact
that the transition economies' trade had been severely restrained and also
diverted to countries within the socialist bloc, increased integration into
the world economy may also be usefully indicated by trade diversification, measured by exports to OECD countries divided by total exports, or
additionally by increment in the ratio of their exports of manufactures
(now increasing in volume) to their total exports to OECD markets. In
fact, I rank the countries according to their OECD market penetration via
manufactured goods exports during 1991–95. The second indicator that I
use is based on FDI inflows. It ranks the countries according to their FDI
inflows as a proportion of gross fixed investment in the latest available
year.[17]

## Going Global: Ranking by Policy Outcomes

### *Ranking by Exchange Rate Regime in 1995*

I begin with an analysis of the transition economies' effectiveness in
making their currencies convertible. A unified exchange rate and fully
convertible currency are necessary for facilitating efficient trade flows and
promoting foreign investment (although, as I shall argue later, FDI can
flow in as long as profits and the principal are allowed to be repatriated
freely). How do the countries rank in that regard?

The information on currency convertibility and the rankings of the exchange rate regime are presented in Table I.1. (Recall that East Germany
and Finland are omitted from the entire comparative analysis in this Introduction. It may be noted, however, that the East German currency was
converted one-for-one with the fully convertible deutsche mark in a single
step. As for Finland, as soon as the bilateral trade arrangements with the
FSU were terminated in 1991, the Finnish markka started functioning as
a convertible currency in trading activity with the East, as it had done

with the West.) Four clarifications about the methodology underlying the country rankings by their foreign exchange regimes in Table I.1 are necessary before I discuss the countries in some depth.

First, effective inflation control in line with the inflation rate of trading partners and of rival suppliers translates into a stable and fully convertible currency. This fosters foreign trade competitiveness and, barring exogenous shocks (such as the sudden loss of COMECON markets by the East-Central European transition economies), is an invaluable aid in creating and sustaining a healthy current account balance. Therefore, the ranking by the indicator of exchange rate convertibility is not independent of the ranking of the country by the efficacy of its macroeconomic policies. Since my view is that by and large, the five policy reforms that I have distinguished above tend to reinforce each another's efficacy in promoting efficient transition, this also holds true for such other policies as privatization, which can help external accounts by attracting FDI flows.[18]

Second, I should stress that the ranking is independent of whether the nominal exchange rate is fixed or whether an economy has alternative arrangements (such as a preannounced crawling peg or a managed float) that allow its policy makers flexibility in the conduct of monetary policy.[19] In fact, only the Baltic economies currently operate under a fixed exchange rate regime supported, if necessary, by central bank intervention. The Czech koruna is fixed within a band (which was widened in February 1996). Thus, a variety of exchange rate regimes is compatible with the presence of convertibility.

Third, we need also to take into account the possible fragility of the exchange rate management before assigning ranks to countries based on their relative success. Thus, for example, aggressive macroeconomic management to control inflation may encourage policy makers to adopt a fully convertible currency. However, the resulting higher unemployment (as I discuss in a later section) or real wage decline may in turn generate political pressures forcing them to reverse the decision down the transition road.

Therefore, an economy with a fully convertible currency may be grouped in the same class as another with a fully convertible currency; it is, however, ranked lower if its unemployment rate is higher even though its real GDP growth rate is similar or slightly higher.

Fourth, the ranking, which I ultimately report in the final column of Table I.1, is influenced by pointers to fragility of the exchange rate regime that are suggested by "external" indicators such as the current account balance and debt servicing ratio (both listed in Table I.1). The Mexican peso debacle, precipitated by a combination of circumstances including a deteriorated current account balance and a huge short-term debt overhang, provides a solid example in support of such a procedure (which I state below).

Effective foreign exchange management and the progress to currency convertibility in these reforming economies have been hampered by widely differing exogenous factors, such as the legacy of high foreign debt and by the collapse of the COMECON export market, which was not compensated for by exports to Western Europe because of recession.[20] Again, as growth and imports have picked up, the trade balance has been put under varying stress. Export growth, ceteris paribus, has had to be unusually robust to make up for lost markets, to cover foreign debt obligations, and to finance growing import needs. The final ranking of countries by the 1995 exchange rate regime in the last column of Table I.1 is thus adjusted informally by these "fragility concerns" where relevant.

Thus, the central point in the context of comparing the cross-national currency covertibility performance is that although inflation has been brought down everywhere (as I noted earlier), the impact of the macroeconomic policies on the real economy—that is, on the real GDP growth and unemployment rates—has differed from country to country, with varying implications for the policy makers' ability to launch full currency convertibility by slashing inflation further. Therefore, I begin with an analysis of the impact of inflation control policies on the real economy, which in turn slowed the adoption of full currency convertibility (via a slackening, for example, of budget deficit control). I then discuss the role of the external factors that, interacting with the appreciating real exchange rates and growth-led import demand, put excessive stress on the foreign exchange regime, resulting once again in the postponement of full currency convertibility.

### The Real Economy and the Uneven Progress Toward Convertibility by 1995

Take the East-Central European and Baltic economies first. They have bounced back to positive GDP growth rates but the unemployment rate has varied. (These details are in Table I.1. Country GDP growth and inflation rates are also presented in Figures I.1 and I.2.) As a result, the policy makers' ability to press on with macroeconomic tightening has varied from country to country.

The Czech Republic is ahead of the rest in this group because its GDP growth rate was 5.2 percent in 1995 and its unemployment rate was a

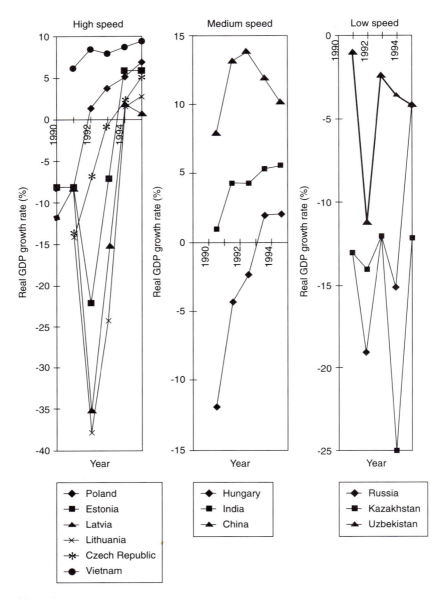

**Figure I.1**
GDP growth rates of countries grouped by reform speed, 1990–95
*Source:* Table I.1.

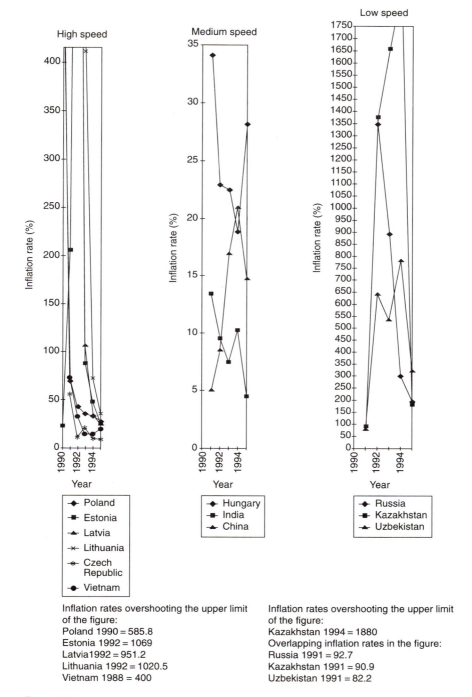

**Figure I.2**
Inflation rates of countries grouped by reform speed, 1990–95
*Source:* Table I.1.

low 3 percent of the workforce, in fact a remarkably steady 3 percent through 1995. By contrast, Poland's high growth rate, rising to 7 percent in 1995, was accompanied by an unemployment rate escalating from 6.1 percent in 1990 to 16 percent in 1994. In the Baltic states the situation was similar, with rising unemployment: Estonia dominated with a 6 percent GDP growth rate in 1995. Hungary performed worst on all scores: a low GDP growth rate (2 percent), a high unemployment rate (10.4 percent) and an inflation rate of 28.2 percent in 1995. In consequence, it gets the lowest ranking on foreign exchange regime within the European (including the Baltic) group.

China, India, and Vietnam, the three Asian economies, have high GDP growth rates (with China having a double-digit 10.2 percent), relatively low inflation rates, and manageable unemployment (which is disguised in the rural areas but has to be monitored carefully with regard to the urban workforce). Another major contrast is that the three economies have grown through the transition without a recession, except for a 1991 dip in India. I therefore rank China, Vietnam, and India in that order, on the basis of their macroeconomic management and the resulting 1995 foreign exchange regime.

Finally, among the three post-Soviet states, Russia, Kazakhstan, and Uzbekistan have continued to have negative growth rates, triple-digit annual inflation, and rising unemployment. Kazakhstan's record of inflation control under a painful IMF regime of shock therapy has brought it to the forefront, with a current account convertible exchange rate regime in 1995, achieved in less than a year. The ranking in this subset is therefore led by Kazakhstan, followed by Russia, and Uzbekistan.

### External "Fragility" Factors and the 1995 Foreign Exchange Regime Rankings

These rankings must be adjusted for the "fragility" factors on the external front: the state of the current account balance and the debt servicing ratio.

As I have already noted, exogenous factors such as the legacy of high foreign debts and the sudden loss of COMECON markets in 1991, stretching into 1992, have affected different countries differently. (Details are in country chapters.) For example, Russia, India, and Hungary continued struggling with market transition while confronting inordinately high foreign debt burdens. Some of Poland's debt was written off. Much of Russia's Soviet debt had been rescheduled. Hungary sharply added to its foreign debt as the transition proceeded.

The negative effects of the breaking of trade links continued throughout the period for the post-Soviet states, especially Kazakhstan and Uzbekistan. The appreciating real exchange rate strained the foreign trade balance for every country except China. (Brada and Kutan, and Desai assess its impact for the Czech Republic and Russia, respectively, with the aid of export-supply and import-demand equations.) Economic recovery added to the stress via increased import demand.

How do the countries finally rank with regard to their exchange rate regime in 1995 when the impact of these influences, as reflected in the current account balance and the debt servicing ratio in 1995, are factored in?

Take first the current account balance as a percent of GDP. Omitting Uzbekistan and Kazakhstan (for which, along with Russia, I present separate non-FSU and FSU balances from IMF sources and discuss the problems of consolidating these accounts), Hungary had the worst record: Its current account deficit had deteriorated to almost 10 percent of GDP in 1994, then recovered to 5.3 percent in 1995. By contrast, the Asian economies fared better, with the exception of a negative showing by Vietnam of 8 percent in 1995. Hungary therefore comes after the Asian economies in the final ranking of exchange rate regime management.

The remaining European economies (including the Baltic states) had an uneven but reasonably manageable current account record that is difficult to distinguish from country to country. Poland's rank remains behind the Baltic states because, with an almost similar inflation and real growth record, its unemployment rate escalated during the five years, constraining the adoption of more rigorous macroeconomic policies. Furthermore, the Baltic currencies, unlike the Polish zloty, are fully convertible.

Next take the record of debt servicing. Hungary performs worst, with a debt servicing ratio of 45 percent in 1995, preceded by Russia and India, in that order. But for frequent rescheduling of debt repayment obligations, Russia's record would have been worse. Poland's ratio is only little worse than the Czech ratio because much Polish debt was written off. The Baltic states remain ahead of Poland in the final ranking because of their low debt servicing ratios.

In conclusion, I have judged the final ranking of the economies' 1995 foreign exchange regime, from best to worst, as follows: the Czech Republic, Estonia, Latvia, Lithuania, China, Vietnam, Poland, India, Hungary, Kazakhstan, Russia, and Uzbekistan.

### Country Ranking by Trade and FDI Policy Regime in 1995

A fully convertible currency enhances global interaction by promoting trade and attracting capital flows. But this clearly is not sufficient. The trade regime has to be free, and the investment environment needs to be positive. I now rank the countries according to their 1995 foreign trade regimes (using the information in Table I.2) and by the policies for attracting foreign direct investment by year-end 1995 (on the basis of the information in Table I.3).

### Ranking by Foreign Trade Regime

I use three criteria for judging the pro-globalization characteristics of the trade regime. The first relates to the agents (e.g., private parties or state organizations) who undertake foreign trade; the second, to the continuing prevalence or elimination of nonmarket measures, including QRs and licensing requirements, for regulating trade; and the third, to the height and dispersion of import duties.

In the European and Baltic economies, private companies had replaced the former state trading organizations (STOs) more effectively than in the post-Soviet states. In Russia and (less so in) Kazakhstan, former STOs had been converted into joint stock companies in which the former party bosses were mostly in charge. Private traders (with a substantial role in Russia) had appeared in both countries.

In Uzbekistan, STOs still dominated foreign trade activity, and private trade was being controlled via export quotas and licenses. State orders in Uzbekistan dominated exports of cotton (which was bought by state agencies from domestic producers and sold at a higher price on the world market) and imports of grain (which was bought at the world price and sold at a lower price to domestic mills). Among the Asian economies, government agencies at various levels continued to be most active in China, less so in Vietnam, and least in India.

Nonmarket interventions also had diminished. They had disappeared in the European and Baltic economies except in Hungary, where import quotas remained on some consumer goods. Among the post-Soviet states, export quotas were allocated directly to private parties in Uzbekistan, whereas they were increasingly auctioned off in Kazakhstan. In Russia, quotas were being removed but they still operated in oil shipments via selective access to pipelines. Among the Asian economies, import controls were used in China to protect specific industries, and licenses, which applied to a quarter of imports in 1992, were necessary. Import quotas had ceased to exist in Vietnam and in India as well, except that in India licenses were still necessary to import consumer goods. In Vietnam, state agencies were active in foreign trade and private traders faced bureaucratic hurdles.

If one goes only by two indicators—the continuing role of government trading agencies and the presence of quotas and licenses—then India was the most liberalized among the post-Soviet and Asian economies because it had the fewest state trading and nonmarket restrictions by 1995. It was followed by Kazakhstan, Russia, Vietnam, China, and Uzbekistan. Kazakhstan and Russia rank ahead of Vietnam and China because, under persistent IMF pressure, they had (by the end of 1995) moderated their restrictive trade regimes, whereas Vietnam and China had not. Hungary ranks as least liberalized among the European economies (including the Baltic states) because some import quotas still prevailed in 1995. The remaining (five) European economies had hardly any nonmarket interventions and rank at the top.

On the other hand, on the indicator of trade taxes and subsidies, the Baltic and post-Soviet states did not do so well. Export taxes (and quotas) were used to prevent the outflow of goods, especially to the neighboring states, and to maintain their local availability. These were being phased out in Russia, and had already disappeared in Estonia and Latvia. Lithuania had retained some export licensing, which placed it below the other Baltic states.

By contrast, import duties were much more important and had acquired a dominant role in trade policy management in 1995, especially because the real exchange rate had appreciated everywhere except in Uzbekistan and Vietnam. (The import duties are shown in Table I.2.) Note, however, that the rates are simple averages and generally unweighted by import shares of specific items or groups.

Even so, the pattern is unmistakable. In the European economies, except the Czech Republic, import duties had gone up, with the highest average rate in Hungary (which, as already noted, had also retained some import restrictions). Lithuania, among the Baltic states, had the highest import duty rates (especially on agricultural items) with large dispersion, again qualifying it for the lowest rank among the Baltic states. Among the post-Soviet states, Russia was marked by increasing import duties and escalating pressures from agricultural and food processing lobbies to raise them further. By contrast, Uzbekistan and Kazakhstan, both importers of essential consumer goods, had fewer import duties (but their trade regime, as noted earlier, was marked by a dominant role of state agencies and export controls; moreover, in Uzbekistan there were subsidies on the sale of imported grain for domestic users and taxes on domestic producers on exports of cotton).

The Asian economies had, on average, high import duty rates in 1995: 15 percent (average, unweighted, with massive dispersion) in Vietnam, 27

**Table I.2**
Foreign trade arrangements in transition economies: 1990–95

| | Import-export regime | Import tariff rates | Trade policy ranking in 1995 |
|---|---|---|---|
| Czech Republic | No quantitative trade restrictions. Regional trade agreements | 5% + 20% surcharge (1991)<br>5% + 10% surcharge (1992)<br>5% (surcharge abolished in 1993) | 1 |
| Hungary | Global quotas on imports of some consumer goods from hard currency sources gradually enlarged and commodity coverage reduced. Nonbinding auto import quotas. Some export subsidies. Regional trade agreements | 10.9% + 8% import surcharge introduced in March 1995. The surcharge was to be reduced by 2% in 1995 and eliminated by July 1, 1997 | 5 |
| Poland | Most quantitative restrictions abolished in January 1990, and import duties removed from 4,500 items in June 1990. Reappearance of some import restrictions. Export promotion program adopted in 1994. Regional trade agreements | 5.5% (up to August 1991)<br>18.4% (1992)<br>18.4 + 6% import surcharge (1993)<br>9.3% average tariffs on industrial goods +5% import surcharge for all items from January 1995 | 4 |
| Estonia | No quantitative trade restrictions. Trade licenses for export and import activity remain for Social Security and health reasons. Regional trade agreements | 10–16% import tariffs on selected items in 1995 were subsequently abolished | 2 |
| Latvia | No quantitative trade restrictions. No import licensing except for agricultural commodities. Regional trade agreements | Export taxes varying from 2 to 3.0%, and higher on exports to CIS states and on barter trade. 10% average import tariff with wide dispersion | 3 |
| Lithuania | No quantitative trade restrictions. Some export licensing remains. Regional trade agreements | Frequent changes in import tariffs (which were varied 13 times between February 1993 and February 1995) resulted in higher tariffs on agricultural items and wide dispersion. Consumption-weighted average tariff on agricultural items is 35% | 6 |

| Country | Trade arrangements | Import tariffs | |
|---|---|---|---|
| Russia | Quotas on major exports and export taxes were abolished in April 1995. Export quotas on oil trade are maintained via selective access to pipelines. Import subsidies abolished by January 1, 1994. IMF recommendation in early 1996 that the remaining export taxes on oil be replaced by excise taxes. Trade with CIS states subject to administrative controls and barter agreements | 5 to 15% (to July 1994) New schedule with a higher average rate of 12.5% and wider dispersion (to July 1995) Average tariff on a number of commodities at 15% in 1995 | 9 |
| Kazakhstan | Export quotas abolished in 1995 except for oil and oil products. These quotas increasingly distributed via auctions. No quantitative restrictions on imports. Duty-free trade agreement with Russia | 5% or less (on furniture, carpets, and leather goods) except on autos and alcohol, for which it is higher | 8 |
| Uzbekistan | 60 to 65% of trade carried out through state channels in early 1995. Private trade controlled via export licenses and quotas, and import licenses. Bilateral trade agreements with 17 countries in 1994 | Import duties adjusted or removed to increase supplies of essential items. New import tariff schedule introduced in October 1995. Tariffs reduced to a maximum of 40%, with the exception of autos (up to 60%), on March 20, 1996. Many 5% and 10% rates introduced then | 12 |
| China | Some imports continue to be canalized through specific FTOs and licensing. Licensing applied to a quarter of imports in 1992. Specific import controls used to protect domestic agriculture and industry | Trade-weighted mean tariff of 31.9% (implying a much higher unweighed rate) in 1992. High variance of rates. Average (unweighted) tariff rate reduced to 23%, involving 5,000 items, on April 1, 1996 | 11 |
| Vietnam | FTOs continue trading in major items. Import restrictions, in order of decreasing transparency, include tariffs, reference prices, excise taxes, quotas, and import licenses. Trade agreements with EU and US | 15% average rate combined with 28 different rates dispersed from zero to over 100% | 10 |
| India | Raw materials and machines can be imported without a license. Licenses necessary for imports of consumer goods. Export incentives continue | Rate on liberalized consumer goods is 50%. Average import-weighted tariff reduced from 87% in 1990/91 to 27% in 1994/95. 1995 tariff structure less dispersed | 7 |

*Source:* The table is put together from details on the foreign trade arrangements for each country in the Appendix.
*Note:* The import tariff rates are simple averages unless stated otherwise.

**Table I.3**
Foreign direct investment in transition economies: environment and performance, 1991–95

| | | Infrastructure | Progress on restructuring of large state-owned enterprises (SOEs) | Investors' perception (IP) at the end of 1995 | Ranking of IP by end of 1995 | FDI flows | | |
|---|---|---|---|---|---|---|---|---|
| | | | | | | As percent of FDI flows to non-OECD countries | As percent of gross fixed investment | Ranking of FDI as % of gross fixed investment in latest year |
| Czech Republic | 1991 | Financial and investment activity supported by well-drafted laws and their slow but effective implementation | Lengthy bankruptcy procedures. Case-by-case approval of restructuring plans of SOEs | Positive because of a stable, low-inflation economy. Selective approach of policymakers to FDI participation | 4 | — | 9.1 | 6 |
| | 1992 | | | | | | 14 | |
| | 1993 | | | | | 0.59 | 7 | |
| | 1994 | | | | | — | — | |
| | 1995 | | | | | — | — | |
| Hungary | 1991 | Same as in Czech Republic | Implementation of bankruptcies on track. Speedy approval of SOE restructuring plans with FDI participation | Sharp improvement by 1995 because of a stabilizing economy | 3 | — | 21.4 | 1 |
| | 1992 | | | | | — | 20.2 | |
| | 1993 | | | | | 2.7 | 33.2 | |
| | 1994 | | | | | 1.3 | 13.7 | |
| | 1995 | | | | | 5.2 | 68.7 | |
| Poland | 1991 | Same as in Czech Republic and Hungary | Steady progress on restructuring SOEs because of continuing enforcement of hard budget constraints | Improving because of targeted incentives and a growing economy | 6 | — | 0.75 | 8 |
| | 1992 | | | | | — | 2 | |
| | 1993 | | | | | 0.66 | 4.2 | |
| | 1994 | | | | | — | — | |
| | 1995 | | | | | — | — | |
| Estonia | 1992 | Compares favorably with that in Czech Republic, Hungary, and Poland | Speedy restructuring à la Treuhand model aided by direct sale of enterprises, vigorous implementation of bankruptcies, and hard budget constraints | Positive due to location, and incentives to foreign investors | 2 | — | 24.2 | 2 |
| | 1993 | | | | | 0.18 | 43 | |
| | 1994 | | | | | 0.18 | — | |
| | 1995 | | | | | — | — | |

| Country | Year | | | | | | | |
|---|---|---|---|---|---|---|---|---|
| Latvia | 1992 | Same as in Estonia | Some progress because of restructuring emphasis on strategic investors, including foreigners, rather than on factory insiders. However, ineffective bankruptcy implementation and soft budget constraints | Less enthusiastic than for Estonia | 5 | — | 28.1 | 3 |
| | 1993 | | | | | 0.06 | 16.4 | |
| | 1994 | | | | | 0.18 | 28.2 | |
| | 1995 | | | | | — | — | |
| Lithuania | 1992 | Least developed among Baltic economies. Conflicting, unclear laws and ineffective implementation | Insider stock ownership has hobbled restructuring. Ineffective bankruptcy procedures | Discouraged by lack of restructuring opportunities | 8 | — | 4.2 | 7 |
| | 1993 | | | | | 0.03 | 3.3 | |
| | 1994 | | | | | 0.07 | 5.1 | |
| | 1995 | | | | | — | — | |
| Russia | 1992 | Conflicting legal signals from presidential decrees and parliamentary legislation as well as between federal and republic levels. Slow progress on adoption of civil code | Few actual bankruptcies. Insider ownership plus selective budgetary support of defense and coal industries. Otherwise budget constraints have hardened. Parliamentary opposition to sale of government stocks to outside investors | Negative because of unpredictable and shifting taxation and ownership environment | 9 | | | |
| | 1993 | | | | | | | |
| | 1994 | | | | | | | |
| | 1995 | | | | | | | |
| Kazakhstan | 1992 | Laws exist but may not be enforced. In general, weak institutions and inadequate physical infrastructure | Bankruptcy laws and labor layoff regulations not fully in place. Soft budget constraints still in operation | Potentially positive response undermined by the disadvantages of a landlocked economy | 10 | | | |
| | 1993 | | | | | | | |
| | 1994 | | | | | | | |
| | 1995 | | | | | | | |
| Uzbekistan | 1992 | Laws, often in the form of executive decrees, exist but are badly drafted and not enforced. Poor institutional and physical infrastructure | No bankruptcies because of insider ownership and political risks of large-scale labor layoffs. Soft budget constraints exist | Weak response because of a bureaucratized, infrastructurally underequipped and landlocked economy | 12 | | | |
| | 1993 | | | | | | | |
| | 1994 | | | | | | | |
| | 1995 | | | | | | | |

**Table I.3** (continued)

| | | Infrastructure | Progress on restructuring of large state-owned enterprises (SOEs) | Investors' perception (IP) at the end of 1995 | Ranking of IP by end of 1995 | FDI flows | | |
|---|---|---|---|---|---|---|---|---|
| | | | | | | As percent of FDI flows to non-OECD countries | As percent of gross fixed investment | Ranking of FDI as % of gross fixed investment in latest year |
| China | 1991 | FDI concession are codified in 500 pieces of legislation with unclear rules to be enforced by different authorities. Therefore, delays and arbitrary enforcement. Inadequate financial and physical infrastructure | Nil in state-owned enterprises | Decidedly positive because of well-targeted incentives to foreign investors in open economic zones | 1 | — | 4.3 | 5 |
| | 1992 | | | | | — | 7.8 | |
| | 1993 | | | | | 31.4 | 13.3 | |
| | 1994 | | | | | 45.6 | 19.7 | |
| | 1995 | | | | | — | — | |
| Vietnam | 1991 | Meddlessome bureaucracy, overlapping legislation, tax code under constant revision, and underdeveloped financial and physical infrastructure | Only 3 out of an estimated 6,000 SOEs have been privatized. None have been subjected to effective restructuring | Positive response by ASEAN investors may be slackening | 7 | — | 15.2 | 4 |
| | 1992 | | | | | — | 14.7 | |
| | 1993 | | | | | 0.34 | 11.2 | |
| | 1994 | | | | | 0.74 | 17.4 | |
| | 1995 | | | | | 1.6 | 28.2 | |
| India | 1991/92 | Financial sector reform firmly in place. Rules to attract FDI need to be liberalized further. Inadequate physical infrastructure | Extremely slow because of political risks of labor layoffs and complicated procedures | Negative so far because of lack of clear guidelines and decisive incentives to attract FDI | 11 | — | 0.30 | 9 |
| | 1992/93 | | | | | — | 0.66 | |
| | 1993/94 | | | | | 0.71 | 1.4 | |
| | 1994/95 | | | | | — | — | |
| | 1995/96 | | | | | — | — | |

*Sources:* Information on infrastructure and restructuring of large SOEs is summarized from details relating to foreign direct investment, the institutional infrastructure, and industrial restructuring for each country in the Appendix. Data on FDI flows and gross fixed investment are put together from IMF sources and EBRD, *Transition Report 1995* (1995), p. 68.

*Notes:* FDI flows to non-OECD countries defined as net equity investment are available in *Capital Flows to Emerging Economies and Prospects for 1996,* (Washington, D.C.: Institute of International Finance, January 12, 1996). These are estimated at $87.6 billion, $87.7 billion, and $86.6 billion for 1993, 1994, and 1995, respectively.

Indian years run from April 1 to March 31.

percent (average, trade-weighted) in India, and 31.9 percent (average, trade-weighted) in China. However, the Indian system, as already noted, was relatively the least encumbered by state trading and direct controls among the three.

Taking all features into account,[21] I judge the final ranking of the 1995 trade policy regime (with the almost free Czech Republic at the top and the least liberalized Uzbekistan at the bottom) to be as follows: the Czech Republic, Estonia, Latvia, Poland, Hungary, Lithuania, India, Kazakhstan, Russia, Vietnam, China, and Uzbekistan.

**Ranking by Receptivity of FDI Environment (end of 1995)**
Finally, I use the information in Table I.3 for ranking countries in terms of factors that would influence and shape foreign investors' perception of the investment environment as 1995 ended.

An important consideration in this regard is the ease with which foreign investors can repatriate their profits and initial investment should they choose to do so. A fully convertible currency automatically guarantees such transfers. Repatriation of the invested principal was legally guaranteed everywhere, especially in countries in which the currency was convertible only for current account transactions. (Occasionally foreigners were not able to take profits out because of a shortage of foreign exchange, as in Kazakhstan and Uzbekistan.)

Other criteria that are relevant for potential foreign investors are the level of country infrastructure, physical and financial, and progress on restructuring of state-owned enterprises (SOEs) in industry. Infrastructure includes not only roads, railways, and telecommunications but also the investment underpinning provided by banks, stock markets, and financial intermediaries. More relevant are legal guarantees to investors, a predictable and transparent tax system, and tax incentives. (These details are collected in the Appendix.)

Take infrastructural features first. The European and Baltic economies were ahead of the Asian economies, followed by the post-Soviet states. The three European economies in turn dominated the Baltic states. Among the post-Soviet states, Kazakhstan and Uzbekistan were further handicapped by their landlocked position. Russia, therefore, leads Kazakhstan and Uzbekistan.

Industrial restructuring, on the other hand, among the European-Baltic group was speediest in Estonia, followed by Hungary and Latvia. Lithuania had made the least progress. Toward the end of 1995, Hungarian policy makers' midyear austerity program and the strengthening forint had revived foreign investors' interest in seizing attractive investment opportunities in the economy. The Czech policy makers, blessed with low inflation and an appreciating koruna, encouraged FDI selectively for upgrading technologies. The three post-Soviet states continued to be hampered by insider ownership and soft budget constraints. Among the Asian economies, India had made a slow start in the sale of state-owned assets but faced problems of labor layoff in privatized units. Neither China nor Vietnam had begun the process of restructuring SOEs.

Absence of enterprise restructuring need not deter foreign investors if they can find profitable opportunities supported by large markets for new ventures. China, in sharp contrast with India, successfully played the market-size card by offering concessions to foreign investors in new projects and joint ventures in the special economic zones. Thus investors' negative perception with regard to infrastructural handicaps and slow SOE restructuring in China was overcome at the outset by the size of the market accompanied by decisive investment incentives.

Increasingly, however, infrastructural bottlenecks, procedural red tape, and political pressures to overstaff (all of which are pervasive in state industries) can deter foreign investors from remaining engaged. Thus the FDI momentum, fed by incentives and investment opportunities in new industries, needs to be sustained by subsequent infrastructure buildup and SOE restructuring. In China and Vietnam, the initial phase was marked by positive incentives to foreign investors up to the end of 1995; India, by contrast, continued giving mixed signals. The next phase of infrastructure creation and SOE overhaul is only emerging in the Asian economies. By contrast, the European and Baltic policy makers sought FDI to simultaneously promote SOE restructuring and infrastructural upgrading (especially of telecommunications and the financial sector) at the start of the transition. Desire for speedy entry into the European Union prompted this pattern.

Past contacts, physical location, and cultural-ethnic affinity also have contributed to a varying assessment of FDI potential by would-be investors. Note the dominance of overseas Chinese investors in China via Hong Kong; the Finnish groups in the Baltic states, especially in Estonia; the West Germans in East Germany; and the ASEAN countries in Vietnam.

Finally, the reforming policy makers' view of the role of foreign investors in the local economy, which is conditioned by complex economic and political factors, is relevant. The Baltic policy makers' assessment of Western European investment participation in industrial restructuring is benign, more so to obliterate the malign impact of the Soviet-era exploitation. The Czech reformers have been rather selective, compared with the Hungarian, in offering restructuring opportunities to foreign investors, out of a sense that local business can manage the task. The approach of Kazakh authorities is pragmatic and well-focused, in contrast to the chaotic policy mess in Russia and the small, selective start in Uzbekistan. The Chinese and Vietnamese Communist leadership pursued an aggressive early strategy of inviting foreign investors, in contrast to the "you can, you can't" approach of India's policy makers.

Taking all aspects into account, I judge that the country ranking of foreign investors' perception of investment environment toward the end of 1995 was most favorable for China, followed by Estonia, Hungary, the Czech Republic, Latvia, Poland, Vietnam, Lithuania, Russia, Kazakhstan, India, and Uzbekista.

Having thus ranked countries according to the three policy indicators —their 1995 exchange rate and trade policy regimes, and the policy-led foreign-investor perception by the end of 1995—I turn now to an assessment of the two performance indicators regarding globalization: one relating to trade flows and the other concerning FDI inflows.

### Going Global: Ranking by Flows

All countries, according to the contributors, have oriented their foreign trade away from intra-CPE confines.

### Country Ranking by Foreign Trade Flows in 1995

Noting that all countries have reoriented their foreign trade away from intra-CPE confines, and have moved away from autarkic orientation that crippled their trade in many cases, I present three indices in Table I.4 for measuring successful globalization in trade, reflecting these transition economies' trade participation ratios and diversification in trade toward the hitherto neglected and highly competitive OECD markets by 1995.

Trade participation in terms of the familiar $(X + M)/GDP$ ratio is well known to be problematic because exports and imports in the numerator are measures of gross output, whereas GDP is gross value added; the ratio thus has incommensurate items in the numerator and the denominator. Here, this conceptual problem is compounded by insufficient information for the chosen countries. The ratios that could be calculated show a definite trend toward increased globalization for Hungary in Europe, and for China, Vietnam, and India in Asia. Compared with 1990, Hungary's trade partic-

**Table I.4**
Export performance of transition economies: 1990–95

| | | $X+M/$ GDP index | X to OECD/ total X (%) | Manufactured goods X to OECD/ X to OECD (%) | Export performance ranking |
|---|---|---|---|---|---|
| Czech | 1991 | 1.00 | 55.14 | 59.75 | 4 |
| Republic | 1992 | 1.29 | 67.50 | 65.98 | |
| | 1993 | 1.39 | 55.48 | 68.84 | |
| | 1994 | — | 60.23 | 71.50 | |
| | 1995 | — | — | — | |
| Hungary | 1990 | 1.00 | 53.87 | 52.26 | 3 |
| | 1991 | 1.56 | 67.29 | 57.00 | |
| | 1992 | 1.45 | 70.56 | 63.98 | |
| | 1993 | 1.42 | 67.06 | 62.60 | |
| | 1994 | 1.61 | 71.19 | 66.63 | |
| | 1995 | 1.72 | — | — | |
| Poland | 1990 | 1.00 | 66.05 | 48.85 | 2 |
| | 1991 | 1.11 | 74.08 | 50.44 | |
| | 1992 | 0.97 | 72.64 | 59.46 | |
| | 1993 | 1.08 | 75.80 | 68.61 | |
| | 1994 | 1.17 | 75.85 | 71.64 | |
| | 1995 | — | — | — | |
| Estonia | 1991 | — | — | — | |
| | 1992 | 1.00 | 52.91 | 31.70 | |
| | 1993 | 1.22 | 57.93 | 38.73 | |
| | 1994 | 1.24 | 55.05 | 42.20 | |
| | 1995 | — | — | — | |
| Latvia | 1991 | — | — | — | |
| | 1992 | 1.00 | — | — | |
| | 1993 | 0.72 | — | — | |
| | 1994 | 0.51 | 43.16 | 49.60 | |
| | 1995 | — | — | — | |
| Lithuania | 1991 | — | — | — | |
| | 1992 | 1.00 | 23.04 | 28.94 | |
| | 1993 | 1.09 | — | — | |
| | 1994 | 0.58 | 32.03 | 45.56 | |
| | 1995 | — | — | — | |
| Russia | 1990 | 7.00 | 35.96 | 17.60 | |
| | 1991 | 0.73 | 56.50 | 10.20 | |
| | 1992 | 3.06 | 58.61 | 9.30 | |
| | 1993 | 1.90 | 59.59 | 6.80 | |
| | 1994 | 1.41 | 52.85 | 9.30 | |
| | 1995 | — | 49.84 | 11.10 | |
| Kazakhstan | 1990 | 1.00 | 5.00 | 33.50 (average 1989–90) | |
| | 1991 | 1.73 | 5.30 | — | |
| | 1992 | 3.81 | 17.00 | — | |
| | 1993 | 2.03 | 16.50 | — | |
| | 1994 | 1.89 | 23.50 | 4.50 | |
| | 1995 | — | 27.77 | 4.80 | |

**Table I.4** (continued)
Export performance of transition economies: 1990–95

| | | X + M/ GDP index | X to OECD/ total X (%) | Manufactured goods X to OECD/ X to OECD (%) | Export performance ranking |
|---|---|---|---|---|---|
| Uzbekistan | 1991 | — | — | — | |
| | 1992 | — | — | — | |
| | 1993 | — | — | — | |
| | 1994 | 1.00 | 20.33 | 8.30 | |
| | 1995 | 0.68 | 20.43 | 2.60 | |
| China | 1990 | 1.00 | 34.78 | 53.61 | 1 |
| | 1991 | 1.14 | 34.81 | 59.68 | |
| | 1992 | 1.17 | 35.57 | 65.15 | |
| | 1993 | 1.16 | 52.45 | 77.89 | |
| | 1994 | 1.50 | 51.60 | 79.33 | |
| | 1995 | — | — | — | |
| Vietnam | 1991 | 1.00 | — | — | |
| | 1992 | 1.18 | — | — | |
| | 1993 | 1.12 | 66.00 | — | |
| | 1994 | 1.38 | — | — | |
| | 1995 | 1.58 | — | — | |
| India | | | | | |
| Apr. 1'90/Mar. 31'91 | | 1.00 | 56.70 | 73.66 | 5 |
| | 1991/92 | 1.08 | 58.13 | 72.10 | |
| | 1992/93 | 1.11 | 60.83 | 74.16 | |
| | 1993/94 | 1.42 | 57.20 | 73.33 | |
| | 1994/95 | 1.30 | 59.03 | 74.10 | |
| | 1995/96 | — | — | — | |

*Sources:* (X + M/GDP) ratios are computed from trade data and GDP estimates in IMF reports; (X to OECD/Total X) and (Manufactured Goods X to OECD/X to OECD) ratios for the Czech Republic, Hungary, Poland, Latvia, Lithuania, China, and India are computed from information in World Trade Organization sources. Ratios for Russia, Kazakhstan, and Uzbekistan were supplied by the World Bank.

*Notes:* Manufactured goods exports include SITC categories 6 (manufactured goods, classified chiefly by material), 7 (machinery and transport equipment), and 8 (miscellaneous manufactured articles).

Export performance ranking is based on the average annual rate of growth (average of the annual growth rates) of (manufactured goods X to OECD/X to OECD) ratios. These rates are: China, 10.5%; Poland, 10.25%; Hungary, 6.4%; the Czech Republic, 6.2%; and India, 0.2%. The remaining countries are not ranked.

(X + M) in (X + M/GDP) ratios for Russia, Kazakhstan, and Uzbekistan represent FSU *and* non-FSU exports and imports. FSU values are converted into dollars via the average annual exchange rate.

(X to OECD/Total X) ratios for Russia, Kazakhstan, and Uzbekistan represent the relative share of exports to non-FSU industrial countries in total non-FSU exports (which include shipments to developing countries and non-FSU transition economies as well).

(Manufactured goods X to OECD/X to OECD) ratios for Russia, Kazakhstan, and Uzbekistan represent relative share of manufactured goods exports to non-FSU industrial countries in total non-FSU exports defined above.

ipation had gone up by 72 percent in 1995, Vietnam's by 58 percent in 1995, China's by 50 percent in 1994, and India's by 30 percent in fiscal 1994/95.

I measure the economies' trade orientation toward OECD markets with two other ratios. The first represents the share of an economy's exports to OECD markets relative to its total exports. The available data show a rising share for all countries except India (for which, having long been trading with OECD countries, the ratio is not a helpful guide because India already had a very high share of 57 percent at the outset), and Russia (for which the ratio shows a declining trend from 1991).

The second trade orientation ratio measures the share of manufactured exports to OECD in a country's total exports to OECD. These ratios (with adequate information only for Russia among the Baltic and post-Soviet states) again show a rising trend (again except for India, which began and ended with a high ratio of 74 percent), and Russia, which stagnated in a low range of 7 to 11 percent during 1991–95).

In the end, lack of adequate data for all the three indicators handicapped the ranking of a sufficient number of the countries studied to enable me to say anything meaningful for comparative analysis. Nonetheless, Table I.4 presents an export performance ranking for five countries, based on the second orientation indicator described above, and the ranking is according to the rate at which a country increased its share of manufactured goods exports in its total exports to OECD markets in the first half of the 1990s. In other words, I measure a country's effective trade orientation in terms of the speed with which it has diversified its OECD export basket toward manufactured goods. Such a shift provides an appropriate index of an economy's ability to push exports in OECD markets toward manufactured products, in which competition is acute and from which the earlier autarkic policies had particularly diverted trade. China ranks at the top (with an annual growth in its ratio of manufactured goods exports to OECD/ exports to OECD of 10.5 percent), followed by Poland (10.25 percent), Hungary (6.4 percent), the Czech Republic (6.2 percent), and India (0.2 percent). But, frankly, little of value can be inferred from this fragmented set of statistics, and so, beyond claiming the advantage of this and the other two indicators set out above, I must refrain from making any inferences about the comparative pace of globalization on this dimension.

### Country Ranking by FDI Flows in 1993–1995

Actual FDI flows are presented in Table I.3 in terms of two indicators: each country's share of total FDI flows to non-OECD countries and FDI contribution to gross fixed investment in the economy.

China clearly has a lion's share of FDI flows into non-OECD countries at 31.4 percent in 1993. Contrast that with India's share of 0.71 percent! Hungary claimed 2.7 percent of non-OECD FDI in 1993 and reached 5.2 percent in 1995. Vietnam's share in 1995 was 1.6 percent. All other shares are below 1 percent.

FDI's relative contribution to gross fixed investment in the economy, which therefore adjusts for a country's scale, provides a more meaningful comparison. The share was 68.7 percent in Hungary (in 1995), 43 percent in Estonia (in 1993), 28.2 percent in Latvia (in 1994), 28.2 percent in Vietnam (in 1995), 19.7 percent in China (in 1994), 7 percent in the Czech Republic (in 1993), 5.1 percent in Lithuania (in 1994), 4.2 percent in Poland (in 1993), and 1.4 percent in India (in fiscal 1993/1994).

In the end, given these two globalization indicators of FDI outcomes, I have chosen the latter as the more apt. I have therefore ranked the countries in the order suggested by that indicator, with Hungary leading the pack.[22]

**Comparative Performance: Some Key Results**

We now have the rankings of the countries by their policy outcomes in regard to exchange rate and trade policy regimes, as well as the foreign investors' (end of 1995) perception of FDI opportunities offered by the host country policies. We also have the performance index for the FDI share in gross fixed investment (for the latest year).[23] They are pulled together in Table I.5, which also rank-orders the countries by their GDP growth rates in 1995, the unemployment rates in 1995, and three indicators of the inflation rate: in 1995, decline over the entire reform period terminating in 1995, and decline in a year from its peak during the period (to gain some rough-and-ready insight into whether inflation was slashed more readily at the outset in one country than in another).

The pairwise rank correlation coefficients, in the final rows of Table I.5, are computed between the rank order of the countries on the speed of their reforms and the nine indicators in the other columns just described. Armed with these, and the qualitative knowledge gained from the country analyses, I can now reach some key conclusions.

*Reform Speed and Growth, Inflation, and Unemployment*

The 1995 GDP growth rates and decline in the inflation rate over the transition period—remember that the period terminates in 1995 but the

**Table I.5**
Reform speed and transition record: 1991–95

Country ranking in terms of:

| Speed of reform | GDP growth rate in 1995 | Unemploy- ment rate in 1995 | Inflation rate | | | Foreign exchange regime in 1995 | Trade policy regime in 1995 | Foreign investor perception by end 1995 | FDI as share in gross fixed investment in latest year |
|---|---|---|---|---|---|---|---|---|---|
| | | | in 1995 | Decline over reform period | Decline from peak to next year | | | | |
| I. High speed | | | | | | | | | |
| 1. Poland | 3 | 9 | 5 | 4 | 4 | 7 | 4 | 6 | 8 |
| 2. Estonia | 4 | 6 | 3 | 1 | 1 | 2 | 2 | 2 | 2 |
| 3. Latvia | 9 | 3 | 4 | 2 | 3 | 3 | 3 | 5 | 3 |
| 4. Lithuania | 7 | 4 | 7 | 3 | 7 | 4 | 6 | 8 | 7 |
| 5. Czech Republic | 6 | 1 | 1 | 8 | 5 | 1 | 1 | 4 | 6 |
| 6. Vietnam | 2 | — | 2 | 5 | 6 | 6 | 10 | 7 | 4 |
| II. Medium speed | | | | | | | | | |
| 7. Hungary | 8 | 7 | 6 | 10 | 10 | 9 | 5 | 3 | 1 |
| 8. India | 5 | — | — | — | — | 8 | 7 | 11 | 10 |
| 9. China | 1 | — | — | — | — | 5 | 11 | 1 | 5 |
| III. Low speed | | | | | | | | | |
| 10. Russia | 10 | 5 | 9 | 7 | 9 | 11 | 9 | 9 | 9[+] |
| 11. Kazakhstan | 12 | 8 | 8 | 6 | 2 | 10 | 8 | 10 | 11[+] |
| 12. Uzbekistan | 11 | 2 | 10 | 9 | 8 | 12 | 12 | 12 | 12[+] |
| Correlation coefficient with reform speed ranking | 0.48(12), 0.66* (11, without China), 0.87* (9, without Asia) | −0.25 (9, without Asia) | 0.62** (10, without India and China) | 0.75* (10, without India and China) | 0.50 (10, without India and China) | 0.74* (12) | 0.78* (12) | 0.52** (12) | 0.58* (12) |

| | | | |
|---|---|---|---|
| Correlation coefficient with 1995 foreign exchange regime ranking | 0.69* (12) | 0.66* (12) | 0.61* (12) |
| Correlation coefficient with 1995 trade policy regime ranking | | 0.46 (12) | 0.48 (12) |
| Correlation coefficient with (1995-end) foreign investor perception ranking | | | 0.85* (12) |

*Sources:* Country rankings of GDP growth rate, unemployment and inflation rates, and foreign exchange regimes (all four in 1995) are from Table I.1. 1995 trade policy ranking is from Table I.2. Rankings based on foreign investor perception (by end of 1995) and on FDI share in gross fixed investment (in the latest year) are from Table I.3.

Rank 1 is assigned to the country with the *highest* 1995 GDP growth rate and FDI share in gross fixed investment (in the latest year), *most* liberal 1995 foreign exchange and trade policy regimes, and the *most* positive foreign investor perception by 1995. Rank 1 is assigned to the country with the *lowest* 1995 unemployment and inflation rates, and the *sharpest* decline of the inflation rate during the period and from its peak to next year.

The decline in the inflation rate for each country over the reform period is calculated from Table I.1 as the proportionate difference between the highest inflation rate and the 1995 inflation rate. Inflation rate decline from peak to next year is measured from Table 1 as the proportionate drop between the highest and next year's inflation rates.

China, Vietnam, and India are omitted from the sample in estimating the correlation coefficient between reform speed ranking and 1995 unemployment rate ranking because the unemployment problem in these Asian economies is not comparable with that in the remaining countries. The former is essentially structural, whereas the latter resulted from macroeconomic stabilization and privatization measures.

India and China are omitted from the sample in estimating the correlation coefficient between reform speed ranking and the three inflation rate rankings because these two economies were not marked by the extreme initial inflation rates prevailing in the remaining countries. By contrast, Vietnam's inflation rate in 1988 was 400 percent.

*Notes:* The correlation coefficients are the pairwise Spearman rank correlation coefficient estimates. The sample size is stated in parentheses under each estimate.

*These estimates are statistically significant at the 5 percent level.

**These estimates are statistically significant at the 10 percent level.

+These rankings are not based on any calculations. I have assumed that the Russian share of FDI in gross fixed investment in 1995 was higher than that in India, Kazakhstan, and Uzbekistan, in that order.

transition is often not complete, hence the question of "fragility" that is raised pointedly in this Introduction—happen to correlate nicely with speed of reform. The coefficient of correlation between reform speed and 1995 GDP growth rate rankings is 0.87 when the three Asian economies (which did not experience an output decline) are omitted. (See Figure I.3.) That between reform speed ranking and country ranking in terms of inflation decline over the period is 0.75 when China and India (which did not experience high inflation) are omitted. These conclusions also are reached in the *World Development Report 1996*, which independently ends on the same general note.[24]

On the other hand, the conclusion must be qualified somewhat in regard to inflation control. Alternative associations of reform speed with country ranking according to the 1995 inflation rate (with a coefficient of 0.62) and according to decline in the inflation rate from its peak to the next year in a single swoop (with a coefficient of 0.50) are rather weak. Thus, speedy liberalization strategy goes well with declining inflation during the transition in a gradualist mode, but not so well with knocking it cold in a single year or bringing it down to low levels in the final year. In other words, reform speed may bring down the inflation rate but still not adequately tackle the job relative to gradualist policies.

But the real problem is that speedy reform and lower unemployment rates in the final year do not go together. The rank correlation coefficient between reform speed and 1995 unemployment rate rankings (omitting the three Asian economies, which present problems of defining and measuring unemployment) is negative at $-0.25$ (although statistically not significant). (This relationship is presented in Figure I.4.) Thus speed is good for growth turnaround but may result in higher unemployment, raising problems for policy makers who must weigh the alternative reform agendas.

Indeed, on a closer look at country analyses, one can argue that the speedy reform countries have generally experienced higher unemployment rates, whereas the gradualist reformers, especially when confronting acute stabilization problems, seem to have had lesser growth rates but better unemployment outcomes. Thus, the rank correlation coefficient between the 1995 growth rate and unemployment rate rankings is negative at $-0.15$ (although it lacks statistical significance). Figure I.5 suggests this tendency, indicating the presence of a trade-off, when the rankings of countries on GDP growth rates are related to their rankings on unemployment rates in 1995.

Such a trade-off implies two things: First, speedy reforms may produce better outcomes, like growth and globalization (which I analyze below),

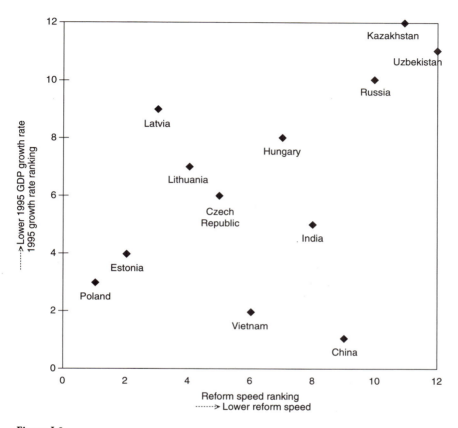

**Figure I.3**
Country rankings by reform speed and 1995 GDP growth rates
·*Source:* Table I.5.
*Note:* The rank correlation coefficient between the two rankings with the full sample of twelve countries, statistically not significant, is 0.48. When China is omitted, it rises to 0.66 and is statistically significant at the 5 percent level. It is 0.87 and statistically significant at the 5 percent significance level when the three Asian economies, which did not experience a transition GDP growth turnaround, are excluded.

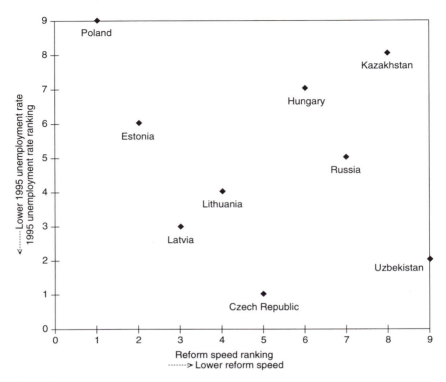

**Figure I.4**
Country rankings by reform speed and 1995 unemployment rates
*Source:* Table I.5.
*Notes:* The three Asian economies—China, Vietnam, and India—are omitted because their unemployment, which is structural, differs from that in the remaining economies, which evidently experienced labor layoffs associated with macroeconomic stabilization and privatization measures.

The rank correlation coefficient between the two rankings, statistically not significant, is −0.25.

but they may come at the cost of short-run unemployment; second, rising unemployment may itself engender the sustainability of the reforms by provoking a political reaction.

To underline this conclusion, consider the case studies of two contrasting sets of high-speed reformers, the Czech Republic, Vietnam, and East Germany, on the one hand, and Poland, Estonia, Latvia, and Lithuania, on the other. The former group either avoided the trade-off or managed it due to special circumstances, whereas the acute trade-off between GDP growth and unemployment rates in the latter group may still be persisting.

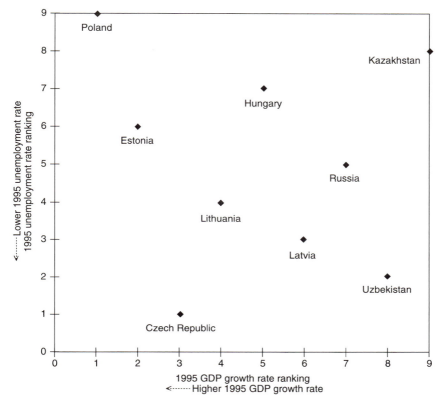

**Figure I.5**
Country rankings by 1995 GDP growth and unemployment rates
*Source:* Table I.5.
*Notes:* The rank correlation coefficient between the two rankings, −0.15, lacks statistical significance.

The speedy growth turnaround of the Czech Republic, marked by a steady and low unemployment rate, resulted from the initial favorable macroeconomic conditions, which helped policy makers immeasurably. Brada and Kutan warn against drawing hasty conclusions from the Czech experience with a view to transplanting it elsewhere. Vietnam emerged as a high-growth performer with a manageable unemployment rate bypassing the output decline of high-speed transition because of benign initial circumstances of a different order. According to Dollar and Ljunggren, the large agricultural, private service, and manufacturing sectors (which traditionally did not receive any credit from the formal banking sector or subsidies from the budget) responded energetically to the incentives of price liberalization and inflation decline of 1989. Finally, the fast and full economic, monetary, and social union of East Germany with West Germany, described by von Hagen, was predicated on the willingness of West German taxpayers to bear the costs of the safety net provisions for the East German unemployed via massive transfers that were to be made available immediately, as specified in the Unification Treaty. No other transition economy could count on such a well-timed, credible, and substantial resource transfer from a "rich uncle" next door for overcoming the resistance of the unemployed to fast-paced reforms.

By contrast, Poland and the Baltic states, the celebrated cases of shock therapy, traveled from negative to positive GDP growth rates in the midst of rising unemployment and sagging macroeconomic stabilization as 1995 ended. In fact, the rank correlation coefficient between GDP growth rate and unemployment rate rankings in 1995 for the four economies is negative at $-1$! The two rankings get perfectly reversed. (Also see Figure I.5.) Indeed, the combination of high inflation (ranging from 25 to 35 percent) and high unemployment rates leaves one wondering if these so-called star performers have left the transition trade-offs behind them and emerged as the hoped-for high-growth-rate, fast-job-creating economies.

### Reform Speed and Globalization

I finally consider the correlation between ranks by reform speed and ranks by the four indicators of globalization in Table I.5. These are the foreign exchange and trade regimes in 1995, the FDI environment by the end of 1995, and FDI share in gross fixed investment in the latest year.

The first question relates to the association between the speed of reform and of globalization: does speedy reform lead to speedy globalization? The second issue focuses on the nature of globalization itself: Do its four components move together? An important caveat qualifying this analysis is that it is based on the three policy outcomes in 1995 and a single indicator of FDI flows representing actual integration. Recall that I had to drop the trade penetration index because of insufficient information.

First, the estimated, pairwise correlations between reform speed ranking and the globalization performance rankings (ranging from 0.52 to 0.74 in Table I.5) are reasonable, enabling me to conclude that speed pays off in terms of increased globalization. This is not surprising because the policy package that qualifies a country to be assigned to a higher-speed category typically consists of policies that can be argued to lead together to increased and efficient integration of the transition economies into the world economy. And reformers are judged to be high-speed not only when they have attempted to go fast but also when they have stuck to their policies in the teeth of transition trials.

Next, has globalization proceeded in lockstep? Note that each indicator cannot be expected to correlate strongly with every other. But the pairwise coefficients (in the final three rows of Table I.5) suggest that globalization outcomes of policies and of FDI flows by 1995 are well coordinated. The exception here is the small and (statistically) insignificant impact of trade policy regime on FDI environment and flows. (The coefficients are 0.46 and 0.48.) In other words, foreigners' perception of investment opportunities and FDI flows do not seem to depend on the host country's trade liberalization successes (witness China and Vietnam). On the other hand, an exchange rate regime marked by a convertible currency in place evidently plays a role in enhancing foreign investors' positive view and actual response. (The coefficients are 0.66 and 0.61.) The exercise also suggests a link between the foreign exchange and trade regimes in 1995. (The estimate is 0.69.) In other words, transition economies, which were ranked ahead in terms of their foreign exchange regimes in 1995 (for example, the Czech Republic and the Baltic states), were more or less similarly placed in the sequence with regard to their trade regimes.

In conclusion, the policies of the sample countries that opened them into the world economy were, on the whole, well coordinated by 1995.

**Summing Up**

Let me recapitulate the principal conclusions:

• Speedy reforms, with comprehensive policy changes in tandem, appear to promote both higher growth and faster inflation control while also increasing globalization.

• But speedy reforms also seem to create a short-run trade-off via an adverse impact on employment.

• Thus, speedy reforms, once such a trade-off is present, are not necessarily superior to less ambitious, gradualist reforms that impose fewer short-run difficulties and hence create a smaller risk of reversal.

• Where this risk is judged to be unimportant, and the short-run costs are also deemed to be socially acceptable in the pursuit of successful transition, the choice of speedier reforms is desirable.

• In that instance, rapid globalization also turns up as a distinct possibility.

These general conclusions emerge from the rich details that each country analysis offers. At the same time, they complement these analyses, providing the textured backdrop against which each country's transition experience can be studied and savored.

## Appendix

### The Czech Republic

### 1 Main Features of the Transition Reforms and Their Outcomes

Wholesale and retail prices were liberalized in January 1991. By mid-1991, goods that made up 90 percent of GDP value were freed. It is estimated that 5 percent of prices are currently regulated.

An elaborate system of wage tariffs (which allowed some flexibility) was retained to forestall an inflationary price-wage spiral. Wage controls were enforced via taxes levied on excessive wage increases. Real wages at the end of 1992 were lower than at the start of 1990. These wage controls were removed in July 1995.

The consolidated budget of the government showed a surplus in 1991 and a small deficit in 1992.

A restrictive monetary policy in 1991 was implemented via ad hoc and quantitative measures. It was followed by the adoption of indirect market instruments, and eased in 1992 leading to a real growth in M2. Interest rates were completely liberalized in April 1992.

In January 1990, the commercial and noncommercial rates of the koruna were unified and the currency was made convertible for trade transactions a year later. At the same time, the koruna was devalued in late 1990 and early 1991.

As a result of the restrictive fiscal and monetary measures, real GDP declined by 14.2 percent in 1991 and 6.6 percent in 1992. Exports and imports declined (in real terms) in 1991, with the real trade balance improving sharply in 1991 by 16 percent. By 1992, real exports had risen considerably and real imports had almost recovered to 1989 levels. At the same time, the Czechoslovak economy (while maintaining a trade surplus under a liberalized trade regime) had oriented its exports to the West.

By the end of 1992, the Czechoslovak economy was showing signs of revival, with GDP growing in the last two quarters, direct foreign investment increasing, and the balance of payments in good shape. However, the aggregate numbers masked differences between the two republics. In Slovakia, unemployment at 12 percent was at least three times higher than in the Czech Republic. The Slovak budget was under strain despite subsidization by the Czech Republic. Social and political pressures led to the partitioning of Czechoslovakia into two independent states at the beginning of 1993. The result was a substantial decline in bilateral trade.

The separation freed the Czech Republic to follow more conveniently the macroeconomic policies that had been the hallmark of 1991 and 1992.

Real GDP decline of 14.2 percent in 1991, 6.6 percent in 1992, and 0.3 percent in 1993 was reversed in 1994, with a growth rate of 2.6 percent and a projected growth rate of 4 percent in 1995. The low unemployment rate, averaging 3 percent of the labor force since the beginning of the reform, continued at that level in 1995. The inflation rate measured in consumer price index had declined from 56.5 percent in 1991 to 20.8 percent in 1993, and dropped to 10 percent in 1994 and 9.1 percent in 1995. The 1996 budget is expected to record a small surplus (around 1 percent of GDP) as in 1994 and 1995. The current account balance went into deficit, estimated at 4.2 percent of GDP in 1995 (following small surpluses in 1993 and 1994) as a result of accelerating growth.

## 2   The Trade Regime

The institutional changes involved the abolition of state monopoly of foreign trade starting in 1991.

There are no quantitative trade restrictions. The import tariff rate is low at 5 percent. (The surcharge of 20 percent was gradually abolished in 1993.)

Trade with the smaller members of the Council of Mutual Economic Assistance (CMEA), which was dissolved in September 1991, was put on a hard currency basis using world market prices. Among measures to sustain trade with members of the ex-CMEA were the formation of the Central European Free Trade Agreement (CEFTA) with Poland and Hungary in December 1992, and the search for barter agreements with the post-Soviet states in order to continue exporting traditional manufactures and importing raw materials.

Association Agreements (which became effective in March 1992) were also signed with the European Union for mutual lowering of tariffs, and subsequently with the European Free Trade Area (EFTA).

The Czech Republic became a member of the WTO in December 1994. The first post-Communist state, it signed an agreement to join the OECD in November 1995.

## 3  The Foreign Exchange Regime

Since May 1993, the Czech koruna has been pegged to a basket of two currencies with a weight of 65 percent for the deutschemark and 35 percent for the dollar. The koruna's market value is determined in daily auctions between the Czech National Bank (CNB) and the commercial banks. The currency, which fluctuated within a 0.5 percent band around the nominal peg in 1995, was allowed a wider band of $\pm 7.5$ percent from February 1996. As a result, the CNB was ready to use the full width of the band to increase uncertainty in the exchange rate to discourage speculative inflow of capital.

## 4  Currency Convertibility

"The new Foreign Exchange Law, effective on 1 October 1995, provides full current account convertibility and partial capital account convertibility. According to the draft law, Czechs will have the right to convert crowns into hard currency to buy foreign real estate, and Czech companies will have the right to buy foreign currency to make investments abroad. On the side of capital inflows the main restriction will apply to purchase of real estate in the Czech Republic by nonresidents" (European Bank for Reconstruction and Development (EBRD), *Transition Report 1995*, p. 40).

## 5  Foreign Direct Investment

Foreign investors face no limits on equity participation. Nonresidents can fully repatriate their capital and capital gains after paying taxes. Foreign residents in EU countries can invest in the Czech Republic without a license, although they need to report their corporate activities.

The sharp decline in FDI in 1993 was offset by higher portfolio investment. The offer of equity in telecommunications and energy in 1995 to foreign investors was expected to stimulate FDI flows. The strong balance of payments and a strong koruna also attract foreign investors. However, the authorities had moved to a selective approach combining incentives to domestic industry with positive signals to foreigners to invest in key sectors on a case-by-case basis.

Cumulative FDI from 1990 to end of 1995 amounted to $5.8 billion. Japan and other Asian investors, such as South Korea and Taiwan, have been slow to enter the emerging markets of Central and East Europe. The 1996 decision by Matsushita Electric of Japan to invest in a television plant in the Czech Republic for its Panasonic subsidiary plant marks a departure in that regard.

## 6   The Institutional Infrastructure

Laws governing investment activity are clearly drafted and properly implemented, albeit with some delay.

A two-tier banking system was created in 1990. The legal framework defining the functions of the central bank and the commercial banks is currently in place. There were fifty commercial banks at the start of 1994, of which eleven were fully foreign-owned. Despite continuing attempts at strengthening the balance sheets of banks, problems of deteriorating portfolios and undercapitalization persist in small banks. Banks continue to extend loans to failing enterprises because bankruptcy procedures are not enforced energetically. Following the failure of three banks in 1994, the CNB has initiated measures to consolidate the banking sector, restrict the granting of new licenses, and encourage small banks to merge.

By May 1995, there were 365 investment companies, 279 investment privatization funds, and 60 private insurance companies, a few foreign-owned.

Trading on the Czech stock exchange began in April 1993. Its activity is currently constrained by inadequate domestic capital and insufficient information about companies whose stocks are traded. After a year of trading, only 23 of the 1,000 shares were traded and share prices on the stock exchange remained highly volatile. However, by early 1995, automated processing of recording, concluding, and settling direct stock exchange trades had begun.

Standard and Poor, the U.S. debt-rating agency, upgraded its rating of the Czech economy to A-stable in November 1995, the highest in the region.

## 7   Industrial Restructuring

Large state-owned enterprises (SOEs), which have been converted into joint stock companies, are being restructured on a case-by-case basis with participation by local and foreign investors. The bankruptcy procedures are slow, however.

The surge in foreign investment to $2.6 billion in 1995 from $862 million in 1994 and $568 million in 1993 resulted from a series of key restructuring deals involving sale of stakes in the Czech telecommunication and oil-refining sectors.

*Hungary*

## 1  Main Features of the Transition Reforms and Their Outcomes

The post–May 1990 government continued the process of price decontrol and, by the end of 1990, all prices were freed except charges for public transport and household energy use, which were raised.

As a result of the fiscal measures introduced by the government, the 1990 deficit of the state budget (excluding local government activity) showed a surplus of 0.8 percent of GDP. However, the surplus had moved to a deficit of 7.7 percent in 1994, and a projected 5 percent in 1995. (This resulted from reform-related measures in the early years such as issuance of debt to finance recapitalization of commercial bank debts, suspension of tax and social security payments by bankrupt enterprises, the takeover by the budget of subsidized loans for housing from the National Savings Bank and finally, the switch to financing budget deficits by issuing securities at market interest rates from 1991; from increased expenditure from the budget on goods and services and unemployment compensations. The growth in expenditures in 1995 was dominated by a projected 56 percent increase in interest payments reflecting the cumulative burden of past deficits and the rise in interest rates.)

Monetary policy until mid-1993 was marked by lower interest rates to boost domestic demand and secure economic recovery. As the external current account balance deteriorated (from increased import demand), the policy was reversed and a tight monetary control began in 1994 and continued in 1995.

Reflecting the relaxed monetary policy and the central bank financing of the budget deficit, inflation measured by the consumer price index remained at 22.5 percent in 1993, almost the same as in 1992. It was 18.9 percent in 1994 and 28.2 percent in 1995, substantially ahead of world inflation.

As a result, the National Bank of Hungary devalued the forint five times in 1993 and seven times in 1994, altogether by a cumulative 76.6 percent relative to its 1989 level. The unit-labor cost based real exchange rate at the end of 1994 was 20 percent higher than in 1990.

The reform measures resulted in a decline of real Hungarian GDP by 20 percent, of consumpton by 11.7 percent, and of fixed investment by 21.5 percent between 1989 and 1993. Unemployment, measured as the ratio of registered unemployed in the economically active population, had risen to 10 percent in January 1995. GDP grew (for the first time in four years) at 2 percent in 1994 and another 2 percent in 1995. However, the deficit in the state budget at 6.6 and 6.8 percent of GDP in 1993 and 1994 continued to be high; so did the external current account deficit in both years at nearly 10 percent each of GDP. The external debt (net of reserves) was a whopping $21.7 billion at the end of 1994.

The erratic exchange rate policy, which failed to counter the devaluationary expectations and establish firmly the competitiveness of Hungarian exports, was abandoned on March 12, 1995, in favor of weekly devaluations of the forint by the Hungarian National Bank. At the same time, Finance Minister Lajos Bokros announced austerity measures aimed at stabilizing the economy and putting Hungarian public finances on a long-term sustainable basis. As a result, 1995 budget deficit was brought down to 4.1 percent of GDP. So was the 1995 current account deficit, to 5.3 percent of GDP. These improvements were expected to continue in 1996.

## 2  The Trade Regime

There are few quantitative restrictions on export and import transactions that can be undertaken by private companies. Some consumer goods imports are subject to "global quotas" that define separate ceilings for about twenty product groups. Quantitative restrictions on farm product imports were removed in accordance with the new GATT agreement in January 1995.

While import licensing and quotas have been progressively liberalized, a number of industrial and "sensitive" products (among them textiles and agriculture) remain "substantially" protected by tariffs. The nominal average import tariff rate was 10.9 percent in 1994. "On 20 March 1995, Hungary introduced an 8 percent import surcharge on all goods, except primary energy carriers and machinery for investment. The surcharge is to be phased out during the first half of 1997" (EBRD, *Transition Report 1995*, p. 44). The import tariffs on agricultural items and export subsidies (to exporters of grain, meat, and other items) are expected to go down and eventually disappear as a result of the Association Agreement with the European Union.

Hungary became a member of the WTO in December 1994.

## 3  The Exchange Rate Regime

The exchange rate of the forint is based on a basket of currencies. The composition of the basket has been adjusted several times. Prior to December 9, 1991, the basket consisted of eleven currencies weighted to reflect the currency composition of Hungarian foreign trade turnover.

Between December 9, 1991, and August 2, 1993, the basket consisted of equal proportions of the dollar and ECU. Between August 2, 1993, and May 16, 1994, it had equal weights of the dollar and the deutschemark. Since May 16, 1994, it has carried weights of 70 percent and 30 percent respectively of ECU and the dollar. The value of the forint to the basket has been adjusted periodically based on the difference between the domestic and foreign rates of inflation.

## 4 Currency Convertibility

The interbank foreign exchange market was established on July 1, 1992, and the state monopoly of foreign exchange operation was abolished. The foreign exchange operations of commercial banks have expanded steadily since 1988. Banks can lend foreign exchange to domestic enterprises and conduct foreign exchange operations on behalf of their clients.

Registered importers can purchase foreign exchange from banks for bona fide imports of goods and most services. Export earnings must be surrendered to a licensed bank in exchange for Hungarian forints within eight days of the receipt of foreign exchange.

Hungarian enterprises and residents are generally not allowed to hold bank accounts abroad.

Resident and nonresident individuals may open foreign currency bank accounts in Hungary without declaring the source of foreign exchange.

Allowances to Hungarian tourists for foreign travel are restricted to $800 per year. No foreign exchange is made available to students for study abroad. Equally, nonresidents must register their foreign exchange and personal assets so that they can take them out of the country.

## 5 Foreign Direct Investment

The policy of privatizing factories for cash and foreign exchange through auctions and international tenders stimulated FDI. However, the tax incentives to foreign investors since 1989 have been tied to specific criteria such as the size of investment, the sphere of activity, and the share of foreign ownership in the company operating with foreign participation. These measures were calculated to encourage foreign investment in specific production activities and promote advanced technologies.

Instead, given the poor macroeconomic performance and an unstable currency, foreign investors advanced their own agenda with deliberate caution and calculation. They concentrated on the distribution, commercial, financial, and real estate (including hotels) sectors, stepped into protected branches (such as tobacco, beer, vegetable oil, and sugar), acquired a stake in the telecommunication branch, and promoted efficient use of their home production capacities by distributing their products in Hungarian markets. Barring noteworthy exceptions such as the Opel assembly plant of General Motors and the Japanese Suzuki auto factory, FDI until the end of 1994 failed to create new industrial establishments, branches, or products. It went into industries and factories that operated with above average technological productivity and economic efficiency.

Although their role turned out to be contrary to expectations, they provided financial resources for investment (domestic savings were abysmally low), supported the balance of payments by foreign exchange inflows, and pushed the politically constrained Hungarian privatization process forward.

The inclusion of financial institutions (for example, banks), telecommunication, and energy in the privatization program and the stabilization of the economy following the Bokros austerity measures gave a boost to FDI flows in 1995. Total FDI from 1990 to the end of 1995 was estimated at $11.2 billion.

The authorities are, however, careful about liberalizing portfolio flows on capital account. Occasionally, foreigners are allowed to subscribe to special issues of government bonds.

## 6 The Institutional Infrastructure

Laws relating to investment activity are properly drafted and adequately implemented, albeit with delay.

The five large, state-owned banks consist of four commercial banks and the National Savings Bank (NSB). The loan portfolios of the former have continued to deteriorate. (The authorities carried out several rounds of state-financed recapitalizations in these banks in the early 1990s and have announced plans to privatize them.) By contrast, the small and medium-sized private banks, thirty in all (some of which are jointly foreign owned), offer a variety of fianancial services to viable joint ventures and domestic enterprises.

Several investment funds and insurance companies operate in Hungary. The Budapest Stock Exchange, which trades largely in treasury bills, was opened in June 1990.

## 7 Industrial Restructuring

Restructuring of large, state-owned enterprises has continued with participation by local and foreign investors. It had failed to pick up decisively until 1995 because of mixed signals from policy makers and their uncertain management of the macroeconomic situation.

## Poland

### 1   Main Features of the Transition Reforms and Their Outcomes

The Balcerowicz Plan, launched on January 1, 1990, was a comprehensive, stabilization-cum-liberalization program aimed at reducing the rate of inflation and restoring internal equilibrium in the Polish economy.

The plan sought to impose fiscal control by balancing the budget via drastic cuts in subsidies. At the same time, the National Bank of Poland (NBP) imposed monetary discipline by fixing the discount rate (which sets a floor to the interest rate structure) slightly above the anticipated rate of inflation.

Most prices, except charges for domestic utilities, basic medicines, local housing, and alcohol, were liberalized in 1990–91. The excess wage (Popiwek) tax, imposed on state enterprises in 1990, led to an average, yearly decline in real wages of 8.4 percent in the state sector from 1990 to 1993. In 1994, it was abolished and replaced by arrangements that linked enterprise wages to profitability. Since January 1995, wages are set via tripartite negotiations among government, employers, and worker representatives.

The foreign exchange regime was simplified: The zloty was fixed on January 1, 1990, at the rate of 9,500 zlotys in exchange for a dollar for three months, after which the rate could be adjusted if necessary. The foreign trade arrangements were liberalized: Almost all direct controls on external commercial transactions were removed. Barring a few exceptions, Polish enterprises were freed to import and export without obtaining permits.

The restrictive monetary and fiscal policy worked "too well" (until September 1990). The 1990 state budget was in surplus at 0.7 percent of GDP. The volume of credit (in real terms) declined. Real GDP fell by 11.6 percent and unemployment climbed from 0.1 percent in 1989 to 6.1 percent by the end of 1990. Subsequently, real GDP recovered from a further decline of 7.6 percent in 1991 to a positive growth of 5 percent in 1994 and 7 percent in 1995. However, the consumer price index was running at 33.3 percent in 1994 (slightly lower at 27.8 percent in 1995), the unemployment rate had climbed to 16 percent by the end of 1994, and the state budget was in the red to the tune of 3 percent of GDP in 1994 (about the same at 2.8 percent of GDP in 1995).

In the meantime, the negotiations with GATT, the European Union, and EFTA, and the formation of the Visegard trading bloc, took on a "strategic" character. Poland sought to obtain better access to foreign markets. It was willing, albeit reluctantly, to reduce its trade barriers in exchange for concessions.

## 2  The Trade Regime

Poland abolished the state monopoly and administered management of foreign trade in 1990. Most nontariff restrictions were eliminated in January 1990, and tariffs became the main policy instrument. Import duties were removed from 4,500 imported items in June 1990, and the average tariff rate was set at 5.5 percent.

However, the mid-1991 to mid-1993 period was marked by a relative trade stagnation (brought about exogenously by the West European economic slump) and by a return to protectionism. Fiscal stringency also tilted the scale toward higher import tariffs. Quantitative export restrictions also reappeared. The import duty rate was raised to 18.4 percent in August 1991 and was followed by an across-the-board 6 percent import surcharge in December 1992. The need to support the balance of payments and the budget prompted these decisions. The authorities introduced a more protective trade regime in July 1993: They revised the tariff structure, lowered duties on raw materials and semifinished products, and raised rates on finished items. They adopted an export promotion program, which they expected to carry out in 1994.

"In January 1995, the average tariff on industrial goods was reduced to 9.3 percent and the import surcharge was reduced to 5 percent. In May 1995, quantitative restrictions on agricultural imports were converted into tariffs in line with GATT Uruguay Round. In July 1995, Poland became a member of the WTO" (EBRD, *Transition Report 1995*).

In December 1991, the European Union signed the Association Agreement with Poland (Hungary and former Czechoslovakia) and provided for immediate and progressive trade liberalization that was asymmetric. The EU promised to liberalize trade over five years, in contrast to Poland's promise to reciprocate over seven years. As a result, most tariffs and all quantitative restrictions imposed by the EU on industrial goods imports (except on automobiles) were eliminated. However, trade in textiles, coal and steel, and agricultural products is covered by special protocols. The Agreement also permits protectionist measures in infant industries and in industries undergoing restructuring and facing social problems. It allows antidumping actions in accordance with GATT rules.

Poland signed similar agreements with EFTA and CEFTA in December 1992. The agreement with EFTA is more liberal than that with the EU. Tariffs and quotas were eliminated for all industrial goods (except for textiles and steel). In June 1993, the EU improved market access even further by reducing import duties.

## 3  The Exchange Rate Regime

The zloty was unified in January 1990 for current account transactions at the rate of 9,500 zlotys exchanging for a dollar. The exchange rate arrangement was changed on May 17, 1991, from the dollar peg to a peg that included the European currencies in the basket, and the zloty was devalued by 14.4 percent against this basket.

This fixed exchange rate regime was replaced by a preannounced crawling peg on October 16, 1991. The rate of crawl at 1.8 percent per month was set lower than the differential between Polish inflation and the average inflation in the countries whose currencies were included in the basket. The zloty was devalued by about 11 percent against the basket on February 25, 1992. It was further devalued by 7.4 percent on August 27, 1993, and the rate of crawl was reduced from 1.8 percent to 1.6 percent per month. Since May 1995, the zloty fluctuates within a band of 7 percentage points around the central rate, which is devalued at 1.2 percent per month.

## 4  Currency Convertibility

Foreign currency is freely available at the going rate for all current account payments. Citizens are free to buy and sell foreign exchange on the free market. The conversion of export proceeds into zlotys at the official rate was obligatory until the end of 1995. Nor were enterprises and individuals free to hold foreign exchange abroad.

In early 1996, Poland began moving toward full convertibility in view of its forthcoming membership in the OECD.

## 5  Foreign Direct Investment

The hesitant privatization program, the large foreign debt, and the delays in normalizing relations with commercial bank creditors discouraged foreign investors who feared increased taxation for servicing the debt. FDI is expected to accelerate in Poland as privatization picks up speed. Foreign investors are attracted to Poland because of cheap labor cost, substantial domestic demand, and Poland's proximity to the potentially large markets of the former Soviet Union.

The bulk of investment ($4.3 billion through 1994) is in joint ventures because Polish legislation treats such investment favorably. The new 1991 legislation abolished registration of foreign investors (except in priority sectors), simplified taxation and repatriation of investors' profits, lifted limits on profit transfers abroad, allowed repatriation of capital invested in joint ventures and in shares of Polish companies, and gave tax benefits to investors in new joint ventures depending on the size of their investment and its location in areas with high unemployment.

### 6 The Institutional Infrastructure

As in the Czech Republic and Hungary, investment activity is supported by well-drafted laws and their slow but effective implementation.

Nine state-owned commercial banks and four specialized banks accounted for three-quarters of total banking sector assets in 1994. (Two of the nine banks have been privatized.) The Law on Financial Restructuring of Enterprises and Banks of March 1993 announced plans to recapitalize banks, restructure their loan portfolios, and deal with the bad debts of state enterprises to commercial banks.

Private commercial banks (eighty-five in 1993) are generally undercapitalized and at a competitive disadvantage vis-à-vis publicly owned banks. Most are owned by inexperienced private entrepreneurs and investors. Some banks have foreign capital, and foreign banks have opened branches in Poland. However, foreign banks generally approach Poland with caution.

The Warsaw Stock Exchange reopened in July 1991 after being closed for over fifty years. However, shares of a small number of companies are quoted on the exchange, and the stock market does not represent an important source for raising new capital. The absence of intermediaries that can prepare new issues hobbles the process. Foreigners are free to participate on the stock exchange and can repatriate their profits freely. Despite a variety of problems, the Warsaw Stock Exchange is a bustling arena of stock market activity.

### 7 Industrial Restructuring

The continuing enforcement of hard budget constraints has contributed to across-the-board progress on the restructuring of large, state-owned enterprises.

### Estonia

### 1 Main Features of the Transition Reforms and Their Outcomes

Soviet hidden inflation was cracked open by Estonia in the winter of 1990 when the Estonian administration liquidated most wage controls. Prices were subsequently liberalized in October 1990 via the removal of budget subsidies on food purchases by consumers. As a result, average annual consumer prices in 1991 rose by 210 percent. Estonia's price liberalization created shortages in the Baltic neighbors. Subsequently, Russian price decontrol in January 1992 (and the higher cost of energy imports from Russia) pushed inflation further in all the Baltic states. The continuing price rise was restrained by the shortage of cash resulting from the announced blockade of cash by the Russian central bank.

Estonian policy makers stepped out of the ruble zone by introducing a new currency and requiring the immediate exchange of all rubles for the kroon (EEK). The kroon was pegged to the deutschemark on the currency board principle on the basis of the initial reserves of gold (which was frozen in Western banks in 1940 and returned to Estonia in 1992) and the demand-supply situation of foreign currency at 1 DM = 8 EEK. The fixed exchange rate of the kroon, which is fully convertible, is supported by central bank intervention.

Currently, utility charges and housing rents continue to be regulated. Private sector wages are negotiated, but state sector wages are occasionally controlled to contain wage inflation.

Export and import trade restrictions were removed in 1992. Trade licenses for export and import activity remain for social security and health reasons.

The negative impact of the measures to secure an independent, stable currency had tapered off by 1995. The annual growth rate of real GDP in 1994 and 1995, at 6 percent, was in sharp contrast to its decline of 22 percent in 1992 and 7 percent in 1993. Inflation measured in consumer prices had declined from 1,069 percent in 1992 to 89 percent in 1993 and 25 percent in 1995. However, the unemployment rate stood at 8.1 percent in 1994, up from 4.8 percent in 1992. The budget was balanced in 1994, but the current account deficit was 6.4 percent of GDP.

The geographical reorientation of Estonia's foreign trade was dramatic and fast: The share of Estonian exports to the West rose to 40.9 percent in the first quarter of 1992, from 5.1 percent in 1991. However, the commodity structure had not changed much. Estonia continues to export traditional consumer goods and import raw materials and machinery.

## 2   The Trade Regime
Import quotas and licensing requirements (except for products considered essential for national defense, health, and safety), and quantitative restrictions on exports were removed when reforms began. Import tariffs (including a 16 percent tariff on furs and fur products and a 10 percent tariff

on cars, motorcycles, bicycles, and recreational boats), which were in force in 1995, were subsequently abolished. Export tariffs apply to articles of cultural value.

The Free Trade Agreement with the European Union, which became effective on January 1, 1995, freed trade in manufactured items and retained quotas on Estonian exports of agricultural items to the European market. Moreover, the Association Agreement with the EU is expected to promote trade in services, labor mobility, and creation of subsidiaries by companies in each other's territory.

## 3  The Exchange Rate Regime
The Estonian kroon is pegged to the deutschemark at the rate of 1 deutschemark for 8 kroons. Therefore, the Bank of Estonia guarantees the conversion of kroon currency notes and bank deposits in the central bank into deutschemarks and vice versa.

## 4  Currency Convertibility
The kroon is convertible for current and capital account transactions. Estonian citizens can open foreign currency accounts in domestic and foreign banks. There are no requirements to surrender export earnings.

## 5  Foreign Direct Investment
Estonian policy makers have assiduously sought FDI by enacting liberal legislation (the 1991 law gave higher tax advantages to foreign investors, which were removed in 1994) and by implementing a speedy privatization program in which foreigners are encouraged to participate. A stable currency, low labor costs, absence of capital account controls, and historical ties with Western Europe, Finland, and Russia have contributed to substantial FDI flows, which amounted to $253 million in 1994.

## 6  The Institutional Infrastructure
The legal and financial infrastructure has improved steadily and compares favorably with that in the Czech Republic, Hungary, and Poland.

Throughout 1994, the Bank of Estonia was busy drafting and seeking parliamentary approval for legislation to strengthen the commercial banks and bringing the regulatory framework in line with that in the European Union by the year 2000. The regulations specified minimum capital requirements for banks, adequate provisions for problem loans, and strict classification of bank assets. The central bank has firmed up banking supervision and monitoring with technical assistance from the Nordic countries.

The Tallin stock exchange is scheduled to start operating in 1996. In the meantime, enterprise, bank, and investment fund stocks are traded over-the-counter at the computerized depository, which was opened in September 1994.

## 7  Industrial Restructuring
Large enterprises (except those in the energy, transport, and telecommunication sectors) have been restructured according to the East German Treuhand model via direct sale to domestic and foreign investors. Bankruptcy procedures are applied rigorously under a regime of hard budget constraints.

## Latvia

### 1  Main Features of the Transition Reforms and Their Outcomes
By the end of 1992, only prices of energy and utilities for household use, approximately 8 percent in the consumer price index, remained under control.

Unlike Estonia, which introduced a currency right away, Latvia adopted a two-stage currency reform. It introduced a parallel (with the ruble) legal tender rublis in May 1992. The lats, which replaced the temporary rublis, was introduced from March to October 1993. The exchange rate of the (fully convertible) lats, which is currently pegged to the SDR, is supported by central bank intervention.

The trade regime evolved from quantitative restrictions and licensing to moderately high and widely dispersed export taxes and import duties beginning 1992.

Real output decline of 35 percent in 1992, one of the steepest in transition economies, had recovered to a growth of 2 percent in 1994 and a lower 1 percent in 1995. The inflation rate, which was 124.4 percent in 1991, zoomed to 951.2 percent in 1992 (fueled by higher prices of energy imports and currency creation in the ruble zone) but was down to 35.7 percent in 1994 and a still lower 25 percent in 1995 as a result of effective fiscal and monetary control. The budget was in surplus at 1 percent of GDP in 1993 and unemployment was high at 4.9 percent of the labor force. The situation had worsened in 1994: The budget deficit was 1.7 percent and unemployment was 6.4 percent.

Latvia's trade orientation to Western markets has been less effective than that of Estonia.

## 2  The Trade Regime

The trade regime is free from import licensing requirements (except for a few agricultural commodities) and export quotas. However, export quotas and licenses, which were abolished in mid-1992, were replaced by export taxes that varied from 2 to 300 percent and were higher on exports to CIS states and on barter trade. These discriminatory export taxes were calculated to prevent outflow of products to Russia and the CIS states, and redirect trade to the West. (Some rates were reduced by 1994.)

At the same time, import duties were introduced in September 1992 to counter the appreciating real exchange rate. The number of dutiable items and the average (unweighted) rate at 10 percent remained high in 1994.

The tariff law of December 1, 1994, specified basic rates of 1 percent for raw materials and spare parts, 20 percent for final, nonagricultural items, and 53 percent for agricultural products (all weighted by production). The corresponding MFN rates, which apply to "special" trading partners, are 0.5 percent, 15 percent, and 46 percent. The production-weighted agricultural tariffs on European Union imports are expected to decline to 38 percent by the year 2000 as a result of the June 1994 European Free Trade Agreement.

## 3  The Exchange Rate Regime

The Latvian lats, which became the sole legal tender on October 18, 1993, was pegged to the SDR in February 1994 at the rate of 1 SDR exchanging for 0.7997 lats. The exchange rates between the lats and convertible currencies (except the dollar) are based on the rates at which these currencies are traded against the dollar in international markets. (The official rate of the lats against the dollar was 0.512 lats in early 1994.) Banks and authorized exchange dealers are free to trade in these currencies.

The exchange rates between the lats and the currencies of Estonia, Lithuania, Russia, and other post-Soviet states (which are also quoted weekly by the Bank of Latvia) are determined on the basis of their rates against the dollar or the deutschemark.

## 4  Currency Convertibility

The lats is fully convertible for current and capital account transactions. Foreign exchange earnings from exports and service transactions are free from surrender requirements. Residents, individuals as well as enterprises, can hold foreign currencies at home or abroad, in cash or in commercial banks. Similarly, nonresidents can hold bank accounts in Latvia in local or foreign currency.

## 5   Foreign Direct Investment

The Law on Direct Foreign Investments of November 1991, which was amended finally in March 1995, governs FDI in Latvia. There are no restrictions on repatriating capital or profits from investments by foreigners. There are no impediments to the entry of foreign banks, but only one foreign bank operates in Latvia.

## 6   The Institutional Infrastructure

Laws relating to investment activity are as well drafted and implemented as in Estonia.

The Bank of Latvia and a number of commercial banks were established in the first phase of financial reform in 1992. The commercial banks (numbering sixty-three at the end of 1993) lacked adequate capital, sound portfolios, the necessary banking skills, proper accounting procedures, and an effective regulatory framework. The banking crisis of 1994, which led to the closure of one of the largest banks (Banka Baltija), was followed by a series of measures by the Bank of Latvia, among them increased supervision (by outside auditors) of the "core" banks licensed to accept household deposits. Toward the end of 1995, the Bank of Latvia had established its autonomy by implementing a strict monetary policy and by carrying out the supervisory and regulatory functions of a central bank.

A securities market started operating in July 1995 with the creation of the Riga Stock Exchange, the adoption of the necessary legal framework, and the setting up of a securities depository.

In August, Latvia launched a 4 billion yen, two-year international bond issue through Nomura, the Japanese investment bank.

On the whole, banks dominate the financial sector of Latvia. However, they provide meager medium- and long-term credit: Safe investment opportunities are limited; assets that can serve as collateral are hard to come by because factory privatization is slow; banks also lack the expertise to assess risks. As a result, their financing in the form of unsecured, short-term credits accounted for 70 percent of total bank credits in the economy at the end of June 1995.

## 7   Industrial Restructuring

Restructuring has emphasized strategic investment from outsiders including foreigners rather than factory insiders. However, the enforcement of bankruptcy procedures and of hard budget constraints is weak.

## Lithuania

### 1   Main Features of Transition Reforms and Their Outcomes

As a result of the price decontrol (which began in February 1991), prices were freed for 85 percent of the value of items in the consumer goods basket.

As in Latvia, a national currency was introduced in two stages. The temporary legal tender talona circulated with the ruble for almost a year beginning May 1992. The litas replaced the talona over a period from June to August 1993. It was pegged against the dollar in April 1994 under a currency board arrangement and is fully convertible.

Lithuania's trade regime too was liberalized in stages: 1991 witnessed the replacement of state trading by export licenses, quotas (with some items totally banned from export trade), and export taxes. Quantitative restrictions and licenses for export activity were reduced in 1992 and 1993; import duties were moderated from mid-1993 to mid-1994 and changed several times.

Until the introduction of the fixed exchange rate regime in April 1994 under a currency board arrangement, monetary policy was influenced by political pressures to prevent a sharp real appreciation of the flexible litas via increased supplies of the currency which fuelled inflation.

As a result, inflation (measured in consumer prices) was higher than in Estonia and Lithuania—1,020.5 percent in 1992, 410.4 percent in 1993, 72.1 percent in 1994, and 35 percent in 1995. Real GDP, which had declined by 37.7 percent in 1992 and 24.2 percent in 1993, was up by 1.7 percent in 1994 and 3 percent in 1995. But the unemployment rate had also increased from 1 percent at the end of 1992 to 4.2 percent by the end of 1994 and (was projected to rise) to 6.6 percent in 1995.

### 2   The Trade Regime

There are no quantitative restrictions on imports. Export restrictions have been largely eliminated. However, the trade regime with respect to import tariffs has continued to be unstable. Frequent changes in these rates—thirteen times from February 1993 to February 1995—have resulted in higher rates on agricultural imports and wide dispersion in the tariff structure. A three-tier tariff schedule (announced on December 30, 1994) granted (1) MFN status to imports from countries with a "foreign policy priority," (2) preferential treatment to Foreign Trade Agreement partners, and (3) and an "autonomous" rate (5 to 10 percentage points

higher than the MFN rate) to the remaining countries. The average, con-
sumption-weighted tariff rate on eight groups of agricultural products
was raised from 24 percent in April 1994 to 44 percent in July 1994, and
then reduced to 35 percent in October 1994.

As a result of the Free Trade Agreement with the European Union
(which became effective on January 1, 1995), the trading partners abolished quantitative restrictions and tariffs on trade in industrial products
except textiles. The average, weighted tariff on agricultural imports into
Lithuania will remain at 35 percent until the year 2000.

## 3  The Foreign Exchange Regime
Under the currency board arrangement adopted on April 1, 1994, the litas
has been pegged to the dollar at the rate of 4 litas per dollar.

## 4  Currency Convertibility
Foreign exchange earnings from exports of goods and services need not
be surrendered and may be retained abroad. Foreign exchange for imports
of goods and services is available freely. Foreign currency transactions are
carried out by commercial banks licensed for the purpose by the Bank
of Lithuania. Citizens and enterprises can freely operate their foreign exchange accounts with domestic authorized banks. These banks can freely
borrow abroad or loan funds in foreign currencies to residents and nonresidents alike.

## 5  Foreign Direct Investment
The Law on Foreign Investments of December 1990 (which was later
amended) allows unlimited repatriation of after-tax profits and invested
capital. In 1995 the Lithuanian parliament removed the tax incentives to
foreign investors that were granted earlier. The current law requires that
25 percent of the committed funding must be brought in by the foreign
investor when the enterprise is established.

## 6  The Institutional Infrastructure
Laws relating to investment activity, often drafted by unqualified personnel, tend to be unclear. Nor are they administered effectively.

The commercial banking sector in Lithuania is being consolidated with
the number of banks having declined from 28 in 1994 to 20 in 1995.
These banks generally loan short-term funds for trading activity. Banks
have been reluctant to undertake medium- and long-term lending because
of their inability to assess investment risks and because of the inability of

borrowers to provide tangible assets as collateral. Since the passing of the Commercial Banking Law in December 1994, the Bank of Lithuania has intensified its supervision of commercial banks.

Lithuania has a stock exchange, and brokerage firms that deal in stocks, treasury bills, and privatization vouchers.

### 7  Industrial Restructuring
Worker collectives and old managers, who favor job security over restructuring, have substantial stock ownership in corporatized factories. Few firms have been subjected to bankruptcy procedures.

### *Russia*

### 1  Main Features of the Transition Reforms and Their Outcomes
Prices of food items and most consumer goods were released in early 1992. Prices of monopoly products and raw materials (among them oil and gas) were decontrolled gradually. A presidential decree of March 1995 stipulated that all price controls be removed except for items produced by natural and state monopolies. The domestic price of oil, which was about 70 percent of the foreign price by mid-1995, had moved down to 40 percent in early 1996. The gas price differential was bigger. Prices of energy and transport for household use, and of housing (which was being handed over to local administrations) were raised in stages. Some localities continue to subsidize consumer purchases of essential food items.

A tax on average wage of enterprises in excess of the official minimum wage (by a multiple of six times in 1995) was set to be removed in 1996. Pensions and wages of state employees have been raised periodically.

By mid-1993, the central bank refinance rate followed the interbank interest rate. Beginning 1994, real interest rates on credits have been positive, with the exception of the November 1994 to January 1995 period.

The budget deficit was sought to be reduced from its estimated 17 to 21 percent of GDP in 1991 to zero in the first quarter of 1992. The removal of consumer subsidies and cutbacks in industry support, defense expenditures, and state-financed investments were Soviet-style fiats, and did not involve negotiations with the public or the Supreme Soviet (the parliament).

In 1993 and 1994, the fiscal deficit management repeated the pattern of 1992: Deficit control of the early months was reversed in late summer via increased budgetary allocations (to support agricultural activity and prepare the Northern Territories for the winter months). Budgetary management in 1995 broke this pattern with steady control of the deficit through the year. However, the lagging revenues, running at 60 percent of projections in late 1995, forced authorities to enforce arbitrary cutbacks and postponement of discretionary spending, among them wage payments to state employees. Inflation control in 1995 was also helped by a stricter and more effective monetary policy.

The steady control of inflation in 1995 prompted the government to modify the exchange rate policy in mid-1995: The exchange rate was to be maintained until end of the year via central bank intervention within a band of 4,500–4,800 rubles to a dollar (in contrast to the earlier managed float, which shied away from such an explicit corridor). The band was widened to 4,800–5,150 rubles to a dollar for implementation until mid-1996.

The stabilization policies resulted in inflation control (measured in consumer price index) from 1,353 percent in 1992 to 896 percent in 1993, 302 percent in 1994, and 190 percent in 1995. The real GDP decline of 19 and 12 percent in 1992 and 1993 (which reflected, in part, the breakdown of traditional economic and trade ties with the FSU states), and of 15 percent in 1994 (which was largely in response to the stabilization measures and relative price changes) had bottomed out with a 4 percent decline in 1995. Open unemployment as a percent of the labor force was 7.4 percent in January 1995.

The trade balance with non-FSU partners was positive in 1994 and 1995, reflecting improved export performance, which kept ahead of resurgent import demand. Dollar exports of energy products, timber, and metals—70 percent of the total in 1995—grew by 18 percent, reflecting sluggish domestic demand. Toward the end of 1995, official foreign exchange reserves were estimated at $12.5 billion, worth approximately 3 months of imports.

The continuing output decline in the first quarter of 1996 and lagging tax collection coupled with the spending surge on the eve of the June presidential elections raised serious doubts about the fulfillment of the 1996 budget deficit target (at 3.9 percent of GDP) and inflation control (at monthly 1.9 percent by December 1996).

## 2   The Foreign Trade Regime

The state monopoly of foreign trade was dismantled in 1992.

Major exports were subject to quotas and taxes until the end of 1994. Authorities also controlled export activity for these commodities which were classified as "strategically important." (Only special exporters were authorized to export these items.) The phasing of quotas and export taxes (the latter to be replaced by excise duties) began under IMF pressure in early 1996. However, export quotas on oil trade were maintained indirectly by an interagency committee which regulated pipeline access.

Import trade was freed from licensing requirements and quotas in January 1992, but some imports were subsidized until January 1, 1994. Basic rates of 5 to 15 percent import tariffs were introduced on July 1, 1993. A new import tariff schedule with a higher average rate of 12.5 percent, and a wider range was introduced beginning July 1994. The average tariff on a number of commodities was 15 percent in 1995. "Temporary" tariff hikes and export quotas, for example, on fertilizers (the latter to keep domestic prices artificially low) were announced on the eve of the June 1996 presidential elections.

Trade with the FSU states is marked by administrative controls and barter agreements.

Russia has applied for membership to the WTO. In early 1996, it sought entry into the OECD by arguing that it was a democracy, had completed market reforms, and had further reforms on the agenda.

## 3   The Foreign Exchange Regime

The exchange rate for current account transactions was unified on July 1, 1992, and was allowed to float (in terms of the dollar). It followed the quotations, twice a week, of the Moscow Interbank Currency Exchange (MICEX). The Central Bank of Russia (CBR) intervened in the market to prevent wild fluctuations in the exchange rate, which has appreciated in real terms since January 1, 1993.

The policy of managed float was altered in mid-1995, and the nominal exchange rate was allowed to vary within a fixed band of 4,300–4,800 rubles to a dollar. The band was moved up to 4,800–5,150 rubles to a dollar on the eve of the December 15 elections to the Russian Duma (lower house of the parliament) with a view to making exports and import substitutes more competitive.

The CBR announced a further upward shift of the crawling corridor, to begin on July 1, 1996, at 5,000–5,600 rubles to a dollar and end at 5,500–6,100 rubles to a dollar on December 31. It also committed itself to preventing the ruble from falling more than 1.5 percent a month, slightly lower than the monthly inflation pledge of 1.9 percent in the second half of 1996. The CBR would eventually like to land on a stable and realistic nominal exchange rate. Its success en route in switching from a crawling band to a crawling peg (as in Hungary and Poland) and moderating the real appreciation of the ruble (contrary to the earlier pattern) with a view to keeping exports and import substitutes reasonably competitive will depend on whether the steady decline of the inflation rate from 3.2 percent in December 1995 to 2.2 percent in April 1996 can be maintained.

## 4   Currency Convertibility

A flexible, current account convertible and unified exchange rate was in place in Russia at the start of 1994. However, capital account transactions for residents and nonresidents, individuals, and corporate entities continued to be restricted.

On June 1, 1996, the CBR abolished the surrender requirement of foreign exchange earnings from exporters by signing IMF Article VIII on full current account convertibility.

## 5   Foreign Direct Investment

Foreign investors can repatriate their profits. However, they face unclear property rights and contract law, inadequate law enforcement against criminal elements, unpredictable taxes, and excessive regulations that continue to change. FDI in the energy sector is hampered by jurisdictional disputes over the control of natural resources by local, regional, and federal authorities, and lack of a transparent legal framework. The government's announcement of preferential treatment of foreign investors in the oil industry has not been followed by the necessary legislation. As a result, prospective investors have shied away from investing in the Russian oil sector.

From January 1991 to October 1995, FDI had cumulated to $4.9 billion, far below the economy's potential. Some regions such as oil-rich Tyumen in Western Siberia and the Far Eastern port of Vladivostok have attracted foreign investors because of natural resources and good location. Others such as Tatarstan, Nizhny Novgorod, and Samara southeast of Moscow have succeeded with aggressive marketing ranging from tax breaks to water subsidies. The prospects of FDI have improved as result of Yeltsin's reelection as president following on the $10.2 billion three-year credit agreement with the IMF in March 1996, steady inflation decline, and a bulging trade surplus (estimated at $16 billion in mid-1996).

## 6   Institutional Infrastructure

Investment activity, domestic and foreign, is not only hampered by too many conflicting and changing laws, but also by a chaotic financial sector and outdated physical infrastructure.

The Russian economy witnessed an unprecedented and unregulated growth of commercial banks, most of them "pocket-sized parasites" (2,561 on June 1, 1995), investment funds (650 in 1995), insurance companies (2,700 in 1995), and private pension funds (600 in 1995). Several undercapitalized banks were closed in 1995. Investment and pension funds have been subjected to tighter supervision.

Foreign banks are subject to limits on authorized capital; foreigners are not allowed majority ownership in the insurance business.

Seventy authorized stock exchanges and one hundred commodity exchanges (with stock exchange departments) operated in 1995. Credit instruments of a modern market economy, among them government bonds and treasury bills, municipal bonds, corporate and bank shares, and hard currency certificates currently trade in these outlets. The volumes have been increasing, although their prices are volatile and the risks are enormous. Legislation on a full-fledged securities market and joint-stock companies is expected to be adopted in 1996.

### 7  Industrial Restructuring

There have been few actual bankruptcies. Insider ownership of large factories has prevented rapid inflow of outside funding and managerial expertise. Selective budgetary support of the defense sector and the coal industry has continued. But budget constraints have increasingly become hard.

The continuing opposition of the Communist and Agrarian parties to the sale of government stock to outside investors (including foreigners) is likely to slow restructuring in the coming months because of their increased representation in the Duma elected in the December 1995 elections.

### *Kazakhstan*

### 1  Main Features of the Transition Reforms and Their Outcomes

Transition reforms picked up speed in Kazakhstan toward the end of 1993 when an independent currency, the tenge, was introduced on November 15, 1993.

Administered prices of bread, grain products, and fodder were completely freed in October 1994; oil and coal prices were decontrolled in April and May 1995.

The lax financial policies of the first half of 1994 were reversed in the latter half: The budget deficit of 16 percent of GDP was turned into a surplus of about 4 percent in the third quarter.

The severe fiscal adjustment supported by tight credit policies resulted in a sharp decline in inflation from 46 percent in June 1994 to a core monthly rate of 10 to 12 percent toward year's end, positive real interest rates, and a virtually stable real exchange rate.

Real GDP declined by 25 percent, and unemployment was 11 percent of the workforce in 1994. Average real wages by the end of September 1994 were half their level at the end of 1991. The inflation-output performance was projected to improve but remained critical in 1995: The rate of inflation was forecast at 180 percent and output decline at 12 percent.

There was a sharp decline in 1994 trade volume: Exports of oil fell because of major interruptions through the year in the use of Russian pipelines, and imports fell because of tight credit policies and lower export earnings. Non-FSU trade (exports plus imports) was approximately 40 percent of the total.

## 2   The Trade Regime

The trade regime till the end of 1994 was marked by export quotas (which were brought down to include seven items), export licensing, and monopoly of state-owned companies in trading "strategic commodities." Only 20 percent of export quotas were distributed via auctions. The government abolished all export quotas except those on oil and oil products and distributed more export quotas via auctions in 1995.

Oil exports to non-FSU states, however, are constrained by access to Russian oil pipelines and the formidable problems of creating alternative routes of deliveries to the outside world. This issue remained unresolved in 1995.

There are no quantitative restrictions on imports. In April 1994, the authorities removed customs duties on most imports except on alcohol, cars, furniture, carpets, and leather goods. The rates are 5 percent or less except on cars and alcohol.

A Partnership, Cooperation, and MFN Agreement with the EU signed in January 1995 is aimed at establishing closer economic and political ties with the EU and liberalizing mutual trade. Tariffs on imports were abolished by Kazakhstan and Russia as a result of an agreement in early 1995. However, Kazakh authorities unilaterally slashed tariffs on a number of manufactured goods imports from third countries in April 1996 threatening Russian exports.

## 3   The Exchange Rate Regime

The exchange rate of the tenge (the Kazakh currency introduced on November 15, 1993) is determined in weekly interbank auctions. The nominal value of the tenge moved up from 4.68 tenges for a dollar in November 1993 to 50.5 tenges by May 1994. (It remained there until September 1994.) However, the tenge appreciated in real terms because the inflation differential was higher than the rate of decline in the nominal value of the currency. The National Bank of Kazakhstan intervenes in the currency market in a limited fashion to prevent sharp fluctuations or a rapid appreciation in the real exchange rate.

## 4   Currency Convertibility

The exchange rate was unified when the tenge was introduced in November 1993. Centralized allocation of foreign exchange for imports was also removed. The surrender requirement for export earnings was abolished in August 1995. However, there are limitations on foreign exchange allowances to Kazakh citizens for travel abroad and to enterprises for current account transactions. Nonresidents cannot freely convert tenge accounts into foreign currency and transfer it abroad.

## 5   Foreign Direct Investment

Foreign companies, consulting and legal firms, and banks have opened offices in Alma Aty. The government has invited tenders for five-year contracts from foreign companies to mangage eighteen large enterprises. Projects for investing several billion dollars in the Tenghiz and Karachagank oilfields, for construction of an oil pipeline, and for energy exploration in the Caspian Sea have been drawn up by several foreign corporations. A serious obstacle is Kazakhstan's inability to export oil and other industrial raw materials without reaching an agreement with Russia on access to the outside world.

A protocol signed in April 1996 by Russia and Kazakhstan on the construction of a $2 billion pipeline linking the Tengiz oilfields of Western Kazakhstan to the Russian port of Novorossisk promised to unblock numerous foreign-financed oil and gas projects in Kazakhstan, Turkmenistan, and Azerbaijan. As a result, Russian, Kazakh, and Omani negotiators and Western oil companies have begun the process of resolving complex issues of tariffs, taxes, and management control over the pipeline.

The authorities passed new laws in 1994 to make Kazakhstan more attractive to foreign investors by allowing them to repatriate profits and the original investment. In case of nationalization or expropriation, the foreign investors are to be granted prompt, adequate, and effective compensation paid in the currency in which the investment was made. In practice, the implementation of these generous provisions is hindered by foreign exchange shortages. The Tax Code of July 1, 1995—one of the best written and comprehensive among the CIS states—specifies a tax rate of 30 percent for Kazakh enterprises and permanent establishment of foreign companies.

There are no export performance or import content requirements or restrictions on hiring foreign personnel.

### 6  The Institutional Infrastructure

Laws governing investment activity exist, but their implementation is not guaranteed.

Kazakhstan lacks the necessary financial institutions for stabilizing the economy and attracting foreign investment.

Specialized state banks, which hold 80 percent of the banking system assets, continue to channel credit in the economy. In 1994, the National Bank of Kazakhstan began supervising and regulating commercial bank activity by imposing reserve requirements on tenge deposits, introducing a reserve backing of 15 percent on foreign currency deposits, enforcing stricter capitalization requirements for commercial banks, and introducing proper accounting procedures.

The Central Asian Stock Exchange operates in Alma Aty.

### 7  Industrial Restructuring

The process has been stalled by delays in adopting legislation governing the restructuring of 400 large factories. Bankruptcy procedures and labor laws are biased against laying off workers.

### Uzbekistan

### 1  Main Features of the Transition Reforms and Their Outcomes

Prices were freed for all items in 1994 except those for flour, sugar, and vegetable oil (which were also rationed) and for monopoly products. Rationing and price ceilings (except for natural monopolies) were discontinued in 1995. Energy prices are based on costs of supply including changes in world prices and in the exchange rate of the sum, the Uzbek currency. Toward the end of 1995, domestic wholesale prices of oil and oil products were at or above world levels. The difference between industrial and household rates for electricity and gas was being reduced. Local governments, however, continued to subsidize utility prices including those for household energy, transport, and housing.

Wages and pensions are adjusted to keep pace with inflation. The central bank refinance rate has been based, since March 1995, on the interbank money market rates. The monthly refinance rate was 7 percent in December 1995, substantially above the consumer price inflation of 4 percent.

The Uzbek authorities introduced a national currency in two stages. Following the breakdown of negotiations on the formation of a new ruble area in 1993, they issued the sum-coupon (at a par rate of exchange with the ruble) in November 1993. However, with a continuing depreciation of the sum, the link with the ruble was cut and the coupon was allowed to vary beginning April 1994 according to its value in foreign currency auctions. At the same time, financial policies were tightened so as to reduce inflation and stabilize the exchange rate in anticipation of the introduction of a national currency. The Central Bank of Uzbekistan (CBU) raised its rediscount rate several times and cut back credits to unviable enterprises.

The sum was then introduced at an initial exchange rate of sum 7 per dollar on July 1, 1994. The official and market rates were unified in October, and the sum was made legal tender for all internal transactions.

Despite the stabilization measures, the inflation rate remained high and volatile in a three-digit range, finally declining to 325 percent in 1995 from a high of 785.1 percent in 1994. Real GDP growth rate decline of 11.1 percent in 1992 was slowed to 4 percent in 1995. Open unemployment was 4.5 percent of the workforce in 1994. This estimate does not include the 1 million underemployed in the agricultural workforce of about 2.7 million. Finally, the budget deficit was estimated at 4.1 percent of GDP in 1994.

The old state order system, which contributes to production and consumption distortions, has continued into 1996. The below-world-price state procurement targets for cotton and grain of January 1996 were as high as 50 percent of the 1996 crops. The procurement prices for the two crops were also fixed at 70 and 60 percent of the world prices.

Reflecting close production and trade ties with FSU states, Uzbekistan's FSU trade was 55 percent of the total in 1993. Exports were dominated by cotton and cotton fiber, textiles, and textile machinery.

## 2 The Foreign Trade Regime

Foreign trade remains tightly controlled. 60 to 65 percent of trade with FSU and non-FSU partners was carried out through state channels in 1994. The growing private sector was controlled via export licenses and quotas, and import licenses. The Ministry of Foreign Economic Relations continued to register and review contracts and agreements by private parties that required licenses and agreements involving intergovernmental negotiations and centralized deliveries. In 1994, Uzbekistan had bilateral agreements with seventeen countries.

The number of commodities requiring export licenses has been reduced over time from twenty-six to eleven toward the end of 1994. A further reduction was planned by the end of 1995. All licensing of goods, except for cotton, and export bans were to be eliminated by January 1997. Import and export duty rates were to be simplified during 1996. Joint ventures and wholly owned subsidiaries can export their products without a license.

Import duties have been adjusted or removed to increase supplies of essential items such as grain, sugar, machinery and parts, and oil. For example, the January 21, 1994, decree removed all import duties until July 1, 1995.

Uzbekistan has an observer status with the WTO.

## 3   The Foreign Exchange Regime

The exchange rate arrangements were changed several times during 1994.

On July 1, 1994 a national currency was introduced at an exchange rate of sum 7 per dollar. The gap between the official rate of the sum determined by the Republican Currency Exchange and the open market widened over the months. These exchange rates were unified on October 10, 1994, at the rate of sum 22 for a dollar. The CBU intervenes in the exchange market to soften sharp fluctuations in the rate, but does not target it. In view of the uncertainty of the proper level of the real exchange rate and the possibility of unexpected foreign exchange inflows, pegging of the exchange rate is currently ruled out. If the auctions continue to function smoothly, the authorities intend to reduce the surrender requirement of 30 percent of export earnings and eliminate it by the end of 1996. The auction-determined exchange rate between the sum and the dollar is used for all official exchange transactions. The spread between the (higher) cash exchange rate charged by the foreign exchange bureaus and the (lower) auction-determined rate, which was 40 percent in October/ November 1995, had narrowed to 20 percent by mid-December and remained there in early 1996.

## 4   Currency Convertibility

Thirty percent of foreign exchange earnings must be surrendered at the market rate of exchange to the CBU by state as well as private exporters. The CBU passes on half the amount to the Ministry of Finance, which transfers it to the Republican Foreign Exchange Fund, which in turn finances the needs of the government and meets its obligations.

The Ministry of Foreign Economic Relations, having approved the foreign exchange needs for merchandise trade by state agencies, allows the remainder to be used for their current account transactions. (Private importers can acquire foreign exchange from the auctions.)

Residents can buy any amount of foreign exchange, and can take up to $500 out of the country without documentation of how the currency was obtained. Nonresidents can carry foreign exchange brought by them according to customs declaration.

Residents and nonresidents, private individuals, and companies are allowed to open and operate convertible currency accounts with local banks and receive interest on them. These accounts can be used for transferring funds abroad subject to regulations.

## 5  Foreign Direct Investment

Joint ventures with foreign partners must register with the Ministry of Finance and must be licensed by the Cabinet of Ministers. The President must approve large investment projects. Joint ventures enjoy a two-year tax holiday except those in the priority sectors (such as agricultural and textile processing, mining, oil and gas industries, and tourism), which can claim a five-year holiday. Joint ventures can export their products and import inputs without licenses and retain all foreign exchange earnings. One hundred percent foreign equity participation is allowed. Foreign investors may purchase local products for exports in lieu of cash profits, which can be repatriated by joint ventures (with a foreign share of at least 30 percent) after payment of a 10 percent tax. In practice, currency restrictions and bureaucratic hassles persist. Corruption is widespread. The laws also tend to change frequently.

Despite the substantial endowment of mineral resources, among them nonferrous metals, gold, and natural gas, foreign investment is constrained by the difficulties of exporting the materials through the trade routes that run through Russia.

## 6  The Institutional Infrastructure

Laws, often in the form of executive decrees, exist but they are badly drafted and difficult to enforce. The roads, railways, and telephone systems are outdated, creating massive hurdles for investors and traders. The underdeveloped banking, financial, accounting, and data-collecting systems inhibit foreign investment and trade.

Two state banks, the Agroprombank and Promstroibank, dominate banking activity in the industrial sector, and the National Bank for

Foreign Economic Activity continues to channel the flow of foreign exchange.

A Republican Stock Exchange, a National Share Depository, and a National Investment Fund were set up in 1994.

## 7 Industrial Restructuring

Insider ownership of large factories and the political risks of large-scale labor layoffs have prevented the initiation of bankruptcy procedures. Budgetary support of factories has continued.

## *Vietnam*

### 1 Main Features of the Transition Reforms and Their Outcomes

Under the *doi moi* (renovation) reforms, which began in 1989, price controls were largely phased out and the distortionary dual price system was laid to rest.

The budget deficit was reduced via a cutback of government expenditure (with revenue remaining constant) of 6 percent between 1989 and 1991.

The authorities controlled inflation by dramatically raising the lending rate on bank loans above the level of inflation (to 9 percent per month in the spring of 1989, when inflation was about 7 percent), and deposit rates to an even higher level.

They also unified the various controlled exchange rates in 1989 and devalued the unified rate to the level prevailing in the parallel market. This implied a 73 percent real devaluation which, combined with the relaxed administrative procedures for imports and exports, increased the profitability of exporting.

Prior to 1989, external trade was monopolized by a small number of state trading companies. This system was liberalized first by allowing competition among state trading companies and later, by letting private firms engage in trade via quota allotments and import shipment licenses from the Ministry of Foreign Trade. As a result of the stabilizaton measures, inflation declined from 400 percent in 1989 to 72.5 percent in 1991 and 14.5 percent in 1994, rising to 19.8 percent in 1995. GDP growth of 6.3 percent in 1991 had steadily gone up to 9.5 percent in 1996. The budget deficit, which had ranged between 5 to 10 percent of GDP in 1985–1989, was down to 3.3 percent in 1994.

During most of 1989–1994, export growth averaged more than 25 percent per annum, driven by rice and energy (oil and coal) exports.

Liberal FDI policies have promoted substantial foreign investment from ASEAN neighbors (from which Vietnam imports) into manufacturing (oil and tourism in the early years), which has been the leading source of exports in recent years.

## 2  The Foreign Trade Regime

Import restrictions, in order of decreasing transparency, include tariffs, reference prices, excise taxes, quotas, and import licenses (Kokko and Zejan, 1996). The tariff structure currently includes 28 rates ranging from 0 to 100 percent. The average tariff rate is 15 to 20 percent. However, two-fifths of imports, according to the Ministry of Foreign Trade, are subject to rates of 40 percent or higher. Again, tariffs on several goods are levied on reference prices (which are set at higher levels than the c.i.f. prices declared by importers) to counter under-invoicing of imports. Excise taxes, which are levied on imports (at times to counter reduction of import tariffs) also prevail.

The import legislation remains cumbersome: Occasionally, finished products are protected at higher rates than intermediate items, resulting in large and inefficient effective protection. In other cases, the rates are higher on intermediate than on final products, creating negative protection for assembly line operations. The tariff code needs to be simplified before vested interests develop a stake in retaining the current arrangements.

The Agreement with the European Union concluded in 1995 is expected to increase trade with the EU. The normalization of diplomatic relations with Washington also improved prospects for trade and investment flows from the United States. Of greater significance in this regard is Vietnam's entry as a seventh member of the Association of South East Asian Nations (ASEAN) in July 1995. Vietnam has been given a ten-year grace period during which it must moderate tariffs and eliminate trade restrictions. A year later, Vietnam asked to join APEC, the Asia Pacific Economic Co-operation forum, the eighteen-member group formed in 1989 to promote regional trade.

## 3  The Foreign Exchange Regime

The foreign exchange arrangements had three phases. The exchange rate was allowed to devalue during 1990 and 1991 in line with the moderate inflation. In 1992, the authorities pegged the currency against the dollar to bring inflation from the 70 percent range to single digits. Thus, the real exchange rate appreciated as inflation was brought under control in 1992.

By early 1993, the fixed exchange rate was abandoned in favor of a crawling peg policy (of allowing the exchange rate to devalue in line with domestic inflation) because inflation was brought under control. (The authorities did not have enough foreign exchange reserves to support the "anchor" for long.) The resulting real appreciation affected export competitiveness negatively.

## 4  Currency Convertibility

The dong is convertible for current account transactions. Exporters, however, are not allowed to keep foreign exchange abroad and must surrender it at the market rate of exchange by depositing it in local banks. Foreign investors can repatriate profits freely. Vietnamese citizens are not allowed to open foreign exchange accounts abroad.

## 5  Foreign Direct Investment

FDI has taken place in joint ventures with state-owned enterprises in protected sectors of the economy such as heavy industry, transport and communications, financial services, and distribution of agricultural inputs and products. Hong Kong and Taiwan have remained the top investors. However, investment projects actually undertaken have remained far below committed amounts, at about 20 percent by 1995. In fact, about 12 percent of licensed FDI during 1988–1993 was subsequently withdrawn.

While foreign investors were initially attracted to Vietnam by low wages and investment incentives, they have subsequently faced high costs arising from delays, conflicting rules and bureaucratic snafus, and shortages of essential services such as water and power.

Irreconcilable differences with domestic partners have been pushing foreign investors to search for wholly owned ventures. Indeed, some have pulled away from planned high-profile investments: A French company scuttled a $1.2 billion oil refinery project on account of disagreement over where to locate it; an Australian group abandoned plans to develop port facilties in Ho Chi Minh City after protracted negotiations; and two Japanese companies pulled out of prospective funding of a supermarket and a steel plant because the Vietnamese side felt they offered too little investment.

In October 1995, the Vietnamese National Assembly approved the merger of the State Committee for Co-operation and Investment (SCCI) and the State Planning Committee (SPC) with the aim of improving the investment climate in the economy.

## 6 The Institutional Infrastructure

Much time and effort are needed to push a project requiring approval by a meddlesome bureaucracy through a maze of overlapping legislation.

The banking system consists of the State Bank of Vietnam, four state-owned commercial banks (which specialize in trade, development, industry, and agriculture), about fifty private, joint-stock banks, and three foreign, joint-venture banks. Branches or representative offices of sixty foreign financial institutions also operate in Vietnam. Two hundred credit cooperative banks and credit funds serve the financial needs of the rural areas.

However, the state banks lack strict auditing and most of the joint-stock banks are undercapitalized or insolvent. There is a fledgling bond market, but no stock exchange. A secondary market for government securities does not exist. The rural population prefers to keep its savings at home, in foreign currencies or in precious metals. The underdeveloped financial system is not geared to cope with the demands of a growing economy.

## 7  Industrial Restructuring

A major disincentive for Western, market-oriented investors arises from the fact that the bulk of the economy remains publicly owned and government controlled. Only 3 out of an estimated 6,000 state-owned enterprises have been privatized. Investors are also discouraged by 1995 legislation that prevents private ownership of land. State ownership, however, has not daunted ASEAN entrepreneurs from investing in Vietnamese industry.

## *China*

## 1   Main Features of the Transition Reforms and Their Outcomes

When Deng Xiaoping launched reforms in China in 1978, the economy did not have a macroeconomic stabilization problem internally (marked by huge budget deficits) or externally (evidenced in balance of payments deficits). Rather, the problem was lack of microeconomic incentives to households, farms, and factories under the Maoist planned system.

The Deng reforms provided these incentives to farm households during (1978–1984) by virtually dismantling the communes (1979–1981), allowing the households to lease their plots from the state and sell part of their outputs at fixed prices to state procurement agencies and the remainder at market prices in nonstate outlets. Again, town and village administrations were allowed to set up township and village enterprises (TVEs) for the production and sale of manufactured items outside the state plan.

The planners also sought to promote industrial efficiency by giving greater autonomy to state factories to set contract prices, select their inputs and outputs, and pay a corporate tax to the state in place of the earlier automatic contribution of profits to the state budget. This measure, the counterpart of the family household responsibility system in the farms, has failed because these factories have continued receiving support from the budget, which in turn has strained effective budgetary management.

The overall budget surplus of the pre-1978 years was beginning to turn into deficit, which exceeded 10 percent of GDP beginning in 1990. Bud-. getary support, overt and covert, to unviable state enterprises amounted to 3.5 percent of GDP. (For most of 1978–1994, however, inflation remained below an annual 10 percent because the deficit was financed partly by an inflation tax on houeshold savings, in the form of bank deposits, which had evidently climbed from 30 percent of GDP in the 1980s to 40 percent by 1994.)

The fiscal problem in turn was exacerbated over time by the inability of the People's Bank of China (PBC) to impose credit controls and reserve requirements on the banking system, which has operated with substantial excess reserves and has generously responded to the demand for loans. The provincial banks, in fact, are linked to the provincial governments. Since the 1980s, reserve requirements and administered interest rates have become monetary tools, though both have limited effectiveness.

Price decontrol—a necessary policy tool that (combined with fiscal and monetary discipline) can promote microeconomic efficiency—has proceeded haltingly in China. Farm product prices were freed in 1985, followed by decontrol of several manufactured consumer goods in 1988. At that time, however, a two-tier price system was introduced for critical inputs, among them steel, crude oil, cement, coal, and rail transport. Factories bought and sold at official prices for state quotas, but transacted at market prices beyond these amounts. The system promoted distortions penalizing and rewarding factories at random, and led to corruption. Most prices were raised in January 1991, and the dual system was abolished for cement.

In the realm of foreign trade planning, the initial import-substitution policy was abandoned in 1978 in favor of an "open door" orientation marked by gradual relaxation of trade and exchange rate arrangements: Provincial and local administrations (as well as Foreign Trade Organizations or FTOs) were allowed more freedom to retain foreign exchange, set up special economic zones, and attract foreign investment—especially from nearby Hong Kong, which, after an initial trickle, turned into large flows beginning 1991.

The outcome of the policies has been impressive GDP growth and export performance respectively of 9 percent and 14 percent annually from 1978 to 1994. The remarkable growth of new industry in the coastal regions assisted by FDI flows has reduced the share of the moribund state sector. However, the real GDP growth rates have fluctuated in the 1990s (having declined from 11.9 percent in 1994 to 10.2 percent in 1995), and inflation control remains a major battle for policy makers: The consumer price index had jumped by 21 percent in 1994 and by a lower but still large 14.8 percent in 1995. The 1996 growth rate is forecast at a "low" 8.9 percent, the result of strict curbs on fixed-asset investment that began in 1993.

## 2 The Foreign Trade Regime

Chinese trade liberalization has implied gradual freeing of commodity groups from trade restrictions and an enhanced role for provincial and local authorities in foreign trade planning. For at least thirty years (1948–1978), trade policy was shaped by the goal of import substitution.

Foreign trade management during this phase was "import driven": export levels were determined by import targets. The State Planning Commission and the Ministry of Foreign Trade set specific import and export targets. The FTOs sold the exports and bought the imports at domestic prices in types and quantities specified by the plan. Since the yuan was overvalued, the domestic-price revenues of the FTOs from exports did not offset the costs of imports in yuan. The difference was covered by government subsidies to the FTOs at the levels that implemented the import targets. Thus, the foreign exchange rate played no role in equalizing demands and supplies of foreign exchange.

With the announcement of the "open door" policy in 1979, trade policies and practices began to be relaxed. Branch offices of the old FTOs operated independently, provincial and ministerial FTOs proliferated, and provinces and enterprises were allowed to retain part of their foreign exchange earnings. "Restricted" imports were under the control of the Ministry of Foreign Economic Relations and Trade (MOFERT), but "unrestricted" imports could be imported by ministerial and provincial as well as MOFERT FTOs. Quantitative controls were eliminated for about 35 percent of imports in 1984. A system of duties and licenses for both exports and imports was introduced beginning in 1980.

The 1988 reform reduced the coverage of the mandatory plan and priority plan exports. The national FTOs and provincial administrations also entered into three-year contracts with MOFERT in regard to their export targets, the share of foreign exchange to be handed to the central government, and the center's commitment to covering their export losses with subsidies. In 1991, the contracts were converted into annual agreements that were to be developed in negotiations with enterprises and provincial authorities.

Some imports continued to be canalized through specific FTOs and licenses in 1995. (Licensing applied to a quarter of imports in 1992.) Specific import controls were also used for protecting domestic industry. Finally, import tariff rates in early 1996 were among the highest in the world and were distinguished by their high variance.

On April 1 1996, the average (unweighted) tariff rate was reduced from 35.9 percent to 23 percent on about 5,000 items including 380 agricultural products. One third of import quotas were scrapped. (Quotas were, however, retained on thirty-four agricultural items.) The new tariff rates varied from 3 percent on aircraft engines to 50 percent on bicycles, hi-fi systems, and radios, and 100 percent on autos, cigarettes, and alcohol. The tariff cuts, which were higher on raw materials in short supply and on high-tech items than on manufactured goods, were designed to benefit domestic producers of the latter. At the same time, the cuts were not large enough to compensate Foreign Funded Enterprises (FFEs) for the removal of the tax exemption on their capital-equipment imports, thereby pushing up start-up costs of new projects. Despite the cuts, China's tariffs have remained higher, more numerous, and more dispersed than those of other large developing countries.

China's entry into the WTO has been in limbo and has awaited resolution of a number of issues relating to its slow pace of trade liberalization, less than satisfactory market access to partner countries, weak enforcement of market access agreements, and copyright abuses.

## 3   The Foreign Exchange Regime

China had a dual exchange rate regime during 1986–93. The official rate was adjusted periodically. A market-determined rate was set in the swap centers. Domestic enterprises and FTOs were required to surrender their export earnings at the official exchange rate. However, they received a fraction of their export earnings as retention quotas, which entitled the owner to repurchase foreign exchange at the official exchange rate. They could also trade the quotas in the swap market where the exchange rate was depreciated.

This scheme was liberalized in February 1991: Domestic exporters were reimbursed for most exports at the swap market rate for 70 to 80 percent of their export earnings. About 80 percent of trade transactions took place at swap market rates in 1993.

The retention quotas, which involved the official exchange rate, were abolished in April 1994 except for FFEs. Thus, Chinese firms were allowed to buy and sell foreign exchange freely. The retention quotas for FFEs were removed in July 1996, enabling them to deal in foreign exchange with commercial banks at the market rate of exchange. In sum, by mid-1996, Chinese and foreign banks could undertake current account transactions (including profit and capital repatriation by foreign firms) at a single, market-determined rate.

A unified exchange rate to be determined in an interbank market was introduced on January 1, 1994. The People's Bank of China announces a reference rate at the start of each trading day (based on the weighted average of the buying and selling rates of the yuan against the dollar at the close of the previous day), and buys and sells foreign exchange to maintain the reference rate within 0.3 percent on either side of the reference rate. Twelve major cities were linked with the China Foreign Exchange Trading System (CFETS) in Shanghai on April 1, 1994. Domestic financial institutions can buy and sell foreign currency in CFETS on their own account, and foreign banks can use brokers for the purpose.

China's foreign exchange reserves were estimated at $81 billion in March 1996.

## 4   Currency Convertibility

Domestic enterprises must sell foreign exchange earnings from sales abroad to designated financial institutions. By contrast, FFEs can retain all their foreign exchange earnings and deposit them in banks, but must obtain approval from the State Administration for Exchange Control (SAEC) for purchases and sales of foreign exchange. Importers can purchase foreign exchange for trade not subject to quotas, licensing, or automatic registration by presenting commercial invoices or bills. It can be purchased for controlled imports only with appropriate approvals.

Foreign investors can repatriate profits abroad.

Chinese citizens can buy (and sell) foreign exchange and deposit it in local banks.

## 5  Foreign Direct Investment

China's policy makers discarded the strict limits against DFI in 1978. They opened up the economy to foreign investors in 1979 (by enacting the Foreign Investment Law) in four Special Economic Zones (SEZs) in Guangdong and Fujian provinces, which had transportation links to the outside world and connections with overseas Chinese. Decisions in regard to investment, land use, labor policies, finance, taxation, and foreign trade were left to the jurisdiction of local administrations. Foreign investors also enjoyed lower income taxes and tax holidays.

FDI response until 1985, however, was low ($0.5 billion a year, rising to $1.5 billion annually in 1984–1985) because of bureaucratic red tape, poor infrastructure, and a shortage of skilled labor. The overheated economy in the final years also discouraged outside investors.

New measures were introduced and old arrangements were liberalized in the late 1980s. FFEs could deal in foreign exchange in the newly opened foreign exchange swap markets; fully owned foreign enterprises could be set up outside SEZs; indiscriminate levies on foreign enterprises were reduced; foreign investors who stepped into high-tech, exportable industries received higher tax incentives.

Deng Xiaoping's tour of the southern coastal areas in January 1992 gave a further boost to the process. Almost all major cities and provincial capitals set up their open development zones with a variety of tax incentives and local concessions. Consequently, FDI during 1992–1994 amounted to $72 billion, exceeding more than three times the cumulative amount of 1979–1991. The special zones accounted for 20 percent of China's exports in 1995.

In 1995, FFEs continued to be approved and monitored by the Ministry of Foreign Trade and Economic Cooperation or the SAEC. FFEs that created exports or foreign exchange, brought in new technologies, and developed infrastructure were readily approved and received incentives if they were located in the open economic zones. These incentives consisted of lower income and trade taxes, and input costs. Toward the end of 1995, foreign-funded joint ventures paid 15 percent corporate tax in China's special economic zones, 24 percent in some areas "open" for investment, and 30 percent elsewhere. (Chinese state enterprises paid tax at 55 percent.)

By early 1996, the FDI guidelines had begun emphasizing participation in infrastructure development and in China's hinterland. The tax benefits were being phased out. The authorities were becoming choosier.

A special feature of FDI flows in China is the dominance of Hong Kong and Macau, which provided 54 percent of the flows in 1995 in contrast to 8 percent each by Japan, Taiwan, and the United States.

## 6   The Institutional Infrastructure

The arrangements to attract FDI, which apply to numerous zones and include various concessions, are codified in 500 pieces of legislations, which do not, however, specify the exact rules to be implemented by different authorities. They are therefore carried out differently from one region to another, contributing to delays and arbitrariness.

The financial and physical infrastructure are inadequate for the requirements of a rapidly growing economy.

## 7   Industrial Restructuring

There is no progress on privatizing and restructuring the state sector in industry, which is heavily overmanned and subsidized via budgetary outlays.

### India

## 1   Main Features of the Transition Reforms and Their Outcomes

For over three and half decades, India's import substitution industrialization development strategy was marked by investment in capital and intermediate goods (rather than consumer goods), a dominating investment and production role for the government rather than private industry in these sectors, and regulation of private sector decisions on capital formation and foreign trade through quantity controls rather than market instruments.

The policy makers responded to the frequent balance of payments crises by adjusting the policy mix to deal with the immediate problem: Thus it sought to overcome the lack of foreign exchange (for financing machinery imports for investment) during the second and third plans (1956–65) by licensing the use of foreign exchange, relying on foreign aid, and introducing export incentives. It tried overcoming stagnant agricultural production during 1966–68 by introducing the green revolution technology. When higher oil prices created an acute balance of payments crisis in 1974, it increased investment in the oil sector. It liberalized imports of raw materials, then of capital goods and high-tech items to boost capacity utilization and growth of output in industry during 1974–84. But throughout the ups and downs, it continued the policies of regulating domestic investment and imports through direct controls until the 1990/91 (fiscal year April 1 to March 31) balance of payments crisis.

The economy's performance for over three decades was marked by a low but accelerating real growth rate of GNP, from annual 3.4 percent during 1969–73 to 5.6 percent during 1985–89; low inflation rates (between 6 and 8 percent except during the destabilizing oil crisis of 1980–84); accelerating government budget deficit, which climbed from 5.6 percent of GNP in 1969–73 to 11.7 percent in 1985–89. Fixed investment had gone up from 15.1 percent of GNP in 1969–73 to 21.9 percent during 1985–89.

The foreign exchange crisis of 1990/91 was caused by a steep rise in the price of oil and the susbsequent withdrawal from Indian banks of foreign exchange deposits by nonresident Indians. By March 1991, India's foreign exchange reserves could finance an import bill of only three weeks.

The new government, elected in July 1991, agreed with the IMF to reduce the budget deficit from 8.4 percent of GDP in 1990/91 to 5.7 percent in 1992/93; to eliminate government control of foreign trade and foreign exchange management; and in fact, to reduce its direct role in investment activity by allowing private industry to step into sectors that had been reserved for the public sector.

It abolished government licensing requirements for setting up factories and expanding them, for locating industry, and for selecting material use. It raised foreign equity participation, earlier restricted to 40 percent, to 51 percent. It opened up the infrastructure sector for investment by private (including foreign) investors.

The exchange rate was unified and devalued by 50 percent in June 1991. Controls on imports of intermediate and capital goods were eliminated, though they remain on some consumer goods imports. Import tariffs were gradually reduced from a maximum of 400 percent to 55 percent.

As a result, real GDP growth averaged 4.3 percent each in 1992/93 and 1993/94 and 5.3 percent in 1994/95. Export growth was up 22.2 percent in 1993/94 and 17 percent in 1994/95. Foreign exchange reserves of $21.5 billion by the end of 1995 were worth eight months of imports. However, the budget deficit of the entire government was large, 11.9 percent in 1993/94. The post–1996-election government has announced plans to trim the fiscal deficit within five years from 5.9 percent of of GDP in 1995/96 to 4 percent within five years.

## 2   The Trade Regime

Indian trade liberalization has proceeded on three fronts.

First, intermediate and capital goods can be imported without a license. However, licenses are required for imports of consumer goods and agricultural commodities. In 1995, the government allowed free imports of more commodities, among them pulses, sugar, edible oil, butter oil, and skimmed milk powder. Again, the Special Import License (SIL) scheme, which allows importers to buy an import license from exporters (to whom it is given as a proportion of their exports), was liberalized to include more manufactured consumer goods (from 42 to 75). The import duty on the liberalized consumer goods is 50 percent.

Second, 1995 also witnessed enhanced export incentives. The Export Promotion Capital Goods (EPCG) arrangements are extended to the service sector. (Exporters who promise to export four times the c.i.f. value of capital goods imports from the date of issue of the import license can import capital goods at a concessional tariff of 15 percent.)

Finally, import tariffs have been slashed and the tariff structure rationalized. The maximum tariff rate was lowered from 300 percent in 1990–91 to 65 percent at the start of 1994–95. Successive tariff reductions brought down the average import-weighted tariff from 87 percent in 1990/91 to 27 percent in 1994/95. The 1995 tariff structure is less dispersed because peak rates have been lowered to 50 percent and duties on a variety of industrial inputs and raw materials have been reduced. Specific duties have been abolished.

In December 1994, the government signed Market Access in Textiles agreements with the European Union and the United States, allowing a phased access of the Indian market for textile imports.

In March 1996, the government lifted more import licenses, from a total of 190 items.

## 3   The Foreign Exchange Regime

The Reserve Bank of India (RBI) intervenes in the foreign exchange market to maintain a stable nominal exchange rate of the rupee against the dollar.

In 1994 and 1995, the RBI bought excess foreign exchange to prevent the surpluses in the capital account from causing the nominal and real exchange rates to appreciate, thereby reducing the export growth. At the same time, the RBI also announced new measures to reduce the inflow of foreign exchange with a view to reining in its impact on money supply and the inflation rate. Thus, Indian firms could raise money abroad only for physical investment projects and could bring it in for a definite use. It made the foreign exchange deposits by nonresident Indians less attractive by raising the deposit time limit.

In early 1996, the RBI sold foreign exchange to prevent the rupee from depreciating and the momentum of the reform process from deteriorating as a result of a weakening currency. As a result, however, massive amounts of rupees were sucked out of the banking system, forcing the RBI to undertake countermeasures such as lowering the cash reserve ratio of commercial banks to ease the liquidity crisis.

## 4  Currency Convertibility

The Indian rupee is fully convertible for all current account transactions. Foreign investors can readily repatriate their profits.

In view of the substantial foreign exchange reserves, the rules governing the repatriation of foreign exchange earnings from exports have been gradually relaxed. So are the rules governing investment by Indian companies abroad.

Capital account controls continue for Indian citizens. They cannot convert rupees into foreign exchange for deposit or investment abroad. The foreign exchange allowances for travel abroad have been liberalized.

## 5  Foreign Direct Investment

The Indian FDI regime is crawling toward the hospitable environment of open economies. FDI was a mere trickle of less than a billion dollars in 1995.

A decisive turnaround resulted from the amendment of the Foreign Exchange Regulation Act (FERA) in 1993 that removed discrimination between firms with foreign equity and wholly owned Indian companies. As a result, an established foreign investor can invest in a given activity on the same terms as an Indian investor. Again, profits can be remitted abroad without restrictions. However, foreign shareholding cannot exceed 49 percent. Foreigners cannot hold government securities, and can acquire private stock only in the illiquid secondary market.

Joint ventures (with equity participation of 49 percent) and consortia of foreign and domestic companies can participate in the basic and cellular telephone services in twenty regional "circles." FDI in electricity generation has been hampered by limited access to the final market for electricity and the shaky finances of State Electricity Boards with whom a foreign investor may have to collaborate. The RBI automatically approves foreign investment in mining, with a maximum 50 percent equity participation. Such approval is readily granted also in drugs and pharmaceuticals, with a maximum 51 percent foreign participation. A number of drugs have been exempted from price control.

The post–1996-election government announced measures in June 1996 that eased conditions for external borrowing by Indian companies in infrastructure investment. These are aimed at raising $50 billion from all sources in the next five years. As a result, financial and manufacturing companies can raise funds through global depository receipts or foreign-currency-denominated convertible bonds to finance infrastructure investment.

## 6  The Institutional Infrastructure

The financial sector reform, which began in 1992, is designed to regulate capital markets, strengthen commercial bank balance sheets, and deregulate the credit market.

The Securities and Exchange Board of India (SEBI) was established in 1992 with authority to regulate the capital market. Companies can raise capital without prior approval. There are no restrictions at present on bonus issues. Stocks and bonds can be traded on screen-based trading on the National Stock Exchange since June 1994. SEBI has substantial powers to regulate and impose penalties on participants for violations. Brokers are subject to strict guidelines announced by the RBI in March 1995.

Nineteen "nationalized" commercial banks received capital infusion of $3.3 billion in 1994 from the government in exchange for strict financial performance. Some of them have subsequently borrowed from the equity market and become partially private. The improved balance sheets of the banking system prompted the government to deregulate lending rates.

Thus, interest rates on bank loans exceeding Rs. 200,000 ($6,400) were set free in October 1994. Interest rates on smaller, priority loans (for example, in the agricultural sector) and deposit rates continue to be fixed.

In sum, the government's ability to manage a monetary policy and public debt via open market operations is in place.

## 7  Industrial Restructuring

Little progress is evident in privatizing the massive public sector. The closure of sick units is embroiled in procedural wrangles and court battles. Retrenchment, retraining, and retirement of the excess workforce in unviable units is at a standstill. Finally, viable public sector units can be privatized only up to 49 percent of their equity, leaving them in charge of insiders and government bureaucrats.

## Notes

This Introduction was presented at the Davis Center for Russian Studies, the European Bank for Reconstruction and Development, the Kennedy School of Government, the London Business School, and the World Bank. I have benefited from comments of the participants in these seminars.

1. I use the expressions "transition" (of the selected countries into the world economy) and "integration" (implying their increased trade and financial linkages with the global economy) interchangeably in this chapter because the objective on which the authors focus is globalization or its synonym, integration. I should also add that I use the term "liberalization" in the conventional sense, to imply market orientation.

2. *From Plan to Market: World Development Report 1996* (hereafter the *World Development Report 1996*) links time series of annual GDP growth rates (p. 29) and of inflation rates (p. 39) from 1989 to 1995 with liberalization indices, and argues that rapid liberalization leads to quicker output turnaround and inflation control. However, it does not connect these indices with the growth rates of unemployment or of income disparity, or of real wage decline over time, thus ignoring the issue of trade-offs between a quick turnaround of output and a substantial rise in unemployment (or another misery indicator) that reforming policy makers must deal with in the short run. I address this issue at length later on.

3. As a result, the present volume differs from earlier contributions, among them Blanchard, Froot, and Sachs (1994); Bruno (1992); Bruno and Easterly (1995); CEPR (1992); Collins and Rodrik (1991); Gross and Steinherr (1995); Islam and Mandelbaum (1993); Kaminski, Wang, and Winters (1996); Lavigne (1995); Michalopoulos and Tarr (1994, 1996); Rodrik (1995); and Winters and Wang (1994). De Melo, Denizer, and Gelb (1995) and the *World Development Report 1996*, however, include some Asian countries along with several transition economies of Europe and the former Soviet Union in their analysis.

4. So is East Germany, although it is included as an important country study. The reason is that its transition is uniquely special, insofar as it was inherently tied to unification with West Germany.

5. To deal with this problem, the *World Development Report 1996* assigns weights of 0.3 each to liberalization of domestic and of external transactions, and of 0.4 to entry of new firms (p. 14). The problem, of course, is that there is no theoretically satisfactory way to arrive at such weights, and therefore a judgment-based approach, rather than the assignment of arbitrary fixed weights, may be more sensible. I have adopted this procedure in this essay, as in the case of Vietnam just discussed in the text, when I rank countries on their reform speed by weighing the five elements distinguished above. However, judging the five policy elements underlying the concept of reform speed in each case can be fairly tricky. For example, notions such as their being simultaneous run into the difficulty that they cannot be implemented simultaneously. For instance, liberalizing trade normally takes longer than freeing most prices; privatization takes even longer.

Despite these problems, the guidelines for characterizing speedy reform are more or less clear: The budget deficit, if inflationary, should be brought under control; prices, if administered and rigid, should be freed globally (except for the output of natural monopolies); the exchange rate should be unified and made convertible for current account transactions; market instruments should replace direct controls in credit allocation and foreign trade transactions; and these measures should be attempted in a policy package together and with dispatch. The six high-speed reformers in the text have come close to fulfilling these criteria.

Among the studies that discuss different aspects of reforms in transition economies, see Peck and Richardson (1991) and Lipton and Sachs (1990).

6. To claim that shock therapy was "not tried" is to obscure its failure, since the political undoing of this strategy, when attempted, was precisely the reason why gradualists such as myself argued that it would fail.

7. If the political consensus for the necessary fiscal and monetary discipline is missing, the Sachs version of shock therapy, on its prescription that inflation should be slashed by fixing the exchange rate at the start of the stabilization process, is again unworkable. Here again, I believe that the Russian developments support my position, along with that of the IMF, which has had an eclectic view on which exchange rate policy will work best in which country when stabilization from high inflation is required.

8. Another example of the wrong sort of gradualism is the Hungarian New Economic Mechanism of 1968–88, described well by Blahó and Gál in this volume. By contrast, China's gradualism on dimensions such as privatization and import liberalization, which puts China surely into the "middle-speed" group of reformers, has nonetheless been compatible with huge success in growth rates, as studied systematically by McMillan (1995a, 1995b), and McMillan and Naughton (1992), who therefore, with me, reject the view that high speed on every dimension of (say, the five) reforms is either a sufficient or a necessary condition for successful transition. Unfortunately, these issues are glossed over in the *World Development Report 1996*, which, in its uncritical enthusiasm for high-speed reforms, does not even include reference to our numerous writings.

9. Even though trade liberalization was announced by Vietnam, in reality it turned out to be slower than in the European countries; as a result, Vietnam gets a poor ranking (10, in Table 5) with respect to its trade policy regime in 1995.

10. Other indicators are suggested and discussed, but data unavailability has prevented me from using them effectively.

11. Budget deficits for the European and post-Soviet states can be found in the European Bank for Reconstruction and Development (hereafter the EBRD; 1995, 1996). Information for the Asian economies is available from World Bank and IMF reports.

12. In an apparent policy shift following Mexico's devaluation crisis, the IMF said that during times of surges in inflows, a country might consider measures to influence the level and characteristics of capital inflows, such as taxes on short-term bank deposits and restrictions on borrowing from abroad, in order to avoid problems of exchange rate appreciation, a widening current account deficit, and accelerating money and credit growth. Details are in Ito and Folkerts-Landau (1995).

13. For a similar early observation on appreciating real exchange rates, see Halpern and Wyplosz (1995).

14. For a discussion of these concepts, see Desai (1994c, 1995a).

15. Even if the unemployment rate remains low, real wages may have declined. Also, income distribution may have worsened. In the analysis that follows, I adopt the unemployment rate as a proxy for these transition costs.

16. Note that the full convertibility of the Baltic currencies, despite continuing double-digit inflation rates, resulted from their adoption of arrangements resembling currency boards. Their aspirations for independent statehood and for swift integration into the European Union (EU), a hallmark of the Baltic leadership, crystallized from the start into their policy

makers' decisions to junk the Soviet ruble, adopt fully convertible currencies, and re-create trade and investment links with the EU. For variations in their performance, see Chapter 5.

17. Later, I also rank countries according to their GDP growth and unemployment rates in 1995, and their record of inflation control (via three measures) for assessing the merits of speedy reform.

18. When I calculate the pairwise rank correlation coefficients between reform speed ranking (which I decide on the basis of the five policy variables and their implementation) and a policy outcome ranking (for example, the exchange rate regime), I avoid the problem of endogeneity by ranking all outcomes in 1995, thus defining the transition policy package exogenously with a predetermined lag.

19. The distinctions among these arrangements and their policy implications are discussed in Williamson (1996).

20. For a succinct analysis of this issue and estimates of the loss of COMECON markets to East-Central European exporters, see Rodrik (1992).

21. All economies were also part of regional arrangements of one kind or another, as shown in the Appendix and in the country analyses.

22. The ranking remains virtually the same (except that Estonia ranks ahead of Hungary, with the rest ranked identically) when the ratios are averaged over the period. Hungary, however, should remain at the top because it has complete information for the five years and therefore its high performance is more reliable.

23. Unfortunately, as the reader will recall, the trade indicators such as trade participation and trade orientation in OECD markets could not be calculated for all countries, and therefore have to be discarded for the rest of the analysis in the text.

24. It is not clear, however, that the *Report* clearly defines what "speed" means, whereas I have been at pains to emphasize its multidimensionality and hence the necessity for a proper, if judgment-based, approach to determining a country's quickness of reform in a study that seeks to draw conclusions about the efficacy of such speed. Nor does the *Report* adequately address the well-defined question of the relative merits of shock therapy and gradualism in the matter of stabilization itself, as I have already noted.

# References

Blanchard, O., K. Froot, and J. Sachs (eds.). 1994. *Transition in Eastern Europe: A NBER Project Report*. Chicago: University of Chicago Press.

Bruno, M. 1992. "Stabilization and Reform in Eastern Europe: A Preliminary Evaluation." *IMF Staff Papers*, 39, no. 4. Washington, D.C.: International Monetary Fund.

Bruno, M., and W. Easterly. 1995. *Inflation Crises and Long-Run Growth*. Policy Research Working Paper 1517. Washington, D.C.: World Bank.

Centre for Economic Policy Research (CEPR). 1992. *Monitoring European Integration: The Impact of Eastern Europe*. London: CEPR.

Collins, S., and D. Rodrik. 1991. *Eastern Europe and the Soviet Union in the World Economy*. Washington, D.C.: Institute for International Economics.

De Melo, M., C. Denizer, and A. Gelb. 1995. *From Plan to Market: Patterns of Transition.* Policy Research Working Paper. Washington, D.C.: World Bank.

Desai, P. 1994a. "No Megabucks and No Miracles: Russia and Western Aid." *European Brief,* pp. 8–9 (April/May).

Desai, P. 1994b. "Gradualism—What Makes the Reform Tick in Russia." *The World Bank Transition,* pp. 15–16 (May/June).

Desai, P. 1994c. "Aftershock in Russia's Economy." *Current History,* pp. 320–323 (October).

Desai, P. 1995a. "Beyond Shock Therapy." *Journal of Democracy,* pp. 101–111 (April).

Desai, P. 1995b. "Russian Privatization: A Comparative Perspective." *The Harriman Review,* pp. 1–34 (August).

Desai, P. 1995c. "Will 1995 Stabilize Russia's Economy?" *U.S. Relations with Russia, Ukraine and Eastern Europe.* Washington, D.C.: Aspen Institute.

European Bank for Reconstruction and Development. 1995. *Transition Report 1995, Investment and Enterprise Development: Economic Transition in Eastern Europe and the Former Soviet Union.* London: EBRD.

European Bank for Reconstruction and Development. 1996. *Transition Report Update.* London: EBRD.

Gross, D., and A. Steinherr. 1995. *Winds of Change: Economic Transition in Central and Eastern Europe.* London: Longman.

Halpern, L., and C. Wyplosz. 1995. "Equilibrium Real Exchange Rates in Transition." Discussion Paper No. 1145. CEPR (April).

Islam, S., and M. Mandelbaum. 1993. *Making Markets: Economic Transformation in Eastern Europe and the Post-Soviet States.* New York: Council on Foreign Relations.

Ito, Takatoshi, and David Folkerts-Landau. 1996. *International Capital Markets: Developments, Prospects, and Key Policy Issues.* Washington, D.C.: International Monetary Fund.

Kaminski, B., Z. K. Wang, and A. Winters. 1996. "Foreign Trade in the Transition: The International Environment and Domestic Policy." *Studies of Economies in Transformation,* 20. Washington, D.C.: World Bank.

Kokko, A., and M. Zejan. 1996. "Vietnam: At the Next Stage of Reforms." Stockholm School of Economics, April. (Mimeo).

Lavigne, M. 1995. *The Economics of Transition from Socialist Economy to Market Economy.* New York: St. Martin's Press.

Lipton, D., and J. Sachs. 1990. "Creating a Market Economy in Eastern Europe: The Case of Poland." In D. Lipton and J. Sachs (eds.), *Brookings Papers on Economic Activity,* 1: 75–147. Washington, D.C.: Brookings Institution.

McMillan, J. 1995a. "China's Nonconformist Reforms." In E. Lazear (ed.), *Economic Transition in Eastern Europe and Russia: Realities of Reform.* Stanford: Hoover Institution Press.

McMillan, J. 1995b. "Markets in Transition." Symposium address at the Seventh World Congress of the Econometric Society, Tokyo, August. Mimeo.

McMillan, J., and B. Naughton. 1992. "How to Reform a Planned Economy: Lessons from China." *Oxford Review of Economic Policy,* 8, no. 1, pp. 130–143.

Michalopoulos, C., and D. Tarr. 1996. *Trade Performance and Policy in the New Independent States*. Washington, D.C.: World Bank.

Michalopoulos, C., and D. Tarr (eds.). 1994. "Trade in the New Independent States." *Studies of Economies in Transformation*. Washington, D.C.: World Bank.

Peck, M. J., and T. J. Richardson (eds.). 1991. *What Is To Be Done? Proposals for the Soviet Transition to the Market*. New Haven: Yale University Press.

Portes, R. (ed.). 1993. *Economic Transformation in Central Europe*. London: CEPR.

Rodrik, D. 1995. "The Dynamics of Political Support for Reform in Economies in Transition." *Journal of the Japanese and International Economies*, vol. 9, No. 4, (December), pp. 403–425.

Rodrik, D. 1992. *Making Sense of the Soviet Trade Shock in Eastern Europe: A Framework and Some Estimates*. NBER Working Paper (June).

Sapir, A. 1994. "The Europe Agreements: Implications for Trade Laws and Institutions. Lessons from Hungary." Discussion Paper 1024. CEPR (September).

Williamson, J. 1995. "How to Manage Exchange Rates: Lessons from Israel, Chile and Colombia." Institute for International Economics (October).

Winters, L. A., and Z. K. Wang. 1994. *Eastern Europe's International Trade*. Manchester, U.K.: Manchester University Press.

World Bank. 1996. *From Plan to Market: World Development Report 1996*. Washington, D.C.: World Bank.

# I

# Central and East Europe

# 1                           The Czech Republic

Josef C. Brada and Ali M. Kutan

The post-1989 economic policies of Czechoslovakia and, since January 1, 1993, of the Czech Republic have been viewed by many observers as a textbook example of how to open an economy to international trade and capital flows while simultaneously achieving financial and fiscal stability and low unemployment.[1] Although criticism has been raised regarding the level of interenterprise debt; the alleged lack of restructuring, as evidenced by low levels of unemployment; the low level of real wages by international standards; and the concentrated stock ownership that emerged from the voucher privatization, these are largely microeconomic or mesoeconomic problems. In aggregate terms, the Czech Republic is seen as having gotten it right and as having done so by following the classical recipe of liberal economics. The trade regime and domestic prices were liberalized; the currency was made convertible for current account transactions and for capital inflows; a nominal anchor in the form of the exchange rate was set; and monetary and fiscal policies were implemented so as to maintain the exchange rate.

This view of Czech policies is more right than not, but any effort to draw policy lessons from the Czech experience must deal with the peculiarities of the Czech situation and also explain the paradox of a sharp output decline while unemployment remained at low levels. This effort to draw lessons from the Czech experience must also recognize that the exchange rate has not been a nominal anchor; rather, it has been set so low as to make fighting inflation a relatively secondary issue. Finally, it must be recognized that the policies adopted have had some costs.

## 1.1  Background and Liberalization Measures

### 1.1.1  Starting Conditions

The government that assumed power in Czechoslovakia at the end of 1989, in the wake of the "velvet revolution," faced the same fundamental challenges of transition that confronted governments in other formerly Communist countries in the region, although, as is to be expected, the mix of positive and negative environmental factors faced by Czechoslovak policy makers was somewhat different from that faced by policy makers in other countries of the region.

**Advantages**
Czechoslovak policy makers inherited a number of positive economic legacies from their Communist predecessors as well as from the pre-World War II period. In addition, the country had geographic, political, and social advantages that have played an important role in the successful implementation of transformation and stabilization policies.

*Macroeconomic Equilibrium.*  Unlike neighboring Poland and Hungary, not to mention the USSR, in the 1980s Czechoslovakia enjoyed considerable macroeconomic stability. Neither government deficits nor growth of the money stock was high during the decade (Drábek et al., 1994, Fig. 1). With the exception of 1982, inflation, as measured by the Consumer Price Index, did not exceed 3 percent per year, and wages did not grow faster than labor productivity. Thus, with the share of investment in national income eroding from 26 percent in 1980 to 16.5 percent in 1989, the general assessment is that the picture of macroeconomic equilibrium painted by the official data was not far off from the true picture.[2] Trade with developed market economies was balanced and a gross hard currency debt of $7.9 billion was being serviced without evident difficulty.[3]

These favorable macroeconomic conditions were of inestimable benefit to policy makers. First, the post-November 1989 government had the luxury of being able to move slowly, since the policy status quo could safely be maintained while conflicts over reform and stabilization measures were resolved. Indeed, the new regime not only could avoid stabilization measures, but it even appeared to benefit from delaying such measures as the 1990 consolidated budget moved toward a slight surplus without drastic changes in tax and expenditure policies. Second, with internal and external equilibrium more or less secure, the dangers inherent in the liberalization of domestic markets and of foreign trade were much less than in countries where fears of inflationary spirals and the loss of international reserves were serious future possibilities at best and current crises at worst. Moreover, macroeconomic stability meant that reform measures such as price or trade liberalization could be focused toward microeconomics or relative price effects rather than having to do double duty as stabilization measures as well.[4]

A final advantage in the realm of macroeconomic management was the attitude of the public toward price stability and fiscal conservatism. The country's population has had a historic aversion to inflation, and thus retaining price stability in the post-Communist period was a politically popular course. Moreover, the experience of the Polish liberalization of 1990, Hungary's budgetary problems of that year, and the USSR's slide into financial chaos were viewed by the Czech population as solid arguments for fiscal and financial rectitude. In 1992, the claims of the government sector on credit were very small, ranging from 2.9 to 8.5 percent of total domestic credit issued.

***Lack of Economic Reforms.***   The reluctance of the Husák regime to institute any significant economic reforms in the 1970s and 1980s, and to keep the Czechoslovak economy firmly oriented toward the Council for Mutual Economic Assistance (CMEA), also provided a number of positive legacies. First, neither labor unions nor informal workers' movements were important sources of political and economic power after the velvet revolution. Thus there was little organized-labor pressure to lobby for higher wages or for employment-saving subsidies when the transition began. Moreover, the Czechoslovak labor movement did not achieve the kind of independent political role that Solidarity did in Poland.

Equally important was the fact that ownership and control over enterprises had remained firmly in state hands. Therefore Czechoslovak managers enjoyed greater autonomy over enterprises than did, for example, their Polish counterparts, who were subject to control by workers' councils and by labor unions in setting the strategic responses of their firms to the newly emerging market economy (Estrin et al., 1995). This managerial autonomy resulted in a greater willingness and ability of Czechoslovak firms to respond to new conditions and opportunities. Privatization was accelerated because there were fewer obstacles to the use of vouchers for mass privatization. No doubt, the voucher privatization implemented in Czechoslovakia might have met the same fate as Polish privatization proposals had workers' councils been active in Czechoslovakia, just as

Czechoslovak reformers might have steered toward the more time-consuming process of selling enterprises to foreign investors had the fiscal situation been as bad as it was in Hungary.

The CMEA orientation of the Husák regime also facilitated the implementation of a number of policy measures, particularly the sharp devaluation of the koruna. Neither the population's holdings of hard currency in official accounts nor the share of Western goods in the total supply of consumer goods was very significant. Thus, the consequences of devaluation for the population's holdings of domestic and foreign currency did not play the large role in determining the international value of the koruna that they played in deliberations about the value of the Hungarian forint (Blue Ribbon Commission, 1992). With access to Western consumer goods so restricted before the fall of the Communist regime, there was no large consumer lobby to protest against the price increases implicit in the devaluation of the koruna. Indeed, it may be argued that if the pre-revolution implicit quotas on imports of consumer goods are factored in, then, even with a sharp devaluation, the effective price of Western goods fell from the viewpoint of consumers. This was much less the case in Hungary and Poland, whose markets had been penetrated by Western consumer goods to a much greater extent, thus giving consumers a higher stake in keeping the price of imported consumer goods low.

*High Level of Industrialization.* While all East European countries were to some extent deformed by Communist-era industrialization strategies, Czechoslovakia, and especially the Czech lands, had undergone extensive industrialization by the pre-World War II period. This market-based industrialization created a population of firms that was perhaps more diverse in size and product assortment than those in countries where more of the growth of industry was the result of Communist gigantomania. Although the existence of these relatively small firms was masked by means of administrative amalgamations of many establishments into single administrative units, the physical, as opposed to organizational, structure of Czech firms nevertheless resulted in more diversified local industrial bases than was the case, for example, in Slovakia, where towns and villages were economically dominated by the large single-product enterprises located in their vicinity.

*Location and Infrastructure.* The Czechoslovak Republic clearly benefited from its common borders with the Federal Republic of Germany and with Austria. Although rail lines and roads were not strongly oriented toward these markets, adjustments were relatively easy and inexpensive to make. Thus distance and the need to transit through third countries were not barriers in Czechoslovakia's trade with its two principal developed-country markets.

A further, partly geographic and partly historical, element was the city of Prague, which, by virtue of its location and intrinsic appeal as a tourist attraction, became a major international tourist destination with important positive consequences, not only for the balance of payments and for the expansion of the tourist and service industries but also for construction, food processing, and agriculture. Moreover, the benefits of this tourist boom extended beyond Prague.

## Disadvantages

*Economic Stagnation.* As Table 1.1 shows, the 1980s were years of stagnation for the Czechoslovak economy. Despite capital deepening in industry, output grew slowly, especially toward the end of the decade, as did national income. In part, the deceleration was the result of declining demand for Czechoslovak manufactures, especially by the USSR, whose imports from Czechoslovakia declined steadily after 1987. The deceleration was met largely by reducing the share of investment in output so as to maintain the living standard of the population.

**Table 1.1**
Growth rates of main economic indicators for Czechoslovakia, 1980–89 (percent)

| Year | Industry | | | National income produced | Exports to USSR* |
|------|----------|--------------|--------|--------------------------|------------------|
|      | Employment | Capital stock | Output |                          |                  |
| 1980 | 0.7 | 5.8 | 1.7 | 2.9 | — |
| 1981 | 0.6 | 5.5 | 2.0 | −0.1 | 15.7 |
| 1982 | 0.4 | 5.9 | 1.0 | 0.2 | 17.4 |
| 1983 | 0.4 | 4.6 | 2.9 | 2.2 | 12.1 |
| 1984 | 0.5 | 5.2 | 3.8 | 3.5 | 14.2 |
| 1985 | 0.5 | 5.1 | 3.6 | 3.0 | 5.4 |
| 1986 | 0.5 | 5.8 | 3.5 | 2.6 | 1.2 |
| 1987 | 0.0 | 5.2 | 2.5 | 2.1 | 2.3 |
| 1988 | 0.1 | 5.2 | 1.6 | 2.3 | −2.4 |
| 1989 | −0.6 | 4.2 | 0.8 | 0.7 | −11.1 |

*Source:* Federalní Statistický Uřad, *Statistická Ročenka ČSFR* (various years).
*Note:* *Nominal, at current exchange rate.

The costs of reducing the share of GDP devoted to capital formation were an aging capital stock, an inadequate infrastructure, and a lack of structural change.[5] Indeed, whether measured in terms of employment or of value added, the Czechoslovak industrial branch structure of 1989 was virtually the same as that of 1980. Only the machinery, electrical machinery, and transport equipment branches were able to increase their share of industrial value added or employment by more than one percentage point over the decade (OECD, 1994a, Figs. 1.6, 1.7). Ironically, these sectors were among the hardest hit in the transition period, devastated by the collapse of investment, by the loss of CMEA markets, and by competition from Western products.

*Reliance on CMEA Markets.*   The political dependence on the USSR was mirrored by economic dependence on the Soviet economy, both as a source of raw materials and fuels and as a market for Czechoslovak manufactures. In view of the decline in Soviet imports after 1987 and the impending adverse shift in terms of trade and the loss of Soviet markets, Czechoslovakia was, as Table 1.2 shows, more vulnerable to trade shocks from the East than were Hungary and Poland.

Czechoslovak exporters had fewer business contacts in the West, fewer established market niches, and poorer knowledge of Western market environments and commercial practices. Therefore, the reorientation of trade would have to be greater than in other Central European countries; however, both the structure of industrial output and the commercial skills appeared to be less suitable for achieving such a reorientation.

*A Large Defense Industry.*   Under the Communist regime, defense production was expanded both geographically and in terms of product

**Table 1.2**
Central European trade with the USSR and CMEA, 1989

| Country | CMEA's share of total exports (percent) | | Exports to USSR as percent GDP |
| --- | --- | --- | --- |
| | At the bilateral commercial ruble/$ rate | At 2 rubles =$1 | |
| Czechoslovakia | 54 | 47 | 11 |
| Hungary | 39 | 40 | 8 |
| Poland | 35 | 44 | 4 |

*Source:* OECD (1994a), Table 1.2.

assortment. In the Czech lands, traditional emphasis on small-arms production was supplemented by avionics, electronics, and chemical-based products. In Slovakia, the creation of a sizable defense industry was part of the Communist development strategy, and large factories for the production of heavy armaments, tanks, jet engines, and so on were built. By 1988, military production accounted for over 4 percent of Czechoslovak net material product; in the Slovak Republic armaments production accounted for 6 percent of industrial production (OECD, 1994a, pp. 78–80). This sector would prove to be a major drag on the transforming economy, because both domestic and Warsaw Pact demand, which absorbed the bulk of production, collapsed. Adjustment and conversion of production proved difficult, with the sharp declines in activity at the large plants in Slovakia having particularly severe local impacts on employment and incomes.

***Czech-Slovak Tensions and Separatism.*** Although the Czechoslovak Republic was spared the sort of devastating interethnic conflict that shattered Yugoslavia, there were significant historical, social, and economic conflicts between Czechs and Slovaks that slowed the reform process, led to some suboptimal policies, and ultimately forced the breakup of Czechoslovakia into two independent states.[6]

**Assessment**
Overall, Czechoslovakia was probably at a disadvantage in the short run but in a better long-term position for a successful transition to capitalism than were its Central European neighbors. The advantages of macroeconomic and external equilibrium perhaps counted for less in the short run than did the advantages possessed by Poland and Hungary, both of which had an important head start in market-oriented reforms, the development of a small-business private sector, banking reform, and business and investment contacts with the West.

However, in the longer term, policy makers in Czechoslovakia and the Czech Republic have not been constrained in their choices by external indebtedness or current account deficits, by government budget deficits, or by the effects of high domestic inflation on exchange rate policy. Thus, perhaps to oversimplify somewhat, the task of policy makers in the Czech Republic has been more to avoid mistakes in macroeconomic policy that would disequilibrate the economy than to find ways of reequilibrating an overheated and deficit-plagued economy.

### 1.1.2   First Steps Toward Liberalization[7]

**Price and Wage Liberalization**

Although the Czechoslovak economy was closer to macroeconomic equilibrium than many other economies in the region, markets were subject both to some repressed inflationary pressure and to severe relative price distortions. The first liberalizing step was taken in 1990, to eliminate the large subsidies on food and on some industrial raw materials. Households were compensated for higher food prices by means of government-mandated increases in incomes, while budgetary outlays on subsidies decreased from 16 percent of GDP in 1989 to 7 percent in 1991.[8]

A comprehensive liberalization of retail and wholesale prices was implemented in January 1991. This covered goods that made up about 85 percent of GDP, and by mid-1991 goods that made up 90 percent of GDP were free. Price regulations remained largely for some rents, energy and municipal services, and utilities and products in monopolized sectors. The pattern of liberalization has been such that prices of industrial inputs and investment goods are less subject to controls than are goods and services consumed by the household sector. Thus, while perhaps less than 10 percent of GDP remains subject to price controls, perhaps as much as, or even more than, 20 percent of the household consumption basket still may be subject to either administratively determined or formula-based price ceilings.[9]

The effect of the price liberalization was an upsurge in prices of consumer goods and services, but this inflation subsided very quickly, as can be seen in Figure 1.1. By the third quarter of 1991, inflation on a quarter-on-quarter basis had fallen to only a few percent, although it accelerated in 1992:IV as a result of the anticipated breakup of the federation. There were no major regional differences in the rate of inflation.

The pattern of price decontrol, especially in 1991, had implications for foreign trade performance because the liberalization of prices was most thoroughgoing in the goods sector but much less ambitious for food and in the largely nontradable services sector, particularly for services consumed mainly by households. Without minimizing the costs of distortions caused by the underpricing of energy, a major exception to the goods–services distinction proposed here, such a pattern of price liberalization is quite advantageous for foreign trade. This is because tradables' prices are free to approach world market levels, thus leading to efficient decisions about the production and trade of these goods. On the other hand, distortions in nontradables' prices may distort micro choices regarding their

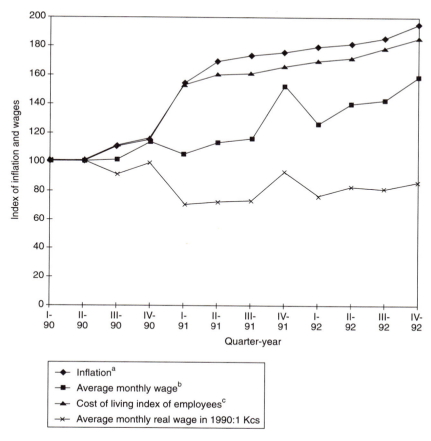

**Figure 1.1**
Inflation and wages in the Czech Republic, 1990–92 (1990 : I = 100)
*Sources:* FSU, *Statistické přehledy* (various issues); Czech Statistical Office, *Quarterly Statistical Bulletin* (2d quarter, 1993).
*Notes:*
a. Inflation is measured in terms of prices of consumer goods and services.
b. Up to 1992, based on enterprises with more than 100 employees; more than 25 employees thereafter.
c. End of quarter.

use, but they do not distort trade flows except insofar as they influence the relative prices of tradables and nontradables and the real wage. In the latter case, controls over services and smaller increases in food prices may be seen as keeping domestic wages higher relative to food and services while, through devaluation, lowering them vis-à-vis tradables.

Partly out of concern that price liberalization might set off an inflationary price–wage spiral, the rather elaborate system of wage tariffs was retained, although with some flexibility built in. The government, labor unions, and employers agreed on maximum and minimum wage changes for 1991, with a proviso that real wages not decline by more than 12 percent in the first quarter of 1991 and by no more than 10 percent in any subsequent quarter. The agreement was renewed for 1992, allowing state-owned firms to raise nominal wages by 18 percent over 1991, but the process of wage regulation was discontinued during the year. The wage controls were enforced by means of taxes levied on excessive increases. Private firms, cooperatives, and joint ventures with at least 30 percent foreign ownership were exempt from these regulations.

As Figure 1.1 indicates, nominal wage growth failed to keep up with price increases in 1991, and even in 1992, when nominal wage growth exceeded inflation, real wages remained appreciably lower than at the start of the period. What role was played by the wage controls is unclear. Reports from the Ministry of Economy suggest that few firms provided wage increases that made them subject to the tax, although this, of course, may have been due to their financial situation rather than to wage controls.

### Privatization

The privatization of state-owned assets was pursued by several means. Small businesses were privatized through small-scale privatization and restitution. This involved returning such establishments to their former owners or auctioning them to the highest bidder. The privatization of large state-owned enterprises was carried out partly by sale to new owners but mainly by means of the mass voucher privatization, the first wave of which, completed in 1992, exchanged the shares of 1,004 Czech firms with a book value of 362.2 billion koruny for vouchers that had been distributed to the population.

The large privatization had a number of consequences for foreign trade. Some of the privatized firms were sold to foreign investors, resulting in both inflows of foreign capital and the creation of business alliances that would help integrate local firms into the global economy. The latter effect was probably more important in the early phase of transition because total investment inflows into the Czechoslovale Republic were only U.S.$180 million in 1990 and U.S.$600 million in 1991, then rose to over U.S.$1 billion in 1992. These sums were considerably less than the comparable figures for Poland and Hungary.

Also important was the requirement that enterprises slated for inclusion in the voucher scheme develop a plan for privatization. One consequence of this was that a number of large state-owned firms to split into independent units in order to pursue different privatization strategies. Thus the number of very large firms decreased, and that of medium-sized ones increased (Charap and Zemplinerová, 1993), creating a more competitive atmosphere. A second important benefit of the privatization process was that it forced enterprise managers to undertake strategic thinking about their firm's future. Research on enterprise behavior in East Europe during the transition (Estrin et al., 1995; Matesová, 1993) indicates that while most firms in the region made some short-term adjustments in output and input utilization in response to changes in their environment, the ability to formulate plans for changing products, technology, markets, and marketing strategy depended critically on the existence of a credible privatization program. To the extent that such changes included responses to opportunities to enter new markets and to respond to emerging competition from imports, this sort of strategic thinking, if successful, should have strengthened foreign trade performance.

### Liberalization of the Foreign Trade and Payments System

*Convertibility.* The Czechoslovak koruna did not become convertible until January 1991, but measures for introducing convertibility were begun in 1990. The commercial (15.05 ks/$) and noncommercial (9.75 ks/$) rates were unified and the koruna was devalued to 16.5 ks/$ in January 1990. Further devaluations occurred in October, to 24 ks/$, and at year's end to 28 ks/$. In January 1991 the koruna became convertible, fixed at first to a basket of foreign currencies and then to a combination of the dollar and the deutsche mark (DM). This rate has been maintained since then.

Under the new regime, the koruna became convertible for trade transactions. Exporters had to sell their foreign exchange receipts to commercial banks, and registered firms were able to obtain foreign exchange from the banks for imports. Residents were permitted to maintain foreign exchange accounts, but households were limited to purchases of 7,500 koruny in foreign exchange per person annually. This limit was raised over time. Residents and nonresidents were treated differently for capital account purposes. Foreign investors faced no restrictions on the repatriation of profits, dividends, or principal. Czechoslovak citizens, on the other hand, could not invest abroad, and firms could do so only with the permission of the National Bank.

***Tariffs and Commercial Policy.*** Liberalizing trade flows required the destruction of old institutions and the creation of new ones. The monopoly on foreign trade of the centrally planned economy was abolished, and starting in 1991, all registered enterprises, a category that initially excluded new private firms, were given rights to engage in foreign trade. A new tariff system was also put into effect at this time. Tariff rates were relatively low, averaging about 5 percent ad valorem. At the outset, they were supplemented with a 20 percent surcharge on consumer goods imports; the surcharge was subsequently reduced to 18 percent in May 1991, 15 percent in June, 10 percent in January 1992, and finally abolished at the beginning of 1993.

Czechoslovakia also undertook a series of measures to integrate itself more effectively into the world economy. The centerpiece of this effort was the negotiation of an association agreement with the European Community (EC) in 1991, coming into effect in March 1992. The agreement called for the mutual lowering of tariffs, though in asymmetric fashion, with EC tariffs being reduced first. So-called sensitive sectors, including textiles, steel, and agricultural products, are subject to special restrictions by the EC. A similar agreement was signed with the European Free Trade Area (EFTA).

As Czechoslovakia was building its commercial ties with the West, its institutional trading ties with the members of the CMEA were dissolving. Trade with the smaller CMEA countries was increasingly placed on a hard currency clearing basis using world market prices. The collapse of trade with the USSR and with other ex-CMEA members prompted the Czechoslovak authorities to seek measures to sustain this trade. One such measure was the negotiation of the Central European Free Trade Agreement, in December 1992, with Poland and Hungary (Slay, 1994). The second, and somewhat more ad hoc, policy was to seek out barter agreements with the Soviet Union and its successor states in order to sustain certain traditional exports of manufactures and to secure the supply of certain raw materials (Brada, 1993).

## Assessment

Taken together, the liberalization measures were coherent and effective. The plan for rapid privatization through the voucher system, when announced, had a positive effect on the behavior of firms even before it was implemented. Trade liberalization and convertibility were introduced very cautiously, with a steep, possibly excessive, devaluation backed by temporary import restrictions. While observers both within Czechoslovakia (see Hrnčír, 1994) and in the West (see, e.g., Portes, 1994) have argued that the devaluation of the koruna was excessive, the short-term benefits of export stimulation and a trade surplus were undeniable. The long-term structural consequences are less clear. It is safe to conclude that a large devaluation served to reduce pressures for restructuring in industry because, with a cheap koruna, more Czech firms in a greater range of sectors were able to export on a profitable basis. The long-term costs may be that investment flows will be directed toward sectors that compete mainly on price rather than on quality, innovation, and other firm-specific advantages, thus trapping the country in a low-wage, low-skill competitive strategy. Alternatively, the return to higher wages and prices will exact the costs of structural change in the future. This, however, may be an advantage in that the deferral of some structural change to the future, when its costs can be better borne, may prove to have been a useful policy.

## 1.2   Policies and Outcomes, 1989–1992

### 1.2.1   The Domestic Economy

#### Fiscal Policy

A key decision in fiscal affairs was to attempt to maintain a balance between government outlays and revenues while simultaneously pursuing a policy of reducing the share of the government in economic activity. The 1991 budget called for a surplus of 6.4 billion koruny, and this target was almost achieved. Profit tax revenues increased quite sharply in 1991, in part because enterprise profits were overstated due to failure to account properly for the effect of inflation on inventories.[10] The government also sought to achieve a balanced consolidated budget for 1992. Spending was to be controlled by reducing subsidies to consumers and by restricting unemployment benefits. Revenues failed to grow at anticipated rates and, particularly in the Slovak Republic, expenditures on unemployment increased faster than anticipated. The Czech Republic ran a deficit of 1.7

billion koruny, the Slovak Republic, of 7.9 billion; and the federal budget had a deficit of 7 billion. There is no evidence that the swing toward a more expansionist stance had any important effect on the macroeconomic situation.

**Monetary Policy**
The banking system was reformed in 1990, with the former State Bank broken up into several commercial banks and the remnant constituted as a Western-style central bank. New private commercial banks, some foreign-owned, were established beginning in 1991. Thus the possibility of using the traditional tools of monetary policy, including the discount rate and reserve requirements, was created, although in 1990 and 1991, ad hoc measures and quantitative restrictions were the main tools of monetary policy, yielding only subsequently to indirect policy instruments. The deposit rate increased to reflect the higher rates of inflation, as did the lending rate (Dittus, 1994). Aside from the first quarter of 1991, the interest rate for borrowers was positive. Credit rationing led to a decline in the real stock of debt in 1991. The outstanding debt of enterprises to banks was marked up to the new interest rates, leading to a net flow of funds from the enterprise sector to banks. The failure to write off these old debts of the enterprises was a rather costly policy mistake. Although the burst of inflation at the beginning of 1991 reduced the real value of enterprise debts, marking up the rate of interest on this debt from 2–3 percent to levels in excess of 15 percent meant that the drain on the enterprise sector's cash flow actually increased in real terms. Moreover, the existence of this debt has continued to complicate the process of separating viable firms from unviable ones.[11]

Given the uncertainties about the effects of the various institutional changes on the demand for money and on velocity, it is difficult to gauge the effect of the tight monetary policy of 1991, or of its loosening in 1992, on output and prices. Indeed, given the large changes in monetary aggregates, real aggregates, and prices between 1990 and 1995, it is not possible either to establish the existence of a causal relationship among these variables or to parameterize it in any reliable way (Hanousek et al., 1995). In any case, the easing of monetary policy in 1992 did lead to real growth of M2. (See Table 1.3.) The real stock of debt also increased, although lending rates declined very little from 1991 levels as banks sought to build up their balance sheets, thus continuing the net flow of financial resources from the corporate to the banking sector (Dittus, 1994).

**Table 1.3**
Monetary indicators for the Czech Republic

| | 1990 | | | | 1991 | | | | 1992 | | | |
|---|---|---|---|---|---|---|---|---|---|---|---|---|
| | I | II | III | IV | I | II | III | IV | I | II | III | IV |
| Discount rate (percent) | 4.0 | 5.0 | 5.0 | 8.5 | 10.0 | 10.0 | 9.5 | 9.5 | 9.0 | 9.0 | 8.0 | 9.5 |
| M2 (percent) | | | — | | | 27.3 | | | | 22.6 | | |
| CPI (percent) | | | 10.0 | | | 57.9 | | | | 10.8 | | |
| Domestic credit (bill. Ks, end of period) | | — | — | 640.2 | 656.0 | — | — | 749.1 | 743.5 | — | — | 876.4 |

*Source:* State Bank of Czechoslovakia, *Annual Report* (1992).

## Households, Enterprises, and Macroeconomic Outcomes

The deflationary effects of policy were augmented by the behavior of households and enterprises. There was an upsurge of buying by households at the end of 1990 in anticipation of the price liberalization of January 1991, and at the end of 1992 in anticipation of the separation of the country and, more important, of the introduction of the VAT system in January 1993. After the price liberalization, consumption dropped sharply, both as a rebound from the buying spree of 1990:IV and due to a longer-term increase in the savings ratio as households sought to rebuild liquid assets.

Firms also decreased investment outlays, in part due to the CMEA shock, which influenced both capital expansion and inventory decisions, and in part to a decline in domestic demand. The data reported in Table 1.4 show a modest rise in stocks and reserves until 1992, and investment behavior that mirrored the buying behavior of households in anticipating price increases in 1991 and 1993. Moreover, it is rather surprising that fixed capital formation held up as well as it did during what was seen by many as a crisis in the enterprise sector.

The story that Table 1.4 tells about the effects of the decline in GDP is relatively straightforward. More complex, of course, is the issue of causality. Some writers have argued that a large part of the decline in output in 1991 was caused directly by monetary and fiscal policy, and that household and investment outlays declined in response to these policies, leading to a larger fall in GDP. This argument seems the least likely. Government expenditures fell by 9 percent, gross investment by 13 percent, and household consumption by 23 percent—well in excess of the decline in income. Consumption and output were driven much more by the effects of the price liberalization than by incomes and expenditures (Brada and King, 1992).

The role of foreign trade, to be taken up in the next section, is also problematic. In a strictly Keynesian sense, the positive trade balances achieved in 1991 and 1992 would suggest that the effect of the foreign trade sector was expansionary. At the same time, the CMEA shock imposed a number of costs on the economy, including worsened terms of trade and the decline in the exports of certain sectors. Rodrik (1993) estimates these income losses at 7.5 percent of GDP or, with Keynesian multiplier effects, 14.9 percent in 1991.

To the extent that autonomous effects, including household and enterprise responses to price liberalization and the CMEA trade shock, as well as the positive effects of the trade surplus, predominated, it is unlikely

**Table 1.4**
Growth rates of components of real GDP of the Czech Republic, 1990–92

| | | GDP (percent Δ) | Consumption of | | Gross investment (percent Δ) | Trade balance[a] |
|---|---|---|---|---|---|---|
| | | | Household (percent Δ) | Government (percent Δ) | | |
| 1990 | I | — | — | — | — | 5.9 |
| | II | 5.3 | 4.9 | 15.8 | 5.9 | 3.5 |
| | III | −0.2 | −2.9 | 7.4 | 0.5 | −1.5 |
| | IV | 6.1 | 20.4 | 24.2 | −15.5 | −0.5 |
| 1991 | I | −7.9 | −37.2 | −34.1 | 74.8 | −1.6 |
| | II | −13.5 | 2 | 3.3 | −46 | 15.1 |
| | III | −2.9 | 2.8 | −10 | −12.4 | 19.6 |
| | IV | −2.5 | 7.9 | 56.1 | −56 | 16.7 |
| 1992 | I | −3.7 | −9.6 | −51.8 | 120.7 | 20.3 |
| | II | −0.3 | 9 | 19.5 | −12.4 | 14.5 |
| | III | 7.7 | 4.9 | −6.7 | 44.4 | 7.7 |
| | IV | 0.8 | 16.6 | 39.7 | −26 | −0.5 |

| | | Yearly changes (percent) | | | | |
|---|---|---|---|---|---|---|
| | GDP | Household consumption | Government consumption | Gross investment | | Trade balance[a] |
| | | | | Fixed capital | Stocks and reserves[a] | |
| 1989 | 4.5 | 1.5 | 4.6 | 2.8 | −17.4 | 26.4 |
| 1990 | −1.2 | 6.7 | 0.9 | −2.1 | 218.4 | −1.8 |
| 1991 | −14.2 | −23.9 | −9.1 | −17.7 | 37.2 | 16.2 |
| 1992 | −7.1 | 11.1 | −22.9 | 3.8 | * | 6 |

*Source:* Czech Statistical Office, *Quarterly Statistical Bulletin* (2nd quarter, 1993).
*Notes:* a. Figures are in billion koruny, 1984 prices.
*in 1992, inventory investment was 8 billion koruny.

that a more expansionary macroeconomic policy could have done much to offset these effects. Indeed, if one accepts the rapid price liberalization and the inevitability of the decline in exports to the USSR, then government policy was virtually powerless.

### 1.2.2 The External Economy

Two events played a key role in the external economy of Czechoslovakia in this period. The first was the CMEA shock, wherein the CMEA trade and payments arrangement was dismantled. Some observers have cited this as a major policy error, one that ought to have been remedied by creation of a regional payments system. In fact, the demise of the system

**Table 1.5**
Czechoslovak trade volumes and prices, 1989–92 (1989 = 100)

|                                      | 1990  | 1991  | 1992  |
|--------------------------------------|-------|-------|-------|
| Export prices                        | 103.3 | 162.2 | 157.8 |
| Import prices                        | 100.7 | 203.1 | 191.5 |
| Exports in                           |       |       |       |
| Current prices                       | 99.0  | 147.6 | 163.4 |
| Constant prices                      | 95.8  | 91.1  | 106.3 |
| Imports in                           |       |       |       |
| Current prices                       | 110.9 | 136.9 | 186.5 |
| Constant prices                      | 109.7 | 67.4  | 97.4  |
| Trade with market economies          |       |       |       |
| (current prices)                     |       |       |       |
| Exports                              | 128.7 | 228.5 | 308.3 |
| Imports                              | 143.8 | 207.3 | 348.0 |
| Trade with planned and transition economies |   |       |       |
| (current prices)                     |       |       |       |
| Exports                              | 79.8  | 95.5  | 69.3  |
| Imports                              | 91.1  | 94.3  | 88.9  |
| CPI                                  | 109.6 | 171.7 | 190.7 |

*Source:* Český Statistický Úřad, *Statistická Ročenka České Republiky, 1993*, 1994.

had more to do with events in the USSR than with the proclamations of East European reformers about basing intra-CMEA trade on world market prices and dollar clearing (Brada, 1993). Unfortunately, the move from transferable ruble pricing within the CMEA has left a very imprecise statistical record of the extent and the effects of the decline in trade with the USSR and with the other ex-CMEA countries.[12]

The results in Table 1.5, which should be viewed as rough approximations, show the general picture. The devaluation of the koruna, the change in the dollar/transferable ruble (TR) exchange rate, and a real shift in trade toward the West are all clearly evident. The terms of trade moved against Czechoslovakia, in large part due to the more realistic pricing of imported fuels and raw materials. Perhaps most important is that by 1992, real exports had risen considerably and real imports had almost recovered to 1989 levels. This suggests either that a rapid change in the structure of production and exports had taken place, a hypothesis not strongly supported by the data, or that a considerable part of the production that had gone to CMEA markets had been redirected toward the West.[13]

By 1992, about two-thirds of trade was with developed market economies, with Germany the predominant trade partner. Trade with the USSR and the successor states held up reasonably well for fuels and raw materials, although policy makers worked hard to reduce trade dependency on the USSR by seeking out alternative sources. Imports of Soviet manufactures largely disappeared, and Czech exports to the USSR declined sharply. Thus, the Czech Republic, in some sense, and now at world market prices, imports Soviet fuels and raw materials for processing into exports destined for Western markets. This is an ironic outcome of market-based processes because it is a trade pattern that in the past was harshly criticized by Western and East European critics of the CMEA as irrational and uneconomic, yet it is now being validated by market-based decisions.

The second major development in Czechoslovak trade was the devaluation of the koruna in late 1990 and early 1991. The devaluation maneuver must be judged as a success in that the government's objectives were met to the extent that the devaluation was sufficiently large to cushion the effect of the price liberalization, and inflation was reined in so that the nominal exchange rate established in 1991 has easily been maintained. There is a tendency in the literature to ascribe the low value of the koruna to the devaluation itself. However, the low value of the koruna is something of a historical phenomenon that was only accentuated by devaluation so that the spread between the official and the purchasing-power-parity (PPP) exchange rate that existed in Czechoslovakia in 1991 and 1992 was much greater than in Hungary and Poland. This in turn led to significant differences among these countries in labor costs and incomes when measured in dollar terms. For example, Richter (1993) calculated total monthly compensation per employee in industry in 1992 as $249 in Czechoslovakia, $402 in Hungary, and $335 in Poland.

However, as Table 1.6 shows, this undervaluation of the koruna was not caused by the devaluation. Indeed, any real devaluation of the koruna was limited to 1991, a year in which it may have been needed. By 1992, the real value of the koruna was, in fact, at or above the levels of 1989, and the gap between the PPP and official rate had returned to its previous level. The argument may be made that the devaluation was excessive, and that, to the extent that large price increases, in part caused by devaluation, affected cash balances and household and enterprise spending in a deflationary way, it was in part responsible for the decline in output (Portes, 1994, p. 1184). At the same time, to the extent that there was some room for the effect of domestic excess demand to raise prices and for the effects of higher prices for energy and raw materials from the USSR to work through into cost-push inflation, a failure to devalue would likely have led to a real appreciation of the koruna in 1991 due to these price increases, a policy that would have been seen as quite risky.

**Table 1.6**
Czechoslovak exchange rates, 1990–92 (end of period)

| | 1990 | | | | 1991 | | | | 1992 | | | |
|---|---|---|---|---|---|---|---|---|---|---|---|---|
| | I | II | III | IV | I | II | III | IV | I | II | III | IV |
| Official exchange rate (Ks/$) | 16.81 | 16.51 | 15.71 | 28.00 | 30.15 | 31.03 | 29.85 | 27.84 | 29.03 | 27.89 | 27.01 | 28.90 |
| Ratio of official/PPP exchange rates | 2.93 | 2.91 | 2.54 | 3.82 | 3.28 | 3.34 | 3.28 | 3.06 | 3.09 | 2.98 | 2.77 | 2.80 |
| Effective real exchange rate (CPI, January 1990 = 100) | 96.5 | 96.9 | 111.2 | 73.9 | 86.2 | 84.5 | 86.2 | 92.3 | 91.5 | 94.7 | 101.8 | 101.0 |

*Source: PlanEcon Report 9, nos. 46, 47, 48 (1993).*

The key point, then, is that it was not the devaluation to 28 ks/$ in 1991 that created a koruna that appeared to be undervalued relative to the dollar and to other East European currencies. The effects of this devaluation on the international value of the koruna were, in fact, largely dissipated by the end of 1991, in part by the forces set in motion by the devaluation. Whether the devaluation was excessive in the short run, then, depends very much on judgments regarding the extent to which prices would have increased without devaluation, whether relative price changes could have been achieved without a general price increase, and whether the shift toward the West could have been as swift without the temporary devaluation effects that were evident in 1991.

The short-term issues raised above are in some sense independent of the longer-term question of the relationship between the PPP and the official exchange rate in the long run. The discrepancy between the two, as we have seen, was not caused by the devaluation of 1991, although, of course, failure to devalue would have closed the gap, with perhaps quite devastating results for Czechoslovakia's ability to maintain balanced trade under a liberalized trade regime and to reorient its exports to the West.

Nevertheless, the failure to close the gap between the official and PPP rates of the koruna has had some costs. These include the failure of the nominal exchange rate anchor to act as a limit to inflation and the existence of large inflows of capital that have caused problems with sterilization; these problems are discussed below. A second alleged cost of the undervalued koruna was a failure of the Czechoslovak economy to adjust structurally. Indeed, the argument made by many Czechoslovak economists is that the undervalued koruna has led to the growth of exports of low value added; material-, resource-, and pollution-intensive products at the expense of "progressive," high-tech, modern products. These arguments, despite the frequency with which they are made, are usually based on impressionistic and subjective evaluations of the factor intensity of exports and of the structure of export flows. Table 1.7 provides more

**Table 1.7**
Structure of Czechoslovak exports to OECD countries (percent)

|      | Resource-based | Labor-intensive | Physical capital-intensive | R&D-intensive | |
|------|----------------|-----------------|----------------------------|---------------|---|
|      |                |                 |                            | Easy to imitate | Difficult to imitate |
| 1988 | 30.3 | 30.1 | 17.0 | 11.3 | 10.5 |
| 1992 | 18.0 | 38.8 | 21.1 | 7.3 | 13.9 |

*Source:* OECD (1995), Table 2-4.

systematic information about the changes in the factor content of Czechoslovak exports, and these suggest that the structure of Czechoslovak
trade in fact did shift away from resource-intensive goods. Indeed, the
major gains were in labor-intensive products, which, given the decline in
real wages and even more in the cost of labor relative to many natural resources, is to be expected. Whether labor-intensive sectors are low-value-
added is questionable.

## 1.3   The Separation of Czechoslovakia

By the end of 1992, the Czechoslovak economy was showing signs of revival, with GDP growing in the last two quarters, foreign direct investment increasing, and the balance of payments in good shape. Demand,
both of consumers and of enterprises, also grew. Real industrial output
continued to decline, albeit at a slower rate; given problems with price
indexes and the inability to capture the output of new private firms, it,
too, may have been higher than official statistics indicate. With the completion of the first round of voucher privatization, it may have appeared
that Czechoslovakia was poised to begin making gains in both output and
institutional change.

However, the aggregate figures masked a number of differences between the two republics. In Slovakia, unemployment of around 12 percent
was at least three times higher than in the Czech Republic. The budgetary
situation of the Slovak Republic was also under strain, despite subsidization by the Czech Republic, and the Slovak government was losing its
access to commercial credit. The benefits of the tourist boom and the bulk
of foreign direct investment accrued to the Czech Republic as well. These,
as well as a number of social and political pressures, led to the partitioning of the state into two independent republics at the beginning of 1993.

Economists in both the Czech Republic and the Slovak Republic believed that trade between the two states would decline, bringing about
considerable costs. In the rather arbitrary prices of the time, in 1987 about
one-third of Slovak industrial output was sold in the Czech Republic,
whereas the latter sold one-tenth of its industrial output to Slovakia
(Martin, 1992). A decline in mutual trade as the result of the separation
was anticipated, and this was expected to lead to a decline in production
estimated by reputable sources as being equal to 3–5 percent of the
Czech Republic's GDP (Janáčková and Janáček, 1993; Šujan, 1992).

To prevent a precipitous decline in mutual trade, a number of measures
were prepared prior to separation (Janáčková, 1994). One of these was a

currency union between the two new states. While such a union might have minimized the decline in trade between the Czech and Slovak Republics, it had no credibility, as both states prepared for currency separation before the beginning of 1993. Indeed, it lasted no longer than one month after the separation. To facilitate payments between the two republics, a new system was put into place. For payment obligations incurred prior to the end of the currency union, clearing was in "old bloc" clearing koruny whose value was determined by the value of the former Czechoslovak koruny against the European Currency Unit (ECU) on February 5, 1993. Since the exchange rate between Czech and Slovak koruny started at 1:1, settlements of these payment obligations were protected against devaluation. This account was to be cleared every three months by means of a hard currency settlement.

For transactions resulting in payments obligations after February 6, 1993, a "new bloc" clearing account was established. Firms would pay for imports in national currencies but clearing would be denominated in ECUs, with each of the currencies able to change its value vis-à-vis the ECU by 5 percent. An automatic credit of 130 million ECUs was created, and amounts over this would have to be settled in convertible currencies. In March 1993, the Czech Republic appreciated the Czech koruna (K) by 5 percent and the Slovak Republic devalued the Slovak koruna (Sk) by 2 percent for clearing purposes. This arrangement continued until the Slovak government carried out a general devaluation of the Sk by 10 percent on July 12, 1993. In December 1993 the Sk was again devalued by 5 percent within the clearing arrangement.

Trade between the two countries was at first subject to no tariff barriers, but over time frictions appeared, largely as the result of Slovak efforts to protect the Sk by means of administrative measures that, in the eyes of the Czech government, constituted nontariff barriers. These and the future of the bilateral clearing arrangement remain in some doubt.

The effect of the separation on the volume of trade between the two republics was negative. In 1993, bilateral trade is said to have declined by 30 percent, and in 1994 Czech exports to Slovakia declined by 22 percent and imports by 10 percent. While the effects of this trade decline must have been adverse for the Czech economy, they are difficult to quantify. For example, in 1993 Slovakia accounted for 21 percent of Czech exports and 17.5 percent of imports. Thus major changes in the volumes ought to have significant economic impacts unless trade lost in this way can be replaced either by domestic sales or by finding new markets. The latter is clearly part of the Czech Republic's turn toward the West. The former can

**Table 1.8**
Structure of Czech–Slovak trade: first six months, 1993 (percent)

|  | Czech | |
| --- | --- | --- |
|  | Exports | Imports |
| Food and live animals | 8.6 | 5.1 |
| Energy and fuels | 14.1 | 6.6 |
| Chemical/pharmaceutical products | 11.7 | 14.7 |
| Iron, steel, wood products | 25.9 | 34.9 |
| Machinery and transport equipment | 23.1 | 23.0 |
| Industrial consumer goods | 10.1 | 10.4 |

*Source:* Frensch (1993).

be facilitated if bilateral trade flows involve considerable intraindustry trade. That this might, indeed, be the case is suggested by Table 1.8, which shows that trade between the two republics is relatively balanced across broad categories of products.

## 1.4   Outcomes Following Separation and Policy Prospects

### 1.4.1   Macroeconomic Survey

The separation freed the Czech Republic to follow more easily the macro-economic policies that had been the hallmark of the previous two years. The government's finances were revamped, with a VAT tax replacing the turnover tax. The effect of this on tax revenues was more or less neutral, but the CPI increased by over 51 percent on an annual basis in the first quarter of 1993; inflation then subsided, and as can be seen in Table 1.9, averaged 20.8 percent for the year. In 1994, without further price shocks, it was about 10 percent, which appears to be the core rate of inflation in the Czech Republic.

The separation had a short-term negative effect on aggregate output as well, although the stagnation of real GDP in 1993 indicated by official statistics is seen by many observers as understating the dynamism of the economy. Noteworthy, however, is that in 1994 the growth of GDP was greater than that of industrial production, in contrast to the pattern in other recovering transition economies. This may suggest that the pressure for downsizing and restructuring in industry continued to exercise a drag on industrial output. The increase in the growth of imports in 1994 reflects in part the continuing real appreciation of the koruna, a pro-

**Table 1.9**
Macroeconomic indicators for the Czech Republic, 1993–94 (growth rates in percent)

|  | 1993 | 1994 |
|---|---|---|
| Real GDP | −0.5 | 3 |
| Real industrial output | −5.3 | 2.5 |
| Real construction output | −7.5 | 6.5 |
| Retail sales—constant prices | −2.1 | 5 |
| Exports (excluding Slovak Republic) | 20 | 11–13 |
| Imports (excluding Slovak Republic) | 2.7 | 15–17 |
| CPI | 20.8 | 10 |
| Real wages | 3.5 | 5–6 |
| Unemployment (percent) | 3.5 | 3.2 |
| Budget surplus (percent of GDP) | 0.1 | 0.9 |

Source: Komerční Banka, *Economic Trends* (February 1995).

cess likely to continue through 1995, when inflation again approached 10 percent.

### 1.4.2  Emerging Policy Problems

With the onset of economic recovery, the Czech Republic appears to have succeeded in its stabilization and transformation efforts despite the effects of the separation of Czechoslovakia. Thus, at this point, it faces the need to deal with neither domestic fiscal deficits nor balance of payments problems. Nevertheless, a number of less immediate but potentially serious problems exist. Since 1993, foreign direct investment in the Czech Republic has held steady, but portfolio investment has grown very rapidly. Part of this involves lending by foreign banks to Czech firms, and the remainder consists of deposits in banks and purchases of Czech securities. From virtually nothing in 1992, portfolio investment grew to $1.06 billion in 1993 and even more in 1994. Inflows of portfolio capital have been augmented by rising foreign exchange deposits of households. These deposits arise in large part from earnings from tourism, which now account for 10–15 percent of export revenues. Foreign exchange deposits of households rose from 239 billion koruny in 1992 to 318 billion in September 1994.

Portfolio inflows into the Czech Republic are driven by a relatively straightforward calculus. At this point, there is little risk of devaluation; indeed, many expect a revaluation of the koruna because it is so far below its PPP rate. Thus foreign investors perceive no exchange rate risk. At the same time, in order to maintain positive interest rates and to help the banking system build up reserves, lending rates remain high—at least 13 percent on bank loans—and bonds carry higher rates. As a result, foreign investors face very attractive opportunities, and they have responded to them. Capital inflows have been so large that they have become a key component of money supply growth, causing M2 to increase faster than targeted in 1994. In 1993 this growth was 19.7 percent, and in 1994 about 19 percent, well above the inflation rate of 10 percent, although with declining velocity of circulation, the inflationary effect of money growth is difficult to judge.

The Czech National Bank (CNB) took measures to sterilize these inflows but, given a positive external balance and a government budget surplus, it was limited to using monetary instruments. It raised minimum reserve requirements from 9 percent to 12 percent in 1994 and increased the discount and Lombard rates. To some extent, these policies were counterproductive, since they raised lending rates and reduced the supply of credit from domestic banks, thus encouraging more capital inflows. Moreover, the CNB has been forced to acquire greater foreign exchange reserves from the domestic banking system. Thus official reserves increased from $824 million on January 1, 1993, to $5,417 million on September 30, 1994. The CNB repaid a $1.1 billion stabilization loan from the IMF, although it carried a lower interest rate than the implicit cost of the foreign exchange reserves being acquired by the CNB.

With the fixed exchange rate not acting as a nominal anchor, and with external pressure on the money supply unlikely to subside, there seems little likelihood that money supply growth, inflation, and thus interest rates can be reduced in the near future. The real costs of this situation are lower levels of investment, of growth, and particularly of development of small and medium-sized firms.

Proposals for dealing with this situation are not encouraging. Revaluation is seen as unacceptable because it would endanger the growth of exports and promote imports, and because its effects would be difficult to reverse. Liberalization of capital outflows offers some hope of reducing the surplus on the capital account, but Czech households lack the financial resources to offset the large capital inflows into the country. To resolve this dilemma, the Czech government adopted two measures. In June 1995 the CNB imposed restrictions on short-term capital inflows into the country. A second measure was to introduce the full-scale convertibility of the koruna by establishing current account convertibility for Czech residents.

The former step, despite some self-interested and ill-informed criticism by Western bankers, is likely to prove the more effective measure in dealing with what had become a potentially serious problem.

Of course, the Czech Republic was under less pressure and had more time to deal with this problem than it would have had with large payments or government deficits. Nevertheless, this experience shows that erring on the side of virtue in following the classical prescriptions for stabilization does carry certain costs of its own. Of course, it can be of some comfort to Czech policy makers that most other countries in the region would only wish to have had the kind of economic problems facing the Czech Republic.

## 1.5   An Econometric Model of Czech Trade

In the foregoing discussion, numerous factors affecting trade during the transition were discussed. In this section, we specify and estimate a model of Czech trade flows with market economies to show how these factors influenced trade performance. In the modeling we were constrained by a number of factors. The first of these was that the Czech Republic's new trade regime was not introduced until January 1991, and estimation of dynamics thus is limited by the small number of observations. Second, there were major structural changes in the commodity composition and geographic orientation of trade. We therefore sought specifications that would stress short-run response and would, in some sense, turn the large reorientation of Czech trade caused by the CMEA shock and the separation of the country into an advantage for specification and estimation. We deal with the former problem by using monthly data for 1990:1 to 1994:8 and assuming relatively short adjustment lags. Such short lags appear to be appropriate in the light of the abrupt trade shocks faced by the economy and of the rapid reorientation of Czech trade toward the West. We are interested in explaining Czech exports to, and imports from, developed market economies. Trade with the former USSR, with East Europe, and, from 1993, with the Slovak Republic are treated as exogenous, thus enabling us to gauge how the CMEA and separation shocks influenced Czech trade with the West.

### 1.5.1   Import Demand

We estimated a relatively traditional import demand equation, with the real volume of Czech imports depending on real domestic income and the relative price of imports and of domestic goods. We proxied real domestic income by real GDP and, to allow a lag between changes in income and imports, we assumed a six-month response period. The usual practice for sorting out price effects on import demand is to enter domestic and foreign prices and the exchange rate separately (Wilson and Tackas, 1979; Warner and Kreinin, 1983). Thus we entered the nominal exchange rate and domestic and import prices separately; however, tests indicated that utilizing a price ratio was acceptable, and we did so to save degrees of freedom. Both the exchange rate and the price ratio variables were lagged six months to capture dynamic effects.

Shocks to the regime, which we regarded as exogenous to the import decisions of agents in the economy, were introduced by a series of dummies. The old, state-directed system and its abolition at the end of 1990 were proxied by a one-zero dummy. A negative value for this coefficient would suggest that the new regime was more open, allowing a greater inflow of Western imports. A second dummy captures the more progressive liberalization of imports that occurred after 1990 as the tariff surcharge was reduced. Thus the regime dummy and the tariff dummy should be considered together to yield the total effect of trade liberalization on imports.

The second set of dummies shows the effects of a decline in imports from the Soviet Union, East Europe, and Slovakia. The dummies take on the value of real imports from these three regions after the onset of events that reduced such imports. Such events include, in part, the breakdown of the CMEA payments and trade system and the separation of Czechoslovakia into two states. These events raised the costs of importing from these regions and, in the case of the Soviet Union, reduced supplies of fuels and raw materials. If Western imports were an important substitute for these imports from the Czech Republic's former trading partners, one would expect the coefficients of these dummies to be negative, since falling imports from the East would stimulate imports from the West.

The specification of the model estimated, with error term suppressed, was:

$$I_t = C + aOR_t + bT_t + cISU_t + dIS_t + eIEE_t + \sum_{i=0}^{6} f_i GDP_{t-i}$$

$$+ \sum_{i=0}^{6} g_i ER_{t-i} + \sum_{i=0}^{6} h_i (P/P_x^*)_{t-i} \tag{1}$$

where all trade and price variables were in logs, and

$I_t$ = real volume of Czech imports from developed market economies (Dm),

C = constant,

$OR_t$ = dummy variable for the effect of the old state-trading regime;
OR = 1 from 1990:1 to 1990:12 and zero thereafter,

$T_t$ = dummy variable for the tariff surcharge. T = 0 to 1990:12,
and then is set equal to 1.2 to reflect the 20 percent surcharge
on imports and subsequently declines to 1.0, the statutory
level of tariffs according to the schedule described previously
in the text,

$ISU_t$ = real imports from the (former) Soviet Union from 1991:1 onward; zero otherwise (Dm),

Ist = real imports from the Slovak Republic from 1993:1 onward;
zero otherwise (Dm),

$IEE_t$ = real imports from Eastern Europe from 1991:1 onward; zero
otherwise (Dm),

$GDP_t$ = real Gross Domestic Product, Czech Republic (in real Kčs or Kč),

P = domestic wholesale price index,

$P_x^*$ = price of imports—calculated as weighted average of partner countries' export price indices, in Dm, converted into an
index.

P = domestic wholesale price index,

$P_x$ = price of imports—calculated as weighted average of partner countries' export price indices (in DM) converted into an
index.

Parameter estimates are reported in Table 1.10. These results indicate a
relatively rapid response to price, income, and regime changes, mostly in
the appropriate direction. The coefficient for $OR_t$, the state-trading regime
that existed prior to January 1991, is negative, indicating that the abolition of this regime increased imports from the West. Because the new system liberalized imports from the West, such a shift is to be expected. Also
negative and significant is the coefficient for $T_t$, the dummy for the new
tariff regime introduced when state trading was abolished. Since its coefficient is smaller in absolute value than that of $OR_t$, the new regime was
less restrictive vis-à-vis imports of Western goods than the previous one

**Table 1.10**
Parameter estimates for Equation 1
Dependent variable $= I_t$

| Variable | Coefficient | t-statistic |
|---|---|---|
| C | 17.18 | 4.99* |
| $OR_t$ | −16.15 | −5.77* |
| $T_t$ | −13.46 | −5.66* |
| $ISU_t$ | −0.01 | −0.11 |
| $IS_t$ | −0.14 | −4.71* |
| $IEE_t$ | 0.14 | 1.16 |

| Variable | | | | ER | | | | |
|---|---|---|---|---|---|---|---|---|
| Lag | 0 | 1 | 2 | 3 | 4 | 5 | 6 | Sum |
| Coefficient | −0.66 | 0.17 | 0.36 | 0.15 | −0.23 | −0.54 | −0.54 | −1.28 |
| t-statistic | −1.70*** | 0.75 | 0.52 | −1.12 | −2.01** | −2.01** | −2.04** | −1.52 |

| Variable | | | | GDP | | | | |
|---|---|---|---|---|---|---|---|---|
| Lag | 0 | 1 | 2 | 3 | 4 | 5 | 6 | Sum |
| Coefficient | 0.21 | 0.06 | 0.05 | 0.11 | 0.19 | 0.24 | 0.19 | 1.05 |
| t-statistic | 1.07 | 0.50 | 0.33 | 0.83 | 1.87** | 2.47** | 2.33** | 1.84*** |

| Variable | | | | $P/P_x$ | | | | |
|---|---|---|---|---|---|---|---|---|
| Lag | 0 | 1 | 2 | 3 | 4 | 5 | 6 | Sum |
| Coefficient | 0.76 | −0.08 | −0.24 | −0.01 | 0.38 | 0.69 | 0.64 | 2.15 |
| t-statistic | 1.45 | −0.28 | −0.70 | −0.03 | 2.74** | 3.31* | 2.74** | 3.20* |

$\overline{R}^2 = 0.874$
Ljung-Box Q-stat for autocorrelation $= 11.43(0.49)$
Jarque-Bera normality statistic $= 5.20(0.07)$***
ARCH test statistic $= 9.44(0.66)$

*Notes:*  *Significant at the 1% level.
           **Significant at the 5% level.
           ***Significant at the 10% level.

had been. The reduction of the tariff surcharge, causing $T_t$ to decline from 1.2 to 1, thus also had a significant impact by increasing the volume of imports. After 1990, the decline in imports from the USSR did not have an impact on imports from the West, indicating that the latter were not a substitute for the former. An examination of the commodity structure of Czech imports from the two regions confirms this. Similarly, the decline in imports from other ex-CMEA countries did little to boost imports from market economies. On the other hand, the decline in Slovak imports after the separation served to increase imports from the West, although the elasticity, 0.14, is rather modest.

Responses to the movements of prices, exchange rates, and income are significant, relatively quick, and in accordance with expectations. For all three variables, responses in the first quarter are generally insignificant. However, in the second quarter, a relatively strong response is evident. In the case of the exchange rate, an increase in the koruna price of the deutsche mark reduces imports significantly, and the elasticity appears to be greater than 1. In the case of GDP, the temporal pattern is the same, although the income elasticity based on the second quarter appears to be less than 1. Finally, despite many observers' expectations that East European buyers would be unwilling to substitute domestic products for well-recognized imports, it would appear that demand for imports is quite sensitive to relative price movements.

We have seen from the results above that Czech imports from developed market economies were "crowded in" by the decline in imports from the Slovak Republic after separation. This issue of regional redirection of trade flows is even more important in the case of exports, where the expansion of exports to the West was not only a response to normal economic factors such as the change in the exchange rate, but also was in part a process of "crowding in" of export supply that was diverted from the former CMEA market and from domestic demand.

To capture these features of supply and demand, we employ a model developed by Beenstock et al. (1994). This model divides the economy into two sectors, one producing tradables and the other, nontradables. Since domestic residents can consume the tradable goods, the supply of exports depends both on the production of tradables and on their consumption by the domestic population. To this framework we add, in a relatively straightforward way that is analogous to the procedure in Equation 1, a series of "supply shocks," which consist of increases in the supply of tradables potentially available for export to the West that result from exogenous declines in exports to the East. These shocks are proxied by the declining level of exports to the USSR, East Europe, and Slovakia. Estimation of this model of exports to the West requires even more stringent assumptions than those required to estimate import demand, because one must assume that the market for exportables clears very quickly. Moreover, estimates are limited to ordinary least squares (OLS) by the paucity of data.

### 1.5.2 *Export Demand and Supply*

The demand for Czech exports by Western countries in real terms, with all monetary and quantity variables in logs, is specified as

$$E_t = A + \alpha OR_t + \beta E_{t-3} + \sum_{i=0}^{6} \gamma_{iD} t - i^* + \sum_{i=0}^{6} \theta (P_x/P_x^*)_{t-i} \tag{2}$$

where

$E_t$ = real Czech exports to developed Western countries (DM)

$D_t$ = volume of world trade, proxied by a weighted sum of German, Italian, and French imports (DM)

$P_x$ = price of Czech tradables (DM)

$P_x$ = price of foreign tradables (DM)

and $OR_t$ as defined above.

In this specification, the demand for Czech exports depends on the volume of world trade, a proxy for the income of partner countries, and on the price of Czech exportables relative to other tradable goods on world markets.

Parameter estimates for Equation 2, estimated on the same monthly sample as for Equation 1, are reported in Table 1.11. Although the change

**Table 1.11**
Parameter estimates for Equation 2
Dependent variable $= E_t$

| Variable | Coefficient | t-statistic |
|---|---|---|
| A | −13.54 | −3.32* |
| $OR_t$ | 0.20 | 1.55 |
| $E_{t-3}$ | 0.55 | 5.97* |

| Variable | | | | $D^*$ | | | | |
|---|---|---|---|---|---|---|---|---|
| Lag | 0 | 1 | 2 | 3 | 4 | 5 | 6 | Sum |
| Coefficient | 1.40 | 0.14 | −0.28 | −0.17 | 0.20 | 0.54 | 0.57 | 2.42 |
| t-statistic | 3.70* | 0.58 | −1.11 | −0.82 | 2.12 | 2.45** | 2.83* | 2.88* |

| Variable | | | | $P_v/P_v$ | | | | |
|---|---|---|---|---|---|---|---|---|
| Lag | 0 | 1 | 2 | 3 | 4 | 5 | 6 | Sum |
| Coefficient | 3.95 | 1.80 | 0.61 | 0.13 | 0.09 | 0.23 | 0.28 | 7.11 |
| t-statistic | 5.28* | 4.28* | 2.64* | 1.04 | 1.05 | 2.19** | 2.93* | 5.01* |

$\overline{R}^2 = 0.841$
Ljung-Box Q-statistic for autocorrelation $= 11.74$ (0.46)
Jarque-Bera normality test statistic $= 3.81$ (0.15)
ARCH test statistic $= 6.04$ (0.91)

in the trade regime had no independent impact on the demand for Czech exports, both the short-term and the long-term elasticities of demand for Czech exports are significantly different from zero and very elastic. Thus Czech devaluation did have an extremely beneficial effect on the volume of Czech exports demanded on world markets.

The supply of Czech exports for Western countries is specified as depending on their production; on "spill-ins" from exports previously directed toward other markets, which are proxied by the declining volume of exports to the East; on production costs; and on the domestic demand for tradables as proxied by GDP. The specification is thus

$$E_t = B + \eta OR_t + \sum_{i=0}^{2} \delta_i XSU_{t-i} + \tau XS_t + \Psi XEE_t + \sum_{i=0}^{6} \rho_i (P_x \cdot ER/P_n)_{t-i}$$

$$+ \sum_{i=0}^{6} \gamma_i (P_{mi} \cdot ER/P)_{t-i} + \sum_{i=0}^{6} \pi_i GDP_{t-i} \qquad (3)$$

where

$XSU_t$ = real exports to the USSR after 1990:12, zero otherwise (DM)

$XS_t$ = real exports to the Slovak Republic after 1992:12, zero otherwise (DM)

$XEE_t$ = real exports to East Europe after 1990:12; zero otherwise

$P_x$ = price of Czech tradables (DM)

$P_n$ = price of Czech nontradables (Ks or K)

$P_{mi}$ = price of intermediate imports (DM)

$P$ = domestic price index (Ks or K)

and other variables as defined above.

Trade shocks are captured by declining exports to the USSR, Slovakia, and East Europe. The ratio of the price of tradables to nontradables is expected to be positive. As the price of exportables increases relative to nontradables, Czech residents will switch to the latter, thus increasing the amount of the former available for export. When the price of imported intermediates increases relative to other prices, then the supply of exportables will decline. Finally, increases in real domestic income, a proxy for output, should increase export supply.

Parameter estimates for Equation 3 are reported in Table 1.12. Because the Soviet trade shock was so large, we lagged the effect for three months, yielding significant coefficients whose net sum is negative, indicating that a decline in exports to the USSR had a significant and independent

**Table 1.12**
Parameter estimates for Equation 3
Dependent variable $= E_t$

| Variable | Coefficient | t-statistic |
|---|---|---|
| B | 9.62 | 7.44* |
| $OR_t$ | 0.19 | 0.69 |
| $XSU_t$ | 0.25 | 1.77*** |
| $XSU_{t-1}$ | −0.26 | −2.91* |
| $XSU_{t-2}$ | −0.24 | −2.82* |
| $XS_t$ | 0.02 | 1.28 |
| $XEE_t$ | −0.25 | −3.29* |

| Variable | | | | $(P_x \cdot ER/P_n)$ | | | | |
|---|---|---|---|---|---|---|---|---|
| Lag | 0 | 1 | 2 | 3 | 4 | 5 | 6 | Sum |
| Coefficient | 1.72 | 0.81 | 0.25 | −0.03 | −0.13 | −0.10 | −0.03 | 2.49 |
| t-statistic | 2.23** | 2.36* | 2.07*** | −0.53 | −2.46* | −2.24** | −0.65 | 2.20** |

| Variable | | | | $(P_{mi} \cdot ER/P)_t$ | | | | |
|---|---|---|---|---|---|---|---|---|
| Lag | 0 | 1 | 2 | 3 | 4 | 5 | 6 | Sum |
| Coefficient | 0.02 | −0.05 | −0.17 | −0.28 | −0.33 | −0.36 | −0.25 | −1.43 |
| t-statistic | 0.06 | −0.60 | −0.99 | −1.85*** | −3.46* | −2.77* | −1.88*** | −4.16* |

| Variable | | | | GDP | | | | |
|---|---|---|---|---|---|---|---|---|
| Lag | 0 | 1 | 2 | 3 | 4 | 5 | 6 | Sum |
| Coefficient | 0.10 | 0.12 | 0.14 | 0.14 | 0.13 | 0.11 | 0.07 | 0.80 |
| t-statistic | 0.49 | 0.83 | 0.88 | 1.21 | 2.03** | 1.69*** | 0.90 | 1.81*** |

$\overline{R}^2 = 0.893$
Ljung-Box Q-stat for autocorrelation $= 20.01$ (0.07)**
Jarque-Bera normality statistic $= 3.13$ (0.20)
ARCH test statistic $= 10.74$ (0.55)

*Notes:*  *Significant at the 1% level.
        **Significant at the 5% level.
        ***Significant at the 10% level.

"crowding in" effect on Czech exports to developed market economies. The same is true for exports to Eastern Europe. Thus, the results offer evidence that the Czech Republic was, indeed, able to redirect goods from ex-CMEA markets to the West. In the case of the disruption of trade with Slovakia, no such crowding in is evident.

The coefficient for the relative price of exportables to nontradables is positive, although it tends to dissipate with the passage of time. This means that Czech consumers are quite willing to switch between exportables and nontradables in response to changes in their relative price, at least in the short run. In contrast, a change in the price of imported intermediates, such as fuels and raw materials, while having a large and correct sign for the sum of coefficients over the six months, takes longer to make itself felt in export flows. These dynamics of response to price changes are consistent with expectations. Because the sum of the coefficients on the intermediate imports variable is greater in absolute value than the sum of the coefficients on the exportables—nonexportables prices variable, we conclude that a devaluation of the koruna would expand the supply of exports more by suppressing domestic demand for them than it would reduce their supply by increasing production costs. Nevertheless, given the pattern of these two responses, a longer-term analysis might suggest that the net effect would be negligible, a result in accord with theory. Finally, although the sum of GDP coefficients is positive, the main effect is felt in the second quarter, suggesting that a positive supply effect makes itself felt with a lag.

The results of the econometric exercise lead to several conclusions. The first is that despite the short time span covered by the sample period, it is possible to estimate a model of Czech trade with the West that is quite robust and plausible in terms of its economic implications and its dynamics. Second, the model confirms that the redirection of Czech trade toward the West was in part the result of trade liberalization and of the price and exchange rate policies followed by the Czech government. Finally, the shocks caused by the collapse of CMEA trade were qualitatively, although not quantitatively, less difficult for the Czech economy than was the separation of Czechoslovakia. At the same time, the CMEA shock played a large, exogenous role in redirecting Czech exports toward Western markets.

## Notes

1. See Banerjee (1995) and Drábek (1995) for favorable assessments.

2. Drábek et al. (1994) discuss at length the available literature on this point.

3. For a favorable assessment of Czechoslovakia's macroeconomic and international situation in the framework of a regional comparison, see Bruno (1993).

4. Ironically, these advantages were largely the result of the fact that the classical system of planning and financial control remained relatively intact up to the demise of the Communist regime (Kaminski, 1994).

5. The effects of the aging of Czechoslovakia's capital stock were exacerbated by the reluctance to import Western technology and to permit a significant role for joint ventures with Western firms.

6. OECD (1994b), Table I.2, summarizes differences between Czech and Slovak public opinion on various economic issues.

7. For surveys of early reform measures, see Dyba and Švejnar (1991) and Brada (1991). For details on the early period, see Křovák (1994).

8. This ability to remove a major price distortion by means of a compensated relative price change is an example of the benefits bestowed by macroeconomic stability and a balance between budgetary outlays and expenditures.

9. The effects of price controls on consumer goods and services also have a regional character. For example, state-owned housing, telephone services, and municipal services all tend to be more extensive in cities such as Prague, and thus the effects, both beneficial to consumers and dysfunctional for markets, tend to be most evident there.

10. The corporate profit tax rate was reduced in 1991 by ten–twenty percentage points. Subsidies also were sharply reduced and frozen in nominal terms. The effect on revenues and expenditures was to some extent offsetting, but it did serve to reduce the size of the government sector.

11. Some cleaning up of debts was undertaken through the Consolidation Bank, but these operations were small relative to the total debt of the enterprise sector.

12. In the case of the Czech Republic the usual problems of dealing with the abolition of transferable ruble (TR) trade and the devaluation of the TR vis-à-vis the dollar are compounded by a change in the methodology for collecting trade data and by the conflation of Slovak and Czech trade (see U.S. International Trade Commission, 1993).

13. See OECD (1994a), Table 3–8, for changes in the structure of Czech industrial exports between 1990 and 1991.

# References

Banerjee, Biswajit. 1995. "Czech Republic: A Progress Report on the Transformation Program." Paper presented at the Annual Meetings of the Allied Social Science Associations, Washington, D.C.

Beenstock, Michael, Yaakov Lavi, and Sigal Ribon. 1994. "The Supply and Demand for Exports in Israel." *Journal of Development Economics,* 44 (Sept.): 333–350.

Blue Ribbon Commission. 1992. *Sustainable Forint Convertibility for Hungary: What Type, and When and How to Introduce It.* Indianapolis: Hudson Institute.

Brada, Josef C. 1991. "The Economic Transition of Czechoslovakia from Plan to Market." *Journal of Economic Perspectives,* 5 (Fall): 171–177.

Brada, Josef C. 1993. "Regional Integration in Eastern Europe: Prospects for Integration Within the Region and with the European Community." In Jaime de Melo and Arvind Panagariya, eds., *New Dimensions in Regional Integration*. Cambridge: Cambridge University Press.

Brada, Josef C., and Arthur E. King. 1992. "Is There a J-Curve in the Transition from Socialism to Capitalism?" *Economics of Planning*, 25:37–53.

Bruno, Michael. 1993. "Stabilization and Reform in Eastern Europe: A Preliminary Evaluation." In O. J. Blanchard, Kenneth A. Froot, and Jeffrey D. Sachs, eds., *The Transition in Eastern Europe*. Chicago: University of Chicago Press.

Charap, Joshua, and Alena Zemplinerová. 1993. *Restructuring in the Czech Economy*. European Bank for Reconstruction and Devolopment Working Paper No. 2. London: European Bank for Reconstruction and Development.

Dittus, Peter. 1994. "Bank Reform and Behavior in Central Europe." *Journal of Comparative Economics*, 19 (December): 335–361.

Drábek, Zdeněk. 1995. "IMF and IBRD Policies in Czechoslovakia." *Journal of Comparative Economics*, 20 (April): 235–264.

Drábek, Zdeněk, Kamil Janáček, and Zdeněk Tůma. 1994. "Inflation in the Czech and Slovak Republics, 1985–1991." *Journal of Comparative Economics*, 18 (April): 146–174.

Dyba, Karel, and Jan Švejnar. 1991. "Czechoslovakia: Recent Economic Developments and Prospects." *American Economic Review*, 81 (May): 185–190.

Estrin, Saul, Alan Gelb, and Inderjit Singh. 1995. "Shocks and Adjustment by Firms in Transition: A Comparative Study." *Journal of Comparative Economics*, 21 (October): 131–153.

Frensch, Richard, 1993. *Wirtschaftliche Folgen der Teilunng der Tschechoslovakai*. Osteuropa-Institut München Working Paper 162. Munich: Osteuropa-Institut München.

Hanousek, Jan, Vratislav, Izák, and Otakar Klokočník. 1995. "Monetary Policy During Transformation." *Eastern European Economics*, 33 (January–February): 5–53.

Hrnčír, Miroslav. 1994. "Economic Recovery and Foreign Exchange Rate Regime in the Transition Economies: The Case of Czechoslovakia." In J. Krovák, ed., *Current Economics and Politics of (ex-) Czechoslovakia*. Commack, N.Y.: Nova Science Publishers.

Janáčková, Stanislava. 1994. "Parting with the Common State and Currency." *Eastern European Economics*, 32 (March–April): 6–22.

Janáčková, Stanislava, and Kamil Janáček. 1993. "Après la Partition de la Tchécoslovaquie: Les Perspectives des nouveaux États." *Revue du Marché commun de l'Union européene*, 398 (June): 11–14.

Kaiser, Phillip J. 1994. "The Czech Republic: An Assessment of the Transition." In Joint Economic Committee, Congress of the United States, *East-Central European Economies in Transition*. Washington, D.C.: U.S. Government Printing Office.

Kaminski, Bartolomiej. 1994. "The Legacy of Communism." In Joint Economic Committee, Congress of the United States, *East-Central European Economies in Transition*. Washington, D.C.: U.S. Government Printing Office.

Krovák, Jiří (ed.). 1994. *Current Economics and Politics of (ex-)Czechoslovakia*. Commack, N.Y.: Nova Science Publishers.

Martin, Peter. 1992. "Slovakia: Calculating the Cost of Independence." *RFE/RL Research Report*, 1 (March): 12–20.

Organisation for Economic Co-Operation and Development. 1994a. *Industry in the Czech and Slovak Republics*. Paris: OECD.

Organisation for Economic Co-Operation and Development. 1994b. *Economic Review of the Czech and Slovak Republics*. Paris: OECD.

Organisation for Economic Co-Operation and Development. 1995. *Review of Industry and Industrial Policy in Hungary*. Paris: OECD.

Portes, Richard. 1994. "Transformation Traps." *Economic Journal*, 104 (September): 1178–1189.

Richer, Sandor. 1993. "East-West Trade Under Growing Western Protectionism." Mimeo. Vienna: Institute for International Economic Comparisons.

Rodrik, Dani. 1993. "Making Sense of the Soviet Trade Shock in Eastern Europe: A Framework and Some Estimates." In Mario Blejer et al., eds., *Eastern Europe in Transition: From Recession to Growth?* World Bank Discussion Paper 196.

Slay, Ben (ed.) 1994. "Free Trade in Central Europe." *Russian and East European Foreign Trade*. 30: (Spring): 1–106.

Šujan, Ivan. 1992. "Economic Outlook of the SFR: Estimation of the Consequences of the Czecho-Slovak Divorce." *Hospodaské noviny* (13 August), p. 2.

United States International Trade Commission. 1993. *International Economic Review* (June): pp. 6–7.

Warner, D., and Mordechai Kreinin. 1983. "Determinants of Trade Flows." *Review of Economics and Statistics*, 65 (February): 96–104.

Wilson, J., and Wendy Tackas. 1979. "Differential Responses to Price and Exchange Rate Influences in the Foreign Trade of Selected Industrial Countries." *Review of Economics and Statistics*, 61 (May): 267–279.

Winters, L. Alan. 1994. "The Europe Agreements: With a Little Help from Our Friends." In *The Association Process: Making It Work*. CEPR Occasional Paper no. 11. London: CEPR.

# 2        Hungary

András Blahó and Péter Gál

## Promising Start

The economic policies of Hungary since 1968, the year of the start of the New Economic Mechanism (NEM), have attracted much attention as an attempt to reform the rigid system of a planned economy. As a result of the NEM, the national planning system was changed. Natural indicators of plan fulfillment were discarded. Company management was decentralized. The isolation of the domestic from the foreign economy was gradually lessened, and Hungary was opened up to the global economy. Gradually, monetary and fiscal policy started receiving much greater attention and the exchange rate became an important tool for the policy makers.

These policy measures, until 1988, have been analyzed extensively. Among the results, analysts noted that direct administrative controls over enterprises were reduced and managers' flexibility in influencing economic policy had increased. The financial results of the enterprises were affected through price, wage, and exchange rate regulations as well as through taxes and subsidies. Generally, indirect policy instruments rather than direct controls governed entry, exit, and the selection of lines of activity of enterprises. The macroeconomic policy in the 1970s and 1980s managed to achieve a balance on the whole: major disequilibrium, especially chronic shortages and inflationary pressures in consumer markets, were avoided in the domestic economy. Growing indebtedness in the convertible currency area, however, could not be averted. Liberalization of private and small-scale activities and a more pronounced role for foreign trade and foreign direct investments improved supplies in domestic markets and contributed to a substantial increase in consumer satisfaction. Living standards improved until 1987, a process in which significant imports of consumer goods from the developed market economies played a role. Unemployment had never been a serious issue before 1990, and income differentials appeared to have decreased at least until 1987.

These results notwithstanding, the rate of economic growth in Hungary was very slow in the 1980s; the share of accumulation in net material product (NMP) fell from 25–28 percent in the mid-1970s to 10–12 percent by the end of the 1980s. Capital stock became obsolete and was poorly maintained. Between 1970 and 1989, the gross hard-currency debt rose sharply from $1 billion to $21 billion. It was obvious that further domestic and external adjustments were needed.

Based on the pre-1988 achievements of the reform process, many observers hoped for a fast and efficient transformation of Hungary. Post-1988 economic policies and results, however, did not fulfill these expectations. Beginning in 1989, the trade regime and domestic prices were liberalized further. The Hungarian forint was made convertible for current account transactions and for capital inflows. An active exchange rate policy, which involved stabilizing the currency with monetary and fiscal policies, was followed. These attempts, however, were not systematically thought through and carried out. Political goals and aims sidetracked important policy measures, as in the case of compensation schemes. The almost complete liberalization of foreign trade and the deliberate attempt to let the forint appreciate against the basket of currencies ended in serious deficits in the trade and balance of payments accounts. Hungary had to increase its indebtedness in order to finance these disequilibria. As a result, debt servicing became an important burden on the national budget. Fiscal deficits, especially interest payments, have been on the rise. Consequently, macroeconomic policy was buffeted by domestic and external pressures. Aggressive stabilization measures were called for. Harsh monetary and fiscal measures were introduced on 12 March 1995 that called for a dramatic decrease in the budget deficit and a reversal of exchange rate policy aimed at enhanced exports and reduced imports.

Throughout this period, and especially after 1988, the inflow of foreign direct investment (FDI) in Hungary has been substantial. Hungary has been the principal target of FDI in East-Central Europe as a result of its liberal legislation. The stock and flow of FDI were on the rise until 1996,[1] in which year the FDI inflow was less than in the previous years.

Efforts to draw policy lessons from the Hungarian transition experience must deal with the peculiar macroeconomic situation and explain the paradox of high-level FDI inflow. The discouraging macroeconomic balances partly reflect the fact that beginning in 1991, the exchange rate had ceased to be a nominal anchor; it was set so high as to make inflation control a

priority issue. This policy was changed in March 1995. Expectations for
the positive effects of the new exchange rate policy are based partly on
FDI considerations. Long-term swings in exchange rates can affect the
volume and pattern of FDI. If exchange rate risk were to be reduced, FDI
would be attracted to Hungary. However, variability in input costs may
offset the risk premium on foreign investment, and FDI may be reduced.
As microeconomic analysis will show later, the spatial allocation of investment can be dominated not so much by efficiency as by exchange rate
considerations. Investments may not be concentrated in areas with lower
costs and higher efficiency but, rather, be diversified so as to minimize the
exchange rate risk. Hungary's experience with FDI in the period 1991–96
clearly bears out these remarks. The high exchange rate risk, with a certain time lag, led to a more cautious attitude on the part of foreign direct
investors.[2]

## 2.1  Background and Liberalization Measures

### 2.1.1  Starting Conditions

The Antall government that assumed power in Hungary in May 1990
faced fundamental challenges of transition similar to those faced by other
governments in the region. There were, however, positive and negative
environmental factors in Hungary that differed significantly from those in
other transition economies.

**Advantages**
Hungarian policy makers inherited a number of positive economic legacies from the pretransition governments. In addition, the country had other
geographic, political, and social advantages that have played an important
role in the partial success of the transformation. Negative economic and
political factors, however, contributed to the mixed overall results of
transformation and stabilization.

*Long History of Economic Reforms.*   The initial conditions for systemic
transformation in Hungary were favorable. The share of the private sector
in the gross domestic product (GDP) was small but increased substantially
after 1986. Private activities mushroomed not only in agriculture and
related manufacturing but also in services. Earlier limitations on land and
real estate ownership were abandoned in mid-1989, and small-scale private production activity began to emerge in industry as well. The Private

Enterprise Act of January 1990 offered similar opportunities to individual entrepreneurs and business organizations. Economic activity was substantially decentralized and the overly concentrated structure of industry was partly broken. Large-scale state enterprises, however, dominated the industrial landscape although important legal prerequisites of antimonopoly legislation were put in place.

The price and wage system began to provide reasonable guidance in economic decision-making. Relative prices, together with the continuously updated system of interest and exchange rates, adjusted the economy to the international economic environment to a great extent. Foreign trade and payment regimes were modified, the isolation of domestic producers in hard currency trade relations was reduced,[3] and the regulations governing foreign trade were substantially liberalized. As a party to the General Agreement on Tariffs and Trade (GATT) since 1973, Hungary conducts its foreign trade with market economies on a most-favored-nation (MFN) basis. Its trade with other CMEA members and centrally planned economies was based, until the end of 1990, on annual protocols calling for deliveries of fixed quantities at fixed prices within the framework of five-year bilateral trade and payment agreements. This system of trading and payments was abolished on 1 January 1991.

The legal and institutional basis for a market economy began to take shape. Since 1989 Hungary has allowed the establishment of Western style corporations. The rights, guarantees, and privileges of foreign investors are protected by a special act providing the legal framework for the activities of economic units that are partly or fully foreign-owned. A comprehensive banking reform was launched as early as 1985. Commercial credits began to be extended from one enterprise to another; in 1987 a two-tier banking system—with six commercial banks—was put in place. In late 1989 these banks were allowed to accept foreign currency deposits of residents without asking for the origin of these funds. From 1 January 1990, the commercial banks were authorized to finance convertible currency transactions in foreign trade. Various forms of savings and investment instruments—bonds, stocks, treasury bills, certificates of deposit, and commercial bills—have proliferated since then.

Fiscal arrangements began to undergo positive changes in the 1980s. The strict administrative separation of households' financial transactions from those of enterprises ceased to exist. Fiscal policy, which was put under the control of the Parliament, began to acquire market economy features. The value-added tax was introduced in the production sphere, and individuals began to be taxed on their personal incomes. Currently enterprise and private profits are taxed in a uniform manner. The share of consumer and producer subsidies in the state budget was reduced substantially, and the basic elements of a social safety net were put in place. Having joined the International Monetary Fund (IMF) and the International Bank for Reconstruction and Development (IBRD) in early 1982, Hungary was able to secure the necessary external funds throughout the 1980s. The short-term economic program, worked out by the Németh government, and accepted by the Parliament in December 1989, was supported by an IMF standby agreement of $200 million.

***Consumer and Investor Behavior.*** With a long history of economic reform, the Hungarian population got used to the impact of policy instruments such as price hikes, interest rate changes, and differentiated incomes. Investors faced similar developments. Company managers freely employed modern management styles; their personal responsibility increased, as did their incomes. As a result, by the end of the 1980s both the general public and the economy were in a constant state of reform. The 1988 reform wave had a substantial impact. It seemed easier to introduce fundamental changes in the Hungarian economy than in the economic systems and management of neighboring countries.

***External Trade and Foreign Direct Investment.*** Since the early years of the NEM, Hungary has followed a multifaceted foreign trade and FDI policy. The export and import monopoly of the state was dismantled and an increasing number of companies received direct access to external trade. A revised, more flexible exchange rate policy was introduced over time; legislation regulating FDI was introduced as early as 1972.[4] The economy was opened up, resulting in deeper adjustments to the Western international economy.

***Political Advantages.*** The NEM received wide international recognition and Hungary began to be studied as the "laboratory test" of the reforms in Central and Eastern Europe. As the political and foreign policy relations of the country expanded, the special qualities of Hungarian domestic economic and general policy attracted the interest of a number of transition economies. Partial change in the economic system brought Hungary closer to Western creditors and international financial institutions, thereby creating benefits for Hungary. It was hoped that the systemic change of 1990 would follow the "philosophy" of Hungarian macroeconomic management and in turn speed the change.

## Disadvantages

*Macroeconomic Disequilibrium.* Unlike neighboring Czechoslovakia, Hungary did not experience macroeconomic stability in the 1980s. Government deficits and the growth of money stock were high during the decade, as was inflation measured by the CPI.[5] Investments developed sporadically in particular after 1985, when, under the influence of politicians, an acceleration of the growth process was accepted by the Hungarian Socialist Workers' Party. In the country's external relations, the situation was almost the same. Trade with the developed market economies was unbalanced, and a gross hard currency debt of $20.4 billion was being serviced with considerable difficulty.

These unfavorable macroeconomic conditions were of concern to policy makers. First, the post-May 1990 government had to move fast because the policy status quo could not safely be maintained while conflicts over reform and stabilization measures were resolved. In 1990 several stabilization measures and changes in macroeconomic policy were implemented. The new regime introduced stabilization measures and even appeared to benefit from them; the 1990 consolidated budget showed a much smaller deficit.[6] Second, given internal and external disequilibrium, the dangers inherent in liberalization of domestic markets and of foreign trade were much more than in countries where inflationary spirals and the loss of international reserves were not serious future possibilities. Moreover, macroeconomic instability meant that stabilization measures could not be focused on microeconomic or relative price effects because the stabilization effects were of primary importance.

*Long Period of Economic Reforms.* Paradoxically, the long period of economic reforms has had negative consequences. First, the labor unions became important sources of political and economic power after the 1989–90 changes in the ownership structure of the Hungarian economy. The introduction of the personal income tax increased the cohesion of these organizations. Organized labor lobbied for higher wages, employment-saving policies, and a wide social safety net when the transition began.

Equally important in this respect was the fact that managerial behavior and ownership structure changed substantially by 1989; a small-business private sector evolved. Managerial autonomy had started earlier, but managers were neither willing nor able in 1990 to respond to new conditions and opportunities. Clearly, they feared a new wave of political interference in company affairs. At the same time, their readiness to implement the new macroeconomic policy was rather weak. Privatization had started earlier but could not be accelerated because of the political ramifications of the issue. Slow privatization procedures were adopted because privatization met heavy resistance in the Parliament. Sale of government-owned company stock for political reasons interfered with privatization. For example, the voucher-based privatization method was firmly rejected by the general public and the Parliament.

Consumers feared further price increases, especially of Western goods that were imported after the new wave of import liberalization. Several political parties put this issue on their agenda and defended consumer interests against price increases, thereby helping to establish a consumer lobby.

### 2.1.2   Assessment

Overall, Hungary had long-term advantages arising from its long history of economic reforms, the development of a small-business private sector, the banking reform, and business and investment contacts with the West. There were, however, short-run problems associated with its macroeconomic and external disequilibria. In resolving these immediate concerns, Hungarian policy makers could count on substantial assistance from the market economies, the willingness of foreign investors to participate in the country's privatization projects, the existence of trade relations with the West, and Hungarian business's awareness of market economy business practices. The policies that were adopted to resolve the short-term issues and their results are discussed below.

## 2.2   Main Economic Results of the Transition: 1990–96

### 2.2.1   Macroeconomic Development

As a result of severe stabilization and transformation policies, gross domestic product (GDP) in Hungary declined by about one-sixth between 1989 and 1995,[7] and final consumption by 9 percent. The output slump was spread across consumption by households and government, and fixed investment. The aggregate decline in fixed investment of 8.5 percent in these years resulted in a further fall in the investment share of GDP to approximately 11 percent. Important modernization projects had to be postponed. Only the most important investments could be financed from domestic sources. Therefore, the demand for external investment resources was substantial.

One important source of investment, net savings of the population, behaved erratically in the period. After a substantial increase in 1991 and 1992—the ratio reached 10.9 percent in the latter year—it declined to 6.5 percent in 1993, followed by another fall in 1994 to about 4 percent. In 1995 the ratio reached again the level of 1992. More worrisome than the actual drop in the ratio was the substantial change in savings in favor of foreign exchange deposits. In fact, there was a strong connection between the expected devaluation of the forint and the increase in foreign exchange deposits of the population. Devaluation expectations were high throughout the period.

With an 28.2 percent price increase in 1995,[8] inflation was still high. Domestic and external pressures played a role in this performance. The exchange rate had to be adjusted several times because domestic inflation clearly ran ahead of world inflation. The usual one-step devaluation(s) did not correct the full inflation differential and led to a real appreciation of the forint. In other words, domestic inflation ran ahead of the rise in the nominal value of the forint. While this policy was important to counter the large inflow of FDI, it led to increased imports. Moreover, expectations of inflation led to excessive wage pressures, but above-quota wage increases were usually punished by a tax.

Unemployment has been one of the most troubling developments in recent years. Measured as the ratio of registered unemployed in the economically active population, unemployment at present is 10.8 percent.[9] The number of registered jobs available fell dramatically: At the beginning of 1990, the number per 100 unemployed was 161; a year later, it was 13, declining to 3.5 in December 1992 and 4.4 in December 1993 in 1995 this indicator increased to 5.4.[10]

Industrial output and sales began to recover in 1993, following the continuous decline that began in 1989.[11] Industrial growth, which improved in 1994 with an output increase of 9.2 percent,[12] continued in 1995. The growth in the output of small businesses employing a maximum of 50 people was particularly dynamic in both years (24 and 22.7 percent, respectively). The share of small business in overall industrial output reached 14 percent by 1994. An increasing share of production was accounted for by Hungarian-foreign joint ventures.

As a result of several negative factors,[13] the gross output of agriculture fell continuously between 1989 and 1993, reaching an aggregate decline of about 30 percent. In 1995, however, gross agricultural production increased again by 15 percent.

### 2.2.2 External Trade and Payment Issues

There were two distinct phases of foreign trade development between 1989 and 1995. As a result of the reform measures of 1987–88, the trade balance showed a declining but still positive balance in 1989–91. Stabilization measures, however, left their mark on foreign trade: the period 1992–95 registered a cumulative $9.5 billion trade deficit.[14] The volume of imports increased by 23.5 percent, whereas that of exports increased by 1.6 percent in 1989–95. Thus the impact of the transformation policies resembled that in other transition economies and increased imports much more than exports. The role of the internal and external factors in the severe deterioration of the balance of trade cannot be determined accurately, but some contributory factors can be singled out. Among these were the deepening recession in the important Western European economies (in which economic activity picked up slightly in 1994), the structural weaknesses of Hungarian export supplies, the stimulation of domestic demand, and the deteriorating (or sluggish) price competitiveness of Hungarian exports in external markets. An import duty surcharge of 8 percent was introduced on 20 March 1995 to counter this strong import surge.[15]

Significant changes occurred in the trade of the main product groups.[16] As can be expected, imports of consumer products and technological items such as machinery and equipment increased mainly in the early years of the transition process. Later, imports of basic materials, spare parts, and semi-finished products surged. The most important growth on the export side resulted from commission work.[17] Partial results, especially in the first phase of the period, could be observed with regard to agriculture, but this proved to be temporary.[18]

The geographical composition of external trade changed as well during 1989–95. The share of developed market economies in the turnover increased further, to about 72 percent. The share of the European Union in imports was 61 percent, and in exports, 63 percent. The share of the former socialist economies in Hungary's exports was 20 percent, and in imports, 22 percent. Developing countries accounted for only 4–5 percent of the external trade turnover.

By the end of 1995, Hungary's gross foreign debt increased to $31.65 billion from $21.27 billion in December 1990, according to the National

Bank of Hungary. At end of 1995, international assets (reserves) stood at $14.8 billion, of which the National Bank's convertible foreign exchange reserves totaled $12.0 billion and the claims abroad amounted to $2.8 billion.

### 2.2.3  *Exchange Rate Policy and Development*

Hungarian policy makers adjusted the exchange rate several times between 1990 and 1995. The purpose was twofold: to influence domestic prices by keeping the exchange rate under control and to maintain the competitiveness of Hungarian exportables by adjusting the exchange rate (Hajdu, 1994 p. 38). The exchange rate was fixed in terms of currencies that were most important for Hungarian foreign trade.[19] In the course of 1990–95, the forint was devalued by 102.2 percent, relative to its 1989 level, against the basket of currencies used to determine its exchange rate. The nominal devaluations of the period under review were aimed at preventing the deterioration of the competitiveness of Hungarian products. This objective was attained in 1990, 1992, 1994 and 1995. By contrast, the forint appreciated in real terms (signaling a deterioration of price competitiveness) in 1991 and (slightly less) in 1993.

In contrast with this erratic exchange rate policy, the Hungarian government decided on 12 March 1995 to devalue the forint by 9 percent and introduce a new exchange rate policy. Accordingly, the National Bank of Hungary announces weekly devaluations in order to counter the strong expectations of devaluation in the domestic economy. The forint was devalued monthly by 1.9 percent until 30 June 1995; since 1 July 1995 this monthly devaluation has been 1.3 percent (*Népszabadság*, March 15, 1995, p. 5). In August 1995, the National Bank of Hungary announced 1.2 percent as the monthly rate of depreciation for the first half of 1996.

### 2.2.4  *Assessment*

It is clear from the above analysis that the Hungarian economy is fragile. Domestic capital accumulation is weak; the large state sector is "decapitalized" through deep cuts in investments, and the budding private sector is not yet strong enough to counter this decline. Import propensity is still very high, and the savings propensity of the population is rather low. Economic policy measures aimed at transformation in the past years have been slow and inconsequential. Policy makers made optimistic assumptions about the economy's potential, but its shortcomings turned out to be greater than anticipated.

The critical problem, however, was that since 1990 the governments led by successive prime ministers[20] did not act decisively and rationally. Macroeconomic stabilization did not take place effectively. Structural issues and industrial modernization received inadequate attention. Privatization dragged on, and the compensation programs further complicated the not-too-transparent schemes of privatization. The long-awaited reform of the state budget was postponed until March 1995. The margin of economic growth was too narrow to counter negative factors in the economy and push it forward (Kornai, 1993). This was amply demonstrated by the results of 1994: Mild economic growth was followed by a worsening balance of payments, increasing both domestic and external indebtedness.

It was clear by early 1995 that the policy focus should be on the export-oriented sectors of the economy. If exports show a dynamic upward trend and if imports support better export performance, an external imbalance can be avoided. An export drive must take priority in policy making.

Harsh austerity measures taken in March 1995 have laid the foundations for a sustainable recovery. In the period of March 1995–December 1996, interest rates have fallen, as have deficits and debt levels and price inflation. True, there was also a steep fall in real incomes,[21] and domestic consumption shrank.[22]

The benefits, however, are already visible: the state budget deficit has been reduced from 7.4 percent of GDP in 1994 to about 4 percent in 1996.[23] The share of GDP distributed by the state budget has been reduced from 61 percent in 1994 to 48 percent in 1996. The dangerously high current account deficit in 1994 ($3.9 billion) was reduced to $2.5 billion last year and to between $1.6 and $1.8 billion in 1996. Unit labor costs had also been drastically reduced. In manufacturing this indicator was reduced in 1995 by 8.7 percent, and in the first quarter of 1996 alone by a further 10.3 percent.[24]

The resulting increase in exports of between 8 and 10 percent in both 1995 and 1996 had helped to avoid a drop into recession. 1996 closed with a 1 percent growth of GDP.

Hungarian liberalization did not create genuine competition between domestic producers and foreign suppliers. Rather, the production activities of the firms that were wholly or majority foreign-owned continued without domestic rivals.[25] As a result, issues governing FDI gained critical importance. These are discussed below.

## 2.3    Transformation and FDI in Hungary

### 2.3.1    *Growth of FDI*

The opportunity to attract foreign direct investment through various forms of joint venture has existed in Hungary since 1972, and the rules have been updated several times.[26] Hungarian policy makers have been using the advantages of FDI in various forms. They expected that FDI would increase export potential, raise the level of technological development, lead to more efficient company and management behavior, and stimulate structural changes. In addition, the positive effects of FDI on the balance of payments have not escaped attention. Generally, balance of payments receipts increase with FDI inflow (in cash),[27] whereas profit repatriations on these investments usually decrease. It is necessary to counter the monetary pressures arising from incoming FDI by means of prudent monetary policies.

A basic assumption throughout the reform process in Hungary has been the need to manage an annual flow of FDI that covers interest payments and amortization of the international debt. As will be argued later, as this goal received priority attention, other effects of FDI on the national economy were often pushed into the background.

Two phases may be clearly distinguished in the history of FDI in Hungary. The first phase, before 1989, witnessed the launching of economic transformation under the influence of reforms initiated in 1968, under the central control of a planned economy, that created the economic and political conditions for the gradual opening up of foreign trade. FDI could legally be undertaken in Hungary since 1972. The legal framework governing FDI improved steadily until 1988. In 1988 alone, two important acts, the Act on Companies and the Act on Foreign Direct Investment, were passed by the Parliament.

Initially, foreign venture capital was limited to minority ownership and basically to the service sector. All direct restrictions were lifted by 1989. The fact that enterprises with foreign ownership were operating in Hungary for more than twenty years gave Hungary a substantial edge in the initial period of transformation. Toward the end of 1989, the cumulative total of FDI, most of it in the service sector, amounted to approximately $0.5 billion.

Since 1972, but especially since the 1988 Act on Foreign Direct Investment, the growth of FDI and the number of foreign-Hungarian joint ventures has been spectacular. (See Table 2.1.) The stock of accumulated FDI

**Table 2.1**
Value of foreign direct investment and number of joint ventures, 1974–1996 (million U.S. dollars)

| Period | Number of JVs | Flow of FDI | Stock of FDI | Share of foreign capital* |
|--------|---------------|-------------|--------------|---------------------------|
| 1974–1984 | 28 | | 13 | |
| 1985–1986 | 32 | 6 | 19 | |
| 1987.I.1 | 44 | −1 | 18 | |
| 1988.I.1 | 104 | 5 | 23 | 8.4 |
| 1989.I.1 | 208 | 188 | 215 | 24.0 |
| 1990.I.1 | 1350 | 54 | 569 | 34.0 |
| 1991.I.1 | 5693 | 1538 | 2107 | 45.0 |
| 1992.I.1 | 9117 | 1317 | 3424 | 56.0 |
| 1993.I.1 | 17182 | 2152 | 5576 | 60.0 |
| 1994.I.1 | 20999 | 1511 | 7087 | 76.0 |
| 1995.I.31 | 25430 | 244 | 7231 | 78.0 |
| 1996.I.1 | 29150 | 4688 | 11919 | |

*Source:* National Bank of Hungary, *Annual Report, 1955*, Budapest, p. 214; Központi Statiszti-kai Hivatal (1995), p. 8, Table 1.
*Note:* *Share of FDI in the total of statutory capital in Hungary.

at the end of January 1996 seems modest compared with the stock of foreign indebtedness of Hungary; however, compared with the FDI stock of other transition economies of Central and Eastern Europe, the Hungarian performance is noteworthy. (See Table 2.2; see also Horváth, 1993, pp. 37–40.) The table shows that FDI volume invested in Central and Eastern Europe increased by 41 times during 1989–95, starting from a rather low level. Annual growth of FDI flow, however, has slowed substantially (growth rates are in parentheses): 1990 (436 percent); 1991 (239 percent); 1992 (47 percent); 1993 (41 percent); 1994 (−9 percent); (ECE, 1995). In 1995, however, FDI investment in the region more than doubled.

There are two reasons for the high Hungarian figures, a general one and a specific one. The general explanation is that, compared with the situation in the other countries of the region, the Hungarian economy reached its most advantageous position regarding international integration and attractiveness in 1992 and 1993. The earlier two-decade liberalization process reached its climax at the start of the 1990s and created a positive environment. For example, the association agreement with the European Economic Community generated advantageous market conditions for activities performed in Hungary. On the other hand, the high

**Table 2.2**
Foreign direct investment in Central and Eastern Europe (million U.S. dollars, annually)

| Country | 1989 | 1990 | 1991 | 1992 | 1993 | 1994 | 1995 | 1989–1995 | Share |
|---|---|---|---|---|---|---|---|---|---|
| Bulgaria | 10 | 4 | 56 | 42 | 40 | 105 | 115 | 372 | 1.4 |
| Czech Republic | 10 | 426 | 511 | 1004 | 568 | 862 | 2500 | 5881 | 21.6 |
| Hungary* | 120 | 526 | 1459 | 1471 | 2339 | 1146 | 4453 | 11514 | 42.2 |
| Poland | 60 | 55 | 291 | 678 | 1715 | 1875 | 1892 | 6566 | 24.0 |
| Romania | 20 | 0 | 40 | 80 | 87 | 341 | 419 | 987 | 3.6 |
| Slovakia | 5 | 28 | 82 | 100 | 144 | 170 | 180 | 709 | 2.6 |
| Slovenia | 5 | 7 | 65 | 111 | 113 | 84 | 150 | 535 | 2.0 |
| Ukraine | 10 | 0 | 0 | 200 | 198 | 151 | 150 | 709 | 2.6 |
| Central and Eastern Europe | 240 | 1046 | 2504 | 3686 | 5204 | 4734 | 9859 | 27273 | 100 |

*Source:* Economic Commission for Europe (ECE): *Economic Survey of Europe in 1995–1996.*
United Nations publication (Sales no.E.96.II.E.1), New York, 1996, p. 151.
*Note:* *The stock of FDI in Table 2.1 is different because it contains only FDI in cash; here it
includes FDI in kind as well.

investment flow in 1993 and in 1995 resulted from a specific privatization
project, the offer of shares to foreign investors in the Hungarian Telecommunication Company (MATÁV).

Evidently, from 1990 to 1995, the value of FDI was higher than the
deficit in the current trade balance.[28] From a short-term perspective, the
positive feature of FDI consisted in the fact that investments made in cash
were increasing, and those in kind, which provided technical services and
technological innovation, were decreasing.[29]

The FDI pattern in Hungary has been marked by a positive relationship
between foreign trade liberalization, FDI regulation, and FDI dynamism.
Along with the rapid and peaceful political transition and the general
liberalization of the economy after 1989, the fast-paced, radical deregulation of FDI obviously contributed to its spectacular growth. FDI per
capita reached $331 during 1990–95 in the entire Central and East Euro-
pean region. Figure per capita FDI in Hungary was $1118; in the Czech
Republic, $619; and in Slovenia, $297. FDI in the region (cumulated from
its start) was 2.38 percent of GDP; in Hungary (1995), it was 12.4 percent.
Hungary attracted 42 percent of the total FDI of the region; 47 percent
if only the Visegrád countries[30] are considered. It must be noted, however, that Hungary's attraction was stronger in the first period, 1988–90,
during which 66 percent of the region's FDI flowed into Hungary. This

**Table 2.3**
Hungary: change in the structure of company assets

|  | 1989 | | 1995 | |
|---|---|---|---|---|
|  | All companies | Joint ventures | All companies | Joint ventures |
| Number of companies | 14242 | 1350 | 220449 | 24950 |
| Statutory capital (bill. forint) | 1780.1 | 124.4 | 4932.0[a] | 1973.0 |
| Foreign investment (bill. forint) | 30.0 | 30.0 | 1308.0 | 1308.0 |
| Share of FDI in statutory capital (percent) | 1.7 | 24.1 | 26.5 | 66.3 |
| Statutory capital/company (mill.forint) | 125.0 | 92.1 | 22.4 | 79.1 |

Source: KSH: *Külföldi tőkével működő vállalkozások*, Budapest, 1996, Table 1, p. 5.
Note: a. Estimate based on partial official data.

share in 1991–95 dropped to 42 percent, clearly showing that other countries were able to attract substantial FDI.[31]

The number of joint ventures with majority foreign ownership increased substantially during 1990–95, measured in terms of the increasing share of wholly owned foreign companies in the total number of joint ventures and in their investments. Only 2 percent of joint ventures were wholly owned by foreigners in 1989. This ratio had climbed to 44 percent by the end of 1995. The opposite trend is revealing as well: 87 percent of the joint ventures had Hungarian majority owners in 1989. This share was only 37 percent in 1993. (There is no data for 1995.) The share of majority foreign-owned joint ventures (in all joint ventures) increased from 12 percent in 1989 to 28 percent in 1993.[32] Altogether, half of foreign-owned firms are majority owned, a third are wholly owned, and a fifth have majority domestic ownership.

FDI share in the assets of Hungarian companies increased from 2 percent in 1989 to 17 percent in 1995. Important changes occurred in the structure of company assets as well. (See Table 2.3.) The average size of both domestic-owned and foreign-owned companies decreased between 1989 and 1995. There was, however, an interesting change within this overall development. Joint ventures were substantially smaller than the average Hungarian company in 1989; in 1995, they had 3.5 times more average statutory capital than the average Hungarian company.

FDI distribution varies greatly among the sectors of the Hungarian economy. Half of cumulated FDI operated in manufacturing industry at the end of 1995. The second largest sector was trade, with only 14 percent of total FDI stock. Majority of the manufacturing FDI stock was concentrated in three branches: food industry (13 percent), machine industry (65 percent), and chemical industry (9 percent). The share of FDI increased from 2 percent to 9 percent in two years in the transportation, storage, post, and telecommunication branches as a result of the partial privatization of MATÁV, the Hungarian Telecommunication Company.[33] The FDI share in financing, insurance, and real estate has decreased since 1991. Foreign investors have little interest in Hungarian agriculture, electric power, gas, and water supply projects.[34]

The structure of foreign direct investments in Hungary has become more favorable in recent years: 57.5 percent of the total (cumulated) investments operate in industry (mostly in machine building, including the automobile and food industries), 14 percent in telecommunications, 8.5 percent in the financial sector, 8.5 percent in the commercial sector, and 7 percent in the real estate and hotel sector. The current structure is more favorable than the structure in 1990–1993 and reflects the positive structural effects of the investment flows. New investments in 1994 and 1995 followed this trend. A significant part of commercial activities and services is beginning to come under the control of foreign capital.[35]

The transition economies that faced agonizing transformation problems gradually liberalized FDI legislation, decreased red tape, and stimulated FDI with macro- and microeconomic measures. As a result, the significant differences among these economies relating to FDI flows have narrowed. Hungary has lost its initial advantage of the 1980s because other reforming economies will successfully redirect FDI flows to themselves.[36]

### 2.3.2   *Effects of FDI on the Balance of Payments*

FDI helped to stabilize the economy from year to year. Through a positive effect on the balance of payments, it contributed to the easing of increased external debt service burdens without the immediate siphoning of resources from the Hungarian economy. There has been a growing improvement, supported by FDI, in the balance of payments since 1989. (See Table 2.4.) The positive impact of FDI on the balance of payments in 1991 was almost five times greater than in 1990: The 1991 balance of payments closed with a $267 million net surplus. (Cash FDI in that year was slightly more than the net balance of interest payments.) In 1992 this pattern was almost copied: The FDI flow of $1,272 million exceeded the $1,216 million in net interest payments. And 1993 was exceptional in

**Table 2.4**
The effect of foreign direct investment on the balance of payments in Hungary, 1989–1994

|                                               | 1989 | 1990 | 1991 | 1992 | 1993 | 1994 | 1995 | 1996 Jan.–June |
|-----------------------------------------------|------|------|------|------|------|------|------|----------------|
| FDI in cash                                   | 187  | 311  | 1459 | 1471 | 2339 | 1146 | 4453 | 734            |
| Net income outflow on FDI                     | 0    | −24  | −32  | −45  | −56− | −117 | −194 | −125           |
| Short-term improvement in balance of payments | 187  | 287  | 1427 | 1272 | 2283 | 1029 | 4259 | 609            |
| FDI in kind                                   | 20   | 50   | 92   | 160  | 160  | 200  | 250  | 170            |

*Source:* National Bank of Hungary, *Monthly Report*, no. 8. 1996; Table III/11 and Table III/12, pp. 91 and 93.
*Note:* FDI in kind is estimated on the basis of Tables 2.1 and 2.2 and partial official statistics.

this respect: Although the balance of trade—and with it the balance of payments—worsened substantially,[37] there was a short-term improvement in the balance of payments of $2,283 million, supported by FDI, which was substantially above net interest payments of $1,130 million. But 1994 could not repeat this: The balance of payments closed with a deficit of $3,911 million; the FDI flow, which was less than net interest payments, amounted to $1,029 million.

1995, however, was exceptional again. Although the current account closed with a U.S.$2.4 billion deficit, FDI inflows came to U.S.$4.4 billion. This amount was more than twice the level of net interest payments in that year alone, allowing substantial reduction in the level of net debt.[38] In the first ten months of 1996, the trend continued. The combined balance of payments deficit for these ten months came to U.S.$1.124 billion, while FDI flow in the same period brought into the country U.S.$1.47 billion. Net debt was further reduced to U.S.$13.7 billion.[39]

### 2.3.3  Effects of FDI on the Balance of Trade

The process of opening up an economy entails import liberalization. Allowing FDI in kind contributes to the deterioration of the balance of trade by "increasing" imports. The export performance expected from these assets follows several years later. However, FDI in cash may compensate for the deterioration of the balance of trade in the intervening period.

Hungarian import liberalization took place simultaneously with the elimination of barriers to FDI. However, the opening of the economy was not followed by an immediate import boom; moreover, the balance of trade was increasingly in surplus until 1991, with joint ventures playing a substantial role in the process.[40] Their foreign trade activity in exports and imports grew more dynamically each year than that of national companies. (See Table 2.5.) In fact, the foreign trade balance of joint ventures constitutes a dominant share of the Hungarian trade balance except in 1993, 1994, and 1995. The share of joint ventures in the export earnings of Hungarian companies was 40 percent in 1992 and rose to 65 percent in 1995. The dominant role of joint ventures in Hungary's foreign trade is related to these companies' extensive Western market relations, the greater competitiveness of their products, and their sophisticated marketing. High interest rates on loans, increasing liquidity problems of companies, and government delay in developing a financial, credit, and information network to assist small and medium-sized businesses in export markets led to the dominance of subcontracting and joint ventures in foreign trade. The superior knowledge of markets and the flexible organization of economic and production activity, supplemented by the financial muscle of FDI, gave an edge to these operators over traditional Hungarian companies.

At the same time these maneuvering abilities gave an advantage to joint ventures in avoiding large tax burdens (including social insurance, wage-related taxes, and the profit tax). Interviews with joint ventures revealed that these companies often employed transfer pricing[41] to repatriate additional revenue by using the price margin differences of exports and imports (Hamar, 1993, p. 16). This practice and the change in the system of compiling the foreign trade statistics[42] pose problems in accurately measuring the role of subcontracting and the impact of joint ventures' foreign trade activity on export profitability and the balance of trade. Although the trade data are marred by uncertainties, they nevertheless suggest a substantial and increasing role of joint ventures in foreign trade activity and in shaping market processes, thereby creating tensions and uncertainties for domestic exporters. Some experts estimate the contribution of joint ventures' exports to overall Hungarian exports to be around 70 percent.[43]

## 2.4   Microeconomic Issues Relating to FDI in Hungary

The role of FDI in the restructuring of Hungarian companies and the criteria in terms of which FDI contribution can be assessed are analyzed in this section. For a long time Hungarian companies were left out of the internationalization of production, which started rather late and reluctantly.

**Table 2.5**
Joint ventures and foreign trade, 1988–95

| Year | Foreign trade, total (billion forint) | Growth of foreign trade (percent) | Foreign trade of joint ventures (billion forint) | Growth of foreign trade of joint ventures (percent) | Share of JVs' foreign trade in total (percent) |
|---|---|---|---|---|---|
| | | | Export | | |
| 1988 | 499.4 | 112.7 | 32.7 | N.A. | 6.5 |
| 1989 | 587.2 | 117.5 | 46.3 | 141.8 | 7.9 |
| 1990 | 615.1 | 104.7 | 69.4 | 149.9 | 11.3 |
| 1991 | 764.1 | 124.2 | 189.7 | 273.3 | 24.8 |
| 1992 | 843.6 | 110.4 | 325.9 | 171.7 | 38.6 |
| 1993 | 819.9 | 97.2 | 438.9 | 134.9 | 53.5 |
| 1994 | 1128.7 | 137.6 | 629.8 | 143.5 | 55.8 |
| 1995 | 1622.0 | 143.7 | 1049.4 | 166.6 | 64.7 |
| | | | Import | | |
| 1988 | 469.0 | 104.1 | 17.3 | N.A. | 3.7 |
| 1989 | 535.2 | 114.1 | 33.5 | 194.0 | 6.3 |
| 1990 | 556.0 | 103.9 | 50.5 | 150.6 | 9.1 |
| 1991 | 855.4 | 153.8 | 232.7 | 460.7 | 27.2 |
| 1992 | 878.5 | 102.7 | 358.4 | 154.0 | 40.8 |
| 1993 | 1162.5 | 132.3 | 584.9 | 163.2 | 50.3 |
| 1994 | 1537.0 | 132.2 | 804.0 | 174.3 | 52.3 |
| 1995 | 1936.4 | 126.0 | 1196.7 | 148.8 | 61.8 |
| | | | Balance | | |
| 1988 | 30.5 | | 15.4 | | 50.4 |
| 1989 | 52.1 | | 12.8 | | 24.5 |
| 1990 | 59.0 | | 18.9 | | 32.0 |
| 1991 | −91.3 | | −43.0 | | 47.0 |
| 1992 | −34.9 | | −32.5 | | 92.7 |
| 1993 | −342.6 | | −146.0 | | 42.6 |
| 1994 | −408.3 | | −174.2 | | 42.7 |
| 1995 | −314.4 | | −147.3 | | 46.9 |

*Source:* For 1988–92, see J. Hamar (1993), p. 70; 1993–94 foreign trade total data are from National Bank of Hungary, *Monthly Report*, no. 4 (1995). 1994–95 joint venture trade data are estimates, based on partial information from the Hungarian Joint Venture Association. 1995 foreign trade data are from National Bank of Hungary, *Annual Report, 1995*, Annex A, Table III/3, p. 157.

The organizational and managerial systems that were distorted by the strict separation of production and foreign trade shielded the Hungarian economy from the world market.

Joint ventures brought important changes in this respect. They encouraged changes in the traditional production and organization systems by integrating these separated activities and by creating new opportunities. In this context the political stability and the positive attitude of government helped, but the uncertainties and stagnation of an economy marked by declining effective demand were disincentives to producers that could not be compensated for by tax allowances or depressed wages. Barring noteworthy exceptions such as the Opel assembly plant of General Motors and the Japanese Suzuki auto factory, FDI failed to create new industrial establishments, branches, or products. FDI was directed mainly toward those industries and factories which operated above the average technological productivity and economic efficiency levels. Firms that urgently needed technological reconstruction, management changes, and new markets were neglected by FDI partners (Szentes, 1995, p. 20).

The privatization of Hungarian industrial enterprises was expected to attract large FDI flows. The important aspects of this interaction are discussed below.

### 2.4.1 Privatization and FDI in Hungary

The obvious way in which FDI could contribute to the privatization of Hungarian state assets was financial. Private savings, as noted above, were eroded in the transition years by inflation, and in any case were inadequate to provide the fianancial resources for effective privatization. Foreign financing could bridge the gap. It need not be in the form of direct investments. Privatization opened up opportunities for transnational corporations to make major acquisitions in Hungarian industry.

The development of a significant private sector rests not only on the denationalization of state-owned assets but also on the creation of new units through the growth of private enterprise. The initial, joint-venture phase of FDI in Hungary created entities that were legally independent but operated largely within the administrative and operational framework of the local partner: the state enterprise. However, they initiated the evolution of the hitherto solely state-owned sector toward mixed ownership. Recently a second phase, in which the acquisition of former state-owned assets became possible through privatization, has enlisted FDI more directly and on a larger scale. A third phase legally allows foreign firms

**Table 2.6**
Foreign direct investment in Hungarian privatization (as of September 30, 1996)

| Origin of FDI | Number of companies | Billion HUF | Share in total |
|---|---|---|---|
| Germany | 83 | 82.26 | 25.07 |
| United States | 30 | 79.35 | 24.20 |
| Austria | 111 | 45.78 | 13.96 |
| France | 37 | 22.91 | 6.98 |
| Great Britain | 34 | 28.13 | 6.96 |
| Netherlands | 12 | 16.04 | 4.89 |
| Belgium | 8 | 14.24 | 4.34 |
| Sweden | 10 | 9.97 | 3.04 |
| Switzerland | 14 | 7.78 | 2.37 |
| Italy | 22 | 6.68 | 2.04 |
| Commonwealth of Independent States | 15 | 6.81 | 2.08 |
| Other | 43 | 19.79 | 4.10 |
| Total | 419 | 339.74 | 100.0 |

Source: Hungarian Privatization and State Holding Company, *Privatization Monitor*, September 1996, Budapest, p. 4.

increasingly to establish entirely new "greenfield" investments. This process started in the late 1980s.

As of September 30, 1996, through a variety of such privatization transactions, about 782.6 billion forint worth of Hungarian private ownership has been acquired by foreign companies since 1991 (ÁPV Rt: *Privatization monitor*, Budapest, September, 1996, p. 4). As of Seprember 1996, more than half of state-owned property had been privatized. About 500 companies, mostly small ones, have not yet been privatized.[44]

In the initial phase FDI pushed the process of privatization forward. As of September 1996, there were 472 privatized companies with foreign interest having an aggregate value of 782.63 billion forint, approximately $5.1 billion at the going exchange rate. (See Table 2.6.) Austria leads in the number of established foreign firms in Hungary. In terms of the stock of invested capital, Germany is at the top, followed closely by the United States. The leading foreign companies, each investing above $60 million, provided two-thirds of the accumulated FDI so far. (See Table 2.7.)

Foreign exchange receipts through privatization increased between 1990 and 1992 but declined quite rapidly thereafter until 1995, when a substantial revenue increase took place.[45] The sharp decline in foreign

**Table 2.7**
Important foreign investors in Hungary, 1996

| Company | Origin | Value (mill. $) | Method of FDI* | Location in Hungary | Industry |
|---|---|---|---|---|---|
| Deutsche Telecom | D | 863 | P | national | telecomm. |
| Ameritech | USA | 863 | P | national | telecomm. |
| General Electric | USA | 550 | P | Budapest Nagykanizsa | lightbulbs |
| General Motors | USA | 500 | G | Szentgotthárd | car assembly |
| Suzuki | Japan | 250 | G | Esztergom | car assembly |
| US West | USA | 330 | GC | national | telecomm. |
| First Hungarian Concession Motorway Co. | France, Austria, Germany | 200 | GC | M1, Győr Hegyeshalom | motorway |
| Audi | Germany | 550 | G | Győr | car engines |
| EBRD | London | 170 | PG | Budapest | stock investment in private computer company |
| Pannon GSM | Finland, Denmark, Sweden | 150 | GC | national | telecomm. |
| Siemens | Germany | 150 | P | Budapest Bicske | switch centers |
| FOTEX | USA | 130 | P | Budapest Ajka Győr | retail trade, glass industry |
| Allianz | Germany | 220 | P | national | insurance |
| Ford | USA | 120 | G | Székesfehérvár | car industry |
| Sanofi | France | 120 | P | Budapest | medicine |
| Guardian Glass | USA | 110 | G | Orosháza | sheet glass |
| Prinzhorn | Austria | 110 | P | Budapest Kiskunhalas | paper industry |
| First Hungarian Fund | USA | 100 | M | Budapest | portfolio investment in retail chain |

| | | | | | |
|---|---|---|---|---|---|
| Hungarian Investment Co. | Great Britain | 100 | M | Budapest | protfolio investment in finance and trade |
| Sara Lee | USA | 100 | P | Budapest | coffee, tea |
| Unilever | Great Britain, Netherlands | 100 | P | Budapest, Baja | food, detergents |
| Aegon | NL | 100 | P | national | insurance |
| International Finance Corporation | USA | 100 | G | Budapest | mixed |
| Ferruzi | Italy | 100 | P | Martfű Budapest | vegetable oil |
| Amylum | Belgium | 90 | P | Szabadegyháza | alcohol |
| Alcoa | USA | 80 | P | Székesfehérvár | aluminum |
| Linde | Germany | 75 | P | Répcelak | industrial gas |
| Mariott | USA | 75 | P | Budapest | hotel |
| Reemsta | Germany | 75 | P | Debrecen | tobacco |
| Agrana | Austria | 70 | P | Petőháza | sugar, alcohol |
| Al Italia | Italy | 70 | P | Budapest | air transport |
| Beghin Say | Italy | 70 | P | Szolnok | sugar |
| Corvinus-Lufthansa | Germany | 70 | G | Budapest | hotel |
| Coca-Cola | USA | 70 | G | Dunaharaszti Győr Budapest | soft drinks |
| Shell | Netherlands, Great Britain | 70 | PG | Budapest and country side | oil trade |
| Electrolux | Sweden | 70 | P | Jászberény | cooling industry |
| South African Breweries | South-Africa | 70 | P | Budapest | beer |
| Tengelmann | Germany | 70 | P | Budapest | retail trade |
| Heidelberg-Swenk | Germany | 65 | P | Vác Beremend | cement |
| Henkell | Germany | 65 | P | Budapest Szolnok | chemicals |
| Institutional Investors | Great Britain | 60 | P | Budapest | medical industry |
| Hungarian-American Enterprise Fund | USA | 60 | PG | Budapest | portfolio investment in finance |

**Table 2.7** (continued)

| Company | Origin | Value (mill. $) | Method of FDI* | Location in Hungary | Industry |
|---|---|---|---|---|---|
| Pepsi Cola | USA | 60 | PG | Budapest | soft drinks |
| Messer Griesheim | Germany | 60 | P | Budapest | industrial gases |
| PTT Telcom | Netherlands | 410 | G | Budapest | telecomm. |
| RWE-EVS | Germany | 350 | P | Budapest | electricity production |

*Source: Figyelő* (1995), p. 13, and October 17, 1996, p. 11.
*Notes:* *Methods of FDI are the following:
P     privatization
G     greenfield investments
GC    greenfield investments/concessions
M     mixed investments
PG    privatization/greenfield investments

exchange receipts in the earlier years was only partly due to lessened interest on the part of foreign investors. Another recent element in this development is the establishment by foreign owners of companies with Hungarian headquarters that are registered as Hungarian companies, allowing them to act in the privatization market as Hungarian and not as foreign companies.[46]

In the early phase of privatization, previous state monopolies and oligopolies were typically acquired by transnational corporations due to lack of state control. This was the case with the vegetable oil and sugar industries. Later such anomalies became fewer and the role of the Hungarian Office of Competition became more visible (as in the beer and tobacco industries). Substantial capital investments in the country have been initiated by FDI since the transformation, largely due to the shortage of domestic capital. The cash position of several domestic enterprises that were struggling for survival early on has improved since the takeover. Privatization has been followed in many cases by technological and organizational modernization.

In the early phase, FDI in Hungary focused on standard Western distribution and production chains. These chains were perhaps necessary for modernizing the Hungarian production base, but they crowded several domestic producers from the market and endangered some supplier industries as well (Vissi, 1994, p. 351). Hungarian suppliers using their intercompany delivery and supply services experienced smaller demand for their products. For example, the share of Hungarian suppliers in Opel's assembly plant was 3–5 percent in 1995; that of Suzuki was 15 percent.[47]

There is a fundamental difference between privatization-induced FDI activity in Hungary and in other developed and developing market economies. Foreign companies that bought an FDI stake in Hungarian units via privatization acquired new markets, new distribution and production chains, new production capacities, and new business relations without facing intensive competition on the investment market. This is relevant from the microeconomic point of view as well because company-specific advantages were not decisive for acquiring a new market in Hungary, as is the case in other market economies. The close interaction in Hungary between FDI and privatization assured a substantial new market to foreign investors who did not face competition from domestic companies.

Indeed, Hungarian privatization has attracted foreign investors whose agenda consists of distribution of foreign products in the Hungarian market and more efficient utilization of their home production capacities. The general economic effect of a substantial part of FDI in Hungary is not entirely positive in generating a competitive environment. Several foreign investors not only import new products into Hungary but narrow the domestic commodity supplies by narrowing the product variety of the privatized enterprise.[48] Although the resulting industry concentration on the national level is currently not dangerous,[49] it tends to dominate in certain branches and geographical regions.

The interaction between FDI and privatization of state-owned assets creates problems at the enterprise level that spill into macroeconomic decision making. Among these problems are the potential loss of asset values of the enterprises being privatized, their physical survival, and their cash flow potential. The sale price of these assets is low because the contract specifies that the foreign investor will handle these problems.

In conclusion, the following specific aspects of FDI activity in relation to Hungarian privatization are noteworthy.

First, it was not necessary for Hungarian companies to have exceptional microeconomic advantages for FDI entry; in fact, their privatization guaranteed such advantages to foreign participants. In other words, fewer company-specific advantages could bring about a successful business venture in Hungary than would be the case in a developed market economy.

Second, foreign firms preferred industries with a high level of protection. As a result, participation in privatizing industries such as tobacco, beer, vegetable oil, and sugar was highly popular with foreign direct investors. Later, telecommunication was added to this list.

Third, privatization was necessary but not sufficient for attracting FDI flows into efficiency-creating activities in Hungary. In other words, restructuring a privatized enterprise was perhaps more difficult than setting up a new "greenfield" investment. On the other hand, privatization attracted FDI, which enhanced Hungarian trade in Western markets (Árva, 1994, p. 48).

### 2.4.2  Motivation of Foreign Investors in Hungary

The foremost motivator for foreign investors was market presence, followed by profit (and "extra profit") considerations (*Invest in Hungary*, 1995 p. 4; also see Table 2.8).

### 2.4.3  Changes in the Main Features of Joint Ventures

The analysis of data from 1974 to 1994, based on the number of joint ventures and FDI flow, indicated the role of FDI in stimulating improved

**Table 2.8**
Objectives of foreign investors in Hungary

| Objectives | Motivation (% of all answers) |
|---|---|
| Domestic market presence | 24 |
| Profit, extra profit | 16 |
| Expanding in neighboring countries | 13 |
| Breaking Hungarian competitors | 11 |
| Obtaining cheap labor, cost reduction | 10 |
| Good investment prospects | 10 |
| Obtaining intellectual and production capacity | 8 |
| Tax benefits in host country | 4 |
| Long-term cooperation | 4 |

Source: *Invest in Hungary* (1995), p. 4.
Note: The survey covered 125 statistically representative joint ventures.

corporate structure and performance in Hungarian enterprises, and in their production and market organization.

The catalyzing role of joint ventures and small enterprises in the Hungarian transformation process was evidenced in integrating activities that were rigorously separated earlier, such as production and trade, domestic as well as foreign. Also, joint ventures involving transnational companies promoted conditions for implementing higher production-line efficiency by developing domestic and international intercompany relations.

## Size Structure

FDI played a considerable role in the development of small business, an activity absent from Hungary for a long time. The process of setting up small-scale entrepreneurship in Hungary accelerated in 1990. The disintegration of old companies and the establishment of new ones was of extraordinary importance for the national economy. Indeed, the number of companies doubled within a year. The dynamic role of joint ventures was obvious: Their number more than quadrupled. More than one-fifth of all Hungarian companies and 23 percent of small businesses functioned with foreign capital; 10 percent of large firms claimed foreign equity. By 1995 the foreign presence had become even stronger.

## Employment Effects

The number of jobs associated with foreign capital in Hungary was reported to be around 400,000 at the end of 1993 (KSH, 1995, p. 12). This included both direct and indirect jobs. The number of persons directly employed increased rapidly in the period 1990–1996. While overall employment of all Hungarian companies increased only slightly between 1990 and 1994,[50] that of joint ventures increased dramatically—by 53.8 percent in 1992 and 21.1 percent in 1993. Evidently employment growth in joint ventures slowed somewhat in 1994 but was still higher than overall employment growth in the economy. Although data are not available, FDI-related employment must have increased substantially both in 1995 and in 1996. Of course, not all FDI has been job-creating. Mergers and acquisitions and corporate restructuring have resulted in employment absorption rather than employment creation. The service sector, in which FDI is substantial, has been an important employment creator. In 1992, 16 percent of workers in all companies were in joint ventures; this figure grew to 20 percent in 1993.

Foreign investors generate indirect employment through linkages with enterprises in the host country. Backward linkages, such as the purchase of raw materials and parts and components, are the main channels through which employment is affected indirectly. Indirect employment effects vary depending on the nature of the investment, the industry involved, the sourcing strategy of the investor, and the conditions in the Hungarian economy. Affiliates targeting the Hungarian market had a greater ripple effect. Assemblers of final products usually had negligible indirect employment effects. However, over time, major foreign investors tended to increase linkages with local Hungarian firms, evidently in response to local-content rules.

Foreign investors generally provide employment under conditions that compare favorably with those prevailing in domestic firms. However, there are significant exceptions to this general rule, when the benefit packages offered by foreign investors do not follow the regulations. Work contracts in particular suffer from this type of deficiency. However, average wages in foreign-related businesses are on average 30 percent higher than those in Hungarian national companies.

In general, FDI-related businesses produce more with fewer employees and in a more cost-effective way.[51] Efficiency per employee is the best in joint ventures with 100 percent foreign ownership. Net company income per employee in these ventures is 75 percent higher than in national companies. Value added per employee for joint ventures with 100 percent foreign ownership is 14 percent higher rate than in national companies.

## Efficiency Results

FDI is expected to exert positive pressures on company performance, resulting in improved efficiency. These positive effects, however, are realized only with a substantial time lag. Efficiency results, therefore are very sensitive to the time over which the venture has existed. Despite this caveat, the performance of joint ventures is better than that of national companies.

Companies with foreign participation invest actively. According to the latest available information, the share of joint venture investment in the total rose from 18 percent in 1989 to 34 percent in 1993 (Központi Statisztikai Hivatal, 1995, p. 13). By 1993, their investment dynamism seemed to have slowed down: Perhaps the early heavy investments were no longer necessary and profits were repatriated for investment elsewhere. Thus the share of investments by exclusively foreign entities increased from 3 percent in 1992 to 5.5 percent in 1993, and majority-owned foreign companies (having more than doubled their share in the total investment growth between 1992 and 1993) decreased this share in 1993. In 1993 fully foreign-owned companies excelled in their performance in terms of per employee wages, net company income, and value added (see Table 2.9) despite slowed investment growth. Based on partial statistical evidence, the trend continued in 1994 and 1995.

## Tax Allowances

The most effective instrument for encouraging and regulating FDI in Hungary has been the system of company tax incentives since 1989. This

**Table 2.9**
Wages, net company income, and value-added per employee, 1993

| Companies | Average wage per employee (forint) | Indicator (per employee) | | |
|---|---|---|---|---|
| | | Net company income | Export revenue | Value-added |
| | | Million forint | | |
| All business units | 374,080 | 3.30 | 0.43 | 0.74 |
| Foreign-related businesses | 487,656 | 5.26 | 1.08 | 1.12 |
| 100 percent foreign-owned | 534,290 | 8.00 | 1.11 | 1.19 |
| Majority foreign-owned | 476,920 | 4.74 | 0.98 | 1.04 |
| Hungarian majority-owned | 479,790 | 4.57 | 1.11 | 1.15 |

*Source:* Központi Statisztikai Hivatal (1995), p. 14.

system regulated the tax incentives of foreign investments between 1989 and 1994. These incentives depended on the size of investment, the percentage of foreign ownership in the company operating with foreign participation, and the sphere of activity. They were calculated to encourage foreign investment in specific production activities and to promote use of advanced technologies. The arrangements were amended in 1991 and in 1994.

In 1991, the range of incentives to companies operating with foreign participation was reduced and made stricter. Beginning that year, tax incentives were granted to companies operating with foreign participation subject to the following conditions:

1. The initial capital of the company must be greater than 50 million forint ($500,000).

2. The share of foreign ownership in the company operating with foreign participation must be at least 30 percent.

3. More than 50 percent of the sales revenues must originate from manufacturing activity.

If all three conditions were met, the tax relief could reach 60 percent in the first five years of operation and 40 percent in the next five years. (With a company tax rate of 40 percent, the actual tax payments would be 16 percent and 24 percent in the two quinquenniums).

In addition, the company could be supported by 100 percent tax exemption in the first quinquennium and 60 percent reduction in the next if it operated with foreign participation in "particularly significant" branches of the economy. The branches that received this concession were electronics and related activities; motor vehicles and parts; machine tools; agricultural and food-processing machinery; construction; packaging technology; medical preparations, agricultural chemicals, and intermediate products; food processing; development of protein livestock feed; production of goods that stimulated leasing in above activities; artificial insemination; tourism; public telecommunications; goods and equipment serving environmental purposes.

Although the incentives encouraged foreign investors to enter a variety of new sectors, the conditions were general and excluded specific targets, such as export sales or increased productivity or employment. The incentives were available only until 31 December 1993. Consequently, the companies concerned could enjoy them until 2003.

These normative tax incentives, which were designed to encourage FDI, were replaced by new arrangements in 1994, when the government was authorized to grant tax concessions based on capital expenditures by companies that operated with foreign participation. These incentives were defined in terms of specific conditions:

1. The initial capital must be at least 500 million forint (approximately $5 million).

2. The taxpayer must initiate a capital outlay of at least 200 million forint such that at least 50 percent of sales revenues would accrue of environmentally sound products, or of a product manufactured by modern technology, or from the sale of products manufactured by the application of scientific research.

3. Sales revenues must increase or new jobs must be created.

4. Companies must apply to the proper authorities in order to receive the tax concessions for capital expenditures. Applications were approved on a case-by-case basis. The new system was expected to encourage productive activities.

The arrangements, however, suffer from multiple taxes and lack transparency. As a result, they discourage foreign investments. A variety of taxes—municipality taxes, (federal) budgetary taxes, personal income taxes, and property taxes—are sometimes levied independently. The taxation system is confused, and occasionally taxed income is included in the tax base.

In 1993 alone, foreign businesses in Hungary experienced an after-tax loss of 30 billion forint, 25 percent of the total after-tax losses. (This income loss, however, was half of 1992 losses.) Foreign businesses made profits in the food-processing, chemical, and nonferrous metals industries. Food processing generated profits worth 4.5 billion forint for foreign businesses, whereas income loss for industry as a whole was 2 billion forint. Approximately 68 percent of all after-tax income losses of the machine-building industry occurred in foreign-related businesses. However, the overall profitability[52] of foreign businesses was higher than that of Hungarian companies. (See Table 2.10.) The share of reinvestment in distributed dividends of foreign businesses increased from year to year, reaching over 50 percent in 1993. Only 3 percent was reinvested outside Hungary.

## 2.5  Summary

Two decades of economic reforms had helped to change the macroeconomic and institutional environment in Hungary. By 1988 the country

**Table 2.10**
Profitability indicators, 1993 (percent)

| Indicator | All business ventures | Foreign-related businesses |
|---|---|---|
| Total profitability of capital | 1.1 | 1.5 |
| After-tax profit/own assets | −0.02 | −0.03 |
| Cash flow/net receipts | 1.5 | 0.7 |
| Cash flow/own assets | 2.1 | 1.5 |
| Share of stocks | 30.2 | 26.4 |
| Share in exports | 13.0 | 22.0 |
| Share of wages in costs | 16.0 | 12.0 |
| Own assets + long-term liabilities/invested assets | 1.1 | 1.1 |
| Liquid assets/short-term liabilities | 1.2 | 1.2 |

*Source:* Központi Statisztikai Hivatal (1995), p. 16.

was attracting substantial foreign direct investment. In 1989–1990, further improvement in macroeconomic management, and extensive liberalization of external relations and of the foreign exchange regime, contributed to substantial increase in FDI in those years.

However, beginning in 1990, hasty stabilization policies, halfhearted economic policy measures, and overpoliticization of economic issues changed the macroeconomic setting drastically. Compared with other transitional economies, Hungary started to lose its advantage as the risk to foreign investors increased substantially due to worsening domestic and external balances. FDI soon reacted to these changes: The annual flow of FDI to Hungary started to decline in 1993 and only resumed growth in 1995.

The macroeconomic and microeconomic effects of FDI have been positive for the Hungarian economy. Foreign investors brought modern technologies and management to Hungary and helped to revamp the rigid company structure. Companies with FDI have shown much better economic performance in terms of cost efficiency, export performance, and employment although the foreign-trade-related advantages of FDI have been felt throughout the economy with a time lag.

Reacting to the loss of the head start in attracting FDI flows, Hungarian authorities have changed FDI legislation since 1988. These changes attracted FDI until 1992, but thereafter legislative measures were not enough. Thorough macroeconomic measures were called for in order to reestablish the country's standing among foreign investors. The strong stabilization measures of March 1995 were accompanied by a policy to devalue the forint by 1.3 percent on a monthly basis, in order to encourage exports and limit imports. Changes in privatization policy are calculated to involve foreign investors in industries that were closed or restricted to FDI. The latest Act on Privatization, of 9 May 1995, which opened up electric power generation, the oil industry, and telecommunications, further enhanced the interaction between internal restructuring and the world economy. As a result, the much-needed technical, managerial, and financial expertise of foreign investors is already improving Hungary's prospects in its continuing transition to an open, market economy.

## Notes

1. The stock of FDI increased from $569 million to $13,227 million between 1991 and 1996 June. Magyar Nemzeti Bank (hereafter MNB), *Monthly Report*, no. 8 (1996): 108, Table III/22.

2. Hungarian FDI policies also had negative consequences. Policy discussions regarding privatization of state-owned assets with an FDI role showed vividly the sensitivity of the public on this issue.

3. In 1989 alone, 35–40 percent of imports were freed from licensing requirements.

4. After Romania, Hungary was the second country in Central and Eastern Europe to allow FDI in the country in the form of joint ventures.

5. On deficits and money stock, see MNB, *Monthly Report*, no. 5 (1995): Table V/1. Between 1980 and 1989 the inflation was 215 percent. See MNB, *Monthly Report*, no. 8 (1996): p. 76. Table II/4.

6. While the 1989 deficit was 54 billion forint, that of 1990 was 1.4 billion. MNB, *Monthly Report*, no. 4 (1995): p. 98, Table V/1.

7. See MNB, *Annual Report 1995*, p. 146, Table Annex A/I/1.

8. The highest inflation rate was 1991, at 35 percent, followed by 23 percent in 1992, 22.5 percent in 1993 and 18.8 percent in 1995. MNB, *Monthly Report* no. 8 (1996): 76.

9. The latest available data are for July 1996. MNB, *Monthly Report*, no. 8 (1996): 65.

10. MNB, *Annual Report '95* (Budapest, 1996), p. 170.

11. The 1993 industrial output was still 30 percent below the 1989 level.

12. Központi Statisztikai Hivatal, *Tájékoztató*, no. 12 (1994): 7.

13. The continuous deterioration of the financial position of farm producers, the low profitability of production, uncertainties associated with the transformation of ownership and organization, and the controversial privatization and restitution practices affected production.

14. MNB, *Monthly Report* no. 8 (1996): 84.

15. *Hungarian Economic Review*, April 1995, p. 24. The general surcharge is a payment obligation similar to the customs duty and must be paid with the duty. Exemption from the surcharge is applied to assets invested by foreigners in Hungary as noncash contributions, which are exempt from customs duty.

16. Issues relating to industrial restructuring and trade reorientation of East and Central Europe are analyzed in Michael A. Landesmann and István p. Székely, eds., *Industrial Restructuring and Trade Reorientation in Eastern Europe* (Cambridge: Cambridge University Press, 1995). For Hungary, see A. Blahó and L. Halpern, *"Stabilization, Crisis and Structural Change,"* in Landesmann and Székely.

17. Commission work (*bérmunka* in Hungarian) is an export deal in which the material, such as cloth, is imported, reworked with Hungarian labor, and exported. Therefore Hungarian value added is exported.

18. In 1994, for example, the smallest import item, food and agricultural products, increased by 29 percent in volume, covering the gap in the domestic market.

19. The exchange rate of the forint was fixed until 8 December 1991 on the basis of the foreign exchange composition of the trade turnover of the preceding year. The weights from 9 December 1991 were 50 percent U.S. dollar and 50 percent ECU; from 2 August 1993, 50 percent U.S. dollar and 50 percent deutsche mark; from May 16, 1994, in 70–30 percent of European Currency Unit (ECU) and U.S. dollars.

20. The prime ministers were József Antall (until December 1993), Péter Boross (until June 1994), and Gyula Horn (since June 1994).

21. Real wages had dropped by 12 percent in 1995 and by a further 3–4 percent in 1996 (authors' estimate based on partial official information).

22. Domestic consumption declined in 1995 by 5 percent and by a further 3 percent in 1996 (authors' estimate based on partial official information).

23. See NBH, *Monthly Report*, no. 8, 1996, p. 124.

24. See European Bank for Reconstruction and Development (EBRD), *Transition report 1996*, London, 1996, Table 8.6, p. 118.

25. Issues of competition in the context of FDI in Hungary are discussed in F. Vissi, "A külföldi működötöke-beruházások és a verseny" (Foreign Direct Investment and Competition), *Közgazdasági szemle*, 41, no. 4 (1994): 349–359.

26. The latest, extensive revision was Act XXIV of 1988 on Foreign Direct Investment in Hungary. See the official text in *Magyar közlöny* (Official Gazette), no. 69 (1988) or National Bank of Hungary, *Market Letter*, no. 1–2 (1989): 1–7.

27. There are great disparities in the estimates of FDI, depending on the statistical sources used. Some calculations are based on registered investments expressed in cash, as they appear in the balance of payments, whereas others are based on registered investments received in cash and in kind, as recorded by the Court of Registration. Yet another calculation is based on the amount to be invested, according to the contracts and letters of intent. Most of the information used in this chapter is based on calculations of the second type: They are derived from registered values expressed in cash and in kind. Reports of the United Nations Economic Commission for Europe, which are referred to later, present information that is based on the third type of calculation, which generally results in higher amounts.

28. The cumulated current account deficit in 1989–1995 amounted to U.S. $10.56 billion. See NBH *Monthly Report*, no. 8, 1996 p. 91.

29. *Figyelő*, March 30, 1995, p. 17.

30. The Czech Republic, Hungary, Poland, and Slovakia.

31. The declining attraction of Hungary over time is also brought out by comparing the FDI flow into Hungary with that in the Visegrád region as a whole. The ratio dropped from 61.5 percent in 1989 to 50.8 percent in 1990, climbed to 62.3 percent in 1991, and fluctuated thereafter from 45.2 percent in 1992 to 49.0 percent in 1993 and 28.3 percent in 1994.

32. Unless Otherwise noted, the data are from Központi Statisztikai Hivatal, *A külföldi Működötőke Magyarországon, 1993* (Budapest, 1995).

33. The American Telecommunication Co. bought a package of shares of MATÁV for $827 million in late 1993; another 40 percent share [U.S. $900 million] was acquired in late 1995, making the foreign partner the majority owner.

34. The attitude may change due to the newly enacted Privatization Law, which focuses on electric power and gas companies. Thirty-five percent of the increase in FDI in 1995 was invested in these sectors, the share of which in total FDI stock increased to 13 percent. See, KSH: *Kütföldi tőkével műdökő vállalkozások*. Budapest, 1996, p. 3.

35. This pattern has both positive and negative effects. The fact that the majority of Hungarian department store chains, which enjoyed a monopolistic position and consequently a permanent market share in domestic trade, have practically all come under the control of foreign-owned companies has negative implications. Thie development discourages participation in manufacturing activity or efficient international cooperation. See Vissi, 1994, p. 358.

36. In 1994, for example, the Hungarian and Polish FDI flows were almost equivalent; the Czech Republic's FDI flow shows high growth rates as well. See Economic Commission for Europe, *East—West Joint Ventures, 1989–1994* (Geneva: United Nations, 1995), pp. 41.

37. The balance of payments deficit was $3,455 million. National Bank of Hungary, *Monthly Report*, no. 4 (1995): 78.

38. Net interest payments in 1995 were U.S. $1.599 billion, short-term improvement in the balance of payments due to FDI U.S. $4.259 billion. See National Bank of Hungary: *Monthly Report* no. 8. Table III/15, p. 98, and Table 2.4 in this chapter.

39. *Népszava*, Budapest, December 23, 1996, p. 9.

40. Their role was larger than their weight in the economy.

41. The use of intracompany prices instead of arms'-length prices is fairly widespread among subsidiaries of multinationals.

42. It is difficult to accurately measure the cost of imported material that is used for producing a finished product (which is then exported) when the material is imported from a parent company. Again, recent trade statistics compiled by customs authorities differ from earlier information supplied by trading companies.

43. Estimate of Mr András Inotai, Director of the Institute of World Economy of the Hungarian Academy of Sciences, as reported by the *Financial Times*, London, Survey, December 16, 1996, p. II.

44. According to the new Law of Privatization, enacted by the Parliament on 9 May 1995, 40 percent of asset ownership will remain in state hands.

45. Foreign exchange earnings from privatization (in billion forint) were 0.53 in 1990, 24.61 in 1991, 40.98 in 1992, 25.50 in 1993, 6.10 in 1994, *Népszabadság*, June 7, 1995, p. 4. In 1995 the hard currency examings was 412.054 billion forint; in the first nine months of 1996, 54.033 billion forint. See, A'PV Rt: *Privatization monitor*, Budapest, December 1995. p. 5 and September 1996, p. 5.

46. Foreign investors who discovered the favorable features of compensation vouchers started to use them as well.

47. *Figyelő*, March 30, 1995, p. 9.

48. However, it is difficult to establish clearly whether Hungarian products were squeezed from the domestic market because they were not competitive or because the foreign investors changed the production structure according to their company policy.

49. The share of such privatized distribution and production chains in Hungary is 10–20 percent of the total turnover.

50. There are no detailed statistics for all the transition years. The employment figures for 1991–1993 are as follows: 2.134 million in 1991, 2.227 million in 1992, and 2.172 million in 1993. FDI employment was 233,900 in 1991, 359,600 in 1992, and 435,600 in 1993. Központi Statisztikai Hivatal, *A külföldi működőtőke Magyarországon, 1993* (Budapest, 1995), p. 35, Table VI.

51. As discussed above, net income and value added per employee are 59 and 51 percent higher than in exclusively Hungarian-owned companies. See Központi Statisztikai Hivatal, 1995, p. 13.

52. Results of business activity/value of capital assets.

## References

Árva, László. 1994. "A működőtőke-mozgás elméleti és gyakorlati kérdései." (Theoretical and Practical Questions of Foreign Direct Investments). In Magyar Nemzeti Bank, *Műhelytanulmányok*, 6: p. 75.

Blahó, András, and László Halpern. 1995. "Stabilization, Crisis and Structural Change in Hungary." In Michael Landesmann and István P. Székely, eds., *Industrial Restructuring and Trade Reorientation in Eastern Europe*. Cambridge: Cambridge University Press.

Economic Commission for Europe. 1995. *East–West Investments and Joint Ventures, 1989–1994*. Geneva: United Nations.

European Bank for Reconstruction and Development (EBRD). *Transition report 1996*, London, 1996.

*Financial Times*, 1996.

*Figyelő*, March 30, 1995, p. 13; October 17, 1996. p. 11.

Hajdu, Györgyné. 1994. "Árfolyamrendszer és árfolyampolitika Magyarországon." (Exchange Rate System and Exchange Rate Policy in Hungary). Magyar Nemzeti Bank, *Műhelytanulmányok*, 7: p. 61.

Hamar, Judit. 1993. *Foreign Direct Investment and Joint Ventures in Hungary*. Budapest: KOPINT-DATORG.

Horváth, László. 1993. "Működőtőke-beáramlás néhány közép- és kelet-európai országban." (Foreign Direct Investment in Some Central and Eastern-European countries). Magyar Nemzeti Bank, *Műhelytanulmányok*, 4: p. 43.

Hungarian Chamber of Commerce. 1995. *Hungarian Economic Review*. Appendix: *Investment opportunities in Hungary*, pp. 24–25.

Hungarian Chamber of Commerce 1995. *Invest in Hungary.* no. 2. pp. 3–6.

Hungarian Privatization and State Holding Company. 1996. *Privatization monitor.* Budapest, September.

Kornai, János. 1993. "Transzformációs visszaesés." (Decline in Transformation). *Közgazdasági szemle,* 40, no. 7–8: 569–599.

Központi Statisztikai Hivatal (KSH). 1995. *Külföldi működőtőke Magyarországon, 1993.* (Foreign Direct Capital in Hungary). Budapest: KSH.

Központi Statisztikai Hivatal. 1994. *Tájékoztató,* 12.

Landesmann, Michael, and István P. Székely. eds. 1995. *Industrial Restructuring and Trade Reorientation in Eastern Europe.* Cambridge: Cambridge University Press.

*Magyar közlöny.* (Official Gazette). 1988. no. 69.

National Bank of Hungary. *Market Letter.* 1989. no. 1–2.

National Bank of Hungary. *Monthly Report.* 1995. no. 4.

National Bank of Hungary. *Annual report. 1995.*

National Bank of Hungary. *Monthly report.* 1996. no. 8.

*Népszabadság.* 1995. March 15, p. 5

*Népszabadság.* 1995. Supplement *Privatizáció,* 7 June. *Népszava* 1996.

Szentes, Tamás. 1995. "Structural Adjustment in the Contemporary World Economy: The Case of Hungary." Invited paper for the conference Structural Change in Eastern Europe and Transition." Jena, Germany, 27–29 April. (Manuscript).

Vissi, Ferenc. 1994. "A külföldi működötöke-beruházások és a verseny." (Foreign Direct Investments and Competition). *Közgazdasági szemle,* 41, no. 4: 349–359.

# 3          East Germany

Jürgen von Hagen

The transition of East Germany from socialism to a market economy is unique. Following the opening of its border with West Germany in November 1989 and the first free elections in more than fifty-five years, East Germany entered into an economic, monetary, and social union with West Germany on 1 July 1990. Soon afterward, on 3 October 1990, the five reconstituted states of East Germany (Mecklenburg-Vorpommern, Brandenburg, Sachsen, Sachsen-Anhalt, and Thüringen) and East Berlin were granted accession to the Federal Republic of Germany. Rather than opting for the foundation of a new Federal Republic (i.e., the writing of a new constitution for a united Germany), the *Länder* used the faster option of entering the Federal Republic by extending West Germany's existing constitutional and legal order to their territory.

What made East Germany's position unique compared with other former socialist countries was the fact that under West German law, East Germans were citizens of West Germany with all the rights and privileges this implies, and that West Germany never gave up its constitutional mandate for unification. Thus, upon opening their borders and expressing their will to shed socialism, East Germans held the asset of kinship: the advantage of having a rich uncle obliged and—though at times grudgingly—willing to support the poor nephew's start of a new life.

Given West Germany's commitment to unification throughout the postwar period and the popular demands for unification in the East, it is clear that unification was going to happen at some point. Less obvious is why West Germany opted for *rapid* unification with the East rather than a transition period during which East Germany might have been rebuilt economically while retaining its political autonomy and its monetary and fiscal system. Figure 3.1 illustrates the point from the *rich uncle's* perspective. With the opening of the iron curtain and the tearing down of

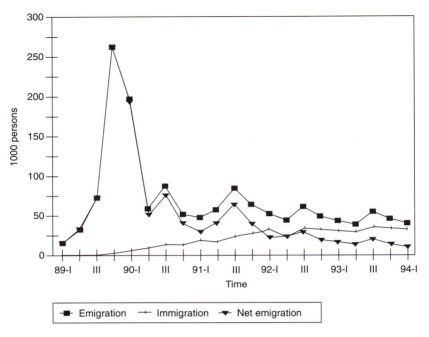

**Figure 3.1**
Migration from East to West Germany
*Source:* Ministry of Interior.

the Berlin Wall, West Germany faced a huge wave of immigration from East Germany: 2.3 percent of East Germany's population migrated to West Germany in 1989 alone. When Chancellor Helmut Kohl made the first announcement of monetary union early in 1990, about half a million immigrants had already arrived. Thus, the *uncle's* part in the deal that followed was to halt immigration and rebuild the East rather than to pay for the settlement of large numbers of immigrants in the West.[1]

Turning to the *nephew's* side, assessments of the East German transition commonly focus on the size of the *uncle's* wallet—that is, on the size of financial transfers from the West to the East. Such a narrow perspective implies that there is little to learn from the East German experience, precisely because it is so unique. However, the transfers are only a part of the *economics of kinship,* and perhaps not the most interesting one. Of more relevance to other cases of transformation is the fact that *kinship* implies living by the *family rule*: East Germany was immediately brought into the trading and financial system of the world economy and immediately

**Table 3.1**
Foreign trade

| | Trade with FRG[1] | | Trade with EC[2] | | Trade with USSR[3] | |
|---|---|---|---|---|---|---|
| | Exports | Imports | Exports | Imports | Exports | Imports |
| 1985 | 8458 | 9174 | 4000 | 2200 | 7.60 | 7.38 |
| 1986 | 7704 | 8651 | 3400 | 2300 | 7.34 | 7.78 |
| 1987 | 7473 | 8481 | 2900 | 2300 | 7.25 | 7.41 |
| 1988 | 7763 | 8294 | 2800 | 2600 | 7.15 | 7.09 |
| 1989 | 8429 | 9221 | — | — | 7.18 | 7.18 |

*Source:* DIW (1990b, 1990c).
*Notes:* 1. Trade with West Germany (FRG), mill. DM, including services.
2. Mill. of DM, excluding services and trade with FRG.
3. Bill. Transfer-rubles.

adopted Western legal and administrative structures. Section 3.1 focuses on these broader aspects.

Section 3.1 briefly lays out East Germany's starting position at unification. Section 3.2 relates the main elements of the German union and describes the process of East Germany's economic integration into the Federal Republic. Section 3.3 considers the political economy of East–West *kinship* in Germany.

## 3.1   The Starting Position

Toward the end of the 1980s, the East German economy was not doing well (see DIW, 1989). The targets for economic growth laid down in the Five-Year Plan for 1986–90 had not been reached in 1986 and 1987; and 1988 brought a growth rate of 2.7 percent compared with a targeted 4.1 percent. While about half of the discrepancy was due to weather-related production shortfalls in the agricultural sector, other sectors of the economy showed severe structural weaknesses: shortages of labor, energy, and raw materials, and outdated capital stock. Labor productivity grew more slowly than targeted. At the same time, the rate of investment rose significantly, implying that private consumption was even more sluggish than output. The consumption component of *produced national income* grew by 1.7 percent annually in real terms between 1985 and 1989, but stagnated in 1988 and 1989.

Table 3.1 summarizes East Germany's foreign trade record since the mid-1980s. Calculated in *valutamark*, the country's unit of account in foreign trade, the USSR was East Germany's largest trading partner, accounting for 37.5 percent of its foreign trade in 1988 (see Stamm, 1990). Another 28.9 percent of East Germany's foreign trade was with the other CMEA countries, and 27.6 percent was trade with Western industrialized countries, mainly West Germany. Exports to and imports from West Germany fell between 1985 and 1988, then picked up in 1989. Exports to the rest of the European Community (EC) declined similarly, whereas imports from the EC grew somewhat between 1985 and 1988.

The declining trend in East Germany's trade with the West was due to two structural factors. On the one hand, East Germany had increased the share of fuel and fuel products in its Western exports during the early 1980s and was now affected by the decline in world market prices of oil. Second, East Germany's competitiveness in other industrial products was faltering because the quality of its investment goods was not sufficient to penetrate Western markets, and competition from developing countries in other industrial markets was increasingly harder to withstand. East Germany's trade with the West was characterized by the outdated paradigm of *interindustry* trade (the exchange of raw materials and consumption goods for investment goods) rather than *intraindustry* trade; its trade was relatively unspecialized in terms of goods exported and imported, and did not reflect the comparative advantage expected from a country with a relatively highly educated workforce (DIW, 1990a). Trade with the USSR also declined slightly over the five years prior to unification. The same was true for trade with the other CMEA countries (DIW, 1989, p. 59).

Overall, then, the external picture of the German Democratic Republic (GDR) economy was bleak. In 1988 economic analysts of the socialist government came to the conclusion that the GDR would be forced to reschedule its external debt within four or five years. A secret government document completed in 1989 flatly concluded that "just stabilizing the [external] borrowing would require a reduction of the standard of living by 25 to 30 percent in 1990" (Schürer et al., 1989, cited in Fischer and Schröter, 1993, p. 20).

In summary, unification hit an ailing economy that suffered from severe structural weaknesses. The economic developments following unification have to be viewed against this background: The counterfactual of no unification, even of survival of the socialist regime, would have included either a continued economic decline or a major structural overhaul of the economy, creating a need for people to move to more productive industries and including further efforts to modernize the East German capital stock.

## 3.2   German Unification

### 3.2.1   Main Elements

The process of German unification can be divided into four main elements. The first, immediately visible one was the monetary union between East and West Germany. Second, with the accession to the Federal Republic, East Germany entered a fiscal union with the West. Third, by virtue of the same act, the territorial domain of West Germany's constitution was extended immediately to East Germany, resulting in administrative and legal union. Finally, a rapid privatization program was introduced under the auspices of an independent federal agency, the Treuhand Trust Company. Rather than going through a process of transformation, East Germany was taken under the wings of a modern, Western economic system in one bold step. Thus, East Germany's transformation emphasized speed, the strong influence of external decision-making power determined to introduce reforms, and the availability of a large financial cushion.

**Monetary Union**
On 1 July 1990, East and West Germany formed a monetary union that had the Deutsche Mark (DM) as the only legal tender and the German Bundesbank as the sole monetary authority in the unified currency area. For East Germany, monetary union meant the introduction of a modern financial and banking system together with the adoption of a stable, convertible, and reputable currency.

Under the socialist regime, the only financial assets available to East Germans had been cash, interest-paying savings deposits also usable as transactions accounts, and a basic form of life insurance that was, however, quantitatively negligible.[2] The ratio of cash holdings to bank deposits was smaller than in West Germany—6.1 percent in May 1990, compared with 51 percent in West Germany—in part because East German businesses were obliged to execute payments on a non-cash basis through the state banking system.[3] East German banks were essentially bookkeeping operations for the state bank, without any autonomous financial activity.

Apart from small coins remaining in circulation until July 1991, only bank deposits of East German residents at East German banks were eligible for conversion into DM. The immediate cash supply came about by withdrawing cash from accounts converted into DM balances. To prepare for this step, the Bundesbank gave East Germans the opportunity to convert Mark balances into claims on DM cash for some time before 1

**Table 3.2**
Conversion rates (mark per DM)

| Assets | Rate | Liabilities | Rate |
|---|---|---|---|
| Loans to domestic borrowers | 2.2 | Deposits of domestic nonbanks | 1.6 |
| Firms | 2.0 | Private nonbanks | 1.48 |
| Housing sector | 2.0 | Firms | 2.05 |
| Foreign assets | 1.2 | Foreign liabilities | 2.74 |
| Participations | 1.0 | Currency | 2.00 |
| Average | 2.03 | Average | 1.82 |

*Source:* Bundesbank (1990a).
*Note:* Total asset volume as of May 31, 1990: M 446.6 bill or DM 246.0 bill.

July; these claims were redeemed in the first few days of monetary union (Bundesbank, 1990b).

Following the example of the West German monetary reform of 1948, the treaty on monetary union applied different rates of conversion to bank assets and liabilities. These rates are reported in Table 3.2. Bank loans to domestic borrowers were converted at a rate of 2:1 to 2.2:1. The main consideration behind this was that the banking sector should not be forced to hold large amounts of nonperforming loans, thereby endangering its financial viability under the new regime. Furthermore, East German businesses would otherwise have carried excessive financial liabilities, the service of which would have endangered their competitiveness. Domestic nonbank deposits were converted at an average rate of 1.6:1, leaving East German citizens a greater part of their savings than would have resulted from applying the rate used for bank assets. Depending on their age, East Germans could convert DM 2,000, 4,000, or 6,000 per person at a rate of 1:1. On average, the conversion rate was 1.8:1 for bank liabilities. The gap between the asset and the liability side of the banking sector's balance sheet was bridged with compensation claims, that is, interest-bearing, nontradable claims on the newly created federal Monetary Conversion Equalization Fund. In addition, banks received compensation claims sufficient to assure that they met the 4 percent minimum capital—asset ratio.

With the rapid move of West German commercial banks into East Germany—by the end of 1991, 22 percent of all bank branches in East Germany were owned by West German or foreign banks—and the transfer of Western bank management know-how through personnel and training, the whole array of financial assets available to West Germans quickly became available to East Germans. To adjust the hybrid, East German type of bank deposits to the West German bank law, the treaty on monetary union ruled that these deposits had to be converted into either demand deposits, which pay no or only a nominal fixed interest rate, or savings deposits, which pay higher interest but have limitations on withdrawal. Most of these conversions took place as of 31 December 1990; a smaller, final adjustment occurred as of 30 June 1991.

With monetary union, it is obviously difficult to study the demand for money in East Germany, since residents in both parts of Germany can hold deposits in either part.[4] Empirical studies have, therefore, focused on the properties of the combined money demand function following unification (von Hagen 1993, 1995a; Kole 1994). The general result of these studies is that the demand for narrow money, M1, has remained stable since unification, while the stability of broad money demand, M3, is more in doubt. This makes sense because M1 includes transaction balances that existed previously in East Germany, whereas broad money includes types of deposits that were unknown before unification, such as time deposits, and broad money is closely substitutable with nonmonetary financial assets that also did not exist prior to unification. Thus, learning about the new financial environment seems to have focused on non-transactions and nonmonetary assets.

Since the end of the Bretton Woods era, the West German money supply process has centered on central bank loans to domestic banks as the main channel of the base money supply (see Neumann and von Hagen, 1993). Banks use trade bills in discount operations, securities in Lombard operations and open market operations with repurchase agreements as collateral for central bank loans. While the discount rate is used as a floor for market rates and banks are encouraged to use up their predetermined discount quotas, the rate on REPOs has become the main instrument to control short-term interest rates in the German money market.

To facilitate their market entry and improve their competitiveness in the unified monetary system, East German banks were initially granted special conditions in loan operations with the Bundesbank. In particular, banks were allowed to discount trade bills drawn on themselves in discount and Lombard operations in order to compensate for the fact that East German businesses were not used to this financing instrument. These special regulations expired at the end of 1991, so the East German banking system now functions like the West German system. Empirical analysis of money multipliers suggests that bank portfolio behavior has become somewhat more volatile since unification (von Hagen, 1993).

In summary, East Germany was equipped with a Western-style banking sector within a short time after unification. This implies the availability of modern business financing, including trade financing in relation to Western markets, and the avoidance of disruptive credit market turbulence. Although this is hard to quantify, it seems plausible that the availability of a financial infrastructure will be an important factor in the competitiveness of East Germany's economy.

With unification, the Bundesbank continued its policy of a strict commitment to price stability. As prices started to rise more rapidly in the unified currency area due to the unification shock to aggregate demand and subsequent, excessive wage policies, the Bundesbank turned to a more restrictive monetary policy in 1991, ultimately inflicting a recession on Germany and its partners in the European Monetary System (EMS). Not surprisingly, the fixed-rate regime turned out to be inadequate for German unification, though for very different reasons than in other cases of transformation: As German interest rates began to rise, the other European central banks followed suit to keep their exchange rates fixed to the DM, pushing their economies into recession. For the EC, the macroeconomic consequences of German unification might have been more positive with a flexible rate regime (see von Hagen, 1995b).

**Fiscal Union**
With unification, East Germany entered a federal system. Federalism in Germany is a balanced system of local, state, and federal government power. The constitution defines the responsibilities of each level of government. To meet their responsibilities, local and state governments have their own tax bases and are allowed to borrow in the capital market; compared with other federations, federal grants to state governments are quite small in Germany. The constitution also provides for a system of equalization payments among state government (*Länderfinanzausgleich*) by which the richer states make payments to the poorer states. The federal fiscal system is complemented by a centralized Social Security system (pension fund and unemployment insurance) administered by independent federal agencies, financed by contributions of the insured citizens, and separate from the federal government budget.

In principle, the five new *Länder* should have stood on their own feet financially to meet their new responsibilities, drawing, however, from the equalization system and from EC structural funds while the new citizens became members of the Social Security system and, as such, eligible for benefits. The absence of a developed tax base in the new *Länder* and the

**Table 3.3**
Public transfers to East Germany (bill. of DM)

| Gross transfers | 1991 | 1992 | 1993 | 1994 | 1995 |
|---|---|---|---|---|---|
| Federal government | 73 | 88 | 114 | 114 | 151 |
| Unity Fund | 31 | 24 | 15 | 5 | 0 |
| EC | 4 | 5 | 5 | 6 | 7 |
| Pension Fund | — | 5 | 9 | 13 | 15 |
| Federal Labor Agency | 24 | 29 | 28 | 28 | 24 |
| State governments (West) | 5 | 5 | 10 | 14 | 14 |
| Total | 139 | 152 | 168 | 170 | 200 |
| Additional federal tax revenue | 31 | 35 | 37 | 42 | 48 |
| Administrative revenue | 2 | 2 | 2 | 2 | 2 |
| Total extra revenue | 33 | 37 | 39 | 44 | 50 |
| Net transfers | 106 | 115 | 129 | 126 | 150 |
| Net transfers as percent of GDP | 52 | 44 | 42 | 37 | n.a. |

*Source:* Bundesministerium der Finanzen (1995a, 1995b).

unbalanced Social Security situation made this approach nonviable. As the West German states refused to provide broader financial support for the new states, the Federal government shouldered the bulk of the responsibility by paying huge transfers to the new *Länder* and their citizens.

Table 3.3 reports the volume of gross and net transfers to East Germany from 1991 to 1995. Federal government payments more than doubled from DM 73 billion to DM 151 billion in the five years considered. The German Unity Fund was set up under the Economic, Monetary, and Social Union Treaty to compensate East Germany for not participating in the equalization system until it was appropriately redesigned; the Unity Fund ceased to exist after 1994. The fund was financed by contributions by the West German *Länder* (10 percent), the federal government (31 percent), and borrowing in the capital market. Thus, the Unity Fund indirectly allowed the new *Länder* to borrow in the (international) capital markets at the same rate as the federal government and the Western *Länder* governments, avoiding the payment of high-risk premiums. Payments from the fund were proportional to the populations of the new *Länder*. Among the other contributors to the new transfers, the Federal Labor Agency stands out as particularly significant. EC funds have not exceeded 4 percent of the total transfer volume.

Total gross transfers grew from DM 139 billion to DM 200 billion in the five years from 1991 to 1995. Taking into account the additional federal revenues generated by German union, net transfers amounted to

**Table 3.4**
Federal government spending in East Germany (bill. of DM)

|                                           | 1991 | 1992 | 1993  | 1994  | 1995  |
|-------------------------------------------|------|------|-------|-------|-------|
| Contributions to state and municipality budgets | 21.0 | 24.7 | 28.2  | 33.0  | 20.4  |
| Transfers to individuals                  | 30.1 | 35.7 | 50.6  | 41.7  | 47.0  |
| Regional policies and other federal programs | 23.5 | 27.8 | 34.8  | 39.7  | 48.1  |
| Total                                     | 74.6 | 88.2 | 113.6 | 114.4 | 115.5 |

*Source:* Bundesministerium der Finanzen (1995a, 1995b).
*Note:* Discrepancies with table 3.3 arise from differences in the accounting base.

DM 106 billion in 1991 and 150 billion in 1995. They corresponded to more than 50 percent of East German GDP in 1991 and almost 37 percent of GDP in 1994.

Table 3.4 shows how federal government spending in East Germany was distributed between 1991 and 1995. Transfers to individuals held the largest share until recently. Most of these payments relate to social assistance. Federal contributions to state and local government budgets peaked at DM 33 billion in 1994; they have been replaced (and effectively augmented) by giving the new *Länder* a larger part in the shared taxes.[5] Spending for regional and other federal policies in East Germany more than doubled from DM 23.5 billion to DM 48.1 billion. About 50 percent of this was used to finance infrastructure projects such as highways and railways.

Table 3.5 reports transfers to East Germany in connection with social assistance. Labor market policies—unemployment insurance, retraining programs, and wage subsidies—account for the largest part of these payments, 80 percent in 1991 and 51 percent in 1994.

Since 1995, new rules apply to the financial relations among the federal states (see Bundesbank, 1995). At least 75 percent of the states' share in VAT is now distributed according to population, and a maximum of 25 percent is distributed to those states whose total tax revenue (from state taxes and the states' share in income taxes and business taxes) falls below 92 percent of the average state tax revenue per capita. In addition, equalization payments are used to assure that no state receives less than 95 percent of the average state tax revenue per capita. The federal government complements these payments by covering 90 percent of the difference between a state's postequalization tax revenue and the average state tax revenue per capita. Over the coming ten years, the new *Länder* will

**Table 3.5**
Transfers connected to Social Security, 1991–94 (bill. of DM)

| Transfers | 1991 | 1992 | 1993 | 1994 | 1995–1997[1] |
|---|---|---|---|---|---|
| 1. Retirement | 8.2 | 14.7 | 21.2 | 28.1 | 96.0 |
| Pension fund | — | 4.5 | 8.8 | 12.8 | 41.9 |
| 2. Labor market policy | 31.5 | 45.2 | 48.7 | 40.7 | 104.1 |
| Unemployment insurance | 25.3 | 38.5 | 39.5 | 27.6 | 69.0 |
| 3. Veterans' pensions | 0.3 | 0.9 | 1.7 | 1.4 | 5.4 |
| 4. Total | 40.0 | 60.8 | 71.6 | 70.2 | 205.5 |
| Social security funds | 25.3 | 43.0 | 48.3 | 40.4 | 110.9 |
| Current federal budget | 14.7 | 17.8 | 23.3 | 29.8 | 94.6 |

Source: Bundesministerium der Finanzen (1995a, 1995b).
Note: 1. 1995–97 as projected by the federal government.

**Table 3.6**
Fiscal performance, 1991–94

| | 1991 | 1992 | 1993 | 1994 |
|---|---|---|---|---|
| Total revenues (DM bill.) | 66.1 | 73.0 | 76.4 | 79.3 |
| Taxes | 16.0 | 22.4 | 24.6 | 29.3 |
| Total expenditures (DM bill.) | 76.9 | 13.1 | 15.9 | 16.5 |
| Personnel cost | 14.9 | 19.0 | 22.2 | 23.2 |
| Deficit (DM bill.) | 10.8 | 13.1 | 15.9 | 16.5 |
| Taxes/GDP (percent) | 7.7 | 8.5 | 8.1 | 8.5 |
| Expenditures/GDP (percent) | 37.3 | 32.8 | 30.2 | 27.9 |
| Deficit/GDP (percent) | 5.2 | 5.0 | 5.2 | 4.8 |

Source: Deutsche Bundesbank (1995).

receive an additional DM 11.5 billion annually to compensate for the lack of tax resources of their local communities, and DM 5.5 billion annually in special grants.

Table 3.6 reports the budgetary developments of the new *Länder*. From 1991 to 1994, tax revenues grew from 7.7 percent to 8.5 percent of their combined GDP, while spending declined from 37 percent to 28 percent. This compares with a tax–GDP ratio of 9.3 percent and a spending–GDP ratio of 12 percent of the old *Länder* in 1994. Thus, the fiscal situation is particularly dramatic on the expenditure side. Interestingly, personnel cost is only around 24 percent of total spending in the East, compared with 40 percent in the old *Länder*, while transfers to local governments amount to

around 40 percent in the East and 20 percent in the West. This reflects the
fact that the financial picture of the communities in the East, which rely
mostly on revenues from local business and property taxes, is still bleak.
State debt rose from 2.4 percent of state GDP in 1991 to 16.2 percent in
1994 in East Germany, compared with 13.2 percent and 13.9 percent,
respectively, in the West. This shows that the new states were able to
raise substantial funds in the capital markets following unification.

**Administrative and Legal Union**
Under the socialist regime, East Germany had lost its traditional administrative structure, consisting of a tier of local governments (municipal-
ities and villages) and a separate tier of state governments below the
central government. The *Länder* had been completely abolished as administrative units in 1952 (Stamm, 1990). Local administrations continued to
exist, but had deteriorated to purely executive bodies taking orders from
higher administrations and, more important, Communist party structures.
The GDR had introduced the county as a more important administrative unit dealing with the concerns of the individual citizen. The counties
had become the main units of local administrative power and centers of
influence-peddling.

With the entry into the Federal Republic of Germany (FRG), *Länder* and
local governments had to be reinstituted according to the constitution of
the FRG. Local government is traditionally quite autonomous in Germany,
being responsible for a wide array of public services, such as schools, hos-
pitals, streets, and energy supply. The FRG's constitution acknowledges
and protects the position of local governments as a branch of government
in their own right. The core of the reform was, therefore, to turn local
authorities from administrative units into governments in the proper
sense of the word. This included the reinstitution of local parliaments and
other forms of citizen participation. Since a simple re-creation of the old
structure of local government resulted in a very large number of small
local entities, a sweeping administrative reform was initiated to redraw
boundaries and design more viable local units. Similarly, state governments had to be rebuilt in order to be able to cope with their new rights
and responsibilities as autonomous entities.

To facilitate these reforms, partnerships were formed between the West
German and East German *Länder* that provided the latter with technical
legal advice. As a result, administrative structures in the new *Länder* now
reflect the structures and experiences of their West German partners,
which are quite diverse.

**Table 3.7**
Public sector personnel transfers to East Germany

| Date | Federal employees delegated to federal administration | | Federal employees delegated to state administrations | | State employees delegated to state administrations | |
|---|---|---|---|---|---|---|
|  | Total | Long-term | Total | Long-term | Total | Long-term |
| 11/30/91 | 12905 | 4976 | 965 | 107 | 7682 | 388 |
| 01/31/92 | 12608 | 5635 | 1175 | 165 | 8104 | 625 |
| 04/30/92 | 13679 | 4637 | 1322 | 299 | 8375 | 858 |
| 10/01/92 | 15485 | 5898 | 1384 | 558 | 8403 | n/a |
| 01/01/93 | 14772 | 6426 | 1365 | 691 | 8217 | 1987 |
| 06/01/93 | 15015 | 7152 | 1587 | 815 | 8337 | 2633 |

*Source:* Federal Ministry of the Interior.

East German state and local governments obviously lacked adequately trained personnel to manage their administrative functions under the Western legal system and federalism. There was, thus, a danger that the new regime would be only a formal veil with no real power, and that the old political and administrative decision-making structures would survive, hidden under the cover of the new legal structure. This danger was reduced by the fact that the West German·public authorities delegated personnel to East Germany to help build up the new public sector there. Table 3.7 illustrates this by showing the number of public-sector employees sent to East Germany by the federal and state governments in 1991 and 1993, together with their destinated place in the public sector.[6] The federal government sent between 13,000 and 15,000 employees to East Germany to staff federal administrations there, and up to an additional 1,600 to staff state governments. West German state governments sent around 8,000 employees to help state governments in the East. It is noteworthy that the share of long-term delegates increased over time. Not contained in this data is a large number of West German local government employees sent to local East German authorities—over 10,000 at the last date of recording in 1993. Furthermore, judges and law enforcement personnel was sent to the new *Länder* to help with the rebuilding of the legal system.

As a result of these efforts, East Germany had adopted, within a few years, a widely decentralized form of government. Unification allowed the swift adoption of a legal order and an administration compatible with a market economy and providing administrative and legal security.

**Privatization**

Already during the last phase of the GDR, privatization of public enterprises was entrusted to the Treuhandanstalt. (See *Gesetzblatt der DDR*, 8 March 1990 and 19 March 1990. For a history of the foundation of Treuhand, see Fisher and Schröter, 1993.) Treuhand was founded as a trust fund holding ownership of the East German state-owned companies and firms upon the conversion of the latter into limited-liability companies or common-stock companies. Treuhand was authorized to sell shares of these companies to the public. Between March and July 1990, it was mainly occupied with disentangling the large conglomerates and the conversion of existing firms into corporations to facilitate the presentation of DM-denominated balance sheets as required by the monetary union treaty with West Germany. Lack of adequate expertise and personnel made the work of the Treuhand very slow in this period (Fischer and Schröter, 1993; see also Treuhandanstalt, 1990). Although the idea of a *third way* between socialism and market economy still had support, the Treuhand Act of 17 June 1990 declared the goal of curtailing the state's economic activities as quickly and extensively as possible. For this purpose, Treuhand was charged with the task of privatization, as well as of producing an active competition and industrial policy, including the restructuring of conglomerates as well as the liquidation of nonviable ones.

Under the Unification Treaty (Art. 25), Treuhand became an independent federal agency.[7] Rapidly staffed with several thousand Western managers and granted the right to raise funds in the capital market, Treuhand became the largest industrial holding company in the Western world. When, in early 1991, public dissatisfaction with mounting unemployment rose in East Germany, Chancellor Kohl pushed for a more active involvement of Treuhand in regional, sectoral, and labor market policies in collaboration with the *Länder* governments and the trade unions (Pilz and Ortwein, 1992). Similarly, the Federal Finance Ministry, Treuhand's supervising ministry, insisted that Treuhand make more active use of its instruments of industrial policy, mostly of long-term subsidies, to keep noncompetitive firms alive. For a while, therefore, a possibility existed that Treuhand would become a giant ministry of industry (Pilz and Ortwein, 1992).

Probably the main factor preventing that from happening was the German Parliament's decision to dissolve Treuhand by 1994. The limited time horizon made the agency emphasize speed of privatization before other goals. Thus, by the end of 1993, only 7 percent of the original 13,384 firms remained in the hands of Treuhand (Ditges, 1994). Of the latter, 49 percent had been privatized, 12 percent reprivatized, and 24 percent liquidated. By December 1994, 257 firms remained in the hands of Treuhand: of these, 65 were offered for privatization; 30 percent of the original number of firms had been liquidated. Privatization had brought a total revenue of DM 65 billion as of December 1994; but much more than that had been spent on investment subsidies, assumption, and servicing of old loans, and guarantees.[8] The total Treuhand debt raised in the capital market amounted to DM 203.5 billion as of December 1994.

Overall, rapid privatization implied that economic restructuring was left mainly to the new investors. While there are important economic arguments for that approach, there was also a significant price (Ditges, 1994). On the one hand, East Germany might face the risk of deindustrialization as much of the old industrial sector was closed down. On the other hand, the goal of helping an East German middle class of firm and business owners to come into existence clearly was not met: 75 percent of the privatized firms went to West German entrepreneurs, 6 percent to foreigners, and only 19 percent to East German entrepreneurs.

## 3.3   Economic Performance since 1991

### 3.3.1   Output, External Performance, and Prices

Table 3.8 summarizes the performance of the East German economy from 1991 to 1994. In these four years, East German GDP expanded by 25

**Table 3.8**
Real GDP and components (billions of DM, 1991 prices)

|                              | 1991 | 1992 | 1993 | 1994 |
|------------------------------|------|------|------|------|
| GDP                          | 206  | 222  | 235  | 258  |
| Consumption                  | 180  | 197  | 202  | 211  |
| Investment                   | 91   | 121  | 139  | 162  |
|   Machinery & equipment | 42   | 46   | 49   | 52   |
|   Structures       | 50   | 72   | 85   | 104  |
|     Residential structures | 17   | 23   | 28   | 38   |
| Government expenditure        | 88   | 94   | 93   | 94   |
| Exports                      | 47   | 52   | 55   | 67   |
| Imports                      | 199  | 241  | 254  | 278  |
| External deficit             | 152  | 190  | 199  | 211  |
| Domestic absorption          | 359  | 412  | 434  | 467  |

*Source:* Bundesministerium der Finanzen (1995a, 1995b).

percent in real terms, much more than West German GDP, which increased by only 2.2 percent during the same time period and fell in 1992–1993, in what proved to be Germany's worst recession after World War II. Most of the expansion was driven by a very strong investment boom, gross investment expanding by 78 percent over this period. This, in turn, was mainly carried by a strong increase in the building of new structures. In contrast, real consumption rose more moderately (17 percent over the entire period), and real government expenditures on goods and services were almost constant.

The most astonishing fact shown in Table 3.8 is the huge difference between domestic absorption (consumption plus investment and government spending) and GDP, that is, East Germany's external deficit, which increased from 74 percent of GDP in 1991 to 82 percent of GDP in 1994. Thus, after unification, the East German economy was able to attract almost as much in resources from abroad (West Germany and other countries) as it was able to produce itself. Subtracting the net public-sector transfers reported above from the external deficit yields an estimate of the total resources the East German economy was able to attract from the external nongovernment sector: DM 46 billion in 1991, DM 75 billion in 1992, DM 70 billion in 1993, and DM 75 billion in 1994. This compares with private domestic savings of DM 14.5 billion, 32.2 billion, 34.4 billion, and 30 billion in the same four years. External nongovernment financing was thus much larger than private domestic savings.

"Foreign" investment is increasingly difficult to measure in East Germany due to the fact that much of this investment is by East German branches of West German firms. Table 3.9 provides some estimates of investment in machinery and equipment. From 1991 to 1994, roughly half of all investment was foreign. Comparing Tables 3.8 and 3.9 suggests that the share of foreign investment in the total external deficit increased substantially, thus strengthening East Germany's ability to pay back its foreign liabilities in the future. Table 3.9 also shows that the share of the manufacturing sector in total investment declined by 8 percent from 1991 to 1994, while investment flowing into the service sector has more than doubled in relative terms. Interestingly, the same pattern is not observed in foreign investment, where the share of manufacturing remained higher and the share of services was much lower.

Table 3.10 reports East and West Germany's industrial production. After a drop of around 30 percent upon unification and two years of stagnation, industrial production finally started to pick up rapidly in 1994. The comparison with West German industrial production suggests that to some

**Table 3.9**
Total and foreign investment

| | Total investment[1] | | | | Foreign investment[2] | | | |
|---|---|---|---|---|---|---|---|---|
| | 91 | 92 | 93 | 94 | 91 | 92 | 93 | 94 |
| | Percent | | | | | | | |
| Manufacturing | 41.9 | 39.3 | 36.5 | 33.5 | 40.6 | 42.9 | 40.9 | 38.7 |
| Construction | 4.6 | 4.3 | 3.6 | 3.7 | 4.4 | 3.8 | 2.7 | 3.2 |
| Trade | 5.6 | 5.1 | 4.6 | 4.1 | 8.8 | 7.6 | 6.8 | 6.2 |
| Transportation, communication | 20.8 | 21.5 | 20.1 | 18.2 | 38.1 | 34.3 | 30.3 | 27.4 |
| Services | 20.5 | 33.1 | 37.8 | 43.2 | 12.5 | 15.2 | 22.0 | 27.7 |
| Dwellings | 20.5 | 22.8 | 25.3 | 30.6 | 3.1 | 4.8 | 6.8 | 11.6 |
| | Billions of DM | | | | | | | |
| Total private sector | 77.6 | 104.6 | 124.0 | 146.8 | 32.0 | 52.5 | 66.0 | 77.5 |
| Government | 14.9 | 23.3 | 26.5 | 32.1 | | | | |

*Source:* Neumann (1994).
*Notes:* 1. Includes only investment in machinery and equipment.
2. Including investment by West German firms.

**Table 3.10**
Output and prices in East Germany, 1990–94

| Year | Consumer prices | | Producer prices | | Industrial production | |
|---|---|---|---|---|---|---|
| | East[1] | West[2] | East[1] | West[3] | East[4] | West[3] |
| 1991 | 108.3 | 103.5 | 63.2 | 103.4 | 77.2 | 121.0 |
| 1992 | 120.4 | 107.6 | 63.8 | 104.8 | 78.7 | 119.4 |
| 1993 | 131.0 | 112.1 | 64.3 | 104.8 | 86.9 | 111.0 |
| 1994 | 135.7 | 116.3 | | | 110.8 | 121.7 |

*Source:* Statistisches Bundesamt (1995a, 1995d).
*Notes:* 1. July 1990–June 1991 = 100.
2. 1990 = 100.
3. 1985 = 100.
4. July 1990–December 1990 = 100.

extent, at least, the sluggish behavior of East German industrial output can be attributed to the German recession that also brought West German industrial output down by 8 percent between 1991 and 1993. The parallel movement of both outputs in 1994 suggests that East German industry had the same cyclical pattern as West Germany's industry.

The high level of aggregation in Table 3.10 is, to some extent, deceiving. Normalizing output levels of 1991 (first quarter) to 100 in a sample of 29 industries, output levels in 1994 (last quarter) varied from 18.2 (production of leather) to 592.1 (plastics) (see Statistisches Bundesamt, 1995). Hidden behind the initial decline and the subsequent upswing in aggregate production is a massive restructuring of East Germany's industrial sector.

Table 3.10 also reports the main price movements in the two parts of Germany. Consumer prices went through a strong rise upon unification, which was much more pronounced in the East than in the West. In East Germany, the increase in consumer prices reflected large shifts in relative prices, particularly for services and housing. For example, the average gross rental price for dwellings increased from DM 0.90 per square meter in mid-1990 to DM 6.00 per square meter in January 1994. During the same period, the average cost of heating and water supply rose from DM 0.50 to DM 1.85 per square meter. All the while, industrial producer prices remained flat in both parts of Germany. In particular, the relative price of East German industrial products remained constant after an initial drop in 1990.

With unification and the beginning of the transformation process in the other East and Central European countries, East Germany's external trade situation changed dramatically. Figure 3.2 illustrates the development of the trade volumes—excluding intra-German trade—after 1990. East German export markets literally fell apart, and traditional import relations broke down. Exports and imports fell to 50 percent of the 1990 volume in 1991, and to around 40 percent in 1992. Undoubtedly, one important factor in this was the large real exchange-rate shock East Germany experienced upon unification, particularly due to the postunification wage policies. The real exchange-rate shock alone, however, would lead one to expect a decrease in exports together with stable or increasing imports. The fact that both exports and imports shrank suggests that the collapse of the traditional CMEA markets was at least of equal importance in explaining East Germany's external performance in the early 1990s.

Table 3.11 reports the regional structure of East German trade—not including intra-German trade—between 1990 and 1994.[9] It shows that the

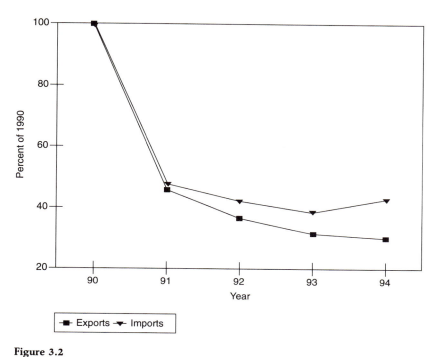

**Figure 3.2**
External trade, 1990–94

**Table 3.11**
Regional structure of foreign trade (percent)

|                                                  | 1990 | 1991 | 1992 | 1993 | 1994[1] |
|--------------------------------------------------|------|------|------|------|---------|
|                                                  |      |      | Exports |   |         |
| Western industrialized countries                 | 13.4 | 25.5 | 33.7 | 31.7 | 41.4    |
| European Union                                   | 7.7  | 17.1 | 23.0 | 16.0 | 22.4    |
| East and Central European countries[2]           | 78.3 | 65.5 | 52.1 | 52.4 | 41.5    |
|                                                  |      |      | Imports |   |         |
| Western industrialized countries                 | 24.8 | 36.2 | 46.9 | 50.5 | 55.8    |
| European Union                                   | 11.7 | 21.5 | 25.8 | 29.8 | 34.0    |
| East and Central European countries[2]           | 65.0 | 56.2 | 48.1 | 45.3 | 39.2    |

*Source:* Sachverständigenrat (1994).
*Notes:* 1. First two quarters.
            2. Including former USSR.

share of the traditional trading partners of East Germany declined dramatically on both sides of the trade relation. Today, Western industrialized countries are as or more important as trade partners than the former CMEA countries, and the European Union is gaining importance as a trade partner. Here, of course, the fact that East Germany gained immediate entrance into the European Union, including free trade with its members, is an important factor. Still, Russia remains the single most important trade partner, accounting for 18.8 percent of East Germany's imports and 19.4 percent of its exports.

Sales figures for East German industries (DIW, 1995) paint a similar picture. In 1994, East German manufacturing industries sold about 55 percent of their output to East German customers and another 27 percent to customers in West Germany. Of the rest, 44 percent went to East and Central Europe.

Table 3.12 shows the commodity structure of East Germany's foreign trade from 1990 to 1994. Four years after German unification, the trade pattern did not yet indicate any specialization according to comparative advantage other than the loss of importance of oil and fuel exports (SITC 3). If anything, it is noteworthy that the manufacturing sector became more important in exports despite the general decline of that sector in the East German economy.

Again, the high level of aggregation is deceiving. A more detailed picture emerges through examining sales figures of eleven individual industries (DIW, 1995). In 1994, iron and nonferrous industries and foun-

**Table 3.12**
Commodity structure of foreign trade (percent)

| SITC | 0 + 1 | 2 | 3 | 4 + 5 | 6 | 7 | 8 |
|------|-------|-----|------|-------|------|------|------|
|      |       |     |      | Exports |    |      |      |
| 1990 | 3.5   | 1.6 | 2.2  | 10.5  | 13.2 | 53.2 | 14.6 |
| 1994 | 6.5   | 2.0 | 0.5  | 12.4  | 13.7 | 56.3 | 8.0  |
|      |       |     |      | Imports |    |      |      |
| 1990 | 7.1   | 6.2 | 24.2 | 6.0   | 17.1 | 29.1 | 6.5  |
| 1994 | 5.8   | 4.8 | 265. | 4.9   | 17.2 | 32.3 | 8.4  |

*Source:* Sachverständigenrat (1994).
*Note:* SITC codes are: 0 food and live animals, 1 beverages and tobacco, 2 crude materials inedible except fuels, 3 mineral fuels and lubricants, 4 animal and vegetable oils and fats, 5 chemicals and related products, 6 basic manufactures, 7 machinery and transport equipment, 8 miscellaneous manufactures.

dries sold 76 percent of their output outside the area of the former East Germany, 55 percent of which went to West Germany. Textiles, electrical products, plastics, office machinery, and chemical products ranked next: 66 (39 to West Germany) percent, 65 (36) percent, 59 (40) percent, 50 (19) percent, and 50 (39) percent, respectively. Combining these data with industry data for productivity change reveals an interesting point. Productivity gains in these eleven industries between 1991 and 1994 ranged from 178 percent (food processing) to 670 percent (plastics). The rank correlation between the share of exports in total sales and the increase in productivity is 0.77 (with a standard error of 0.21), and rises to 0.86 (with a standard error of 0.17) if sales to the former East European markets are left out. Both are statistically significant. Thus, export shares were higher in industries where productivity gains had been most pronounced. Given the commodity structure of world trade, this is compatible with the Ricardian conjecture that East Germany should export products of those industries where productivity differentials are relatively favorable.

### 3.3.2  Factor Markets

Table 3.13 shows the development of employment in East Germany from 1989 to 1994. Overall, the number of dependent workers, that is, those who are not self-employed, declined by 40 percent. The largest drops occurred in 1990 and 1991, with 19 percent and 13 percent, respectively. Even factoring in a preunification *hidden unemployment rate* of 15 percent, as calculated by Treuhand (1995), the East German economy lost about a third of its full-time, dependent employment between 1989 and 1993. The unemployment rate jumped from 4.7 percent in 1990 to 10.1 percent in 1991; it peaked at 14.5 percent in the first half of 1994. In the second half of 1994, a turnaround occurred and employment increased by two percentage points over the level of the first six months of that year. Meanwhile, the number of self-employed increased by 155 percent, but it remained a mere 7.6 percent of the employed labor force compared with 10.7 percent in West Germany (1994).

In addition to full-time employed persons, Table 3.13 shows the number of workers in partial layoffs, in government-managed training programs, and in subsidized workplaces. This number peaked at almost 2.1 million workers, or 23.1 percent of the workforce, in 1991. It dropped sharply in 1992 and 1993 due to the end of special federal assistance programs, reaching about 650,000 workers, or 7.5 percent of the workforce, in late 1994. While the majority (78 percent) of these were in partial layoffs in

**Table 3.13**
Employment (1,000 persons)

| Year | East Germany | | | | | West Germany |
| | Dependent workers | Self-employed | Labor market programs[5] | Early retirement | Unemployment rate | Dependent workers |
| --- | --- | --- | --- | --- | --- | --- |
| 1989 | 9560 | 187 | | | | 24647 |
| 1990 | 8568 | 252 | 1562[1] | 344 | 4.7 | 25453 |
| 1991 | 6950 | 371 | 2079 | 511 | 10.1 | 26136 |
| 1992 | 6046 | 417 | 1249 | 808 | 13.3 | 26385 |
| 1993 | 5821 | 452 | 901 | 849 | 13.4 | 25930 |
| 1994[2] | 5773 | 474 | 630 | 692 | 14.5 | 25502 |
| 1994 | 6389[3] | | 649[4] | 604[4] | 12.5[4] | |

Source: Statistisches Bundesamt (1995b, 1995c), Bundesministerium der Finanzen (1995a).
Notes: 1. Second half.
2. First half.
3. November and December.
4. Second half.
5. Subsidized training programs, subsidized workplaces, and workers in partial lay-offs.

1991, 44 percent were in subsidized workplaces, and 40 percent were in training programs in late 1994. Finally, the table shows that a large part of the workforce (9.2 percent in 1992, 7.2 percent in late 1994) moved into early retirement programs.

Part of the decline in East German employment can be attributed to the loss of external markets. But Table 3.14 leaves no doubt that a very aggressive wage policy is the main explanatory factor. Average monthly earnings in East German industry started at 47.1 percent of West German earnings in 1991. In 1994, they reached almost 72 percent. In 1991 and 1992, years of the recession in Germany, there were wage increases of 30 percent and 17 percent, respectively. Only in 1994 was a more moderate wage growth reached. In the trade, commercial, and financial sector, salaries increased from 46.7 percent to 72.8 percent of the West German level. Meanwhile, productivity in East Germany, measured as GDP per employed member of the labor force, rose from 31 percent of the West German level (DM 90,702) in 1991 to 52.7 percent of the West German level (DM 104,046) in 1994. Unit wage cost[10] declined from 158 percent of the West German level (DM 54.02) to 135.7 percent (DM 52.71) during the same period (Bundesministerium der Finanzen, 1995a).

**Table 3.14**
Wage trends

|  | 1991 | 1992 | 1993 | 1994 |
|---|---|---|---|---|
| Average monthly earnings (DM) | | | | |
| Industrial workers and employees, East Germany | 1963 | 2561 | 2989 | 3261 |
| Industrial workers and employees, West Germany | 4168 | 4401 | 4550 | 4547 |
| Trade, commercial, and financial sector employees, East Germany | 1819 | 2499 | 2999 | 3308 |
| Trade, commercial, and financial sector employees, West Germany | 3892 | 4182 | 4398 | 4547 |
| Relative productivity of East German labor (percent) | 31.0 | 43.1 | 50.1 | 52.7 |
| Relative unit wage cost in East Germany (percent) | 158.0 | 145.4 | 136.2 | 135.7 |

*Source:* Bundesministerium der Finanzen (1995a) and own calculations.

**Table 3.15**
Sectoral structure of employment

|  | 1989 | 1993 | Change (%) | West Germany |
|---|---|---|---|---|
| Farming, mining | 10.0 | 3.9 | −75.2 | 3.0 |
| Manufacturing, construction | 45.0 | 34.9 | −50.0 | 37.2 |
| Trade, transportation | 15.5 | 18.0 | −25.3 | 19.3 |
| Services | 6.4 | 17.6 | 78.7 | 20.6 |
| Government | 23.1 | 25.6 | −28.7 | 19.8 |

*Source:* Statistisches Bundesamt (1995b, c), own calculations.

Thus, even allowing for a large degree of uncertainty in picking the correct initial wage level for East German labor in terms of DM, the wage and productivity movements following unification clearly were not conducive to maintaining a satisfactory level of employment. In a nutshell, East German labor was priced out of the market, and the bill was picked up by the unemployment insurance and the pension funds.

Table 3.15 reports the sectoral structure of employment. Before unification, a relatively large share of East Germany's workforce was employed in the farming and manufacturing sectors, compared with West Germany. In contrast, the trade and transportation and the services sectors were comparatively small. Overall, the structure of East German employment in 1989 was very similar to that of West Germany in 1971 (Treuhand, 1990). Table 3.15 also shows that the farming and manufacturing sectors experienced the largest relative reductions in employment, 75.2 percent and 50 percent, respectively, between 1989 and 1993. Only the services sector showed a growth in employment during that period. It is interesting to note that a disaggregation of employment by the five new states reveals the same developments in all states. At the same time, there was very little movement of employment between the five states. Thus, the restructuring had not induced, as of 1993, any pattern of sectoral specialization among the five new states.

Less aggregated data provide further interesting information. Normalizing employment levels of 1991 (first quarter) to 100, employment levels in 1994 (last quarter ) varied from 7.2 (production of leather) to 94 (steel structures) in a sample of twenty-nine industries (Statistisches Bundesamt, 1995). Thus, the structure of industrial employment changed dramatically after unification. These structural shifts were accompanied by changes in labor productivity ranging from 59 percent (shipbuilding) to 819 percent (stones and quarries) of the productivity level in 1991 (first quarter). The rank correlation between output and employment changes across industries is 0.76 (standard error 0.13); the rank correlation between output and productivity changes is 0.48 (standard error 0.17). Both are statistically significant. In contrast, the rank correlation between employment and productivity changes is not significantly different from zero. This indicates that the productivity gains are not simply due to labor shedding.

A similar impression arises from the following regression:

$$L_i = 29.3 + 0.014P_i + 0.19YR_i$$
$$\;\;\;\;\;(8.2)\;\;\;\;(0.009)\;\;\;\;\;\;(0.016)$$
$$R^2 = 0.85$$

where $L_i$ is the index of employment in industry $i$, $P_i$ is the index of productivity, $YR_i$ is the residual of a regression of the index of production on the index of productivity, and the numbers in parentheses are standard errors. We use $YR_i$ instead of raw production levels in 1994 as a regressor in this equation to account for the positive and significant correlation between the changes in production and changes in productivity.[11] The interpretation is that $YR_i$ reflects the responses of industrial output to changes in relative prices following unification. With this interpretation, the regression suggests that the restructuring of the labor force has been driven mainly by the response to relative price changes and to a smaller extent by the distribution of productivity gains across industries.

**Table 3.16**
Demographic structure of employment

|  | 1991 | 1993 | West, 1993 |
|---|---|---|---|
| All male | 59.9 | 55.7 | 58.9 |
| Male, 55–60 | 72.8 | 39.5 | 80.4 |
| Male, 60–65 | 26.8 | 12.3 | 33.7 |
| All female | 50.0 | 47.7 | 39.4 |
| Female, unmarried | 27.6 | 28.5 | 36.3 |
| Female, 20–25 | 82.9 | 80.8 | 75.0 |
| Female, 55–60 | 35.0 | 26.2 | 75.1 |
| Female, married | 73.0 | 68.9 | 48.1 |
| Female, 20–25 | 94.7 | 89.3 | 67.9 |
| Female, 55–60 | 36.5 | 26.6 | 42.5 |
| Female, widowed or divorced | 30.7 | 27.7 | 22.9 |
| Female, 20–25 | 96.3 | 94.8 | 69.5 |
| Female, 55–60 | 40.0 | 25.7 | 56.5 |

*Source:* Statistisches Bundesamt (1994).
*Note:* Labor force participation rates in percent.

Table 3.16 describes the demographic structure of employment in terms of labor force participation rates. At the start of the transformation process (1991), male participation was similar in both parts of Germany, and female participation was considerably higher in the East. This was particularly true for young women: unmarried, married, divorced or widowed. The table indicates that participation was very different across age groups in the two parts of Germany. The data for 1993 reveal two things. First, much of the employment reduction in East Germany was achieved by shifting workers—male and female—above age fifty into early retirement. Participation rates in the older age groups are now dramatically lower in East Germany than in West Germany. This strategy of dealing with the destruction of East German employment compounded the severe aging problem the German Social Security system faces over the next decades (see von Hagen and Walz, 1995).

Second, there are some indications that participation patterns in East Germany may approach those of West Germany in the future. This applies particularly to women. This, together with the evidence in Table 3.15, suggests that much structural adjustment will be needed in the years to come and that structural unemployment will remain high as a consequence.

A large part of the federal government's response to the wage trends in East Germany was to give massive financial support to existing firms and investment opportunities. Investment support includes allowances for movable and depreciable fixed assets, investment grants, and special depreciation provisions. In addition, various forms of liquidity aid and equity support are available (see Sinn, 1995). The economic effect of these programs was to lower the cost of capital for investment in East Germany. Sinn (1995) estimates that the cost of capital might have become negative for industrial investment and the renovation of buildings, and substantially lower, though still positive, for other types of investment.

Two observations are noteworthy. First, subsidizing capital implies that factor price distortions in East Germany were increased rather than reduced —the more appropriate strategy would have been to subsidize the cost of labor (see Akerlof et al., 1991). By inducing the choice of overly capital-intensive technologies, this policy has aggravated East Germany's employment problems, although the income effect of the subsidies has likely increased total investment and, hence, helped increase employment.

Second, the capital subsidies were largely embedded in the West German tax system, which, with unification, was extended to East Germany. An important characteristic of this system is that the more a firm can use losses and depreciation from subsidized investment projects to offset taxable profits from other business activities, the larger the benefit of capital subsidies. Sinn (1995) shows that this created a bias of the capital subsidies in favor of West German businesses acquiring East German production facilities. East German investors without offsetting incomes found little or no advantages in the support programs. This is consistent with the results of a recent poll (DIW, 1995). They indicate that the scarcity of capital and liquidity is a more pressing problem for East German businesses, particularly among small and medium-sized businesses, than for businesses owned by West German or foreign companies.

### 3.4    The Political Economy of Kinship in Germany

#### 3.4.1    *Transformation and Uncertainty*

Pure and straightforward economic analysis of the transition problem generates a clear picture: Transition reforms should aim at opening up goods and factor markets to introduce competition and a relative price structure reflecting true comparative advantages and disadvantages, and relative scarcities of goods and factors. In doing so, the economy is first moved to the frontier of its production possibility space, and then to a point corresponding to its utility-maximizing participation in world trade (von Hagen,

1992). Since both movements imply aggregate efficiency gains, the economist would expect countries to opt for rapid transition, the big-bang strategy.

In light of this, observers of the transformation processes in the former socialist countries have been puzzled by the sluggishness of the actual reforms. Apart from East Germany, no other country seems to have adopted a big-bang strategy. The clue to solving the puzzle is in the fact that reform programs entail distributional consequences that are uncertain. Though the Pareto-improving quality of reform programs assures that opposition against reform can be bought out *in principle*, the potential losers in a reform cannot always be sure that they will receive compensation when the gains and losses are realized, because the appropriate transfer mechanisms may not be in place at the start of the reform and because, from the point of view of the individual, it is not always clear, ex ante, who is on the winning and who is on the losing sides of the reform.

The existence of appropriate transfer mechanisms early in the reform, assuring that losers receive compensation, is important for two reasons. First, because distributional consequences may occur quickly, so that potential losers want the assurance of quick assistance. Where this is not certain, potential losers may resist reform until a safety net has been installed.

Second, one might argue that a transfer *mechanism* is not needed and that transfers can be granted on a discretionary basis. Discretion, however, raises problems of credibility. Once the reform has been implemented and the actual winners and losers have been identified, the incentive for the winners to keep the promise of paying compensation to the losers may be small. Thus, the winners may simply decide to keep the gains for themselves and leave the losers behind. This credibility problem is compounded if those who were relatively well off under the prereform regime are more likely to be among the losers than among the winners. A transfer mechanism based on legal rules and automaticity helps overcome this credibility problem because it limits the scope of discretion.

The importance of uncertainty in the reform process has been discussed in two dimensions. Alesina and Drazen (1991) consider a scenario where the costs of reform (prereform economic privileges forgone under the reform) are distributed unevenly among different groups of society, and no group knows exactly how large the costs of the other groups are. In their analysis, a reform is stuck unless a group in society agrees to accept paying the cost of reform. Ex ante, several groups could make that decision. A group will do that if the expected cost of postponing reform exceeds the cost it anticipates having to bear under the reform. Postponing the reform increases the total cost to society, but each group has an incentive to hold out and see if the others give in first. Thus, reform is not started although it is beneficial for society as a whole to go ahead with it.

Fernandez and Rodrick (1991) and Dewatripont and Roland (1993) consider a scenario where the costs and benefits of reform are spread unevenly across individuals ex ante. Fernandez and Rodrick show that if the net gains are more concentrated than the losses, the median voter may be among the ex ante losers and vote against the reform. The point here is that a sufficiently equitable distribution of the gains is needed ex ante for reform to win enough political support.

Dewatripont and Roland look at the issue from a more positive angle. They argue that gradual reform may be instrumental in resolving distributional uncertainty in small steps and in keeping the option of reversing reform programs that are found unacceptable in their distributional consequences. In this way, gradualism helps win political support along the way and facilitates reform that would have been politically impossible otherwise.

What do these arguments imply for East Germany? A first, important aspect of German union in this regard is the social union, the immediate introduction of the West German social safety net into the East. East Germans could be assured that their claims for redistribution of the gains from reform would be treated on the basis of highly developed social legislation rather than discretion. West Germany's willingness to provide the initial funding for Social Security in East Germany, laid down in the Unification Treaty, assured the immediate availability of transfers. Thus social union helped solve the timing and credibility problems of the transfers needed to overcome resistance to reform.

A second aspect of this is that with unification, the decision to begin and pursue a reform course was no longer left to the East Germans alone. Given the general perception that West Germany would benefit from rapid reform in the East, the political support for swift and comprehensive reform was increased by the fact that the decision-making power was shared by East and West Germany, and in some cases, such as the early management of Treuhand, was left primarily in the hands of West Germans.

A third aspect of relevance is the administrative and legal union. The introduction of West Germany's legal system and of federal government dissolved the traditional centers of power and created new ones. In addition, new and competing forms of interest representation were created, often with West German leadership or advice (see the papers in Schmid, Löbler, and Tiemann, 1994). As the new structures cut across the boundaries of the old ones, those who had been at the centers of power before unification most likely found it much harder to organize political support against reform among potential losers than had the old political structures survived. Thus, the risk of distributional struggles slowing down the reform was reduced. In addition, the introduction of a Western legal and administrative infrastructure reduced individual distributional uncertainty by securing the citizens' rights and by giving individuals the possibility to challenge administrative decisions.

These points lead to the conclusion that the circumstances of the East German transformation created unique conditions favoring a big-bang reform strategy. Quite apart from having a *rich uncle*, East Germany's case may remain an outlier for the study of transformation processes simply by being the only case where this strategy was politically feasible.

### 3.4.2  Union Responses to Unification

Kinship implies the risk of being drawn into the middle of family fights and facing disaster. The picture of German unification would not be complete without showing how this happened to East German workers.

For East German workers, economic union with West Germany created the opportunity to migrate to the West and seek the better-paying employment prevailing there. We have seen above that a wave of immigration did indeed enter West Germany in late 1989. West German unions were quick to realize the threat they faced with unification: The entry of several million new workers would likely have destroyed the stability of the highly cartelized, overregulated West German labor market, undermining the unions' economic and political power. It might have been the death blow to unions whose main preoccupation, throughout the 1980s, had been to reduce work time and secure the benefits of highly paid labor-market insiders, creating ever higher long-term rates of unemployment in West Germany.

The unions' response to the threat of immigration was the aggressive wage strategy documented above. In fact, West German union leaders took over the leadership of East German unions immediately—a takeover that was facilitated by the fact that the old union leadership was politically discredited after unification—and conducted the wage bargaining on behalf of the East German workers. Following West German practices, wage agreements in East Germany were negotiated on an industry basis between unions and employers' associations. According to German labor-market legislation, such agreements are binding on all employers who are members of the relevant association, regardless of whether their work-forces are unionized.

Pushing for excessive wages in East Germany had one main purpose: With unemployment compensation tied to exit wages in factories from which the workers were laid off, the goal was to make being unemployed in East Germany sufficiently attractive that workers laid off in the East would forgo the option of seeking employment in the West. The benefit structure of unemployment insurance and its immediate extension to East Germany are obviously a critical part of this strategy: Without the avail-ability of sufficiently generous benefits, higher unemployment due to exces-sive wage demands would have increased rather than reduced the incentive for migration (Sinn, 1995). The strategy worked when it turned out that West German employers were willing to go along with it, valuing the stability of West German corporatist industrial relations more than the potential wage reductions from hiring East German immigrants.

West German unions thus willingly embarked on a course of risking the mass destruction of East German employment to save their own posi-tions.[12] Section 3.3 showed that their wage policy destroyed employment in the East while the unemployment insurance and the pension fund picked up the cost. Through increasing Social Security contributions and the *solidarity* income-tax surcharge, West German workers were forced to pay for maintaining a union system hostile to employment. By increasing the cost of labor, including in West Germany, it is likely that this policy increased long-term unemployment in the West even further.

Much was written in the early 1990s about the wisdom of the conver-sion rate of Mark- to DM-denominated wage contracts. Many suggested that a lower conversion rate would have helped preserve employment in East Germany. In retrospect, it is clear that these considerations miss the crucial point: The only difference a lower conversion rate would have made would have been faster wage growth in the period immediately after unification, to jack up exit wages to a level sufficient to keep East German workers from competing in the West German labor market.

The really fatal decision was, therefore, not the conversion rate but the immediate extension to East Germany of West German labor-market leg-islation and an unemployment insurance system tying benefits to exit wages. It gave the West German unions the opportunity of a free ride on the Social Security system to safeguard their economic and political power, while pretending to care about the welfare of the East German workers. With labor market institutions that favor insider–outsider behavior, unions were allowed to turn a third of the East German workforce into outsiders. This large externality of the traditional West German system of industrial relations for the East German labor market is another unique factor in East Germany's transition.

East Germany is now beginning to react to these harmful developments by pulling itself out of the traditional system of industrial relations. This is most visible on the employers' side. According to a 1995 study by DIW, East German employers have left their associations in large numbers, freeing themselves from having to pay excessive wages. Only 27 percent of all employers were still members of an association in the spring of 1995. The tendency to leave was particularly strong among small and medium-sized companies. 40 percent of all companies with fewer than twenty employees, 30 percent of all companies with twenty to one hundred employees, and 20 percent of all companies with one hundred to two hundred employees paid wages lower than the union wage in the spring of 1995. Disconnecting themselves from the collective bargaining process has helped these businesses to survive. With mounting dissatisfaction about the traditional system of industrial relations in West Germany, these developments may eventually turn out to be the beginning of a radical overhaul of German labor-market institutions—a rather unanticipated version of the old insight that neither part of the family remains the same when new members join the clan.

## 3.5   Conclusions

German union created a unique environment for transformation in East Germany. Macroeconomically, it promoted East Germany's integration into the Western trading system and gave East Germany relatively privileged access to international capital markets to finance its transition. These factors may help in the longer run to overcome the huge terms-of-trade shock implied by monetary union and the loss of the traditional external markets. On a politicoeconomic level, German union created an environment favorable for a big-bang strategy of reform by reducing the distributional problems reform processes may face. At the same time, however, the East German labor market was drawn into the West German pattern of industrial relations, resulting in massive destruction of employment. *Kinship* has, therefore, had its pluses and its minuses for East Germany. It is still too early to tell which of these will prevail in the longer run.

# Notes

This paper was prepared for the UNU/WIDER project on the Integration of Transition Economies into the World Economy, I thank Padma Desai for very helpful comments, and Stephan Monissen and Jürgen Stanowsky for competent research assistance.

1. Rapid unification allowed West Germany to finance about two-thirds of unification-related expenditures through savings and restructuring of separation-related expenditures. Such savings might not have been available without unification.

2. As of May 1990, the volume of life insurance contracts amounted to 7 percent of the financial assets of private nonbusiness residents.

3. The West German ratio of cash holdings to demand deposits plus savings deposits, which may be more comparable with the East German figure than the ratio of currency to demand deposits, was 0.20 in May 1990—it still exceeded the East German figure substantially.

4. Initially, the Bundesbank published balance sheet data for East German banks separately (see von Hagen, 1993, for an analysis).

5. Federal and state governments share VAT and income tax revenues. In 1995, the new *Länder* obtained an extra DM 35 billion through reduction of the federal government's share in these taxes.

6. Similar data were not collected after June 1993.

7. The Treuhand Act of 17 June 1990 remained valid after unification.

8. By mid-1993, Treuhand had spent DM 55 billion in investment subsidies, other subsidies, and payment of losses; DM 56 billion for old loans and their service; DM 15 billion on payments of equalization claims; and DM 19 billion on guarantees (see Ditges, 1994, p. 50).

9. Because many East German enterprises are owned by West German companies that do not report shipments from their East German subsidiaries, intra-German trade is difficult to measure statistically.

10. Unit wage cost is measured as 100 times gross income from employed work divided by GDP.

11. We regress the change in output on the change in productivity in the first step to account for the correlation between the two. This regression is

$$Y_i = -61.3 \ (98.3) + .508 \ (.11) \ Pr_i; \ R^2 = 0.44.$$

Since functional misspecification and simultaneity bias are matters of concern here, the regression reported in the text was repeated, replacing the index variables by their respective rank scores. Here, a high rank means a relatively large increase in productivity, output, and employment. The resulting regression is

$$L_i = -5.2 \ (3.2) + 0.8 \ (0.07) \ YR_i + 0.54 \ (0.07) \ PR_i; \ R^2 = 0.87.$$

12. Naive partisans of union policies in Germany argue that the wage excesses were initiated by West German employers who feared the competition of low-wage East German industries. This argument makes no sense for several reasons. First, because privatization implied that a large part of East Germany's industry would be owned by West German companies; thus, West German employers had every reason to advocate wage restraint. Second, it was clear from the beginning that, due to their outdated technologies and low-quality products, East German industries would not pose a serious competitive threat to West German

manufacturers. Third, the resulting increases in Social Security constributions have deteriorated the international competitiveness of West German manufacturers. All this is not to deny the obvious: Ultimately, the excessive wage increases constitute an equilibrium that was possible because employers chose not to oppose the unions' strategy more vehemently.

# References

Akerlof, G., Andrew K. Rose, Janet L. Yellen, and H. Hessenius. 1991. "East Germany in from the Cold. The Economic Aftermath of Currency Union." *Brookings Papers for Economic Activity*, pp. 1–101.

Alesina, Alberto, and Alan Drazen. 1991. "Why Stabilizations Are Delayed." *American Economic Review* 81, pp. 1170–88.

Bernet, Wolfgang. 1993. "Gemeinden und Gemeinderecht im Regimewandel." *Aus Politik und Zeitgeschichte* B36:93, pp. 27–38.

Bundesministerium der Finanzen. 1995a. "Datensatz Ausgewählte Wirtschaftsdaten zur Lage in den neuen Ländern' Februar 1995." Bonn: Bundesministerium der Finanzen. (Mimeo).

Bundesministerium der Finanzen. 1995b. "Beitrag zur Fortschreibung der Materialien zur deutschen Einheit und zum Aufbau in den neuen Bundesländern." Bonn: Bundesministerium der Finanzen. (Mimeo).

Deutsche Bundesbank. 1990a. "Die Währungsunion mit der Deutschen Demokratischen Republik." *Monatsbericht* 42:7, pp. 14–29.

Deutsche Bundesbank. 1990b. "Technische und organisatorische Aspekte der Währungsunion mit der Deutschen Demokratischen Republik." *Monatsbericht* 42:10, pp. 25–32.

Deutsche Bundesbank. 1995. "Die Finanzentwicklung der Länder seit der Vereinigung." *Monatsbericht* 47:4, pp. 35–49.

Dewatripont, Mathias, and Gérard Roland. 1993. *The Design of Reform Packages Under Uncertainty*. Working Paper 860. London: CEPR

Ditges, Johannes. 1994. "Privatisierungsstrategien in den neuen Bundesländern." In Gernot Gutmann and Ulrich Wagner, eds., *Ökonomische Erfolge und Mißerfolge der Deutschen Vereinigung—Eine Zwischenbilanz*. Stuttgart: Fischer.

Deutsches Institut für Wirtschafts forschung (DIW). 1989. "Die Lage der DDR—Wirtschaft zur Jahreswende 1988/89." *Wochenbericht* 5:89, pp. 53–61.

DIW. 1990a. "Handelsbeziehungen der DDR zum Gemeinsamen Markt." *Wochenbericht* 9:90, pp. 103–13.

DIW. 1990b. "Außenwirtschaftliche Verflechtung zwischen DDR und UdSSR." *Wochenbericht* 21:90, pp. 285–93.

DIW. 1990c. "Innerdeutscher Handel im Übergang." *Wochenbericht* 25:90, pp. 327–39 .

DIW. 1995. "Gesamtwirtschaftliche und unternehmerische Anpassungsfortschritte in Ostdeutschland." *Wochenbericht* 27–28:95, pp. 461–95.

Fernandez, Raquel, and Dani Rodrick. 1991. "Resistance to Reform: Status Quo Bias in the Presence of Individual-Specific Uncertainty." *American Economic Review* 81, pp. 1146–55.

Fischer, Wolfram, and Harm Schröter. 1993. "Die Entstehung der Treuhandanstalt." In Wolfram Fischer, Herbert Hax, and Hans Karl Schneider, eds., *Treuhandanstalt—Das Unmögliche wagen*. Berlin: Akademie Verlag.

Kole, Linda. 1994. "Inside the Holy Grail." Washington, D.C.: Board of Governors, Federal Reserve System. (Mimeo).

Neumann, F. 1995. "Investitionen in den neuen Bundesländern: Dienstleistungsbereiche weiter expansiv Industrieinvestitionen erhalten konjunkturelle Impulse," *IFO Schnelldienst* 5, pp. 3–10.

Neumann, Manfred J. M., and Jürgen von Hagen. 1993. "Germany." In Michele Fratianni and Dominik Salvatore, eds., *Handbook of Monetary Policies in Developed Economies*. Westport, Conn.: Greenwood.

Pilz, Frank, and Heike Ortwein. 1992. *Das vereinte Deutschland*. Stuttgart: Gustav Fischer.

Sachverständigenrat zur Begutachtung der gesamtwirtschaftlichen Lage. 1994. "Zur Lage in den neuen Bundesländern." *Gutachten*.

Schmid, Josef, Frank Löbler, and Heinrich Tiemann, eds. 1994. *Organisationsstrukturen und Probleme von Parteien und Verbänden*. Probleme der Einheit 14. Marburg: Metropolis.

Schmidt-Eichstädt, Gerd. 1993. "Kommunale Gebietsreform in den neuen Bundesländern." *Aus Politik und Zeitgeschichte* B36:93, pp. 3–17.

Schneider, Herbert. 1993. "Der Aufbau der Kommunalverwaltung und der kommunalen Selbstverwaltung in den neuen Bundesländern." *Aus Politik und Zeitgeschichte* B36:93, pp. 18–28.

Schürer, Gerhard, Gerhard Beil, Alexander Schalck, et al. 1989. "Geheime Verschlußsache b5 1158/89." *Vorlage für das Politbüro des ZK der SED*. 30 October. Reprinted in *Deutschland Archiv* 10 (1992), pp. 1112–20.

Sinn, Hans-Werner. 1995. *Factor Price Distortions and Public Subsidies in East Germany*. CEPR Discussion Paper 1155. London: CEPR.

Stamm, Eugen. 1990. "Die Länder der DDR." In Günter Fischbach, ed., *DDR Almanach 90*. Bonn: Bonn Aktuell.

Statistisches Bundesamt. (1994). *Statistisches Jahrbuch für die Bundesrepublik Deutschland*. Wiesbaden: Statistisches Bundesamt.

Statistisches Bundesamt. 1995a. Fachserie 4, *Produzierendes Gewerbe*, Reihe 4.1.1., Reihe 2.1., Wiesbaden Statistisches Bundesamt.

Statistisches Bundesamt. (1995b). Fachserie 1, Beschäftigte Reihe 4.3, Wiesbaden.

Statistisches Bundesamt. (1995c). Fachserie 1, Beschäftigte Reihe 4.2.1, Wiesbaden.

Statistisches Bundesamt. (1995d). Fachserie 17, Preise und Preisindizes für gewerbliche Produkte, Wiesbaden.

Treuhandanstalt. (1990). "Tätigkeitsbericht vom 2. Juli." Berlin: Treuhandanstalt. (Mimeo).

von Hagen, Jürgen. 1992. "German Unification: Economic Problems and Consequences. A Comment." *Carnegie Rochester Conference Ton Public Policy* 36, pp. 211–22.

von Hagen, Jürgen. 1993. "Monetary Union, Money Demand, and Money Supply: A Review of the German Monetary Union." *European Economic Review* 37, pp. 803–27.

von Hagen, Jürgen. 1995a. "Inflation and Monetary Targets in Germany." In Lars Svensson and Guido Tabellini, eds., Inflation Targeting. London: CEPR.

von Hagen, Jürgen. 1995b. "Credible Ways to EMU." In Marc Uzan, ed., *Reinventing Bretton Woods*. London: Routledge.

von Hagen, Jürgen, and Uwe Walz. 1995. "Social Security and Migration in an Ageing Europe." In Jeffrey Frieden, Barry Eichengreen, and Jürgen von Hagen, eds., *Politics and Institutions in an Integrated Europe*. Heidelberg: Springer-Verlag.

# 4  Poland

Stanislaw Wellisz

The East-Central European Communist regimes that came into power at the close of World War II sought to eradicate the market mechanism and to insulate their countries from the capitalist West. Poland was no exception: most of its exports were directed to, and most of its imports were obtained from, other COMECON members, in particular from the Soviet Union. Gradually, however, the leadership of PZPR, the Polish United Workers (Communist) Party, realized that the command system and isolation from the world spelled stagnation. Sporadic attempts at reform were made as early as 1956, but the system remained virtually unchanged for the next twenty-four years.

In the 1970s, growth slowed down while social opposition to the regime gained in strength. The Communist Party made an abortive effort to improve economic performance by importing foreign technology. This strategy having failed, the July 1981 Communist Party Congress adopted a reform program calling for increasing reliance on the market mechanism and for the opening of the economy (see World Bank, 1987). But the November 13, 1981, declaration of the "state of war" by Wojciech Jaruzelski, who combined the offices of prime minister, defense minister, and first secretary of PZPR, delayed implementation. After the return to "normalcy," various measures were taken to decentralize economic decision-making. The scope of central allocation of raw materials was reduced. Enterprises were granted more freedom of decisions concerning production, marketing (including foreign sales), and investment. The market was allowed a greater role in price determination. Yet progress was slow: the ruling party was clearly aware of the risk that economic reform would lead to the loss of power (see Fallenbuchl, 1988; Poznański, 1988).

The Solidarity-led regime that was formed in the autumn of 1989 inherited a partially liberalized and half-dismantled command system, and an economy hovering on the verge of a hyperinflation.[1] It also inherited a staggering foreign debt, the result of the ill-conceived modernization policy, financed by foreign loans, of the 1970s.

The new regime faced two immediate tasks: to bring down the rate of inflation, and to restore internal and external market equilibrium. January 1, 1990, heralded the implementation of a bold, comprehensive stabilization-cum-liberalization program, known as the "Balcerowicz Plan."[2] The budget was balanced by making drastic cuts in subsidies. Virtually all direct controls limiting internal and international commercial transactions were swept away. The currency was made "internally convertible" (see Section 4.1). The door was open wide to foreign investment. Though a number of key issues, among them the problem of foreign debt, remained to be settled, Poland seemed to be well on the way to full integration into the world system.

The reforms ran into social and political obstacles. Interest groups, among whom the farmers were the most important, pressured the government to retreat from extreme liberalism. The centrist governments, formed after the first completely free parliamentary elections (October 1991), were weak and lacked clear economic vision; hence, they were fearful of further change and ready to compromise.[3] Victory in the next parliamentary election (September 1993) went to a Social Democratic (neo-Communist)–Peasant Party alliance. The neo-Communist–Peasant government asserted its commitment to the continuation of reform, the tempo of change slowed even more, and, in some important respects, there was retrogression.

Poland's current position vis-à-vis the world economy was thus largely determined by the Balcerowicz reforms. The changes that occurred toward the end of the Communist regime constitute, as it were, a prelude. What has happened since is a postlude. A discussion of Poland's international position must, therefore, pay special attention to the 1990–91 period.

The balance of this chapter is organized as follows. Section 4.1 is devoted to a discussion of the evolution of the foreign exchange regime. Section 4.2 discusses foreign trade; Section 4.3, the debt problem; and Section 4.4, the treatment of foreign investment. Section 4.5 appraises of the degree of integration that has been achieved and looks into the future.

## 4.1   The Foreign Exchange Regime[4]

During the 1980s the "classical" Communist system of direct allocation of foreign currency was replaced by a multiple exchange system. Less than a third of the available foreign currency continued to be allocated directly to high-priority imports at the official rate. Enterprises were permitted to retain a portion of their foreign exchange earnings that could be deposited in foreign-exchange-denominated accounts at Polish banks or utilized for the purchase of approved imports. Starting in May 1987, enterprises were also permitted to sell and purchase foreign exchange at currency auctions held by the Export Development Bank. The proportion of earnings that could be retained was specified by industry, and the auction mechanism was controlled by the government; hence the exchange rate varied from product to product. There was also a free rate: individuals were permitted to buy and sell foreign currency on a semilegal free market.

### 4.1.1  The Foreign Exchange "Anchor": January 1, 1990–September 30, 1991

The Solidarity-led government took immediate steps to simplify the system and narrow the gap among the three rates. During the autumn of 1989, the official price of the dollar was raised, in steps, by 390 percent; the zloty was devalued in real terms by 75 percent. In September 1989, the free market price of the dollar was six times higher than the official rate. By the last week of December 1989, the official rate stood at 5,600 zl/$, the average auction rate at 6,000 zl/$, and the free rate at 8,000 to 9,000 zl/$.

The exchange rate regime appropriate for the transition period was the subject of an exhaustive discussion. The need to restore confidence dictated the establishment of a realistic, sustainable parity. On the other hand, it was argued that, given the difficulty of determining the appropriate parity level, it would be preferable to adopt a flexible system. The government opted for a compromise course. Within the framework of the reforms instituted on January 1, 1990, foreign currency was made freely available at the official rate for all current account payments. The retention accounts and the auction system were abolished. The conversion of export proceeds into zlotys at the official rate was made obligatory. Enterprises were permitted to retain, but not to replenish, their foreign-denominated accounts, and they were not allowed to establish accounts abroad. Consumers remained free to buy and sell foreign exchange on the free market.[5] They were permitted to hold foreign-exchange-denominated accounts, in Polish banks and, up to a limit, they could take the foreign exchange out of the country for personal use. The government pledged to maintain a fixed exchange rate of 9,500 zl/U.S.$ for three months, after which the rate could be adjusted, if necessary.

The announcement that the initial exchange rate was to hold for a specific period opened the door to potentially destabilizing speculation. In its fight against inflation, the National Bank of Poland (NBP) set its discount rate (which constitutes a floor of the interest rate structure) slightly above the anticipated rate of inflation. The monthly rates for January, February, and March were set respectively at 36 percent, 20 percent, and 10 percent. Since the rate paid on zloty deposits closely tracked the discount rate, depositors who switched from dollars to zlotys at the beginning of January and back to dollars at the end of March could have earned a 70 percent return on their dollar savings. Large-scale speculation could have precipitated a collapse of the exchange rate.[6] However, the government's declaration that the rate would remain fixed for three months seemingly lacked credibility: very little switching and reswitching took place, and the initial undervaluation of the zloty permitted the government to adhere to its pledge despite the liberalization-induced price rise.

Within a few months inflation appeared to be well under control.[7] If anything, the restrictive monetary and fiscal policies seemed to be working too well. There was excessively rapid accumulation of foreign reserves. The fiscal budget was in surplus.[8] There were signals that the stringent policy measures were about to precipitate a serious recession: the volume of credit (in real terms) declined; output fell; and unemployment began to rise.

To stimulate the economy, the government relaxed its monetary policies and raised the fiscal expenditures.[9] The immediate results were positive. The economy picked up temporarily and inflation continued to abate.

By September 1990, however, the rate of inflation accelerated and the general economic situation continued to worsen. In 1991 there was a sharp decline in the profits of state-owned enterprises (SOEs), depriving the government of a major source of revenue.[10] The budget was again in deficit, thus feeding inflation (see Gomułka, 1994). The zloty appreciated in real terms until May 17, 1991, when its rate was lowered to 11,000 zl/$. Indices of the quarterly inflation rates (in terms of the consumer price index) and of the real exchange rate are presented in Table 4.1 and in figure 4.1. At the same time the zloty was delinked from the dollar, and linked to a foreign exchange basket in which the dollar was assigned a weight of 45 percent, the DM 35 percent, the pound sterling 10 percent, and the French and Swiss francs 5 percent each.

The shift to a currency basket was not unjustified. As long as the dollar linkage was maintained, the fluctuations in the dollar-ECU exchange rate introduced an extraneous disturbing factor in the trade between Poland

**Table 4.1**
Indices of consumer prices and to the real effective exchange rate, 1991–94 (1900 = 100)

| Year | Quarter | C.P.I. | Real effective exchange rate* |
|------|---------|--------|-------------------------------|
| 1991 | I | 153.6 | 145.5 |
|      | II | 171.5 | 160.6 |
|      | III | 181.9 | 154.9 |
|      | IV | 199.7 | 154.7 |
| 1992 | I | 225.6 | 154.6 |
|      | II | 246.1 | 147.9 |
|      | III | 264.6 | 148.8 |
|      | IV | 290.0 | 158.0 |
| 1993 | I | 319.0 | 165.7 |
|      | II | 339.8 | 165.8 |
|      | III | 357.2 | 160.6 |
|      | IV | 390.0 | 159.4 |
| 1994 | I | 419.3 | 164.3 |
|      | II | 447.3 | 165.2 |
|      | III | 475.9 | 164.1 |
|      | IV | 516.4 | 168.3 |

*Source:* IMF.
*Note:* * In U.S.$/zloty, adjusted for changes in relative price levels.

and Western Europe, Poland's main trading partner. The relative weights in the basket seemed well chosen. Though trade with the United States is of little significance, dollar-priced imports, such as oil, amount to a substantial proportion of Poland's imports; hence the assignment of the major weight to the dollar. The second highest weight attached to the DM reflects the fact that Germany is Poland's single largest trading partner. The weights attached to the other currencies also are defensible. But the linkage to a basket does not have the transparency, and it does not carry the credibility, of linkage to a single, strong currency. The abandonment of the dollar standard looked like a signal of retreat from the fixed exchange rate policy.

### 4.1.2 The "Crawling Peg" Regime: October 1, 1991–May 15, 1995

In the face of a continuing price rise,[11] the government announced, on October 1, 1991, the replacement of the fixed parity with a "crawling peg." Henceforth the nominal exchange rate of the zloty was to decline at a preannounced rate. Under such a policy, called by Dornbusch "the PPP-oriented exchange rule," the nominal exchange rate is adjusted to take

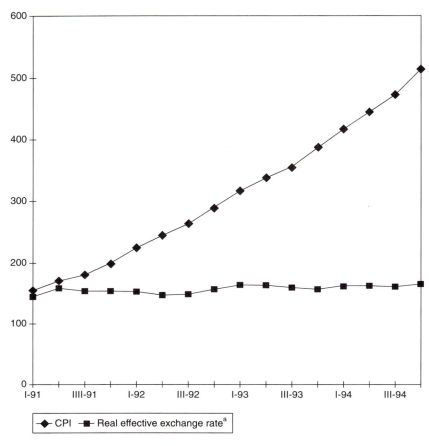

**Figure 4.1**
Indexes of consumer prices and of the real effective exchange rate, 1991–94 (1900 = 100)
*Source:* International Monetary Fund.
*Note:*
a. In U.S.$/zloty, adjusted for changes in relative price levels.

**Table 4.2**
Fiscal deficits and domestic reserves of the National Bank of Poland, 1991–94

| Year | (A) Fiscal budget surplus or deficit (percent of GDP) | (B) NBP claims on general government (trillion 1990 zlotys) |
|------|-------------------------------------------------------|-------------------------------------------------------------|
| 1990 | +0.4 | 0.60 |
| 1991 | −7.0 | 2.47 |
| 1992 | −6.0 | 4.74 |
| 1993 | −2.7 | 4.47 |
| 1994 | −3.2 | 4.17 |

*Sources:* (A) Ministry of Finance and World Bank estimates. The fiscal deficit estimate for 1994 was reported in *Rzeczpospolita* no. 259 (3908) (Sept. 7, 1994); (B) IMF.
*Note:* The constant 1990 zloty values were calculated by deflating the current zloty values by the consumer price index (1990 = 100).

into account the differential between the rate of inflation in the home country and the rate of inflation of the major trading partners. The initial rate of "crawl" was set at 1.8 percent per month (about 24 percent per year). The rate of inflation outstripped the rate of "crawl," however, and the zloty was devalued by an additional 12 percent on February 26, 1992. Another devaluation (this time by 8 percent) came on August 27, 1993, but since the rate of inflation appeared to be slowing down, the rate of the "crawl" was cut to 1.6 percent per month.

In 1993–94 the inflationary pressure exerted by budgetary deficits subsided. The fiscal deficit declined, and the shortfall in government revenue was covered to an increasing extent through sale of government obligations on the financial market. As a consequence, the NBP claims on the general government, expressed in constant 1990 zlotys, began to decline (see Table 4.2).

Starting in mid-1993, however, the NBP had to cope with the inflationary effects of a rapid accumulation of foreign reserves. These rose from $3.3 billion at the end of the second quarter of 1993 to $5.7 billion at the end of the fourth quarter of 1994. The sources of this growth are yet to be determined;[12] it is clear, however, that the accumulation is related to the undervaluation of the zloty. To remedy the situation, the NBP reduced the rate of crawl to 1.4 percent per month in mid-1994, and to 1.2 percent per month in January 1995. At the same time, seeking to contain credit expansion, the NAP set the 1993 discount rate at 35 percent per year. Inflation subsided in 1994, and the discount rate was lowered to

33 percent, but a year-end resurgence of inflation induced the NAP to rescind the reduction in February 1995. (Because inflation seemed to be calming down, the cut was reinstated two months later.)

The simultaneous enforcement of a slow crawl and a high nominal interest policy created the danger of destabilizing speculation. Once again it became attractive to switch from dollars to zloty accounts and back to dollars. Aware of this danger, the NBP announced a major policy shift on May 15, 1995. Henceforth the zloty would be permitted to fluctuate within the upper and lower crawling limits set by the NBP. The system is a variant of the familiar "snake in the tunnel." The floor and ceiling values provide an indication of the points at which the central banking authorities are ready to intervene. The behavior of the zloty would in turn, provide a signal for the setting of the rate of crawl. The new system has yet to pass the test of time, but the first indications are that the rate of foreign exchange inflow has diminished, and the inflation is subsiding. Thus, after a "crawling peg" detour, Poland may be moving toward the monetary stability that was sought by the 1990 reformers.

## 4.2   Foreign Trade

### 4.2.1   Trade under the Communist Regime

As in all the Soviet bloc countries, Poland's trade under the Communist regime was a state monopoly. Exports and imports were strictly subordinated to the plan, and the direction and composition of trade were determined as much by political as by economic considerations. The trade was carried out under three different regimes. The highest priority was given to trade with the Council for Mutual Economic Assistance (CMEA) partners, conducted in "transferable rubles." Most of the trade with the West was conducted in terms of convertible currencies. There were special barter agreements, mainly with developing countries.

Stalinism was a period of virtual economic isolation in Poland. In the 1960s, however, imports expanded faster than "national income produced"; exports grew, too, albeit at a slower rate.[13] Between 1970 and 1978, imports were further boosted by a modernization drive that called for the acquisition of Western technology and Western capital goods,[14] undertaken under the leadership of Edward Gierek, then first secretary of the PZPR. In 1978, burdened with foreign debt and unable to obtain further loans, the government was forced to reduce imports and expand exports (see Table 4.3).

**Table 4.3**
Indices of national income produced, imports, and exports in constant 1970 prices (1970 = 100)

| Year | National income produced | Imports | Exports |
|------|--------------------------|---------|---------|
| 1960 | 56  | 41  | 64  |
| 1970 | 100 | 100 | 100 |
| 1978 | 184 | 229 | 198 |
| 1980 | 169 | 222 | 203 |
| 1981 | 149 | 185 | 164 |
| 1982 | 141 | 159 | 179 |
| 1988 | 182 | 239 | 262 |

Source: GUS (1990).

The attempt at austerity added fuel to political discontent, leading to the rise of Solidarity (1980–81). The imposition of martial law on November 12/13, 1981, permitted the government to renew its retrenchment efforts, resulting in a sharp fall in income and an even sharper fall in imports.

After reaching a nadir in 1982, the Polish economy recovered, although the "national income produced" in 1988, the penultimate year of Communist rule, was still slightly below the 1978 peak. In 1988 imports were, however, 4 percent higher, and exports 32 percent higher, than ten years earlier.

The modernization drive of the 1970s marked the beginning of reorientation of trade away from CMEA. Western machinery purchased with Western credits required Western inputs, which had to be paid for with hard currency earned by exporting. When the regime attempted to inject market elements into the decision-making process in the 1980s, Western orientation became even more apparent. In 1981–82 the state-owned enterprises (SOEs) were granted a degree of marketing autonomy. On October 30, 1988, the Council of Ministers approved the introduction of a nondiscriminatory structure of customs duties patterned, broadly speaking, after the tariff schedules of semi-industrialized countries.[15] Trade monopolies were abolished by an ordinance of December 23, 1988, that became law in January 1989. Though political considerations continued to play a key role, the proportion of Polish exports to the CMEA countries declined from 64 percent in 1970 to 54 percent in 1982 and to 41 percent in 1988, the last full year of Communist rule (GUS, 1990).

### 4.2.2 The 1990 Trade Liberalization

January 1, 1990, saw the elimination of virtually all quantitative trade barriers. Polish enterprises were free to import and to export on their own account without obtaining permits. There were only three exceptions to this rule: (1) the reexport of raw materials imported from other CMEA countries (mainly from Russia) at lower than world prices was prohibited;[16] (2) coal exports were subject to quota restrictions (the domestic price of certain grades of coal continued to be maintained below the world price levels); (3) Poland had to abide by import quotas set by Western Europe and by the United States on Polish textiles, steel, and several other products.

The goal was to achieve a trade balance for the year 1990 as a whole. Liberalization was expected to result in a rapid rise in imports and a more gradual expansion of exports. The current account would be in deficit during the first half of the year, but this deficit would be compensated by a surplus accumulated in the course of the next six months.

As expected, consumers took advantage of liberalization to build up a stock of hitherto unavailable durables. But as the household stocks of durables rose, purchases declined. The undervaluation of the zloty kept purchases of imported consumer durables in check. With the passing of socialism, there was increasing anxiety about job security, which also reduced demand for imported consumer durables. As the economy went into recession, imports of producer goods declined. The domestic slump and the undervaluation of the zloty spurred exports. The trade balance turned positive as early as February 1990, leading, as mentioned earlier, to an undesired rise in foreign exchange reserves.[17]

To slow the accumulation of reserves, about two-third of all customs duties were reduced or suspended. The unweighted average tariff declined from 11.7 percent to 5.8 percent, and the average trade-weighted tariff dropped from 11.4 percent to 5.8 percent. In mid-1990 Poland came to enjoy a remarkable degree of free trade (see Nogaj, 1992).

### 4.2.3 The Return to Protectionism

The mid-1991 to mid-1993 period was marked by relative trade stagnation and by a return to protectionism. The two phenomena were doubtless connected, but exogenous factors played a key role in each case. The stagnation of trade reflected, to a large extent, the West European economic slump. The return to protectionism marked the victory of dirigiste political elements.[18]

Though trade liberalization was at the heart of the 1990 reforms, the customs duty reductions and suspensions were looked upon as interim measures. It was necessary to completely rewrite the tariff system inherited from the Communist regime. The number of tariff brackets was confusingly large. Similar products often fell into different tariff categories, complicating clearance procedures and encouraging customs fraud and bribery. The duty on some intermediates was higher than that on the final products. The nomenclature was idiosyncratic and not readily translatable into the standard international system.

The revision process, which began in 1991, soon revealed a clash of conceptions and of interests. Technical advisers to the government favored sweeping away all protective measures except for a revenue tariff. To minimize tariff-induced distortions, they proposed a broad-based, flat 10 percent duty to which there would be few or no exceptions.

The free traders found themselves in opposition to a broad array of specific interests, of whom the farmers were the most powerful. Paradoxical as it may seem, Poland's small private farmers had fared well under communism. Under a policy instituted in the 1970s and 1980s, agricultural inputs were available at stable, subsidized prices, and the home market was tightly protected. The last years of Communist rule brought exceptional prosperity to the peasants. The average income of members of peasant households surpassed that of workers' households by 16 percent in 1987, by 23 percent in 1988, and by 16 percent in 1989 (Dąbrowski and Kwieciński, 1994).

The 1990 reforms brought hardship to the farmers. Agricultural subsidies declined from 5.6 percent of GDP in 1989 to 1 percent in 1990. The freeing of all consumer goods prices, and the opening of the home market to competition from better-quality foreign dairy products, fruits, and meats, led to a precipitous decline in the farmers' terms of trade. Although the first years of transformation affected virtually all strata of society, farmers fared especially badly. The average farm income fell by 1991 to 84 percent of the average income of the nonagricultural workers' households. The decline in their fortunes led the farmers to organize a vigorous campaign for the restoration of their lost privileges, including demands for protection and for duty-free importation of agricultural inputs such as protein-rich fodder and machines that were not produced in Poland.

Powerful manufacturing interests also sought special favors. Poland has a comparative advantage in basic products; on the other hand, highly fabricated, technology-intensive products compete with foreign products with difficulty. The manufacturing sector favored a tariff structure in which the rates increase steeply with the degree of fabrication. Such a structure also found favor among government policy makers interested in fostering high-tech industries. Paradoxically, even the Ministry of Co-operation with Foreign Countries pressed for higher tariffs. Poland had just entered into talks with the European Economic Community (EEC) and with the European Free Trade Area (EFTA) countries, and it wanted to participate in the General Agreement on Tariffs and Trade (GATT) Uruguay Round. What could it give away in exchange for foreign concessions if its tariffs were already low?

Fiscal stringency was yet another factor that tilted the scales in favor of protectionism. It became evident in 1991 that all possible sources of revenue had to be tapped to keep the fiscal deficit at an acceptable level— an argument used by advocates of high duty rates on "luxury" goods that are presumed to have highly inelastic demand.

The protectionists won a clear victory. With the August 1, 1991, introduction of the new tariff schedule, the unweighted average tariffs rose from 5.82 percent to 16.83 percent, and the weighted average from 5.49 percent to 14.27 percent[19] (see Table 4.4). The new schedule comprised nine customs duty brackets; the lowest two (0 percent and 5 percent) applied to raw materials, and the highest (ranging from 35 percent to 45 percent and over) to highly sophisticated and "luxury" products. Most of the semifabricates were subject to a 15 percent, and most of the finished industrial products to a 30 percent, duty. A separate schedule applied to automobiles. Polish cars, inexpensive but inefficient, competed with used, foreign-made cars rather than with the (much more expensive) new foreign cars. To protect the Polish car industry, the tariff on used car imports was

**Table 4.4**
Import tariff rates prior to and after the August 1, 1991, tariff reform (percent)

|                      | Before Aug. 1, 1991 | Since Aug. 1, 1991 |
| -------------------- | ------------------- | ------------------ |
| Unweighted averages  |                     |                    |
| Nominal rates        | 11.7                | 17.0               |
| Actual rates*        | 5.8                 | 16.8               |
| Weighted average     |                     |                    |
| Nominal rates        | 3.4                 | 16.2               |
| Actual rates*        | 5.5                 | 14.3               |

Source: Nogaj (1992), p. 65.
Note: * Taking into account temporary tariff reductions and suspensions.

set at a higher level than on new cars, the rate rising with the age of the car. Importation of cars more than ten years old was prohibited.

Farmers scored the greatest victory. Even before the general tariff revision they were granted special favors. Now they obtained higher protection than industry (see Table 4.5). The next four years saw the banning of some food imports (e.g., of chicken thighs and legs), the introduction of seasonally varying tariffs, and the appearance of "compensatory" tariffs equalizing the cost of selected agricultural imports with domestic reference prices.

The new tariff schedule represented a compromise between the protection-seeking domestic producers and the purchasers of their products. Not surprisingly, a differentiated tariff could not satisfy everybody. A commission for tariff revision, formed in September 1992, considered thirteen hundred petitions for change, of which it accepted three hundred (Nogaj, 1994). Most of the changes involved greater tariff rate differentiation, but they had no significant effect on the average rate of protection (see Table 4.5).

Imports at the new, higher tariff rates generated more government revenue, but in view of the persistent deficit, the government imposed an additional 6 percent tax on the value of all imports, inclusive of customs duties. This tax was converted on July 5, 1993, into a 6 percent customs duty. The duty was calculated on the value of imports, inclusive of all other duties and taxes, such as the newly introduced value-added tax and the excise taxes applicable to certain commodities (e.g., alcohol and tobacco). The duty remained in force in 1994; it was lowered to 5 percent in 1955 and, fiscal conditions permitting, is to be phased out gradually. The problem was that under very optimistic assumptions, the 1995 fiscal deficit would amount to 10.7 percent of the fiscal revenues and to 3.3 percent of the GNP. The budget projections assumed that the 5 percent, tax would contribute 3 percent, and all customs duties and taxes 9.7

Table 4.5
Actual industrial and agricultural average weighted tariff rates (percent)

|  | Before Dec. 12, 1993 | Since Jan. 1, 1994 |
| --- | --- | --- |
| Agricultural products | 18.5 | 18.3 |
| Industrial products | 10.7 | 10.7 |
| All products | 11.7 | 11.6 |

Source: Press release of the Ministry for Foreign Cooperation, reported by Nogaj (1994).
Note: Exclusive of the 6% percent "border tax" levied on all imports.

percent, of all fiscal revenues. Weaning the government from dependence on import tax revenue would be a problem.

With the retreat from liberalism, trade policy came to be seen more and more as a tool of industrial policy (Nogaj, 1994, pp. 73–86). The first measures were modest in scope. In order to help the leather industry, which was hurt by a rise in rawhide prices, the government raised the turnover tax levied on rawhide exports from 20 percent to 50 percent in 1992, and a year later, it suspended import duties on rawhides. In mid-1993, the scope of ad hoc measures was greatly expanded. Customs duties that were levied on a long list of products "needed for the reconstruction of the national economy" were reduced or suspended (*Dziennik Ustaw*, 1993, no. 53, item 245). The list included raw materials such as nonferrous ores and concentrates, and machinery (large tractors, which were not produced in Poland, gas turbines, and textile machinery). The new auto assembly industry obtained a duty-free component import quota; the electronics industry obtained a similar privilege, as did a number of other industries, including some, such as the silk industry, most unlikely to survive foreign competition. A duty-free quota was set for products needed by the military and the police. A quota was also set for duty-free importation of equipment and vehicles needed for oil and gas prospecting. A somewhat longer list of temporary reductions and suspensions applied in 1994 (*Dziennik Ustaw*, 1993, no. 128, item 592). In the same year the government created a sugar producers' cartel. A tax was imposed on domestic sugar sales; its proceeds were to be used to subsidize exports needed to dispose of the sugar surplus created by the artificially high domestic sugar prices.

Quantitative export restrictions also reappeared. Poland exports steel; it also exports scrap iron and steel used in steelmaking. Exports of scrap in 1991 amounted to sixteen hundred tons, and in 1992 to thirteen hundred tons. A six hundred-ton limit was placed on scrap exports in 1993, under pressure from the Polish steel industry. The exporters were granted additional quotas in the course of the year, and total exports reached 1,011.7 tons. Despite the quota expansion, the price of scrap in Germany was twice as high as in Poland toward the end of 1993. Not content with this result, the steel interests pressured the government to reduce the 1994 scrap export quota to four hundred tons (Woklodkiewicz-Donimirski, 1994).

The trend toward quantitative trade restrictions is spreading: such restrictions are built with increasing frequency into joint venture agreements, and many new contracts with foreign firms (e.g., in telecommunications) contain a domestic content provision.

### 4.2.4    Change in the Direction of Trade

The transition years (1990–93) witnessed a striking reorientation of the direction of trade. As noted earlier, CMEA accounted for over 40 percent of Poland's trade (exports plus imports) in 1988; in 1990, for only 25 percent. The CMEA was dissolved in 1991. The dissolution was followed by transition difficulties in the former USSR, CMEA's dominant partner. By 1993, Eastern Europe accounted for less than 14 percent of Poland's trade, whereas 71 percent was with the EEC and with EFTA. Gradually, however, normal links with Russia and the Ukraine are being reestablished: preliminary figures for 1994 show that Poland's trade with its Eastern partners is gaining in importance.

### 4.2.5    Trade Agreements

The 1990 Balcerowicz reforms had one overriding goal: integration of Poland into the world economy. Poland opened up its markets and sought access to markets for Polish goods. To this end it undertook negotiations with GATT, with the European Economic Community, and with EFTA. It formed a Central European Free Trade Area (CEFTA or the Visegrad Group) with Hungary and Czechoslovakia.

Despite Poland's retreat from free trade, these efforts did not slacken in subsequent years. The goals changed, however. The negotiations took on a strategic character. Poland sought to obtain better access to foreign markets. It was willing, albeit reluctantly, to reduce its trade barriers in exchange for concessions.

#### General Agreement on Tariffs and Trade

Poland joined the General Agreement on Tariffs and Trade in 1967 and obtained the status of a most favored nation. In exchange for admission to the GATT, the member countries are usually asked to lower their tariffs. But tariff concessions are meaningless in centrally planned economies. In lieu of such concessions, Poland agreed in the Act of Accession to increase its imports from GATT member countries at a 7 percent annual rate. This pledge was not honored after the mid-1970s.

The implementation of the Balcerowicz reforms called for a redefinition of conditions of GATT membership. Poland joined the Uruguay Round of talks in November 1993. Along with other countries, it submitted a schedule of base duty rates that were to serve as a starting point for negotiations on multilateral reductions.

In the course of the negotiations, Poland agreed to reduce the average level of tariffs on industrial goods by 40 percent, and on agricultural goods by 35 percent, relative to a base level by the year 2000. It also pledged to "bind" 96 percent of the eight-digit industrial import categories[20] and all the agricultural import categories on the new, lower level.[21] Poland also agreed to reduce the average mean support (AMS) to domestic agriculture by 20 percent,[22] to cut export subsidies by 36 percent, and to refrain from imposing new quantitative import restraints. The concessions are of the same order of magnitude as those made by highly industrialized countries, but in the case of Poland they overstate the degree of promised liberalization, especially with regard to agriculture. Thus, in 1990–93, the AMS of Polish agriculture was approximately 40 percent lower than in 1986–88, the period used as a basis for the Uruguay Round reduction. As a consequence Poland may raise the degree of support and yet adhere to its Uruguay Round schedule of "cuts." The same holds for the export subsidies, most of which (sugar and powdered milk being the major exceptions) were swept away in 1990. However, the Uruguay commitments of most of the developing and some of the highly developed countries were similar.[23]

### Treaty of Association with the European Economic Community

Poland, Czechoslovakia, and Hungary signed a Treaty of Association with the European Economic Community on October 16, 1991.[24] The treaty calls for the harmonization of trade practices and the establishment of free trade in industrial products. It also outlines the conditions that the three (now four, since the division of Czechoslovakia) countries have to meet to qualify for full EC membership without specifying, however, the time period within which such membership may be granted. Pending the completion of the ratification process, an Interim Agreement came into force on March 1, 1992, and the Agreement itself on February 1, 1994.

Under the treaty the EEC agreed to eliminate (between 1992 and 1996) all barriers limiting the importation of Polish industrial products.[25] All quotas on industrial products other than those limiting the entry of coal, iron and steel, and textiles were eliminated by the end of 1994. Full liberalization of import of products that are covered by the European Coal and Steel Community was to be accomplished by the end of 1995, and the removal of quotas on textiles and clothing by the beginning of 1998.

As the "weaker partner," Poland was given ten years to eliminate all trade barriers against industrial imports from the EEC. The liberalization of imports of raw materials and of capital goods in 1992 was a first step. All other restrictions, except those applying to automobiles, are to be removed in a phased manner during 1995–99. A duty-free automobile import quota, established in 1992, is to be increased by 5 percent per year between 1994 and 2002, by which year all restrictions (including the prohibition of importation of cars more than ten years old) are to be removed.

Both sides may reimpose import restrictions under conditions specified by the GATT. Poland is permitted to take protective measures if imports from the EEC endanger its infant industries, industries in the process of transformation, and industries that encounter serious economic or social problems. Poland also may grant special protection to EEC enterprises located in Poland. Thus Poland is free to pursue an independent industrial policy during the transformation period.

The treaty does not call for the establishment of a free market in agricultural goods. However, Poland gave the EEC exporters a customs tariff preference of ten percentage points on 246 agricultural products, and the EEC undertook to enlarge its import quotas. Both sides retain the right to conduct an independent agricultural protection policy.

## Poland–EFTA Treaty

On November 15, 1993, Poland and the member countries of the European Free Trade Agreement concluded a treaty whose provisions closely matched those of the Poland–EEC agreement. As in the latter arrangements, restrictions on Polish products were to be lifted more rapidly than those imposed by Poland. Since EFTA countries did not pursue a common agricultural policy, partial liberalization of trade in agricultural goods was covered by bilateral treaties.

## The Visegrad Group

Under the "Visegrad Agreement," signed on December 21, 1992, Poland, Czechoslovakia, and Hungary agreed to form the Central European Free Trade Area (CEFTA), a common market in industrial products. The implementation schedule called for a drastic reduction of barriers during the first five-year period; the entire process was to be completed by the year 2001.

The agreement, however, has purely symbolic significance. In recent years Czechoslovakia accounted for less than 4 percent of Poland's foreign trade, and Hungary for about 1 percent. The three countries are to become gradually integrated in the broader European community; thus CEFTA will have, at most, a marginal impact on the direction of trade.

### 4.3  Foreign Debt

When the Solidarity-led government came to power in 1989, Poland was unable to meet its foreign financial obligations. Though the country was in default, its program to restore democracy and free enterprise found favor in the West. Poland was offered aid and support by the IMF and the World Bank. Yet a settlement of the debt issue was an essential prelude to full access to international financial markets. Negotiations with the creditors predated the Solidarity takeover; they were resumed by the Solidarity regime, but the final settlement was not reached until 1994.

#### 4.3.1  The Genesis of the Debt Crisis[26]

Poland's foreign debt problem dates to the 1970s. The Communist regime, threatened by popular revolt, attempted simultaneously to increase the availability of consumer goods and to lay the foundations of future prosperity through the modernization of the economy. Foreign borrowing was to be the key to this strategy. Foreign credit was to be used to finance the purchase Western technology and Western equipment. Given the expected improvement in productivity, loan repayment would be no problem.

The ambitious program raised indebtedness from $200 million in 1970 to $12 billion in 1976. About 15 percent of the loan proceeds were used for consumer goods imports; indeed, the availability of such goods was the one visible benefit of the program. Twenty percent of the credits were utilized to retool the economy (foreign credits financed nearly 25 percent of gross investment). There was little improvement in productivity because of misdirection of investment and of the misuse of the new equipment. The utilization of the new equipment required the use of Western raw materials and semifabricates; 65 percent of the loan money went for such imports.

As the debt mounted, the government found it increasingly difficult to borrow new money and to refinance old loans. Interest rates rose and the repayment periods grew shorter. As early as 1977, Poland had trouble meeting its Western obligations. Attempts to rein in the economy precipitated a sharp recession and fueled popular discontent, but they did not solve the problem. The convertible currency debt surpassed $24 billion in 1980, the year in which the Solidarity movement almost succeeded in toppling the regime, and debt service payments amounted to 96 percent of total exports to the convertible currency countries (World Bank, 1987,

p. 5). About 70 percent of the debt was to become due for repayment between 1981 and 1983. The creditors recognized the fact that the repayment of $17 billion far surpassed the country's capability.

In April 1981, Poland reached an agreement with the "Paris Club" (the lender governments) delaying, until 1986–89, 90 percent of the payments of principal and accumulated interest on long- and medium-term loans. Negotiations were also started toward a comprehensive debt restructuring agreement, but these were interrupted when the government declared a "state of war" suspending civil liberties and jailing Solidarity leaders. As a consequence of this declaration, Poland was cut off from obtaining credits guaranteed by foreign governments. Negotiations with the "London Club" (the commercial lenders), which were initiated prior to the "state of war," ultimately led to a rescheduling of repayment of 95 percent of the principal, although Poland continued to be responsible for meeting its interest payment obligations. Poland also obtained access to short-term revolving credits.

Negotiations with both clubs resumed in 1984 and led to a series of piecemeal arrangements that gave temporary relief. Nevertheless, Poland was constantly in arrears on payments of its obligations and the country continued to be cut off from contracting new foreign-government-guaranteed loans. The foreign debt kept mounting. During the 1980s Poland failed to meet two-thirds of its interest obligations. The value of the debt surpassed 500 percent of the annual value of exports in 1989. The debt to Western creditors (including capitalized unpaid interest) amounted to $40.8 billion, of which close to 70 percent was due to the "Paris Club." In addition, Poland owed 7 billion convertible rubles to its former COMECON partners.

### 4.3.2 Agreement with the "Paris Club"

The advent of the Solidarity-led government brought much-needed debt relief. As early as October 1989, commercial lenders (the "London Club" members) agreed to delay the repayment of the principal and 85 percent of interest payments due in the fourth quarter of the year. Following the adoption of the IMF-backed liberalization-cum-stabilization program, the "Paris Club" granted Poland a payments moratorium until the end of March 1991. Negotiations aiming at a comprehensive solution were resumed.

The April 1991 agreement between Poland and the seventeen "Paris Club" members involved a scaling down of the principal, recapitalization, and the rescheduling of payments. The program was to be implemented in two phases. The first phase (April 1, 1991–March 31, 1994) coincided with the stabilization agreement reached between Poland and the International Monetary Fund. Poland's payments of interest on the loans outstanding were reduced by 80 percent. The overall net present value of the debt (due account being taken of the interest payment reduction) was cut by 30 percent. The net present value of the debt was to be reduced by another 20 percent of the initial amount in the second phase. The implementation of the second phase was to be contingent upon three conditions: (1) the government was to adhere to an IMF-approved stabilization program; (2) the government would meet the (reduced) debt servicing obligations; (3) no agreements would be concluded giving other creditors more favorable treatment than was given to the "Paris Club" members (Ministry of Finance press release).

The first two conditions were readily met. Negotiations with the "London Club" took four years; an agreement fulfilling the third condition was signed on October 27, 1994.

### 4.3.3  Reduction and Conversion of the "London Club" Obligations

Poland reached an agreement with the "London Club" in the autumn of 1994 that resulted in the scaling down of Poland's $14.39 billion commercial debt by 49.2 percent.[27] The sum of $870 million in overdue interest payments was canceled outright; the Polish government agreed to buy back its debt worth $3,250 million at a cost of $1,324.6 million.[28] And $10.27 billion of the old debt was converted into a new debt instrument with a nominal value of $7.98 million. The operation called for an immediate outlay of $1,324.6 million,[29] a major part of which was covered by the IMF, the World Bank, and the reserves of the National Bank of Poland.[30]

The cost of debt service under the agreements was to rise gradually from $400 million in 1995 to $600 million by the turn of the century. The entire debt is to be repaid by the year 2024, and the average annual payment over the thirty years amounts to $561.7 million.

The reduction agreements notwithstanding, Poland continues to bear a heavy burden of external debt. According to the Ministry of Finance, Poland owed foreign creditors $47.5 billion as of September 30, 1994. Of this amount, $27.1 billion (57 percent) was owed to the "Paris Club," $14.2 billion (30 percent) to the "London Club," and $2.4 billion (5 percent) to the former USSR and other COMECON countries;[31] the balance consisted of other government-guaranteed and short-term loans. The total cost of debt servicing in 1995 and 1996 will amount to $1.5–$1.6 billion per year; if no additional debt is contracted, the cost will rise to $2.3 billion in 2000, $2.9 billion in 2002, and $3.5 billion in 2004 ("Strategia dla eksportu," *Rzeczpospolita*, Nov. 23, 1994, based on Urszula Płowiec, "Sprostać wyznaniom konkurencyjności" [Match Competition], a paper presented at a Central Planning Office conference held on November 18, 1994). The payments, even under the assumption of a moderate rate of growth, should be well within the country's capability.

## 4.4   Direct Foreign Investment

### 4.4.1   *Direct Foreign Investment under the Communist Regime*

Foreign capital played a major role in Poland's industrialization before World War II (see L. Wellisz, 1938). However, following the Communist takeover, the government nationalized all privately owned (including foreign) means of production[32] and barred new direct foreign investment (DFI).

A small chink in the anti-DFI armor was made in 1976 with the adoption of a Council of Ministers' regulation concerning the licensing of foreign and Polish-foreign partnerships ("Rozporządzenie Rady Ministrów w sprawie wydawania zagranicznym osobom prawnym i fizycznym zezwoleń na prowadzenie niektórych rodzajów działalnosci gospodarczej" [Regulation of the Council of Ministers Concerning the Licensing of Foreign Physical and Legal Persons to Engage in Certain Types of Economic Activity], *Dziennik Ustaw*, 1976, no. 19, item 128). The conditions were far from benign, however. The regulation was, technically speaking, not a law and could be amended or repealed at any time. The tax system was unclear and was administered in a highly arbitrary fashion. The licenses were issued at the pleasure of the authorities, and the rights of the licensees were severely circumscribed. The partnerships were required to deposit 30 percent of the proposed investment in a noninterest-bearing account in a Polish bank, and they were barred from receiving credit from Polish banks. The annual rate of profit repatriation was not to exceed 9 percent of the foreign capital investment plus 50 percent of the net surplus of direct exports over direct imports.[33]

A series of modest measures adopted in the course of the next decade made foreign investment somewhat more welcome. In July 1982, Parliament turned the 1976 regulation into a law, thus giving a modicum of security to DFI though retaining all the restrictive rules ("Ustawa o zasadach prowadzenia na terytorium Polskiej Rzeczpospolitej Ludowej działalnosci gospodarczej w zakresie drobnej wytwórczosci przez zagraniczne osoby prawne i fizyczne" [A Law on the Principles of Conducting Business on the Territory of the Polish People's Republic by Foreign Physical and Legal Persons], *Dziennik Ustaw*, 1982, no. 19, item 146). The rules were gradually relaxed. However, during the decade following the introduction of the regulation, licenses were granted only to very small firms formed with the participation of expatriate Polish capital ("Polonia" firms), and the total volume of investment was insignificant.

The first comprehensive foreign investment law, adopted by Parliament on April 23, 1986, swept away all previous regulations ("Ustawa z dnia 23 kwietnia 1986 roku o spółkach z udziałem zagranicznym" [The Law of 23 April 1986 on Companies with Foreign Participation], *Dziennik Ustaw*, 1986, no. 17, item 88). No new licenses were to be issued under the 1982 law (most of the licenses were to expire in 2000 or in 2010). Foreign investors gained permission to acquire minority interest in joint stock or limited liability companies. The law put some restrictions on the fields of activity open to foreigners and on profit repatriation, but these were eased toward the end of 1988 ("Ustawa z dnia 22 grudnia 1988 roku o prowadzeniu działalności z udziałem podmiotów zagranicznych [The Law on Economic Activities in Which Foreign Enterprises Participate], *Dziennik Ustaw*, 1988, no. 41, item 325).

Despite the gradual relaxation of restrictions, the volume of foreign investment remained quite low until the very end of the Communist regime. Total DFI at the end of 1988 was variously estimated between $70 and $130 million.[34] According to Breitkopf, firms with direct foreign participation employed 130,000 workers in 1989; 100,000 of these workers were employed by about 700 "Polonia" firms,[35] and 30,000 worked in the fifty-odd firms licensed under the 1982 law.[36] Enterprises with foreign participation thus gave employment to 0.7 percent of the 17.5 million labor force, and accounted for 1.6 percent of total sales and 3.0 percent of total exports (see Breitkopf, 1990).

In 1989, the year of transition from a Communist to a Solidarity-led government, there was further liberalization. The most important measure was the removal of the ceiling imposed on foreign participation. The licenses issued in one year rose to over 800,[37] seventeen times the number in the previous two years; 214 of these actually became operational (Kubielas, 1994). The liberalization of the foreign exchange law (December 1990) and the law on privatization (1990) further encouraged DFI.

### 4.4.2  DFI Since the Introduction of the Balcerowicz Reforms[38]

Since the introduction of the Balcerowicz reforms, the legal framework for the functioning of enterprises with direct foreign participation has been defined by the Polish Commercial Code of 1934 (as later amended) and by the 1991 Law on Corporations with Foreign Participation ("Ustawa o spółkach z udziałem zagranicznym," *Dziennik Ustaw*, 1991, no. 61, item 253).

Foreign enterprises are required to establish a Polish legal entity to do business in Poland. Exceptions are allowed for foreign trade, transport, tourism, and cultural services, in which foreign firms are permitted to operate directly. Under the 1991 law, foreigners may invest in corporations and in limited liability companies, and they may hold up to 100 percent of the equity. The Ministry of Finance stands ready to issue, at the request of the foreign firm, a guarantee against loss resulting from expropriation or similar action.

Foreign investment may take the form of a new enterprise ("greenfield investment"), or a joint venture with an existing private or public-sector Polish enterprise, or the acquisition of shares in an enterprise that is being privatized.[39] All foreign persons, whether physical or legal, are required to obtain a government license to acquire real estate. The procedure is complex (see Taradejna, 1991), and it may be costly and lengthy, thus reducing the attractiveness of greenfield investment. Permission is also required to form a joint venture with a state-owned enterprise.

A government license (issued by the Ministry of Ownership Transformation) is needed to engage in the management of harbors and airfields, real estate brokerage, the defense industry, and wholesale trade; to import consumer goods; and to provide legal services.[40] A license is also required when the Polish partner in a joint venture is a government-owned corporation, and when that Polish partner's contribution to the joint venture consists of capital in kind.[41] Finally, the permission of the NBP is necessary for establishing a bank with foreign participation. At least one of the directors has to be a Polish citizen. Foreign investors may participate in Polish insurance companies, provided foreign investment amounts to at least 50 percent of the reserve requirements. Foreign insurance companies are not permitted to open branches in Poland until 1999.

### 4.4.3  Taxation of Foreign Investment

Under the 1991 law, foreign investments exceeding 2 million ECU could be granted tax-exempt status for a specified time if they satisfied any one of the following conditions: (1) the investment was located in an area of structural unemployment; (2) the investment brought in new technology; (3) exports amounted to 20 percent or more of the production.

Tax relief was granted by the Ministry of Finance on a discretionary basis, creating numerous conflicts and suspicion of corruption. The special internal privileges were abolished in January 1994 and all firms, regardless of the origin of capital, are now subject to the same tax laws.[42] However, the machinery and equipment paid for by the foreign partners can be imported duty-free during the first three years of a firm's existence. Foreign employees are subject to a 20 percent income tax (or a tax specified in a bilateral tax treaty), and they may repatriate their earnings.

### 4.4.4   The Scope and Role of DFI

Since the collapse of the Communist regime, the volume of DFI has rapidly increased, its annual inflow having risen from $20 million in 1989 to a peak of $1.5 billion in 1993 (the inflow declined slightly in 1994), and the stock having risen from less than $70 million in December 1989 to over $4 billion in September 1994 (see Table 4.6).[43] There was a slight decline in the rate of inflow in 1994, but the total DFI surpassed $4.3 billion at the end of the year.[44]

The size of the average investment in 1989 was under $100,000 (see Table 4.6). Liberalization brought a flood of small-scale Polish expatriate capital. Larger investors came to play a more important role in subsequent years. Though the average size of the foreign holding was still under $400,000 in December 1993, investments of $1 million or over amounted to $2,828 million, thus accounting for over 90 percent of the total.[45] A major share of foreign investment was in joint ventures. Typically, foreign investors initially took a minority share and then enlarged their

**Table 4.6**
Foreign investment in Poland, 1989–94

| Year | 1989 | 1990 | 1991 | 1992 | 1993 | 1994 |
|------|------|------|------|------|------|------|
| Number of enterprises | 946 | 1,849 | 2,649 | 6,180 | 8,335 | 8,775 |
| Cumulative investment (mill. $) | 67 | 180 | 459 | 1,408 | 3,071 | 4,400 |
| Investment per enterprise (thou. $) | 71 | 97 | 173 | 227 | 368 | 501 |

Source: Foreign Trade Research Institute, Foreign Investment in Poland (various issues), cited in Kubielas et al. (1994), and GUS (1995).
Note: The 1994 data are not strictly comparable with earlier years.

holdings to assume control. Thus, between 1990 and 1993, the share of foreign holding in joint ventures rose from 40.7 percent to 72.8 percent (Foreign Trade Research Institute data cited in Kubielas, Markowski, and Jackson, 1994). Industry accounts for 75 percent of cumulative DFI, and trade for 12 percent.

How big a role does DFI play in the Polish economy? According to GUS, aggregate DFI accounted for 3.3 percent of all corporate equity capital as of December 31, 1993, and firms with foreign participation for 5.1 percent (calculated on the basis of data in GUS, 1994a, Table 1.4). Such firms employed 310,000 workers, about 2.1 percent of the total labor force. However, foreign presence is growing in importance. DFI amounted to 2.2 percent of total gross investment in 1991, 6.3 percent in 1992, and 11.1 percent in 1993.[46] Estimates of the percentage of investments in plant and equipment undertaken by enterprises with foreign capital participation, are not fully consistent with the above figures but show a similar trend (see Table 4.7).

## 4.5 How Far Is Poland Along the Road to Integration?

Poland was an almost closed economy in 1988, the penultimate year of the Communist regime. The ratio of the value of internationally traded goods and services (the sum of imports and of exports) to GDP equaled only 0.39. Moreover, the Polish producers were shielded from foreign competition. The exporters to the CMEA countries had a guaranteed market,[47] and imports of goods competing with domestic products were strictly controlled. By 1992 the trade/GDP ratio rose to 0.49 (based on IMF data). The change is not dramatic, but it is significant. The change in the character of trade is, however, even more significant. Polish products now have to compete with foreign products at home and abroad. The effects of increased competition are striking, albeit difficult to document:

**Table 4.7**
Investment in buildings and machinery by source (in trillion zlotys at current prices)

|  | 1990 | 1991 | 1992 | 1993 |
|---|---|---|---|---|
| (A) Total | 107.4 | 142.7 | 179.5 | 229.7 |
| (B) Enterprises with foreign participation (B) | 1.4 | 4.2 | 9.4 | 14.1 |
| (C) (B) as percent of (A) | 1.3 | 2.9 | 3.6 | 6.1 |

Sources: (A) GUS (1996), (B) PAIZ.

the quality of a broad range of Polish products is rapidly improving and already matches some Western items.

The integration of Poland into the world economy is largely the effect of the reforms introduced in 1990–91 by the Solidarity-led government. Hyperinflation was brought under control in 1990. The zloty was made convertible and linked to the dollar. Production and consumption prices were freed, and most of the subsidies were eliminated. The economy was opened to world trade and foreign investment. A Treaty of Association was signed with the EEC. Much remained to be done, but the foundation of integration was firmly in place.[48]

The tempo of reforms slowed in 1991, and there was considerable retrogression in the area of trade policy. This raises a question: Were the initial reforms too radical? Perhaps a gradual opening up of the economy would have given more time for adjustment and mellowed the opposition to liberalization. A slower tempo of reform thus might have led, in the longer run, to greater freedom of trade.

There is no doubt that the severe trade shock suffered by Poland in 1990–91 strongly contributed to the public's reaction against reform. Gradual liberalization of trade would not have reduced the distress of manufacturing industries that were most adversely affected by the transition, those dependent on CMEA or on military orders, or both.[49] On the other hand, it may be argued that the sudden liberalization of trade in agricultural products was a mistake. The shock turned the peasants, who constituted a stronghold of private enterprise under communism, into enemies of reform.

It can also be argued that it was incorrect to treat liberalization as a policy tool rather than as a goal in itself. Under the Balcerowicz regime customs duties were temporarily reduced or suspended in lieu of currency revaluation, thereby setting a precedent for the subsequent increase in tariffs for fiscal purposes. The 1991 tariff revision presented an opportunity to put into effect a structure that would minimize distortions; instead, the new schedule deliberately took into account the interests of individual branches of industry. Subsequent regimes carried this policy one step further: import and export controls were employed to win friends and influence people.

The retreat from free trade is, however, a passing phenomenon. The degree to which the Polish government can manipulate trade is subject to a decisive external check. Poland is firmly committed to a political and economic integration with Western Europe, and Polish industry and financial services (if not Polish agriculture) will be fully integrated with the European Economic Community by the year 2000.

# Notes

1. In the parliamentary election of June 1989, 65 percent of the seats in the Sejm (the lower chamber) were reserved for the PZPR and for two satellite parties, the United Peasant Party (PZPL) and the Democratic Party (SD). Solidarity won all the seats it was allowed to contest and ninety-nine of the one hundred Senat (upper chamber) seats. As a compromise between Solidarity and the PZPR, General Jaruzelski, first secretary of the PZPR, became president and Tadeusz Mazowiecki, a ranking member of Solidarity, became prime minister. Mazowiecki's government included members of Solidarity as well as of PZPR, PZPL, and SD. When the new government was formed, the satellite parties distanced themselves from the PZPR.

2. So called after the finance minister and vice premier, Leszek Balcerowicz. For a comprehensive discussion of the Balcerowicz Plan, see, Kierzkowski, Okólski, and Wellisz, 1993.

3. The 1991 election was contested by a large number of small parties, none of which won enough votes to form a stable government.

4. A more detailed analysis of the evolution of the foreign exchange regime is in Wellisz, 1995.

5. The official rate and the free market rate were, however, never allowed to deviate by more than a few percentage points.

6. Guesstimates indicate that private dollar hoards totaled $6 to $9 billion, surpassing the official reserves by a factor of three or more.

7. The monthly rate of increase of the consumer price index declined from 79.6 percent in January 1990 to 4.6 percent in May and to 3.6 percent in June. Price stability by year-end seemed to be a feasible goal.

8. The IMF-approved stabilization plan called for the fiscal deficit of the first half of the year to be compensated by a second half-year surplus.

9. Measures for slowing the accumulation of reserves also included a temporary reduction or suspension of customs duties. See Section 4.2.

10. The high paper profits registered by SOEs during the 1990 inflation reflected lags in the revaluation of inventories and of depreciation allowances. Enterprises also made paper profits as a result of the increase in the zloty value of their foreign exchange accounts. The SOEs as a whole recorded losses in 1991 and beyond.

11. The consumer price index rose by 59.1 percent and the GDP deflator by 55.3 percent in 1991.

12. According to the official trade and capital transaction statistics, Poland's balance of payments was negative in 1993 and 1994. The accumulation of reserves may have arisen as a consequence of a surplus on unrecorded border trade or of an unrecorded influx of speculative capital.

13. Though "national income produced" in the Soviet-type economies differs from GDP, the intertemporal movements of the two series are closely correlated.

14. The modernization drive was masterminded by Edward Gierek, then first secretary of PZPR.

15. Raw materials were exempt from duties or subject to a low rate; finished products were more heavily protected. The unweighted average rate was less than 12 percent.

16. The reexport provisions lapsed with the dissolution of the CMEA.

17. The accumulation of foreign exchange reserves was unwanted (1) because of its inflationary effects and (2) because Poland had just entered into negotiations with its creditors. The rapid rise in reserves was harmful to Poland's claim that the country was unable to meet its debt obligations.

18. Poland is not the only post-Communist country to retreat from trade liberalism. For a comparative study of Poland, Hungary, and the Czech and Slovak Republics, see Gacs (1994).

19. These figures take into account temporary reductions and suspensions.

20. Automobile tariffs are the most important exception.

21. "Binding" implies an undertaking to refrain from future increases in the scheduled tariffs except under specific circumstances enumerated in the protocol of the agreement.

22. The AMS is calculated as follows: $AMS = Q(P - P^*) + S$, where $Q =$ quantity produced, $P =$ domestic price, $P^* =$ import or export price, and $S =$ direct subsidy.

23. For the highly developed countries as a group, the tariffs prior to the Uruguay Round were "bound" at 6.0 percent trade-weighted average. The actual average was 5.0 percent. After reduction the tariffs were bound at 5.0 percent on average. In the case of the United States and of the European Economic Community, the actual protection rates are the same as the base period rates, but the averages for Australia are 20.1 percent, 10.0 percent, and 12.2. percent respectively. See Kirmani et al. (1994).

24. The 1991 treaty supplanted and enlarged the agreement for trade cooperation concluded by Poland and the EEC in 1989.

25. For the purpose of satisfying the EEC domestic content clause, Poland, Hungary, and Czechoslovakia (later the Czech and Slovak Republics) are treated as one country.

26. This section draws heavily on "Ciężar starych długów" (The Burden of Old Debt), *Nowa Europa*, November 19–21, 1994.

27. The agreement with the "London Club" was signed on September 14, 1994, and came into force on October 27 of the same year. Unless otherwise indicated, the discussion that follows is based on Ministry of Finance press releases.

28. $2.93 billion of the debt was to be bought back at 41 cents on the dollar and $320 million at 31 cents on the dollar.

29. $1,324.6 million of this sum was needed for the debt buyback and $623 million for the purchase of U.S. Treasury obligations. These were deposited with the Federal Reserve Bank of New York and were to be used (at the end of thirty years) for repurchasing $4.8 billion of the new obligations.

30. The loans advanced by the IMF and the World Bank amounted, respectively, to $900 million and $400 million; $440 million came out of the reserves of the National Bank of Poland; $137.7 million was obtained under the "new money agreement"; and $70 was provided in the 1994 budget.

31. The COMECON debt issue was subsequently settled via multilateral negotiations and the cancellation of mutual debts.

32. Small rural holdings were an exception. Large holdings were divided into smaller parcels; some (especially in former German-owned territories) were collectivized.

33. For a discussion of private foreign investment prior to 1990, see Breitkopf, 1950.

34. The low estimate is given by Kubielas (1994b). Breitkopf (1990) gives the high estimate.

35. Breitkopf (1990) states that there were 727 "Polonia" firms; Kubielas (1994b) puts their number at 688. The temporary existence of many such firms and reporting inaccuracies account for the differences in estimates.

36. According to Breitkopf (1990), fifty-two permits were issued under the 1982 law; Kubielas (1994a) states that fifty-three enterprises (thus licensed) operated in 1989.

37. Breitkopf (1990) puts the number at 867; Kubielas (1994a), at 814.

38. This section is based primarily on Instytut Koniunktur i Cen Handlu Zagranicznego (1994a).

39. An investor (whether Polish or foreign) who wants to acquire through the stock market more than a 10 percent holding in any enterprise is required to make public his or her intentions.

40. The ministry must communicate its decision within two months of the filing for a license.

41. No license is needed if the Polish partner is a fully government-owned corporation.

42. Profits currently are subject to a 40 percent tax; in addition, dividends are taxed at a 20 percent rate. The tax on dividends may be reduced in accordance with bilateral treaties concluded between Poland and its major trading partners for eliminating double taxation.

43. The PAIZ (the Polish State Agency for Foreign Investment) figures are among the highest of the various estimates of DFI. For a comprehensive discussion of the data issue, see *Economic Bulletin for Europe* (1994).

44. According to PAIZ, investments of $1 million or over amounted to a total of $4,080 million by November 1994. Investments under $1 million amounted to $200 to $400 million.

45. Data on investments of $1 million or more (large-scale investments) are collected by PAIZ. GUS gives data on aggregate investment (large-plus small-scale). The PAIZ data, which are cited here, are more detailed (and appear to be more reliable) than the GUS data.

46. These estimates were obtained by expressing DFI as a percentage of total gross investment in current dollars, which was calculated by converting the current zloty gross investment figures for 1991, 1992, and 1993 (GUS, 1994a) at midyear dollar-zloty exchange rates.

47. Most of the highly differentiated products, for which quality plays a major role, were exported to the CMEA; exports to the West were largely confined to standardized commodities such as basic chemicals.

48. In particular, the debt reduction negotiations were barely initiated.

49. For estimates of the short-run costs of the dismantling of CMEA, see Rodrik (1992).

# References

Breitkopf, Mikołaj. 1990. "Foreign Direct Investment in Poland." *Institute of Finance Working Papers*. Warsaw: Institute of Finance.

Dąbrowski, Jerzy, and Anrdzej Kwieciński. 1994. "Skutki protekcjonizmu rolnego w Polsce dla transformacji rolnictwa" [The Impact of Protection of Agriculture on the Process of Agricultural Transformation in Poland]. Warsaw University, Department of Economics. MIMEO.

*Dziennik Ustaw*. Various issues.

*Economic Bulletin for Europe*. 1994. 46, no. 4.

Fallenbuchl, Zbigniew. 1988. "Present State of the Economic Reform." In P. Marer and W. Siwinski, eds., *Creditworthiness and Reform in Poland: Western and Polish Perspective*. Bloomington: Indiana University Press.

Foreign Trade Research Institute. *Foreign Trade in Poland*. Various issues.

Gacs, Janos. 1994. "Trade Policies in the Czech and Slovak Republics, Hungary and Poland 1989–1993: A Comparison." *Case Studies and Analyses* 11 (January).

Główny Urząd Statystyczny (GUS). 1990, 1996. *Rocznik statystyczny* [Statistical Yearbook]. Warsaw: GUS.

Główny Urząd Statystyczny (GUS). 1995. *Wyniki finansowe podmiotów gospodarczych z udziałem kapitału zagranicznego w r. 1994* [Financial Results of Companies with Foreign Participation]. Warsaw: GUS.

Gomułka, Stanisław. 1994. "Budget Deficit and Inflation in Transition Economies." *Case Studies and Analyses* 13 (February).

*Institute of Finance. Working Papers*. Various issues.

Instytut Koniunktur i Cen Handlu Zagranicznego. 1994a. *Inwestycje Zagraniczne w Polsce* [Foreign Investment in Poland]. Warsaw: Instytut Koniunktur i Cen Handlu Zagranicznego.

Instytut Koniunktur i Cen Handlu Zagranicznego. 1994b. *Polski handel zagraniczny w 1993 roku* [Polish Foreign Trade in 1993]. Warsaw: GUS.

Instytut Koniunktur i Cen Handlu Zagranicznego. 1994c. *Polska polityka handlu zagranicznego 1993–1994* [Polish Foreign Trade Policy 1993–1994]. Warsaw: GUS.

Kierzkowski, Henryk, Marek Okólski, and Stanisław Wellisz, eds. 1993. *Stabilization and Structural Adjustment in Poland*. London: Unwin.

Kirmani, Naheed, et al. 1994. *International Trade Policies: The Uruguay Round and Beyond*. Washington, D.C.: International Monetary Fund.

Kubielas, Stanisław. 1994a. *The Attractiveness of Poland to Foreign Direct Investment*. In Polish Policy Research Group, Warsaw University, PPRG Discussion Papers, no. 33.

Kubielas, Stanisław. 1994b. "Opening up the Polish Economy and Foreign Direct Investment Inflow in 1989–1993." Warsaw University. Mime.

Kubielas, Stanisław, Stefan Markowski, and Sharon Jackson. 1994. *Atrakcyjność Polski dla zagranicznych inwestorów po pięciu latach transformacji* [The Attractiveness of Poland to Foreign Investors After Five Years of Transformation]. Warsaw: PPRG, December. Mimeo.

Marer P., and W. Siwiński, eds. 1988. *Creditworthiness and Reform in Poland: Western and Polish Perspectives.* Bloomington: Indiana University Press.

Nogaj, Mieczysław. 1992. "Cele i założenia nowej polityki celnej" [Goals and Assumptions of the New Tariff Policy]. *Kontrola Państwowa* 1. Reprinted in his "Polityka celna." In Instytut Koniunktur i Cen Handlu Zagranicznego. *Polski handel zagraniczng w 1993 roku.* Warsaw: Instytut Koniunktur i Cen Handlu Zagranicznego.

Nogaj, Mieczysław. 1994. "Polityka pozacelna" [Non-Tariff Policy]. In Instytut Koniunktur i Cen Handlu Zagranicznego. *Polski handel zagraniczng w 1993 roku.* Warsaw: Instytut Koniunktur i Cen Handlu Zagranicznego.

*Nowa Europa.* Various issues.

Poznański, Kazimierz. 1988. "The Competitiveness of Polish Industry and Indebtedness." in P. Marer, and W. Siwinski, eds., *Creditworthiness and Reform in Poland: Western and Polish Perspectives.* Bloomington: Indiana University Press.

Rodrik, Dani. 1992. "Making Sense of the Soviet Trade Shock in Eastern Europe: A Framework and Some Estimates." Paper prepared for the World Bank/IMF Conference on the Fall of Output in Eastern Europe. Washington, D.C.

*Rzeczpolspolita.* Various issues.

Taradejna, R. 1991. "Acquisition of Real Estate by Foreigners." *Polish Foreign Trade* (December).

Wellisz, Leopold. 1938. *Foreign Capital in Poland.* London: Allen and Unwin.

Wellisz, Stanisław. 1993. "Macroeconomic Policies." In Henryk Kierzkowski, Marek Okolski, and Stanisław Wellisz, eds., *Stabilization and Structural Adjustment in Poland.* London: Unwin.

Wellisz, Stanisław. 1995. *Inflation and Stabilization in Poland 1990–1994.* Columbia University, Department of Economics, *Discussion Paper Series* (September).

Wokłodkiewicz-Donimirski, Zdzisław. 1994. "Wyroby przemysłu metalurguicznego" [Products of the Metalworking Industry]. In Instytut Koniunktur i Cen Handlu Zagranicznego, *Polski handel zagraniczny w 1993 roku.* Warsaw: GUS.

World Bank. 1987. *Poland: Reform, Adjustment, and Growth.* Washington, D.C.: World Bank.

# II    The North European Economies

# 5      The Baltic States: Estonia, Latvia, and Lithuania

Kalev Kukk

In the official version, the Baltic economies were said to be flourishing in the 1980s. That had to be taken at its face value because a variety of statistical growth statements such as "Industrial output increased in the Lithuanian SSR [Soviet Socialist Republic], Estonian SSR and Latvian SSR by 73, 55 and 53 times respectively between 1941 and 1985" (*Narodnoe khozyaistvo SSSR za 70 let,* 1987) confirmed this. The "truth" of that time was meant not only for Estonians, Latvians, and Lithuanians; it was for the whole world. And it was accepted, at least partially. Actually, the economic distortion grew so great that any sense of proportion was lost. Take, for example, the claim of a high official of the Estonian SSR State Planning Committee in 1980, addressed to Estonians in exile, that Estonia ranked among the top ten countries in the world in terms of national income per capita, ahead of advanced industrial countries such as the United Kingdom, Norway, and Finland. The myth of the welfare country was thus created.

Much has changed in the Baltic economies in the course of time.

For their eastern neighbors, too, the Baltic states were mythical. They had higher wages, housing with all conveniences readily available, shops full of goods, and polite service. Estonia, Latvia, and Lithuania were said to be genuine "eldorados" compared with the vast Russian hinterland. These neighbors were convinced that the Baltic states' well-being was created by their generous help.

Before Christmas 1990, the West included the Baltic states de jure or de facto as constituent parts of the Soviet Union that needed food assistance. The annexation of the Baltic states by the Soviet Union during World War II had signified the liquidation of a self-managing economy. It was replaced by a fetishistic "planning" regime in which economic development was measured by expenditure (marked by waste) that served as a

basis for awarding prizes and honorary ranks. The labels "Made in Estonia," "Made in Latvia," and "Made in Lithuania" disappeared from the
world market. For example, only 0.6–0.7 percent of Estonian industrial
production reached the developed market economies in the early 1980s.
It consisted mostly of raw materials and less processed goods with their
consumer utility fortunately untouched by Soviet work.

Two distinct periods, which began in the second half of the 1980s as a
result of several objective and subjective factors, marked the economic
transition of the Baltic and other Central and East European countries.
They were characterized by different political environments and development goals.

The first period searched for a "humane socialism" (coined in the
"Prague spring" of 1968) or a socialist market economy. The second
phase destroyed previous ideas and values, and opened the road to a
market economy. The beginning of this period coincided with the reestablishment of independence in the Baltic states in August 1991.

The search for economic independence and elaboration of the concepts
of economic autonomy during the first period resulted in the enactment of
the necessary legislation by the Supreme Councils in 1989: in Estonia on
May 18, in Lithuania on May 19, and in Latvia on July 27. The second
period was marked by a rapid acceptance of the principles of economic
deregulation and market economy. The events that followed resembled
the beginning of capitalism against the background of Western rules and
economic ethics.

The shifts in the direction of a market economy were far from homogeneous. There were differences in the degree of radicalness of solutions and
in the speed of processes. Specific differences also appeared in institutional
development, ownership reform, government intervention, and methods
chosen for the purpose. The most important and quantitatively the most
noticeable changes in the three Baltic countries concerned money circulation and restructuring of markets. The former was expressed in the monetarization (i.e., transition from a nonmonetary to a monetary economy),
and the latter in the opening of the Baltic states into the world economy.

## 5.1   Monetary Development

Monetary development in the Baltic states must be discussed in the context (1) of macroeconomic stabilization and (2) of the introduction of
national currencies. The former is concerned with inflation control and

formation of European price structures, and the latter with the transition from rubles to real money and secession from the ruble zone.

### 5.1.1 From Hyperinflation to Monetary Stabilization

In the official Soviet view, the ruble, the most stable currency in the world, could be shaken neither by international currency and energy crises nor by domestic inflation. The ruble in fact was convertible only in exceptional cases at the official exchange rate fixed by the Soviet central bank, and inflation could not ideologically exist in a socialist economy. The "stable" domestic value of the ruble was secured by fixed prices and appropriate methods of calculating the price indices. Repressed inflation, increasing shortages, and deteriorating product quality were accompanied by increasing budgetary subsidies and structural price distortions. The average retail prices of consumer goods rose by 11 percent in the Soviet Union between 1981 and 1989, and by 34 percent in Estonia.

Such stable prices lasted for decades and were associated with a simultaneous rise in nominal income that, however, could not be spent on goods, which were in short supply. The resulting accumulation of cash, the monetary overhang, contained the seeds of hyperinflation if prices were to be liberalized (see Desai, 1989; McKinnon, 1991; Nordhaus, 1990). Over time the divergence of the fixed prices from the actual production costs, as well as from the equilibrium prices, increased.

Soviet hidden inflation was first cracked open by Estonia in the winter of 1990, when the Estonian administration abolished most wage restrictions. Estonia thus made an unprecedented economic decision: wages were freed before prices. Estonia added a new model: frozen prices-free wages to the list of currently known models: free prices-free wages, free prices-frozen wages, and frozen prices-frozen wages. The decision, which seemed absurd at first, did not prove absurd in practice. This step helped Estonia survive the subsequent liberalization of prices relatively painlessly.

The liberalization of prices in Estonia, which occurred in October 1990 via removal of state budget subsidies to foodstuffs, began the Estonian transition to cheap rubles while elsewhere in the Soviet Union, including in Latvia and Lithuania, prices and wages were essentially frozen. Consumer prices rose by 79 percent in Estonia in 1990. By contrast, they rose by 29 percent in Latvia and by 9 percent in Lithuania. According to official statistics, Soviet consumer prices, excluding the black market, rose by 5.3 percent. Estonia retained the lead in the universal inflation race during

1991 as well. As a result of the reestablishment of national independence, wages and prices in Estonia were almost twice those elsewhere in the ruble zone.

The cheap ruble proved to be a rather effective safeguard for the Estonian domestic market against rubles from other ruble zone countries; at the same time, local relative prices approached the European price structure. Although there was a relative abundance of goods, people had to spend their savings because prices rose. These savings were not indexed. It was astonishing that the Soviet central authorities did not react to the sabotage of the ruble by Estonia. Only 3 million rubles were emitted through the Estonian branch of the Soviet State Bank in 1989, compared with 589 million rubles in 1990. However, the arbitrary behavior of Estonia, in which Latvia and Lithuania could not join promptly, created friction in the relationship among the Baltic states. For example, Prime Minister Ivars Godmanis of Latvia repeatedly attacked Estonian policy makers, saying that Estonia's cheap rubles created shortages in the Latvian market. Average annual consumer prices in 1991 rose by 211 percent in Estonia, 125 percent in Latvia, and 225 percent in Lithuania. In the CIS countries, by contrast, this indicator remained between 79 and 140 percent.

Inflation peaked in the independent Baltic states (which were still in the ruble zone) between November 1991 and March 1992, when consumer prices rose by 508 percent in Estonia, 436 percent in Latvia, and 407 percent in Lithuania. While inflation in 1990 and 1991 was mostly pushed by demand, the sharply accelerating inflation at the end of 1991 was expectational inflation, which was generated by the anticipated price liberalization in Russia. At the beginning of 1992, Russia sharply raised the prices of energy and raw materials (for example, the prices of oil products rose by fifty to seventy times in Estonia in January), which gave a sharp upward push to the general price rise via higher costs of imported energy. The continuing price rise was restrained by the shortage of cash resulting from the unannounced blockade of cash by the Russian central bank.

However, the subsequent slowdown of inflation was directly connected with the rigid monetary policies carried out in the Baltic states after the currency reforms. These monetary policies were the most effective means of macroeconomic stabilization. The rate of inflation (based on consumer prices) in 1992, 1993, and 1994 (from December to December) was 954 percent, 35.6 percent, and 41.6 percent in Estonia; 959 percent, 34.9 percent, and 26.1 percent in Latvia; and 1,163 percent, 189 percent, and 45.1 percent in Lithuania. The underlying monthly rates of inflation for the three countries are presented in Figure 5.1.

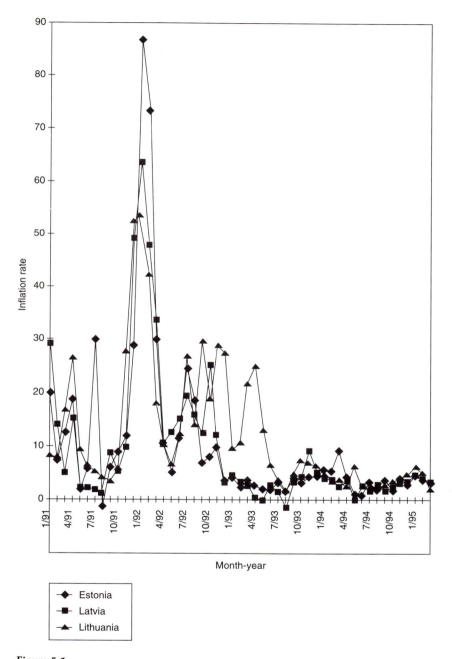

**Figure 5.1**
Monthly inflation rates in Estonia, Latvia, and Lithuania, January 1991–March 1995 (percent)
*Source:* Official statistics of the Baltic states.

### 5.1.2   Currency Reforms

Estonia was the first Baltic state to propose a national currency in 1987 (Kallas et al., 1987). During the next two to three years, discussions about a national currency in Estonia, Latvia, and Lithuania were aimed primarily at gaining independence from the increasingly irresponsible monetary policy of the Soviet central bank. From a broader perspective, a national currency was to serve the goal of economic autonomy. Suggestions to introduce the "convertible ruble" in the administrative regions of the Soviet Union, which would apply for the status of free economic zones (as in China), occasionally surfaced from Moscow. These seemingly harmless ideas were supported by several Russian perestroika-minded economists but were ignored by the increasingly assertive Baltic administrations.

The idea of Baltic national currencies was legalized in 1989 in the concept of economic autonomy, which was adopted as law by the Supreme Councils. There were, however, no states in which to introduce this national currency. The transitional parliaments elected in 1990 and the first non-communist governments nominated by them moved to the next stage in initiating Baltic national currencies. The initial covert movement toward independence was replaced by a direct demand to restore national independence, one component of which was separate money circulation and, consequently, the introduction of a national currency. As a result of the discussions in economic and political groups, the first official ideas about concrete implementation of the currency reforms were developed in 1990–91. For example, two alternative currency reform concepts were worked out in Estonia by the end of 1990, one of them under the leadership of Bo Kragh (an officer of Svenska Handelsbanken and counselor to the Estonian government) and the other under the leadership of Rein Otsason, then the president of Eesti Pank (Bank of Estonia) (*Oma rahale üchmineku kontseptsioonid*, 1990).

Though Estonia was still de facto a constituent part of the Soviet Union, both concepts essentially represented the idea of introducing a parallel money. The convertibility and stability of an independent currency seemed unattainable in the beginning. For example, Bo Kragh offered the following view:

One may say with 100 percent certainty now that for many years after the implementation of the Estonian currency reform, Estonia will not have sufficient gold and foreign currency reserves (not to mention economic power) to make the Estonian kroon internationally convertible. Estonia is incapable of protecting a fixed exchange rate of the kroon against the U.S. dollar, the deutsche mark or some other internationally convertible currency by using its foreign currency or gold reserves. (*Oma rahale ülemineku kontseptsioonid*, 1990, p. 51)

Though many suggestions could not be implemented during the currency reform, they contained positive elements. For example, the disputes about the "best" currency reform were over and done with when the time for the currency reform arrived, and the Eesti Pank introduced the reform without major public discussions.

In preparation for abandoning the ruble, an intensive dollarization occurred in the Baltic states. The currency black market was legalized in Estonia at the beginning of 1990 through the first private newspapers, which, as intermediaries between sellers and buyers, began quoting exchange rates. The Estonian government also began to favor dollarization publicly and, based on the Polish experience of the 1980s, started a special dollarization program at the beginning of 1991. It was aimed at the creation of alternative money circulation and accumulation of foreign currency in Estonia. Polls of that time showed that 15 percent of the Estonian families possessed or had possessed foreign currency, and 23 percent of the population had used it in their purchases. Eesti Pank started to quote the Soviet ruble separately in March 1991, on the basis of black market rates, thus influencing the exchange rates. This implied a local devaluation of the Soviet ruble by five to six times against the tourist exchange rate. The fast increase in the foreign currency reserves of Eesti Pank after the currency reform was due to the foreign currency (mainly Finnish, Swedish, and U.S. currency) accumulated during this period. For example, receipts from the sale of convertible foreign currency accounted for 8.3 percent of the net money income per average household in June 1992 (the month of the currency reform), 3.3 percent in July, and 4.8 percent in August. In the three months preceding the currency reform, it had been 1.7 to 2.6 percent (Kuddo 1994).

The use of foreign currency in domestic circulation helped the Baltic states adjust their economies to the world economy via the adoption of world market prices and the orientation of their production costs to outside competition. While Estonia managed to get rid of the high dollarization unexpectedly fast (the currency reform liquidated all foreign currency shops by converting all shops into "currency shops"), the dollarization culminated in Latvia and Lithuania in a transition phase of rublis and talonas, the temporary currencies.

At the beginning of 1992, induced by the shortage of cash, direct preparations began in all three Baltic states for the introduction of their national currencies. In order to alleviate the shortage of cash, Lithuania and Latvia introduced parallel legal tenders—couponlike talonas in Lithuania (on May 1) and rublis in Latvia (on May 7). Their initial exchange rates against the ruble were 1 : 1. Estonia managed to avoid the introduction of the cash-shortage-induced parallel money mainly by increased clearing of bank checks and other cashless clearing accounts, as well as by delaying the payment of wages, pensions, and benefits. Other abnormal solutions were invented. Tartu, the second largest town in Estonia, for a short time introduced its "city money." Less than a month before the currency reform, Prime Minister Tiit Vähi attempted to introduce the one-kroon banknote as a surrogate money of high nominal ruble value. It was not successful. However, the government's attempt had another objective, which out-weighed the first one: in the absence of a state budget approved by the Parliament, the government hoped to cover the budget deficit with the help of such emission.

In Latvia and Lithuania, the rublis and talonas at first circulated along with the Soviet ruble and a variety of foreign currencies. The introduction of the rublis and talonas as additional legal tenders, which arose from the cash deficit, turned out to be the first stage of the stepped-up currency reform in these countries. After that, all rubles in circulation in Latvia were exchanged without restrictions for rublis at the rate of 1 : 1 between July 7 and July 15, 1992; the ruble accounts in Latvian banks were converted into rublis by July 20. The rublis thus became the national currency in Latvia, although a temporary one. Lithuania converted to the tempo-rary talonas currency by October 1.

The introduction of these new banknotes implied only conditional cur-rency reform. Subsequently, the rublis and the talonas started strengthen-ing against the ruble due to the lower inflation than in Russia (consumer prices rose by twenty-six times in Russia in 1992). Meanwhile, the exchange rate of the rublis and the talonas against convertible foreign currencies depended on demand and supply without interference from the newly established central banks: Latvijas Banka (Bank of Latvia) and Lietuvos Banko (Bank of Lithuania).

The introduction of the temporary national currencies, which pulled Latvia and Lithuania gradually from the ruble zone, allowed them to carry out their own monetary policies, which soon became very restrictive in Latvia. As a result, the exchange rate of the rublis began to strengthen against foreign currencies at the beginning of 1993. By their very nature, the rublis and the talonas were "everyday money," primarily fulfilling the function of a legal tender. This was also emphasized by the low quality of the banknotes. For example, their color faded quickly and they could easily be counterfeited. The rublis and the talonas also influenced the restructuring of the Latvian and Lithuanian economies and foreign markets less than in Estonia, which introduced the permanent currency immediately.

Estonia also had an interim currency, the ordinary Soviet ruble, with a purchasing power two times lower than elsewhere in the ruble zone thanks to the earlier legalization of hidden inflation and the anticipated inflationary policies at the time independence was restored. Estonia, however, was the first Baltic state to introduce a permanent currency. The currency reform began there on June 20, 1992, exactly forty-four years after the German currency reform. Although the impact of the German reform on the technological side of the Estonian currency reform was minimal, its philosophy had considerable influence (see Dornbusch and Wolf, 1990). In order to avoid parallel ruble circulation, almost all rubles that circulated in Estonia were exchanged for kroons at the rate of 10:1 between June 20 and 22. Every permanent resident of Estonia could change 1,500 rubles into kroons. The same exchange rate, with provisional restrictions, was used for legal persons and bank accounts. The Estonian kroon was pegged to the deutsche mark, on the basis of the initial reserves of the reserve currency and the demand-supply situation of foreign currency at 1 DM = 8 kroons (EEK). The initial reserve currency consisted mainly of the gold that had been frozen in Western banks in 1940 after the occupation of Estonia by the Soviet Union and was recovered from them immediately before the currency reform. Between 1992 and 1993, the Bank of England, Sveriges Riksbank, the Bank for International Settlements, and the Federal Reserve Bank of New York returned to Estonia 11.3 tons of gold, in the form of metal or of money for a total of DM 193 million. Latvia and Lithuania also recovered their gold that had been frozen in Western banks in 1940.

Externally, the Estonian currency reform represented the denomination of the kroon along with some devaluation: the official buying and selling rates of the kroon were "devalued" by 9.6 percent and 2.4 percent, respectively, during the reform. At the same time, the foundation of the financial system on currency board principles signified an essential shift in monetary policy. This choice best satisfied the ultimate goal, which was macroeconomic stabilization with the help of the fixed exchange rate of the kroon.

The currency board regime was chosen for the technological implementation of monetary policies primarily for two reasons (see Hanke, Jonung, and Schuler, 1993, pp. 63–80). First, the economy needed an autonomous and automatic arrangement that would guarantee the stable exchange rate of the kroon. Second, Estonia lacked the necessary skills and experience for implementing the classical, money-supply-regulating central bank policies. If mistakes were made under political pressure, they would have cost the country very dearly. Several experts had feared that the young national governments of the Baltic states, having acquired access to printing presses, would start solving social and environmental problems under strong political pressure by printing empty money (see, e.g., Vilks, 1992).

In turn, a stable exchange rate was calculated to create preconditions for structural changes in the economy via its ready acceptance by the market and by economic agents in their strategic decision-making. It not only would integrate Estonia into the world economy by being fully convertible but also would promote long-term economic growth under competitive conditions.

The world reacted to Estonia's choice of the currency board regime with suspicion. Earlier regarded as an extravagant and dubious step, it was later held up as an example to the successor states of the Soviet Union. Such suggestions may have been off the mark. The currency board system is suitable only for a small and open economy that can avoid protectionism in its foreign economic arrangements.

The choice of the currency board system was also influenced by international discussions about an appropriate currency reform and monetary system for Estonia. Hanke, Jonung, and Schuler proposed a strict currency board regime in 1991 linking the Estonian currency with the Swedish kroner (see Hanke, Jonung, and Schuler, 1992). Because Sweden had to take the entire responsibility with the right of veto for the classical currency board they suggested, their idea was not taken seriously at first. The final decision in favor of the modified currency board regime was made immediately before the currency reform and was influenced by the opinion of Ardo Hansson, an Estonian in exile.[1]

There were four main features of the currency board regime: the complete backing of the base money with gold and convertible foreign currency; an exchange rate of the kroon against the deutsche mark fixed by law; a fully convertible kroon; an absolute preclusion of crediting the government.

Estonia also opted for the currency board system because of the uncertainty prevailing in the prereform money market. The Soviet ruble, called the "occupation ruble," had been discredited; and the Finnish markka, the Swedish krona, and the U.S. dollar had become idols (the deutsche mark, which was chosen as the reserve currency to support the kroon, was not popular in Estonia). These doubts were voiced by Siim Kallas, president of Eesti Pank, in his speech on the first anniversary of the currency reform:

We were far from sure whether the Estonian people and the international public would take seriously a piece of paper we called money, which was backed by the blessing of the Estonian government and of Eesti Pank, but completely unknown in the world. We wanted something more serious, simple and understandable to back our currency. Therefore we returned to the 100 percent guarantee. This decision made the Estonian kroon trustworthy, and faith in the kroon has been constantly increasing. (Kallas, 1993, p. 10)

Thus, the banknotes issued by Eesti Pank had a solid backing; they were, and are, backed sufficiently with convertible foreign currency reserves. The Estonian kroon is a derivative of the deutsche mark, interpreted by Buch (1993) as the direct de facto taking over by the deutsche mark.[2]

In Latvia and Lithuania, the introduction of the lats and litas was actually the second stage of the evolutionary currency reform. Latvia exchanged the rublis gradually for the lats between March 5 and October 18, 1993, at the rate of 200:1. The transition from the talonas to the litas in Lithuania occurred between June 25 and August 1, 1993. Latvia and Lithuania (until April 1, 1994) used a floating exchange rate. When Lithuania later introduced the modified currency board regime (the third stage of the currency reform), the exchange rate of the litas was fixed against the dollar at 4:1. At the beginning of 1994, the Latvijas Banka pegged the lats informally to special drawing rights (SDR) and allowed for the central bank's intervention in the money market. Estonia and Lithuania differ primarily in that the Estonian kroon was pegged to the deutsche mark under the currency board arrangement, with the aim of introducing stability into the Estonian monetary system, whereas in Lithuania, where these principles were adopted with hesitation, the strict pegging that they involved caused heated discussions (lasting to this day). Though the validity of the currency board regime in Estonia and Lithuania continues to be disputed, it has at least proved effective in the economic and political context in Estonia and has met with the approval of foreign commentators (see, e.g., Buch, 1993; Lainela and Sutela, 1994; Träumer, 1994).

### 5.1.3 Monetary Policies

The monetary policy performance of the Baltic states in the period following the currency reforms has been determined mostly by the monetary system chosen. Having opted for the currency board regime, Estonia uses an automatic exchange rate system for regulating the base money supply. Latvia and Lithuania, on the other hand, opted for the classical central bank system, although Lithuania switched to a currency board system similar to the Estonian model on April 1, 1994. The Estonian and Lithuanian arrangements are modified currency boards because their central banks specify obligatory reserve requirements against commercial bank deposit liabilities—10 percent in Estonia and 12 percent in Lithuania.[3] Again, the Estonian and Lithuanian currency boards are endogenous rather than classical exogenous systems.[4] As a result, Hanke, Jonung, and Schuler (1993) do not regard the Estonian arrangement as a currency board.

The monetary policy aspects that have been critical in the monetarization of the Baltic economies are exchange rate policy, money supply, and interest rate policy.

**Exchange Rate Policy and Export Performance**
Though the monetary policies of the three Baltic states have been aimed primarily at maintaining full convertibility of the national currency at stable exchange rates, the important differences in the Estonian, Latvian, and Lithuanian monetary policies concern exchange rate management. Estonia and Lithuania (beginning April 1, 1994) operate under a fixed exchange rate regime. However, the working of the currency board system under a fixed exchange rate system (following the logic of Bretton Woods) is still conditional in Estonia and Lithuania. That is, the exchange rates of the kroon and the litas fluctuate against third currencies to the same extent as the deutsche mark and the dollar. The external value of the Latvian lats, which has been kept by the Latvijas Banka at the level 1 SDR = 0.7997 lats (LVL) since March 1994, also changes against third currencies. The classical view about fixed versus floating exchange rate has to be modified with respect to the monetary systems of Estonia, Lithuania, and Latvia: they have a fixed exchange rate supported by central bank intervention. The monthly exchange rates of the Estonian kroon (against the dollar, the Finnish markka, and the Swedish krona), of the Latvian lats (against the deutsche mark and the dollar), and of the Lithuanian litas (LTL; also against the deutsche mark and the dollar) from June 1992 to December 1994 are presented in Figure 5.2, which also shows the variations in the quarterly exchange rates of the three currencies from mid-1992 to December 1994.

Monetary management has clearly influenced the nominal exchange rates of the Baltic currencies to varying degrees. For example, the exchange rate of the Estonian kroon against the dollar in December 1994 was about the same as in December 1992; however, it was only 65.8 per-

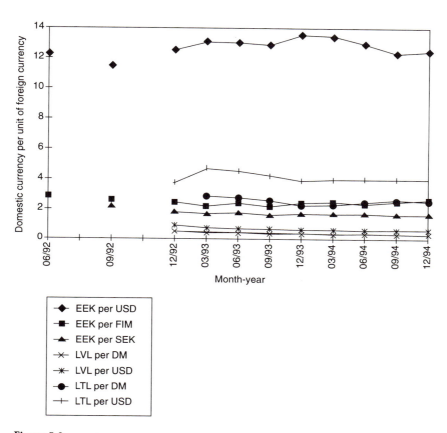

**Figure 5.2**
Average monthly exchange rates of the Eesti Pank, Latvijas Banka, and Lietuvos Banko, June
1992–December 1994
*Note:* EEK = Estonian kroon; FIM = Finnish markka; SEK = Swedish krona; LVL = Latvian
lats; DM = Deutsch mark; LTL = Lithuanian litas.
*Sources:* Eesti Pank, *Bulletin;* Latvijas Banka, *Monetary Statistics; Bulletin of the Bank of
Lithuania.*

cent for the Latvian lats, which had risen against the dollar. By contrast, the Lithuanian litas continued to decline against the dollar before it was pegged against the dollar in April 1994.

All currencies have appreciated in real terms, depending on the rate at which domestic inflation has run ahead of the rate of change in their nominal values. The real appreciation, in turn, has had varying impacts on export performance.

The fixing of the Estonian kroon at the level 1 DM = 8 EEK at the time of the currency reform, which was highly overdevalued with respect to domestic purchasing power, provided the economy with the time and opportunity for restructuring. The arrangement guaranteed the long-term competitiveness of the economy's productive resources, and the under-valued fixed exchange rate worked as a strong barrier against competing imports. The policy was objective in the sense that it corresponded to demand and supply in the money market. True, the demand for foreign currency was excessive in the entire ruble zone. Foreign currency was, after all, a liquid and inflation-free means of saving, on the one hand, and on the other hand, the rubles were plentiful relative to the supply of for-eign currency, which was limited. The fixed exchange rate of the kroon against the deutsche mark excluded its revaluation as a result of the increase in the supply of foreign currencies. This happened as the deut-sche mark strengthened against other currencies, primarily the Swedish krona and the Finnish markka. Though the real exchange rate of the kroon rose gradually, Estonia continued to maintain its competitiveness, which was marked by a sustained increase in exports in both dollars and deutsche marks.

The floating exchange rate of the lats (until March 1994) and, to a lesser extent, of the litas (until April 1994) caused these currencies to appreciate considerably, which affected Latvian and Lithuanian exports. Latvian exports decreased between the first quarter of 1993 and the first quarter of 1994 from 204.4 million lats to 120.9 million lats (40.9 percent), which, when calculated in terms of dollars and deutsche marks, could not be compensated for even by the heavy revaluation of the lats. Only the cessation of the revaluation of the lats by pegging it to SDR in March 1994 contributed to an increase in Latvian exports. There is also a direct connection between the "floating" revaluation of the litas and the decline in Lithuanian exports. The quarterly dollar exports for 1993 and 1994 for the three countries are presented in Figure 5.3.

The free convertibility of the kroon, lats, and litas under IMF Article VIII and liberal foreign exchange transactions have guaranteed the Baltic

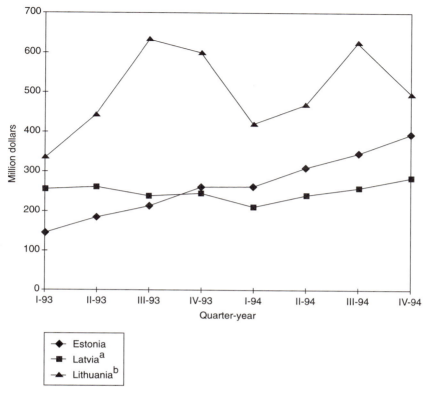

**Figure 5.3**
Exports of the Baltic states in 1993–94 (million dollars)
*Source:* Official statistics of the Baltic states. Turnover in U.S. dollars calculated by the author.
*Notes:*
a. Excluding reexports reported in customs declarations.
b. 1994 preliminary data.

states perfect competition in their foreign exchange markets. The difference between the selling and buying rates has been reduced to a minimum, especially in Estonia, thereby demonstrating great confidence in the
domestic currency. Foreign exchange policies have been most liberal in
Latvia, where foreign currency is treated as an ordinary good. In Estonia,
only licensed banks and foreign exchange bureaus are allowed to sell and
buy foreign currency. Commercial banks need a license from Eesti Pank
for trading in foreign exchange, though only a few small banks cannot
obtain a license. Following the currency reform, Estonia applied a few
restrictions (such as obligatory conversion of foreign currency in bank

accounts and restrictions on opening foreign currency accounts) on the use of foreign currency in order to limit heavy dollarization; these restrictions, however, were fully removed at the beginning of 1994. The limit on the open net foreign exchange position in deutsche marks also was removed for commercial banks. Some restrictions on foreign currency transactions remain in Lithuania.

A difference among the Baltic states is that Eesti Pank quotes only the currencies quoted in Frankfurt (excluding the lats, litas, and Russian ruble), whereas Latvijas Banka and Lietuvos Banko have a wider scope of activity. The central bank of Lithuania, for instance, quotes the national currencies of all post-Soviet states.

Theoretically, the different exchange rate policies should have had different effects on the rate of inflation. The revalued exchange rate of the lats has probably helped to curb inflation in Latvia, but the difference from Estonia is not great, especially from a long-term perspective. For example, the consumer price index rose by 293 percent in Estonia and 307 percent in Latvia between July 1992 and February 1995.

## Money Supply

The Baltic states have oriented their monetary policies to limiting money supply. The central banks that were founded on the currency board principles in Estonia and Lithuania can influence only the base money supply, and even that depends on the changes in foreign currency reserves. However, these countries can, in principle, influence the money supply through a change in the mandatory reserve requirement for commercial banks, which has not been tried. For example, in order to curb inflation and influence the interest rates on loans, Eesti Pank treats the mandatory reserves as the commercial banks' reserves with Eesti Pank, which may be used in a crisis for maintaining the solvency of the banks rather than for regulating banks' loan resources. Eesti Pank is prohibited by law from crediting the central government and local governments. Commercial banks can raise only short-term liquidity loans in the amount of capital and reserves of the Eesti Pank. Thus, Eesti Pank can influence the money supply only with regard to cash in circulation, which has to be fully backed with gold and convertible foreign currency. The Latvijas Banka also can influence the money supply rather moderately, though it has ample opportunities for doing it as the central bank. The mandatory reserve requirement for commercial banks is 8 percent in Latvia. The Latvijas Banka can also refinance the money market and credit the government, but only to a limited extent.

The Baltic states are characterized by a relatively fast increase in money supply resulting from the excessive inflow of foreign currency. Data for selected months in 1993 and 1994 are presented in Figure 5.4. In 1994, the cash in the economy increased by 28.5 percent in Estonia, by 39.5 percent in Latvia, and by 68.6 percent in Lithuania, and the broad money supply (defined as currency outside banks plus all deposits) by 30.8 percent, 47.4 percent, and 73.0 percent, respectively. In Latvia and Lithuania, the money supply increased faster than inflation.

The Baltic states are also characterized by the relatively high importance of cash in the total money supply. The share of cash is especially strong in Latvia, where the ratio of cash in M1 (defined as currency outside banks plus demand deposits) was over 70 percent in 1993. In Estonia, this indicator has been between 40 and 50 percent, and in Lithuania between 50 and 55 percent. A peculiarity of the money supply in Latvia and Lithuania has been the extremely high share of foreign currency deposits (25 to 30 percent since 1993), which is a result of the continuing dollarization and, to some extent, the lack of confidence in the national currencies. The lower share of foreign currency deposits in Estonia was due to the obligatory conversion of foreign currency in bank accounts after the currency reform. The removal of this requirement has increased the share of foreign currency deposits in Estonia. Some enterprises that have frequent contacts with foreign markets refrain from converting their foreign currency despite higher interest on kroon deposits.

The relatively high variability over time of the indicators of money supply suggests that the young money markets of the Baltic states are not yet fully developed. Evidently the currency board is inherently characterized by the high share of cash, because the obligations of the central banks with respect to the commercial banks under the currency board arrangement are limited mainly to cash. That is, deposits are converted into foreign currency in two steps under the currency board system: first, into base or central bank money, and then into reserve money.

### Interest Rate Policies

The Baltic states have no restrictions on interest on deposits and interest on loans, which are determined according to demand and supply in the money market; however, an important component of marginal interest rates is the credit risk. The latter is increased by the general economic uncertainty and by insufficient experience of banks in evaluating credit-worthiness of projects. However, interest rates also vary by countries. Latvia and Lithuania have extremely high (especially when evaluated

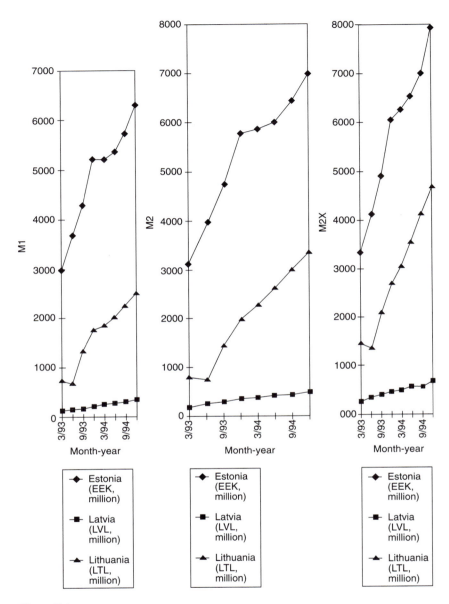

**Figure 5.4**
Money supply in the Baltic states
*Sources:* Eesti Pank, *Bulletin;* Latvijas Banka, *Monetary Statistics; Bulletin of the Bank of Lithuania.*
*Notes:* M1 = currency outside banks + demand deposits; M2 = M1 + time deposits + savings deposits; M2X = M2 + foreign currency deposits.

against the background of the stable exchange rate of the lats and litas) and positive real interest rates; Estonia has relatively moderate and clearly negative real interest rates. Even larger differences occur in the interbank overnight loan rates. They are around 5–6 percent in Estonia. The interbank rate was 25–46 percent in 1994, when the interbank money market was nascent and was restricted for various reasons. The refinancing interest rates of the Latvijas Banka fell from 120 percent in January 1993 to 25 percent in December 1994.

## 5.2 Foreign Economic Relations

The Soviet incorporation of the Baltic states in 1944 marked their forced entry into the unitary economic system of the Soviet Union. Past relations with the world economy were disrupted and were replaced by those with other Soviet republics. Moreover, economic relations with the Soviet East implied a destruction of the traditional production structures and the integrity of the Baltic economy. Under the slogan of socialist reconstruction of the Baltic economies, extraterritorial structures (subordinated to the Soviet Union) were established and, through departmental relations, were detached from the local economy. According to Taagepera (Misiunas and Taagepera, 1983),

It was industry based on Russian investment and Russian labour, managed by Russians according to goals set by Russians, importing a large part of the raw materials from Russia, and exporting most of its products. The whole show was called "Baltic" industrial growth because the Soviets decided to run it on Baltic soil. (p. 333)

The economic relations between Estonia and Latvia (or Lithuania or some other Soviet republic) did not indicate autonomous relations between them as republics but the sum total of deliveries by enterprises located in the territories of Estonia and Latvia (or some other republic) in the form of funds and quotas allocated from Moscow. The relations of enterprises and organizations with foreign countries were managed via all-Union foreign trade associations. Estonian, Latvian, and Lithuanian enterprises exported in world markets not so much on the basis of the fitness of their production as on the export policies of the Soviet Union. Moreover, the overcentralized and detailed organization of foreign trade relations excluded initiatives of producers to enlarge export production. Isolation from the world economy brought about accommodation of enterprises in the domestic market of the Soviet Union. Full protection from possible competition from the world market, which was secured by the foreign trade state monopoly and the nonconvertibility of the ruble, led to the technical backwardness of the Baltic economies, deterioration of their production culture, and a massive decline in their competitiveness in the world market.

### 5.2.1   Reorienting to the West

As recently as 1991, both West and East were pessimistic about the Baltic states' strivings for independence. The share of the Soviet regions was 90 to 95 percent in Baltic exports and about 80 percent in their imports in the 1970s and 1980s. Contacts with the West, which were minimal, were mediated by about a hundred all-Union foreign trade associations, which were centralized monopolies. For example, the exports of Estonia outside the Soviet Union accounted for 2 to 3 percent of its GDP in the second half of the 1980s, and two-thirds was to COMECON countries. Latvia and Lithuania had a similar foreign trade structure.

Under such conditions it was difficult for an outsider to visualize the Baltic economies outside the Soviet Union and the ruble zone, although the Baltic states, in the view of some, had ideal economic preconditions for independent development (see, e.g., Deutsche Bank, 1990). The pessimism was increased by the economic blockade applied by the Soviet central power against Lithuania in 1990. Even after the Baltic states regained independence, open skepticism dominated the thinking of politicians and sovietologists. Take the following view of Jürgen Nötzold (1993):

The destruction of a unitary monetary system and an economic area with an integral economic system leads to the decline in production and income and to increasing socioeconomic destabilization caused by the collapse of the planned economy. It may be assumed that at least half of the decline in outputs has been caused by the interruption of trade between the descendant countries of the Soviet Union. ... The marketing of their [Baltic states'] products remains dependent on the CIS markets. The exports of animal products can be reoriented to Western Europe but only if open markets can be found there. In industrial goods exports, nothing can replace the CIS markets. The continuing economic decline in the CIS countries and the insufficient qualification of industry for export in the West leads the Baltic states to continuous economic stagnation. The maintenance of economic relations with the successors of the Soviet Union, primarily with Russia, needn't mean membership in some economic or monetary alliance, but association agreements with Russia are still indispensable. (p. 55)

The decline in GDP by 40 percent and in industrial output by 60 percent that the Baltic states experienced in 1994 compared with 1990 resulted from the collapse of the Soviet economic system, which disrupted economic relations. However, the separation from the former Soviet economic system was an indispensable precondition for macroeconomic stabilization and structural changes in the Baltic states. This is borne out by a comparison of the rates of inflation (in Figure 5.5) in Estonia, Latvia, and Lithuania, which were lower than those in the CIS nations.

The reestablishment of the independence of the Baltic states, coupled with their withdrawal from the ruble zone, brought rapid shifts in their foreign trade geography. Detailed information is presented in Tables 5.1–5.3.

In 1991 the former USSR accounted for 94.8 percent of Estonian exports and 84.7 percent of imports, but during 1992 its share dropped to 47.0 percent of exports and 45.4 percent of imports. The respective figures for Latvia were 96.8 and 49.9 percent for exports and 87.2 and 47.1 percent for imports. Lithuanian performance was more conservative: the share of the former Soviet Union decreased from 94.5 percent in 1991 to 71.5 percent in 1992 in exports, and from 90.2 percent to 82.0 percent in imports. The slow Lithuanian transition to a new geographical trade structure might have been caused by the slow pace of economic reforms in Lithuania compared with Estonia and Latvia. Actually, these shifts in the foreign trade geography of Estonia and Latvia happened in an even shorter period of one to two months. The share of Western partners, which was 5.1 percent of Estonian exports in 1991, increased to 40.9 percent in the first quarter of 1992.

From a broader perspective, the reorientation to Western markets resulted from several factors: the accelerating inflation and the sharp decline in the exchange rate of the ruble (from the end of 1991), which made export for convertible currency (i.e., outside the former Soviet Union) extremely tempting for Baltic enterprises; the introduction of a national convertible currency and withdrawal from the ruble zone; sharply increasing risk in trade with Eastern markets caused by the insolvency of consumers and payment arrears; explosive economic decline in the CIS countries; and the administrative restrictions imposed by Russia on the Baltic, especially Estonian, foreign trade, often resembling an economic blockade.

The introduction of freely convertible national currencies with stable external value pushed trade to Western markets. The kroon, lats, and litas, which were undervalued in terms of purchasing power, made Baltic producers competitive in Western markets. At the same time, exports to the ruble zone were restricted by the rapidly increasing appreciation of the Baltic currencies against CIS currencies. As the ruble and other CIS currencies cheapened, the competitiveness of Baltic goods declined in Eastern markets. In principle, this situation favored imports from the East, but

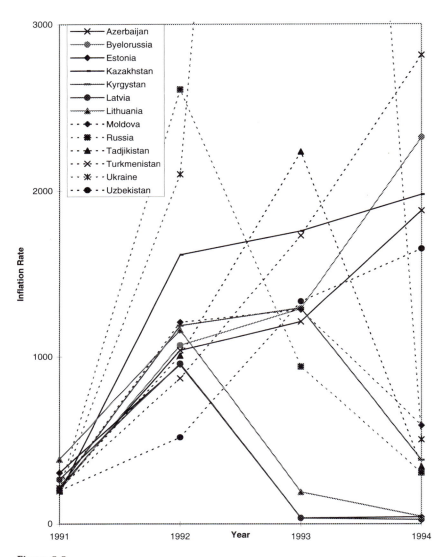

**Figure 5.5**
Consumer price index in the Baltic and the CIS states (annual average, 1990 = 100; data for
Russia and the Baltic states are from December to December)
*Source: Sodruzhestvo nezavisimykh gosudarstv v 1994 godu, 1995*; official statistics of the Baltic
states.
*Note:* 1993: Ukraine = 10,256.

**Table 5.1**
Foreign trade geography of Estonia, 1990–1994 (percent)

| | Exports | | | | | Imports | | | | |
|---|---|---|---|---|---|---|---|---|---|---|
| | 1990 | 1991 | 1992 | 1993 | 1994 | 1990 | 1991 | 1992 | 1993 | 1994 |
| Western | 5.9 | 5.1 | 53.0 | 57.4 | 56.0 | 18.0 | 14.7 | 54.2 | 72.4 | 75.6 |
| EU | | 3.9 | 43.2 | 48.3 | 47.8 | | 6.0 | 44.6 | 60.3 | 63.2 |
| Germany | 0.3 | 0.2 | 3.9 | 8.0 | 6.8 | 2.3 | 0.8 | 8.3 | 10.7 | 10.0 |
| Finland | 1.1 | 2.3 | 21.2 | 20.7 | 17.8 | 1.6 | 2.0 | 22.6 | 27.9 | 29.9 |
| Sweden | 0.4 | 0.5 | 7.7 | 9.5 | 10.8 | 0.1 | 0.8 | 5.9 | 8.9 | 8.9 |
| USA | 0.2 | 0.1 | 1.9 | 1.9 | 1.8 | 0.9 | 3.5 | 2.4 | 2.7 | 2.5 |
| Baltic States | 8.8 | 11.5 | 12.1 | 12.3 | 13.6 | 7.9 | 11.4 | 5.3 | 5.6 | 4.0 |
| CIS | 85.3 | 83.3 | 34.9 | 30.3 | 30.4 | 74.1 | 73.3 | 40.1 | 21.7 | 20.4 |
| Russia | 55.0 | 56.5 | 20.8 | 22.6 | 23.1 | 51.8 | 45.9 | 28.4 | 17.2 | 16.8 |
| Country unknown | | 0.1 | 0.0 | 0.0 | | | 0.6 | 0.4 | 0.3 | |
| Total | 100.0 | 100.0 | 100.0 | 100.0 | 100.0 | 100.0 | 100.0 | 100.0 | 100.0 | 100.0 |

*Source:* Official statistics of Estonia.

**Table 5.2**
Foreign trade geography of Latvia in 1990–1994 (percent*)

| | Exports | | | | | Imports | | | | |
|---|---|---|---|---|---|---|---|---|---|---|
| | 1990 | 1991 | 1992 | 1993 | 1994 | 1990 | 1991 | 1992 | 1993 | 1994 |
| Western | 4.8 | 3.2 | 50.1 | 46.2 | 49.1 | 25.5 | 12.8 | 40.9 | 34.0 | 52.6 |
| EU | | | 39.9 | 33.4 | 39.2 | | | 29.5 | 27.4 | 40.6 |
| Germany | | 0.8 | 7.9 | 6.6 | 10.5 | | 1.3 | 15.0 | 10.0 | 13.5 |
| Finland | | 0.2 | 3.7 | 2.0 | 2.4 | | 0.8 | 2.6 | 4.2 | 8.5 |
| Sweden | | 0.6 | 7.5 | 6.5 | 6.9 | | 0.4 | 3.8 | 5.3 | 6.4 |
| USA | | 0.0 | 0.4 | 0.6 | 1.2 | | 0.4 | 2.6 | 1.2 | 2.0 |
| Baltic States | 8.3 | 8.6 | 4.9 | 6.2 | 8.2 | 10.6 | 15.3 | 9.5 | 13.5 | 9.5 |
| CIS | 86.9 | 88.2 | 45.0 | 47.6 | 42.7 | 63.9 | 71.9 | 37.6 | 38.2 | 30.4 |
| Russia | 50.7 | 54.4 | 26.0 | 29.6 | 28.1 | 41.9 | 44.5 | 27.9 | 28.5 | 23.6 |
| Country unknown | | | | | | | | 12.0 | 14.3 | 7.5 |
| Total | 100.0 | 100.0 | 100.0 | 100.0 | 100.0 | 100.0 | 100.0 | 100.0 | 100.0 | 100.0 |

*Source:* Official statistics of Latvia.
*Note:* * Excluding re-exports and re-imports reported in customs declarations.

**Table 5.3**
Foreign trade geography of Lithuania in 1990–1994 (percent)

|  | Exports | | | | | Imports | | | | |
|---|---|---|---|---|---|---|---|---|---|---|
|  | 1990 | 1991 | 1992 | 1993 | 1994* | 1990 | 1991 | 1992 | 1993 | 1994* |
| Western | 10.3 | 5.1 | 28.5 | 25.1 | 42.5 | 21.6 | 9.8 | 18.0 | 14.6 | 45.5 |
| EU |  |  |  | 16.8 | 30.1 |  |  |  | 8.1 | 32.3 |
| Germany | 1.3 | 0.6 | 4.6 | 6.0 | 11.5 | 3.3 | 2.5 | 4.6 | 3.8 | 13.8 |
| Finland | 0.7 | 0.3 | 1.3 | 1.1 | 1.0 | 0.3 | 0.1 | 0.9 | 0.8 | 2.9 |
| Sweden | 0.1 | 0.3 | 2.7 | 2.1 | 3.1 | 0.2 | 0.0 | 1.1 | 0.3 | 2.4 |
| USA | 0.1 | 0.0 | 0.3 | 0.4 | 0.7 | 0.8 | 1.5 | 2.7 | 1.9 | 2.0 |
| Baltic States | 5.0 | 9.0 | 5.9 | 12.4 | 11.0 | 5.9 | 6.4 | 2.9 | 1.6 | 4.3 |
| CIS | 84.7 | 85.5 | 65.6 | 62.5 | 46.7 | 72.5 | 83.8 | 79.1 | 83.8 | 50.2 |
| Russia | 50.1 | 56.5 | 31.8 | 43.5 | 28.2 | 42.7 | 49.6 | 57.7 | 74.0 | 39.3 |
| Total | 100.0 | 100.0 | 100.0 | 100.0 | 100.0 | 100.0 | 100.0 | 100.0 | 100.0 | 100.0 |

*Source:* Official Statistics of Lithuania.
*Note:* *1994 preliminary data.

the increasing risk of Eastern trade and the trade barriers established by Russia forced Baltic enterprises to avoid those markets.

Despite the stabilization in the foreign trade geography of Estonia and Latvia (which lags by two to three years in Lithuania), the markets are not yet fully formed. For example, the unnaturally high share of Nordic countries in Estonian trade is temporary. This, however, is not surprising. For geographical-cultural reasons, the Estonian economy "discovered" the West for itself, first in Finland and Sweden, which opened up Estonia for the West. At the same time, the share of the large economies—among them the United Kingdom, France, the United States, Germany, and Japan —is unusually low in Estonian foreign trade.

Finally, Baltic foreign trade, despite a striking geographical restructuring, is nowhere close to its structure in the 1930s. In 1936, the Soviet Union took 3.3, 3.0, and 5.3 percent of Estonian, Latvian, and Lithuanian exports. The rest (including intra-Baltic transactions) were exports to the West (including Poland and Danzig). Similarly, Estonia, Latvia, and Lithuania obtained 5.8, 2.9, and 9.4 percent of their imports from the Soviet Union. The rest (including intra-Baltic shipments) came from the West (including Poland and Danzig).

### 5.2.2 Commodity Composition of Trade

While the trends in the geographical distribution of Baltic foreign trade are currently distinct, the commodity structure of exports and imports is only in the initial formative stage. The Baltic states export almost everything that can be sold because the purchasing power of the domestic market is small. Besides, the restructuring of production in its adjustment to the production costs and prices of world market is still under way. It is too soon to speak of comparative advantage in a situation of insufficient and distorted information. The structure of imports is influenced by abnormally strong noneconomic factors and preferences, including prolonged, administratively suppressed consumption. Traditional articles of export of the Baltic states have been, and still are, foodstuffs, textiles, timber, and wood products. Raw materials and machinery dominate their imports.

### 5.2.3  Main Features of Foreign Trade Policies

The foreign trade policies of the Baltic states so far have been influenced by obligatory steps rather than by strategic planning (see Hansson, 1994; Hansen and Sorsa, 1994; Sorsa, 1994). The primary aim of the Baltic states has been to exit from the ruble zone and to integrate into the European economies while fulfilling the role of a bridge between the East and the West. The most distinct trends so far have been in Estonia. In 1992, Estonia started to move unambiguously toward a liberal and open market economy. It has adopted the most liberal foreign trade policy among the Baltic states, with the aim of joining the European Union as soon as possible. Estonia's preparedness for that objective is proved primarily by its rejection of a transition period in its association with the European Union.

Two periods can be distinguished in the foreign trade policies of the Baltic states. When they were in the ruble zone, they tried to protect their domestic market from aggressive ruble penetration by restricting exports and promoting imports.

Thus, they applied quotas and licenses on exports in 1990 and 1991. These were abandoned gradually, Estonia being the first to give them up in the first half of 1992. The remaining export restrictions specify conditions for particular goods (such as alcohol, cultural artifacts, hunting trophies, and explosives). Estonia also established a state monopoly for metal trading in 1993, in order to regulate commerce that had acquired criminal aspects. In 1994, the export of gravel and hard-melting clay was prohibited. The only export duty was applied to rapeseed oil. Metal export is also a state monopoly in Latvia. Lithuanian export restrictions combined export taxes (removed in November 1994) and export quotas, which in 1993 and 1994 applied to pigs, grain, bread, clover seed, unprocessed oak and ash wood, pesticides, and some other goods.

Essential differences prevail in import policies. Estonia has generally avoided import restrictions. By contrast, Latvia, and Lithuania in particular, have applied extensive protectionist measures. Import duties in Lithuania, for instance, are defined as a combination of tariff rates from 5 to 100 percent and a fixed minimum absolute tariff. These import policies often express, quite clearly, the role of specific interest groups. For example, on May 28, 1993, the government levied a temporary import duty on potatoes in the amount of 5,000 talonas per ton in order to provide producers with opportunities to sell their previous year's output as late as possible in the summer (until July 1). Import duties, which in Estonia were applied only to particular goods (such as alcohol, tobacco products, furs, cars, motorboats, yachts, and some other goods) have been replaced by excise duties. An experiment was the establishment of an import duty on flour in 1993, which ruined the local macaroni industry because the local products were not competitive—products made with imported flour, due to the higher price; products made with local flour, due to low quality.

## 5.3  Conclusions

Half a century of Soviet planned economy in the Baltic states resulted in the demonetarization of their economies (by 1990 the ruble at the officially fixed price had become the worst currency); their isolation from the world economy (foreign exports accounted for only a small percentage of GDP); and the anonymity of property ownership (if people are the owners, who, specifically, is the owner?).

The Baltic states thus faced a threefold challenge of economic monetarization, integration into the world economy, and denationalization of public property. They have succeeded in accomplishing the first two.

First, the Baltic states have introduced fully convertible national currencies with stable external values, an accomplishment that has evaded most postsocialist countries. However, the Estonian kroon lost 75 percent of its initial internal value during the macroeconomic stabilization between July 1992 and March 1995. The Latvian lats and Lithuanian litas lost 75 percent and 94 percent, respectively (including the rublis and talonas, which were the predecessors of the lats and litas, and circulated at the time of the Estonian currency reform as parallel currencies), of their internal value.

Second, the Baltic states have managed to reorient their economies to the West. The former USSR accounted for 94.8 percent of Estonian and Lithuanian exports and 94.5 percent of Latvian exports in the year preceding the reestablishment of independence; three years later, in 1994, the share of the former USSR had dropped to 44 percent of Estonian exports, to 50.9 percent of Latvian exports, and to 47.8 percent of Lithuanian exports (CIS states accounted for 30.4 percent, 42.7 percent, and 46.7 percent, respectively, of Estonian, Latvian, and Lithuanian exports). The integration of the Baltic states into the world economy is also marked by overall economic openness. The exports of goods and services accounted for 65 percent of Estonian GDP in 1993. This figure for Latvia was 73 percent, and for Lithuania, 86 percent (compare these shares with 55 percent for the Czech Republic, 35 percent for Bulgaria, 30 percent for Hungary, 24 percent for Poland, and 23 percent for Romania). However, these indicators are not fully comparable because of the differences in price levels and proportions of tradable and nontradable economic sectors.

Finally, ownership reform is by its nature slower than monetarization and foreign trade participation. The quantitative progress there is much less noticeable.

Based on the results of their economic reforms, the Baltic states, especially Estonia and Latvia, rank among the successful Central and East European postsocialist countries. Schrader (1994) sums up the Estonian "interim balance sheet" in the context of economic monetarization and globalization in the spring of 1994 as follows: "GDP is decreasing at a decreasing rate, the monetary situation is stable by East-European standards, trade orientation to Western markets shows a recovery" (p. 36). Similar judgments on the performance of the Baltic economies appear in the reports of the international agencies. The Baltic states have indeed made an effective transition to an open market economy.

The reforms, however, as in other Central and East European countries, have not occurred painlessly. The transition from a moneyless economy to one based on monetary regulation, removal of state subsidization, and opening to the world economy has involved decline in production and structural changes in these economies. Yesterday's full employment, guaranteed by ineffective production and inflationary emission, is being replaced by moderate overall and high sectoral unemployment (highest in heavy industry, which produced for the Soviet market, and in agriculture). The abandonment of the cheap Soviet ruble and the choice of restricted monetary and budgetary policy has helped to differentiate current income of the population. The Baltic states, however, prefer to promote long-term objectives (such as creating preconditions for economic growth and increased investment) rather than serve interests of the moment (marked by higher wages in the state sector and higher pensions today). As for the resulting phenomena of high unemployment, income differentiation, and decline in the birth rate, they are not specific to the Baltic states. They represent the unavoidable price of the economic mismanagement of the Soviet era and the inevitable cost of moving to independent statehood.

## Notes

1. The difference between the classical and modified currency board arrangements is presented in note 4.

2. However, as explained in note 4, the Estonian currency board arrangement is endogenous.

3. By contrast, commercial banks under a strict currency board choose their reserve levels to cover deposit liabilities.

4. An endogenous currency board can be subjected to political pressures by the national legislature, whereas an exogenous currency board can be made independent of local political maneuvering.

Thus, commenting on the Estonian currency board arrangement, Hanke, Jonung, and Schuler write:

… in Estonia institutional protection for the exchange rate and for the reserve ratio [100 percent backing of the monetary base by gold and foreign currency assets] is weak. The Bank of Estonia cannot devalue the kroon by itself, but the legislature can authorize the Bank of Estonia to devalue the kroon. Advisors to the Estonian government on the monetary reform have characterized the exchange rate as a "peg" … rather than a fixed rate, and the governor of the Bank of Estonia has warned that he would have to devalue the kroon if the Estonian parliament approved a high minimum wage. (1993, pp. 76–77)

By contrast, the same authors had proposed an exogenous currency board for Estonia and suggested that the kroon be linked to the Swedish krona. They provide the following details:

To protect the proposed Estonian currency board from political pressure to convert it into a central bank, we suggested that it operate according to a strict constitution; that it be legally independent from the Estonian government; and that the Swedish government appoint non-Estonian directors to the currency board, who would have veto power over the Estonian directors. The actual Estonian monetary reform included none of these features. (ibid., p. 76)

## References

*Baltic Independent.* 1993–95.

*Das Baltikum in Zahlen. Estland, Lettland, Litauen, Memelgebiet.* 1995. Königsberg: Institut für Osteuropäische Wirtschaft.

Buch, C. M. 1993. "Das erste Jahr der Krone—Estlands Erfahrungen mit der Währungsreform." *Die Weltwirtschaft* no. 4, pp. 441–465.

*Bulletin of the Bank of Lithuania.* 1993, 1994.

Czech National Bank. 1994. *Annual Report 1993.* Prague: Czech National Bank.

Desai, P. 1989. "Perestroika, Prices and the Ruble Problem." *Harriman Institute Forum* 2, no. 11, pp. 1–11.

Deutsche Bank. 1990. *Die Sowjetunion im Umbruch. Fakten zu den Sowjetrepubliken.* Frankfurt am Main: Deutsche Bank.

Dornbusch, Rudiger, and Holger Wolf. 1990. "Monetary Overhang and Reforms in the 1940s." Cambridge, Mass.: Department of Economics, MIT. (Mimeo).

Eesti Pank. *Bulletin.* 1993–95.

Hanke, S. H., L. Jonung, and K. Schuler. 1992. *Monetary Reform for a Free Estonia. A Currency Board Solution.* Stockholm: SNS Förlag.

Hanke, S. H., L. Jonung, and K. Schuler. 1993. "Estonia: It's Not a Currency Board System!" *Transition* no. 1. vol. 4, p. 12.

Hansen, J., and Piritta Sorsa. 1994. "Estonia: A Shining Star from the Baltics." In Constantine Michalopoulos and David Tarr, eds., *Trade in the New Independent States.* Washington, D.C.: World Bank.

Hansson, A. 1994. "The Political-Economy of Macroeconomic and Foreign Trade Policy in Estonia." In Constantine Michalopoulos and David Tarr, eds., *Trade in the New Independent States.* Washington, D.C.: The World Bank.

International Monetary Fund. 1993. *Latvia.* IMF Economic Review 6. Washington, D.C.: IMF.

Kallas, S. 1993. "Pros and Cons of the Reintroduction of the Estonian Kroon." Paper presented at Conference on the Reintroduction of the Estonian Kroon. Tallinn, June 18, 1993.

Kallas, S., T. Made, E. Savisaar, and M. Titma. 1987. "Ettepanek: Kogu Eesti NSV täielikule isemajandamisele." [Proposal: The Whole Estonian SSR to Full Self-management]. *Edasi*, September 26, p. 3.

Kuddo, A., ed. 1994. *Eesti sotsiaalstatistikat.* [Estonian Social Statistics]. Tallinn.

Lainela, S., and P. Sutela. 1994. *The Baltic Economies in Transition.* Helsinki: Bank of Finland.

Latvijas Banka. 1993, 1994. *Monetary Statistics.* Riga: Latvijas Banka.

McKinnon, R. 1991. *The Order of Economic Liberalization: Financial Control in the Transition to a Market Economy.* Baltimore: Johns Hopkins University Press.

Misiunas, R. J., and R. Taagepera. 1983. *The Baltic States: Years of Dependence, 1940–1980.* Berkeley: University of California Press.

*Narodnoe khozyaistvo SSSR. Statisticheskii ezhegodnik.* [National Economy of the USSR. Statistical Yearbook]. 1986–91. Moscow: gosudarstvennyi komitet SSSR po statistike.

*Narodnoe khozyaistvo SSSR za 70 let. Jubileinii statisticheskii ezhegodnik.* [National Economy of the USSR During 70 Years. Jubilee Statistical Yearbook]. 1987. Moscow: gosudarstvennyi komitet SSSR po statistike.

Nordhaus, W. 1990. " Soviet Economic Reform: The Longest Road." *Brookings Papers in Economic Activity* 1: 287–308.

Nötzold, J. 1993. "Können wirtschaftliche Interessen die Nachfolgestaaten der Sowjetunion Zusammenhalten." *Europäische Rundschau* 2, pp. 51–55.

*Oma rahale ülemineku kontseptsioonid.* [Concepts for Introducing National Currency]. 1990. Tallinn.

Schrader, K. 1994. *Estland auf dem Weg zur Marktwirtschaft: Eine Zwischenbilanz.* Kiel Discussion Papers 226, Kiel: Institute for World Economics.

Shik, O. 1972. *Der dritte Weg. Die marksistisch-leninistische Theorie und die moderne Industriegesellschaft.* Hamburg: Albrecht Knaus Verlag.

Shik, O. 1979. *Humane Wirtschaftsdemokratie. Ein Dritter Weg.* Hamburg: Hoffmann und Campe Verlag.

*Sodruzhestvo nezavisimykh gosudarstv v 1994 godu. Kratkii spravochnik predvaritel'nykh statisticheskikh itogov.* [Cooperation of Independent States in 1994]. 1995. Moscow: gosudarstvennyi komitet rossiskoi federatsii po statistike.

Sorsa, P. 1994. "Lithuania: Trade Issues in Transition." In Constantine Michalopoulos and David Tarr, eds., *Trade in the New Independent States.* Washington, D.C.: World Bank.

Träumer, F. 1994. "Währungsreformen in den baltischen Ländern." Bulletin, Deutsche Bank Research. Frankfurt am Main (April 11), pp. 13–20.

Vilks, A. 1992. "Zur Frage der Währungsordnung in den baltischen Staaten." In *Die Wirtschaft der baltischen Staaten im Umbruch.* Cologne: Verlag Wissenschaft und Politik.

# 6         Finland

## Urpo Kivikari

The revolutionary process in Eastern Europe, culminating in the disappearance of the Second World and its transition to democracy and a market economy, has not left the First World untouched. Naturally the demise of the Soviet Union and other socialist countries had varying effects on the rest of the world. Apart from reunified Germany, these changes probably had the greatest economic impact on Finland. The trade with the CMEA member countries was far more important to Finland than to any other Organization for Economic Cooperation and Development (OECD) member (see Table 6.1). The Finnish framework for trade relations with the socialist countries also was unique.

Finland's trade with the socialist countries, especially the Soviet Union, was often described as a success story compared with the poor progress of other East-West trade and the distortions of intra-CMEA trade. Finland's exports to the Soviet Union had experienced a slight decline since the mid-1980s, and in 1991 they dropped by two-thirds. This meant that Finnish-Soviet trade experienced an abrupt normalization just before the end of the Soviet Union.

Finland was the Western country most affected by the transition's "shock treatment." However, it quickly managed to overcome the setback in East-West trade. In 1993, the growth rate of Finland's exports to the transition economies was higher than that of any other OECD member. The explanation for this rapid recovery can be found in part by looking at a set of characteristics unique to Finland that led to the earlier successes and failures in Finnish-Soviet trade. Although some of the special features of this development are unique to Finland, the case is also applicable in a wider context and provides a basis for general conclusions on the external effects of transition.

**Table 6.1**
The significance of exports to the East (CMEA member countries) for the national economy measured by the share (%) of the exports to the East in total exports (1), and in gross domestic product (2)

| | 1970 | | 1975 | | 1985 | | 1988 | | 1989 | | 1990 | |
|---|---|---|---|---|---|---|---|---|---|---|---|---|
| | (1) | (2) | (1) | (2) | (1) | (2) | (1) | (2) | (1) | (2) | (1) | (2) |
| Finland | 15.7 | 3.32 | 23.9 | 4.64 | 23.4 | 5.84 | 16.4 | 3.45 | 16.2 | 3.19 | 14.0 | 2.71 |
| Austria | 12.9 | 2.53 | 17.0 | 3.41 | 11.0 | 2.91 | 9.7 | 2.37 | 9.9 | 2.54 | 10.4 | 2.71 |
| FRG | 3.8 | 0.70 | 7.2 | 1.55 | 4.0 | 1.18 | 4.5 | 1.22 | 5.0 | 1.42 | 4.9 | 1.31 |
| Sweden | 5.0 | 1.01 | 6.3 | 1.51 | 2.5 | 0.77 | 2.2 | 0.61 | 2.4 | 0.65 | 2.3 | 0.59 |
| France | 3.6 | 0.45 | 5.0 | 0.76 | 3.0 | 0.55 | 2.2 | 0.38 | 2.1 | 0.38 | 1.9 | 0.33 |
| Great Britain | 3.2 | 0.50 | 3.0 | 0.55 | 1.5 | 0.34 | 1.6 | 0.27 | 1.6 | 0.29 | 1.4 | 0.27 |
| OECD | 2.9 | 0.30 | 4.6 | 0.62 | 2.7 | 0.39 | 2.5 | 0.36 | 2.7 | 0.40 | 2.6 | 0.39 |

*Source:* OECD statistics.

## 6.1 Trade with the Soviet Union

### 6.1.1 Background

At the end of World War II, into which Finland was drawn because of the separate "Winter War" (1939–40) with the Soviet Union, Finland was among the defeated nations. However, the country was not occupied by a foreign army or under foreign rule. Hence, after the war Finland was able to continue its development as a Western democracy and market economy.

Finland's foreign trade and payments were gradually liberalized after it joined the IMF in 1948 and GATT in 1950. In 1958, the Finnish markka became freely convertible in commercial exchanges. Finland also became a member of other international communities and organizations compatible with its outlook and policies. For example, Finland has participated in the cooperation of Nordic countries (Nordic Council, 1951), in Western European integration through the European Free Trade Association (from 1961), and in the work of global organizations of developed market economies such as the OECD. Finland became a member of the European Union in 1995.

A central prerequisite for Finland's Western orientation and neutral policy was formed by good and stable relations with the Soviet Union. The basis for Finnish-Soviet political relations, beginning 1948, was established by the Treaty of Friendship, Cooperation, and Mutual Assistance. A major requirement of the treaty was that Finland repel any attack on the Soviet Union through Finnish territory. This treaty and the Soviet

**Table 6.2**
The development of Finnish-Soviet trade

| Years | Share (%) of Finnish-Soviet trade in | | |
| --- | --- | --- | --- |
| | Total Soviet foreign trade | Western-Soviet foreign trade | Total Finnish foreign trade |
| 1951–55 | 3.9 | 25.5 | 14.4 |
| 1956–60 | 3.1 | 18.1 | 16.4 |
| 1961–65 | 2.7 | 14.4 | 14.7 |
| 1966–70 | 2.6 | 12.2 | 14.2 |
| 1971–75 | 3.1 | 11.0 | 15.0 |
| 1976–80 | 3.5 | 11.2 | 13.6 |
| 1981–85 | 3.9 | 13.2 | 23.4 |
| 1986–90 | 2.9 | 11.5 | 14.1 |
| 1991 | 2.9 | 5.2 | 6.6 |

*Source:* Soviet and Finnish trade statistics.

view of a linkage between its interests and Finland's policy had restrictive effects on Finland. For example, Finland did not participate in the Marshall Plan and could not proceed with Western integration at the same pace as its neighbors Sweden and Norway.

The war reparations that Finland had to pay from 1946 to 1952 created the basis for exports to the Soviet Union. When Finland and the Soviet Union initiated five-year trading agreements in 1951, they became important trading partners (see Table 6.2).

Due to the large volume of trade with the Soviet Union, total Finnish trade with the CMEA member countries was important in comparison to trade with other Western countries (see Table 6.1). Until the second half of the 1960s, Finland was the largest Western trading partner of the Soviet Union, and thereafter usually the second largest, surpassed only by West Germany.

The high level of Finnish-Soviet trade cannot be explained by the trading potential of Finland, which has a population of five million people, nor by the geographical closeness of the two countries. The most important factors that led to the development of the special Finnish-Soviet trade relationship are outlined below.

Politics promotes trade. Soviet foreign trade was a servant of foreign policy rather than of the economy. Soviet striving for friendly and stable political relations with Finland resulted in preferential treatment of trade with Finland. Finland's official position, which was expressed in Finnish trade policy, also favored good political relations and promoted the utilization of the neighboring superpower's trading potential. Imports from the Soviet Union received the same treatment as the goods imported tariff-free from the EFTA member countries and later from the European Community. The policy was to avoid any discrimination against the Soviet Union arising from Finland's Western integration. Nevertheless, Finland's trade with the Soviet Union was not in contradiction to the embargo policy of Co-Ordinating Committee for Multilateral Export Controls (COCOM), which Finland observed but did not join because of the country's policy of neutrality.

Soviet preferential policy toward Finland resulted in a special system of agreements and institutions, since effective tariffs did not exist in the Soviet centralized economy. The basis of the preferential position rested on a bilateral trading system until 1991, twenty years longer than with any other developed Western country. The main elements of the bilateral trading system included clearing accounts in the Bank of Finland and in the Foreign Trade Bank of the Soviet Union, as well as five-year agreements and annual protocols concerning mutual trade. The five-year agreements consisted of estimated quotas of goods to be exported from each country during the agreed period. More detailed lists of goods to be traded were specified in annual trade protocols. Within the framework of the government trade agreements, Finnish companies and Soviet foreign trade organizations agreed on actual deals, which for various reasons often deviated substantially from the anticipated trade flows.

The ruble was the clearing unit of account, but payments to Finnish exporters were made in the Finnish markka. The payments were made in cash, even in large transactions such as ship deliveries and construction projects, until the mid-1980s, when customary international payment practices were gradually adopted. One of the rules of the clearing system was that a certain percentage of each commodity had to be of Finnish origin. The share of imported Western input on average had to be below one-fifth.

The main principle of bilateral trading was to keep the clearing account as balanced as possible. The balance was achieved primarily by adjusting trade flows. If Finland had a deficit, Finnish companies increased their deliveries to the Soviet Union. If Finland had a surplus, it could be transferred from an interest-free clearing account to a special interest-bearing account as a credit. A common device, which was used to adjust trade flows, was crude oil trading between Russia and third countries via the Finnish company Neste. At the end of the 1980s, for example, Soviet oil imports into Finland amounted to about one-fifth of Finland's exports to the Soviet Union. At the same time, the share of payments in convertible currencies increased to one-fifth of total payments (Kajaste, 1993, p. 116).

Although business on the Finnish side was managed at the company level, some features of the state trading system can be seen. One of the conspicuous features was the high concentration of trade. More than half of all imports from the Soviet Union was handled by a single company, the state-owned oil and chemical corporation Neste. Some six hundred to seven hundred firms exported to the Soviet Union in the 1970s, compared with more than three thousand exporters to Sweden. By the end of the 1980s, the total number of Finnish exporters to the USSR had increased by about one thousand, but the five largest exporters still accounted for 40 percent of Finland's total exports (Sutela, 1991, p. 304).

In addition to traditional commodity trade, operations like industrial cooperation, construction projects, and joint ventures (since their approval in 1987) played a role in Finnish-Soviet economic relations. In the 1970s and 1980s several big projects were completed by Finnish companies, mostly near the Finnish border, including hydroelectric plants, paper industry complexes, a mining complex, and hotels. The most significant Soviet projects in Finland were deliveries to two nuclear power stations and to the steel industry. Operations other than traditional trade of goods and services increased considerably in the second half of the 1980s. However, their frequency remained low and the pattern differed from that in other markets. Activities such as direct investments, requiring greater financial and managerial commitment, were adopted more slowly in the Soviet market than elsewhere (Hirvensalo, 1993, p. 114).

Bilateralism, including the clearing mechanism, did not favor the establishment of joint ventures. However, the number of operating joint ventures, exceeding two hundred in 1991, as well as the size of Finnish joint ventures, were comparable with those of other big Western trading partners of the USSR (Nieminen, 1991).

### 6.1.2  The Functioning of the Clearing System

**The Cyclical Impact**

The primary source of cyclical fluctuations in Finnish-Soviet trade was the one-sided commodity structure of Finnish imports. The share of crude oil and oil products was remarkably high, representing 50–80 percent of the total imports from the USSR after the first oil crisis in the 1970s. Hence, the value of total imports was heavily dependent on the oil price, which under the bilateral trade system decisively affected Soviet purchasing power (and consequently Finland's exports). The dominant position of oil had a countercyclical impact on the Finnish economy. A rise in the price of oil increased the exports of Finnish products to the Soviet Union, but it generally decreased the demand in Western and domestic markets. From the first oil crisis until 1991, exports to the USSR had a balancing impact on the cyclical development of exports and production in Finland (Kajaste, 1993, pp. 114–15). For many companies, however, it was more important to level seasonal fluctuations with deliveries to the USSR than to balance cyclical developments. The timing of the production process could be adjusted between the exports to the East and the West, which improved the capacity utilization rates, especially in the clothing and footwear industries (Kivikari, 1985).

The countercyclical impact of Soviet trade was noted by many macroeconomic and microeconomic observers. However, the five-year agreements and annual protocols did not dampen the cycles or contribute to more balanced development of Soviet-Finnish trade than those in Western trade. Trade ex post often deviated substantially from trade ex ante. Soviet five-year planning cycles affected trade flows (Dahlstedt, 1975, p. 105), but the oil price was much more significant. Because of the bilateral trading system, the fluctuations of exports to the USSR were greater than the fluctuations of Finnish exports to the West. Moreover, Finland's exports usually varied more sharply than other OECD exports to the USSR (Hukkinen, 1991; Kivikari, 1989; Hirvensalo, 1993; Kajaste 1993). There were wide variations in the exports of shoes and clothing, which could rapidly adjust their deliveries when a rise in the price of oil unexpectedly gave "room" for Finnish exports. On the other hand, these industries also had to be more flexible in giving up exports than the traditional exporters in the metal and paper industries when the USSR reduced its imports.

In the first half of the 1980s the expansion of exports to the East created a "gray" financial market (interfirm banking transactions), which contributed further to the overheating of the domestic economy.

It was not surprising that the authorities' concern about the balance of the clearing account and the Finnish firms' concern to increase exports to the USSR were in direct conflict. From a macroeconomic point of view, due to the striving for balanced trade, the choice was often either to profit from maintaining an interest-free debt to the USSR (resulting from the rise of oil prices) or to increase Finnish employment by rapidly expanding exports to the USSR. Domestic pressures on the government usually led to the latter, which often caused a quick surplus in Finland's clearing account

(Kivikari, 1985). During 1981–89 approximately one-fifth of exports to the USSR was financed by the Bank of Finland (Kajaste, 1993, p. 116).

## The Structural Effects

The Government Trade Commission and the trade protocols succeeded at least partly in providing Finnish companies with information and signals about the Soviet market and buying intentions. On the other hand, the system of state trading in the Finnish market economy created a potential for distortions and rigidities in the economy. In annual negotiations concerning the commodity group quotas, Finnish industrial associations, industry branches, and subbranches competed to win the largest possible quotas. The setting of guidelines for future commodity exchanges was not based on normal market competition. The system favored large, traditional exporters, who had a strong position in the institutional triangle of economy, politics, and administration (Salminen, 1981; Hirvensalo, 1993). Discrimination against small firms was systematic in the sense that as a matter of administrative expediency it was easier to keep the group limited. On a practical level, small firms were unable to deliver the large orders, and therefore large Finnish companies were generally used. However, many medium and small firms were involved as subcontractors in the clearing trade. There was also border trade involving small firms; however, this trade never amounted to more than 2–3 percent of the total clearing trade (Laurila, 1995, p. 95).

The commodity structure of Soviet exports to Finland did not deviate much from its exports to the rest of the West. Despite some efforts on the Finnish side to diversify and upgrade the structure of imports from the Soviet Union, the share of finished products remained rather low. Nevertheless, Finland was the biggest Western buyer of Soviet machines and equipment.

Finland's exports to the East were more diversified than its exports on average. In particular, exports to the USSR and to other countries diverged strongly during the 1980s. As a result of the second oil crisis in 1979–81, the expansion of exports to the USSR involved both trade creation and trade diversion. In some sectors totally new capacity was created for exporting to the East. Trade creation emerged in the textile and clothing industries, in the metal and engineering industries, and to a lesser extent in the chemical industry. During the 1970s and 1980s the rigidities in Finland's export industries slowed their adaptation to the structural changes in Soviet imports from the West. A comparison of the structure and development of Finland's exports in 1970–86 to the

East with Soviet imports from the West in terms of constant market share suggests that the structure of Finland's exports to the Soviet Union was relatively rigid. The contribution of structural factors to Finland's performance in Soviet markets was negative (Hukkinen, 1990).

**Profitability**
In principle, the prices used in Finnish-Soviet trade were world market prices. In practice, the world market prices for energy products, raw materials, and relatively homogeneous manufactured goods were easily checked to eliminate significant and systematic deviations. In other sectors, however, it was easier to discriminate between prices in the Soviet and Western markets.

According to a cross-sectional study of the relative prices of 250 items in 1985, the prices of Finnish exports to the USSR were on average 9.5 percent higher than comparable export prices to Western markets. The analysis also indicated that 60 percent of the exports to the East had higher export prices than to the West. For example, the difference was 16 percent in timber and paper products, and 11–13 percent in engineering products, textiles, and clothing. This result supports the commonly held view that exports to the USSR were exceptionally profitable. On the other hand, prices of commodities like chemicals and metals were, on average, about 10 percent lower than for exports to the West. The profitability of exports to the USSR was in all likelihood supported by the cash payment practice, low unit costs resulting from scale economies, and low marketing expenditures (Kajaste, 1993, p. 119). In a 1983 survey, Finnish textile, clothing, and shoe manufacturers regarded their Eastern exports to be the most profitable (Kivikari, 1985).

The clearing system has also been mentioned as one of the central factors contributing to the profitability of exports to the East. Obláth and Péte (1990) have argued that quoting prices in clearing rubles, which were as overvalued as the official Soviet ruble-dollar rate, caused high prices, excess supply, and the high profitability of Finnish exports. However, a closer study of the clearing mechanism casts doubt on this argument. The clearing ruble was merely an accounting unit in the system, and the markka-dollar rate of exchange alone was relevant for most of the trade (Sutela, 1991, pp. 305–7).

The traditional view is that the reparations after World War II supported sunrise industries, diversified exports, and strengthened Finland's international competitiveness. In fact, the Soviet Union was a stepping-stone to a Finnish firm's internationalization in only a few cases. However, profitable exports to the USSR often helped existing Finnish firms to retain competitiveness in the Western market (Gabrisch, 1985). When the Soviet demand diminished or ended in the 1980s, the finances of many firms deteriorated; some withdrew from the Western market and even went bankrupt. It is possible that in many cases Soviet trade had actually sustained sunset industries, and thus contributed to the deterioration of the competitiveness of Finnish manufacturing. Even if this conclusion is justified by factual evidence, the firms are not to be blamed for doing profitable business within the established framework.

### Dependence on the Soviet Market

Finland's president Juho Paasikivi (1946–56) is said to have warned Finland against letting trade with the Soviet Union exceed 20 percent of the country's total foreign trade. There was a common fear of trade-induced dependence in the cold war world. At times, the Soviet share of Finnish foreign trade exceeded 20 percent, and created considerable economic and political dependence on the Soviet Union.

Although Finnish companies had substantial sales to the Soviet Union and sought to adapt their products to the buyers' requirements, the trade did not integrate Finland into the Soviet economy because the bulk of Finnish exports, 75–90 percent, went to the market economies. Moreover, the dual pattern separating East-East and East-West trade in the CMEA member countries was absent in Finland. The Soviet Union was interested in buying high-quality Western products from Finland.

Many companies and at least two industry branches, shipbuilding and footwear, developed a strong dependence on the Eastern markets during the 1980s. With the decline of Soviet demand, these industries faced serious adaptation requirements (see Table 6.3).

**Table 6.3**
The share of exports to the Soviet Union as a percentage of total production

| Industry | 1981 | 1985 | 1990 | 1991 |
| --- | --- | --- | --- | --- |
| Paper, paperboard | 9.5 | 7.2 | 4.8 | 0.7 |
| Pulp | 2.5 | 1.6 | 1.0 | 0.3 |
| Metal industry | 12.1 | 13.8 | 7.5 | 2.8 |
| Shipyards | 40.6 | 66.4 | 19.5 | 1.8 |
| Clothing | 34.1 | 19.9 | 11.4 | 3.2 |
| Shoes | 41.8 | 44.9 | 19.6 | 9.6 |

*Source:* Eronen-Orpana 1993.

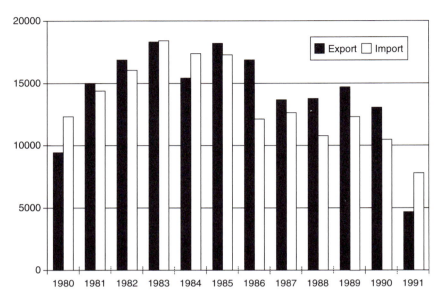

**Figure 6.1**
Finnish-Soviet trade in current Finnish markka prices (millions)
*Source:* Finnish trade statistics.

### 6.1.3   The Decline and Collapse of Finnish Exports to the USSR

A decline in trade between the Soviet Union and Finland started in the mid 1980s (see Figure 6.1). At first it was commonly believed that the decline was caused by the fall in the dollar price of oil, which earlier had temporarily reduced Finnish imports and Soviet purchasing power in the Finnish market. In the mid-1980s, however, the decline turned out to be a longer-term trend that ended in a total collapse of Finnish exports in 1991.

The reasons for the trade decline were primarily of Soviet origin. The changes in the economic and political system and economic decision making affected the entire Soviet foreign trade with the beginning of perestroika in 1985. The development of Finnish trade was not, however, solely attributable to general and common factors. In 1991, Soviet imports from Finland diminished by 77 percent, compared with the decline of 38 percent in imports from Germany, 21 percent from France, 10 percent from Italy, 73 percent from Poland, 68 percent from Hungary, and 58 percent from Czechoslovakia (Foreign Trade, 1992).

There were also specific reasons for the decline of Finland's trade with the Soviet Union since 1985 and its total collapse in 1991. The favorable

**Table 6.4**
Finland's special preconditions in competition with other Western countries for trade with
the Soviet Union (Russia)

|  | Under the old regime 1951–85 | During Perestroyka 1985– | In "New Europe" 1990– | Abolition of bilateral clearing 1991– | In Russia 1992– |
|---|---|---|---|---|---|
| Foreign policy | +++ | ++ | + | + | ? |
| Trade policy | +++ | ++ | ++ | ? | ? |
| Institutions | ++ | +? | ? | ? | ? |
| Experience | ++ | ++ | + | + | + |
| Geographical proximity | ++ | +++ | ++ | ++ | ++ |

*Note:* The number of plus-signs indicates the factor's positive impact on trade.

position of Finland compared with other Western countries was gradually
eroded when revolutionary developments began in the Soviet Union and
Eastern Europe (see Table 6.4).

The final breakdown came at the beginning of 1991, when the bilateral
trade system was abolished. Despite clear signals, there were authorities
and enterprises in Finland (as late as the autumn of 1990) that did not
expect the bilateral system to be terminated so suddenly, without a transition period. As the Soviet crisis deepened, the trading practices of the
past could not be changed quickly. During the 1980s the Finnish economy
adopted a more dual pattern. The divergence between the open (exports
to the West) and closed (domestic economy, exports to the East) sectors
increased. The lack of competitiveness in the closed sector forced the
authorities to devalue the markka by 14 percent in November 1991
(Kajaste, 1991, p. 124). An adequate response to the changing market
situation was further hindered by the fact that the Finnish economy
and many companies had their financial and mental resources tied up in
bilateral trade. In 1991 the accounts receivable from the Soviet Union
amounted to approximately 5.5 billion markka. In addition, Finland's
position in Soviet trade had been weakened by its having to compete on
the same ground as other Western nations.

The decline of exports to the USSR had a substantial impact on production and employment in Finland. The real GDP declined by 6.5 percent in
1991. Macroeconomic model simulations by the Ministry of Finance indicate that two percentage points of this decline can be attributed to the
drop in exports to the USSR, which also caused a corresponding rise in
the unemployment rate (Kajaste, 1993, p. 124).

Again there were considerable differences in the effects of export variations on total production because the importance of trade with the Soviet
Union varied greatly between industries (see Table 6.5). In the metals and
engineering industries, and especially shipbuilding, textiles, clothing, and
processed food industries, the biggest drop occurred in the late 1980s,
whereas other industries experienced the heaviest decline in 1990–91.
Surprisingly, the abolition of the clearing system reduced paper exports
the most (77 percent), although the reverse could have been expected
because of the industry's competitiveness in hard-currency exports.

With respect to economic fluctuations in Finland, the collapse of Soviet
trade occurred at the worst possible moment because it exacerbated the
country's depression caused by the decline of domestic demand and the
stagnation of exports to the West.

### 6.1.4  Conclusions on Bilateral Clearing Trade with the Soviet Union

The evaluation of Finnish-Soviet trade relations will depend heavily on
the weight given to the different stages. A long-term perspective, from
the beginning of the postwar trading system in 1951 to the breakup of the
Soviet Union in 1991, will give a different impression from that of the
final years. The declining trade between Finland and the Soviet Union
during the perestroika years of 1985–91 had few positive features. The
overall view is different if the experience of a longer period is considered.
The positive and negative aspects of Finnish-Soviet trade relationships
can be summarized from a Finnish perspective as follows:

1. At the start of the Finnish-Soviet trade in 1951, Finland did not have
the option of conducting its export and import trade with the Soviet
Union under free market incentives. Its imports were financed by exports
under arrangements in which trade was required to balance bilaterally.

2. The trade was adapted primarily to the Soviet system's requirements,
creating abnormal and even detrimental political and administrative elements in the Finnish market economy.

3. As a result of the political support for mutual trade in both countries,
Finland managed to exploit the economic potential of the Soviet Union to
a much greater extent than did other Western countries.

4. Finland's imports from the Soviet Union (oil was the main commodity)
only included articles that were available from other sources, too. The
most important role of imports was to secure an equivalent reciprocal
demand for Finnish products.

**Table 6.5**
The contribution of exports and domestic demand to changes in manufacturing volumes in Finland (volume change in percent)

| Industry | Domestic demand | Exports to the West | Exports to the East |
|---|---|---|---|
| Processed food | | | |
| 1985–1989 | 16.0 | 4.5 | −10.1 |
| 1990 | −8.8 | −0.4 | 9.0 |
| 1991 | −1.5 | 0.3 | −1.0 |
| Textiles and clothing | | | |
| 1985–1989 | −8.9 | −7.3 | −11.9 |
| 1990 | −7.9 | −4.9 | −0.7 |
| 1991 | −10.8 | −5.6 | −6.2 |
| Timber industry | | | |
| 1985–1989 | 22.2 | −3.0 | −0.3 |
| 1990 | −7.4 | −2.6 | −0.2 |
| 1991 | −25.0 | −3.4 | 0.1 |
| Paper industry | | | |
| 1985–1989 | 3.8 | 12.6 | −2.2 |
| 1990 | 0.3 | 1.5 | −1.0 |
| 1991 | −5.9 | 2.0 | −3.4 |
| Chemicals | | | |
| 1985–1989 | 9.0 | 4.2 | −1.9 |
| 1990 | 1.4 | 2.6 | — |
| 1991 | −10.6 | 4.2 | −1.3 |
| Non-metallic minerals | | | |
| 1985–1989 | 25.6 | 1.7 | −0.2 |
| 1990 | −2.3 | 0.2 | −0.7 |
| 1991 | −18.9 | 0.4 | −0.5 |
| Basic metals | | | |
| 1985–1989 | 3.6 | 12.9 | −2.6 |
| 1990 | −8.3 | 14.8 | −3.1 |
| 1991 | −7.9 | 5.1 | −0.2 |
| Metal and engineering | | | |
| 1985–1989 | 15.6 | 8.5 | −9.2 |
| 1990 | −4.9 | 4.4 | −2.2 |
| 1991 | −4.6 | −3.4 | −6.5 |
| Total manufacturing | | | |
| 1985–1989 | 11.7 | 6.2 | −4.5 |
| 1990 | −3.4 | 2.1 | −0.7 |
| 1991 | −7.5 | −0.1 | −3.1 |

*Source:* Kajaste, 1993.

5. Trade with the Soviet Union created demand for Finnish products during recessions, such as the oil crises, and thus increased employment and balanced economic fluctuations.

6. The trade patterns favored traditional exports of large industrial enterprises, thus deferring the necessary structural changes rather than supporting new industrial activity.

7. The profitability of exports to the Soviet Union, as long as it lasted, strengthened the overall competitiveness of Finnish companies and improved their chances in Western markets.

8. The occasional preference of exports to the Soviet Union may have created elements of a dual economy, and the decline in the 1980s and 1990s therefore could not be entirely compensated for with increased exports to the West.

9. When Soviet foreign trade started to move in a "normal" direction during perestroika, the special preconditions supporting Finnish exports since 1951 were gradually removed, and Finland had to develop its trade with its eastern neighbor on a new foundation.

## 6.2   Trade with the Successor States of the Soviet Union

### 6.2.1   Rapid Recovery

At the start of the 1990s, Finland's trade with its eastern neighbor was decentralized in two stages. In 1991 the bilateral clearing system was replaced with a conventional multilateral trading system based on convertible currencies. The coordinating role of government authorities was abolished and trade was reestablished on company-level business contacts. The second stage of decentralization occurred one year later as the Soviet Union was split into fifteen independent states that had their own trade frameworks and practices that had to be dealt with individually. The first stage of decentralization in 1991 involved a collapse of the trade volume, contributing in part to the severe depression of the Finnish economy. The second stage of decentralization, involving the redistribution of trade among the independent states of the former Soviet Union, did not seem to have such adverse effects on trade volume. Exports to the former Soviet territory in 1992 and 1993 induced demand growth in all the major industrial branches (see Table 6.6). Despite declining income levels in all the successor states of the Soviet Union, Finland recorded solid growth rates in its exports to the former Soviet republics.

**Table 6.6**
Contribution of exports and domestic demand to the growth of the main industry branches in Finland (volume change in percent)

| Industry | Domestic demand | Exports to the West | Exports to the East |
|---|---|---|---|
| Processed food | | | |
| 1990–1991 | −10.3 | −0.1 | −8.0 |
| 1992–1993 | 3.3 | 0.4 | 1.3 |
| Textiles and clothing | | | |
| 1990–1991 | −18.7 | −10.5 | −6.9 |
| 1992–1993 | −11.6 | −3.0 | 4.4 |
| Timber industry | | | |
| 1990–1991 | −32.4 | −0.6 | −0.1 |
| 1992–1993 | −7.9 | 23.2 | 1.7 |
| Paper industry | | | |
| 1990–1991 | −5.6 | 3.5 | −4.4 |
| 1992–1993 | −3.2 | 8.6 | −0.5 |
| Chemicals | | | |
| 1990–1991 | −9.2 | 6.8 | −1.3 |
| 1992–1993 | −2.2 | 6.2 | 0.0 |
| Non-metallic minerals | | | |
| 1990–1991 | −21.2 | 0.6 | −1.2 |
| 1992–1993 | −21.8 | 2.9 | 0.9 |
| Basic metals | | | |
| 1990–1991 | −16.2 | 19.9 | −3.3 |
| 1992–1993 | 8.8 | 9.7 | 0.2 |
| Metals and engineering | | | |
| 1990–1991 | −9.5 | 1.0 | −8.7 |
| 1992–1993 | −8.1 | 20.6 | 3.3 |
| Total manufacturing | | | |
| 1990–1991 | −10.9 | 2.0 | −3.8 |
| 1992–1993 | −3.2 | 9.5 | 1.2 |

*Source:* Calculations made by Ilkka Kajaste, Finnish Ministry of Finance.

The majority of Soviet-Finnish trade, approximately 80 percent, in the Soviet days had its source or destination within the territory of the Russian Federation. The situation did not change in this regard because Russia became the heir of Soviet-Finnish trade (see Table 6.7). In 1993, Russia spent the same amount of money on purchases from Finland as the United States: U.S. imports from Finland amounted to 40 markka per capita. A considerable increase in trade was also recorded between Finland and its southern neighbor, Estonia. Despite its small size, Estonia ranks as Finland's second biggest trade partner among the former Soviet republics, with its per capita imports of 1,174 markka, only slightly below that of its

**Table 6.7**
Finland's trade with the republics of the former Soviet Union in 1993

|            | Exports (million FIM) | Imports (million FIM) | Share in trade with former USSR (%) | Exports per capita (FIM) | Imports per capita (FIM) |
|------------|-----------------------|-----------------------|-------------------------------------|--------------------------|--------------------------|
| Russia     | 6037                  | 7807                  | 76.5                                | 41                       | 53                       |
| Other CIS  | 430                   | 515                   | 5.1                                 | 3                        | 4                        |
| Lithuania  | 204                   | 79                    | 1.7                                 | 55                       | 21                       |
| Latvia     | 253                   | 131                   | 2.1                                 | 94                       | 49                       |
| Estonia    | 1879                  | 759                   | 14.6                                | 1174                     | 474                      |
| Total      | 8803                  | 9291                  | 100.0                               | 31                       | 32                       |

Source: Finnish foreign trade statistics.

rich western neighbor Sweden, whose imports in 1993 amounted to 1,730 markka per capita. The other two Baltic republics, Latvia and Lithuania, rank much higher in trade statistics than the rest of the former Soviet republics, indicating the important role of proximity and a progressing transition toward a market economy in foreign trade intensity.

As Finland's trade partners, Russia, the Baltic states, and other successor states of the Soviet Union differ not only in terms of trade volume but also in terms of commodity structure. Finnish exports to Russia and the Baltic states have changed substantially since the Soviet era, compared with the other former Soviet republics (see Table 6.8). With regard to imports to Finland, the supply structure from the Baltic states is completely different from that of the former Soviet Union. Not surprisingly, the current composition of imports from Russia and the other successor states of the Soviet Union remains similar to the past Soviet pattern.

With over 90 percent of the total trade between Finland and the successor states of the Soviet Union concentrated in Russia and Estonia, and no foreseeable changes occurring in this respect, the following analysis focuses on these two countries in more detail.

### 6.2.2  Commodity Trade with Russia and Estonia

The upheavals of Finnish trade with the former Soviet Union at the beginning of the 1990s can also be seen in the changing commodity compositions of trade flows. In 1988, when the Soviet share in Finland's total trade amounted to 14.7 percent, the composition of exports to the East did not differ significantly from the composition of exports to the West (see Table 6.9). The cosine coefficient[1] that measures the similarity of dis-

**Table 6.8**
The commodity structure of Finland's trade with the former Soviet Union (in percent)

| | Exports | | | | |
| --- | --- | --- | --- | --- | --- |
| | 1990 | 1991 | 1993 | 1993 | 1993 |
| Commodity group (SITC) | USSR | USSR | Russia | Baltic states | Other |
| Food and beverages (0–1) | 6.2 | 7.2 | 16.7 | 12.9 | 4.7 |
| Raw materials and energy (2–4) | 3.6 | 3.7 | 1.8 | 5.8 | 4.2 |
| Chemical products (5) | 7.6 | 14.3 | 6.2 | 5.9 | 10.7 |
| Machinery and vehicles (7) | 45.2 | 38.8 | 42.7 | 38.6 | 45.6 |
| Paper and paperboard (64) | 17.4 | 8.4 | 2.4 | 2.9 | 7.7 |
| Textiles and clothing (65, 84, 85) | 5.9 | 5.7 | 5.3 | 11.5 | 1.2 |
| Other manufactured goods (6, 8, 9) | 14.2 | 21.8 | 24.8 | 22.5 | 26.0 |
| Total | 100.1 | 99.9 | 99.9 | 100.1 | 100.1 |
| Million FIM | 12888 | 4522 | 6037 | 2336 | 430 |

| | Imports | | | | |
| --- | --- | --- | --- | --- | --- |
| | 1990 | 1991 | 1993 | 1993 | 1993 |
| Commodity group (SITC) | USSR | USSR | Russia | Baltic states | Other |
| Food and beverages (0–1) | 0.2 | 0.3 | 0.1 | 4.9 | 0 |
| Cork and wood (24) | 7.6 | 7.5 | 11.4 | 13.3 | 5.2 |
| Metalliferous ores, scrap (28) | 1.5 | 3.1 | 5.4 | 17.6 | 10.1 |
| Energy (32–35) | 69.2 | 72.0 | 60.1 | 0.7 | 57.6 |
| Other raw materials (2–4) | 0.6 | 0.3 | 0.5 | 1.8 | 1.6 |
| Chemicals (5) | 3.6 | 4.8 | 8.5 | 1.8 | 8.9 |
| Machines, transport equipment (7) | 7.9 | 5.4 | 2.5 | 6.2 | 1.7 |
| Metal manufactures (67, 68, 69) | 3.9 | 3.4 | 7.3 | 7.2 | 13.6 |
| Textiles and clothing (65, 84, 85) | 0.4 | 0.8 | 1.1 | 29.3 | 0.2 |
| Other manufactured goods (6, 8, 9) | 5.2 | 2.4 | 3.1 | 17.2 | 1.2 |
| Total | 100.1 | 100.0 | 100.0 | 100.0 | 100.1 |
| Million FIM | 10196 | 7461 | 7807 | 969 | 516 |

Source: Finnish foreign trade statistics.

Table 6.9
Commodity structure of Finland's exports to the USSR, Russia, and Estonia (in percent)

|  | 1988 | 1988 | 1993 | 1993 | 1993 |
|---|---|---|---|---|---|
|  | USSR | World | Russia | Estonia | World |
| Commodity groups (SITC) | (1) | (2) | (3) | (4) | (5) |
| Food (0) | 2.0 | 1.7 | 15.0 | 11.8 | 2.8 |
| Beverages and tobacco (1) | 0.02 | 0.2 | 2.0 | 1.3 | 0.3 |
| Crude materials (2) | 3.0 | 12.4 | 0.4 | 0.9 | 8.7 |
| Mineral fuels (3) | 0.7 | 1.7 | 1.3 | 5.4 | 2.7 |
| Animal, vegetable oil, fat (4) | 0 | 0.1 | 0.1 | 0 | 0.1 |
| Chemicals (5) | 5.0 | 5.7 | 5.4 | 5.7 | 6.5 |
| Basic manufactures (6) | 25.9 | 42.6 | 13.7 | 17.7 | 40.6 |
| Machines, transport equipment (7) | 49.7 | 27.5 | 43.6 | 38.5 | 31.4 |
| Miscellaneous manufactured goods (8) | 13.8 | 8.2 | 18.6 | 18.6 | 6.8 |
| Other (9) | 0 | 0 | 0 | 0 | 0 |
| Total | 100 | 100 | 100 | 100 | 100 |
| Cosine coefficient | 0.76 |  | 0.81 | 0.47 | 0.47 |
| (2-digit level data) | (1), (2) |  | (3), (4) | (4), (5) | (3), (5) |

Source: Finnish foreign trade statistics.

tributions was 0.76 on 2-digit SITC-classified data. A notable exception to the general structure of exports was caused by the 64 percent Soviet share in Finland's export deliveries of ships (SITC 79), which largely explained the dominant role of machinery and transport equipment (SITC 7) in Finland's exports.

Compared with the exports to the Soviet Union in 1988, the commodity structure of Finnish exports to Russia and Estonia in 1993 differed significantly from the general structure of Finnish exports, although the structure of exports to these two countries was very similar.

Compared with 1988 Eastern exports and 1993 total exports, the biggest differences arise from the high shares in Russian and Estonian trade of food (SITC 0) and miscellaneous manufactured goods (SITC 8). In the group of basic manufactures (SITC 6), the share of paper (SITC 64) represented only 2 percent of Finnish exports to Russia and Estonia, compared with the 25 percent share in total Finnish exports.

The structural change in Finnish exports is explained primarily by changes in the target countries' circumstances and demand patterns. Compared with the situation in 1988, the commodity structure of Finnish exports to the East has diverged from the export composition determined

**Table 6.10**

Commodity structure of Finland's imports from the USSR in 1988, Russia and Estonia in 1993 (percent)

|  | 1988 | 1988 | 1993 | 1993 | 1993 |
|---|---|---|---|---|---|
|  | USSR | World | Russia | Estonia | World |
| Commodity groups (SITC) | (1) | (2) | (3) | (4) | (5) |
| Food (0) | 0.2 | 4.9 | 0.1 | 6.1 | 5.7 |
| Beverages and tobacco (1) | 0 | 0.4 | 0 | 0 | 0.6 |
| Crude materials (2) | 9.8 | 6.3 | 17.6 | 31.9 | 7.0 |
| Mineral fuels (3) | 70.4 | 9.6 | 61.1 | 0.1 | 12.6 |
| Animal, vegetable oil, fat (4) | 0 | 0.1 | 0 | 0 | 0.2 |
| Chemicals (5) | 2.8 | 10.8 | 8.6 | 1.6 | 13.3 |
| Basic manufactures (6) | 4.4 | 15.9 | 8.5 | 20.0 | 14.2 |
| Machines, transport equipment (7) | 11.9 | 39.3 | 2.6 | 6.9 | 33.9 |
| Miscellaneous manufactured goods (8) | 0.5 | 12.7 | 1.4 | 33.4 | 12.3 |
| Other (9) | 0 | 0 | 0 | 0 | 0 |
| Total | 100 | 100 | 100 | 100 | 100 |
| Cosine coefficient | 0.42 |  | 0.20 | 0.38 | 0.52 |
| (2-digit level data) | (1), (2) |  | (3), (4) | (4), (5) | (3), (5) |

*Source:* Finnish foreign trade statistics.

by the country's general competitiveness. In 1993 the value of Finland's tropical fruit exports to Russia exceeded the value of paper exports! The present composition of Finland's exports reflects the competitive situation in the Russian and Estonian markets, but the situation will inevitably change and the exports will adjust accordingly. Large-scale exports of food from Finland to Russia and Estonia, for instance, can be explained by the underdeveloped food supply network in the two countries, the subsidies to food exports in Finland, and the fact that Finnish companies are ready and able to sell in neighboring markets. Direct investments by foreign food manufacturing companies, including Finnish firms, in Russia and Estonia will gradually reduce the exports of foodstuffs from Finland.

Energy products had a dominant position in Finnish imports from the Soviet Union in 1988 (see Table 6.10). In 1993, the share of energy products in Finnish imports from Russia was significantly lower due to difficulties in delivering oil products of specified quality to Finnish buyers. An even bigger decline has occurred in Finnish imports of machinery and transport equipment (SITC 7), which now lack the administrative support and preferential treatment offered by the trade clearing practice.

As can be expected, the imports from Russia and Estonia are significantly different in structure. One-third of the imports from Estonia are consumer goods. They are largely based on the Finnish clothing industry's subcontracting operations in Estonia, where clothes are prefabricated before being reexported to Finland for finishing and delivery to the markets. Imports from Estonia have also included metals and scrap materials (SITC 28), mainly of CIS origin. However, the imports of metals and scrap were greatly reduced in 1994.

The quotas and licenses of the pre-1991 trade-clearing arrangements prevented problems of cheap imports and other market disturbances. Recently Finland has had to impose restrictions on some Eastern imports (e.g. on concrete, chemicals, and fish products) to protect its own industries.

When one compares the commodity structures of Finnish exports and imports, the traditional interindustry nature of Eastern trade is seen to characterize trade with Russia. By contrast, the trade between Finland and Estonia has clearly an intraindustry pattern. Finnish companies have established in Estonia many subsidiaries and joint ventures (e.g., in textiles, clothing, and metal industries) in which the international division of labor takes place inside the production process. This arrangement, combined with subcontracting in Estonia, is increasing intraindustry trade between Finland and Estonia. The weighted Grubel-Lloyd indexes[2] (calculated from 2-digit SITC data) that describe Finland's trade in 1988 and 1993 from this perspective are shown below.

|                      | 1988 |       | 1993   |         |       |
|----------------------|------|-------|--------|---------|-------|
|                      | USSR | World | Russia | Estonia | World |
| Grubel-Lloyd index   | 0.14 | 0.53  | 0.11   | 0.32    | 0.56  |

### 6.2.3   Trade Policy

Finland quickly managed to create a network of trade policy agreements with Russia, Estonia, and other post-Soviet states. The Most Favored Nation Treaty and a special agreement on cooperation with the neighboring regions of Russia were signed in 1992. An economic commission was established with Russia to deal with intergovernmental trade policy and other trade-related questions. A free trade agreement between Estonia and the two other Baltic states was signed in 1992.

Finland's entry into the European Union (EU) at the beginning of 1995 gave it a new position as a customs union member. The trade policy of the

EU concerning Russia and the Baltic states was thus enforced in Finland. For example, Finland immediately adopted the Generalized System of Preferences (GSP) that applies to Russian imports into the European Union.

Although Finland's EU membership has changed customs regulations and may affect the imports of some articles, the overall impact of the membership on Finland's trade with the East has been judged to be positive. After all, Finland now has its own markets, as well as access to the huge EU markets, to offer its trade partners in both the East and the West.

Even as an EU member, Finland has the option to continue the work of the Finnish-Russian Economic Commission. In addition, the special cooperation with the neighboring regions of Russia will be continued. This involves joint activities with the Russian regions on the Finnish border: the province of Murmansk, the Republic of Karelia, St. Petersburg, and the province of Leningrad. The goal of the cooperation is to advance the economic development of the neighboring regions, to promote cooperative action between Finland and Russia, and to develop industrial and commercial relations between the regions. Mutually agreed priorities include environmental protection, energy management, nuclear safety, traffic and communications, food supply, education, social work, health care, and forestry. Ten Finnish ministries are involved in implementing the cooperation policies.

Expectations have now been raised about linking the cooperation with the neighboring regions to a wider international context covering the regions of the Baltic and the Barents seas. As a member of the EU, Finland can bind its mutual cooperation programs with the neighboring Russian regions to its own contribution in the framework of the Technical Assistance for the Commonwealth of Independent States (TACIS) program of the EU.

Export promotion activities have been aimed at securing equal competitive conditions for Finnish companies facing Western competition in the former Soviet markets. A central task for export promotion has been to solve problems of financing exports and guaranteeing their deliveries. Export deliveries are mainly based on advance payment arrangements that are well suited for trade in consumer goods, foodstuffs, and minor investment articles. New arrangements for financing and guarantees need to be developed to improve the opportunities, especially for small and medium-sized enterprises operating in Russia and the Baltic states.

### 6.2.4   Business Attitudes

Although trading in the former Soviet territory is problematic and demanding, the proximity of the markets in St. Petersburg and Estonia has especially attracted Finnish companies that have started export and import activities and have established subsidiaries. About six hundred Finnish companies operated in St. Petersburg, and over two thousand in Estonia, in 1994. With respect to the number of foreign investments in Finland's neighboring regions, Finnish companies clearly have the leading position but investment usually remains small. In fact, there is more American and German capital in St. Petersburg, and more Swedish capital in Estonia, than Finnish capital.

Several recent studies have shown that Finnish companies believe in the growing importance of the Russian and Estonian markets for their overall business activity. If the Russian economy stabilizes and investments begin in the Arctic regions, Finnish companies are expected to find significant new market opportunities, especially in energy and food supply, environmental protection, and construction.

According to several Russian and Estonian surveys, Finnish companies enjoy a good reputation compared with other Western enterprises. Positive experiences from the Soviet era are still remembered. However, the reputation has recently suffered as some Finnish businessmen, who are poorly prepared and have the wrong attitudes, undertake business activity in the new markets.

### 6.2.5   Conclusions

Finnish exports (in markka) to Russia grew by 100 percent in 1993 and by 32 percent in 1994. Exports to Estonia grew by 72 percent and 79 percent in 1993 and 1994, respectively. The number of Finnish companies operating in Russia and Estonia has grown remarkably. This growth is based on the developments in the successor states of the Soviet Union and on the epoch-making changes in the content and operation of Finland's trade with its eastern neighbors.

The post-Soviet states have begun moving toward normal markets. During the Soviet regime, the entire economy's foreign trade transactions were concentrated in Moscow. Now St. Petersburg, which is developing as a business center, is functionally as close to Finland as it was in the pre-Soviet era. The same is true of Estonia. Economic geography has been revalidated in Russia and Estonia, which naturally affects the trade of neighboring Finland.

Trade with Russia and Estonia is divided into small deals, compared with the large deliveries of the Soviet state-directed trade. There are many players on both sides, a large number with no experience of the former Finnish-Soviet trade system.

Finland's export success has been supported by the fact that the proximity of Russia and Estonia, together with long familiarity and relatively low transaction costs, have made it easier for the Finns to respond to changing Russian and Estonian conditions. Even doing business on a small-scale can be beneficial to Finns because of closeness to the markets.

An adaptation to unstable circumstances implies that current Finnish trade rests on a more temporary basis than in the Soviet era. The situation is not entirely consistent with Finland's actual advantage in international competition. For example, the subsidized exports of Finnish food products to Estonia can constitute an unfair practice against Estonian production. Such distortions are symptoms of the transition period during which trading opportunities of the moment are exploited.

The degree of domestic input in Finland's current exports to the East is undoubtedly lower than the required level of 80 percent under the Soviets. Demands for competitive production and changing trade patterns have outstripped the requirements for a high level of domestic input in Finnish exports to the East.

No other former socialist country has experienced a complete reorientation of foreign trade comparable with that of Estonia. Over 90 percent of the commodity exchange in the past took place with other Soviet republics. In 1993 only 20 percent of Estonia's foreign trade was with Russia; Finland was the biggest trade partner, accounting for 25 percent of Estonian trade. In 1994 the Finnish share of Estonian imports had risen to 40 percent. The change is explained not only by Estonia's economic reforms but also by Russian policies toward Estonia. It also reflects the role of physical and mental proximity in market-based foreign trade. As a close "godfather" Finland has quickly achieved a leading position in Estonia's foreign trade after its start from scratch.

## 6.3  Trade Relations with Eastern European CMEA Countries

Finland pursued a unique trade policy not only with the Soviet Union but also with other socialist countries. Agreements on the reciprocal removal of obstacles to trade, commonly referred to as the KEVSOS agreements, were concluded with Bulgaria, Czechoslovakia, Hungary, the German Democratic Republic, and Poland. Finland implemented the first tariff reductions on imports from these countries in early 1975, and the final stage was reached in 1984, when the tariff-free status of all goods was put into effect.

Reciprocity in the agreements meant that the socialist countries had to use the means permitted by their economic systems to favor imports from Finland. The safeguard clauses of the KEVSOS agreements, however, enabled partners to employ special measures when the exports of either party caused or threatened to cause disturbances in the production or employment of the other party.

The possibilities provided by the reciprocal reduction of trade obstacles with the socialist countries can be evaluated as part of a comprehensive trade policy solution for Finland, a neutral country's way of balancing relations with the East and the West. As another part of this solution, the free trade agreement negotiated with the EEC was approved in 1973.

From a socialist country's standpoint, the KEVSOS agreement created a new framework for trade with one capitalist country in the West. The agreement entailed a change in the competitive situation of Finland's trade, but it also gave an indication of the general impact of the removal of tariffs and other obstacles to trade between a socialist and a capitalist country. Finland's trade with the KEVSOS countries was an experiment designed to analyze the extent to which tariffs and other obstacles affect trade between socialist and capitalist countries, and how East-West trade might be freed from these obstacles.

Finnish exports to the socialist countries in question were—or at least should have been—in a privileged position vis-à-vis other Western imports due to the KEVSOS agreement. Finland's KEVSOS exports might thus have been expected to account for an increasing share of Western exports to the East. The growth of Finland's KEVSOS trade in the years 1974–83 was compared with Austria's eastern trade by Kivikari (1983). Traditionally, Austria was a more important trade partner of the KEVSOS countries than Finland, and it kept its eastern import tariffs at a relatively high level in comparison with those of the rest of Western Europe. The trade between Finland and the KEVSOS countries developed more positively in terms of both market shares and the growth of intraindustry trade when compared with the corresponding trade figures of Austria. Nevertheless, it seems that the free trade agreements between Finland and the five socialist countries were neither successful nor significant in light of the changes during 1974–88 (see Table 6.11).

**Table 6.11**
The share of KEVSOS trade of total Finnish foreign trade (1), and Finland's share of the total
trade of OECD countries with KEVSOS countries (2)

|      | Exports | | Imports | |
|------|-----|-----|-----|-----|
|      | (1) | (2) | (1) | (2) |
| 1974 | 2.3 | 1.3 | 3.5 | 3.5 |
| 1988 | 1.4 | 1.7 | 2.5 | 3.1 |

The elimination of tariffs did not make Eastern European products competitive in the Finnish market. Finnish companies, on the other hand, did
not actively seek to enter the KEVSOS markets even with the administrative preferential treatment afforded to Finish imports. The KEVSOS countries did not have tariffs; instead they relied on administrative measures
to encourage Finnish imports. However, the KEVSOS markets were
regarded by Finnish companies as distant and difficult to access. The attitudes concerning the potential KEVSOS benefits changed as a result of
the changes of the 1990s, however. Finnish companies retained their preferential position when the transition economies implemented effective
tariff reductions in the early 1990s.

## 6.4   Trade with the Visegrád Countries

The tariff-free exports of Finnish industrial products to Bulgaria, Poland,
Czechoslovakia, and Hungary entered a new stage of development as
these four countries shifted to a market economy at the beginning of
the 1990s and adjusted their foreign trade accordingly. The German
Democratic Republic was dropped from the KEVSOS framework when it
was reunified with West Germany. The following examination also
excludes Bulgaria, whose trade with Finland was insignificant. The analysis focuses on the three Visegrád members: Hungary, Poland, and (former)
Czechoslovakia. The exemption of Finnish products from tariffs and
import duties gave them an advantage of 15 percent, on average, in the
countries concerned.

Finland was the only country exempted from tariffs in the markets of
the above-mentioned countries since the 1970s. However, the real benefits of this position did not materialize until the countries shifted to a
market economy. The growth of Finnish exports in the 1990s can probably be attributed to two major factors. First, it can be argued that the

**Table 6.12**
Finland's exports to Poland, Hungary, and the former Czechoslovakia, 1988 and 1993, measured by (1) percentage share of Finland's total exports, and (2) percentage share of total OECD exports to these countries

|                            | 1988 | | 1993 | |
|----------------------------|------|------|------|------|
|                            | (1)  | (2)  | (1)  | (2)  |
| Poland                     | 0.31 | 1.38 | 1.50 | 2.35 |
| Hungary                    | 0.27 | 1.48 | 0.56 | 1.63 |
| Czechoslovakia             | 0.31 | 1.87 | —    | —    |
| Czech Republic and Slovakia| —    | —    | 0.33 | 1.05 |
| Total                      | 0.89 | 1.55 | 2.56 | 1.73 |

*Source:* OECD statistics.
*Note:* Data for 1993 refer to the Czech Republic and Slovakia.

competitiveness of Finnish products increased in comparison with other Western imports, which added to the "suction" effect for imports from Finland. Second, the awareness of the strengthened competitive position increased the "pressure" to supply Finnish goods to these markets, and thus the success may also be attributed to increasing marketing efforts in the area.

Table 6.12 shows that Finnish exports to the area increased substantially in 1993, compared with exports in 1988, the last year of CMEA's normal activity. The share of these countries in Finnish total exports increased threefold between 1988 and 1993. Similarly, Finland managed to strengthen its position among the OECD countries by increasing its share of total OECD exports to the new market economies during the tariff-free period.

It is difficult to differentiate the "suction" and "pressure" effects on the overall development. All of these effects have been strongly influenced by the underlying marketization of economies in the Visegrád countries. It seems that the speed of transition correlates with the export success of Finland. The Polish shock therapy created new opportunities for Finland to exploit the tariff-free trade quickly. Hungary's advanced gradualism also opened up markets effectively. Czechoslovakia's slow start and its subsequent division did not offer equally favorable conditions for exploiting the preferential position.

One can distinguish two features common to all the countries on the basis of the structural changes in Finnish exports (see Table 6.13). In 1988 the share of raw materials (SITC 2) exports to all four countries exceeded

**Table 6.13**

The composition of Finland's exports to Poland (PL), Hungary (HU), the former Czechoslovakia (CS) in 1988 and 1993

| Commodity group (SITC) | 1988 | | | |
| --- | --- | --- | --- | --- |
| | PL | HU | CS | World |
| Food and live animals (0) | 6.5 | 2.7 | 2.0 | 1.7 |
| Beverages and tobacco (1) | 0 | 0 | 2.7 | 0.2 |
| Crude materials, excl. fuels (2) | 18.9 | 23.4 | 33.7 | 12.4 |
| Mineral fuels etc. (3) | 0 | 0 | 0 | 1.7 |
| Animal, vegetable oil, fat (4) | 2.0 | 1.1 | 0 | 0.1 |
| Chemicals, related products (5) | 13.0 | 10.6 | 4.1 | 5.7 |
| Basic manufactures (6) | 28.9 | 42.8 | 37.4 | 42.6 |
| Machines, transport equipment (7) | 28.7 | 17.1 | 15 | 27.5 |
| Miscellaneous manufactured goods (8) | 1.5 | 2.1 | 5 | 8.2 |
| Goods not classified elsewhere (9) | 0 | 0 | 0 | 0 |
| Total | 100 | 100 | 100 | 100 |
| Cosine coefficient (2-digit level) | 0.66 | 0.85 | 0.31 | 1.00 |

| Commodity group (SITC) | 1993 | | | | |
| --- | --- | --- | --- | --- | --- |
| | PL | HU | CZ | SK | World |
| Food and live animals (0) | 13.9 | 2.7 | 3.0 | 1.7 | 5.6 |
| Beverages and tobacco (1) | 0 | 0.4 | 1.09 | 1.8 | 0.6 |
| Crude materials, excl. fuel (2) | 1.1 | 2.6 | 1.1 | 0.9 | 7.0 |
| Mineral fuels etc. (3) | 9.8 | 0 | 2.5 | 0 | 12.8 |
| Animal, vegetable oil, fat (4) | 0 | 0.1 | 0 | 0 | 0.2 |
| Chemicals, related products (5) | 7.6 | 10.1 | 5.9 | 4.6 | 13.3 |
| Basic manufactures (6) | 34.7 | 49.1 | 26.4 | 28.0 | 14.2 |
| Machines, transport equipment (7) | 23.9 | 26.9 | 42.5 | 54.2 | 33.9 |
| Miscellaneous manufactured goods (8) | 8.9 | 8.1 | 7.6 | 8.7 | 12.3 |
| Goods not classified elsewhere (9) | 0 | 0 | 0 | 0 | 0 |
| Total | 100 | 100 | 100 | 100 | 100 |
| Cosine coefficient (2-digit level) | 0.89 | 0.91 | 0.80 | 0.74 | 1.00 |

*Source:* OECD statistics.

*Note:* Data for 1993 refer to the Czech Republic (CZ) and Slovakia (SK).

**Table 6.14**
Exports of selected industrial products from Finland to Poland, Hungary, and the former Czechoslovakia in 1988 and 1993 measured in million USD, by the share of total exports of the relevant product group

| Commodity | 1988 | | 1993 | |
|---|---|---|---|---|
| | Mill. USD | % | Mill. USD | % |
| Plastics (58) | 4 | 2.2 | 22 | 8.7 |
| Paper (64) | 22 | 0.4 | 155 | 2.6 |
| Machinery for special industry (72) | 12 | 1.0 | 34 | 2.6 |
| Telecommunication (76) | 0 | 0.0 | 53 | 4.3 |
| Prefabr. buildings; sanitary etc. (81) | 0 | 0.0 | 11 | 3.9 |
| Furniture (82) | 2 | 1.0 | 11 | 5.6 |
| Miscellaneous manufacturing (89) | 1 | 0.2 | 19 | 3.7 |

*Source:* OECD statistics.
*Note:* Data for 1993 refer to the Czech Republic (CZ) and Slovakia (SK).

that of Finnish exports as a whole, whereas the share of consumer goods (SITC 8) exports remained below the average level. In 1993 the opposite was true in all the four countries. The tariff advantage for raw materials (pulp and wood) was small or nonexistent. The advantage was generally higher for consumer goods. In this respect, the observed development supports the hypothesis of the increasing effectiveness of tariff reductions resulting from the transition process.

Another indication of the orientation of the Visegrád markets toward the Western competition model is given by the cosine coefficients in Table 6.13. These show that Finland's exports to the Visegrád countries have become very similar in structure to its total export structure, implying that the exports are determined by the general competitiveness of Finnish production.

Table 6.14 lists examples of industrial products with strongly growing export volumes in Finnish trade with the KEVSOS countries. Apart from two categories (SITC 64 and 72), Finnish exports of these product groups have increased remarkably (almost from zero) despite heavy competition from Western suppliers. These growth rates undoubtedly show the effectiveness of the tariff advantage to Finnish products in the changing KEVSOS markets.

Finland's imports from the former socialist Central European countries were not expected to change as strongly as its exports. After all, there were no changes in the Finnish markets that would have enhanced the

**Table 6.15**

Finland's imports from Poland, Hungary, the former Czechoslovakia in 1988 and 1993 measured by (1) the percentage share of Finland's total imports and (2) and the percentage share of total OECD imports from these countries

|                              | 1988 | | 1993 | |
|------------------------------|------|------|------|------|
|                              | (1)  | (2)  | (1)  | (2)  |
| Poland                       | 0.97 | 3.57 | 1.34 | 2.19 |
| Hungary                      | 0.42 | 2.14 | 0.31 | 0.84 |
| Czechoslovakia               | 0.51 | 2.79 | —    | —    |
| Czech Republic and Slovakia  | —    | —    | 0.38 | 0.74 |
| Total                        | 1.90 | 2.92 | 1.36 | 2.03 |

*Source:* OECD statistics.

*Note:* Data for 1993 refer to the Czech Republic (CZ) and Slovakia (SK).

treatment of already tariff-free imports. On the contrary, the depression of the Finnish markets and the incremental import-promoting measures of other Western European countries reduced the comparative advantage of Finland as a market for the KEVSOS countries. On the other hand, it can be assumed that the increasingly market-oriented companies of the KEVSOS countries aim at better exploiting the opportunities of free trade than had the state-owned companies in the socialist era.

Only Poland's share of Finnish total imports increased between 1988 and 1993; Hungary and the successor states of Czechoslovakia lost their market shares in Finland (see Table 6.15). The decline in Finland's share of imports from all Visegrád countries, compared with the OECD member countries' total, has been truly dramatic.

The commodity structure of Finnish imports changed relatively little between 1988 and 1993. Nearly all deviations from the composition of total Finnish imports have remained unchanged (see Table 6.16). The imports from Poland, in particular, differ greatly from the total import composition, as indicated by the low value of the cosine coefficient. This is explained by the dominant role of one product, coal (SITC 32), in Finnish imports from Poland. It accounted for 39 percent of Finnish imports from Poland in 1988 and 60 percent in 1993.

The trade between Finland and the Visegrád countries has mostly retained the character of interindustry trade. The weighted Grubel-Lloyd indices calculated from two-digit data give the low values shown below.

**Table 6.16**
The composition of Finland's imports from Poland (PL), Hungary (HU), and the former Czechoslovakia (CS) in 1988 and 1993 (in percent)

| Commodity group (SITC) | 1988 | | | |
| | PL | HU | CS | World |
|---|---|---|---|---|
| Food and live animals (0) | 4.2 | 13.1 | 0.9 | 4.9 |
| Beverages and tobacco (1) | 0 | 1.6 | 0.1 | 0.4 |
| Crude materials, excl. fuel (2) | 12.6 | 2.5 | 2.2 | 6.3 |
| Mineral fuels (3) | 40.6 | 0.9 | 0 | 9.6 |
| Animal, vegetable oil, fat (4) | 0 | 1.6 | 0 | 0.1 |
| Chemicals, related products (5) | 10.1 | 9.8 | 8.6 | 10.8 |
| Basic manufactures (6) | 9.8 | 41.7 | 36.1 | 15.9 |
| Machines, transport equipment (7) | 15.4 | 12.5 | 24.7 | 39.3 |
| Miscellaneous manufactured goods (8) | 7.4 | 16.2 | 27.3 | 12.7 |
| Goods not classified elsewhere (9) | 0 | 0 | 0 | 0 |
| Total | 100 | 100 | 100 | 100 |
| Cosine coefficient (2-digit level) | 0.24 | 0.48 | 0.57 | 1.00 |

| Commodity group (SITC) | 1993 | | | | |
| | PL | HU | CZ | SK | World |
|---|---|---|---|---|---|
| Food and live animals (0) | 4.5 | 15.7 | 2.2 | 0.3 | 5.7 |
| Beverages and tobacco (1) | 0 | 4.9 | 2.2 | 0.3 | 0.6 |
| Crude materials, excl. fuels (2) | 5.4 | 2.2 | 4.0 | 1.8 | 7.0 |
| Mineral fuels etc. (3) | 61.4 | 0.3 | 4.6 | 0 | 12.8 |
| Animal, vegetable oil, fat (4) | 0 | 0 | 0 | 0 | 0.2 |
| Chemicals, related products (5) | 4.7 | 17.3 | 6.3 | 8.2 | 13.3 |
| Basic manufactures (6) | 8.9 | 28.8 | 31.3 | 37.3 | 14.2 |
| Machines, transport equipment (7) | 9.5 | 14.3 | 20.1 | 3.2 | 33.9 |
| Miscellaneous manufactured goods (8) | 5.5 | 16.5 | 29.3 | 49.1 | 12.3 |
| Goods not classified elsewhere (9) | 0 | 0 | 0 | 0 | 0 |
| Total | 100 | 100 | 100 | 100 | 100 |
| Cosine coefficient (2-digit level) | 0.16 | 0.48 | 0.49 | 0.29 | 1.00 |

*Source:* OECD statistics.
*Note:* Data for 1993 refer to the Czech Republic (CZ) and Slovakia (SK).

|      | Poland | Hungary | Czechoslo-vakia | Czech Republic | Slovakia |
|------|--------|---------|-----------------|----------------|----------|
| 1988 | 0.17   | 0.27    | 0.16            | —              | —        |
| 1993 | 0.14   | 0.19    | —               | 0.24           | 0.08     |

## 6.5   Finland as a Gateway

### 6.5.1   The Usefulness of the Gateway

The radical change in the Soviet Union, followed by its collapse and the birth of the successor states, was a shocking experience for the outside world. The shock hit Finland especially hard as a neighbor and led to the collapse of the extensive mutual trade. The challenge for Finland was further exacerbated by the fact that the forms of economic interaction and the underlying attitudes had to be changed completely. The Finns were used to doing business with the Soviets bilaterally.

Now that Russia and the other successor states of the Soviet Union are striving to move toward a market economy, multilateralism has been substituted for the bilateral relationships. A natural goal for Finland is to act as a mediating agent for Russia's internationalization. It therefore has an important role as a gateway between Russia and the outside world.

The gateway concept may involve two different operating models in practice. On the one hand, the gateway refers to a natural nodal position in international transport and communications, with good connections and adequate logistics infrastructure. This kind of position is offered by Singapore in Asia and several locations in Europe. On the other hand, the gateway concept may serve to reduce or avoid various functional obstacles between different market areas. This kind of gateway offers a well-developed infrastructure and high-quality services, know-how, and so on to help cross the boundaries between different markets and to aid operations in those markets. Examples of this type include Hong Kong, which provides a gateway between China and the rest of the world, and Austria, which was a popular intermediary station between socialist Eastern Europe and the West.

The latter type of gateway offers ways to improve "matching,"[3] which leads to a shorter business distance between two markets. The Soviet system alienated the national economy from the international economy and its operations. This is still a major source of transaction costs and makes business especially difficult and risky for companies operating between the markets of the former Soviet territory and the outside world. Of course, matching is improved as the former Soviet Union advances toward a market economy. It is also promoted on the international and global level by organizations such as the IMF, GATT, WTO, EBRD, OECD, and ECE. Bilateral or country-specific agreements relating to (free) trade, tariffs, taxation, investment protection, and aid programs also lower the barriers. Business contacts between individual companies are the most efficient learning-by-doing method in adopting the institutions and customs of the market economy.

Despite these measures to promote matching, Russia and the other successor states of the Soviet Union will remain a foreign and uneasy business environment for Western companies for a long time. Likewise, the Western markets are not easily accessible to most Eastern enterprises. Therefore, a gateway is needed as a business basement for implementing foreign trade operations between Russia and other countries.

### 6.5.2 Finland's Special Prerequisites as a Gateway

Two favorable prerequisites for Finnish trade relations with Russia survive from the era of Finland's bilateral trade with the East (see Table 6.4). First, the Finns are used to interacting with the Russians, whereas their Western colleagues seldom had business contacts with them. Although the *Homo Sovieticus* has passed into history, knowledge of its characteristics and personal acquaintances made in that era are still important in Russian business practice. The *Homo Sovieticus* carried the Russian soul, which is known to the Finns because they have lived as neighbors and were citizens of the Russian grand duchy during the tsarist period.

Second, only Finland among the developed Western countries has the real advantage of a common border with Russia. Norway's importance as Russia's western neighbor is limited by the shortness of the common border in the arctic region as well as by Norway's military commitment to NATO. Finland also has a special position among Russia's numerous neighbors because of its well-developed infrastructure and economy, political stability, and good relations, devoid of foreign policy problems, with Russia. It is uniquely located at the mouth of the main route (Moscow–St. Petersburg) and the principal port of Russia (St. Petersburg). A new dimension is added by Finland's membership in the EU since the beginning of 1995, which gives Finland the role of linking the economic might of Europe with the post-Soviet states. It is now possible to get from the EU to Russia with one step in Finland and vice versa.

### 6.5.3  The Functions of Finland's Gateway

**Gate for Transportation**

During the Soviet era Finland's position as a gate for transit traffic was at times significant. Railway transport was facilitated by the gauge being the same in Finland and the Soviet Union (and is different from that in the rest of Europe).

The disintegration of the Soviet Union created a new situation in Russia and the post-Soviet states. As a result of the independence of the Baltic states, Belorus, and Ukraine, Russia was driven further from Western Europe than it had been for several centuries. The Baltic ports in Estonia, Lithuania, and Latvia belong to the newly independent states. The only maritime connections for Russia to Western Europe are Kaliningrad and St. Petersburg and its surroundings. Ordinarily, the Baltic ownership of important ports (Talinn, Talinn-Muga, Riga, Ventpils, Klaipeda) would not necessitate the rearrangements of traffic flows, but political tensions have hampered neighborly relations between the Baltic states and Russia. Hence, from a Russian perspective, the routes via the Baltic ports are considerably less attractive than they were during the Soviet era. The alternative routes via Finland have proved to be very competitive under the new circumstances.

Transit traffic via Finland offers the advantages of reliability, rapidity, and minimum dislocation. International studies have shown that Russia's export and import deliveries via the Baltic states incur longer operating and delivery times and higher disturbance costs in contrast with the deliveries via Finland. In an openly competitive situation, the transit deliveries via Finnish ports can be expected to rise from 5 million tons to 11.5 million tons. On the other hand, if traffic conditions in Russia and the Baltic states are developed to a level corresponding to Finland's, transit deliveries via Finland may decrease from the current level. Russia's economic recovery, however, may increase the transit deliveries considerably.

The main flow of transit deliveries is by sea via Finnish ports and by land between the ports and Russian destinations. However, even air traffic receives a major source of income from transit deliveries, currently representing 16 percent of Finnair's annual turnover (Gateway, 1994). Total direct income from transit traffic has been estimated at $500 million in 1993. On the whole, the prospects of transit traffic in Finland are good.

## Business Basement

Compared with operating as a transport gate between Russia and the outside world, the role of a basement for business with Russia is relatively new
for Finland. This operation takes various forms. In some multinational corporations, Finnish subsidiaries are responsible for Baltic markets and parts
of the Russian market. So far, however, it has been more common to use
other alternatives to participate in production processes in the Russian
territory from a Finnish basement. In particular, the construction industry,
transportation and forwarding, wholesale and retail trade, communications, consultancy, and education have been involved in these operations.
Juridical and accounting service companies are developing similar operations. Finnish companies such as insurance companies (Pohjola, Sampo),
department store chains (Stockmann's), banks (Merita-Bank, OKO-Bank,
PSP-Bank), and oil distributors (Neste) are present in the Russian and Baltic
markets.

Traditional commodity trade may also involve gateway operations. It is
estimated that up to one-third of Finnish exports to Russia now come from
gateway operations. For example, bananas and other tropical fruits are
refrigerated, ripened, stored, and distributed by Finnish companies as they
pass from Central American producers to Russian consumers. In 1994,
exports of bananas from Finland amounted to more than 300 million
markka. Russians also use Finnish services to reach foreign markets.
Investments in Finnish businesses and real estate, the new offices of some
Russian banks in Finland, and the shopping tours of well-off Russian citizens in Finland signify the growing importance of the Finnish gateway in
the East-West direction.

## Acting as Solder Between East and West: A Challenging Role

A traffic gateway denotes the movement of commodities and people,
including accommodating them in stores and in hotels. A business basement involves traffic and other business operations as well as auxiliary services required for their management. The next step is the most demanding
and involves efforts to minimize the negative effects of differences and
borders between the various markets in business (see Figure 6.2). The
location decisions and the international division of labor within the production processes can then take place flexibly within the gateway and its
neighboring regions.

Currently it is possible to flexibly locate and manage operations of
wholesale and retail trade, banking, and other service businesses in
Finland and in Russia or the Baltic states. The production processes with

**Figure 6.2**
The development of Finland's gateway functions

| "GATE" | ⇒ | "BUSINESS BASEMENT" | ⇒ | "SOLDER" |
|---|---|---|---|---|
| Transportation of goods and people and caring for them in stores and at hotels | | Auxiliary services and other inputs for various East-West business operations | | Flexible division of labor within production processes in different markets |

manufacturing operations, subsidiaries, subcontracting units, and marketing agencies can be located on either side of the Finnish and Russian or Estonian borders, depending on logistical and economic considerations. This kind of operation would be greatly promoted by the cooperation of public authorities and officials in Finland, Russia, and Estonia. It has been suggested, for instance, that the countries build common customs facilities and conduct passport and customs inspections on trains traveling between Helsinki and St. Petersburg.

The gateway can act as solder that links two economic areas with different constitutions in a way that minimizes the friction caused by border-crossing activities. The differences between the areas do not disappear, but their negative effects on business and trade are eliminated. The common gauge of Finnish and Russian railways would then truly symbolize the ease of crossing the border between the two countries.

### 6.5.4   Gateway: Competition and Cooperation

There are many regions in Russia and in other countries near the Russian borders that wish to act—and some already do—as a gateway. The gateway is no honorary position that can be proclaimed by the EU, Russia, or any other authority. Nor can Finland claim the right to the gateway position, however tempting it may be. Instead, there is open competition to attract the gateway users, not only to get the first deal but to retain them for each individual transaction.

But Finland's natural advantages as a gateway need not be overdrawn. Only systematic investments and other development efforts can guarantee the opportunities for exploiting the country's natural conditions. The Finnish gateway will be successful only if foreign companies consider its services competitive and if the Russians accept Finland in this role. If companies operating in Russia do not know or appreciate Finnish services, the gateway has no leg to stand on. The Finnish gateway cannot end at the Russian border, which means that cooperation with Russia cannot be

**Figure 6.3**
The basis of the Finnish-Estonian dual gateway

|   | | Finnish contribution | | Synergistic factors | | Estonian contribution | |   |
|---|---|---|---|---|---|---|---|---|
| W | ⇔ | Western economy with well-developed economic, institutional, and technical infrastructure | ⇔ | Coherent cultural and linguistic background | ⇔ | Long experience of Soviet system and good understanding of transition in former USSR | ⇔ | C |
| E | | | | | | | | |
| | ⇔ | Western market knowledge and participation in European integration | ⇔ | Active Finnish-Estonian economic relations | ⇔ | Good market knowledge and extensive networks in CIS area | ⇔ | I |
| S | | | | | | | | S |
| | ⇔ | Western CIS neighborhood | ⇔ | Finnish-Estonian neighborhood | ⇔ | CIS neighborhood | ⇔ | |
| T | | | | | | | | |

neglected. Russians may dislike the Finnish gateway for reasons of prestige or the anticipated reductions of earnings and investments, especially in the St. Petersburg region. Although the competitive situation cannot be entirely denied, it should be remembered that the Finnish and Russian regions form the gateway together, and neither party is able to accomplish the required outcome on its own.

Besides partnership with Russia, the Finnish gateway between East and West should include Estonia. By combining their strengths and compensating for their weaknesses, it would be possible for Finland and Estonia to form a dual gateway that has the versatility and expertise required for fully serving the East-West connections. The basis of the dual gateway is described in Figure 6.3.

The experience of half a century under Soviet rule, followed by the rapid transition to democracy and a market economy, provides Estonia with excellent conditions for understanding and even predicting the developments in Russia and other parts of the former Soviet Union. Although political events have broken traditional ties between Estonia and the Commonwealth of Independent States, there are still a good knowledge of the Russian language, valuable market information, and networks of useful contacts.

The special relationship between Finland and Estonia is manifested by the language that survived the Soviet impact. Estonian and Finnish are closely related languages. Watching Finnish television has greatly improved the Finnish language skills of the people of northern Estonia during the last decades. Estonian independence also brings out other cultural similarities between the two countries—the Estonian national anthem has the same tune as the Finnish one. Comparative research also shows that despite Soviet pressure for uniformity, the managerial culture of Estonian enterprises resembles that of Finnish firms much more than of Russian companies (Liuhto, 1991).

Finnish-Estonian economic and other contacts have experienced an explosive growth in the 1990s. Direct transport connections are busy. Finland, now a member of the EU, is Estonia's closest contact in the West and the most convenient route farther to the west.

Finland's extensive support of Estonia in education and consultancy has directly improved the prerequisites for the dual gateway. Some Finnish companies—including a few multinationals—already operate in the spirit of the dual gateway. However, until Russian and Estonian relations become more stabilized, the Finnish-Estonian dual gateway will remain an idealized model rather than a realistic alternative.

### 6.6  Prospects for Commodity Trade

At its height, eastern trade accounted for more than 20 percent of the total foreign trade of Finland. In the shift of the 1990s, however, the share of eastern trade was dramatically reduced. Subsequent growth has not raised the share to nearly the level of the 1970s and 1980s. The question arises if there exists a "right" level at which trade with the new market economies will settle during the coming years.

Predictability has generally been reduced in the international economy. Forecasts may prove to be reliable if the principal characteristics of the economic system remain unchanged. This is not the case in transition economies, which means that their external economic relations are difficult to predict.

There are, however, methods that help in assessing the development of East-West trade on the basis of existing statistics. In particular, the so-called gravity model, introduced in 1966, is relevant (Baldwin, 1994). The model's explanation of bilateral trade relations is based on the partners' population (or per capita GDP), total GDP, and the geographic distance between the partners with possible dummy variables. The model, which is estimated from trade flows between the developed market economies, may be used to assess the market-based trade flows of the former socialist countries when the frictions of the socialist system and the impact of East-West trade barriers are eliminated. The populations and distances can be measured exactly, but the GDP estimates for the countries in transition are still quite vague.

In his application of the gravity model, Baldwin presents actual and potential (gravity model) trade flows for all European countries. According to these results, the actual exports in 1989 from every Western European country to the Soviet Union or to the rest of the CMEA territory were much below the potential, except Finland's exports to the Soviet Union, with an actual value of $3.1 billion and a potential of $2.3 billion. Finland's potential exports to other former socialist countries were estimated at 3.2 times the actual level. Partly because of the KEVSOS tariff advantage, Finland has quickly attained the trade potential estimated in the gravity model.

Baldwin's model estimated the potential for 1989 exports from Sweden to the Soviet Union at $2.2 billion, only slightly below Finland's $2.3 billion. In 1993, the actual exports from Finland to the former Soviet Union amounted to $1.5 billion, whereas Sweden's exports remained at $0.7 billion. So far, Finland has succeeded quite well in restructuring its eastern trade.

Favorable economic relations based on the geographical closeness of Finland and Russia, the size of the Russian market, and the gateway position, reinforced with Finland's membership in the EU, can be expected to further increase trade between Finland and Russia. Russia's 5 percent share of Finland's total exports in 1994 is low when compared with the 1.5 percent share of exports to Estonia, which has a population that is only 1 percent of the population of Russia.

If Finnish trade with Russia is still too small, it is perhaps too large with Estonia. A large part of Finland's trade with Estonia probably results from forms of dual gateway operations, with Estonia as an intermediary between Finnish trade with the CIS countries and with countries of the West. The competitiveness of other Western countries in Estonian markets will gradually improve, and Finland's market shares will be reduced in many branches. However, with the anticipated growth of Estonia's foreign trade volume, it is still possible that the trade between Finland and Estonia will grow in terms of export volumes.

The special prerequisites of Finnish trade with the Visegrád countries were lost on January, 1, 1995. Possible growth opportunities still exist in trade with Poland, which together with Finland belongs to the newborn Baltic Sea economic region.

In 1993 Finland, in contrast with past decades, was no longer the OECD country most heavily dependent on eastern exports. Exports to the former socialist countries accounted for 9.4 percent of Finland's total exports; the corresponding figure was 12.7 percent for Austria, 12.0 percent for Greece, and 11.4 percent for Turkey. The OECD average was 3.1 percent (Vienna Institute, 1994). Baldwin's model estimated the potential of Finland's and Austria's exports to the former socialist countries at slightly below 20 percent of total exports. If the best transition economies reach the level of Spain in terms of national income, and the other former socialist countries level up with Portugal and Greece by 2010, the estimated share of the former socialist countries would rise to almost 30 percent of Finland's and Austria's exports (Baldwin, 1994).

## 6.7 Conclusions

Finland had a special position among the democratic market economies in relation to the Soviet Union. The rapid recovery of trade in 1993—94 after the decline in the Soviet era shows that Finland managed to create and exploit a new special position that is no longer based on the preferential treatment provided by political and trade policy privileges. The new position is based primarily on the utilization of neighborhood and acquaintance.

The development of the market economy in Russia and Estonia implies that they are now united, although not integrated, with the Finnish economy. The supply and demand conditions in Russia and Estonia have a direct impact not only on commodity trade but also on production and the division of labor within the production processes. Because of large wage differences, Finland needs adaptation strategies for the national economy, industry branches, and enterprises. Some uncompetitive parts of the production processes could be transferred to the East, which would reduce employment in Finland. If the competitiveness of the entire process is improved, however, the final impact on employment may turn out to be positive. Finland is thus at the forefront in facing the problem that remains to be solved in Europe as a whole: how to manage the all-European redistribution of labor in a way that benefits all the parties involved in healthy trade relationships.

A related question is Finland's position as a gateway promoting matching and trade contacts between the former Soviet Union and the West. The gateway is Finland's new strength, a potential for expanding trade relations with Russia and Estonia. Finland's role could be as a solder between Russia and the European Union. Perhaps the new common border between these two big powers will help them find new economic domains of common interest.

Thanks to special trade policy arrangements, Finland has been reaping the benefits associated with the opening up of the Visegrád countries. Despite the more advantageous geographic locations of other OECD countries like Austria, Germany, and Italy, Finland has managed to increase its market share in the countries of East-Central Europe at the same pace as their progress toward a market economy.

Finally, country size, supply and demand, and geographic distance have become increasingly important attributes of the foreign trade of the former socialist economies. In this context, the Finnish experience emphasizes the role of cultural proximity and tariff-free trade for the development of external economic relations.

## Notes

1. The cosine coefficient is calculated as follows:

$$\text{Cos}\, X_i X_j = \left( \sum_n x_{in} x_{jn} \right) \left( \sum_n x_{in}^2 \sum_n x_{jn}^2 \right)^{-1/2},$$

where $X_i$ and $X_j$ denote the vectors of total exports to the selected countries and $x_{in}$ and $x_{jn}$, the corresponding exports of commodity group $n$. When the two distributions are completely similar, the value is 1; if they are completely dissimilar, it is 0.

2. One of the basic and popular indicators of intraindustry trade is the Grubel-Lloyd index:

$$\bar{GL} = \sum_{i=1}^{n} GL_i \left[ (X_i + M_i) \Big/ \sum_{i=1}^{n} (X_i + M_i) \right],$$

where $X_i$ denotes the exports of commodity group $i$ and $M_i$, the imports of the commodity group $i$.

$$GL_i = \frac{X_i + M_i - |X_i - M_i|}{X_i + M_i}.$$

The Grubel-Lloyd index has the value 1.00 when the exports and imports are equal within each commodity group (i.e., the share of intraindustry trade is the highest possible). The value is 0 when the exports or imports are 0 in each commodity group (i.e., there is no intraindustry trade).

3. Matching is offered as a concept for understanding how the development of business relations can be facilitated—by means of appropriate adaptation—between two countries that are culturally, politically, legally, and economically dissimilar.

## References

Baldwin, Richard E. 1994. *Towards an Integrated Europe*. London: CEPR.

Dahlstedt, Roy. 1975. *Cycles in the Finnish Trade with the Soviet Union*. Unpublished licensiate thesis at Helsinki School of Economics.

Eronen, Jarmo, and Orpana. Mika. 1993. *Neuvostoliiton markkinat ja niiden romahtaminen Suomen vientiteollisuuden kannalta*. (The Collapse of the Soviet Markets from the Finnish Export Industry's Perspective). Lappeenranta: Lappeenranta University of Technology.

*Foreign Trade*. 1992. No. 4–5. (Moscow).

Gabrisch, Hubert. 1985. *Finnish-Soviet Economic Relations*. Forschungsberichte no. 109. Vienna: Vienna Institute for Comparative Studies, pp. 1–23.

Gateway Toimenpideohjelma. 1994. (Gateway Action Program). Helsinki: Finnish Ministry of Foreign Affairs.

Grubel, H. G., and P. J. Lloyd. 1975. *Intra-Industry Trade: The Theory and Measurement of International Trade in Differentiated Products*. New York: Macmillan.

Hirvensalo, Inkeri. 1993. *Adaptation of Operation Strategies to Radical Changes in Target Markets*. Helsinki: Helsinki School of Economics and Business Administration.

Hukkinen, Juhana. 1990. "Suomen vientimenestys Neuvostoliiton markkinoilla." (The Export Success of Finland in the Soviet Markets). *Finnish Economic Journal*, Vol. LXXXVI. 3/1990: 268–284.

Kajaste, Ilkka. 1993. "Finland's Trade with the Soviet Union: Its Impact on the Finnish Economy." *Economic Bulletin for Europe* 44:111–125.

Kivikari, Urpo. 1983. *The Free Trade Agreement Between Finland and the East European Countries*. Helsinki: Unitas 3/1983:79–86. Publisher Union Bank of Finland.

Kivikari, Urpo. 1985. "Finnish-Soviet Trade in the Light Industries." Forschungsberichte no. 109, pp. 25–100. Vienna: Institute for Comparative Economic Studies.

Kivikari, Urpo. 1989. "An Appearance of Dual Attachment in the Soviet Union's Imports: Variations in Imports from the West in Relation to Imports from CMEA Countries." In Michael Marrese and Sándor Richter, eds., *The Challenge of Simultaneous Economic Relations with East and West*. London: Macmillan.

Laurila, Juhani. 1995. *Bilateral Clearing Trade and Payment Between Finland and the Soviet Union. History and Experiences*. Helsinki: Bank of Finland.

Liuhto, Kari. 1991. *The Interaction of Managerial Cultures in Soviet-Finnish Joint Ventures*. Turku: Institute for East-West Trade, Turku School of Economics and Business Administration.

Nieminen, Jarmo, ed. 1991. *Foreign Direct Investment in the Soviet Union: Experiences and Prospects for Joint Ventures*. Turku: Institute for East-West Trade, Turku School of Economics and Business Administration.

Obláth, G., and P. Péte. 1990. "Mechanism and Institutional System of the Finnish-Soviet Economic Relations." In M. Friedländer ed., *Foreign Trade in Eastern Europe and Soviet Union*. Boulder, Colo.: Westview Press.

Salminen, Ari. 1981. *Institutional Relations of East-West Cooperation—The Finnish Experience*. Tampere: Finnpublishers.

Sutela, Pekka. 1991. "Exporting to the Soviet Union: Microeconomic Aspects for Finland." *Osteuropa Wirtschaft* 4:301–15.

Vienna Institute for Comparative Economic Studies. 1994. *Monthly Report* no. 12.

# III

The Post-Soviet States

# 7    Russia

Padma Desai

The literature on the various aspects of Russia's transition to an open market economy is substantial. In fact, no aspect of the process has been left outside the scope of scholarly inquiries or the watchful scrutiny of governmental and multinational agencies. In particular, the impact of the uncontrolled inflation on the exchange rate, the continuously changing trade and foreign exchange arrangements, the structure and orientation of Russia's trade with the post-Soviet states and the rest of the world—and more—has been analyzed thoroughly by Easterly and da Cunha (1994), Drebentsov (1994), Illarionov (1994), Konovalov (1994), Kuznetsov (1994), Lucke (1994), Panich (1994), Rogovski (1994), Sarafanov (1994), and Sutela (1994), and in *Economic Bulletin for Europe* (1994, hereafter *Bulletin*) and *Economic Survey of Europe in 1994–1995* (1995, hereafter *Survey*). From this perspective, there is little to add to the existing material on Russia's trade and financial interaction with the outside world as it moves toward a stable market economy.

The focus of this chapter is different. It starts from the available information on and policy changes in the exchange rate, foreign trade, and institutional arrangements (section 7.1); describes Russia's foreign trade performance with regard to its pattern and orientation (in section 7.2); and then develops a model (in section 7.3) for estimating the ruble-dollar real exchange rate. Import demand, export supply, and net export equations in which the observed real exchange rate (with a lag) is used are also presented in section 7.3.

The estimates (in section 7.4) of the monetarist model of the exchange rate adjustment indicate that the real exchange rate was not very sensitive with respect to the gap between the available real cash balances (in a given month) and the demand for real cash in the next month during 1992–94: the estimated elasticity is 0.15. The trade equations (in section 7.4) suggest that during the period, the exchange rate had no role in the emerging pattern of Russia's exports to the non-FSU (former Soviet Union) countries but that imports were influenced by the exchange rate. In particular, the export control and licensing arrangements with respect to Russia's major exports seemed to have influenced its export performance. On the other hand, imports increased with a steadily appreciating real exchange rate despite rising but low average tariffs on imports.

While the results need to be improved, they represent the very first attempt to construct a (monetarist) model of exchange rate determination for Russia and to analyze the role of the exchange rate in Russia's foreign trade performance.

## 7.1   The Exchange Rate, Foreign Trade, and Institutional Arrangements

Three factors are relevant for analyzing Russia's interaction with the world economy beginning 1992.

The first relates to the policy makers' efforts to dismantle the remnants of the multiple exchange rates (which were inherited from the Soviet days) and manage an exchange rate policy that can effectively promote export competitiveness and contribute to inflation control. The second is the emerging regime of import and export policies that govern Russia's foreign trade. The institutional arrangements under which the Soviet Foreign Trade Organizations were increasingly replaced by private exporters and importers constitute the final feature.

### 7.1.1   The Exchange Rate Regime

A variety of exchange rates prevailed in early 1992 (see Sutela, 1994, p. 13).

### Arrangements with Regard to Current Account Transactions

Among the major rates were those at which exporters were required to sell foreign exchange earnings and importers could acquire critical items such as food and medicines for centralized imports of the state. From January to June 1992, exporters could legally keep half of their foreign exchange earnings[1] and had to sell 40 percent to a Republican Hard Currency Fund of the government at the rate of 55 rubles to the dollar and the remaining 10 percent to the Central Bank of Russia (CBR) at an "official" rate that fluctuated between 120 rubles and 200 rubles to the dollar (*Bulletin*, p. 78). Importers, on the other hand, were reimbursed by the government at varying rates for the foreign exchange they spent for essential imports on the government account that were subsequently sold to final users at less than their import price. (Details of the scheme are given below.) Clearly, this arrangement penalized exporters and subsidized imports of critical items.

Foreign exchange auctions, which appeared in Moscow in early 1991, provided alternative dollar sources for importers and sales outlets for exporters. The Moscow Interbank Currency Exchange (MICEX) began trading the dollar once a week on January 8, 1991.[2] Initially, a few banks participated with small offerings and the CBR operated with substantial intervention. The resulting interbank exchange rate, hardly a market rate of exchange, was influenced by enterprises[3] limited access to the auctions, CBR restrictions, and CBR intervention in the auctions.

Despite these limitations, the proliferating currency exchanges opened alternatives for exporters and importers. Having carried out the mandatory surrender at a less than favorable rate, exporters could sell their remaining holdings on the MICEX, or spend them on imports, or deposit them, as required by law, in their resident bank accounts. Importers could buy foreign exchange at the market rate from the MICEX, or at a subsidized rate from the government for importing essential items.

A major change in these arrangements was introduced by the government of Acting Prime Minister Yegor Gaidar when, on July 1, 1992, it enacted measures to unify the exchange rate for current account transactions. Furthermore, the exchange rate of the ruble in terms of the dollar was allowed to vary and followed the quotations, twice a week, of the MICEX.

A critical implication of a flexible exchange rate for the exchange rate adjustment model (which is specified in section 7.3) is that the exchange rate is influenced by policy-driven decisions with regard to the level of money supply in the economy. Since the observed exchange rate is thus endogenously determined, it is used with a lag as an instrumental variable for estimating the export supply and import demand equations for Russia (see section 7.4).

While the new arrangements marked the first step toward a unified and market exchange rate, the 50 percent surrender of export earnings continued. Exporters were required to sell 20 percent of their foreign exchange in the market through authorized commercial banks and 30 percent to the CBR (and not to the government) at the market rate (and not at the unfavorable fixed rate of 55 rubles to a dollar). (Furthermore, the export transactions were subject to export quotas and licensing, as will be discussed below.)

Progress toward a unified exchange rate, however, was absent from importing activity. Organizations that imported critical items—including food products, medicines, industrial raw materials and machinery—at MICEX rates of exchange sold them to domestic traders or final users (of the machinery, for example), who paid these organizations in foreign exchange (or the equivalent amount in rubles)—the amounts were 20 to 80 percent less than the prices at which they were imported from abroad. The importing organizations were reimbursed in foreign exchange from the off-budget, hard currency fund of the government. The subsidization of imported items at varying rates implied the use of multiple exchange rates.

Changes occurred on all fronts in 1993 and continued in 1994. Beginning June 1, 1993, MICEX auctioned currencies five days a week, thus providing daily quotations of the ruble-dollar exchange rate. The CBR's reference exchange rate, which is currently published twice a week, is based on the closing rates of the Tuesday and Thursday MICEX auctions and comes into effect the following day. From July 1, exporters were required to surrender half their export earnings directly to the market through their banks.[3] Despite this compulsory surrender requirement, the repatriation of foreign exchange earnings continued to be a major concern of policy makers. With a view to closing the gap between the declared value of an export contract to the customs authorities and the export earnings deposited in commercial bank accounts, the CBR and the Customs Committee introduced a passport system requiring exporters to record details of export transactions (from January 1, 1994, for "strategically important exports" [hereafter strategic exports] and from March 1, 1994, for all exports). Finally, the exchange rate coefficients applicable to imports were abolished in December 1993.

Thus, a flexible, current account convertible and unified exchange rate was in place in Russia at the start of 1994. The managed float and the crawling corridor regimes have operated under a limited current account convertibility of the ruble in which exporters have been required to convert foreign exchange into rubles. However, capital account transactions for residents and nonresidents, individuals and corporate entities have continued to be retricted. (These arrangements were in place until the end of 1995 but were evidently to be brought under gradual and selective relaxation in 1996.)

### Arrangements with Regard to Capital Account Transactions

Let us consider residents first. Citizens were allowed to open foreign exchange accounts and deposit foreign exchange (which they could buy from authorized foreign exchange bureaus operating in large cities) in resident banks. They could also buy foreign exchange from such banks for legitimate transactions, such as repaying a foreign debt. Bona fide documents were necessary for the purpose. A person could take out any amount of foreign banknotes upon presenting a certificate from an authorized bank to the customs authorities about the origin of the funds. Residents traveling abroad could take out a maximum of half a million rubles in banknotes. (The amount was raised from time to time.) Russian citizens were allowed foreign bank accounts only during their stay abroad. Otherwise, they must get permission from the CBR for the purpose.

Resident corporate entities—enterprises, for example—needed to acquire a license and approval from the CBR in order to borrow abroad. An additional license from the Ministry of Finance was necessary if the foreign loan required a guarantee from a state agency. Enterprises were not allowed to keep accounts in foreign banks, including branches of Russian banks, without CBR authorization.

Finally, Russian commercial banks that had a general foreign exchange license did not require a license to borrow abroad, maintain a foreign account, or import and export foreign currency, banknotes, bonds, and securities.[4] These banks also could carry out all these transactions for other authorized banks.

Detailed rules existed also for foreign exchange transactions by nonresidents. Nonresident individuals were allowed to take out rubles purchased in Russia with foreign exchange. They also could freely convert their income into foreign exchange.

Restrictions abounded with respect to corporate nonresidents.[5] They could take out foreign exchange in their possession that they brought in. If they earned foreign exchange from service activities, such as consulting or provision of shipping and insurance, they could transfer the earnings abroad after having converted half of the hard currency into rubles (which they might keep in their "T" accounts in an authorized Russian bank. In other words, foreign exchange earnings of nonresident suppliers of invisible items on current account were subject to the surrender requirement, just as the earnings of resident exporters were). Beginning September 1, 1994, corporate nonresidents were allowed to use their "I" accounts with Russian banks freely for buying and selling foreign exchange for investment activity. However, foreign investment itself was restricted in Russia (besides being deterred by legal uncertainties and a chaotic securities market): foreigners could not own a bank; they needed a license for owning and exploiting Russia's natural resources; they could not own land.

The limited foreign exchange activity by residents and nonresidents, individual and corporate, in a world of Hobson's choice on capital account transactions suggests that the ruble was not freely convertible beyond current account transactions. Since capital could not move freely in and out of Russia, the equilibrating impact (on the exchange rate) of real interest rate differentials, by inducing the flow of funds in desirable directions, can be assumed to be absent.[6] In other words, the real interest rate differential does not feature in the money demand equation in our model for estimating the exchange rate. (Following the familiar Cagan formulation, however, the expected rate of inflation is introduced in the money demand equation.)

Finally, which currency was used by Russia for trade payments and for debt settlement (including rescheduling and accumulation of arrears) depended on the group of countries under consideration. (These practices continue to the present day.)

A useful distinction emerged in this context between Russia's dealings with the FSU and the non-FSU countries.[7] All transactions with non-FSU countries (except those covered by special agreements with the former CMEA and with developing countries) were conducted in freely convertible currencies (such as the dollar). Trade payments and debt settlements by private traders and trading organizations among FSU countries were conducted in freely convertible currencies, or rubles, or the national currency of the state in question. The correspondent accounts of authorized banks were used for the purpose. The central banks of the FSU states, including the CBR, also maintained correspondent accounts that were used to carry out bilateral, intergovernmental transactions; these accounts were not to be used to settle balances multilaterally.[8] Foreign trade payments were settled with members of the former CMEA on the basis of contractual agreements; the major exception was oil and energy exports by Russia on centralized government account (to be explained below), which had to be paid for by the importer in hard currency.

### 7.1.2  The Foreign Trade Regime

A major challenge facing Russia's policy makers with respect to foreign trade arrangements was to shed the restrictive features of the Soviet planned economy. Another was to narrow the gap separating the trading arrangements between non-FSU and FSU countries, which differed at the start.

## Non-FSU Export Arrangements

The regime of Russia's main exports from early 1992 to the end of 1994 was marked by quotas, licenses, and export taxes that were gradually relaxed during the period. Moreover, strategic goods could be exported only by special exporters.[9]

*Export Quotas.*  Export quotas prevailed on several commodity groups (including fuels, ferrous and nonferrous metals, basic chemicals) in 1992; the arrangements under which they operated became elaborate and bureaucratized as the year advanced. The new scheme, which came into force on January 1, 1993, laid down the methods of working out and enforcing four types of subquotas.

The Ministry of Economy predicted non-FSU exports of each strategic commodity by calculating its domestic production at the start of the year and subtracting from it domestic consumption and the claims of the FSU states, based on their needs and current agreements.

In the next step, export subquotas were allocated to four groups.

The first claimant was the Ministry of Finance, which needed adequate foreign exchange to meet its hard currency obligations and finance imports of essential items under the Centralized Import Scheme. Under the Centralized Export Scheme of subquota allocation, the ministry received the foreign exchange from licensed exporters who bought the items from the domestic market and exported them on its behalf. These special exporters received a fee of 5 to 7 percent of the export proceeds.[10] The special exporter licenses were auctioned to bidders who offered to pay the amount of foreign exchange (guaranteed by an authorized commercial bank) to the ministry in advance.

The next set of subquotas was auctioned to enterprises that needed foreign exchange for importing high-tech items.

Joint ventures received automatic subquotas up to the full amount of their projected production levels.

Finally, some regions, such as Tatarstan, received export subquotas based on agreements with the federal government.

The regime of restrictive export quotas came under severe pressure in 1993 as the ruble appreciated in real terms via-à-vis the dollar. In fact, it was no longer necessary to maintain export quotas in order to protect domestic consumption because the appreciating ruble reduced the relative competitiveness of export sales (at given foreign prices) in relation to domestic sales. As a result, export quotas on a number of commodities, such as timber, fertilizers, coal, and meat products, were removed in June and November 1993. From January 1, 1994, twelve commodity groups, including oil and oil products, gas, electric energy, some ferrous metals, and food products, were retained on the quota list. The presidential decree of May 23, 1994, announced the abolition of all export quotas and licenses, but in a later reversal, they were retained to the end of the year for crude oil and petroleum products, and for aluminum and textiles, to restrict their sales in the European Common Market (*Bulletin*, p. 76).

In any case, centralized export subquotas continued to diminish over time: they accounted for 33 percent of total exports in 1992, 30 percent in 1993, and only 15 percent in the first half of 1994 (*Bulletin*, p. 77). Oil export quotas and oil export subquotas under the centralized export scheme continued to be a contentious issue between the Russian policy makers and the IMF. As argued immediately below, the centralized export subquotas provided an implicit export tax (in dollars, measured approximately as the difference between the higher foreign price and the lower domestic price) to the federal budget. By early 1996, Russia's oil prices were approximately 70 percent of world prices and oil shipments were effectively constrained by pipeline allocations rather than by quotas.

*Non-FSU Export Taxes.* These export taxes, which were introduced on January 1, 1992, changed frequently over the years in their rates and coverage of commodities. As domestic supply prices continued to move up (because of rising costs and production shortfalls), the profit margin from export sales at a given nominal exchange rate and world price declined; the real appreciation of the ruble cut further into the earnings. As a result, the export taxes were reduced steadily on all commodities except crude oil, for which it was 30 ECU per metric ton on September 1, 1994, compared with 26 ECU on January 1, 1992. For the same period, it went down (per ton) from 24 ECU to 5 ECU on natural gas, 51 ECU to 30 ECU on diesel fuel, 30 ECU to 3 ECU on nitrogenous fertilizers, 45 ECU to 8 ECU on timber, 215 ECU to 12 ECU on stainless steel, 500 ECU to 10 ECU on aluminum, and 2,000 ECU to 640 ECU on nickel (*Bulletin*, p. 75, Table 3.3.9).[11]

The centralized exports on government account were exempt from explicit export taxes. They were, however, subject to an implicit export tax because the federal budget automatically earned the difference (excluding special exporters' commission and transport costs) between the foreign price and the domestic price of oil (which was regulated and had moved to 70 percent of the world price toward the end of 1995, from about 40 percent a year earlier). The IMF's recommendation that the authorities remove the remaining energy export quotas and switch from an export tax to an excise tax on energy products in 1996 was calculated to stimulate exports and slash wasteful domestic consumption.

To sum up, the Russian export trade regime edged forward from early 1992 to less extensive export quotas, lower export tariffs, and fewer taxed items. Did this imply that market incentives of sorts were beginning to operate in Russia's export performance? Not really. Export quotas on major items comprising 70 percent of exports continued through 1993; quotas on oil and oil products, constituting about half of exports, continued until the end of the period under consideration. Their exports were determined by the residual amounts left after domestic consumption and claims of partner countries (covered by special agreements) were met. The rest of the exports, where price incentives could play a role, were constrained by market disruptions and rising domestic costs that could not be fully offset by the declining export taxes, in view of the constraints of given foreign prices and an appreciating ruble. The exportable surpluses that emerged from declining outputs after (declining) domestic use was met were sold abroad.[12] It was as though the supply-constrained Soviet regime of residually planned exports, untouched by foreign demand and the real exchange rate, was still in place. This conundrum is explored via the export supply equation with respect to non-FSU markets in section 7.4.

### Non-FSU Import Trade Regime
By contrast, the import trade regime, though marked by higher and more diversified tariffs across commodities, created incentives for domestic demand and relative prices to operate.

Russia's import trade arrangements continued to be free from quotas and licenses throughout the period. Moreover, there were no import duties between January and July 1, 1992, because all import tariff levies of the former Soviet Union were abolished on January 15. Subsequently, the tariff rates were differentiated by commodity groups and by source.

For example, the basic rate of 5 percent of July 1, 1992, was raised to 15 percent on September 1, 1992. Nonessential items such as alcohol, cars, and TVs were subjected to rates varying from 15 to 25 percent. There were no duties on food and medicines.

A new tariff scheme came into force on July 1, 1993: food, medicines, medical equipment, children's clothes, and other "socially important" items were exempt from duties.[13] "For other goods, the basic tax rate varied from 5 per cent (intermediate goods, metals, transport equipment) to 15 per cent (capital goods, consumer durables). The highest rate applied to strong alcoholic drinks (100 per cent)" (*Bulletin*, p. 75). The simple average tariff resulting from these arrangements was 8.1 percent.

At the same time, the tariff schedule was differentiated by import source. The basic rate (5 percent) applied to countries (their number increased over time) with most-favored-nation status; half the basic rate applied to imports from developing countries and twice the rate to the remaining countries.

Increasing protectionist pressures appeared from the agricultural sector and some industries at the start of 1994 as the ruble continued to appreciate in real terms. The new schedule of levies with seventeen bands, which came into force on July 1, 1994, had an average duty rate of 12.5 percent. Food products, which were previously duty free, were taxed at the rate of 15 to 20 percent. The rates were raised on a range of manufactured and investment goods.

Finally, imported consumer goods—among them hard liquors, cars, furs, and leather goods were subjected to excise taxes and a value-added tax (VAT) of 20 percent beginning February 1, 1993.

In effect, the policy makers sought to counter or weaken the impact of the appreciating ruble on imports by successive hikes and selective differentiation of import tariffs. Protectionsist pressures continued throughout 1995 and escalated on the eve of the December 1995 elections for the Russian Duma and later on the eve of the Russian presidential elections of June 1996. The devaluationary shifts in the crawling corridor of the ruble were calculated to counter these demands. The possibility of a connection, ceteris paribus, between the real exchange rate and real imports is explored in the import demand equation of section 7.4.

### Trade Arrangements with FSU States

How did the arrangements of export quotas, licensing, and taxes, and of import tariffs that prevailed in Russia's trade with non-FSU countries differ from those which emerged in Russian-FSU trade?

By early 1993 the export regimes, marked by export quotas, licensing, and tariffs,[14] resembled those which prevailed with non-FSU countries; imports were exempt from tariffs (but were subject to VAT and excise taxes). Russia had trade agreements with the Central Asian republics and Kazakhstan, and with Azerbaijan and Armenia, that specified these features; similar agreements were signed with Ukraine in February 1994 and with Georgia in May 1994.

### 7.1.3  Institutional Arrangements

The elaborate system of export quotas and licensing was operated by several ministries. The Ministry of Economy calculated the production and consumption (including the needs of FSU states that were covered by special agreements), and the potential exportable surpluses to non-FSU destinations of the strategic commodities that were subject to quotas and licensing. The centralized export subquotas of these items were worked out jointly by the Finance and Economy ministries. Quotas for nonenergy products were auctioned by the Ministry of Foreign Economic Relations. Export subquotas, which were auctioned to enterprises so that they could earn foreign exchange to import technologies and know-how, were issued by the Operational Issues Committee of the government.

The special exporters who implemented the quotas of strategic commodities were registered by the Ministry of Foreign Economic Relations, which eliminated former participants on grounds of bad performance and invited fresh blood to energize the scheme. The situation was ripe for distribution of largess in return for bribes. The number of special exporters declined to 497 on August 1, 1994, from 800 at the end of 1993. As of July 1, 1994, quotas and licenses were replaced by registration of export contracts with the Ministry of Foreign Economic Relations. The special exporters were to be abolished as of January 1, 1995. As late as March 1995, that decision had not been implemented. It was difficult to get rid of the system of top-heavy and selective decision-making in which ministry bureaucrats, managerial elites, and trade groups participated to their mutual benefit. The arrangements lacked market incentives and promoted corruption.

## 7.2  The Results

The regime of the unified ruble exchange rate, which was made convertible for current account transactions and was allowed to fluctuate in terms of the dollar, influenced the ruble's nominal and real value. As already noted, the policy makers' "exogenous" decision to incur budget deficits and finance them via borrowing from the CBR and currency emission contributed to the exchange rate movements by aggravating domestic inflation. The exchange rate was thus influenced by the overpowering macroeconomic outcomes of budgetary (and monetary) policies. The purpose of the monetarist model of section 7.3 is to measure the impact of the adjustment of money demand to the exogenous money supply on the ruble-dollar exchange rate. In fact, the model is formulated with the real (rather than the nominal) exchange rate, with a view to assessing ex post the impact of the monetary imbalance on the exchange rate during 1992–94, rather than designed as a policy exercise.

At the same time, the substantial production declines in the economy (especially in the export industries, including oil) and the structural output shifts influenced the overall non-FSU and FSU trade balances and the direction and composition of Russia's foreign trade. Thus, the evolving export and import trade regimes (described earlier) contributed to the changes in the external trade balance and its structure in the midst of turmoil in the domestic economy. It is difficult to incorporate fully these disturbances in the export supply and import demand equations of section 7.3. For example, the declining domestic production and consumption of oil and other export commodities (among them minerals and metals) generated different amounts of exportable surpluses for the period under consideration. However, appropriate monthly measures of domestic supply constraints are hard to construct.

The ruble-dollar exchange rate, both nominal and real, took the full brunt of the policy makers' domestic macroeconomic agenda. These exchange rate movements are discussed immediately below, followed by an analysis of Russia's non-FSU trade balance and its changing trade structure and orientation.

### 7.2.1 The Ruble-Dollar Exchange Rate

The connection between the monthly ruble-dollar exchange rate, the money supply, and the price level (here measured in terms of the Russian consumer price index, CPI) is explored in Easterly and da Cunha (1994). The high correlation between the nominal exchange rate and the money supply (appropriately lagged) suggests a monetary model of the ruble-dollar exchange rate determination. The data of the nominal exchange rate, the ruble money supply, and the Russian CPI are therefore used in section 7.3 to estimate a ruble-dollar exchange rate model, the first such attempt incorporating the familiar Cagan (1956) specification of money demand. The significant feature of the monthly nominal and real exchange rates is that the nominal exchange rate, defined as rubles per dollar, depreciated throughout the period (Table 7.1), whereas the real exchange rate depreciated from June to November 1992 and appreciated thereafter until the end of 1994 (Table 7.2).

Thus, the nominal value of the ruble in MICEX depreciated rapidly from July 1992 to December 1994 (with the trend continuing in 1995), having declined to 3,402.5 rubles per dollar in December 1994 from 143.3 rubles per dollar in July 1992 (ER in Table 7.1). The CBR intervention in MICEX, which was calculated to balance the goal of export and import-substitute competitiveness with inflation control, nevertheless resulted in a real appreciation of the ruble because inflation differential at home and abroad ran ahead of the rate of nominal devaluation: the real exchange rate of the ruble (RER in Table 7.2) of 55.74 rubles per dollar in December 1994 was eight percent of its value in January 1992.[15] The rate of real appreciation moderated somewhat in 1995 as the monthly inflation rate declined. Indeed, the CBR switched from a regime of managed float to that of crawling band *and* tilted the band toward a devaluationary mode from July 1, 1995. The July–December band of 4,300–4,800 rubles to the dollar was lifted to 4,800–5,100 rubles to the dollar on the eve of the elections for the Russian Duma on December 19. With inflation evidently under control (running at 2.2 percent in April 1996), the band was raised again to 5,000–5,600 rubles to the dollar on July 1 and was targeted to reach 5,500–6,100 rubles to the dollar on Decemebr 31.

We turn next to the important issues in Russia's trade performance. They are its trade balances with the non-FSU and FSU trading partners, and the changing composition and orientation of its trade.

### 7.2.2   Non-FSU Exports and Imports: Size and Pattern

Russia's non-FSU exports declined from $71.1 billion in 1990 to $44.3 billion in 1993, an average annual decline of 21 percent (*Bulletin*, p. 70). However they climbed by 16.1 percent in 1994 and an estimated 25 percent in 1995 (EBRD, 1996, p. 42). Imports also declined sharply, at an annual average rate of 11 percent from 1990 to 1993 (*Bulletin*, p. 70), but picked up by 12.7 percent in 1994 and an estimated 12.5 percent in 1995 (EBRD, 1996, p. 42). As a result, the net trade balance turned from a negative $10.6 billion in 1990 to positive levels thereafter.

Trade balance with the FSU states also registered a sharp positive increase, from 6.7 billion rubles in 1990 to 5.2 trillion rubles in 1993, the positive balances continuing in 1994 and 1995.

It is, however, difficult to aggregate these two balances and arrive at a definite picture of Russia's overall trade balance with the outside world.[16] This exercise presents insurmountable conceptual problems that are discussed below.

**Table 7.1**
Monthly monetary and financial data

| Date | CPI (1992-07 = 100) | INF (percent) | ESTINF (percent) | RM2 (bill. rubles) | ER (rubles/$) | USCPI | WOILP | WCOMP (1992-07 = 100) | EXPRICE | WCPI |
|---|---|---|---|---|---|---|---|---|---|---|
| 1991-12 | 9.00 | | | 1004.00 | 148.80 | 98.14 | 85.87 | 100.61 | 93.98 | 90.66 |
| 1992-01 | 31.08 | 245.33 | | | 199.70 | 98.28 | 84.06 | 101.33 | 93.56 | 91.70 |
| 1992-02 | 42.97 | 38.26 | | | 175.70 | 98.64 | 85.59 | 102.12 | 94.68 | 93.21 |
| 1992-03 | 55.76 | 29.76 | 29.50 | 1325.00 | 148.40 | 99.14 | 84.76 | 100.79 | 93.58 | 94.78 |
| 1992-04 | 67.83 | 21.65 | 25.49 | | 152.70 | 99.28 | 91.55 | 99.45 | 95.90 | 96.11 |
| 1992-05 | 75.94 | 11.96 | 19.68 | 1398.00 | 122.30 | 99.50 | 95.98 | 99.82 | 98.09 | 97.37 |
| 1992-06 | 90.09 | 18.63 | 12.72 | 1731.00 | 123.60 | 99.78 | 103.88 | 100.61 | 102.08 | 98.77 |
| 1992-07 | 100.00 | 11.00 | 17.67 | 2169.00 | 143.30 | 100.00 | 100.00 | 100.00 | 100.00 | 100.00 |
| 1992-08 | 109.90 | 9.90 | 12.05 | 2994.00 | 169.70 | 100.27 | 96.40 | 99.10 | 97.89 | 101.33 |
| 1992-09 | 123.42 | 12.30 | 11.33 | 3888.00 | 225.30 | 100.56 | 98.61 | 99.55 | 99.13 | 102.99 |
| 1992-10 | 154.32 | 25.04 | 13.09 | 4953.00 | 353.00 | 100.92 | 99.30 | 97.33 | 98.22 | 104.48 |
| 1992-11 | 188.28 | 22.01 | 22.33 | 5103.00 | 426.90 | 101.06 | 93.49 | 96.89 | 95.36 | 105.78 |
| 1992-12 | 236.93 | 25.84 | 19.99 | 6084.00 | 414.60 | 100.99 | 88.64 | 97.77 | 93.66 | 107.04 |
| 1993-01 | 298.55 | 26.01 | 22.81 | 7221.00 | 489.20 | 101.48 | 84.06 | 98.39 | 91.94 | 108.83 |
| 1993-02 | 373.15 | 24.99 | 22.89 | 7820.00 | 569.50 | 101.85 | 89.61 | 97.61 | 94.01 | 110.57 |
| 1993-03 | 447.83 | 20.01 | 22.15 | 9081.00 | 663.70 | 102.20 | 91.27 | 96.89 | 94.36 | 112.31 |
| 1993-04 | 532.61 | 18.93 | 18.54 | 11251.00 | 766.10 | 102.49 | 91.41 | 95.11 | 93.45 | 114.20 |
| 1993-05 | 628.82 | 18.06 | 17.80 | 13653.00 | 911.70 | 102.63 | 89.88 | 93.87 | 92.07 | 116.04 |
| 1993-06 | 754.59 | 20.00 | 17.18 | 15957.00 | 1078.70 | 102.77 | 86.29 | 91.92 | 89.39 | 117.89 |
| 1993-07 | 920.63 | 22.00 | 18.60 | 18656.00 | 1019.60 | 102.77 | 80.74 | 94.93 | 88.54 | 119.67 |
| 1993-08 | 1156.48 | 25.62 | 20.04 | 21396.00 | 986.00 | 103.05 | 81.57 | 94.67 | 88.78 | 121.71 |

| 1993-09 | 1426.75 | 23.37 | 22.65 | 22043.00 | 1077.30 | 103.27 | 78.39 | 94.22 | 87.10 | 123.90 |
| 1993-10 | 1712.07 | 20.00 | 20.97 | 24872.00 | 1188.20 | 103.70 | 81.16 | 94.31 | 88.39 | 126.06 |
| 1993-11 | 1986.03 | 16.00 | 18.55 | 27345.00 | 1196.30 | 103.76 | 74.51 | 97.42 | 87.11 | 128.48 |
| 1993-12 | 2244.14 | 13.00 | 15.67 | 32601.00 | 1245.20 | 103.76 | 64.96 | 99.82 | 84.13 | 130.93 |
| 1994-01 | 2648.10 | 18.00 | 13.53 | 33980.00 | 1428.70 | 104.05 | 73.08 | 101.27 | 88.58 | 133.86 |
| 1994-02 | 2939.45 | 11.00 | 17.20 | 36439.00 | 1584.50 | 104.40 | 72.36 | 102.83 | 89.12 | 136.74 |
| 1994-03 | 3145.22 | 7.00 | 12.06 | 39550.00 | 1718.70 | 104.77 | 72.36 | 102.21 | 88.78 | 139.46 |
| 1994-04 | 3459.72 | 10.00 | 9.22 | 46401.00 | 1793.70 | 104.91 | 80.36 | 101.59 | 92.04 | 142.57 |
| 1994-05 | 3736.48 | 8.00 | 11.45 | 52253.00 | 1878.30 | 104.97 | 87.17 | 104.29 | 96.59 | 144.78 |
| 1994-06 | 3885.94 | 4.00 | 9.96 | 59414.00 | 1961.80 | 105.33 | 89.56 | 106.06 | 98.64 | 147.78 |
| 1994-07 | 4080.27 | 5.00 | 7.07 | 64363.00 | 2027.70 | 105.61 | 94.10 | 108.97 | 102.28 | 150.37 |
| 1994-08 | 4243.42 | 4.00 | 7.84 | 70970.00 | 2136.90 | 106.04 | 89.44 | 108.03 | 99.66 | 151.46 |
| 1994-09 | 4582.88 | 8.00 | 7.11 | 77063.00 | 2361.10 | 106.33 | 84.78 | 112.19 | 99.86 | 152.76 |
| 1994-10 | 5316.21 | 16.00 | 10.02 | 80359.00 | 2993.80 | 106.40 | 85.98 | 111.67 | 100.11 | 153.89 |
| 1994-11 | 6007.29 | 13.00 | 15.80 | 84348.00 | 3142.90 | 106.54 | 90.87 | 113.23 | 103.17 | 154.81 |
| 1994-12 | 6992.52 | 16.40 | 13.53 | 96200.00 | 3402.50 | 106.54 | 85.26 | 115.00 | 101.62 | 155.44 |

*Sources:* CPI: Consumer price index is from *Statisticheskoe obozrenie,* 1994, no. 1,2; *Finansovaya izvestiya,* 6–12 August 1993, no. 40; and various issues of *Kommersant*; INF: Inflation rate is calculated as $100 \times (CPI - CPI[-1])/CPI[-1]$; ESTINF: Estimated inflation rate is calculated using the regression results in Table 7.2; RM2: Ruble money supply (M2) is from Goskomstat; ER: The nominal exchage rate is from Goskomstat; USCPI: U.S. consumer price index is from *International Financial Statistics* of the IMF (July 1992 = 100); WOILP: World oil price index is from *International Financial Statistics* of the IMF (July 1992 = 100); WCOMP: World commodity price index (excl. petroleum) is from *International Financial Statistics* of the IMF (July 1991 = 100); WOILP: World oil price index is from *International Financial Statistics* of the IMF (July 1992 = 100); EXPRICE: Export price index is computed as $.45 \times$ WOILP $+ .55 \times$ WCOMP (July 1992 = 100); WCPI: World consumer price index is from *International Financial Statistics* of the IMF (July 1992 = 100).

**Table 7.2**
Monthly export, import, and exchange rate data

| Date | EXP (million dollars) | IMP (million dollars) | REAL EXP (in July-1992 million dollars) | REAL IMP (in July-1992 million dollars) | RER (rubles/$) | ln (RER) | eln (RER) | REAL NX (REAL EXP - REAL IMP) (in July-1992 million dollars) |
|---|---|---|---|---|---|---|---|---|
| 1991-12 |      |      |         |         | 1622.58 | 7.39 |      |         |
| 1992-01 |      |      |         |         | 631.48  | 6.45 |      |         |
| 1992-02 |      |      |         |         | 403.33  | 6.00 |      |         |
| 1992-03 |      |      |         |         | 263.85  | 5.58 |      |         |
| 1992-04 |      |      |         |         | 223.50  | 5.41 |      |         |
| 1992-05 |      |      |         |         | 160.24  | 5.08 |      |         |
| 1992-06 |      |      |         |         | 136.89  | 4.92 |      |         |
| 1992-07 | 3340 | 2875 | 3340.00 | 2875.00 | 143.30  | 4.96 | 4.85 | 465.00  |
| 1992-08 | 3456 | 2916 | 3530.67 | 2877.73 | 154.83  | 5.04 | 5.00 | 652.94  |
| 1992-09 | 3665 | 3215 | 3697.28 | 3121.66 | 183.57  | 5.21 | 5.13 | 575.62  |
| 1992-10 | 4057 | 3114 | 4130.67 | 2980.47 | 230.85  | 5.44 | 5.30 | 1150.20 |
| 1992-11 | 4369 | 3161 | 4581.59 | 2988.28 | 229.14  | 5.43 | 5.40 | 1593.31 |
| 1992-12 | 4758 | 3520 | 5080.00 | 3288.49 | 176.72  | 5.17 | 5.39 | 1791.51 |
| 1993-01 | 2200 | 950  | 2392.83 | 872.92  | 166.28  | 5.11 | 5.10 | 1519.91 |
| 1993-02 | 2200 | 1300 | 2340.18 | 1175.73 | 155.44  | 5.05 | 5.02 | 1164.45 |
| 1993-03 | 2600 | 1300 | 2755.38 | 1157.51 | 151.46  | 5.02 | 4.94 | 1597.87 |
| 1993-04 | 3600 | 1900 | 3852.53 | 1663.75 | 147.42  | 4.99 | 4.95 | 2188.78 |
| 1993-05 | 3800 | 1700 | 4127.09 | 1465.01 | 148.80  | 5.00 | 4.95 | 2662.08 |

| | | | | | | | |
|---|---|---|---|---|---|---|---|
| 1993-06 | 3800 | 1800 | 4251.20 | 1526.85 | 146.91 | 4.99 | 4.96 | 2724.35 |
| 1993-07 | 3100 | 1500 | 3501.06 | 1253.45 | 113.82 | 4.73 | 4.93 | 2247.61 |
| 1993-08 | 3679 | 1834 | 4144.18 | 1506.86 | 87.86 | 4.48 | 4.64 | 2637.32 |
| 1993-09 | 4085 | 2272 | 4690.20 | 1833.74 | 77.98 | 4.36 | 4.33 | 2856.46 |
| 1993-10 | 3730 | 2412 | 4219.82 | 1913.37 | 71.97 | 4.28 | 4.21 | 2306.45 |
| 1993-11 | 4609 | 2730 | 5290.98 | 2124.84 | 62.50 | 4.14 | 4.16 | 3166.14 |
| 1993-12 | 5480 | 3147 | 6513.50 | 2403.57 | 57.57 | 4.05 | 4.04 | 4109.93 |
| 1994-01 | 2522 | 1825 | 2847.00 | 1363.36 | 56.14 | 4.03 | 4.02 | 1483.64 |
| 1994-02 | 3027 | 2087 | 3396.60 | 1526.25 | 56.28 | 4.03 | 3.90 | 1870.35 |
| 1994-03 | 3518 | 2528 | 3962.72 | 1812.71 | 57.25 | 4.05 | 3.96 | 2150.01 |
| 1994-04 | 3766 | 2027 | 4091.85 | 1421.76 | 54.39 | 4.00 | 3.96 | 2670.09 |
| 1994-05 | 4026 | 2223 | 4168.31 | 1535.43 | 52.77 | 3.97 | 4.03 | 2632.88 |
| 1994-06 | 4486 | 2522 | 4548.08 | 1706.59 | 53.18 | 3.97 | 3.97 | 2841.49 |
| 1994-07 | 3912 | 2028 | 3824.85 | 1348.67 | 52.48 | 3.96 | 3.96 | 2476.18 |
| 1994-08 | 3599 | 1903 | 3611.12 | 1256.44 | 53.40 | 3.98 | 4.02 | 2354.68 |
| 1994-09 | 4363 | 2304 | 4369.31 | 1508.25 | 54.78 | 4.00 | 4.00 | 2861.06 |
| 1994-10 | 4193 | 2609 | 4188.41 | 1695.37 | 59.92 | 4.09 | 4.04 | 2493.04 |
| 1994-11 | | | | | 55.74 | 4.02 | 4.03 | |
| 1994-12 | | | | | 51.84 | 3.95 | 4.01 | |

Sources: Trade data are from Statisticheskoe obozrenie, 1994, no. 1; Sotsial'no-ekonomicheskoe polozhenie Rossii, yanvar'-octyabr' 1994 (Moscow: Goskomstat, 1994), p. 55; REALEXP: Real exports are computed as X/EXPRICE; REALIMP: Real imports are computed as IMP/WCPI; RER: Real ruble/U.S. dollar exchange rate is computed as ERxUSCPI/CPI; ln(RER): Log of the real exchange rate is computed as log of RER; eln(RER): Predicted log of real exchange rate is computed from equation 12.

**Conceptual Problems of Aggregating non-FSU and FSU Trade Data**
Four conceptual issues arise in working up a consolidated account of Russia's balance of payments position with the outside world.

The first issue is whether Russia can settle its net overall debtor position with the non-FSU group by using its net creditor position with the FSU trading partners. The net non-FSU debtor situation was sustained through 1992–94 by measures undertaken by official and private creditors rather than by the flow of private investment. (Foreign direct investment from January 1991 to October 1995 was estimated at a disappointing $4.9 billion. See *Wall Street Journal*, April 30, 1996, p. A13.) In fact, this support, which was estimated at $59 billion in 1992 and 1993, consisted of $27 billion in bilateral and multilateral official loans, $15 billion in debt relief, and $17 billion in debt rescheduling.[17] Similar measures have continued to date: the $10.2 billion, three-year IMF credit agreement approved in March 1996 was followed by a rescheduling over a period of twenty-five years of more than $40 billion official debt by the Paris Club of sovereign creditors in April 1996.[18] At the same time the London Club of commercial creditors rescheduled $32.5 billion of commercial credits. The restructuring of the official and commercial debt opened up opportunities for Russia to begin borrowing in international markets. By contrast, the net debtor position of the FSU states with Russia was increasingly reflected in accumulated arrears of interstate and interenterprise liabilities owed to Russia. These were settled with credits from the Russian budget (CBR credits to FSU partners were discontinued in July 1993), settlement of some debts (with the Baltic States) in hard currency, and trade agreements allowing rescheduling of debts and future barter deals.

Russia, however, could not be regarded as borrowing from one group and lending to another because these debt instruments were not viewed as exchangeable by finanacial markets; even if they were, Russian financial institutions were not sufficiently developed to carry out such a swap.

A similar "nonequivalence" problem arose with respect to goods sold by Russia (with the exception of energy products) to the FSU states. They could not be sold freely at world prices in non-FSU countries because of poor quality and lack of servicing with respect to manufactured items.

Third, the conversion of ruble earnings on items sold by Russia to FSU states into dollars was problematic because of daily shifts in the nominal ruble-dollar exchange rate. The averaging method would seriously influence the estimates.

Finally, the prices charged by Russia until the end of 1993 for energy products sold to FSU states were lower. It was not clear if Russia charged lower prices with a view to giving assistance to FSU states. In that case, Russia's trade account in oil could be valued at market prices with a capital account entry registering the aid.

In view of these problems, no attempt is made here to aggregate Russia's trade balances with the two groups of trading partners. In any case, monthly data on foreign trade with FSU states are not available.

Clearly, the aggregate non-FSU exports and imports conceal critical shifts in Russia's commodity trade: the destinations of exports and the origins of imports. This information is not available on a monthly basis and is briefly described below on the basis of annual features.

### Geographical and Commodity Structure of Russian Trade

The most significant change in Russia's non-FSU trade took place with regard to the sources of imports and the destinations of exports. The most dramatic shift occurred in trade with the former CMEA countries: their share in Russia's total exports dropped from 43 percent in 1990 to 14 percent in January–August 1994. Their share in Russia's imports dropped from 44 percent in 1990 to 8 percent in the first half of 1994 (*Bulletin*, p. 70). The share of the OECD countries in Russia's declining exports and imports increased: they took 67 percent of Russia's total exports in the first eight months of 1994, compared with 36 percent in 1990. Similarly, their share in Russia's imports went from 40 percent in 1990 to 69 percent in January–August 1994. The developing countries' share in Russia's exports was stable at 12–14 percent, but their contribution to Russian imports rose from 10 percent in 1990 to 17 percent in 1994.

Russia thus had managed to forge new trade ties with the developed and developing market economies and loosened those with its former CMEA trade partners.

The commodity composition of Russian trade showed a high concentration of crude oil, natural gas, and petroleum products in exports (46 percent of exports in January–June 1994); in fact, ten commodities accounted for 74 percent of Russia's exports. Thus, exports failed to diversify toward manufactured goods. By contrast, the commodity composition of imports registered a shift away from machinery (which dropped from 44 percent in 1990 to 30 percent in the first eight months of 1994) and toward consumer goods and food items (*Bulletin*, p. 73).

Russia's trade structure with the non-FSU countries thus changed significantly in commodity composition and orientation. Moreover, this trade was carried out in hard currency under a unified, convertible, and flexible exchange rate; the export quotas and licenses were progressively relaxed, although the passport system, beginning January 1, 1994, put exporters under surveillance. At the same time, import tariff rates were progressively raised and became more diversified.

The critical question to address in the context of these developments is whether the emerging changes in Russia's trade pattern proceeded under market-type incentives. In particular, was the trade performance with the non-FSU countries a response to the real exchange rate and certain other variables, such as the growth of real GDP (which, ceteris paribus, could be expected to influence import demand) or exportable surpluses of oil (which, given the foreign demand, could spill into exports)?

These questions are rigorously examined via the models presented below, beginning with the model for estimating the real ruble-dollar exchange rate.

### 7.3   The Models

#### 7.3.1   The Exchange Rate Model

Following Cagan (1956), I define the demand for cash balances as follows:

$$L_t = k P_t y_t^{\eta} e^{-\alpha \pi_t^* + \mu_t} \tag{1}$$

Where $L_t$ represents demand for nominal ruble cash balances in (month) $t$, $P_t$ is the price level (defined as the consumer price index, CPI) in $t$, $y_t$ is real output or GDP in $t$, $\pi_t^*$ is the expected rate of inflation in $t$, and $\mu_t$ is the error term.

Note several features about the equation. First, the demand for cash balances, ceteris paribus, rises in proportion to the rise in the price level, thus exhibiting the absence of money illusion. Next, the demand depends positively on $y$ taken by itself reflecting the need to finance more transactions. Third, the demand declines ceteris paribus with respect to the expected rate of inflation reflecting the higher opportunity cost of holding cash if inflation is expected to go up. This feature of $\pi^*$ representing the opportunity cost of holding ruble cash in Russia during 1992–1994 is appropriate because inflation far exceeded the nominal rate of interest due to interest rate ceilings. Finally, $\eta$ is the income elasticity of demand for money, and $\alpha \pi^*$ is the absolute value of the elasticity with respect to the expected rate of inflation.

The demand for real money balances is derived from (1):

$$\frac{L_t}{P_t} = k y_t^{\eta} e^{-\alpha \pi_t^* + \mu_t} \tag{2}$$

The expected rate of inflation $\pi_t^*$ is estimated on the basis of a two-period, backward adjustment process as follows:

$$\pi_t^* = a + b\pi_{t-1} + c\pi_{t-2} + \text{error term} \tag{3}$$

Here, $b$ and $c$ are estimated as weights to the observed inflation rates $\pi_{t-1}$ and $\pi_{t-2}$ in $t-1$ and $t-2$ to determine the expected inflation rate $\pi_t^*$ in $t$. The estimated, expected inflation rate series is presented in Table 7.1.

The long-run demand for real cash balances in the (natural) log formulation is given as

$$\ln\left(\frac{L_t}{P_t}\right) = \ln k + \eta \ln y_t - \alpha \pi_t^* + \mu_t \tag{4}$$

In the short run, however, the actual real supply of money may not correspond to the real demand because of lags in adjustment. The net excess supply of real balances can in turn influence the exchange rate because individuals, banks, and enterprises can convert them into foreign exchange. (Net excess supply implies excess supply of cash if it is positive, and excess demand for cash if it is negative.) Now, assume that any net excess supply of real balances gets reflected in the real exchange rate, that is, the market for real balances clears through variations in the real exchange rate.

First, define the real ruble exchange rate as

$$\varepsilon_t = \frac{E_t P_t^*}{P_t} \tag{5}$$

where $E_t$ is the nominal exchange rate of the ruble per dollar in $t$, and $P_t^*$ is the U.S. consumer price index in $t$.

Next, define the net excess supply of real cash balances as

$$z_t = \ln\left(\frac{M_t}{P_t}\right) - \ln\left(\frac{L_{t+1}}{P_{t+1}}\right) \tag{6}$$

This defintion implies that the real money supply relevant for period $t+1$ is determined at the end of period $t$.

Finally, assume that the demand for foreign exchange in $t$ depends on the traders' expectation of the net excess supply of real ruble balances in period $t + 1$. Thus, defining the equilibrium real exchange rate as $\varepsilon^*$, and the difference $\ln \varepsilon_t - \ln \varepsilon_t^*$ as $x_t$, one can write

$$x_t = \lambda z_t \tag{7}$$

Here, $\lambda$ will have to be different from zero in order for the exchange rate to reflect disequilibrium in the market for real balances. Eliminating $\ln \varepsilon^*$ by differencing, one gets

$$x_t - x_{t-1} \equiv \ln \varepsilon_t - \ln \varepsilon_{t-1} = \lambda(z_t - z_{t-1}) \tag{8}$$

Now assume that the monetary authorities aim at reducing the net excess supply of real balances asymptotically to zero. Accordingly, they carry out the adjustment of real balances as follows:

$$z_t - z_{t-1} = -\mu z_{t-1} \tag{9}$$

or

$$z_t = (1 - \mu)z_{t-1} \quad \text{where} \quad 0 \leq \mu \leq 1 \tag{10}$$

This adaptive adjustment process converges asymptotically to equilibrium implying zero net excess supply of real cash.

Substituting (6) and (9) in (8), and setting $\theta = -\lambda \mu$, we get:

$$\ln \varepsilon_t - \ln \varepsilon_{t-1} = \theta \left[ \ln \left( \frac{M_{t-1}}{P_{t-1}} \right) - \ln \left( \frac{L_t}{P_t} \right) \right] + \text{error term} \tag{11}$$

where $\theta$ is the speed with which the net excess supply of real cash gets reflected into a change in the real exchange rate. The speed with which the demand for real cash adjusts to the available supply implies three possibilities with regard to the exchange rate adjustment. The exchange rate may adjust instantaneously to its equilibrium value; or it may fail to adjust from its previous level; or it may adjust with a delay. The parametric constraints and interaction between $\lambda$, $\mu$, and $\theta$ relevant for the three possibilities are specified below.

I first take the instantaneous adjustment of $\varepsilon_t$ to $\varepsilon^*$. The real exchange rate deviates from its equilibrium value in (7) only if there is disequilibrium in the market for real balances. Therefore, the real exchange rate is $\varepsilon^*$ if the latter is in equilibrium, that is, if $z_t = 0$. Now if $\mu = 1$, $z_t = 0$ regardless of $z_{t-1}$. This implies that any disequilibrium in the market for real balances is removed in one period (in effect instantaneously) by real money stock adjustment. Therefore, via (7), $\varepsilon_t = \varepsilon^*$, so that there is instantaneous adjustment in the real exchange rate, regardless of the value of $\lambda$ or, equivalently of $\theta$, since $\lambda = -\theta \mu$.

I next turn to the case of lack of adjustment in the real exchange rate. If $\mu = 0$, which implies $\theta = 0$, it follows from (10) that any disequilibrium in the market for real balances persists forever. This in turn means, via (7), that the real exchange rate will deviate from its equilibrium value forever. Thus, there is no adjustment in the real exchange rate.

Finally, I consider the case of delayed adjustments in the exchange rate. Let $0 < \mu < 1$; this means $z_t > 0$ asymptotically. Assume that a positive, net excess supply of real money, that is, $z_t > 0$, leads to a rise in $P_t$. Then, assuming that the foreign price level $P_t^*$ does not change and the rate of devaluation in the nominal exchange rate $E_t$ lags behind the domestic rate of inflation (as has been the case in Russia), equation (5) implies a reduction in $\varepsilon_t$ below its equilibrium level. Thus, $x_t < 0$, if $z_t > 0$ so that $\lambda < 0$. Therefore, $\theta > 0$, if $\mu > 0$ because $\theta = -\lambda\mu$. This means that the real exchange rate moves to its equilibrium value, not instantaneously, but asymptotically, as $z_t$ goes to zero. This is the case of delayed adjustment in the real exchange rate.

It is clear that $\mu$ rather than $\lambda$ determines the nature of adjustment. Since $\lambda \neq 0$ by assumption, $\theta = -\lambda\mu$ can be zero only if $\mu = 0$. With $\mu = 0$ and hence $\theta = 0$, there is no adjustment in the market for real balances and the real exchange rate regardless of $\lambda$. On the other hand, if $\mu = 1$, any disequilibrium in the market for real balances is instantaneously eliminated so that the real exchange rate also jumps to its equilibrium value, again regardless of $\lambda$. This is the case of instantaneous adjustment in the markets for the exchange rate and cash balances. Now if $0 < \mu < 1$, any disequilibrium in the market for real balances is eliminated only asymptotically, that is, in the long run. And until it is eliminated, the real exchange rate will also deviate from its equilibrium value regardless of $\lambda$. Thus, there is delayed adjustment in both markets.

Why is the model specified in terms of the real exchange rate and cash balances? For the period under consideration, Russia had a floating exchange rate managed by the CBR. This implied that the money supply was exogenously determined by the policies of the authorities, and the purchase (or sale) of dollars in exchange for rubles by individuals and enterprises resulted in a depreciation (or appreciation) of the ruble in turn influencing their *real* cash balances through a change in the price level.

Finally, (12) below for estimating the real exchange rate is derived by substituting (3) and (4) in (11), and stated as:

$$\ln\varepsilon_t - \ln\varepsilon_{t-1} = \alpha + \beta\ln(M_{t-1}/P_{t-1}) + \gamma\ln(y_t) + \delta\ln(\pi_t^*) + \text{error term} \quad (12)$$

where $\alpha$, $\beta$, $\gamma$, and $\delta$ are the transformed parameters. $\gamma$ is expected to be $<0$, and $\delta < 0$. The equation is estimated with the variables as stated in Table 7.1. The series of $\ln\varepsilon_t$ predicted from equation (12) without the constant term, is presented in Table 7.2, and graphed in Figure 7.1 along with the observed real exchange rate, also defined in log.

### 7.3.2 The Import Demand, Export Supply, and Net Export Trade Models

The observed real exchange rate is used for analyzing Russia's foreign trade performance via three relationships.

At the outset, a few general observations that are relevant in formulating these models, which are based on the monthly import and export data from July 1992 to December 1994, are in order. These data are presented in Table 7.2 and in Figure 7.2.

A dominant feature of Russia's trade performance on exports (valued FOB) and imports (valued CIF), both in dollars, with non-FSU countries is the systematic peaks and valleys in exports and imports in January and July. The unification of the exchange rate in July 1992, the launching of the elaborate export quotas and licenses in January 1993, the import tariff hikes in July 1993 and July 1994, the start of the passport system for exporters in January, 1994 and the abolition of the import subsidies in December 1993 all these seem to be reflected in the sharp discontinuity in the export and import series in those months. January and July are critical months for changes in the export and import regime in Russia.

It is impossible to incorporate all these features, via appropriate dummies, in the trade equations. Also, the real exchange rate appreciated decisively beginning May 1993. There was also a sharp decline in the trade series in January 1994. Therefore, the estimates of the import demand and export supply equations are based on data from May 1993 (the earlier observations were omitted) and on the use of a dummy from January 1994, representing (the shift in the intercept caused by) the sharp decline in exports and imports in that month.

It is also assumed that Russia's exports are constrained by domestic supply rather than world demand. Monthly oil production is used as a proxy representing supply difficulties. The ideal explanatory variable of supply difficulties in oil and some major items (such as metals and precious stones, which contributed 20 and 23 percent of total exports in 1992 and 1993; *Bulletin*, p. 72) is not readily available. The estimated parameter

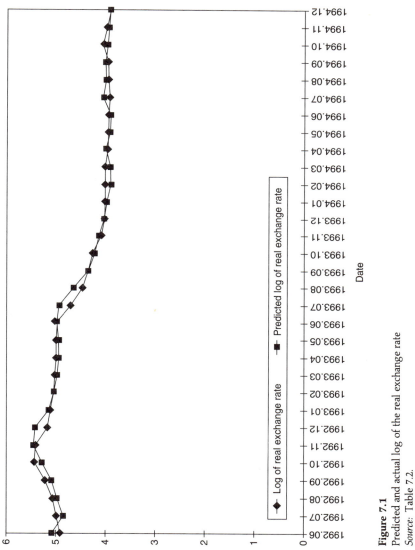

**Figure 7.1**
Predicted and actual log of the real exchange rate
*Source:* Table 7.2.

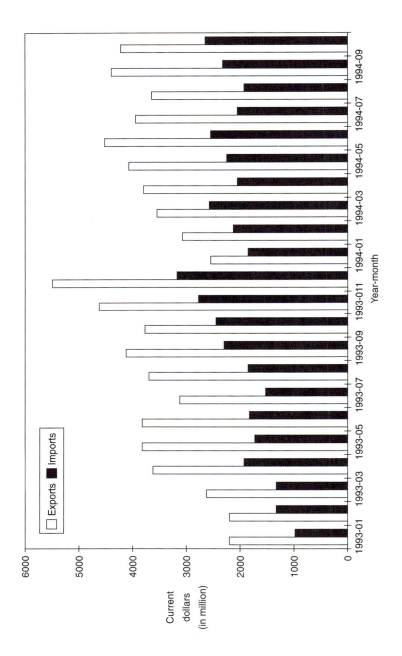

with respect to oil production in the export supply equation was, however, statistically not significant and was omitted in the final round. Similarly, real GDP, which remained more or less constant throughout the period (see Figure 7.3), was removed from the import demand equation.

Finally, the dollar exports are converted into real values through dividing them by a reconstructed monthly international commodity price index. The price indices of commodities and of fuels (Table 7.1) are aggregated by applying weights of 0.45 to the fuel price index and of 0.55 to the commodity price index. (The aggregated price index is stated in Table 7.1.) Russia's exports of fuels were, on average, 45 percent of its total exports during 1992–94. The dollar imports are converted into real magnitudes by dividing them by the CPI of industrial countries (also presented in Table 7.1). This choice is dictated by the increasing share, reaching 69 percent in January–August 1994, of developed market economies in Russian imports (*Bulletin*, p. 70).

The export and import series, both in real terms, and the real net trade balance (exports minus imports) derived from them are presented in Table 7.2.

## 7.4   The Equations and Interpretation of the Estimates

The import demand, export supply, and net export equations are as follows:

**Figure 7.2**
Monthly export and import data in current U.S. dollars (millions)
*Source:* Table 7.2.
*Note:* The monthly export (f.o.b.) and import data (c.i.f.) from July 1992 to October 1994 (used in the estimates) are in billion current dollars. These are reported by Goskomstat (the State Committee on Statistics) in dollars on the basis of information supplied by trading enterprises to Goskomstat's regional offices. Goskomstat's methods conform to international standards for classifying and valuing goods.

The coverage of the reporting enterprises worsened as the trading activity became decentralized especially with regard to imports. In 1994, the collection of trade statistics was transferred to the Customs Committee, which supplied the information on imports to Goskomstat. Some cross-border trading activity escaped the coverage of the Customs Committee.

There are also problems of comparing the trade data from year to year. Exports may occasionally include gold and arms sales and some services; imports sporadically include some services, and items financed with humanitarian aid.

The adjustments of the yearly data carried out on the basis of partner country data and reports provided by representatives of the Ministry for Foreign Economic Relations suggest underreporting of the Goskomstat export and import data, although the relative underreporting is smaller for export than for import statistics. Details of the data collection problems and such adjustments are in *Bulletin*, p. 69.

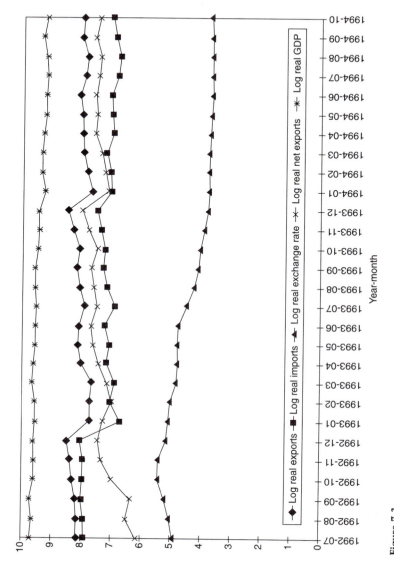

**Figure 7.3**
Trade, real exchange rate, and real GDP in logs
*Source:* Table 7.2.

**Table 7.3**
The log-linear real exchange rate equation

$\ln \varepsilon_t - \ln \varepsilon_{t-1} = \alpha + \beta \ln(M_{t-1}/P_{t-1}) + \gamma \ln(y_t) + \delta \ln(\pi_t^*) + \text{error term}$

| Parameter | Estimated value | t-Ratio |
|---|---|---|
| $\alpha$ | 2.3022 | 0.9693 |
| | (—) | (—) |
| $\beta$ | 0.1869 | 2.3175 |
| | (0.1515) | (2.1092) |
| $\gamma$ | −0.2477 | −0.9644 |
| | (0.0004) | (0.0212) |
| $\delta$ | −0.1831 | −3.4059 |
| | (−0.1790) | (−3.3434) |
| $R^2$ | | 0.3214 |
| | | (0.2978) |
| Adjusted $R^2$ | | 0.2460 |
| | | (0.2476) |
| Durbin-Watson statistic | | 1.4344 |
| | | (1.4531) |
| Number of observations | | 31 |

*Notes:* The data underlying the equation are stated in Table 7.1. The equation was estimated with positive signs of parameters on the right hand side. Estimates of the equation without the constant term $\alpha$ are stated in parentheses. The constant term $\alpha$, and the parameter $\gamma$ with respect to ln GDP are poorly estimated. $\ln \varepsilon_t$, in Figure 7.1 and Table 7.2, is predicted by using the bracketed estimates without the constant term.

$$\log(\text{real imp}) = \alpha_1 + \beta_1[\log(\text{real ER})_{-1}] + \gamma_1 \log(\text{real GDP}) + \gamma_1 DV_{94} + w_t \tag{13}$$

$$\log(\text{real exp}) = \alpha_2 + \beta_2[\log(\text{real ER})_{-1}] + \gamma_2 DV_{94} + \eta_t \tag{14}$$

$$\log(\text{real NX}) = \alpha_3 + \beta_3[\log(\text{real ER})_{-1}] + \gamma_3 DV_{94} + u_t \tag{15}$$

The estimates of equations (3), and (12) to (15) are presented in Tables 7.3–7.7.

The estimate of $\beta$, the adjustment parameter of equation (12), is low (0.15), suggesting a small impact of the gap between real cash supply and real cash demand (the next month) on the real ruble-dollar exchange rate. This result is not surprising. Foreign exchange transactions in Russia (which are officially accounted for) continue to be confined to current account activity, although by September 1994, dollars sold in the MICEX (which determines the exchange rate) had reached 81.8 percent of registered exports for that month (*Bulletin*, p. 79). More to the point, the CBR

**Table 7.4**
Estimate of the relationship between inflation, lagged inflation, and double-lagged inflation

$\pi_t^* = a + b\pi_{t-1} + c\pi_{t-2} + \text{error term}$

| Parameter | Estimated value | t-Ratio |
|---|---|---|
| a | 4.2496 | 2.1870 |
| b | 0.7270 | 5.9729 |
| c | −0.0105 | −0.4278 |
| $R^2$ | | 0.6225 |
| Adjusted $R^2$ | | 0.5981 |
| Durbin-Watson statistic | | 1.9001 |
| Number of observations | | 34 |

**Table 7.5**
Estimate of import demand equation

$\ln(\text{real imp}) = \alpha_1 + \beta_1 \ln(\text{real ER}_{-1}) + \gamma_1 DV_{94} + w_t$

| Parameter | Estimated value | t-Ratio |
|---|---|---|
| $\alpha_1$ | 10.3251 | 14.7624 |
| $\beta_1$ | −0.6245 | −4.0714 |
| $\gamma_1$ | −0.5063 | −4.9626 |
| $R^2$ | | 0.6914 |
| Adjusted $R^2$ | | 0.6202 |
| Durbin-Watson statistic | | 1.8445 |
| Number of observations | | 17 |

*Notes:* DV94 = 1 if year ≥ 94; otherwise DV94 = 0; first-order autocorrelation was corrected using the Cochrane-Orcutt method.

intervenes in the MICEX in order to regulate its movement: the real exchange rate is allowed to appreciate within limits so that the tradable sector of the economy is not hurt excessively.

The estimates of the foreign trade equations, if they are to be believed, have parametric values suggesting that the real exchange rate did not influence export performance but did have an impact on import flows. The estimated parameter in the export equation (Table 7.6) is statistically significant but has the wrong sign; it is statistically significant in the import demand equation (Table 7.5) with the correct negative sign. The parameter linking import demand to real GDP was not statistically significant. Therefore, it was dropped from the equation. (Note that the log

**Table 7.6**
Estimate of export supply equation

$\ln(\text{real exp}) = \alpha_2 + \beta_2 \ln(\text{real ER}_{-1}) + \gamma_2 DV_{94} + \eta_t$

| Parameter | Estimated value | t-Ratio |
|---|---|---|
| $\alpha_2$ | 12.3552 | 8.5255 |
| $\beta_2$ | −0.8521 | −2.5672 |
| $\gamma_2$ | −0.7202 | −4.6700 |
| $R^2$ | | 0.5759 |
| Adjusted $R^2$ | | 0.4781 |
| Durbin-Watson statistic | | 1.8678 |
| Number of observations | | 17 |

*Notes:* DV94 = 1 if year ≥ 94; otherwise DV94 = 0; first-order autocorrelation was corrected using the Cochrane-Orcutt method.

**Table 7.7**
Estimate of the relationship between net real exports and lagged real exchange rate

$\ln(\text{real NX}) = \alpha_3 + \beta_3 \ln(\text{real ER}_{-1}) + \gamma_3 DV_{94} + u_t$

| Parameter | Estimated value | t-Ratio |
|---|---|---|
| $\alpha_3$ | 10.4204 | 3.7060 |
| $\beta_3$ | −0.3510 | −0.5517 |
| $\gamma_3$ | −1.0709 | −5.6708 |
| $R^2$ | | 0.4775 |
| Adjusted $R^2$ | | 0.3569 |
| Durbin-Watson statistic | | 2.0280 |
| Number of observations | | 17 |

*Notes:* DV94 = 1 if year ≥ 94; otherwise DV94 = 0; first-order autocorrelation was corrected using the Cochrane-Orcutt method.

of real GDP in Figure 7.3 is more or less constant for the period under consideration.)

The conclusion that the real exchange rate had no impact on export performance carries over in the estimate of the relationship between the real exchange rate and the net positive trade balance defined by real net exports (Table 7.7). The system of extensive quotas and licensing of exports during the period, supplemented by the passport system for exporters during 1994—rather than the appreciating real ruble—seems to have constrained exports. As a result, it is difficult to establish a connection between the real exchange rate and the net trade balance. (The sign of the estimated parameter, which is statistically, not significant, is "perverse.")

## 7.5    Conclusions

The unified and convertible ruble on current account represented a major step in Russia's foreign exchange management. The monetarist model adopted here (which gives a robust estimate of the real exchange rate) suggests that the impact of the gap between cash supply and cash demand (in the next month) on the real ruble-dollar exchange rate (for the period beginning July 1992) was small. Perhaps this parametric value reflects the restrictions on foreign exchange transactions and the intervention of the CBR in the MICEX.

In contrast to the unification and current account convertibility of the ruble, progress during 1992–94 in the foreign trading arrangements was halting. Export trading was hobbled by export quotas, licensing, and passport surveillance. There were no quantitative restrictions on import activity, which nevertheless was subjected to steadily rising import tariffs (evidently calculated to counter the impact of the appreciating real ruble). The estimates of the trade equations suggest that the real exchange rate had no impact, ceteris paribus, on export performance, but it influenced import flows. The changing pattern of Russia's trade, in terms of both (export-import) commodity composition and orientation, has to be judged in the context of the asymmetrical impact of the exchange rate on that pattern.

## Notes

Thanks are due to Eugene Beaulieu and Devashish Mitra for research assistance, to Michael Connolly and Dani Rodrik for insightful suggestions, and to Vladimir Mikhalev for putting together some of the information used in the paper. The paper was presented in July 1995 before a research group of the Russian Finance Ministry organized by Jochen Wermuth.

1. Foreign exchange may be earned from merchandise exports or services, just as it may be spent for importing goods or services or both. Thus, current account activities were not distinguished from merchandise trade in the arrangements.

2. MICEX, which was formed as a joint stock company by the CBR, Russian banks, and enterprises, took over the currency trading of the Soviet Vneshekonombank by April 1991 and soon expanded its activity: it traded dollars on a daily basis beginning September 20, 1993; by the end of 1993, it had 139 member banks, none of which were foreign. Over time, more currencies were included in its activity.

MICEX was soon followed by several currency exchanges formed by banks, among them the St. Petersburg Currency Exchange, the Urals Interbank Currency Exchange in Yekaterinberg, the Siberian Interbank Currency Exchange in Novosibirsk, the Asian-Pacific Ocean Interbank Currency Exchange in Vladivostok, and the Rostov Interbank Currency Exchange in Rostov-on-Don. The frequency of auctions and the number of currencies traded increased over time. However, the regional markets remained segmented because the local credit markets were underdeveloped and domestic settlements were slow.

The CBR intervenes in each market with dollars, with a view to keeping the regional dollar-ruble exchange rates in line with the MICEX rate.

3. The CBR administers exchange control regulations and monitors the foreign currency transactions of authorized commercial banks. The repatriation of the foreign exchange based on the surrender requirements, which continued into early 1996, is enforced by authorized commercial banks.

4. The CBR currently issues three types of licenses to Russian commercial banks. An internal license allows a bank to deal in foreign exchange transactions, such as opening a foreign exchange bureau inside Russia and opening a correspondent account abroad in banks of the former Soviet Union (such as Moscow Narodny). A limited license allows a bank to open up to six correspondent accounts and deal in up to six currencies. A general license allows a bank to carry out all foreign exchange transactions, including portfolio investments.

5. Nonresident corporate entities at present can operate accounts with authorized Russian banks for servicing their export-import activities (the "T" accounts) or for financing their investment activities, including purchase of stocks of Russian privatized companies (the "I" accounts). Foreign banks also can operate correspondent accounts in Russia.

6. This is not to minimize the critical need for the emergence of a positive real interest rate in Russia, which began in 1994.

7. Non-FSU countries include the OECD market economies, the (former) CMEA, and developing countries.

8. On July 25, 1993, the CBR, under the stewardship of Viktor Gerashchenko, demonetized all pre-January 1993 ruble notes. The substantial ruble surplus that the CBR held with the FSU central banks was subsequently revalued via agreements among the banks. Following the Russian currency reform, all post-Soviet states introduced their own currencies as plans by Armenia, Belarus, Kazakhstan, Tajikistan, and Uzbekistan to form a monetary union with Russia did not succeed.

9. Barring exceptions noted below, all strategic commodities were subject to quotas and licensing. The list of strategic items included all energy and petrochemical products, electric energy, nonferrous metals, alkaline metals and alkaline earths, cellulose, hard and soft wheat, soybeans and sunflower seeds, unmethylated ethyl alcohol, fish and caviar, timber, nitric and phosphoric fertilizers, and uncut diamonds. Of these, nitric and phosphoric fertilizers and diamonds were not subject to quotas and licenses.
   Strategic goods constituted up to 70 percent of Russia's exports.

10. These excluded transport costs. The special exporters were also exempted from paying export taxes on a portion of their noncentralized export subquotas.

11. Export taxes were specific rather than ad valorem because tariff revenues were difficult to calculate with constantly changing domestic prices and exchange rates (*Bulletin*, p. 75).

12. In fact, there were frequent complaints that Russia was dumping aluminum, nickel, and fertilizers in world markets.

13. More items were subsequently exempted from import duties, including imports of gas- and oil-extracting equipment, some imports by joint ventures, and centralized imports. Centralized imports not only were duty free but also were sold to final users at varying rates of subsidies that were finally abolished in December 1993.

14. Items that were exported on the basis of intergovernmental agreements were exempted from export taxes.

15. This appreciation was necessary in view of the fact that in January 1992, the nominal value of the ruble was far too low in relation to the ruble/purchasing power parity estimate, the latter based on the composition of Russian GDP. In fact, "at the exchange rate of January 1992, the entire GDP of Russia in 1992 would come to less than $20 billion, while the value of oil output alone was more than $50 billion in that year" (*Bulletin*, p. 80).

16. Despite formidable problems, these trade balances are aggregated at a market exchange rate in the *Bulletin* (p. 71) revealing exports of $264.7 billion in 1991, which declined to 57.7 billion in 1993, and imports of $209.8 billion, which fell sharply to $17.1 billion! Estimates based on purchasing power parity are also provided there.

17. In April 1996, Russia's total liabilities of $120 billion to $130 billion in outstanding interest and principal payments consisted of $90 billion owed to governments and the rest to commercial bank creditors (*Wall Street Journal*, April 29, 1996, p. 118).

Debt relief (in contrast to debt rescheduling) consists of lowering of outstanding debt via write-offs or of interest charges or both. Debt rescheduling involves stretching repayment schedules, capitalizing unpaid interest payments, and allowing a grace period that did not feature in the original contract. For example, the massive $40 billion debt restructuring agreement with the Paris Club of official creditors in April 1996 offered Russia a six-year grace period on principal payments (*Wall Street Journal*, April 30, 1996, p. A7).

18. The debt repayment obligations to sovereign creditors in 1996 amounted to $8 billion. Instead, Russia will pay between $2 billion and $3 billion (*Financial Times*, April 20, 1996, p. 2).

# References

Cagan, Philip. 1956. "The Monetary Dynamics of Hyperinflation." In Milton Friedman, ed., *Studies in the Quantity Theory of Money*. Chicago: University of Chicago Press.

Drebentsov, Vladimir. 1994. "Russia's Commercial Policy in 1992–1994: Liberalization Versus Protection." Paper presented at the Conference on International Trade Issues of the Russian Federation at IIASA, Luxembourg, May 5–7. Moscow: World Bank. (Mimeo).

Easterly, William, and Paulo Vieira da Cunha. 1994. *Financing the Storm: Macroeconomic Crisis in Russia, 1992–93*. Policy Research Working Paper. Washington, D.C.: World Bank.

Economic Commission for Europe. 1994. *Economic Bulletin for Europe* 46: 68–82. (Cited as *Bulletin*.)

Economic Commission for Europpe. 1995. *Economic Survey of Europe in 1994–1995*. New York: United Nations. (Cited as *Survey*.)

European Bank for Reconstruction and Development. 1996. *Transition Report Update: Assessing Progress in Economies in Transition*. London: EBRD.

Illarionov, Andrei. 1994. "Foreign Trade of Russia in 1992–1993." Paper presented at the Conference on International Trade Issues of the Russian Federation at IIASA, Luxembourg, May 5–7. Moscow: Center for Economic Reform. (Mimeo).

Konovalov, Vladimir. 1994. "Russian Trade Policy." In Constantine Michalopoulos and David G. Tarr, eds., *Trade in the New Independent States*. Washington, D.C.: World Bank.

Kuznetsov, Yevgeny. 1994. "Conditional Comparative Advantage: Development of Russian Firm-Level Organizational Capabilities to Enhance Manufacturing." Paper presented at the

Conference on International Trade Issues of the Russian Federation at IIASA, Luxembourg, May 5–7. Moscow: Institute of Economic Forecasting, Russian Academy of Sciences. (Mimeo).

Lucke, Matthias. 1994. "Competitiveness of Russian Commodities and Industrial Products in Foreign and Domestic Markets." Paper presented at the Conference on International Trade Issues of the Russian Federation at IIASA, Luxembourg, May 5–7. Kiel: Institut für Weltwirtschaft an der Universität Kiel. (Mimeo).

Panich, Vladimir B. 1994. "The Instability of Political Regimes, Prices and Enterprise Financing and Their Impact on the External Activity of the Russian Enterprises." Paper presented at the Conference on International Trade Issues of the Russian Federation at IIASA, Luxembourg, May 5–7. (Mimeo).

Rogovski, Yevgeny. 1994. "Competitive Capacity of Russian Industry." Paper presented at the Conference on International Trade Issues of the Russian Federation at IIASA, Luxembourg, May 5–7. (Mimeo).

Sarafanov, Michael. 1994. "Russia's Actual and Potential Role in International Capital Flows Including Foreign Direct Investments." Paper presented at the Conference on International Trade Issues of the Russian Federation at IIASA, Luxembourg, May 5–7. (Mimeo).

Sutela, Pekka. 1994. "The Instability of Political Regimes, Prices and Enterprises Financing and Their Impact on the External Activity of the Russian Enterprises." Paper presented at the Conference on International Trade Issues of the Russian Federation at IIASA, Luxembourg, May 5–7. Helsinki: Unit for Eastern European Economies, Bank of Finland. (Mimeo).

# 8         Kazakhstan

Heiner Flassbeck,
Lutz Hoffmann, and
Ludger Lindlar

The Republic of Kazakhstan is a large, landlocked country in Central Asia with a substantial natural resource base. It became independent with the dissolution of the Soviet Union in December 1991 and simultaneously joined the Commonwealth of Independent States (CIS). Because of Kazakhstan's strong economic integration with Russia, its government pursued from the outset a reform course closely oriented toward the development of its large northern neighbor, Russia. The country remained a member of the ruble zone until November 1993. It was only after the introduction of its own currency—the tenge—and the sustained decay of Russia's economy that Kazakhstan started to reorient itself toward the West, defining its own path from a planned economy to a market economy.

A focal point of Kazakhstan's economic policy following the transition to independence is monetary stabilization. First within the ruble zone, and then under its own management, the government tried on the one hand to push ahead with price liberalization and on the other hand to take steps against the escalating inflation. The resulting internal and external economic conflicts of these efforts, as well as appropriate possible solutions, are analyzed in this chapter. One cannot understand the process of transformation and its obstacles, and the integration of a transition country into the world economy, without having analyzed the process of monetary stabilization. This process shapes—as the experience of almost all the Eastern European countries shows—the economic policy of the government, at least during the first years of the transition. It also influences the conditions under which foreign assistance is given.

One of the astonishing developments in Eastern Europe is that monetary stabilization is increasingly viewed as part of the globalization of a country. After the failure of many attempts to fight inflation with only domestic policy measures, the idea of creating a nominal anchor by linking the nominal exchange rate to the currency of a stable Western economy has gained widespread acceptance. This is intended to break inflationary expectations. The most consistent form of such a monetary globalization of a national economy is the currency board, as it is practiced in Estonia. But the stabilization of the nominal exchange rate is also suggested for less open economies like Russia, Ukraine, and Kazakhstan. It appears to us, however, that this will drive the globalization of a reforming economy too far. Many Western and developing countries with generally well-functioning market systems cannot fulfill the conditions for stabilizing their exchange rate vis-à-vis the U.S. dollar or the deutsche mark. How can countries in transformation, with rudimentary market economy institutions, meet these demands?

The analysis of this chapter centers on three themes: macroeconomic stabilization, internal reforms, and introduction of a liberal foreign trade and payments regime. It is divided into five parts: (1) the initial conditions; (2) the process of transformation; (3) the attempt to stabilize the price level after the currency reform; (4) policy-oriented suggestions for stabilization; and (5) the prospects of Kazakhstan's economy.

## 8.1   Initial Conditions

### 8.1.1   Geography, Resource Endowment, People

Kazakhstan is located between the Caspian Sea to the west, China to the east, the west Siberian regions of Russia to the north, and the group of central Asian transition economies (Kyrgyzstan, Tajikistan, Turkmenistan, Uzbekistan) to the south. With a territory nearly the size of Western Europe, Kazakhstan is the largest landlocked country in the world and one of the most sparsely populated, having only 6.2 inhabitants per square kilometer. Kazakhstan has a population of 17 million; 43 percent are Kazakh, 37 percent are Russian, and the remaining 20 percent consists of more than 100 ethnic groups. More than half of Kazakhstan's border is shared with Russia. All major transportation routes—railway lines, roads, and pipelines—connect Kazakhstan with Russia. This is so because to the south and the east, Kazakhstan and the smaller central Asian transition economies are surrounded by a chain of mighty mountain masses forming a natural border with China, India, Afghanistan, and Iran. As a landlocked country in the backyard of the Russian Federation, Kazakhstan thus differs significantly from most other transition countries in Eastern Europe and Asia.

Kazakhstan has a vast area of arable land, dry barren steppes, and a substantial natural resource base encompassing rich deposits of coal, oil, gas, iron ore, copper, chrome, wolfram, zinc, uranium, and gold. After Russia, Kazakhstan is the second largest oil producer of the former Soviet Union (FSU). Recoverable oil reserves are estimated at 12 billion barrels; the international petroleum industry considers this potential to be exceptional. A major share of Kazakhstan's oil production is exported to western Russia, and crude oil for its refineries is imported from central Siberia.

### 8.1.2   Level of Development and Economic Structure

Kazakhstan is a middle-income economy. In 1992, the GDP per capita—measured in purchasing power parity—was 21 percent of the U.S. level a figure below that of the Russian Federation (27 percent) but similar to the entire CIS (23 percent) and Eastern Europe (20 percent). In 1987, Kazakhstan had a (post transfer) GDP per capita similar to that of Poland and Malaysia (27 percent). The main products are agricultural goods, coal and other mineral resources (chrome, crude oil, gas), heavy industrial products (metallurgy, heavy machinery, petrochemicals), food processing, textiles, and footwear. Industry accounted for about 40 percent of GDP in 1992, and agriculture for about 34 percent. As a result of Soviet central planning, industrial production is heavily concentrated and geared toward mining and processing activities, primarily intended to exploit Kazakhstan's natural resources. The central authorities belief in the importance of scale economies is responsible for many industries that are local or even Unionwide monopolies.

Fixed assets per capita were in 1989 around 70 percent higher than in other Central Asian republics, the Ukraine, and the Caucasus, but 20 percent lower than in Russia or the Baltic republics. The capital stock is technologically outdated. Kazakhstan's infrastructure is not sufficient for a market-oriented economy due to the widespread shortages of equipment and parts, insufficient investment during the last decades, administrative difficulties in planning and construction of an efficient infrastructure, and outdated technological standards.

### 8.1.3   Kazakhstan's Role in the Soviet Division of Labor

As was part of the Soviet system of state trading, Kazakhstan was among the republics with the highest share of interrepublic trade in total trade, 86 percent in 1988 (Langhammer and Lücke, 1995, p. 4). Russia is by far Kazakhstan's most important trade partner, accounting for more than

**Table 8.1**
Sectoral trade structure before transition (percent shares in total trade; average for 1989 and 1990)

|  | Exports | Imports | Balance | Balance with FSU |
|---|---|---|---|---|
| Resource-intensive industries | 51.0 | 25.2 | 25.4 | 18.7 |
| Agriculture | 15.7 | 2.4 | 13.3 | 15.6 |
| Ferrous metallurgy | 11.5 | 5.7 | 5.7 | 1.1 |
| Oil and gas | 9.1 | 7.4 | 1.6 | 0.8 |
| Nonferrous metallurgy | 8.5 | 1.5 | 7.0 | 3.8 |
| Power | 2.5 | 2.2 | 0.2 | 0.0 |
| Coal | 3.4 | 0.9 | 2.5 | 2.6 |
| Sawmill and lumber industry | 0.3 | 5.1 | −4.9 | −5.2 |
| Capital-intensive industries | 22.1 | 42.2 | −20.0 | −28.3 |
| Chemicals and petroleum | 11.9 | 9.7 | 2.3 | 0.9 |
| Machinery and metal works | 8.8 | 30.7 | −21.9 | −23.5 |
| Building materials | 1.4 | 1.8 | −0.4 | −0.5 |
| Labor-intensive industries | 27.0 | 32.4 | −5.5 | 1.3 |
| Light industry | 17.1 | 18.3 | −1.2 | 4.1 |
| Food production | 6.7 | 10.6 | −3.9 | −2.1 |
| Other industries | 0.9 | 2.2 | −1.3 | −1.5 |
| Other material production | 2.3 | 1.3 | 0.9 | 0.8 |
|  | 100.0 | 100.0 |  |  |

*Source:* World Bank, unpublished data; authors' calculations.

half of its total trade. Within the Soviet system of interrepublic trade, Kazakhstan supplied raw materials to processing factories in Russia and other republics, as well as unprocessed and semiprocessed agricultural goods and some engineering goods. It bought refined petroleum products, processed food, most consumer products, and advanced industrial equipment (Table 8.1). Kazakhstan had one of the highest recorded interstate trade deficits relative to GDP within the Soviet Union.

The system of interrepublic trade had two characteristics. First, it was part of a system of Unionwide state orders. Production levels and flows of inputs and outputs were imposed by central authorities in Moscow. Under the plan, enterprises had to trade with state organizations at fixed prices and meet their delivery targets, regardless of whether payment had been received. Trade with COMECON and Western countries was conducted on the basis of mostly bilateral barter agreements. Hence, the sectoral and regional division of labor, as well as the level and the terms of trade, were largely politically determined and only partly influenced by factor endowments, geographical proximity, and the size of markets of the trading partners. Second, due to trade restrictions and lack of incentives, goods were manufactured with outdated technologies. The quality and design of those goods were—except for military equipment—below the standards of Western countries at a similar level of development.

### 8.1.4   Political Change After Independence

Kazakhstan has adopted a political constitution similar to that of the Russian Federation, with a legally powerful presidency and a rather weak parliament. The president appoints the prime minister and his cabinet and has a profound influence on government policies. However, in contrast to Russia's Boris Yeltsin, the leadership of President Nursultan Nazarbayev has not been seriously challenged. Nazarbayev strongly supports economic reforms as well as more stable relations with Russia and other FSU republics, although the political relationship with Russia has been clouded by several conflicts. The government is also fostering closer relations with foreign countries. Despite his authority, Nazarbayev was not successful in speeding up the implementation of reforms through parliament. Consensus between government and parliament is often difficult to reach, but it has not hindered the process of reform. In March 1995, Nazarbayev dissolved the parliament and now governs by decree.

## 8.2   The Process of Transformation

The process of transformation was inaugurated by the disintegration of the Soviet Union. It was characterized by (1) a sharp and sustained decline in production that started in 1991 and has continued in 1995; (2) a marked acceleration of inflation in 1992–94 but with good prospects of stabilization in 1995; (3) a rather slow process of institutional reforms; and (4) a sharp and sustained decline in interrepublic trade, accompanied by a structural and regional adjustment of trade patterns. Enterprises try to survive in an environment of decline and insecurity; investment to modernize and restructure production is hardly undertaken. The process of transformation is worsened not only by adverse external developments but also by incomprehensible domestic economic policies.

### 8.2.1   Breakdown of Production

Between 1991 and 1995, production dropped to 43 percent of the pre-transition level.[1] The breakdown of production followed a more or less steady path and was particularly pronounced in industry. The decline in

**Table 8.2**
Summary of economic performance, 1989–94

|  | 1989 | 1990 | 1991 | 1992 | 1993 | 1994 |
|---|---|---|---|---|---|---|
| Macroeconomic growth rates |  |  |  |  |  |  |
| GDP | −0.4 | −0.4 | −13.0 | −14.0 | −12.0 | −25.0 |
| Consumer prices (annual average) | — | 4.2 | 90.9 | 1,380 | 1,662 | 1,880 |
| Nominal wages (annual average) | 8.8 | 13.2 | 66.4 | 910 | 1,346 | 1,136 |
| Structure (share of net material product, NMP) |  |  |  |  |  |  |
| Industry |  |  | 37.1 | 46.4 | 44.3 | 40.2 |
| Agriculture |  |  | 34.1 | 30.4 | 31.4 | 38.8 |
| External trade (billion U.S. dollars) |  |  |  |  |  |  |
| Merchandise exports |  |  | 10.2 | 3.6 | 4.8 | 3.3 |
| Merchandise imports |  |  | 13.4 | 4.7 | 5.2 | 4.1 |
| Current account (percent of GDP) |  |  |  |  |  |  |
| Interrepublic |  |  | −1.7 | 0.3 | −15.2 | −2.8 |
| Extrarepublic |  |  | −1.9 | −2.8 | 2.2 | −4.1 |
| Government (percent of GDP) |  |  |  |  |  |  |
| Budget expenditure | 34.5 | 31.4 | 32.9 | 31.9 | 23.5 | 23.5 |
| of which Union transfer |  |  | 4.5 | 1.8 | 0.0 | 0.0 |
| Budget balance | 0.0 | 1.4 | −7.9 | −7.3 | −1.2 | −6.5 |
| Unemployment, population |  |  |  |  |  |  |
| Unemployment rate[1] | 0.0 | 0.0 | 0.0 | 0.5 | 9.3 | 11.0 |
| Population (mill.) | 16.5 | 16.6 | 16.7 | 16.9 | 17.1 | 17.3 |

*Sources:* EBRD (1994), p. 160; unpublished IMF estimates.
*Note:* 1. Percent of total labor force.

agricultural production started only at the end of 1993. Employment declined considerably less than output, causing a substantial deterioration of productivity. Because real wages declined less than productivity, unit labor costs increased sharply. The resulting losses of state firms were financed by an extension of credit lines issued by the Ministry of Finance and the Bank of Kazakhstan. Large state-owned enterprises did not face hard budget constraints because they were responsible for many social services, such as housing, pensions, and health care. In the absence of an economywide social safety net, the government had to finance the social expenditures of the firms in order to prevent an even greater deterioration of the population's welfare. (See table 8.2.)

Three main causes for the breakdown of production in Kazakhstan can be identified: (1) the breakdown of the centrally determined interregional division of labor within the FSU, which deprived Kazakh companies of a substantial part of their customers and suppliers; (2) the insufficient pace of institutional change during and after the breakdown of the system of state orders, especially with respect to privatization, incentives for state managers, and the establishment of capital markets; and (3) the destabilization of the economy via accelerating inflation, which created a situation of tremendous uncertainty and, later, a very tight monetary policy that caused a liquidity crisis for Kazakh firms. (See Figure 8.1.)

### 8.2.2   Inflation Within the Ruble Bloc

The situation before price liberalization—as in all formerly centrally planned economies—was characterized by repressed inflation. Comprehensive price controls created repressed inflation marked by sustained shortages, growing black markets, forced saving by households, increasing nominal wages, budgetary deficits of the state, and a monetary overhang on the side of the firms (see Conway, 1995; Desai 1989; Mckinnon, 1991; Nordhaus, 1990). In April 1991, retail prices in the USSR started to rise as subsidies on many consumption goods were cut and the government tried to control expenditures. The adjustment in relative prices helped to correct the distortions in the price structure, but the monetary overhang and the monopolistic structure of many economic activities in Kazakhstan magnified the rise in prices following the partial liberalization. The growing inflationary pressures were accentuated in 1992 by the monetization of large budget deficits in other ruble zone republics as well as in Kazakhstan. Retail prices rose significantly with further liberalization in January 1992. Until Russia's monetary reform in August 1993, Kazakhstan's monetary policy depended on the developments within the ruble zone. Through the National Bank of Kazakhstan, the government extended large amounts of directed credit to the industrial and agricultural sectors to ease their payment difficulties and to support working capital requirements. Kazakhstan strove to maintain strict budgetary discipline, but its monetary policy depended entirely on that of the Russian Central Bank.

After decades of price stability, inflation started to accelerate in 1991 and was heated further after Russia's monetary reform led to a strong inflow of old rubles into Kazakhstan. Extensive price liberalization in 1992 by Kazakh authorities fueled inflationary expectations. Inflation in turn became inertial because wage increases were more or less linked to price increases from the beginning of the liberalization process, in order to prevent a deterioration of the relative income position of workers. In those areas covered by the public budget, this occurred through formal indexation; in privatized firms through an informal but nonetheless rapid adjustment of wages to prior price increases. This set in motion a wage-price

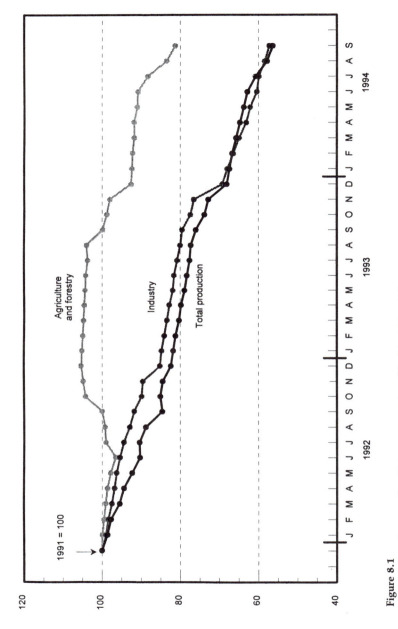

**Figure 8.1**
Volume of production in Kazakhstan, 1991–94 (monthly data, 119 = 100)
*Source*: International Monetary Fund, unpublished data.

spiral that was a determining factor behind the inflationary dynamics. Inflation fed inflation—as long as the monetary authorities provided the necessary finance. A wage-price spiral of this type is a self-sustaining, illusory phenomenon. While this process can be brought to a halt overnight without endangering output and employment by making a "new monetary start," in Kazakhstan it proved impossible to establish the necessary conditions for such a policy.

### 8.2.3   Institutional Reforms

The first, partial economic reforms were initiated in December 1988 when Kazakhstan gained—as part of perestroika—more political autonomy within the Soviet Union. Reforms accelerated with independence because the government was free to pursue liberalization at its own pace and in its own direction. However, the road to a successful market-oriented economy has proved difficult to travel because the macroeconomic situation deteriorated and the power structures in the bureaucracy and state companies resisted change. Institutions were founded to facilitate the reform process and the economic management of the economy.

**Enterprises**
The restructuring and reforms have proceeded slowly. The public sector still dominates the bulk of all economic activity and owns most fixed assets; in 1994, the private sector accounted for no more than 20 percent of GDP. Bureaucratic obstacles at the republic and local levels restrict the development of new private-sector activities. Although the legal basis for private ownership was established by a constitution adopted in January 1993, licenses and the granting of access to land and retail space are still hindered. The National Privatization Program for 1993–95, geared toward medium and large enterprises, was launched, but the government's goal of privatizing 30 percent of the assets of nonagricultural enterprises had not been reached by end of 1995. In the first nine months of 1994 more than two thousand small firms (with fewer than two hundred employees)—out of a total of four thousand firms whose sale had been envisaged—were privatized by means of local auctions. Most of them were retail trade and consumer service enterprises. The medium and large firms, employing two hundred to five thousand workers, have been privatized by means of coupons distributed free of charge to the population.

   Large firms with more than five thousand employees are to be privatized in the way best suited to their individual situation: by direct sale, auction, management contract, or other means. A total of 180 firms were available for such case-by-case privatization. So far, however, very few sales have been completed. The enterprises consist largely of primary goods producers, steel and nonferrous metal works, telecommunications, energy, and transport companies.

## Markets and Trade

Prices were partially liberalized in 1991, and extensive reforms followed in January 1992. In 1993, the remaining price and quantity controls were temporarily enforced by government authorities in order to protect the people's welfare and prevent further deterioration in their standard of living. Intervention occurred by means of the state order system, an anti-monopoly pricing policy, and credit allocation. As of June 1994, only transportation and communication services, some energy products, and a small number of food products were subject to price control. Those prices were liberalized in the fall of 1994 and in January 1995.

The inefficient state order system has been dismantled and replaced by a voluntary state order system, which by design accounted for only one-fifth of output in 1993. This system is to regulate international agreements and the normal government procurement system. It has been cut back significantly since its inception. By 1994, it applied only to agricultural products, and from mid-1994 it was limited to grain purchases. An antitrust law was introduced in September 1992, the aim of which was to limit profit margins and price increases. In mid-1994 the State Price Committee, responsible for monitoring prices, was integrated into the Antitrust Committee: instead of determining prices and profit margins in advance, the new committee was to restrict its activities to the ex post investigation of the prices and profits of monopolistic companies.

## Financial Institutions

Little progress has been made in privatizing the banking sector. The five specialized banks that were in operation under the socialist regime have retained their predominance. The two largest, the Agroprom Bank and the Turang Bank, account for half of the total volume of credit, and the four largest for 80 percent. The remaining banks, numbering more than two hundred, consist primarily of in-house banks of large companies whose prime responsibility is the payment and credit transactions of their respective company. They were set up in order to maintain access to central bank loans and to oversee the payments transactions of the firms. About five hundred banks are privately owned, and their combined market share is negligible.

**The State**

The breakup of the Union gave Kazakhstan independence in fiscal policy, subject only to the constraints imposed by its membership in the CIS. This allowed for reform in the tax and expenditure system. However, Union transfers were phased out when Kazakhstan became independent, forcing the government to cut expenditures drastically; 20 percent of Kazakhstan's state budget was covered in 1989 by transfers from the Union, with the Russian Republic as the main contributor (Langhammer and Lücke, 1995, p. 5). Kazakhstan simultaneously became responsible for expenses formerly shared between the republic and the Union government, such as defense and foreign debt service obligations. This added responsibilities and worsened the fiscal situation further in 1992. At the same time, state companies started a strategy of tax evasion as monetary conditions became more stringent. Despite these difficulties, the Kazakh government was able to reduce its officially reported budget deficit from more than 7 percent of GDP in 1991 and 1992 to 1.1 percent in 1993; in 1994, it rose again to 7 percent according to official sources. These figures, however, do not include the deficits of state enterprises, especially enterprise arrears, which are normally the buffers for an overly restrictive fiscal and monetary policy. Progress on creating a social security system financed by general taxes instead of contributions from the state companies is slow.

### 8.2.4 *International and Interregional Economic Relations*

Under the centralized system, the government ensured that firms acquired the necessary inputs from other enterprises and republics to fulfill their output plans specified by the government. This broke down when the centralized system disintegrated and firms were left with the task of establishing their own trade relations with customers and suppliers. This was very difficult to accomplish due to (1) general scarcities of raw materials and intermediate goods, resulting from production decline and the attempts of other republics to sell their goods to foreign markets; (2) a breakdown of the system of payments because of poorly developed interrepublic payments arrangements and liquidity problems within Kazakhstan, which were accentuated by a phasing out of balance-of-payments credits from the Central Bank of Russia in mid-1993; (3) an increasing reliance on barter trade; and (4) political tensions between the states. Without smooth supply links between enterprises in the republics, extreme shortages of intermediate inputs arose. This was magnified by a collapse of export trade with Eastern Europe since 1991. The disarray in trade and payments within the FSU led to payment difficulties that became acute in 1993. The CIS clearing system ultimately stopped operating. This further deteriorated the trade balance between Kazakhstan and former USSR. The disintegration of the USSR has forced Kazakhstan to seek new markets, but physical access to other markets is difficult due to the country's geographical location.

## Regional Structure

With independence, the Kazakh economy experienced a push toward globalization. Between 1991 and 1992, the share of extrarepublic exports to total exports increased from 10.5 percent to almost 30 percent (see Table 8.3). In terms of imports, the share of extrarepublic in total trade was already relatively high in 1990. China and Germany are the most important trading partners outside the FSU. A large portion of trade with third countries, especially with China, is conducted on a barter basis. A strong bias toward trade with the FSU, especially with Russia, still per-

**Table 8.3**
Geographical structure of trade (percent of total trade)

| | Exports | | | | Imports | | | |
|---|---|---|---|---|---|---|---|---|
| | 1990 | 1991 | 1992 | 1993 | 1990 | 1991 | 1992 | 1993 |
| Interrepublic trade | 90.3 | 89.5 | 70.5 | 75.1 | 80.3 | 92.8 | 75.5 | 77.5 |
| Russia | 45.7 | 55.4 | 50.9 | 52.3 | 50.9 | 61.2 | 56.1 | 54.9 |
| Ukraine, Belarus | 11.9 | 12.8 | 8.8 | 9.8 | 12.5 | 14.1 | 11.3 | 7.9 |
| KTTU* | 24.6 | 14.9 | 8.6 | 9.6 | 8.1 | 13.0 | 7.2 | 12.0 |
| Baltic States | 2.6 | 3.3 | 0.6 | 0.6 | 2.9 | 1.5 | 0.0 | 1.1 |
| Others | 5.6 | 3.1 | 1.6 | 2.8 | 5.8 | 3.0 | 0.8 | 1.5 |
| Extrarepublic trade | 9.7 | 10.5 | 29.5 | 24.9 | 19.7 | 7.2 | 24.5 | 22.5 |
| Industrial countries | 5.0 | 5.3 | 17.0 | 16.5 | 7.7 | 3.1 | 7.9 | 12.0 |
| United States | | | 2.0 | 2.4 | | | 0.3 | 1.8 |
| Western Europe | | | 12.7 | 12.0 | | | 7.0 | 8.7 |
| Japan | | | 1.0 | 0.6 | | | 0.2 | 0.2 |
| Eastern Europe | 3.3 | 2.8 | 4.8 | 3.5 | 4.6 | 1.0 | 3.4 | 4.6 |
| Developing countries | 1.4 | 2.4 | 7.7 | 4.9 | 7.4 | 3.1 | 13.2 | 5.8 |
| China | | | 4.8 | 2.9 | | | 9.2 | 3.8 |
| Total | 100.0 | 100.0 | 100.0 | 100.0 | 100.0 | 100.0 | 100.0 | 100.0 |

*Source:* World Bank, IMF, unpublished data; authors' calculations and estimates.
*Note:* *Kyrgyzstan, Tajikistan, Turkmenistan, Uzbekistan.

sists. In fact, the relative importance of Russia has increased, and more than 50 percent of total trade is with the large neighbor in the north. Measured on a per capita trade basis, Kazakhstan is among the CIS economies with the highest dependence on intra-FSU-trade (UNECE, 1994, p. 87).

For most products the only available trade routes are via Russia. In 1993, more than 85 percent of Kazakhstan's external trade went to or through Russia. Transit trade is subject to political manipulation and arbitrary charges. Difficulties have arisen regarding trade in energy goods, international payments, and incomplete implementation of bilateral trade agreements. A typical example of these difficulties is the trade in energy products. Kazakh oil reserves are located in the west of the country, but the main centers of consumption are in the north, and there are no oil transport routes between the two areas. Therefore, Kazakhstan is forced to import substantial quantities of petroleum and petroleum products from Russia, although it is a major oil exporter. Russia exploits its monopolistic position as a consumer and a transit country for Kazakhstan's oil, with the result that it pays far less for its petroleum than Kazakhstan pays for Russian oil supplies. In the fall of 1993, for example, the export price for Russian petroleum was around 58,000 rubles per ton, whereas Kazakhstan obtained prices of between 20,000 and 40,000 rubles per ton for its sales to Russia. The World Bank estimated that the losses thus incurred totaled $150 million in 1993. In addition, Kazakhstan has faced, and continues to face, refusals by Russian pipeline owners to transport Kazakh oil, with negative effects on Kazakh sales to third countries. Although agreement has been reached with Russia on eliminating such discrimination, it has not been fully implemented. Consequently, the Kazakh government is considering ways to open up new trade routes. However, the choices are few: the construction of new oil and gas pipelines via Russia to Turkey and the opening of overland routes to China.

**Sectoral Structure**
Comparable statistics on the sectoral trade structure before and after transition are not available. Structural changes, in some cases considerable, have occurred in trade with third countries. Energy and primary goods exports have declined, for the reasons given above, whereas food exports have increased sharply. Agricultural imports as a share of purchases from third countries have declined, while those of plant and equipment have increased. Clearly, goods previously purchased from Russia have been replaced by imports from third countries.

**Foreign Trade and Payments Regime**

The trade regime characteristic of the Soviet Union—state commissions, international trade agreements, state foreign trade organizations—has largely been scrapped. The process of liberalization began in the middle of 1993. By the end of 1993, import quotas had been eliminated. Import licenses were required for only eight product categories. The average of import duty is around 13 percent, but there are many exceptions. The duties and other import regulations are not very effective because the customs administration is underdeveloped. The number of goods subject to export quotas was down to seven in May 1994. Exports are subject to duties, which were reduced to an average of 7 to 8 percent at the start of 1994.

In February 1994 a free trade agreement was reached between Kazakhstan, Uzbekistan, and Kyrgyzstan. This agreement provided for the abolition of tariffs, but not of quotas and licenses. Considering that only 10 percent of Kazakhstan's total trade goes to the small transition economies to the south, it is clearly the trading relationships with Russia that need to be improved. Since Kazakhstan cannot match Russia's political and economic strength, the extent of economic cooperation and integration with Russia depends on Moscow's political goodwill and its belief in the mutual benefits of unrestricted economic exchange. However, because of Russia's political and economic strength, it is rational for the Russian government to extract monopoly profits from trade with Kazakhstan—up to the point where it is cheaper for Kazakh firms to trade more with the rest of the world. But since the transportation and transaction costs of transit trade via Russia are under Moscow's influence, even this opportunity is limited. Hence, it is in the vital interest of Kazakhstan to establish smoothly functioning trading relationships with Russia and institutional safeguards against arbitrary interventions. The president of Kazakhstan was one of the leading proponents of the customs union recently announced between Russia, Belarus, and Kazakhstan. Whether it will prove effective remains to be seen, but it constitutes a step in the right direction. Kazakhstan's bargaining power will improve with the participation of more FSU states in a customs union. But a customs union clearly has a price: it means the subjugation of Kazakhstan's external tariff policy to Moscow.

Following the currency reform in December 1993, Kazakhstan adopted a floating exchange rate. As part of the liberalization, currency convertibility was introduced for enterprises. However, international capital transfers are still subject to restrictions. Since mid-1993, a charge of 30 percent has been imposed on export earnings, with currency conversion at the official rate. In January 1994, this charge was raised to 50 percent and currency conversion was allowed via currency auctions. The earlier exemptions from this charge have been abolished except for those applicable to joint ventures. The export duty and the obligation to pay charges on currency earnings have meant that exports have been incompletely reported in company accounts and export earnings have remained abroad. The capital flight thus initiated is estimated at several hundred million U.S. dollars in 1993. The linking of the exchange rate to the auction rate on the foreign currency markets has eased this problem, especially because since mid-1994, the more favorable real interest rate trend has made it more attractive to hold tenge deposits. In addition, since May 1994 the downward pressure on the tenge has eased dramatically; between May and September the currency depreciated by just 20 percent against the dollar and appreciated significantly against the ruble.

### Direct Investment and International Debt

The most important source of foreign direct investment has been the agreements with foreign oil companies to develop Kazakhstan's rich oil and gas fields. During 1990–93, Kazakhstan received twice as much foreign direct investment per capita as Russia but only a fifth of the amount received by Central European countries (EBRD, 1994, p. 123). Kazakhstan has low external debt obligations. On July 1, 1994, external debt amounted to $2.3 billion; Kazakhstan's external debt is among the lowest of all transition economies on a per capita basis. In the past, Kazakhstan ran a trade deficit with other FSU republics and received budgetary transfers from the Union. In 1992, these transfers were replaced by Russia's extension of credit through the central bank correspondent accounts. Net interrepublic credit amounted to approximately 11 percent of GDP in 1992. A part of these credits was cut off in mid-1993. More recently, the trade deficit has been financed by interstate correspondent accounts, other foreign loans, and interstate enterprise arrears.

Kazakhstan's balance of trade with Russia is negative, but in 1993 its trade balance with other countries was positive. In 1994, however, its trade with third countries appears to have slipped into the red due largely to a sharp rise in imports. Its trade deficit vis-à-vis Russia and the other successor states is largely matched by an accumulation of debt. Together with capital inflows in the form of direct investment and trade credits, the trade surplus with third countries has been used to build up national currency reserves. In 1994 there was a further rise in the currency reserves held by the central bank. In the first half of 1994, they amounted to almost double the value of an average month's imports compared with the equivalent of around 1.3 months in 1993. Thus Kazakhstan's overall foreign trade position was noncritical in 1994. But it is important to emphasize the dramatic contraction of domestic output, with its consequences for import trends. Seen in this light, foreign trade developments in Kazakhstan are not without problems. The trend toward declining exports and rising imports poses a serious threat to the balance of payments if it cannot be arrested or reversed.

## 8.3  Stabilization After the Currency Reform

Soon after political independence on September 16, 1991, the parliament of Kazakhstan authorized the government to introduce an independent national currency. The Kazakh government did not take up this option because it was concerned about the likely collapse of economic relations with the other CIS states if it were to leave the ruble zone. Instead, it placed its trust in the Russian government's ability to stabilize the ruble. The International Monetary Fund (IMF) consistently supported this position.

### 8.3.1  The New Currency: An Emergency Measure

It became clear in the course of 1992 that Russia was unable to bring inflation under control. The Russian Central Bank put the blame for this on the ruble credits extended by the other CIS states. Two events in the summer of 1992 speeded the collapse of the ruble zone. First, in June 1992, Russia agreed with the IMF to restrict credit in the second half of 1992, and the Russian Central Bank began limiting financing of republican imports to the amount of rubles it had specifically credited to the central bank of the importing country. Since all transactions between companies in different republics were being channeled through the central banks, the latter were forced to distinguish between rubles granted to them by Russia for financing interrepublic trade and those issued by their commercial banks to domestic companies for their internal transactions. Second, in August 1992, Russia declared that importers in other republics could trade directly with Russian exporters through commercial banks, in order to speed up the payments system. However, companies had to ensure that they had enough "Russian" rubles to buy ruble goods. Rubles lent to companies by local commercial banks were then regarded as "Ukrainian" or "Kazakh" rubles, and each republic in effect had its "own" ruble for use by companies.

The uncertainty about the future of the ruble zone, and the monetary arrangements and policy objectives in 1993 contributed to the disruption of the stabilization efforts. At the same time, supplies of ruble notes failed to keep pace with inflation, giving rise to serious problems with cash payments, particularly of wages, in many CIS countries. A number of republics, Ukraine among them, introduced parallel currencies. At the end of 1993, the Russian Central Bank issued a new ruble, simultaneously declaring that the old ruble notes were no longer valid legal tender in Russia. In effect, this amounted to a unilateral declaration of the end of the ruble zone and the setting of a monetary frontier between Russia and the other CIS countries, which had not yet introduced currencies of their own.

Initially Kazakhstan sought to reverse the decision to end the ruble zone. For this reason, it refrained from immediately introducing a currency of its own despite the fact that the tenge notes had been printed in the spring of 1993. Because Kazakhstan was not provided with an initial endowment of new rubles, it initially had no choice but to allow the old rubles to remain in circulation. These were traded against the dollar at a far lower exchange rate than the new Russian currency. As a result, huge volumes of old rubles flowed from Russia and the other CIS states into Kazakhstan, expanding the money supply significantly and pushing up the inflation rate. The monthly rate of inflation rose from 25 percent to 38 percent between August and November 1993.

Panic purchases of Kazakh goods for old rubles of rapidly declining value forced the Kazakh government to introduce the tenge on November 15, 1993. Currency conversion occurred remarkably quickly—practically within five days. From November 18, 1993, the tenge was the sole legal tender in Kazakhstan. Old rubles were converted into tenge at a rate of 500 to 1, with two exceptions: only amounts of up to 100,000 rubles were converted on the spot; rubles in excess of this amount were frozen for six months in blocked accounts. In view of the fact that prices rose by 400 percent during this period, such deposits were devalued by about 75 percent. Second, savings deposits up to a specific amount were exchanged at a rate of 1 to 10 to partially offset the prior devaluation of savings deposits. This was tantamount to an increase in the money supply. (See Figure 8.2.)

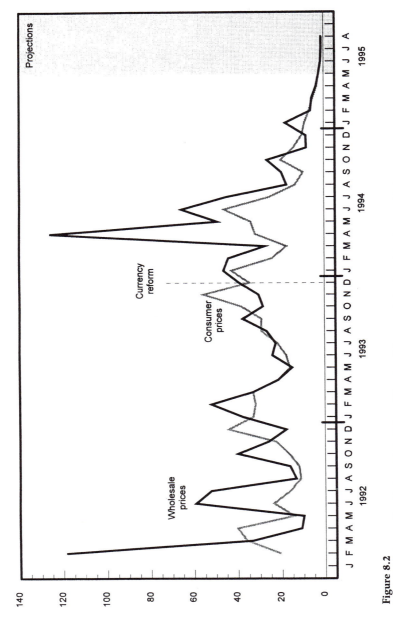

**Figure 8.2**
Rate of inflation in Kazakhstan, 1992–95 (monthly rate of change, wholesale and consumer prices)
*Source:* International Monetary Fund, unpublished data.

## 8.3.2  Failed Stabilization Policy

The introduction of the new currency provided the opportunity for a swift and lasting stabilization of the economy. This opportunity was not taken. Evidently, the government believed that merely by withdrawing from the unstable ruble zone and introducing a currency of its own, it had done enough to stabilize prices. The IMF had pressured Kazakhstan to take this step because the country was unable to implement autonomous monetary and exchange rate policies as long as it remained in the ruble zone. (IMF Background Paper, Kazakhstan, Jan. 10, 1994, p. 16). According to the IMF, stabilization was possible if the policy makers followed a consistently restrictive monetary policy in addition to fiscal discipline. Yet the fiscal and monetary measures envisaged by the IMF for this purpose were hardly adequate.

It was a mistake to raise a range of administered prices for energy, the services of public utilities, transport, communication, and grain and bread simultaneously with the introduction of the tenge. In November 1993, inflation shot up to a monthly rate of 55 percent. The price of bread and grain rose by almost 150 percent, and in December rents and the cost of electricity and water increased by almost 80 percent. Although these price increases were, in principle, justified, they should have been implemented prior to currency conversion, so as not to immediately discredit the tenge as an inflationary currency and initiate an inflationary spiral. Not only prices but also average wages rose sharply: wages were increased by more than 40 percent in November and December combined. It was readily apparent to the population that even the introduction of the new currency would not break the wage-price spiral. It thus proved impossible to generate confidence in the new currency. Until January 1994, the monthly inflation rate remained high at 43 percent, subsequently declined to 17 percent per month in March, then rose again sharply to 46 percent in June. Efforts to stabilize the tenge in the wake of currency reform had failed.

After the introduction of the tenge, the Kazakh Central Bank allowed the exchange rate to be determined by the market. Expectations of lasting inflation led to a rapid decline in the value of the currency. Between November 18, 1993, and December 21, 1993, the tenge depreciated from 4.7 to 6.31 tenge per U.S. dollar, a fairly accurate reflection of the rate of inflation in December. The tenge also depreciated markedly against the ruble. The sharp fall in the value of the tenge led to a corresponding rise in import prices, which served to stoke domestic inflation further.

The central bank initially utilized the opportunity gained by the introduction of the tenge to adopt a more restrictive policy. The rate of expansion of central bank lending to the banks was reduced. In the third quarter of 1993, lending rose by 25 percent; by the fourth quarter the rate of increase was down to 10 percent. At the same time, the minimum reserve requirement for banks was raised from 20 to 30 percent; central bank lending placed via auction increased as a proportion of its total lending, at least temporarily. The central bank refinancing rate, which had reached around 170 percent (simple annual rate, which is 12 times the monthly rate) between September and November 1993, was raised to 240 percent on December 12, 1993, and on January 10, 1994, it peaked at 270 percent. At times, the rate of money supply growth—both base and broad money—fell sharply. However, the effect of these measures was at best marginal. The IMF interpretation that monetary policy exerted a stabilizing effect during this period failed to account for the fact that the restrictive course was maintained only for a short period (IMF Background Paper, Kazakhstan, Nov. 18, 1994, p. 25). Again, the restrictive monetary policy was quickly undermined by enterprises. The fact that credit was in shorter supply and more expensive did not exert an upward pressure on costs and prices, but merely induced firms to chalk up debts with one another. Thus, the impact of the restrictive monetary policy was largely dissipated.

March 1994 saw a renewed, sharp rise in the rate of inflation. The government took the view that corporate debt had reached such proportions that it seriously threatened to undermine the functioning of the banking and payments system. In response, it devised a plan to reduce the gross debts significantly by means of a clearing system and to cover the remaining amount with government credits. The gross volume of debt amounted to 38 billion tenge. The government provided credits of 18 billion tenge to the debtor firms at a simple annual interest rate of 200 percent, of which half was to be repaid in September and the rest at the end of 1994. A number of creditor enterprises in the energy sector were immediately given 1.1 billion tenge, and on April 22, 1994, the other creditor firms were issued one-year treasury bonds with an interest rate of 3 percent and a value index pegged to the tenge-dollar exchange rate. The government earmarked 2.6 billion tenge for this purpose and called on the central bank to make available 7.6 billion by the middle of the year; this amounted to approximately half of the volume of base money then in circulation.

The rapid pace of inflation in the wake of currency conversion and the attempt to pursue a restrictive monetary policy led to payments difficulties not only for firms but also for the government, as tax revenues lagged markedly behind projections. Tax receipts fell to 18 percent of GDP in the first quarter of 1994, compared with 22 percent in 1993. Meanwhile, the government's borrowing requirement was rising rapidly. Approximately half of the decline in tax revenue as a share of GDP was due to unpaid business taxes. In addition, the government allowed a number of large state concerns to spread their taxes due over an extended period. Last but not least, the decision to extend the value-added tax to imports from non-CIS countries and the planned increase in the average rate of import duty were not implemented. Meanwhile, spending was rising faster than planned. The additional spending in the main government budget in the first quarter, compared with the same period a year earlier, amounted to around 5 percent of GDP. Among the contributory reasons were the decision to raise the minimum wage twice within the space of four months; higher petroleum prices; additional defense expenditures, which were necessary because Russian troops were replaced by Kazakh forces on its external borders; and higher subsidies for bread and animal feed because their prices were not fully adjusted for inflation.

On top of the main budget, the government also incurred quasi-fiscal expenses on a number of items. These included the credits offered to firms to manage business debts, only a part of which—10 billion out of a total of 18 billion tenge—was financed by the central bank, and a far lower proportion of which was repaid than had been envisaged. The government continued to service foreign debts that had been incurred by firms in 1992/93 and could not be repaid. The government also assumed part of the debt burden of agricultural enterprises. As a result of these trends, the budget deficit in the first quarter of 1994 amounted to 18 percent of GDP, and in the second quarter to 15 percent.

### 8.3.3  A More Successful Second Attempt at Stabilization Policy

Toward the end of May 1994, monetary policy was tightened significantly. The rate of interest for auctioned credits rose sharply. This did not exert a direct impact on the rate of inflation, however; the inflationary momentum of previous months continued, and the prices for a number of public services and utilities, including energy prices, were increased markedly. Nominal wages rose perceptibly faster than the rate of inflation. The average real wage moved up by 11 percent between March and June 1994. The inflation rate began to subside in July. This was partly due to seasonal effects, as food prices generally tend to stabilize in the summer months. Even so, the fall in the rate of inflation was more pronounced than in the corresponding periods in previous years. The restrictive monetary policy tightened further, as interest rates failed to come down in line with inflation, leading to high positive real interest rates. Calculated on an annual basis, the real rate of interest rose to over 100 percent by September 1994. Fiscal policy, too, was decidedly restrictive in the third quarter of 1994. While tax revenues as a share of GDP remained at approximately the same level as in the previous quarter, spending from the main budget fell by almost five percentage points and quasi-fiscal expenditure dropped by fifteen percentage points, the combined effect of which was a budget surplus of around 4 percent of GDP.

In view of the lack of relevant data, the impact of this extreme turnaround in monetary and fiscal policy on the real economy can be determined only approximately. The output of all economic sectors declined more or less continuously throughout 1994. The decline in GDP for the year as a whole is estimated at more than 25 percent. The slump in fixed capital formation was even more pronounced: during the first half of 1994, investment fell by half of 1993 levels and was equal to just 15 percent of investment in 1991. The contraction was largest in agriculture, down to less than 3 percent of 1991 investment, and in the construction sector it fell to just 8 percent of the 1991 level. It is clearly impossible to restructure an economy under such conditions. Allowing for seasonal components and the influence of administered price increases, inflation cooled further in the fourth quarter. Following a brief stabilization, output again fell in the fourth quarter by around 9 percent. A further decline in output and investment was expected in 1995.

## 8.4  How to Stabilize Kazakhstan's Macroeconomy: A Policy Agenda

### 8.4.1  Inertial Inflation

Kazakhstan failed to seize the opportunity provided by the introduction of a new currency to bring the inflationary process quickly under control. The remaining option was to reduce the rate of inflation steadily. In principle, the approach underpinning the stabilization program negotiated by the government with the IMF in January 1994 was correct. Yet a number of important additional measures should have been implemented in order to achieve the declared goals, and to keep output and employment losses to a minimum.

In principle, it is possible to slash a high rate of inflation in the context of economic transformation, even in the face of major external price shocks following price liberalization. In view of the experiences of Lithuania, Estonia, and Poland, however, a sharp contraction in output should have been anticipated in Kazakhstan following the introduction of the new currency, and not the decline of just 3 percent forecast by the IMF at the start of 1994. In order to avoid a collapse in output, the IMF's orthodox stabilization program should have been complemented by additional measures. In the absence of measures to stabilize business costs, monetary policy in the transforming economies is usually unable to cope with the scale of the inflationary problem, or is totally ineffective.

Phases of persistent rapid inflation, or of hyperinflation, are practically always characterized by a mutually reinforcing process of wage and price increases, a process usually termed inertial inflation.[2] If wages are not adjusted quickly to offset price rises (indexation), large sections of the population quickly descend into poverty and resort to other ways of coping with inflation. These wage increases, in turn, lead to further price increases, while at the same time creating the scope for the price increases to be realized on sales markets. Because cash is required to meet increased nominal transactions, the inflationary process can be maintained only if the money supply is constantly allowed to expand. If the money supply is prevented from growing, production will collapse, because while prices go on rising, purchasing power suddenly is insufficient to purchase the goods produced. In a market economy, many firms suffer losses and go out of business. In a situation in which the majority of enterprises are still state-owned, however, these losses are met by government lending or by firms granting each other additional credits. This cuts the link between a restrictive monetary policy and inflation. As firms' indebtedness and/or that of the government rises, the central bank is usually forced to abandon its restrictive monetary stance. Inflation is then able to proceed unabated.

In order to prevent this from happening, the restriction on purchasing power exerted by monetary policy should be supplemented by direct attempts to dampen rising costs, with their restraining effect on prices— that is, by direct action to break inflationary expectations. The point of departure for such action is nominal wages. They must not be allowed to rise faster than the target rate of monthly inflation plus productivity growth—a target that also applies to monetary policy. The target value for the inflation rate can then be reduced from month to month. This policy can be justified vis-à-vis wage earners provided prices do not on average rise faster than wages. Thus, firms must not be allowed to exploit monopolistic positions in order to increase their profits during a transitional phase by raising prices disproportionately. In order to avoid this, enterprise price policies should be subjected to some form of control or at least surveillance.

### 8.4.2 The Proposal for a Social Contract

In view of this, the German advisory group proposed a social contract in which the leading representatives of government, industry, and trade unions reach agreement on certain guidelines for action. The aim of this stability pact was to reduce the inflation rate without massive loss of output and high unemployment. The central element was to chart a target path for the monthly rate of inflation, a gradual reduction from 20 percent in March 1994 to 3 percent in December 1994. With this aim in view, the targeted wage and price trends were to be brought into agreement with monetary, fiscal, and exchange-rate policies. More specifically, the guidelines discussed below were proposed.

### A Wage Formula
The index of the wage rate may not exceed the product of the target rate of inflation and the expected productivity change. As a result, firms wage cost burden will be stabilized because the monthly rate of wage cost increases will be linked to the targeted monthly rates of inflation. Additionally, it prevents the relative income position of the wage earners from deteriorating during the period of stabilization, which makes it socially more acceptable.

### A Price Formula
The wage trend would be perfectly adequate as a nominal anchor if competitive pressures could be trusted (as in market economies) to force firms to pass the cost reductions on to prices. In view of the monopolistic structures and soft budget constraints characterizing large sectors of the Kazakh economy, price surveillance would be necessary. State enterprises that infringed the price rule without offering a justifiable reason—such as changes in relative prices in the wake of price liberalization or negative price shocks—must face sanctions.

### An Interest Rate Formula
The monetary authorities should set the nominal rate of interest at a level a few percentage points above the target rate of inflation and thus ensure

that real interest rates are slightly positive. The banks should commit themselves to maintaining a certain interest rate margin. The real interest rate should not be allowed to fall far below zero because in that case, the central bank would subsidize borrowers and exacerbate capital flight. On the other hand, a real interest rate substantially higher than zero would deter investors and endanger too many existing firms.

A slightly positive real interest rate in practice can be achieved by fixing the nominal rate in the next month at the target rate of inflation for that month or, alternatively, at the actual rate of inflation in the previous month. In the IMF's "to be on the safe side" view, the latter formulation was preferred because such a link would be independent of an uncertain target rate of inflation. The IMF overlooked the fact that rates of inflation, which have fluctuated widely in the recent past, are irrelevant in providing guidance to firms in their decision-making. Adjusting nominal interest rates to the inevitable fluctuations of ex post inflation rates can lead to significant interest rate fluctuations and thus increase uncertainty for firms. Rather, monetary policy turns out to be "on the safe side" if it links, in combination with appropriate wage targets and a price surveillance policy, the nominal rate of interest to the target rate of inflation. If the actual rate of inflation turns out to be higher than the target rate because of the failure of the wage-price mechanism, the authorities can tighten their monetary policy.

### A Fiscal Policy Rule
The government commits itself to refrain from inflationary price and tax increases. The tax administration will be reinforced so that existing laws can be enforced more effectively. Subsidies for firms will initially be frozen and then steadily reduced.

### Exchange-Rate Policy
The central bank should hold the *real* exchange rate of the tenge against the dollar constant by devaluing the *nominal* exchange rate in line with the preset inflation target. The exchange rate of the tenge against the ruble then results automatically from changes in the ruble-dollar exchange rate. This is likely to imply an appreciation of the tenge against the ruble. Thus, during the stabilization phase, the real exchange rate should remain constant so that irregular fluctuations in the price competitiveness of domestic firms are avoided. A strong real depreciation in the exchange rate, induced by a nominal depreciation in excess of inflation rate differentials, might undermine national and international confidence in the stabilization policy.

This should be avoided as part of the general aim of stabilizing expectations. Yet equally, real appreciation is also to be avoided. It undermines competitiveness, often without indicating a genuine rise in international confidence, because such appreciation often results from the promise of high nominal interest rates in the transforming country in the absence of an expected depreciation of the exchange rate in the short term.[3]

### 8.4.3  Wages Versus the Exchange Rate as a Nominal Anchor

In light of the experiences of smaller transformation countries and a number of newly industrializing countries, many international observers and advisers have recommended that large transforming economies like Russia, Ukraine, and Kazakhstan should employ a fixed exchange rate vis-à-vis Western countries as a nominal anchor.[4] This, it is argued, renders the steering of monetary policy that much easier. In the extreme case of the so-called currency board, monetary policy is deprived of any scope for autonomous action, as money can be generated only in line with changes in the balance of foreign currency holdings.[5]

In view of the logic of inertial inflation, this view cannot be rejected out of hand. A closer look, however, reveals a number of problems with this approach. According to Dornbusch and Fischer (1993), the logic of inertial inflation can be summarized in the following equation:

$$p = p_{-1} + \alpha(w - p_{-1}) + (1 - \alpha)(e - p_{-1}) + y,$$

where $p$ is the inflation rate, $p_{-1}$ is the past price inflation, $(w - p_{-1})$ is the change in real wages plus a lag, $e$ is the rate of depreciation of the nominal exchange rate, $(1 - \alpha)(e - p_{-1})$ represents the lagged change of the real exchange rate, and y is a term for supply shocks. It follows that "Inflation today will be equal to inflation yesterday except for any combination of the following: (i) Wage inflation falls below past price inflation. This requires a break with any implicit or explicit backward-looking indexation. The suspension of indexation, or introduction of an incomes policy, could accomplish this. (ii) Exchange depreciation falls below the rate of past inflation. (iii) Favorable supply shocks lead to disinflation without the need for the exchange rate or wages to take the lead" (Dornbusch and Fischer, 1993, p. 11).

Thus, apparently, the chances of breaking inertial inflation are equally good whether it is the wage regime or the exchange rate regime that is changed. Closer analysis casts doubt on this view, however. In the transforming economies, at least, positive external shocks are virtually out of the question, whereas large-scale negative supply-side shocks in the wake of price liberalization are very much the rule. This exacerbates the problem of stabilization regardless of which variable is used as a nominal anchor. An additional point is that the choice of combining the wage regime and the exchange-rate regime is not mutually independent. Exchange rate stabilization, for instance, makes sense only if the aim is to force greater price and cost discipline on the domestic economy via the competitive pressure of imports. If the exchange rate is to be stabilized successfully, the unit wage costs in the transforming country must be pegged to those in industrialized countries in a credible way; this must be attainable within a limited period of time. As is the case with a strict monetary regime at home, this is possible only with the help of an incomes policy or via high unemployment. Deindexation, that is, a break with backward-looking indexation, must be achieved if exchange-rate stabilization is to be successful. Thus exchange-rate stabilization and a break with backward-looking indexation are not substitutes; they complement each other.

From other perspectives, exchange-rate stabilization is more ambitious and more expensive than direct wage stabilization. Exchange-rate stabilization can be successful in countries emerging from a phase of relatively high inflation only if the domestic currency is devalued substantially—and thus undervalued—at the start of the stabilization phase. This means that an additional, negative, supply-side shock must be overcome at the start of the disinflation phase. This has to be absorbed in the form of a further decline in real wages, which must then link up with trends in the hard-currency countries in a disinflation process determined by the extent of the undervaluation. The task facing those responsible for wage determination is especially difficult given that a disinflation path, once chosen, cannot be abandoned without substantial costs in terms of a loss of credibility in the capital markets. The entire adjustment period, the success of each and every step along the way, and thus each failure in adjustment terms are subject to daily evaluation by the capital markets. It will be difficult to explain reverses in the fight against inflation to investors, even those induced by negative supply-side shocks resulting, say, from bad harvests.

The decisive disadvantage of the strategy of exchange-rate stabilization, however, lies in the potentially destabilizing effect of short-term international capital flows. Exchange-rate stabilization can be successful only if the transforming country offers consistently higher interest rates than hard-currency countries during the disinflation phase. This is inevitable for reasons of sufficient domestic pressure from monetary policy;

otherwise, real interest rates would be negative. The inflation rate differential between the transforming and the hard-currency country is matched by a corresponding interest rate differential, but not—as is normally the case in global capital markets—by a corresponding risk of depreciation. Thus the option of using the exchange rate as a nominal anchor breaks the link between the inflation differential and the risk of depreciation. The assets of a country taking this option are extremely attractive during the disinflation phase, because only the nominal rate of interest and the risk of depreciation are relevant for international investors. This leads to speculative capital inflows. At the same time, the conditions for domestic investment in terms of the medium-term rate of inflation deteriorate due to the extremely high interest rates. Thus investors on the global capital market earn high rates of return in countries in which real incomes and domestic profits are falling dramatically; real-world examples of this constellation are provided by the Baltic republics in 1992 and 1993, Mexico in 1994, and Russia, Ukraine, and Kazakhstan in 1995. At the same time, the transforming country is unable to cut interest rates because this would endanger the credibility of monetary policy at home; in the short term, at least, the political will to achieve economic stability is reflected in the maintenance of high nominal interest rates (see Calvo and Frankel, 1991).

Paradoxically, the inflow of capital associated with this strategy is often taken as evidence of its success. The transforming country is thus perceived as being able to draw on global savings that would not otherwise be available for the reconstruction process. Generally, however, only a fraction of the capital inflow is tied to the transforming country for an extended period, and is thus available for expanding its capital stock. Much of the capital inflow is short-term in nature, simply because the decoupling of the inflation differential and the risk of depreciation holds only for the short term. Such capital can be withdrawn relatively quickly, as a rule initiating a liquidity crisis. In the end, the process of real economic adjustment in the transforming country becomes even more painful, the conditions imposed by investors of capital become even stricter, and the chances of success the second time around are worse than the first time due to the loss of credibility.

## 8.5 Summary and Outlook

Kazakhstan's rich and diverse resource basis provides an excellent foundation for its integration into the world economy. However, its globalization will be impeded for some time to come by the historical legacy of

central planning and its unfavorable geographical location. For many decades, Kazakhstan's sectoral and regional production structure was distorted; its capital stock is physically and technologically outdated; the
workforce lacks knowledge of Western technologies and commercial
practices. Kazakhstan must restructure and redevelop its manufacturing
and mining industries in order to generate sustainable economic growth
for the next decades.

In contrast to most other transition economies, Kazakhstan's access
to world markets is constrained by physical distance: it is landlocked in
Central Asia. On the south and on the east, Kazakhstan and the smaller
Central Asian transition economies are surrounded by a chain of high
mountain masses. Hence, all major transportation routes to the outside
world have to cross the Siberian part of Russia. Eight-five percent of all
trade goes through Russia; more than half of Kazakhstan's trade is directed
to or comes from Russia. Therefore, Kazakhstan has to find an independent entry into the international division of labor that allows it to preserve its special relationship with Russia.

On the other hand, Kazakhstan has to reduce its dependence on the
success of Russia's transition. The most important step in this direction
was the introduction of a national currency in November 1993. This
allowed the Kazakh government, for the first time, to pursue an independent monetary policy and thus end the high inflation originating from the
inflow of cheap ruble notes. This opportunity was missed in the first
round; in the second round, the whole burden of stabilization was shifted
onto the shoulders of monetary policy. On the advice of the IMF, the
macroeconomic policy stance became very restrictive in mid-1994. The
government pushed for a rigorous reduction of the budget deficit and
monetary policy aimed at bringing down the rate of inflation to a low,
single-digit monthly level. Inflation did come down surprisingly quickly,
with a monthly rate of around 2 percent in the summer of 1995. Monetary and fiscal restrictions, supplemented by strong seasonal factors, can
clearly claim part of the success. But the extremely restrictive policy
aggravated the already sustained decline in production. In 1995, domestic
product was expected to fall at a double-digit rate; net investment was
clearly negative.

Currently, there is a stalemate between macroeconomic and microeconomic policies in Kazakhstan. Monetary and fiscal policy makers are
reluctant to relax as long as companies do not start restructuring. But
restructuring can be successful only if the capital stock is renovated by
new machinery and other equipment. However, investment is constrained

by extremely high real interest rates. The nominal refinance rate of the central bank exceeded the rate of inflation in the spring of 1995 by 5 to 10 percent per month, implying an effective annual *real* interest rate of up to 100 percent. Sooner or later, the macroeconomic policy stance has to be reversed to allow for more investment and effective restructuring. But there is no guarantee that inflation will not revive. To break that logjam and the inflationary expectations, it is necessary to complement the orthodox stabilization policy by an income policy using the nominal wage level as an anchor. If such a policy had been implemented at the beginning of 1994, it would have prevented the enormous output loss caused by the orthodox stabilization policy in an economy characterized by strong rigidities of a monopolized, nonprivate industry and marked by the inexperience of the policy makers.

In future, the decisive factor for the success of transformation is whether Kazakhstan will be able to develop suitable domestic conditions for the accumulation of capital. Capital is accumulated by successful enterprise activities that require incentives. The necessary institutional prerequisites for private incentives are private property, profit-oriented salaries of managers, and well-functioning capital markets with reasonably low real interest rates. Fiscal and monetary policies should energetically oppose any new acceleration of inflation, regardless of whether it originates from the cost or the demand side; but they cannot guarantee control of renewed inflation with their instruments alone. Additionally, a wage policy is needed that allows enterprises to earn pioneer profits for productive and innovative activities. If future wage increases are institutionally linked to the average productivity growth of the economy, the resulting cost stabilization will allow the necessary incentives for investment.

Finally, the suggestion that the stability of a country's currency can be guaranteed by linking it to the nominal anchor of a Western currency is unsuitable for a transition economy such as Kazakhstan. As long as the institutional, legal, and administrative conditions in Kazakhstan differ substantially from those in Western countries, the yardstick of a fixed nominal exchange rate is too severe. A crawling peg rate that is regularly adjusted to the inflation differential with the West is more suitable

The most important preconditions for the globalization of Kazakhstan's economy are internal reforms and stabilization. However, if Kazakhstan is to be successful, Russia needs to be successful as well. Without a sustained recovery in the Russian Federation, the economic development of Kazakhstan is likely to be further impeded.

## Notes

This paper relies to a substantial degree on the contents of unpublished background reports of the IMF and the World Bank. Additionally, discussions with leading government officials of the Republic of Kazakhstan provided invaluable insights. Research assistance was provided by Máire Murphy. The manuscript was completed in August 1995.

1. It is difficult to assess to what extent official statistics overstate the decline because firms have incentives to underreport production. Additionally, the newly emerging private sector is not adequately covered by the official data. However, the margins of error are not likely to be large.

2. The theoretical implications of this wage-price spiral leading to hyperinflation were spelled out in a seminal paper by Cagan (1956). Actual examples of such a pattern are discussed in Bruno et al. (1988).

3. One of the earliest analyses of these interrelated issues is in Edwards (1989). Also see Adams and Gros (1986) for a discussion of the impact of real exchange-rate rules on macroeconomic stabilization.

4. The IMF proposed this for Kazakhstan in IMF Background Paper (November 16, 1994), p. 16. A fixed exchange-rate system evidently provides an anchor for domestic price behavior and results in "correct" relative prices, which were seriously distorted in former centrally planned economics. See, for example, Bruno (1992) and Oles and Rubel (1992).

5. Estonia and Lithuania, among the post-Soviet states, have adopted currency board arrangements. The arguments for setting up currency boards in transition economies and the principles of their functioning are stated at length in Hanke et al. (1993).

## References

Adams, Charles, and D. Gros. 1986. "The Consequences of Real Exchange Rate Rules for Inflation: Some Illustrative Examples." *IMF Staff Papers* 33 (September): 439–76.

Bruno, M. 1992. "Stabilization and Reform in Eastern Europe: A Preliminary Evaluation." *IMF Staff Papers* 39 (December): 741–77.

Bruno, M., G. di Tella, R. Dornbusch, and S. Fischer, eds. 1988. *Inflation Stabilization: The Experience of Israel, Argentina, Brazil, Bolivia and Mexico.* Cambridge, Mass.: MIT Press.

Cagan, Philip. 1956. "The Monetary Dynamics of Hyperinflation." In Milton Freedman, ed., *Studies in the Quantity Theory of Money.* Chicago: University of Chicago Press.

Calvo, A. Guillermo, and J. Frankel. 1991. "Credit Markets, Credibility, and Economic Transformation." *Journal of Economic Perspectives* 5 (Fall): 139–48.

Conway, Patrick. 1995. *Saving in Transition Economic—The Summary Report.* Policy Research Working Paper 1509. Washington, D.C.: World Bank.

Desai, P. 1989. "Perestroika, Prices, and the Ruble Problem." *Harriman Institute Forum* 2, no. 11.

Dornbusch, Rüdiger, and Stanley Fischer. 1993. "Moderate Inflation." *World Bank Economic Review* 7, no. 1: 1–44.

Dornbusch, Rüdiger, and Holger Wolf. 1990. "Monetary Overhang and Reforms in the 1940s." Cambridge, Mass.: Department of Economics, MIT. (Mimeo).

European Bank for Reconstruction and Development. 1994. *Transition Report*. London: ERBD.

Edwards, Sebastian. 1989. *Real Exchange Rates, Devaluation, and Adjustment*. Cambridge, Mass.: MIT Press.

Hanke, S., L. Jonung, and K. Schuler. 1993. *Russian Currency and Finance: A Currency Board Approach to Reform*. London and New York: Routledge.

International Monetary Fund. 1993. *IMF Economic Review: Kazakhstan*. Washington, D.C.: IMF.

International Monetary Fund. 1994. *IMF Background Paper: Kazakhstan.) Washington, D.C.: IMF*.

Langhammer, Rolf J., and Matthias Lücke. 1995. *Die Handelsbeziehungen der Nachfolgestaaten der Sowjetunion: Von der Desintegration zur weltwirtschaftlichen Integration?* Kiel Discussion Papers no. 244. Kiel: Institute for World Economics.

McKinnon, R. 1991. *The Order of Economic Liberalization: Financial Control in the Transition to a Market Economy*. Baltimore: Johns Hopkins University Press.

Nordhaus, W. 1990. "Soviet Economic Reform: The Longest Road." *Brookings Papers in Economic Activity* 1:287–308.

Oles, Marek, and M. Rubel. 1992. "Balance of Payments in the Stabilization Program of the Polish Economy." *Russian and East European Finance and Trade* (Fall): 40–60.

United Nations Economic Commission for Europe. 1994. *Economic Bulletin for Europe* 46 (November).

World Bank. 1994. *World Development Report*. Washington, D.C.

# Uzbekistan

## Michael Connolly

Uzbekistan's trade has suffered a major decline in real terms since independence on August 31, 1991. Payments difficulties and recession in the former Soviet Union (FSU) reduced trade with the FSU in 1994 to about one-fourth its 1991 level. The initial lack of correspondent accounts in hard currency, exchange controls, and a rapidly depreciating ruble made the transition to trading on a hard currency basis difficult.

The extent of the decline in trade is dramatic: total exports fell from U.S.$11,829 million in 1991 to U.S.$1,424 million in 1992, U.S.$2,877 million in 1993, and U.S.$2,850.66 million (est.) in 1994. Imports declined correspondingly, from U.S.$11,141 million in 1991 to U.S.$2,784 million (est.) in 1994. In addition, transfer payments from the FSU of U.S.$6,530 million in 1991 virtually halted, declining to U.S.$2 million in 1992 and averaging U.S.$10 million in 1993 and 1994 (figures are from IMF). These negative results were a consequence of severe regional recessions and difficulties in implementing a payments system between the former Soviet republics.

In response to the trade contraction, the government of Uzbekistan firmly maintained its control over trade through the state order system, export licensing, bilateral barter and clearing arrangements, and restricted access to hard currency. In 1994, some of these controls were relaxed but were still in place for most international transactions. The May 1993 imposition of a 35 percent tax on foreign currency receipts discouraged private exports, and encouraged evasion by underinvoicing of exports and capital flight. In February 1994, the tax on foreign currency receipts was replaced by a hard currency surrender requirement; however, the free market rate is not paid to exporters because the central bank foreign exchange auction determining the official price of foreign exchange does not have free entry. As a result, the discount on foreign currency acts as an equivalent tax on foreign exchange. On April 15, 1994, the hard currency surrender requirement was increased to 30 percent and extended to all export receipts, not only non-Commonwealth of Independent States (CIS) countries. On November 17, 1994, a presidential decree reduced the official list of exports requiring licensing to eleven goods effective January 1, 1995. However, natural gas and cotton, still on the list, account for 58 percent of exports. Barter trade has proved to be resilient: Uzbekistan had bilateral payments agreements with seventeen countries at the end of 1994. Some of them, mostly with CIS countries, have lists of commodities to be supplied on a mutual basis.

Uzbekistan now faces a major challenge and opportunity to rejoin the world trading community on a multilateral basis: the country obtained observer status at the GATT in June 1994. A major obstacle to economic reform in Uzbekistan is the pricing of water used for irrigation. As of mid-1995, water was not priced, yet it is used intensively for irrigation of cotton in fields adjacent to the Syr Darya and Amu Darya rivers. Since these rivers flow into the Aral Sea, a saline body of water, intensive irrigation of cotton fields has contributed to the dramatic drawdown of the water level there. From 1960 to 1989, the average level of the Aral Sea fell from 53 meters to 39 meters, half a meter per year. In addition, average salinity rose from 10 to 30 grams liter, suggesting increased harm to the irrigated land (Micklin, 1991). Neighboring countries (Kazakhstan, Kyrgyzstan, Tajikistan, and Turkmenistan) also irrigate from sources that deplete the Aral Sea, in what must be one of the twentieth century's most dramatic examples of the tragedy of the commons (see Ostrom, 1990). An international conference at Tashkent, Uzbekistan, in August 1995 addressed this issue. The problem is that all the cotton in Central Asia, constituting 90 percent of cotton output of the FSU and a third of world production, is irrigated. Consequently, water is overused as an input (in principle, until the marginal product of the last drop is zero).

Cotton, often referred to as "white gold," was brought to Central Asia as a result of the heavy emphasis on converting the area into a cotton bowl that was initiated by "Lenin's May 1918 decree 'About the Organization of Irrigation work in Turkestan' which started work on large-scale irrigation projects here in order to guarantee the USSR's 'cotton independence'" (Micklin, 1991, p. 11). Irrigation is also widely used for Central Asian food crops. However, in October 1995 farmer's still did not pay for water used in irrigation, which represents a considerable input subsidy.

## 9.1   The Macroeconomic Setting

### 9.1.1   *Money and Prices*

As part of the Soviet Union until August 31, 1991, the Republic of Uzbekistan used the ruble as the medium of exchange, and continued to do so even after the issue, initially at par with the ruble, of the sumcoupon on November 15, 1993. On April 15, 1994, restricted auctions of foreign exchange began at the central bank. On July 1, 1994, the sum was issued as the national currency at the rate of 1,000 sum coupons per sum, and as of October 15, 1994, all payments were required to be settled in sum, ending the official use of the Russian ruble as a medium of exchange. During the transition process, the government participated in the ill-fated attempt to establish a ruble zone and a regional central bank with clearing functions. The ruble simply did not prove to be an acceptable medium of exchange due to widespread arrears and nonpayment in the system, and also due to the high rate of depreciation of the ruble, so that as an asset it had a highly negative real rate of return.

The introduction of the sum was mishandled, involving considerable confiscation of existing cash balances through limiting the amounts individuals could exchange, delaying the exchange process during a period in which monthly inflation was high (20 percent a month), and limiting interest on the sums to be converted. Rising fiscal deficits as a percent of GDP (due in part to the elimination of transfers from the FSU to the central budget equal to 18 percent of revenues) led to an inability of the Uzbek authorities to renounce new seigniorage as a means of finance, especially in 1993, when 19.2 percent of the fiscal deficit was financed by domestic bank borrowing. Inflation had accelerated to over 1,134 percent in the twelve months ending June 1994. Table 9.1 reports retail and wholesale price indices in Uzbekistan from 1992 to 1994.

The poor performance of the sum not only as a medium of exchange, both internally and externally, but also as an asset led to a rising velocity

**Table 9.1**
Retail and wholesale price indices: Uzbekistan, 1992–94

|                  | 1/1/92 | 1/1/93 | 1/1/94  | 10/1/94   |
| ---------------- | ------ | ------ | ------- | --------- |
| Retail prices    | 100    | 1,010  | 9,947   | 34,018    |
| Wholesale prices | 100    | 8,963  | 180,950 | 1,522,843 |

*Source:* International Monetary Fund.

**Figure 9.1**
Velocity of broad money: Uzbekistan, 1992–94
*Source:* International Monetary Fund.

of circulation of the sum as individuals and firms economized on its use. (See Figure 9.1.)

### 9.1.2 The Fiscal Deficit

Table 9.2 suggests that Uzbekistan, along with many of the other newly independent states, suffered a major shock in 1991 from the elimination of net transfers from the FSU. The rise in the financing requirements of the fiscal deficit in 1992, to 18.4 percent of GDP, was clearly one of the consequences of the decline in net transfers.

The contribution of the cotton "excise tax"—the difference between the selling price and the procurement price of cotton subject to state order (67 percent of the crop in 1994), times the volume of cotton bought by direct procurement—also provided a declining fraction of finance of the fiscal deficit, falling to one-third its 1992 level in 1994. This was due not only to the lowering of the fraction of cotton production subject to state order but also to increasing the procurement price closer to world levels. Raw cotton output also declined from 4.65 billion tons in 1991 to 4.23 billion in 1993. From January to September 1994, raw cotton output was 4.2 billion tons, so output seemed to be recovering. In 1994, the direct pro-

**Table 9.2**
Fiscal operations: Uzbekistan, 1991–94 (as a percent of GDP)

|                                       | 1991 | 1992 | 1993 | 1994 |
|---------------------------------------|------|------|------|------|
| Fiscal deficit (financing definiton)  | 4.1  | 18.4 | 12.1 | 4.3  |
| Cotton revenue                        | ...  | 6.6  | 5.5  | 2.1  |
| Net transfers from the Union          | 18.5 | —    | —    | —    |
| Domestic bank borrowing (net)         | 3.9  | 0.0  | 19.2 | 4.3  |

*Source:* International Monetary Fund.
*Note:* The financing definition is measured as "the difference between total outlays and total receipts excluding borrowing proceeds (Tanzi, Blejer, and Teijeiro [December 1987, p 715]." It thus includes as outlays amortization payments as well as interest payments on the outstanding stock of public debt since these add to the financing needs of government.
... indicates not available.
— indicates negligible.

curement price for processed cotton fiber paid by Goskomkhlopkopromsbit was 5,770 sum per ton. Goskomkhlopkopromsbit then sold half of the cotton fiber to ministries for 26,000 sum per ton (near world prices). The ministries use the proceeds from cotton exports to pay for imports of wheat, meat, pharmaceuticals, and other commodities.

### 9.1.3   Real Output

Real output is not measured accurately in Uzbekistan, due in part to the legacy of the use of net material product accounting procedures. Nevertheless, real GDP declined from 1991 to 1994 but showed signs of stabilizing in the latter year. (See Figure 9.2.)

On an annual basis, in 1991 Uzbekistan's real GDP fell 0.5 percent; real output contracted a further 11 percent in 1992; and 2.5 percent more in 1993–94. These data compare favorably with declines experienced elsewhere in the FSU. The slow pace of economic reform and the decline in exports suggests that not all difficult times were behind the country by November 1995.

### 9.1.4   Employment and Unemployment

Data on employment are shown in Figure 9.3, suggesting a decline in employment in Uzbekistan of 405,000 workers from 1992 to August 1994. These data are consistent with the real GDP data suggesting that output was down nearly 15 percent over previous peak levels. However, both GDP and employment data may fail to capture emerging private

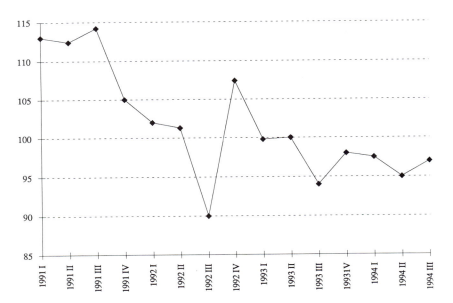

**Figure 9.2**
Real GDP, seasonally adjusted: Uzbekistan, 1991–94 (average, 1992 = 100)
*Source:* International Monetary Fund.

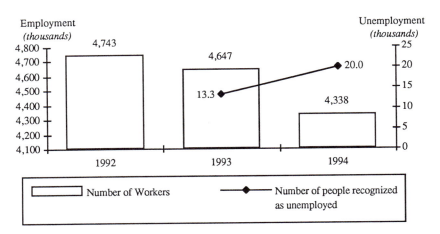

**Figure 9.3**
Employment and unemployment, 1992–94
*Source:* International Monetary Fund.

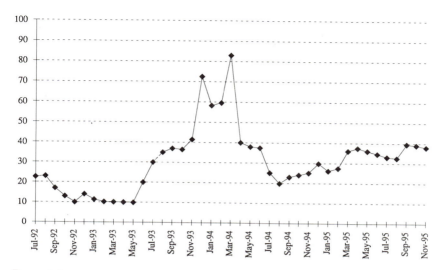

**Figure 9.4**
Average wage, Uzbekistan: July 1992–November 1995 (in U.S. dollars, period average)
*Source:* International Monetary Fund.

activities. The disruption of real economic activity is, however, among the lowest in the FSU because the pace of economic reform has been among the most gradual.

### 9.1.5  Real Wages

For what they are worth, data provided by the International Monetary Fund suggest that real wages in Uzbekistan more than tripled between the first quarter of 1992 and the third quarter of 1994 (See Figure 9.4.) However, the nominal wage was divided by the retail price index, which shows considerably less inflation than the wholesale price index. If anything, there was a significant upward bias in the real wage index (See Table 9.1 for the wholesale price index).

### 9.1.6  The Real Exchange Rate

The real exchange rates of the ruble, the sum coupon, and the sum are plotted in Figure 9.5, where a rise indicates a real appreciation according to the IMF definition.

Following the introduction of the sum coupon on November 15, 1993, there was a strong appreciation from a level around 60 to nearly 100 at

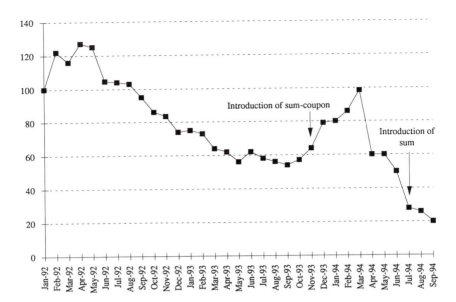

**Figure 9.5**
Real exchange rate: Uzbekistan, 1992–94 (January 1992 = 100)
*Source:* International Monetary Fund.
*Note:* The IMF definition of the real exchange rate (the Multilateral Exchange Rate Index) of
country $i$ is indicated by

$$100 \prod_{\substack{j=1 \\ i \neq j}}^{n} \left( \frac{P_i}{E_{ij} P_j} \right)^{\alpha_j},$$

where $P_i$ is the price level of country $i$ (Uzbekistan in this instance), $E_{ij}$ the local currency
(sum) price of currency $j$, $P_j$ the price level of country $j$, and $\alpha_j$ the weight given to currency
$j$'s bilateral real exchange rate. Consequently, a *fall* in the index indicates a *real depreciation*,
while a *rise* indicates a *real appreciation*.

its peak in May 1994. However, the sum had lost 80 percent of its real
value by September 1994. This evolution reflects, in part, the greater
floating of the currency as more banks were authorized to enter the foreign exchange market. It also reflects the decline in the real value of the
sum as an asset as velocity accelerated. Had the sum been introduced
under tighter fiscal conditions, the currency would not have experienced
such a dramatic decline in real terms.

## 9.2   Patterns of Trade

Uzbekistan primarily exports cotton to the non-FSU nations through state
orders and state trading companies. In this system, the state sets produc-

**Table 9.3**
Uzbekistan's trade pattern (millions of U.S. dollars)

|  | 1990 | 1991 | 1992 | 1993 | 1994 |
|---|---|---|---|---|---|
| Exports to |  |  |  |  |  |
| Rest of world | 1,390 | 1,257 | 869 | 1,466 | 912 |
| Newly independent states | 11,327 | 9,228 | 4,177 | 4,100 | 3,118 |
| Imports from |  |  |  |  |  |
| Rest of world | 2,217 | 2,048 | 929 | 1,280 | 1,106 |
| Newly independent states | 18,818 | 11,715 | 5,818 | 5,243 | 3,322 |

*Source:* Michalopoulos, Constantine, and David G. Tarr (1994) and the World Bank.

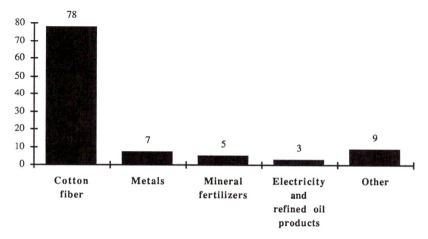

**Figure 9.6**
Composition of exports, 1992 (percent of total)
*Source:* World Bank.

tion quotas, purchases 75 percent of the quota (in 1994; 67 percent in 1995) at a price equal to approximately 15 percent (currently 20 percent) of the world price, and sells it domestically for about 20 percent of the world price and internationally at world prices (which are used in clearing and barter arrangements). Cotton producers may sell the remaining 25 percent of the quota plus any over-quota output; when it is sold internationally, it must be done through state trading companies. (See Table 9.3.) Gold is also a major export commodity, accounting for nearly as much as cotton exports in 1994.

Figure 9.6 illustrates the composition of foreign exports for 1992. Measured in constant rubles, Uzbekistan's exports to the rest of the FSU fell

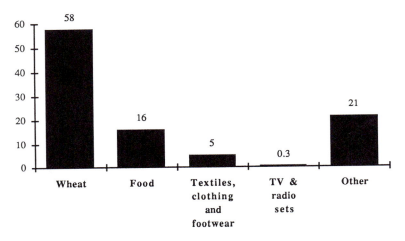

**Figure 9.7**
Composition of imports, 1992 (percent of total)
*Source:* World Bank.

by 18.7 percent in 1991 and by 35 percent in 1992. Import demand in Uzbekistan fell more than exports did, with the end result that the trade balance with the FSU improved from a deficit of 3,695 million rubles in 1990 to 729 million in 1991 and only 441 million in 1992.

Seventy-four percent of Uzbekistan's imports from the non-FSU nations are wheat and food, and another 5 percent are textiles and clothing, as shown in Figure 9.7.

Currently, there are no duties on imports, and there is a considerable consumption subsidy for flour, one of two consumption goods still subsidized. (Later, I will analyze the procurement of grain for sale to domestic flour mills.)

### 9.3   The Payments System

An obstacle to the expansion of Uzbekistan's trade is the payments system, which is characterized by arrears, inconvertibility, and the resort to barter and clearing arrangements to avoid the use of hard currency. The September 7, 1992, agreement to form a new ruble zone collapsed due to the reluctance of Uzbekistan to collateralize 50 percent of new banknotes issued, and 100 percent of banknotes exceeding monetary ceilings, with gold or hard currency. The attempt to establish of the Interstate Bank, a multilateral clearing bank using the ruble as the unit of account and with the governor of the Bank of Russia as the director, was a failure.

The convertibility of rubles and the sum coupon was severely limited within Uzbekistan. Such limited convertibility was backed by a complex system of controls and adhoc arrangements of the central national bank that severely limited the possibilities for trade expansion in Uzbekistan, and also prevented the achievement of macroeconomic stability. The auction of foreign exchange set up April 15, 1994, began with participation by a limited number of buyers, initially the five state banks and more recently the private commercial banks. Typically, the settling price is less than that on the parallel market. Part of the hard currency turned over to the central bank is auctioned in this exchange. Other parts are turned over to ministries via the Republican Monetary Fund (a foreign exchange budget allocated to the Cabinet of Ministers).

The crisis in the Soviet Union affected the economy of Uzbekistan through various channels. Most important was the hyperinflation transmitted by the use of the ruble as the national currency. The run against ruble currency holdings generated abnormally high demands for foreign exchange that put enormous pressure on hard currency markets and depreciated real exchange rates. In the absence of a clearing mechanism and convertible currencies, the payment system among the FSU republics suffered a serious blow. In constant rubles, inter-republic trade fell by 25 percent in 1991 and an additional 34 percent in 1992. Each FSU republic holds a correspondent account at the other's central bank. The instability of the ruble, the lack of political unity, and the existence of inconvertible credit rubles has made clearing between those accounts a subject of bilateral negotiations. Such negotiations are far from substituting for a well-developed clearing system, and the result is that interrepublic trade is severely restricted. The establishment of correspondent accounts in commercial banks has facilitated an increasing amount of trade and is a first step in establishing convertibility in foreign exchange transactions.

Trade among the FSU republics is carried out under three different modalities: monetary settlements in rubles (cash or credit), barter, and clearing. Under barter, commodities are exchanged for commodities with reference to nominal prices set in some unit of account, usually related to domestic prices, and trade proceeds until negotiated global amounts are reached; such trade may include a balance to be settled in some agreed currency. The prices under which clearing agreements are conducted are more closely related to international prices, as in the recent trade agreement between Uzbekistan and Russia. Figure 9.8 shows foreign exports by means of payment in 1992.

Figure 9.9 shows foreign imports by means of payment in 1992.

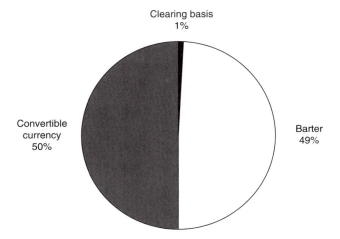

**Figure 9.8**
Exports by means of payment, 1992

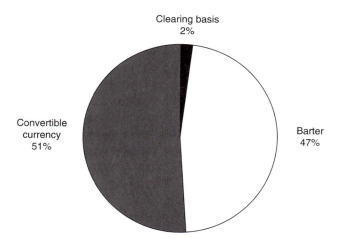

**Figure 9.9**
Imports by means of payment, 1992
*Source: Country Economic Memorandum, 1993.*

Trade with Russia is still governed by a bilateral agreement that provides for a technical balance to settle the net trade transactions. However, there remain significant payments problems because the technical balances can be used to settle only the global trade balance and not individual transactions. Russia demands anticipated cash payment for its exports of many products to Uzbekistan, yet Uzbek exporters cannot obtain similar treatment from Russian importers. Uzbekistan's agricultural exports to Russia normally experience significant loss or deterioration during transport. Under the FSU regime, a settlement court in Russia measured those losses and Uzbekistan abided by its rulings. Since independence, a way has not been found to agree on the evaluation of transport losses, and consequently Russian importers pay only after the merchandise is delivered and fully inspected. Delays in payments are equivalent to payment at a lower real price due to high inflation. Some products are returned due to nonpayment or other payments difficulties.

In the absence of a multilateral clearing system, the members of the ruble area are being forced to settle their transactions with hard currency, finance them by running arrears, or resort to centralized barter trade arrangements that are hard to implement in the present state of confusion about monetary arrangements, relative credit reliability, and relevant relative prices.

## 9.4   The State Order System and Its Implicit Taxes on Trade

### 9.4.1   Implicit Export Taxes

Although abandoned for some goods, the state order system was still in effect in 1995 for cotton, grain, and some industrial goods (gold, copper, and cable wire). Some bilateral trade agreements also involved state orders. Such trade was taxed implicitly when the domestic price of goods imported and exported by Uzbek state trading companies differed from the world price. In fact, it was possible to compute the implicit tax as the additional "wedge" between the domestic and world prices, taking into account transportation and other tariff factors. First, consider an export good for which a Tashkent producer receives $P_p$ from state orders (the subscript $p$ represents "producers," so $P_p$ is the producer price) and for which the FOB Tashkent export price established by a state trading company is $P_w$. The implicit export tax, $t_x$, is readily calculated as

$$t_x = \frac{P_w}{P_p} - 1; \tag{1}$$

that is, the percent by which the FOB price exceeds the producer price. When data are available on the domestic price abroad, $P_f$, the price will include transport costs, $t_c$, and tariffs imposed by the foreign country, $t_f$, so that the implicit export tax is given by

$$t_x = \left[ \frac{P_f}{P_p(1 + t_c)(1 + t_f)} \right] - 1. \tag{2}$$

Equation (2) requires the use of CIF factors and tariff schedules to compute the implicit export tax.

### 9.4.2 Implicit Import Taxes

The equivalent computation can be made for the implicit tax on a good that is imported by a state trading company and sold domestically via state orders. For imports, let $P_w$ indicate the CIF price of the good landed in Tashkent, $P_c$ the CIF/consumer price, and $t_m$ the implicit import tariff. In this case, the implicit wedge is given by

$$t_m = \frac{P_c}{P_w} - 1. \tag{3}$$

When data are available on the foreign FOB price in the exporting country, $P_f$, but not the CIF price at Tashkent, the implicit tax can be estimated by using a CIF factor, $t_c$, for cost of transport, which estimates the transport cost factor. The implicit wedge is then given by

$$t_m = \frac{P_c}{P_f(1 + t_c)} - 1. \tag{4}$$

Since the state order system behaves as an implicit export tax on exported goods, export licensing is clearly necessary to enforce the tax. Otherwise, a competitive, unlicensed exporter would be able to pay a slightly higher price in Tashkent for the good and export it at a slightly lower price, thereby making a profit nearly equal to the rate of the implicit export tax. Restricting entry into exporting by requiring an export license issued by the Ministry of Foreign Economic Relations thus enforces the implicit export tax due to the state order system. The system "hangs together" to keep more raw materials and intermediate inputs within the country at a lower Uzbek price than if there were free trade in these exports. Furthermore, the "export tax revenues" (or profits to the state trading company) generated by the state order system are as real as those that would be collected by an explicit export tax. Indeed, the profits to the state trading company from the export of cotton and other inputs are treated as excise tax revenue in the fiscal accounts of Uzbekistan, and historically are, after the value-added tax, the second highest source of tax revenue. As indicated in Table 9.2 cotton "excise" revenue was 6.6 percent of GDP in 1992, 5.5 percent in 1993, and 2.1 percent in 1994 (through the third quarter).

### 9.4.3 Consumer Subsidies on Imported Goods

Consumer subsidies still existed in 1995, principally on imported grain. Consider the purchase abroad by a state trading company of a consumption good and its sale in Uzbekistan at a lower price. The state trading company incurs losses. Furthermore, since there is an excess demand for the imported good at the subsidized price, the state orders system must ration the quantity imported for sale on the domestic market (through coupons for tea, for example). Furthermore, the lower domestic price discourages Uzbek production of the good. Figure 9.10 illustrates the benefits and costs to Uzbekistan of eliminating consumer subsidies on an imported good. The main loss is to consumers of the imported good, of course, but this loss is more than compensated for by increased profits to domestic producers of the imported good and by Treasury savings. The net triangular benefits result from cost savings due to the lower costs of producing increased amounts domestically and the Treasury savings on the reduction in consumption due to the higher price to consumers. These are small triangular benefits that may involve large transfers from consumers, usually those in the city, who may indicate their displeasure by street demonstrations and the like (see Rodrik, 1994; Connolly and de Melo, 1994). Thus, there may be political costs incurred by the reforming government.

Now consider the case of implicit export taxes that are imposed on exported goods through a combination of the export licensing system and the state order system. The state order system purchases an export commodity from a domestic producer at the procurement price $P_d$ and sells it abroad at the world price $P_w$. Under the assumption that the good is also sold domestically at the procurement price, the net benefits from moving to the world price in both consumption and production are indicated by triangular gains (see Figure 9.11). The main losers are domestic consumers (usually firms, such a flour mills and cotton ginning operations) and the state trading company, which gives up some of its profits on the operation (a significant share of Uzbekistan's tax revenues). Domestic

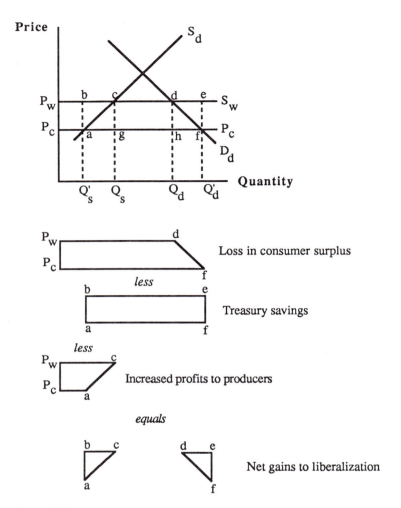

**Figure 9.10**
Benefits to a small country from eliminating consumer subsidies on an imported good

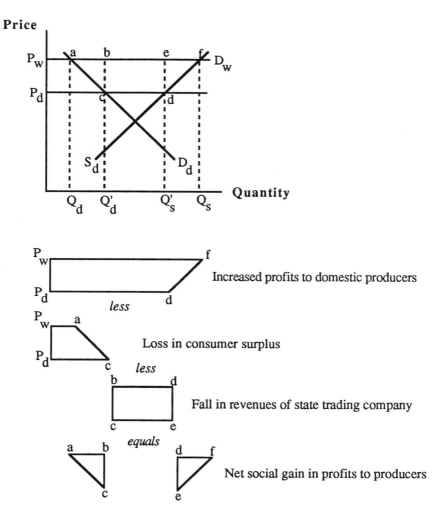

**Figure 9.11**
Benefits to a small country from eliminating implicit export taxes on an exported good

producers are the principal winners, and their supply increases accordingly. The main obstacle to such a reform is likely to come from the export licensing authority and the state trading company, both of which are located in the Ministry of Foreign Economic Relations. As indicated above, two commodities, cotton and natural gas, accounted for nearly 60 percent of exports in 1994 and still required export licensing.

In 1994, Uzbekistan eliminated most price controls on foodstuffs and consumer goods. Only flour, sugar, vegetable oil, and one type of bread remained rationed. In addition, the retail price of meat was 2.7 percent below its wholesale cost (see Table 9.4). Energy prices and communal services still had negative retail margins, suggesting continued subsidization of utilities.

The data in Table 9.4 suggest that considerable decontrol of consumer prices had taken place, with the exception of energy and utility prices, which remained lower than full recovery costs.

**Table 9.4**
Retail prices and wholesale cost of consumer goods and public services (*sums* per unit as of October 1994)

|                          | Unit      | Retail price | Wholesale costs | Retail margin |
| ------------------------ | --------- | ------------ | --------------- | ------------- |
| Consumer goods           |           |              |                 |               |
| Bread                    | kg        | 6.00         | 7.68            | −1.68         |
| Flour                    | kg        | 7.00         | 7.80            | −0.80         |
| Macaroni                 | kg        | 10.00        | 5.60            | 4.40          |
| Rice                     | kg        | 5.80         | 3.58            | 2.22          |
| Vegetable oil            | kg        | 10.00        | 1.34            | 8.66          |
| Tea                      | kg        | 51.00        | 42.21           | 8.79          |
| Sugar                    | kg        | 6.00         | 5.00            | 1.00          |
| Eggs                     | 10        | 13.00        | 8.00            | 5.00          |
| Meat (average price)     | kg        | 15.00        | 17.68           | −2.68         |
| Milk                     | liter     | 2.20         | 1.76            | 0.44          |
| Household soap           | piece     | 2.00         | 1.38            | 0.62          |
| Utilities                |           |              |                 |               |
| City transport           | trip      | 0.40         | 0.70            | −0.30         |
| Nonurban bus transport   | km        | 0.15         | 0.13            | 0.02          |
| Central heating          | $m^2$     | 0.40         | 4.20            | −3.80         |
| Hot water                | residence | 1.76         | 17.63           | −15.87        |
| Water service            | $m^3$     | 0.06         | 0.16            | −0.10         |
| Sewage service           | $m^3$     | 0.04         | 0.12            | −0.08         |
| Telephone service        | line      | 3.00         | 4.22            | −1.22         |
| Postage                  | piece     | 0.08         | 0.11            | −0.03         |
| Telegram                 | word      | 0.15         | 0.15            | 0.00          |
| Rent                     | $m^2$     | 0.35         | 0.88            | −0.53         |

*Sources:* Price Committee of the Ministry of Finance; IMF estimates.

## 9.5   Resource Effects and Transfers Caused by Grain Subsidies

An explicit example of a tradable sector that is distorted due to the state order system and consumer subsidies is grain. Grain is produced domestically, and is imported from both Kazakhstan and the rest of the world. As indicated in Figure 9.12, domestic grain producers are paid $80 a ton, about 43 percent less than the price from the rest of the world. Domestic supply is not large at this price, which discourages domestic production (although inputs such as water for irrigation and energy are subsidized); however, the state order system made nearly $24 million in profit due to the low procurement price of $80 a ton and the resale of grain to domestic flour mills at $124 a ton (a profit of $44 a ton!). In 1993, the state trading companies of Uzbekistan obtained an exceptionally good contract for the delivery of 2 million tons of Kazakh grain at $100 a ton, 29 percent less than the price from the rest of the world. This enabled the state trading companies to make $24 per ton profit on the sale of Kazakh grain to the domestic flour mills at a price of $124 a ton, yielding a total profit on grain imported from Kazakhstan of nearly $49 million. On the other hand, the purchase of 1.4 million tons of grain from the rest of the world at a price of $141 and its sale domestically for $17 less entailed a loss of $24 million dollars, just offsetting the gain from direct procurement from domestic suppliers. The net profits to the state trading companies in the Ministry of Foreign External Relations were thus $48 million. Figure 9.12 summarizes the pattern of grain procurement in Uzbekistan in 1993.

## 9.6   Resource Effects and Transfers Caused by Implicit Taxation of the Cotton Subsector

The cotton subsector in Uzbekistan is another dramatic illustration of the explicit and implicit taxes imposed by the state order and export licensing system. In 1992 cotton represented 78 percent of total foreign exports and the bulk of foreign currency revenues. In earlier days, the government subsidized the draining of the Aral Sea in order to provide water for irrigation of cotton fields. In addition to reducing the level of the sea, the salinity of this brackish water may have harmed the soil on which cotton was grown. This section does not deal in detail with these two issues, except for the overuse of water due to its provision free of charge; rather, it estimates the trade-distorting effects of implicit taxes on cotton exports for 1992. Also developed below are estimates of the tax on cotton farmers, as well as the subsidy to domestic consumers. These, too, are sizable.

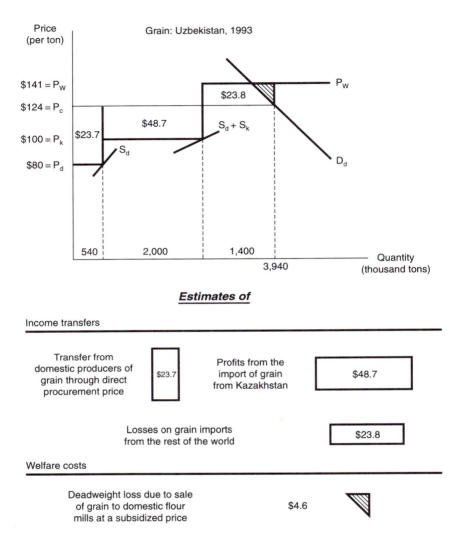

**Figure 9.12**
Income transfers and welfare costs in Uzbekistan's grain sector resulting from direct procurement under the state order system and grain consumption subsidies, 1993
*Source:* Author's calculations.
*Note:* Quantity is measured in tons of grain; prices are in U.S. dollars per ton; and estimated gains and losses are in millions of U.S. dollars.

Farmers transferred $1,034 million to the government, part of which was used to provide a consumer subsidy of $117 million. The methodology and data used to develop these estimates are described below.

The transfer out of the cotton subsector is a gross estimate, since it does not account for the transfer back to farmers through the heavy subsidization of their inputs. Using information developed in Uzbekistan: *Country Economic Memorandum* (1993) to obtain an estimate of the per ton subsidy to farmers, including free water for irrigation and subsidized inputs such as energy and fertilizers, I estimate that cotton farmers received a subsidy of $667.1 million, so that the net transfer was $367 million. This latter figure is a closer estimate of the actual implicit tax on farmers.

As in the system prior to independence, the Uzbek government establishes annual production targets (quotas) for cotton farmers. Of the quota amount, 85 percent (67 percent in 1995) must be sold to a state purchasing agency at a controlled price set below the world price. In 1992, the controlled price was approximately 12 percent of the world price FOB Tashkent. The farmer is free to dispose of the rest of the quota, known as the free quota amount, and any production exceeding the quota. A 5 percent tax is imposed on exports of the free quota and excess over quota to the rest of the world. The Uzbekistan market for cotton fiber is depicted in Figure 9.13.

$D_w$ and $D_d$ are the world and domestic demands for cotton fiber. For simplicity, it is assumed that Uzbekistan is unable to affect the world price of cotton fiber and, to reflect this, the world demand curve is drawn perfectly elastic at $P_w$. The domestic demand is also assumed to be unitary elastic. Over 55 percent of textile mill products are exported, and these external consumers are likely to have ready access to alternative supplies. However, $D_d$ is not perfectly elastic because domestic users' demand for textile products is not highly price insensitive.

Domestic farmers face two prices that form a rising step function. The first price, $P_c$, is the controlled price at which they are required to sell 85 percent of their quota output, $Q_q$. This is represented by a horizontal line at price $P_c$ up to quantity $.85Q_q$. The second, higher price, $P_f$, is the price for the free quota amount. $Q_q - .85Q_q$, and for the excess over quota, $Q_T - Q_q$. The prices faced by consumers thus form a rising step function in Figure 9.13.

The total quantity of cotton fiber supplied, $Q_T$, is determined by the intersection of the domestic supply curve with price $P_f$. This equilibrium arises because domestic farmers increase sales until the marginal cost of

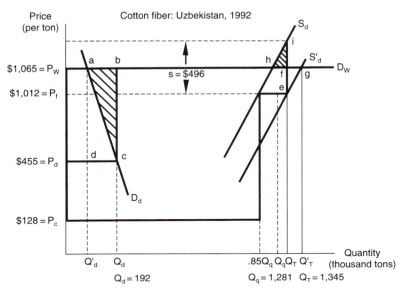

Cotton fiber: Uzbekistan, 1992

$1,065 = P_w$
$1,012 = P_f$
$455 = P_d$
$128 = P_c$

$s = \$496$

$Q'_d$   $Q_d$     $.85Q_q$ $Q_q Q_T$ $Q'_T$   Quantity (thousand tons)

$Q_d = 192$        $Q_q = 1,281$   $Q_T = 1,345$

**Estimates of**

Income transfers

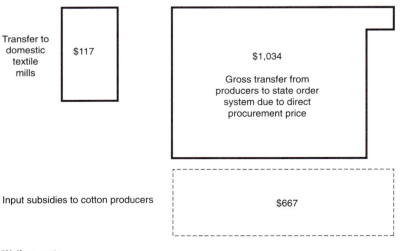

Transfer to domestic textile mills

$117

$1,034

Gross transfer from producers to state order system due to direct procurement price

Input subsidies to cotton producers

$667

Welfare costs

Deadweight loss due to sale of cotton fiber to domestic textile mills at a subsidized price

$31

Deadweight loss due to input subsidies to cotton producers

$14

doing so is equal to the highest price. The quantity of cotton fiber consumed domestically is determined by the intersection of the domestic demand curve with the controlled domestic price for textiles, $P_d$. Finally, total exports equal $Q_T - Q_d$. Figure 9.13 makes it relatively easy to describe the consumption and production effects of Uzbekistan's policies on the cotton sector.

First, by reducing the price received by farmers at the margin from $P_w$ to $P_f$, sales of cotton fiber fall from $Q_T'$ to $Q_T$. $Q_T'$ is the quantity that farmers would supply if they were to receive $P_w$. Second, by charging domestic textile mills a price below the world price, the quantity consumed locally rises from $Q_d'$ to $Q_d$. The sum of these two effects (the increase in local consumption and reduction in supply) is the reduction in Uzbekistan's exports. The attendant decline in export earnings is the sum of $P_w(Q_d'Q_d)$ and $P_w(Q_TQ_T')$. (Note that the efficiency or deadweight losses to the country are contained in this sum; they consist of the triangles above the demand curve, $abc$, and the supply curve, $efg$.) There are two transfers. The first is a consumption subsidy to domestic textile mills, which is $P_wbcP_d$, and the second is the resource transfer from farmers to the government. The latter is the area bounded above by $P_w$ and below by the step function and distance $ef$.

The analysis up to this point has not taken into account the transfer back to farmers through the heavy subsidization of their inputs. Accounting for these subsidies is important not only because we obtain a closer estimate of the actual implicit tax on farmers (the net transfer) but also because these subsidies create an incentive to waste resources, especially water for irrigation, by obscuring the true resource cost of cotton production to farmers. The total cost of the resources used in producing additional units of cotton is reflected in the curve $S_d$. If farmers operated along this curve, production would be at point $h$, where it intersects the world price. However, assuming farmers receive a per unit subsidy of $s$, then $S_d$ shifts down by the amount of the subsidy to $S$, which is now the supply curve on which farmers operate and reflects the (private) costs to farmers of producing an additional unit of output. Since farmers expand production until $S$ intersects $P_f$, resources are wasted because too much

**Figure 9.13**
Income transfers and welfare costs in Uzbekistan's cotton sector resulting from production quotas, direct procurement, and export licensing under the state order system, 1992
*Source:* Adapted from Connolly and Vatnick (1994).
*Note:* Quantity is measured in tons; prices are in U.S. dollars per ton; and estimated gains and losses are in millions of U.S. dollars.

**Table 9.5**
Summary of distortions in the grain and cotton sectors of Uzbekistan

| | | | |
|---|---|---|---|
| GNP per capita (current dollars, 1992) | $2,600 | | |
| Population 1992 (million) | 21 | | |
| GNP | $54,600 (million) | | |
| | | U.S.$ (million) | % of GNP |
| Grain sector: 1993 | | | |
| Transfer from domestic producers of grain | | 23.7 | 0.04 |
| Profits from import of grain from Kazakhstan | | 48.7 | 0.09 |
| Loss on grain imports from rest of world | | 23.8 | 0.04 |
| Deadweight loss due to sale of grain to domestic flour mills | | 4.6 | 0.01 |
| Cotton sector: 1992 | | | |
| Transfer to domestic textile mills | | 117 | 0.21 |
| Gross transfer from producers of cotton to state order system | | 1,034 | 1.89 |
| Input subsidies to cotton producers | | 667 | 1.22 |
| Deadweight loss due to sale of cotton to domestic textile mills | | 31 | 0.06 |
| | | 14 | 0.03 |

*Sources:* GNP and population, *World Development Report* (1994), tables 30 and 25; grain and cotton sectors, author's calculations.

cotton is produced. The waste of resources is reflected in the triangle above $P_w$ (and below $S_d$). At the margin, the cost of the resources embodied in the additional unit of cotton produced exceeds the value at which that additional unit is sold on the world market. Table 9.5 summarizes the distortions in the grain and cotton sectors of Uzbekistan.

## 9.7  Pitfalls in the Use of Partial Equilibrium Harberger Triangles

The analysis summarized in Table 9.5 suggests that the welfare costs of import subsidies on grain and export taxes on cotton can simply be added up to arrive at the total distortion due to these two sectors. This may not be the case, as pointed out by Dani Rodrik (1994). To see his point, consider the following three situations: (1) an export tax, no import duty; (2) an import subsidy, no export tax; and (3) an equal export tax and import duty. With (1), the export tax $t_x$ lowers the domestic relative price of the exportable good, so that the domestic relative price ratio is indicated by

$$\frac{P_x}{P_m} = \frac{(1 - t_x)P_x^*}{P_m^*},\tag{5}$$

which would give rise to a deadweight loss. Now consider (2), an import subsidy of $s_m$ without any export tax, yielding equation (6) for the domestic relative price of exportables in terms of importables:

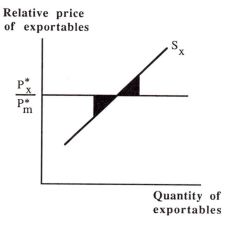

**Relative price of exportables**

**Quantity of exportables**

**Figure 9.14**
Pitfalls in partial equilibrium welfare analysis

$$\frac{P_x}{P_m} = \frac{P_x^*}{(1 - s_m)P_m^*}.$$ (6)

Once again, applied welfare analysis would suggest a similar triangular deadweight loss due to the import subsidy.

What would happen, however, in situation (3), when an import subsidy is combined with an export tax of equal magnitude? Would we not have the sum of the two distortions? The answer is no, due to Abba Lerner's symmetry theorem. An equal export tax and import subsidy just offset one another when trade is balanced. The domestic relative price of exportables in terms of importables is exactly equal to the world relative price ratio because

$$\frac{P_x}{P_m} = \frac{(1 - t_x)P_x^*}{(1 - s_m)P_m^*} = \frac{P_x^*}{P_m^*}$$ (7)

when $t_x = s_m$. There is no distortion whatsoever because relative prices are unchanged. This is a nice example of the theory of the second-best. In the presence of a distortion, a second distortion may be needed to offset the first.

In Figure 9.14, this point is illustrated graphically.

A tax on the export good lowers its domestic relative price below the world relative price ratio indicated by the horizontal line. The export tax taken alone would result in a deadweight loss indicated by the lower left-hand triangle. On the other hand, an import subsidy would raise the relative price of the exportable good, thereby leading to a loss as indicated in the upper right-hand triangle. It is therefore tempting to add the two triangles to estimate the deadweight losses due to an export tax combined with an import subsidy of the same amount. However, from Lerner's symmetry theorem we know that the export tax and the import subsidy just cancel, leaving no net distortion in the allocation of resources. The implication of this result is that it is important to bear in mind the *relative* price effects of the various taxes and subsidies, whether implicit or explicit. In the above analysis on grain and cotton, the presumption is that the relative price distortions are large compared with those elsewhere in the economy.

## 9.8 Conclusion

The trade policy adopted by Uzbekistan should focus on providing a supportive incentive framework that (1) earns foreign exchange by removing restrictions on exports on a multilateral basis (rather than penalizing them by surrender requirements); (2) evens the playing field for all productive activities for domestic and foreign markets by moving toward market and international prices; and (3) raises and maintains government revenue during the transition process toward a social market economy. The trade framework should involve phasing out of export licenses and state orders, their replacement by low uniform taxes on exports combined with no duties on imports, and a convertible currency. These reforms shift the focus toward prices, particularly world prices, as the signal for production and consumption activity. Possible sources of revenue are monies from (1) privatization of trading companies, telecommunications, and transportation companies; (2) a land lease program in agriculture; (3) the imposition of uniform export taxes with few exceptions; and (4) the phasing in after two years of a reduced value-added tax on imports. An important element in the process is the design of a legal framework to ensure property rights and the enforcement of business contracts, domestically and internationally. This effort will require the investment of some resources in the clearing up of international and domestic interenterprise and governmental arrears, and the introduction of a fully convertible currency. These are key factors in the renaissance of international trade on a strictly commercial and multilateral basis rather than on a bilateral clearing and barter basis.

Continued trade liberalization should therefore involve some immediate, medium-term, and long-run reforms that are implemented over a few years. The reasons for a phased approach are twofold: first, to reduce the

adjustment costs associated with the movement of resources from contracting to expanding sectors, and second, to avoid the risk of short-run
reversal of the trade liberalization process. On the other hand, resources
must be encouraged to move, and slowness of pace may permit opponents
of trade reform to mobilize opinion to undercut the program. The target
should be rapid elimination of high tax rates, whether explicit or implicit,
on internal and external trade, combined with a reduction or elimination
of the exemptions and exceptions to these taxes. The reduction of the tax
rates combined with the broadening of the base also encourages greater
voluntary compliance and after-tax incentives, so that the revenue stream
to the government should not fall during the transition process, especially
if combined with a large-scale privatization program.

## Note

The findings, interpretations, and conclusions expressed in this chapter are those of the
author and should not be attributed in any manner to the World Bank, to its affiliated organizations, or to the members of its board of executive directors or the countries they represent.

## References

Connolly, Michael, and Jaime de Melo. 1994. "The Political Economy of Protectionism in
Uruguay." In Michael Connolly and Jaime de Melo, eds. *The Effects of Protectionism on a Small
Country: The Case of Uruguay*. Washington D.C.: World Bank.

Connolly, Michael, and Silvina Vatnick. 1994. "Uzbekistan: Trade Reform in a Cotton Based
Economy." In Constantine Michalopoulos and David G. Tarr, eds. *Trade in the New Indepen-
dent States*. Studies of Economies in Transformation no. 13. Washington, D.C.: World Bank/
UNDP.

Lerner, Abba. 1936. "The Symmetry of Import and Export Taxes." *Economica*, 3. no.11: 306–
13.

Micklin, Philip P. 1991. *The Water Management Crisis in Soviet Central Asia*. Carl Beck Papers
in Russian and East European Studies, 905. Pittsburgh: University of Pittsburgh, Center for
Russian and East European Studies.

Michalopoulos, Constantine, and David G. Tarr. 1994. "Summary and Overview of Developments Since Independence," in Michalopoulos and Tarr, eds., *Trade in the New Independent
States*. Washington, D.C.: World Bank pp. 1–21.

Ostrom, Elinor. 1990. *Governing the Commons: The Evolution of Institutions for Collective
Action*. Cambridge: Cambridge University Press.

Rodrik, Dani. 1994a. *The Rush to Free Trade in the Developing World: Why So Late? Why Now?
Will It Last?*" NBER Working Paper 3947. Cambridge, Mass. National Bureau of Economic
Research.

Rodrik, Dani. 1994b. "Comments on Connolly and Vatnick, 'Uzbekistan: Trade Reform in a
Cotton Based Economy.' (Unpublished).

Tanzi, Vito, Mario I. Blejer, and Mario O. Teijeiro. 1987. "Inflation and the Measurement of Fiscal Deficits." *Staff Papers* International Monetary Fund, Vol. 34 No.4 (December: 711–738.

*Uzbekistan: Country Economic Memorandum.* 1993. Washington, D.C.: World Bank.

World Bank. 1993. *Uzbekistan: An Agenda for Economic Reform.* Report no. 11683-UZ. Washington D.C.: World Bank.

World Bank. 1993. *Uzbekistan: Country Economic Memorandum.* Washington, D.C: World Bank.

# IV

## East, Southeast, and South Asia

# 10       China

Richard S. Eckaus

## 10.1   Patterns of Growth, Trade, and Finance

The expansion of China's participation in international trade since the beginning of the reform movement in 1978, has been one of the most remarkable features of its remarkable transformation. Figure 10.1, presenting the levels and annual growth rates in real GNP from 1951 to 1993, shows a highly uneven, sawtooth pattern of growth before 1978, with the big declines associated with the Great Leap Forward (1960 and 1961) and the effects of the Cultural Revolution (1967 and 1968). As the Cultural Revolution faded and the economic reforms began, the growth rates rose and became less variable.[1] However, Figure 10.1 also shows the higher inflation rates associated with the postreform growth.

While GNP was growing at 9 percent from 1978 to 1994, exports grew at about 14 percent and imports at an average of 13 percent per year. Figure 10.2, which provides quarterly details on foreign trade and the trade balance, also shows clearly that although the growth in trade has been impressive, the course has not been a smooth one. In the late 1980s, China's trade balance passed through a difficult period, but the problems did not spin out of control. Again in 1993 there were large deficits, which were quickly and strongly corrected in 1994. Currently China is building up large foreign exchange reserves.

The successes contradict several customary generalizations about transition economies and large developing countries—for example, that the transition from central planning to market orientation cannot be made without passing through a difficult period of economic disorganization and, perhaps, decline; that very large economies have so much inertia that they cannot transform themselves and grow rapidly; and that the share of international trade in very large economies cannot grow quickly due to the difficulties of penetrating foreign markets on a large scale.

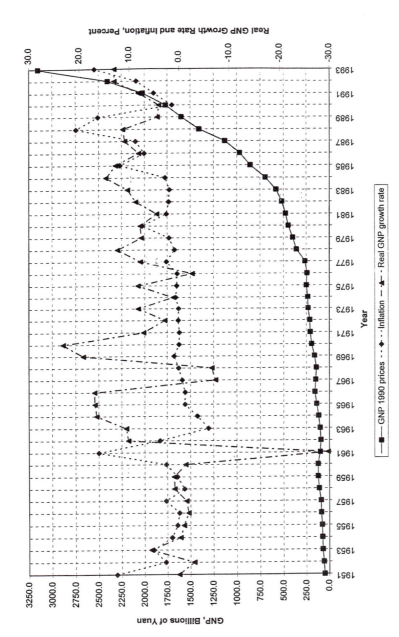

**Figure 10.1**
Levels of real GNP, growth rates of real GNP, and inflation rates
*Source:* International Monetary Fund.
*Note:* Figures for 1951–77 represent national income.

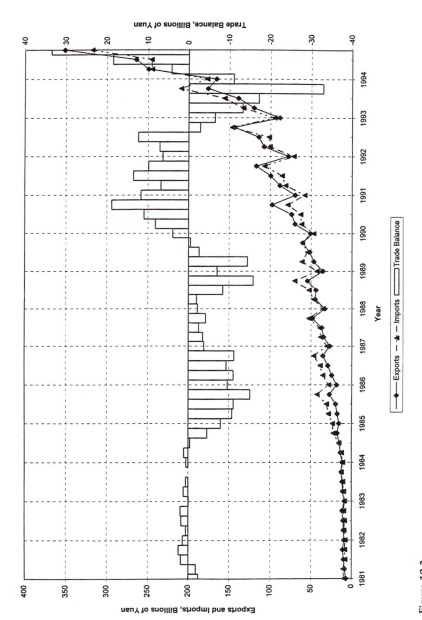

**Figure 10.2**
Quarterly exports, imports, and trade balance, 1981–94
*Source*: International Monetary Fund.

## 10.2   Prereform International Trade and Payments Policies

After the success of the Communist revolution and the founding of the People's Republic of China, the nation's international economic policies were dominated for at least thirty years by the goal of self-reliance. While this was never interpreted as complete autarky, the aspiration for self-reliance profoundly shaped trade policy, especially with the market economies. In particular, it was thought that international prices, being shaped by imperialist and monopolistic forces, should not be allowed to interfere with rational domestic economic planning.[2]

It is clear, from various sources and the manner in which trade was determined, that trade policy was import-driven, with export levels being determined by the import targets (see Eckstein, 1966; Lardy, 1992). Specific import and export targets for particular commodities and manufactured products were determined as part of the overall planning process by the State Planning Commission and the Ministry of Foreign Trade. The targets were then handed to the twelve Foreign Trade Corporations (FTCs) that were established soon after the formation of the People's Republic. These corporations, the sole participants allowed in international trade, acted to sell the exports and buy the imports in types and quantities specified by the plan. However, over time the FTCs came to have some leeway with respect to export composition.

Since domestic prices were distorted and government subsidies covered the deficits of the FTCs, there is no reason to believe that the composition of imports or exports was determined by domestic comparative advantage as revealed by prices. In effect, although for somewhat different reasons than those in other developing countries, China followed an intensive import substitution policy, which was intensified by the U.S. embargo imposed after the Korean War.

The FTCs were required to buy goods for export and to sell imported goods at domestic prices. Import and export values were, of course, determined at international prices. The yuan was, by general consensus, overvalued for much of the prereform period. When foreign prices were converted into domestic prices, the revenues from exports did not offset the costs of imports in yuan. The difference was covered by government subsidies to the FTCs at levels that implemented the import targets.

As a result, between 1948 and 1978 the foreign exchange rate played no role in equalizing demands and supplies of foreign exchange. The balancing mechanism in the foreign trading process was government subsidies. Since exports were import driven and the government subsidies covered any shortfalls, there was never an apparent balance of payments crisis in the prereform days. Yet there are no official data on reserves before 1977, so one cannot be sure.

## 10.3 Foreign Trade in Chinese Economic Reforms

China's foreign trade began to expand rapidly as the turmoil created by the Cultural Revolution dissipated and new leaders came to power. Though it was not done without controversy, the argument that opening of the economy to foreign trade was necessary to obtain new capital equipment and new technology was made official policy. Exports grew rapidly in the 1970s, even before the major domestic economic reforms had started, and exporting firms have been allowed to keep larger and larger shares of their foreign exchange earnings, which previously had to be sold to the Bank of China in their entirety. Special tax benefits and relief from other regulations also have been used to encourage foreign investment.

The foreign trade and investment reforms are conventionally explained as an ideological shift. However, they may also have been the result of short-term pressures. From 1977, the first year for which the IMF published data on China's foreign reserves, to 1978, those reserves fell by more than one-third and the ratio of reserves to imports fell by more than 50 percent. These changes presumably were echoes of the internal disruption created by the Cultural Revolution. The facts were, of course, known to the Chinese leadership and must have been a source of serious concern. For purposes of comparison, in 1978, India's ratio of foreign exchange reserves to imports was almost six times the Chinese ratio.

The creation of an "open door" policy did not mean the end of foreign trade planning. Although Chinese policy became committed to the expansion of its international trade, the decision-making processes and international trade mechanisms of the prereform period continued in full force for several years, to a modified degree for several more years, and still continue to be evident in the licensing controls. Until recently, at least, domestic prices were used for the purchase by the FTCs of the goods for export and for imported goods they sold. This practice has meant that international prices have not been fully translated into the domestic economy, and significant state subsidization in the foreign trade sector has continued for some imports and exports. At the same time, international transactions outside of the state planning system have been growing. Most obviously, enterprises created by foreign investors have been exempt from the foreign trade planning and control mechanisms, although subject to some restrictions on their transactions in foreign currency. In addition, substantial amounts of other types of trade, particularly the trade of the township and village enterprises and private firms, have been relatively free. The clearest evidence is the existence of the swap markets for foreign exchange, created to facilitate transactions between earners and users of foreign exchange.[3]

Starting in 1979, the branch offices of the old FTCs were allowed to operate independently, and provincial and ministerial foreign trading corporations proliferated. In addition, provinces and enterprises were allowed to retain part of their foreign exchange earnings. Nonetheless, it was still true in 1981 that the FTCs under the Ministry of Foreign Economic Relations and Trade (MOFERT) carried on 91 percent of the export trade and 87 percent of the import trade. These proportions declined as the foreign trade operations of the provincial and ministerial FTCs and individual enterprises expanded, and by 1984 exports and imports handled by the FTCs under MOFERT had declined to 79 percent and 65 percent of total trade, respectively (World Bank, 1988, Annex 1, p. 9).

Major changes in foreign trade control policies were made in 1984 and 1985. Provincial governments were, in general, allowed to hold back 25 percent of their foreign exchange earnings, with some provinces permitting a higher retention ratio to local firms. Enterprises that had earned and retained foreign exchange were allowed to use half of that amount. A classification scheme for imports was published, distinguishing "restricted" and "unrestricted" imports. All of the former were under the control of MOFERT, but goods in the unrestricted category could be imported by FTCs in other ministries and at the provincial level, as well as by MOFERT's FTCs, without licensing requirements.

In the planning process the various FTCs submitted to MOFERT estimates of the exports they would generate during the coming year. In a process of iterative review, these estimates were made consistent with import plans. The "command plan" exports were specific with respect to physical quantities of particular goods. There was centralized allocation of particular inputs to producers, who were required to meet quotas for delivery to the designated FTCs for export. These mandatory exports have been estimated to have accounted for 60 percent of total exports in 1986. With respect to exports under the guidance plan, targets were expressed in value terms and there was greater variety of practice. Yet in some provinces guidance plan exports were converted into command exports.

There also appear to have been differences in practice among the provinces in the extent to which contracts were made at official prices or at international prices. In some sectors the FTCs financed export firms and procured goods at negotiated "internal" prices. This indicates the variety of commercial practices that began to flourish during the reform period and that existed side by side with relationships between official institutions and enterprises that antedated the reform period.

On the import side, seven types of raw materials remained under centralized control; these were the "command imports." "Priority investment projects" included centrally financed projects and imports of major and complete plants that received central recognition. "Other priority imports" are described as being determined on an ad hoc basis. These three categories of imports are estimated to account for 70 percent of total imports. Planning for "other imports" consisted of general guidelines for licensing, with the convention of approval for imports for which financing is available.

A system of duties and licenses for both exports and imports was subsequently added to the foreign trade planning process. Export licensing, introduced in 1980, has been used to manage the prices of primary commodities sold primarily in Hong Kong and Macao, so as to exploit China's market power in these commodities in the two areas. Export taxes are also used for this purpose, as well as to limit the exports of goods for which there are domestic shortages. Import licensing is used to control expansion of production capacity for certain types of goods beyond what is deemed economically or socially desirable, smuggling, and imports of consumer luxuries. Import duties are applied to most goods both to raise revenue and as a means of domestic protection.

The 1988 reform reduced the importance of the foreign trade plan with respect to the composition of exports and imports. The coverage of both mandatory plan and priority plan exports was reduced, the former by about half, to 21 commodities, and the latter by about a quarter, from 120 to 91 commodities. However, foreign trade planning continued in a different framework and with different instruments. A system of three year foreign trade contracts was introduced in which targets were established by MOFERT, the Ministry of Finance, and the State Planning Commission for each provincial-level administrative unit and the national FTCs. These units then entered into agreements with MOFERT that specified in value terms their export targets, the share of their foreign exchange earnings to be channeled to the central government, and the central government's commitment to cover losses on export sales through subsidies.

Another major modification of the trading system occurred in 1991, when the contracts were converted to annual agreements and the terms of the contracts were to be developed in negotiations, based on proposals by provincial authorities and enterprises. Currently, while increasing amounts of trade are uncontrolled, a system of overlapping direct controls has evolved for some types of imports that continues the channeling and regulation through specific FTCs and licensing. Specific import controls are also used for protection of domestic industry. Of the 32 percent of total imports subject to channeling in 1992, two-thirds were mandatory imports and one-third in the "other import" category (World Bank, 1994a, p. 64). General import licensing is managed by the Ministry of Foreign Trade and Economic Cooperation (MOFTEC), the successor to MOFERT. This licensing applied to about a quarter of total imports in 1992 (World Bank, 1994a, p. 65).

China's tariffs have become a sophisticated system of protection with rates that are among the highest among developing countries but also are distinguished by their relatively high variance, indicating the specificity of their targets. Tariff exemptions and exceptions are so extensive that tariff collections were only 5.6 percent of the value of imports in 1991. In 1992, with roughly the same tariff rate, the trade-weighted mean tariff was 31.9 percent.(World Bank, 1994, p. 56).

### 10.3.1  The Breakdown of Foreign Trade Management in the Late 1980s

The large trade deficits of the late 1980s are evidence that the trade management system did not avoid very severe balance of payments difficulties in that period. The urgent actions in 1985 to reduce the deficit strongly suggest that intentional international reserve reduction cannot fully account for the very rapid increase in the trade deficits. What went wrong then? Either imports grew more rapidly than expected or exports grew more slowly.

Figure 10.2 shows that imports, measured in yuan, more than doubled from 1984 to 1985.[4] While part of this reflects yuan depreciation and inflation, it is clearly not a sustainable pattern. To some degree the growth in imports reflects the expansion of the domestic economy, yet it is also true that starting in 1985, there was a long-term change in import ratios. Although the growth in imports virtually stopped in 1985 and 1986, import levels did not decline. The import/GDP ratio moved to a distinctly higher level and has not returned to the pre-1985 ratios. In fact, after some reduction of the trade deficits in 1987, they expanded rapidly in 1988 and 1989, and were brought under control in 1991 and early 1992. In 1993 and 1994 imports again rose rapidly.

The category of machinery imports is most revealing with respect to the sources of the breakdown of the foreign trade management system. These imports grew most rapidly in 1984 and 1985 and maintained their relative position in 1986. Machinery imports are not spur-of-the-moment decisions. Either as new capacity or as replacement of old capacity, acquiring new machinery requires planning, which requires time. In addition, while some types of machinery can be purchased "off the shelf," much of it is built to order. Machinery is relatively heavy and shipment by air is expensive, so that, more than most other types of goods, it tends to be shipped by sea. All of this means that the rapid growth in machinery imports in 1985 should not have been a surprise.

It is also possible that the growth of exports was overestimated, since exports did grow more slowly from 1984 to 1985 than from 1983 to 1984. It seems implausible that the authorities would have accepted a projection of a roughly 60 percent growth in exports in one year, from 1984 to 1985, which would have matched the actual increase in imports. Although the mid-1980s was a period of economic expansion in China's major markets, China's exports were becoming less attractive because of domestic inflation. Alternatively, the use of resources for domestic production and consumption became more attractive than exports. There is evidence for both of these explanations. As indicated in Figure 10.1, overall growth of real national income accelerated in 1985 to over 13 percent, from 10 percent in 1984. Price inflation also accelerated to almost 12 percent, as measured by the consumer price index, from 2.7 percent in 1984.

It is most plausible that the extraordinary expansion of imports occurred as a result of the 1984 changes in the foreign trade management system that eliminated quantitative controls for about 35 percent of imports (World Bank, 1988, p. 102). That contributed to the rapid expansion of imports, especially machinery imports, in 1985 and the consequent large deficits. This appears to be the kind of mistake that the system should have been most able to avoid. In this sense, therefore, the system failed. Moreover, the trade management system was not able to bring the deficits under control until 1987, and then for only one year, before they expanded again in 1989 and 1990. In order to understand the changes that did occur and the control policies that came to be used, it is necessary to consider the recent macroeconomic and foreign exchange rate experience in China.

## 10.4  Macroeconomic and Exchange Rate Policy

The economic decision-making process within the Chinese government cannot be known by outsiders, but it is clear that the period starting in 1984 or 1985 was one of new departures in policy, whose lack of coordination, as suggested above, had adverse effects. The new policies implemented in late 1984 reduced the range and power of the direct controls over foreign trade as well as direct management of the economy in general. Existing foreign trade enterprises were made into independent entities, provincial authorities and enterprises were given new authority to engage in foreign trade, and the agency system was adopted, with users of imports responsible for their own accounts. For many types of goods and in some regions, the guidance provided by the central government seems only to have been indicative and not compulsory. For other types of goods and situations, specific targets were maintained. While the huge trade deficits of 1985 led to a partial reversal of these policy changes, their essence remained and they were subsequently extended.

The policy changes of 1984 necessitated new emphasis on and use of indirect macroeconomic instruments of both domestic and foreign trade policy. The fact that the trade balance deteriorated so quickly and to such an extent in 1985, and could not be substantially reversed quickly, suggests that effective macroeconomic policy instruments were not in place when the quantitative controls were reduced, if not eliminated. However, under the pressure of events, there was rapid recourse to such instruments.

Chinese authorities have been aware that tax and expenditure policies have macroeconomic effects, but there is something paradoxical in the fact that fiscal policy is not a readily available tool of macroeconomic policy in China. It might be thought that in a one-party state, this could be a relatively flexible policy instrument. Yet, although China is a one-party state, it is a many-province-power country, and the political power of the provinces has always been substantial. Prior to 1978 the government usually ran a small surplus overall. Taking into account the large government direct investments, there was, in fact, an important contribution to national savings. For most of the years since 1978, however, the government has run deficits, but these have remained in the range of slightly more than 2 percent of GNP. It is possible that 1985 is an exception, since that was the year with the smallest government deficit.[5]

In the Chinese official statistics the swing from deficit in 1984 to surplus in 1985 was almost 1 percent, large enough to have a perceptible effect on total aggregate demand. The deficits in 1991 and 1992, and budgeted for 1994, were noticeably above the average levels. In particular, in 1993, there was a 20 percent difference between the budgeted and actual deficits, indicating in another way that the government's attempts to control expenditures were ineffective at the same time that its public stance was strongly anti-inflationary. Interestingly, over the period during which government savings have been falling, private savings have been rising rapidly, thus becoming the major source of support for the high rates of investment (see Modigliani and Cao, 1993).

The indirect macroeconomic effects of the government debt would be expected to occur through the monetization of the deficit. Although this undoubtedly happened, the direct connection has not been a consistent one, in part because of the increasing resort of the government to bank loans and public placement of its bonds. Figure 10.3 shows the annual government deficits and changes in the money supply, money velocity, and inflation rates, using the definitions of the Chinese government and of the IMF. The closeness of the relationship between government deficits and changes in the money supply is visible until the mid-1980s, after which the direct correlation no longer exists.

But government current deficits are not the only source of increases in the money supply. As noted above, the People's Bank of China (PBC) has had difficulty in imposing credit controls and reserve requirements on the banking system, which has operated with substantial excess reserves. Thus, the banking system itself, in responding to the demand for loans, has had ample opportunity for money creation.

### 10.4.1 Monetary Policy

In such circumstances, it would have been natural for the central government to have relied more heavily on monetary policy, but this, too, has been a blunt instrument. The PBC has not always been a true central bank; only in March 1994 was a bill passed giving it a central bank structure. In particular, the power at the center has been sharply circumscribed by the principle of dual leadership, which links the provincial banks to the provincial governments. That, and the close links between the provincial Communist Party organizations and the provincial governments, have given those governments substantial power over operations of the PBC within the provinces. Only in 1988 was the headquarters of the PBC given the power to appoint the presidents of its provincial branches. It might be inferred that such appointments were subject to political interactions of the center and the provinces.

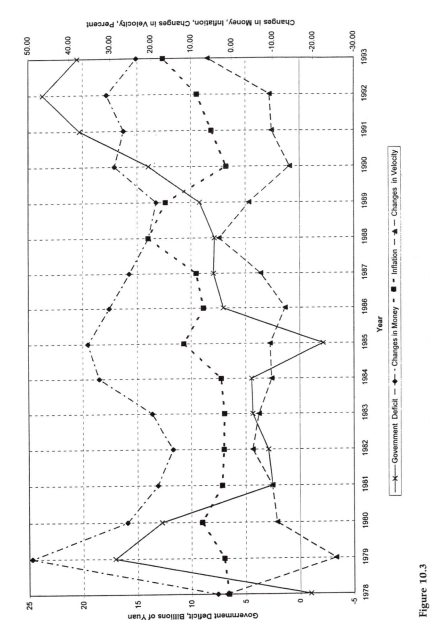

**Figure 10.3**
Changes in government deficits, money supply, velocity, and inflation, 1978–93
*Source:* International Monetary Fund.

It is interesting to note that after the appointment of Zhu Rongji as vice prime minister in 1993, with the announced responsibility of bringing inflation under control, one of the first actions was a reorganization of the PBC to give more control to the center. The fact that the process of implementation has been a long one suggests the difficulty that the center has had in actually exercising control in this arena.

Monetary policy was intended to be implemented through the annual credit plan, which first applied only to both general and specialized banks in China, but since 1988 has been extended to direct financing by enterprises and nonbanking financial institutions. This annual credit plan is part of an overall macroeconomic program that is subject to central monitoring. The major instrument for its implementation has been credit ceilings, set quarterly as well as annually and for specific types of credit (such as fixed investment and working capital) as well as the totals. Since the late 1980s, reserve requirements and administered interest rates have also become monetary policy tools, though both have limited effectiveness. That is true of reserve requirements because of high levels of excess reserves in the banking system. Interest rates have been modestly effective because of soft budget constraints of state enterprises and difficulties in supervising their administration.

It is common for Western economists to complain about the lack of sophisticated tools at the service of monetary policy in China. However, the tool of direct control of the volume of credit can be an effective instrument. Direct credit controls have been a powerful and flexible tool of monetary policy in many countries. In Latin America, they were the most common monetary instrument for many years until the 1980s. There are, no doubt, inefficiencies in their use, compared with monetary instruments that operate through the interest rate, but there is little doubt of their potential effectiveness.

It cannot be presumed, however, that the effects of additions to the money supply in China correspond to analogous changes in market economies. There are no national financial markets through which changes in the money supply would affect interest rates. Although there are local markets, which are increasingly interconnected, they are relatively recent developments, and are limited in scope and intensity. Moreover, while the ventures of private and cooperative enterprises might be affected by the interest charges on their bank loans, it is less obvious that this is true for state-owned enterprises. Their bank loans may be negotiated through the intermediation of the central government or provincial government ministries. This may be also true of some loans to private and cooperative enterprises.

The problem in the use of direct credit controls in China has been the difficulty of enforcing them. The provincial branches of the PBC have not, perhaps until recently, been willing or able to resist the pressures of local enterprises, backed by the provincial governments, for credit, even when that meant breaking through their credit ceilings. The substantial bank excess reserves facilitate their lending, and the difficulties of controlling credit advanced by the rapidly growing nonbank financial institutions have compounded the problem of credit controls.[6]

### 10.4.2  Exchange Rate Policy

Exchange rate policy in China also has been complicated by special administrative and political conditions. Before the reforms, all foreign exchange earnings were collected by the central government and reallocated through the PBC. Although there was nominally one exchange rate until 1981, the multitude of special provisions for balancing trade, in effect, created many different rates. Nonetheless, the foreign exchange rate is unique among macroeconomic and foreign economic policy tools in China in that it appears to be entirely under the administrative control of the central government. That should make it a more flexible tool, which, as will be shown, has sometimes been the case.

At the beginning of 1981 a single exchange rate, below the official rate, was created for the internal settlement of foreign trade transactions. That still left a multiple exchange rate system for external transactions until 1984, when a single rate was established. This did not last long in the face of rapidly growing deficits, and in 1986 a dual exchange rate was created, with an "official" rate pegged to the dollar. Starting in 1985, some enterprises, particularly those created with foreign funds, and some provincial governments were allowed to retain part of their foreign exchange earnings. This system was gradually extended, and Foreign Exchange Adjustment Centers (FEACs) were established in 1986 in which these retentions could, initially, be purchased by foreign-funded enterprises at prices set within the FEACs. This created an unofficial flexible exchange mechanism, although we do not know the extent to which the government intervened in this market. The exchange rate determined in the FEACs was always at a premium in relation to the official rate, with the premium sometimes quite large. After 1986, there were a number of minor adjustments in the official exchange rate, with a major devaluation in December 1989, when the value was reduced by 21 percent, and again in November 1990, when there was a 9 percent devaluation.

Access to the FEACs was extended in 1988 to all firms with foreign exchange earnings or retention quotas, and was increased still further in 1990 and 1991, with individuals being allowed to buy and sell in computerized trading.

On January 1, 1994, a single exchange rate was established at the rate then prevailing on the swap market, and the retention system was eliminated except for foreign enterprises. Foreign-funded enterprises operate under special rules that permit them to retain all of their foreign exchange earnings but require them to obtain approval from the State Administration for Exchange Control (SAEC) for purchases and sales of foreign exchange. The role of the SAEC in approving transactions by domestic enterprises has been eliminated. It is still true, however, that receipts of foreign exchange from sales abroad by domestic enterprises must be sold to designated financial institutions. For trade not subject to quotas, licensing, or automatic registration, foreign exchange can be purchased by importers by presenting commercial invoices or bills. Purchases of foreign exchange for controlled imports requires the appropriate approvals.

Exchange rate determination is now a managed float. The PBC announces a rate at the beginning of each trading day and intervenes in the market to keep it within 0.3 percent of the announced figure. Since the unification of the exchange rates, the yuan/dollar rate has remained virtually stable at about 8.7 yuan per dollar. Figure 10.4 shows the time pattern of the real exchange rate since 1981.

The present system for the determination of the exchange rate is similar to that in a number of market economies. A significant difference remains because important amounts of foreign exchange continue to be allocated by licensing and permits. That is to be reduced in importance by an agreement with the United States Signed in October 1994, in which China will eliminate most of its quota and license controls over a five-year period.

## 10.5   Assessment of China's Trade Policy

China has become a much more open system over the last twenty years and much more is known about it by outsiders. Nonetheless, there are still features of its economy and its economic policy that remain somewhat opaque. While there have been great changes in China's foreign trade policy—from its original character as a planned, managed, channeled, and controlled system—since the economic reform programs began, it would not be accurate to describe the current system as completely free. A substantial amount of trade continues to be channeled through the FTCs and

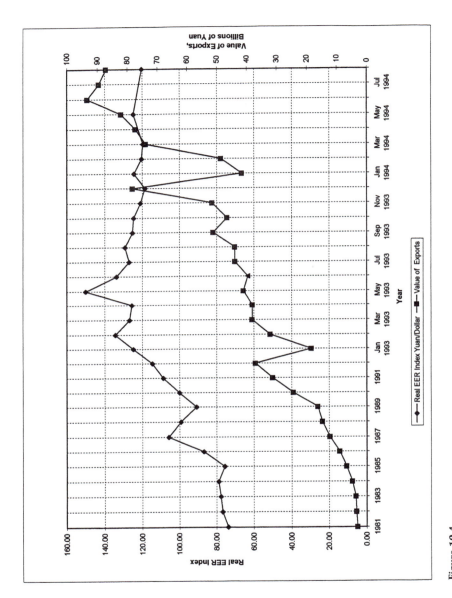

**Figure 10.4**
Real effective exchange rate for exports and value of exports, 1981–94

subject to supervision. A number of centrally imposed licensing and quota requirements for particular goods persist.[7] In addition, there are trade restrictions imposed by provincial officials that are acknowledged but not completely codified, and therefore difficult to assess.

It has been argued that China's international trade has reflected, although perhaps it has not been completely determined by, its comparative advantage in labor-intensive products. There is an apparent transparency in this argument. Much of the growth of exports has been facilitated by Hong Kong, whose enterprises one would expect to be quite sensitive to international prices. Moreover, a careful investigation of the labor intensity of China's exports supports the inference (World Bank, 1994b, Annex 7.2).

The argument poses a puzzle, however. As noted earlier, the distorted prices of the prereform period could not have guided exports along lines of comparative advantage. Since the reforms, the liberalization of prices has been gradual and their relationship to real costs must remain doubtful, especially in the state-owned enterprises. While it is true that wages have been freed from most controls in the Special Economic Zones and in some sectors, wages in state-owned enterprises are still not market-determined. The scope for market pricing has steadily expanded, but for most of the reform period, and even now, important inputs are still subject to price controls. Moreover, we know that, although to a decreasing extent, trade has been channeled through the FTCs and their trade losses have been covered by the government budget.

How is it possible, then, that China's real comparative advantage could have become manifest and determined trade patterns, when most prices have been distorted for most of the reform period and trade has been subject to somewhat arbitrary practices? It is hard to explain this except by denying it. But if it is denied, how can one explain the composition of Chinese exports?

The answer is relatively simple. What else could China have exported in quantity except petroleum, foods (particularly to Hong Kong), textiles, and simple manufactures? The petroleum exports of the early reform period, based on the crude oil reserves, were among the most immediately marketable of China's products. China has only recently developed the expertise and capacity to sell some capital goods in foreign markets. That is also true of sophisticated consumer goods, such as electrical durables. In addition, because of its high rate of investment, China has chosen not to export any of the capital goods that might find a foreign market but has kept them at home.

**Table 10.1**
Township and village enterprise exports

| Year | Exports ($ billion) | Share of total (percent) |
|------|---------------------|--------------------------|
| 1985 | 1.20                | 4.4                      |
| 1986 | 2.67                | 8.6                      |
| 1987 | 4.35                | 11.0                     |
| 1988 | 8.03                | 16.9                     |
| 1989 | 10.00               | 19.1                     |
| 1990 | 12.50               | 20.2                     |

*Source:* World Bank (1994), p. 14.

There is a sense, however, in which real relative factor scarcities have determined Chinese exports. China's manufacturing capacities reflect its relative scarcities. Because of the relative capital scarcity and relatively low levels of skill, much of China's productive capacity is relatively labor-intensive. This is particularly true of the township and village enterprises (TVEs) that have grown extremely rapidly since the beginning of the reform and are now estimated to account for roughly 40 percent of industrial production. Table 10.1 presents estimates of the share of the exports of the TVEs in total exports. As shown, the share increased five times between 1985 and 1990.

The role of comparative advantage in determining exports is, no doubt, increasing as the scope of market-determined prices increases. And, with the help of foreign investors, effective capacities in other types of goods are emerging and making their way into export markets.

## 10.6  Overall Balance, Macroeconomic Policy, and Foreign Exchange Policy

It does not appear that China has ever made a major internal macroeconomic adjustment motivated primarily by the need to correct a payments imbalance (see Tseng et al., 1994, p. 8). On the other hand, international payments issues may have been a contributing influence in some macroeconomic adjustments, for example, in 1988 and 1989. The primary motivation for changes in Chinese macroeconomic policy seems to have been domestic inflation. While domestic economic restraint or stimulation created through monetary policy has undoubtedly affected trade, it appears that greater reliance has been placed on the foreign exchange rate as an instrument of policy.

Estimated changes in the real exchange rate from 1981 to 1994 are presented in Figure 10.4, using the Chinese and U.S. consumer price indices
for the deflation. There was an effective real depreciation from 1981 to
mid-1993, but subsequently, as Chinese prices rose relatively rapidly,
there has been a significant real appreciation in the yuan. That has not yet
elicited an adjustment in the nominal rate, presumably because of the
excellent recent performance of Chinese exports.

The quarterly data in Figure 10.2 on Chinese exports pose another
puzzle. As the estimated real exchange rate has appreciated, exports have
grown. What can account for this apparent paradox? The puzzle is interesting, because the answer might throw some light on trade conditions
and exchange rate policy.

There are not many possible explanations of the puzzle:

1. There may be a delayed reaction of exports to relative prices.

2. There may be some offsets to import and export price subsidies that
have made it possible for Chinese enterprises to continue to export at
higher prices.

3. The statistics may be incorrect.

Unfortunately, it will not be possible to make a definitive distinction
among these alternatives, but some judgment can be applied. The first
answer is not implausible. The J-curve response to currency depreciations
has been observed in other countries at other times. It seems unlikely in
this case, however, because such a large proportion of Chinese exports—
textiles and toys, for example—faces strenuous competition, and the
demands for these goods must be very elastic and respond quickly to
price changes. A second rationale for the first answer is that domestic
costs have not risen so much that Chinese exporters cannot cover the
variable costs of their exports by selling abroad. Finally, the first answer
could be correct if the profit margins on Chinese exports have been very
large. That would have made it possible to maintain the foreign exchange
price by absorbing the increases in domestic costs. That pattern has also
been observed in the past in other countries.

Taking up the second possibility, it is possible that enterprises have
expanded exports, even at a loss, because of domestic offsets to the loss.
For example, state-owned enterprises and FICs might have been exporting at losses, with the expectation that those would be covered by government subsidies. It is somewhat less likely that state-owned enterprise
managers would have done this in 1994, compared with previous years,

since to an increasing extent their bonuses have been tied to their firms' profits. Nonetheless, it is possible to imagine a conjunction of circumstances that would have resulted in an increase in such practices. Since the allocation of foreign exchange is, to some extent, still restricted, there may be a scarcity value for foreign exchange that is above the official rate. That, in turn, could create a temptation that was not fully resisted. The same argument can be made with respect to the FTCs. Another type of export incentive might have arisen from a liquidity shortage created by monetary stringency. Export earnings, even at losses, could have been used to offset this monetary tightness.

Finally, there are at least two ways in which the Chinese statistics could be incorrect. First, there may just be mistakes as the result of incomplete coverage or errors in the measurement of of exports and imports, although it is not clear why mistakes should take the pattern shown in the data. A systematic type of error could have its source in underinvoicing by exporting firms in 1993. Then, when the profits were repatriated in 1994, they would be reported as exports. That is made more plausible by the recognition that the unification of exchange rates on January 1, 1994, was an effective devaluation, which had been preceded by speculation that some type of depreciation would take place. It would have been rational in such circumstances for exporters to have thought of taking advantage of a prospective depreciation by postponing repatriation of profits.

In any case, it is clear that Chinese authorities now consider the foreign exchange rate an important policy tool that is used discreetly but strategically.

## 10.7 Implications of China's Trade Policy for Participation in the World Trade Organization

This is not the place to attempt a review of the all of the issues related to China's potential role in the World Trade Organization (WTO), but some brief implications of the previous discussion can be made explicit. Briefly put, questions about China's entry into the WTO have arisen because its management of trade in the past has caused doubts about its adherence to the nondiscrimination principles of GATT.

As has been pointed out, some aspects of the trading arrangements in China are quite complex, with a number of different participants. The interactions of these different institutions provide opportunities for the granting and for the concealment of subsidies that can support discrim-

**Table 10.2**
Losses of foreign trade corporations financed by central government budget (billions of yuan)

| Year | 1986 | 1987 | 1988 | 1989 | 1990 | 1991 |
|---|---|---|---|---|---|---|
| Losses | 24.96 | 28.21 | 26.85 | 33.64 | 22.44 | 17.61 |
| Total losses of of SOEs within budget | 41.71 | 48.17 | 52.06 | 74.96 | 93.26 | 93.11 |
| Total exports | 108.58 | 147.18 | 176.95 | 195.25 | 293.06 | 375.04 |

*Source:* World Bank (1994a), p. 26.

inatory treatment. Table 10.2 presents data on the magnitude of the losses of the FTCs from 1986 to 1991. To put these losses into perspective, the values of China's total exports in corresponding years are added in a final line.

It can be seen that although the losses of the FTCs declined from 1986 to 1991, they remained, in the latter year, at about 5 percent of the total value of exports. Since the losses were most likely concentrated in certain types of trade, rather than being spread evenly across all trading categories, they were probably a larger fraction of trade of particular types. It should also be pointed out that the table does not include any losses of the FTCs of the provincial governments that might have been borne by those governments.

Table 10.2 proves nothing with respect to government support of exports, since some unknown portion of the losses may have arisen in the subsidization of imports. The table does suggest, however, the difficulties that arise for outsiders in judging the extent to which the central and provincial Chinese governments still play a direct role in trade.

## 10.8   Conclusions

It is striking that as a transition economy, China has managed its international trade and payments as an effective adjunct to its development policy and without persistent problems. Though there have been difficulties, they have not become major obstacles to economic growth. To achieve this, China has moved away from the completely planned and managed international trade and payments policy with which it entered its reform period in 1978 and which it maintained for several years afterward. Increasing freedom has been given to exporters and importers. A dual price system for foreign exchange was created to facilitate trade without imposing all the costs of a full devaluation. Subsequently the exchange rates were unified.

Yet it would be mistaken, as noted above, to consider Chinese foreign trade and payments as completely market-determined. There still is a substantial amount of planning and control, but without more information than is available to outsiders, it is impossible to evaluate its relative importance.

The obstacles to the transformation of China's international economic relations have been formidable. The attitude of irrelevance with which international trade must have been regarded by many enterprises had to be supplanted with trade incentives. The independent attitudes and ventures of provincial leaders had to be tamed. The multiple temptations of international markets had to be both resisted and exploited.

None of this has been done perfectly, to be sure. There are enough imperfections and holes in the policies to have sunk the ship, except for one thing. The expansion of the domestic economy and of exports has been strong enough to overcome any defects without major crises. For this, some credit must be given to the foreign trade and exchange rate policy makers and policy executers, who have managed to steer an unwieldy, if fast-moving, ship. To some extent also the successes of the economic reforms are also reactions to the economic and political failures of the Cultural Revolution. The political excesses and economic turmoil of that period prepared the ground for economic reforms. The injection of some degree of market economics then quickly produced substantial improvements by reducing the profound inefficiencies that had previously prevailed in foreign trade practices and production. The initial successes have been a strong validation of subsequent policies.

## Notes

The author is indebted to Padma Desai for her useful suggestions and to Anna Sokolinski and Christiana Stamoulis for their research assistance.

1. The levels and growth rates before 1978 were based on estimated "national income," which includes only material product. After 1978, the growth rates are based on GNP estimates.

2. World Bank (1988), pp. 95–98. This is of some interest, in view of the more recent argument that China's exports reflect its international comparative advantage.

3. It is understandable that government authorities are reluctant to be explicit about the scope of the planned trade, the relative importance of the FTCs, and the amounts of state subsidies they require. Such subsidies are likely to be inconsistent with the rules of GATT and the new World Trade Organization.

4. There is a puzzle in the data for exports in the mid-1980s. Exports grew by 40 percent in yuan terms, as reported in the Chinese *Statistical Yearbook* and according to IMF statistics. However, the growth rate of exports, measured in U.S. dollars, was about 5 percent. Using

IMF data, about fifteen percentage points are due to depreciation of the yuan, leaving to price inflation a rate that seems on the high side.

5. The percentages are taken from IMF calculations, which have consolidated budgets at all levels and revised them to the definitions of the IMF's *Government Financial Statistics*. The IMF's estimates of deficits are generally about twice the deficits reported in official Chinese statistics. The differences are mainly due to revision of the Chinese government practices of treating some borrowing as revenues, debt repayment as a current expenditure, and shifting revenues and subsidies of state enterprises among government accounts.

6. See Tseng et al. (1994) for discussion of the constraints on use of credit controls and assignment of the problems of monetary policy to the lack of market-based instruments of monetary policy. An unconventional rationale for the development of those instruments is that they would not be subject to the local political pressures that now constrain the use of direct controls.

7. The goods subject to export licensing have been estimated to account for 48 percent of total exports in 1993. See Tseng et al. (1994), p. 5.

# References

Bell, Michael W., Hoe E. Khor, and Kalpana Kochhar. 1993. *China at the Threshold of a Market Economy*. Washington, D.C.: International Monetary Fund.

Eckstein, Alexander. 1966. *Communist China's Economic Growth and Foreign Trade: Implications for U.S. Policy*. New York: McGraw-Hill.

Gorman, T. D. 1986. "China's Changing Foreign Trade System, 1975–1985." In R. Delfs, T. Gorman, and O. Nee, eds., *China*. London: Euromoney Publications.

Hsu, John C. 1992. *China's Foreign Trade Reforms*. Cambridge: Cambridge University Press.

Husain, Athar. 1992. *The Chinese Economic Reforms in Retrospect and Prospect*. CP no. 24. London: Development Economics Research Programme, London School of Economics. Lardy, Nicholas R. 1992. *Foreign Trade and Economic Reform in China, 1978–1990*. Cambridge: Cambridge University Press.

Lardy, Nicholas R. 1994. *China in the World Economy*. Washington, D.C.: Institute for International Economics.

Modigliani, F., and Cao, L. S. 1993. "The Chinese Saving Puzzle and the Life Cycle Hypothesis." Cambridge, Mass.: MIT. (unpublished).

Peebles, Gavin. 1991. *Money in the People's Republic of China*. Boston: Allen & Unwin.

State Statistical Bureau of the People's Republic of China. 1993. *China: Statistical Yearbook: 1993*. Beijing: the Bureau.

Tseng, Wanda, Hoe E. Khor, Kalpana Kochhar, Dubravko Mihaljek, and David Burton. 1994. *Economic Reform in China: A New Phase*. Washington, D.C.: International Monetary Fund.

World Bank. 1988. *China: External Trade and Capital*. Washington, D.C.: World Bank.

World Bank. 1994a. *China: Foreign Trade Reform*. Washington, D.C.: World Bank.

World Bank. 1994b. *China: Internal Market Development and Regulation*. Washington, D.C.: World Bank.

# 11 Vietnam

David Dollar and
Börje Ljunggren

Vietnam has made a remarkable turnaround during the past decade. In the mid-1980s the country suffered from hyperinflation and economic stagnation; it was not able to feed its population; and hundreds of thousands of people were signaling their dissatisfaction by fleeing in unsafe boats. A decade later, the government had restored macroeconomic stability; growth had accelerated to the 8–9 percent range; the country had become the second largest rice exporter in the world; and overseas Vietnamese were returning with their capital to take advantage of expanding investment opportunities. During this period there has also been a total transformation of Vietnam's foreign trade and investment, with the economy now far more open than ten years ago.

Foreign trade, which played a very limited role in the original socialist model, has, together with direct foreign investment (DFI), become a driving force in Vietnam's renovation, known as *doi moi*. In the preparation of the development plan for the period 1996–2000, even the most cautious scenario is based on the assumption that exports will grow by more than 20 percent per year. In the Vietnamese document prepared for the 1994 Consultative Group meeting in Paris, the role of DFI was scaled up further in comparison with earlier government documents. Of the foreign financing projected for the next five years, twice as much private investment as foreign aid is expected (Socialist Republic of Vietnam, 1994). Actually, present policy has a bias in favor of foreign investments compared with domestic private investments (UNDP and World Bank, 1993, p. 6).

Trade as well as foreign investment is now dominated by countries within the region, and Vietnam is rapidly being pulled into the East Asian growth process as a latecomer. In July 1995, Vietnam formally joined the Association of South East Asian Nations (ASEAN) and its trade arrangement (AFTA), and membership in the new World Trade Organization

(WTO) is regarded as a logical objective to be attained during the next few years (*Vietnam Investment Review*, 1995).

This paper examines the interaction between openness to foreign trade and investment and the transition to a market economy in Vietnam. The first section provides an overview of the origins and impact of the reform program. The second section examines in detail macroeconomic management of the transition, and the third part focuses on the structural policies in foreign trade and investment. The final section examines political issues that will have a large impact on whether the program of liberalization and growing openness continues.

## 11.1   The *Doi Moi* Program of Renovation: Origins and Overview

Vietnam has received much publicity for its *doi moi* reform program. The program was formally launched at the Sixth Congress of the Communist Party of Vietnam (CPV) in December 1986. The reforms did not really gain momentum, however, until a series of bold and well-coordinated measures was introduced in 1989. These bold reforms should be seen as the outgrowth of more than a decade of experimentation. In fact, the roots of Vietnam's renovation go back to the deepening socioeconomic crisis following the reunification of the country in 1976, which created a readiness to try certain unorthodox ideas long before the inauguration of *doi moi*.

At the time of reunification, most of Vietnam's economy lay in ruins. In the north the infrastructure had been devastated by years of bombing. The south had relatively good infrastructure as a result of the long American presence. However, much of the skilled labor force fled the country in the years immediately before and after reunification. From a strictly economic point of view, there were nevertheless a number of reasons to be optimistic about development prospects. The economy was starting from a low level but had a good base of human resources: primary education and literacy were nearly universal. Furthermore, the Communist leadership believed that it would get significant financial assistance from the West to rebuild the country's infrastructure. The optimism of the leadership showed in the five-year plan for 1976–80, which projected a 13–14 percent annual growth rate.

Actual economic performance in this early reunification period was very poor. Southern farmers resisted the introduction of the collective system long in place in the north (Woodside, 1989, p. 286). Agricultural output fell. In 1978 Vietnam sent troops into Cambodia. This precipitated a brief war with China and led to a sharp drop in aid from the West. In contrast with the projected 13–14 percent, actual growth during 1976–80 averaged less than 1 percent per year (de Vylder and Fforde, 1988, p. 61). Given the poverty of the initial situation and population growth of more than 2 percent per year, this slow economic growth generated a mounting crisis. New incentive structures were required. (On the Democratic Republic of Vietnam before 1975, see de Vylder and Fforde, 1988, 1996; Beresford, 1988.)

In order to reverse the situation, measures were introduced that may be considered a first phase of the reform process that would follow, even though they were not seen in that way at the time. Two Trojan horse ideas were endorsed by the Central Committee of the CPV when it met in August 1979 "in an atmosphere of mounting crisis" (Beresford, 1988, p. 160): (1) to try a "contract system" in agriculture that would establish a direct link between individual farmers and the state and (2) to allow "fence breaking" by state-owned enterprises, a spontaneous bottom-up adaptation of the Democratic Republic of Vietnam (North Vietnam; DRV) model through which state enterprises "swapped or sold goods on the market in order to raise cash and buy material or pay bonuses to workers" (de Vylder and Fforde, 1988, p. 68). At the time, these initiatives were seen as stopgap measures that would arrest a deteriorating situation and create breathing space for the party—that is, reactive adjustment measures that would rescue the longer-term "socialist project."

However, unorthodoxies were nothing new. The idea of a contract system in agriculture had been tried eleven years earlier in the province of Vinh Phu, but had met serious party disapproval (see Hy Van Luong, 1992). At the time, large-scale mechanized cooperative units rather than "peasantization" was the ideological agenda. Leaders like Le Duan, who in 1969 succeeded Ho Chi Minh as party leader, had a highly centralized, managerial, and statist notion of socialism, of which "large-scale socialist agriculture" formed a crucial part (Le Duan, 1977, p. 514).

While the reform process, hence, did not start from scratch with the launching of *doi moi* at the Sixth Party Congress in 1986, that congress undoubtedly signified a major expansion into a distinct second phase. New space was opened up for development toward a "multisector economy" that recognized the private sector, foreign trade, foreign investments, and peasant agriculture, while the investment structure of the DRV model, with its heavy emphasis on industrial development, was seriously questioned. Most important, central planning was increasingly questioned as a system of resource allocation.

Nevertheless, it was not possible in 1986 to win support for the drastic reform package that was implemented in 1989. Three more years of hyperinflation, reaching 400 percent in 1988, and significant changes in the way the outside world was perceived would be required before the party would be prepared to give up the system of administered prices, undertake an exchange rate reform that would create a unified exchange rate, begin interest rate reform, and declare that the policy of soft budget constraints for state enterprises would come to an end. Until then, various efforts were made to adjust administered prices to the prices prevailing on the parallel market in what amounted to halfhearted reform efforts. In 1989 price controls were largely phased out and a dual price system that had caused severe distortions laid to rest. While 1989 is the year when reforms became indisputably bold, it still seems more correct to talk about a third phase beginning in 1989. The response of the agricultural sector to the 1989 reform package illustrates the importance of applying a long-term perspective when analyzing the Vietnamese reform process.

A decisive reason why the 1989 reform worked was the way the Vietnamese peasantry reacted to the new incentive structure. Between 1988 and 1989 paddy production increased by more than 10 percent (Figure 11.1), and by exporting 1.4 million tons in 1989, Vietnam overnight became the third largest rice exporter in the world (World Bank, 1994, tables 7.1 and 3.2). The same response would have been inconceivable without an agrarian reform that by 1988 had developed into a long-term tenure system granting peasant families use rights. Through the adoption of Politburo decree no. 10, the CPV recognized the peasant family, rather than the cooperative, as the basic unit in the agrarian structure. Such a change is easy to conceive in the context of dramatic political change of the kind that occurred in Eastern Europe, but for a party in the tradition of the CPV, it was exceedingly difficult because it meant moving further away from an established socialist goal. Because of the political and ideological difficulties, the agricultural reform was carried out gradually over the ten years from 1979 to 1989. Each step yielded improvements that encouraged further reform. Since 1989 the return to family-based farming has been further confirmed, first in the 1992 Constitution and then in the land law adopted in 1993. In the latter, peasants are granted five rights that in practice amount to quasi-ownership. According to article 3.2, "Any household or individual shall be entitled to exchange, assign, rent, inherit, and put the right of land use in the pledge [as collateral]."

A similar, though less clear, development can be reconstructed regarding state-owned enterprise (SOE) reform. In the DRV model, the develop-

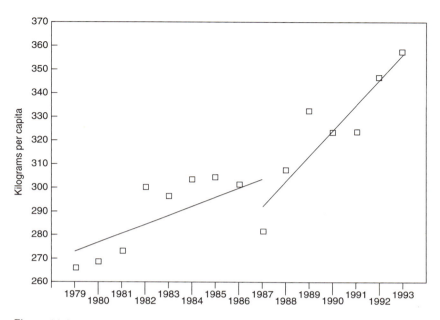

**Figure 11.1**
Per capita food/grain production, 1979–93
*Source:* de Vylder and Fforde (1988) and World Bank (1994).

ment of SOEs and central planning clearly constituted the backbone. The basis of the system was, as de Vylder and Fforde note, "the use of state monopoly power to concentrate resources upon the top priority—state industry" (de Vylder and Fforde, 1988, p. 27). During the First Five-Year Plan (1961–65) a major effort was made to accelerate industrialization. Although impressive rates of growth were reached, expenditure needs grew even faster, reflecting the inefficiency and waste of the system. The tax base could not meet the demands of the emerging "shortage economy." The growing resource constraint had two consequences: the process of industrialization was slowed, and the state failed to discipline SOEs that tried "spontaneous adaptations" in order to manage under the exceedingly difficult conditions caused by the Second Indochina War (1964–75).

It was this "bottom-up" reform tendency that was sanctioned in 1979 after reunited Vietnam (Socialist Republic of Vietnam; SRV) had experienced three years of unsuccessful efforts to achieve rapid growth on the basis of the DRV model. "Fence breaking" became a recognized part of the system.

Under the Three Plan system that emerged two years later, enterprises, in addition to using inputs supplied by the state to produce for the state (Plan A), were legally permitted to acquire resources through their own effort and dispose of the output as they wished to acquire additional inputs (Plan B), as well as diversify their productions by turning out minor products for state trading organs and the open market. (Ljunggren, 1993, p. 79)

As a consequence, SOEs developed dual operations. They operated within the plan but also, increasingly, on the market, and managed through various means to acquire additional raw materials, produce for the market, and pay bonuses to managers and workers. However, many SOEs remained very inefficient, surviving thanks to the soft budget constraint, the lifeline between the state budget and the state banks, on the one hand, and the SOEs on the other. By 1989, after years of experimentation, the CPV was prepared to declare that SOEs had to manage on their own, the objective being to make them operationally autonomous. Until then, physical targets rather than financial results had been what mattered, and firms had been kept afloat regardless of how they performed. Now they would have to perform. In one stroke, the enterprises faced a number of measures that hardened the budget constraint, but also new possibilities as prices were freed and trading was demonopolized. The reform had become comprehensive, creating qualitatively different conditions for the enterprises.

As a result of the 1989 reforms, a few thousand, mainly small, SOEs were forced to close, another two thousand disappeared through mergers with other SOEs, and the number of workers in SOEs was reduced. One cannot deny that Vietnam has been "learning by doing" (Beresford, 1993, p. 11). The experiences of "fence breaking" and the marketization of enterprises that occurred through that process are crucial factors in explaining why Vietnam has been able to avoid a major collapse of its SOE sector. A capacity to improvise and adjust was nurtured in that twilight climate. Also of crucial importance is the fact that the SOE sector never was anywhere near the size it reached in the Soviet Union and Eastern Europe. The SOE sector's share of GDP was about 25 percent in 1989, and its share of the labor force about 8 percent. Furthermore, there were few large firms: in 1989 there were fewer than 250 industrial firms with more than 700 employees (World Bank, 1992). The social costs of adjustment were kept at acceptable levels through the introduction of a number of programs focused on the substantial transitional unemployment that resulted from the elimination of subsidies. To this must be added the fact that an entrepreneurial tradition, which today represents a major asset, survived in the south.

Although Vietnam achieved some progress with enterprise reform, the results should not be exaggerated. Hardly any SOEs have been privatized, and Vietnam in 1995 still has around six thousand state firms (mostly owned by local governments). SOE reform remains one of the most controversial issues of the reform process, being of crucial importance in the debate about how the state should continue to hold the "commanding heights." The supporters of SOEs point to the fact that a number of large, reformed SOEs generate more than 60 percent of state revenue. State enterprise reform remains an Achilles' heel of the renovation process, an issue to which we return later.

Additional themes, such as price reform, could be analyzed in the same manner, and such an analysis would support the conclusion that the reformist "leap" made in 1989 has to be seen in the light of an increasingly open and pragmatic trial-and-error process with its origin in a production crisis that forced measures which could generate economic growth and renewed confidence in the ability of the CPV to be the leading force behind the "national project." By 1989 that process had reached a comprehensiveness that amounted to a system change, central planning and administratively determined prices having been discarded.

Where does the Vietnamese reform stand today? Its major accomplishments—and limitations—may be summarized in the following points (World Bank, 1993, 3–4; Le Dang Doanh, 1994):

*Agrarian reform.* Collective agriculture has been dismantled and replaced by a system in which the individual farming family is the basic unit. Security of tenure has been guaranteed in a land law (1993) defining the rights of the peasants. Peasants are also free to sell their produce on the market.

*Price reforms.* Prices have been liberalized through a sweeping reform that removed virtually all controls. Factor markets have undergone significant development.

*Exchange rate reform.* Since 1989, Vietnam has had one unified exchange rate that is largely determined by foreign exchange trading on the market.

*Interest rate reform.* In the past, bank lending was dominated by lending from the state banks to SOEs. No interest rate policy existed. Real interest rates were highly negative. In 1989 interest rates were raised to positive real levels.

*Fiscal reform.* Revenue as a percentage of GDP nearly doubled between 1991 and 1994 through tax reform and petroleum operations coming on line, and a number of measures have been taken to consolidate the stabilization program. (The number of persons employed in the public sector has been reduced by more than 1.5 million, including 500,000 soldiers.) There remains, however, a need for further tax reform and for a more stable and more substantial public resource base. The introduction of a broadly based value-added tax is envisaged for 1997 at the earliest.

*State enterprise reform.* State enterprise reform is at a critical juncture, with major legislation under way. Significant results have been obtained regarding elimination of subsidies, reduction of the workforce, and decentralization of management, but the reform process is hampered by lack of a determination to reduce the role of the state still further.

*Promotion of the private sector.* After decades of severe discrimination and unpredictable conditions, the private sector has been recognized as being of vital importance to the national economy, even though secondary to the state sector. Institutional conditions for its future growth, in the form of laws, access to bank credit, and so on, are being created.

*Direct foreign investment.* In 1987 Vietnam adopted its first foreign investment law. Since then a system of policies and laws has been developed with the purpose of making foreign private capital a major source of investment capital and technology. A volume of approximately U.S.$12 billion had been contracted by the end of 1994.

*Reform of foreign trade.* The 1989 exchange rate unification and devaluation were key reforms. The government has eliminated many trade barriers, including virtually all import quotas, and rice is the only product subject to export quotas. Decisions about foreign trade have been shifted from the state to the enterprise level, and an increasing number of enterprises are allowed to engage directly in export and import activities. Firms now have easier access to imports and better incentives to export. However, Vietnam's foreign trade remains excessively regulated by cumbersome licensing systems that allow considerable discretion in government decision-making, and maintaining and developing state trading corporations remains a government objective (UNDP and World Bank, 1993, p. 3).

*Legal reform.* In the past, Vietnam was ruled by decrees rather than laws. As a consequence of *doi moi*, the development of company law, bankruptcy law, and other laws required in a market economy has received the highest priority, and legal reform has been made a key element of the renovation. In 1992 the constitution was revised in order to reflect the new realities. The objective is to review the entire body of existing laws.

*Financial sector reform.* Since 1988, when the state banks formed a part of the State Bank of Vietnam (SBV), Vietnam has developed a two-tier banking system and opened up to private shareholding and cooperative banks, joint ventures with foreign banks, and operations of foreign banks in Vietnam. At the same time, a number of efforts have been made to develop banking practices through training programs and modern technology. New instruments (bonds) have been introduced and a stock market is under study.

*Capacity building.* At the time of the launching of *doi moi*, Vietnam hardly had a single person trained in macroeconomics, and the capacity to manage the economy by indirect means was extremely limited. During 1990–95 this changed through a number of efforts, such as scholarship programs, training programs established in Vietnam in collaboration with donor agencies, institutional development, and, not least, experience gained within key institutions.

*Social costs of adjustment.* Major dislocations have been avoided through a number of forward-looking programs to deal with transitional unemployment.

## 11.2  Macroeconomic Policies and Growing Openness, 1988–94

At the same time the government was introducing the *doi moi* structural reform program outlined in the previous section, it was trying to cope with serious macroeconomic problems, including high inflation (over 400 percent in 1988) and the impending cutoff of Soviet aid. The fundamental macroeconomic problem was that the government and state enterprises were spending too much, and this excessive expenditure was being financed by a combination of Soviet aid and central bank credit. Over the next few years the government implemented an effective structural adjustment program to deal with the macroeconomic imbalances, relying on the classic tools of interest rates, domestic credit, fiscal policy, and exchange rate management. Vietnam's structural adjustment experience is unique for several interrelated reasons. First, it did not receive any significant international financial support, either from the IMF or from anyone else, until stabilization was largely completed in 1993. Second, while the government relied on the classic tools, these were not applied consistently at first, and there were episodes of backsliding between 1989 and 1993. Finally, disinflation was achieved without any recession. In fact, real GDP growth during the adjustment period of 1988–93 was higher than during any period since reunification of the country. The country's external policies, and particularly its exchange rate management, were crucial to achieving this latter result.

Vietnam began its serious effort to control inflation by dramatically raising deposit interest rates and lending rates on bank loans (which went almost exclusively to state enterprises). Lending rates were raised above the level of inflation (i.e., to 9% per month in spring 1989, when inflation was about 7% per month). Deposit rates were increased to an even higher level and quickly attracted a flow of resources into the banking system. (see Figure 11.2.) State enterprises are not necessarily sensitive to the price of credit, so the State Bank also exercised its direct control over domestic credit to limit its expansion. This policy, combined with the strong output response in the agricultural sector, brought inflation to a virtual halt by mid-1989. The policy, however, also created severe hardships for state enterprises. Thus, there was strong pressure on the SBV to ease its credit and interest rate policies once some initial success with disinflation had been achieved. Interest rates were lowered, credit growth expanded in the second half of 1989, and inflation resumed at a moderate rate. Looking at 1989 as a whole, the year was one of modest restraint. Domestic credit increased by about 150 percent, down from 400 percent in 1988 (see Figure 11.3).

During 1990–92 the government gradually took additional steps to control the growth of credit, and hence of prices. Credit to finance the budget was stopped by 1991. Loans to state enterprises were controlled more carefully and priced appropriately. This hardening of the budget constraint led to a major restructuring of the sector. Between 1988 and 1992, about eight hundred thousand workers (one-third of the 1988 state enterprise labor force) left the sector, and the number of firms declined from twelve thousand to seven thousand. These policies gradually brought the expansion of credit under control (See Dollar, 1994). As a result, inflation declined from the 70 percent range in 1990–91 to about 10 percent in 1993 and 1994. In 1994 domestic credit increased 21.3 percent, including zero new credit for the budget; credit to state firms, increased 17.2 percent; and credit to the private sector increased 40.7 percent.

The disinflation program required imposing discipline both on state enterprises and on the budget. During 1985–89, the fiscal deficit had ranged between 5 percent and 10 percent of GDP and had been financed

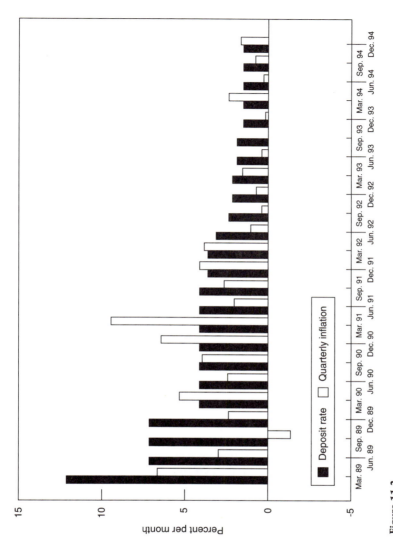

**Figure 11.2**
Inflation and three-month deposit interest rates, 1989–94
*Source:* State Bank of Vietnam.

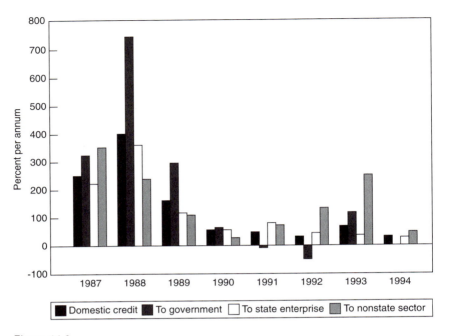

**Figure 11.3**
Growth rate of domestic credit and its components, 1987–94
*Source:* World Bank (1994).

largely by bank credit. The tight credit policies during 1990–92 necessitated a large fiscal adjustment. Revenue as a share of GDP was fairly stable during this period, so that the brunt of adjustment fell on the expenditure side of the budget. Total government expenditure was reduced by six percentage points of GDP between 1989 and 1991 (see Figure 11.4). Part of the savings came from demobilization that returned about half a million soldiers to the civilian labor force. In addition, the government cut back sharply on its investment program. Furthermore, wage increases for civil servants lagged behind the ongoing moderate inflation, which created problems for the provision of social services. Salaries for teachers and health workers had fallen so low by 1991 that it was difficult for communities to get them to perform their duties without additional stipends (World Bank, 1993, ch. 7).

The monetary and fiscal tightening in the early 1990s represents a classic structural adjustment to bring inflation and the fiscal deficit under control. Vietnam's case was unusual in that it did not receive any support from the IMF or the World Bank during this adjustment period, owing to

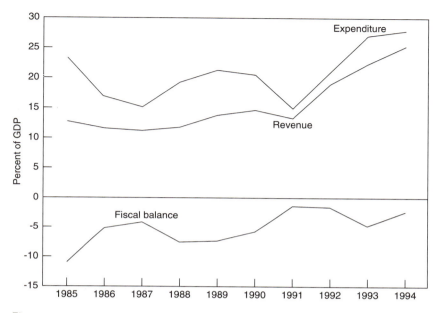

**Figure 11.4**
Government revenue, expenditure, and fiscal balance, 1985–94
*Source:* World Bank (1994).

the opposition of their major shareholders, especially the United States. Vietnam's experience with disinflation was also unusual in that it was not accompanied by a recession. GDP growth in 1989 was 8.0 percent, owing primarily to a strong response from the agricultural sector and from private services. Growth decelerated to the 5–6 percent range during 1990–91, still a healthy rate. Once stabilization was achieved, growth accelerated to the 8–9 percent range in 1992–94. Owing to this rapid growth, and to initial reforms of the tax system, government revenue increased rapidly after 1991, enabling it to restore the investment and social expenditures that were cut during the austerity period. It can be seen in Figure 11.4 that government expenditure as a share of GDP was higher in 1994 than in 1989, at the beginning of the fiscal adjustment. Furthermore, because per capita GDP had increased substantially over this period, real per capita government expenditure was nearly twice as high in 1994 as in 1989. Structural adjustment is usually associated with cutbacks in government services, but Vietnam's experience shows that successful adjustment combined with several good years of growth creates the potential for the government to provide more services than it had previously. In Vietnam there has also been improvement in the allocation of government resources: expenditures that do not promote development (e.g., for the military or to subsidize production) have been reduced relative to development spending for infrastructure, health, and education (World Bank, 1994).

The fact that Vietnam was able to halt high inflation without suffering a recession can be attributed to the dual nature of the economy at the beginning of 1989. As noted, agricultural land had been distributed to peasant families through a series of reforms stretching back over the previous decade. Furthermore, Vietnam had a private sector that was large relative to other socialist economies. This sector had been operating largely underground until 1988. Stabilization is normally a shock to the economy because interest rates are raised, government subsidies are cut, and devaluation makes imported inputs more expensive. Vietnam's stabilization had the predictable effect on the state sector of the economy, which showed negative growth in 1989. What was different in Vietnam was that alongside the state sector, there were large agricultural, private service, and private manufacturing sectors, in total producing about 60 percent of GDP and employing 85 percent of the labor force. These producers were not receiving credit from the formal sector or subsidies from the budget. Thus, for them, 1989 was a year in which inflation was reduced and prices were liberalized, creating a good environment for expansion. That interest rates were much higher and subsidies lower did not matter to firms that were not getting any of the formal credit or budget subsidies to begin with (see Ronnås, 1992). These influences can be seen in the sectoral growth rates for this period. While agricultural value added increased about 8 percent in 1989, industrial growth was negative (see Figure 11.5). The industrial decline is even more striking when the growing crude oil production is removed from that sector. Nonoil industrial value added declined about 12 percent in 1989.

That Vietnam was able to grow throughout its adjustment period can also be attributed to the fact that the economy was being increasingly opened to the international market. As part of its overall effort to stabilize the economy, the government unified its various controlled exchange rates in 1989 and devalued the unified rate to the level prevailing in the parallel market. This was tantamount to a 73 percent *real* devaluation; combined with relaxed administrative procedures for imports and exports, this sharply increased the profitability of exporting. Since 1989 the exchange rate has largely been managed so as to maintain competitiveness. Thus, throughout 1990–91, the exchange rate was allowed to devalue

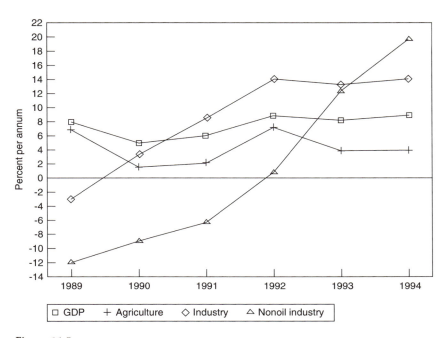

**Figure 11.5**
Growth rates of GDP and major sectors, 1989–94
*Source:* World Bank (1994).

continuously in line with the moderate inflation (see Figure 11.6). There was a shift in the exchange rate regime beginning in 1992, however, when the authorities decided to peg the exchange rate against the U.S. dollar to help bring inflation from the 70 percent range down to single digits. Thus, there was some real appreciation during this period as inflation was brought under control. The policy was relaxed after about a year, however, for several reasons. First, Vietnam did not have sufficient reserves to continue supporting the dong for long. Second, inflation was reduced substantially between 1991 and 1992, so that the importance of the exchange rate as an anchor diminished. Third, the real appreciation appeared to have negative effects on competitiveness and exports, so that there was growing pressure from producers of tradables to amend the policy. By early 1993 the SBV had returned to the crawling peg policy of allowing the exchange rate to devalue in line with inflation.

This exchange rate policy produced strong incentives for export throughout most of the 1989–94 period. During these years real export growth averaged more than 25 percent per annum, and exports were a

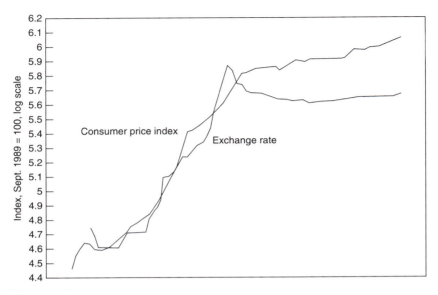

**Figure 11.6**
Inflation and the exchange rate, 1989–94
*Source:* World Bank (1994).

leading sector spurring the expansion of the economy. Rice exports were
a major part of this success in 1989; crude petroleum exports (which were
fortuitous and had nothing to do with the reform program) contributed
in 1990 and 1991; and in 1993–94 there was a wide range of exports on
the rise, including processed primary products (e.g., rubber, cashews, and
coffee), labor-intensive manufactures, and tourist services. Note that in
Figure 11.5 the growth of nonoil industry was extraordinarily rapid
in 1993 and 1994, and this growth included the processing and light-
manufacturing export sectors.

This export surge was important both because it spurred production
and because if financed growing imports for the economy. As anticipated,
Soviet aid declined very rapidly after 1988, and this was not replaced by
financing from other sources. As can be seen in Figure 11.7, the current
account deficit declined from more than 10 percent of GDP in 1988 to
zero in 1992. Normally, the collapse of financing in this way would
required a sharp cutback in imports. However, Vietnam's export growth
was sufficient to ensure that imports could grow throughout this adjustment period. It is also remarkable that investment increased sharply
between 1988 and 1992, while foreign aid was drying up. In response

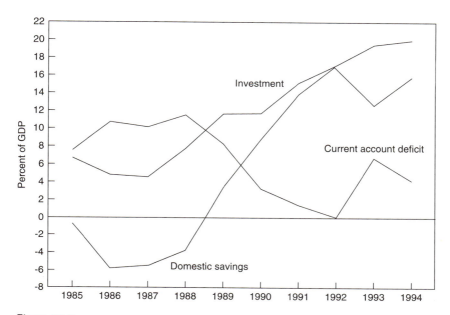

**Figure 11.7**
Savings and investment, 1985–94
*Source:* World Bank (1994).

to stabilization, strengthened property rights, and greater openness to foreign trade, domestic savings increased by twenty percentage points of GDP, from negative levels in the mid-1980s to 16 percent of GDP in 1992.

Lending from the international financial institutions finally resumed in 1993. There was a large increase in both the fiscal and the external deficits that year (see Figures 11.4 and 11.7). However, this development was not the result of the resumption of aid flows. The inflow of official assistance was quite modest in 1993, as it inevitably takes some years for disbursements to build up once aid projects are started. What happened in 1993 was that the government misjudged the situation and anticipated large aid flows to finance its existing expenditure plans. When these flows did not materialize, it resorted to commercial borrowing—both domestic and international—at high interest rates. This excessive reliance on high-cost financing threatened to undermine the macroeconomic stability that had been achieved. The government tightened its fiscal policies in 1994, however, with the result that the fiscal deficit declined from 6.2 percent of GDP in 1993 to 3.3 percent in 1994. Similarly, the external deficit declined to about 5 percent of GDP and was financed largely by direct foreign investment and, to a lesser extent, aid.

In summary, Vietnam's macroeconomic performance has been very good since 1989. The country has reduced inflation from 400 percent to about 10 percent. As in other countries with high inflation, the root problem was a large and inefficient public sector. With military demobilization, state enterprise layoffs, and civil service reductions, about 1.5 million people have left the public sector since 1988, reducing its weight in the labor force from 15 percent to 10 percent. This adjustment was accomplished without a recession because private producers, particularly in agriculture and the service sector, responded quickly to strengthened property rights and price reforms. The fact that the economy was growing made adjustment easier. The Ministry of Labor found in its surveys that most workers laid off from the public sector were absorbed by the rapidly growing private sector within one year (World Bank, 1993, ch. 3). The robust growth has also led to increases in government revenue, with the result that public expenditure increased during this period. The extraordinary devaluation of 1989, and good exchange rate management afterward, resulted in strong effective demand for tradable goods, without which avoidance of a recession would probably have been impossible.

## 11.3  Structural Reforms and Foreign Trade and Investment

While good macroeconomic policies have been key to Vietnam's success in recent years, structural reforms were required to complement those policies. Some of the generic structural reforms have been noted, such as decollectivization, price liberalization, interest rate reforms, and hardening of the budget constraints for state enterprises. This section examines the parallel reforms occurring in foreign trade and investment policies. In general, Vietnam has taken a pragmatic and gradual approach to liberalizing foreign trade and investment. Policies have been revised on virtually a continual basis as experience has been gained.

Concerning foreign trade, Vietnam began with a totally controlled system in which the vast bulk of its trade was organized through bilateral protocols within the context of COMECON. Vietnam in fact had very few exports, and relied on aid, primarily from the Soviet Union, to finance its imports. It depended on the Soviet Union for most of its refined petroleum, steel, and fertilizer—all key inputs for the economy. The limited exports from Vietnam to COMECON partners were primary products (e.g., dried fruit) or labor-intensive manufactures such as clothing. While the trade was limited, it did conform to Vietnam's comparative advantage: exporting products that used natural resources or abundant labor in exchange for more capital- and technology-intensive products.

As noted in earlier sections, the threat of the end of Soviet assistance was a strong impetus to Vietnam's reform. It was clear in the later 1980s that in the future Vietnam would need to finance its imports in a different way, and that in particular it would need to increase its exports and to find new sources of financing. The massive devaluation and generic structural reforms in 1989 created a good basis for exports, but other trade-specific reforms were needed as well. In the COMECON era Vietnam's external trade was monopolized by a small number of state trading companies. In 1989 the system was liberalized, first by allowing competition among state trading companies. Results in 1989 were very good, as hard currency exports doubled. All of this gain, however, can be attributed to two products: crude petroleum and rice. Vietnam was fortunate to have crude oil production coming on line just as Soviet aid went into decline. (The offshore production was from a joint venture with the Soviet Union.) The gain in oil revenue was not a one-for-one substitute for the diminished aid, but it did to some extent cushion the shock of the impending COMECON collapse.

The increase in rice exports—from zero in 1988 to about $300 million in 1989—was a dramatic success resulting from price reform, strengthened property rights, and the trade reforms that allowed more than forty different trading companies to compete for this business. Vietnam's success as a rice exporter has been subtained since 1989, and these exports have increased slowly. There is little potential for them to grow much further, however. Vietnam is a very densely populated country with nine hundred people per square kilometer of agricultural land, three times China's density. Owing to its population density and modest natural resources, Vietnam's comparative advantage lies primarily in labor-intensive activities such as light manufacturing and services (e.g., tourism). The modest trade reforms introduced in 1989 were sufficient to support rice exports, but the resulting regime was not conducive to export of a more diversified set of products. The main problem with the trade regime was that only a small number of firms had certificates from the Ministry of Trade that allowed direct access to the international market. For a country like Vietnam, export of manufactured products requires import of machinery and materials. The control of these imports by a small number of state firms did not encourage development of a dynamic export sector. In addition to limiting the number of firms allowed to engage in foreign trade, the Ministry of Trade had two other control mechanisms: permits that served as unofficial quotas and import shipment licenses that were mostly an accounting tool.

One of the key structural reforms of the past few years has been the gradual dismantling of this complex system of control. First, all firms producing for export were given the right to import machinery and materials directly. Permits regulating the inflow of these products were then dropped, and shipment licenses are being phased out. In practice this means that both state and private firms manufacturing for export can easily import needed inputs; furthermore, the sound exchange rate policy guarantees availability of foreign exchange at the market price.

These policies have encouraged the expansion of manufactured exports, which have been the fastest-growing category of exports in recent years. Analysis of Vietnam's trade is hampered by the weak quality of the import and export data produced by the country. Most of Vietnam's trade now is with countries that report regularly to the U.N. trade data system. Thus, it is possible to reconstruct Vietnam's trade from its partners' data, as is done for exports in Table 11.1. There are obviously some potential pitfalls in this approach, but it nevertheless should indicated broad trends in Vietnam's trade. One serious problem is that Singapore did not report its Vietnam trade to the U.N. database before 1993. In 1988–89 Singapore had virtually no trade with Vietnam, and hence its nonreporting does not distort the comparison between that period and 1993. However, Singapore's trade gradually built up during the early 1990s, so that its nonreporting before 1993 results in an artificial leap in the total from 1992 to 1993.

**Table 11.1**
Vietnam's exports by commodity (U.S.$ million)

|                    | 1988 | 1989 | 1990  | 1991  | 1992  | 1993  |
|--------------------|------|------|-------|-------|-------|-------|
| Primary products   | 466  | 763  | 1,145 | 1,304 | 1,581 | 1,966 |
| Rice               | 0    | 316  | 272   | 225   | 300   | 340   |
| Energy             | 64   | 199  | 403   | 519   | 771   | 983   |
| Manufactured goods | 101  | 137  | 175   | 267   | 598   | 1,085 |
| Clothing           | 34   | 52   | 72    | 142   | 352   | 497   |
| Footwear           | 6    | 13   | 9     | 7     | 32    | 155   |
| Others             | 12   | 6    | 11    | 2     | 16    | 17    |
| Total              | 579  | 906  | 1,331 | 1,573 | 2,195 | 3,068 |

Source: UN trade data base.

The table confirms that there has been an extraordinary increase in Vietnam's exports during this period of adjustment and reform, albeit beginning from a very low base.[1] Most of the increase between 1988 and 1990 came from rice and energy (oil and coal). Since 1990 there has been more diversified expansion. Between 1990 and 1993, rice and energy exports increased by $650 million, out of a total increase in exports of $1.7 billion. The remaining $1 billion increase was primarily manufactured products ($800 million), with $200 million from primary products other than rice and energy (e.g., coffee, rubber, and shrimp). Within manufactured exports, it is no surprise that the big increase was in clothing and footwear. Note also that the table covers *merchandise* trade. Data on tourist earnings are not very good, but their growth probably dwarfs the increase in agricultural exports since 1990.

Vietnam's imports also can be reconstructred from trade partners' data, and the result is reported in Table 11.2 Imports were sustained during the adjustment period because the growth of export earnings compensated

**Table 11.2**
Vietnam's imports by commodity (U.S.$ million)

| Commodity | 1988 | 1989 | 1990 | 1991 | 1992 | 1993 |
|---|---|---|---|---|---|---|
| Food and tobacco | 68 | 85 | 84 | 89 | 143 | 268 |
|   Tobacco and manufactures | 1 | 2 | 1 | 4 | 41 | 88 |
| Intermediate inputs | 1,257 | 1,206 | 1,252 | 1,233 | 1,804 | 2,312 |
|   Textile materials | 65 | 72 | 110 | 159 | 279 | 416 |
|   Petroleum and products | 556 | 449 | 644 | 485 | 615 | 716 |
|   Organic chemicals | 15 | 9 | 20 | 49 | 60 | 110 |
|   Medicinal, pharm. products | 27 | 38 | 54 | 62 | 98 | 118 |
|   Fertilizers, manufactures | 365 | 418 | 223 | 210 | 190 | 130 |
|   Plastic materials, etc. | 11 | 9 | 18 | 65 | 108 | 118 |
|   Iron and steel | 118 | 130 | 90 | 52 | 114 | 146 |
| Capital goods | 346 | 350 | 371 | 532 | 1,364 | 2,044 |
|   Power generating equipment | 67 | 22 | 23 | 36 | 69 | 111 |
|   Industrial machines | 118 | 85 | 98 | 141 | 348 | 473 |
|   Telecomm, sound equipment | 34 | 42 | 62 | 106 | 300 | 280 |
|   Electronic machinery n.e.s., etc. | 26 | 21 | 30 | 55 | 84 | 226 |
|   Road vehicles | 57 | 86 | 89 | 79 | 312 | 615 |
|     Pass. motor vehicles, excl. buses | 2 | 25 | 14 | 10 | 184 | 231 |
|     Road motor vehicles n.e.s. | 4 | 11 | 13 | 5 | 32 | 42 |
|     Motor vehicle parts n.e.s. | 5 | 1 | 2 | 14 | 6 | 14 |
|     Cycles, motorized or not, etc. | 16 | 17 | 36 | 31 | 78 | 271 |
| Others | 20 | 16 | 78 | 9 | 25 | 20 |
| Total | 1,691 | 1,657 | 1,785 | 1,863 | 3,336 | 4,644 |

*Source:* UN trade data base.

for the loss of Soviet aid. Since 1991 there has been a very sharp increase in imports as private and official financial flows have picked up. The pattern of imports is as expected, with 1993 imports divided roughly equally between capital goods and intermediate products. One fact of note is that import of passenger cars and motorcycles amounted to about $500 million in 1993, one-quarter of capital goods imports.

A final point about the import and export data concerns the direction of Vietnam's trade. The country has shifted very rapidly from trading primarily with COMECON countries to trading primarily with countries in its region and with Western Europe. In 1993 two-thirds of Vietnam's exports went to OECD countries, of which Japan was the largest customer. In the same year two-thirds of Vietnam's imports came from the economies of ASEAN plus Korea, Taiwan, and Hong Kong.

While Vietnam has made good progress with reducing direct controls of foreign trade, a remaining problem is the tariff code. The government introduced import taxes as it was dismantling nontariff barriers. The average level of tariffs (about 15 percent) is modest. These tariffs, combined with the spectacular growth of import volumes, have provided the government with an important source of revenue and have been a factor assisting in fiscal stabilization. The problem with the tariff code is that it has twenty-eight different rates ranging from zero to over 100 percent. Furthermore, there is little logic to the code. In some cases, finished products have much higher tariffs than intermediate products, producing large and inefficient effective protection. In other sectors, however, finished products have lower tariffs than intermediate products, creating negative protection for assembly operations. Streamlining this tariff code is an important reform that should be undertaken soon, before vested interests develop that make dismantling of protection difficult.

Vietnam's trade liberalization has been complemented by a similar liberalization of policies toward foreign investment. The move to attract foreign investment began during the very early years of reform, and a foreign investment law was passed in 1987. Vietnam's pragmatism is evidenced by the fact that it has already amended this law and the implementing regulations several times, in light of experience.

Once again the poor quality of Vietnam's data makes it difficult to definitively assess the experience with foreign investment. The State Committee for Cooperation and Investment (SCCI), which licenses and regulates DFI, reports nearly $12 billion of commitments and a much smaller, though still impressively large, $3 billion of cumulative disbursements (inflow) as of the end of 1994. These data are considerably at odds with the balance of payments figures compiled by the SBV and the IMF. For example, in 1994 the balance of payments indicates an inflow of DFI of $600 million, whereas the SCCI figure is over $1 billion. Part of the mystery is that the two figures are not really measuring the same thing. The SCCI figure is for "implementation" of foreign investment projects. Most of these projects are joint ventures with a significant domestic contribution (which should not be counted as foreign investment).

Despite this debate about the underlying data, a number of points are clear. First, the actual inflow of DFI has risen very rapidly and now makes a significant contribution to capital formation. Suppose the true figure for 1994 inflow was $600–700 million: that would amount to nearly 5 percent of GDP and about one-quarter of total investment, a significant amount from a macroeconomic point of view. Second, the inflow of DFI into Vietnam is very small in terms of the region as a whole; it is about 1 percent of the DFI flows in East Asia. Third, implementation of many projects in Vietnam is proceeding slowly, and there are continual complaints from the business community about bureaucracy and corruption. There are also problems with the policy framework; in particular, it is difficult for foreign investors to obtain access to land or to mortgage land use rights. The labor market, on the other hand, is relatively liberal: investors have considerable freedom in hiring and firing, and the minimum wage of U.S.$35/month in foreign-invested firms is close to the prevailing market wage.

A final point is that Vietnam's foreign trade appears to be closely linked to foreign investment. The largest foreign investors are by and large the same nations from which Vietnam imports. The four largest ones are in fact the four tigers: Taiwan, Hong Kong, Singapore, and South Korea (see Table 11.3). Together they account for about half of all the investment (measured by value of commitments). The same four economies account for about half of Vietnam's imports, which, it was shown earlier, are concentrated in capital goods and intermediate products. Furthermore, a growing share of foreign investment is going to manufacturing, which has been the leading source of exports in recent years. In the early years of reform, foreign investment went primarily to the oil sector and to tourism. By the end of 1994, however, industry (excluding oil and gas) was the leading receiving sector (see Table 11.4). Thus, it seems that the four Asian tigers are investing in manufacturing and tourism in Vietnam and contributing to the export boom.

There is an economic logic to these middle-income economies investing in Vietnam. As wages have risen through their successful development, they have lost comparative advantage in the labor-intensive activities. Vietnam's

**Tale 11.3**
Foreign investment by source (commitments, end of 1994)

| Country | Number of projects | Total investment of projects (U.S.$ million) |
|---|---|---|
| Taiwan | 179 | 1,968 |
| Hong Kong | 171 | 1,796 |
| Singapore | 76 | 1,028 |
| Republic of Korea | 98 | 889 |
| Japan | 73 | 789 |
| Australia | 42 | 661 |
| Malaysia | 32 | 585 |
| France | 58 | 510 |
| Switzerland | 14 | 463 |
| England | 15 | 376 |
| Total | 1,201 | 11,992 |

**Table 11.4**
Foreign investment by economic sector (commitments, end of 1994)

| | Number of projects | Total capital (U.S.$ million) |
|---|---|---|
| Licensed projects | 1,201 | 11,992 |
| Industry | 548 | 4,334 |
| Oil and gas | 26 | 1,302 |
| Agriculture and forestry | 74 | 369 |
| Aquaculture | 21 | 62 |
| Transport and telecom. | 128 | 951 |
| Hotels and tourism | 113 | 2,235 |
| Services | 134 | 1,254 |
| Finance and banking | 15 | 177 |
| Housing development | 14 | 70 |
| Export processing zones | 29 | 109 |
| Industrial centers | 2 | 167 |
| Other | 97 | 962 |

*Source:* State Committee for Cooperation and Investment.

excellent location, good human resources, and low wages have attracted producers from the newly industrialized countries (NIC)s. It also is likely that investors from the NICs are less daunted by the weak state of the legal and regulatory framework, compared with investors from OECD countries. In the case of Taiwan, Hong Kong, and Singapore, investors have a link to the still substantial Chinese community in Ho Chi Minh City.

What this picture yields is a balanced assessment of the experience with DFI to date. From a macroeconomic point of view, foreign investment could not have built up much more rapidly, and therefore policies to data must be viewed as largely successful. On the other hand, there is considerable scope for foreign investment to continue to increase. The concerns about slow implementation, bureaucracy, corruption, and land use rights are all relevant for Vietnam' continued development. In this context a significant fact is that 98 percent of all joint ventures are with state enterprises rather than with the domestic private sector. There was a substantial downsizing of the state enterprise sector during the years of fiscal adjustment, 1989–92. More recently, however, the sector has experienced a resurgence, largely owing to partnerships with foreign investors. The main attraction of the state sector to foreign investors is easy access to land and the value of a well-connected local partner in dealing with the bureaucracy.

Linking state enterprises with foreign investors has a positive impact on the firms, leading them to operate on a sound commercial basis. There is a danger, however, that powerful alliances among line ministries, large state enterprises, and foreign investors will create an environment that hampers the development of the domestic private sector. In the East Asian economies that have had sustained growth of exports and *GDP* over a long period, entry of new firms—most starting out as small and medium-sized ones—has been a key element of success. Vietnam can get a certain amount of mileage out of linking its viable state firms with foreign partners. But fairly soon the large gains from this approach will have been achieved, and then the economy will need ongoing entry of small and medium domestic private firms—as well as entry of new foreign investors—to sustain industrial growth. Thus a central question over the next decade is whether a good framework for such an ongoing expansion of the private sector is being put in place.

There are several reasons to be concerned about the alliances between line ministries and foreign investors. First, several of these ministries have crucial roles in developing the basic economic infrastructure, including roads, ports, water supply, and power. However, commercial ventures in hotels or manufacturing are more attractive to these ministries in the current environment of weak accounting and accountability. Aid resources are available to finance the rehabilitation and expansion of infrastructure, but projects are proceeding slowly. The fact that ministries are distracted by commercial activities is one reason for weak implementation. A second and more serious issue is that there is obviously a conflict of interest between ministries and local authorities as regulators and as producers. As regulators, government bodies should favor ease of entry and should promote competition. As partners in producing joint ventures, however, these government agencies have an interest in restrictive arrangements.

In summary, policies toward foreign trade and investment have obviously been sufficiently good to support expansion of GDP and growing integration with the international market in the period 1988–94. That is no guarantee, however, that the policies as they stand now will be sufficient to ensure continued development at a rapid rate.

### 11.4   Political Economy of Openness

Within a few years a crisis-ridden country has emerged "on the trail of the tigers" (Riedel, 1992). The confidence of the CPV, which saw its notion of the world disintegrate as the socialist regimes in the Soviet Union and Eastern Europe collapsed, has naturally grown in the process. At the 1994 Consultative Group meeting, the Vietnamese government announced that it was determined to put the Vietnamese economy, one of the poorest in the world at U.S.$170 GDP per capita, on a growth path that would result in a doubling of GDP per capita during the 1990s. Accomplishing industrialization and modernization has become the basis of the party's claim to legitimacy, and the pursuit of reforms the preoccupation of this survivor of the crisis of socialist regimes.

To catch up has become the essence of the "national project." In the Political Report presented by General Secretary Do Muoi to the mid-term conference of the CPV held in January 1994, four major challenges facing the country were identified. The foremost challenge lay in "the danger of our economy falling further behind those of other countries in the region and the world," that is, the risk of not being able to catch up (Communist Party of Vietnam, 1994, p. 24). In a interview entitled "What Is to Be Done," in one of the country's new economic journals, *Vietnam Economic Times*, Do Muoi reiterated the theme:

Industrialization and modernization are the focus of the transitional period to socialism in Vietnam. This is the leading instruction throughout our activities and the decisive factor to bear in mind if we are to avoid being left behind. The economy must grow to catch up with other economies in the region and with those in the wide world. (*Vietnam Economic Times*. 1995).

The second challenge facing the country, according to Do Muoi, is to accomplish economic development while consolidating "the leading role of the Party." Contemporary development in Vietnam can to a large extent be seen as a complex interplay between these two objectives, between doing what is necessary to generate rapid modernization and doing what is required to ensure that the liberalization process is kept within the boundaries of political stability. As in China, the concept of peaceful evolution is used as a label for different kinds of unacceptable interferences in the political and social life of Vietnam that may threaten stability. *Doi moi* aims at reforming the entire system, not just the economic system; but reform in the political sphere should be in the form of a liberalization process controlled by the CPV. Pluralism and multiparty democracy explicitly are not on that agenda.

According to the 1992 Constitution, Vietnam is in a "transitional stage to socialism." But while the 1980 Constitution said that the economy should be transformed directly into a socialist economy "without going through the stage of capitalist development," the revised constitution foresees "a socialist-oriented multisectoral economy driven by the state-regulated market-mechanism." The market, decollectivized peasant agriculture, and the private sector get constitutional approval, even though in a language reflecting the ideological dilemma of the CPV. During the transition to socialism, "diverse transitional forms" need to be relied upon, again to quote Do Muoi's speech. At the same time, a third major challenge is "to avoid going astray from the socialist orientation" (Communist Party of Vietnam, 1994, p. 23). A balancing act that, it seems, cannot be won unless the meaning of socialism is redefined as circumstances change.

According to Janos Kornai, the distinguished Hungarian economist, there can be no "comprehensive and consistently radical transformation in the other spheres while the key feature of the old classical structure, the Communist party's power, remains" (Kornai, 1992, p. 566). In Vietnam, the fear of falling further behind, and of seeing the legitimacy and power of the party erode the way it did in the Soviet Union and Eastern Europe, has pushed government policies beyond established ideological boundaries. The ambition remains, however, to maintain a leading role for the state or the state sector. That role represents a central element of the searched-for definition of "socialist orientation."

In one form or the other, the state sector is the local partner in all but a few (2 percent) of the eleven hundred joint ventures with foreign investors that were licensed by the end of 1994. Foreign investment clearly also represents an area of rapid expansion where the state sector wants to play a dominating role. Partly this follows from the fact that the private sector has emerged so recently, and has so little to offer in comparison with the state sector in terms of capital, land, and so on. However, it also reflects party and government policy and the nature of the politicoeconomic context in which the potential investor has to operate. High transaction costs are encountered due to cumbersome procedures and the tendency of underpaid officials to put a price on access. Joint ventures represent a source of revenue for state enterprises and the party and state apparatus. This forceful triangle is an important factor in the dynamics of the reform.

A serious dilemma for the CPV and the government, and the fourth of the major challenges identified at the 1994 Party Conference, is the corruption that forms part of emerging structures. The Eighth Plenary Session of the Central Committee of the CPV, held in January 1995, was devoted to administrative reform. By doing so, the CPV moved the reform process into areas that are crucial from a governance perspective. At one extreme is the notion of an efficient civil service recruited and promoted on the basis of merit, and having the capacity to formulate, monitor, and redefine policies in a complex environment and to translate policy into a transparent regulatory framework. At the other extreme is an administration that represents an extension of the party and that lacks defined boundaries. While there is a readiness to move toward the former, in an effort to become a "developmental state," party interests set limits. Legal reform, already a central element of the political dimension of *doi moi*, is also being moved into new spheres as the scope of change in the legal fields is widened to include not only economic legislation required in a market economy (company law, bankruptcy law, etc.) but also the adoption of the first civil code of the DRV/SRV.

The changes taking place in Vietnam are, however, not limited to what is decided by party, government, and bureaucracy. The profound changes that are taking place in the economic field cannot be limited to that sphere. Phenomena such as peasant households, private business, the huge volume of foreign investment, Western aid and aid conditionality, and the rapid spread of a new information technology are bound to have profound effects on the inner workings of the society. The emergence of interest groups such as the Association of Industrialists in Ho Chi Minh City, bar associations (including private law firms) and other professional organizations, semiautonomous research institutes, and embryonic nongovernment organizations in fields such as child protection and the environment suggests that a civil society is taking shape, though slowly, cautiously, and in an atmosphere of continuous uncertainty about where the lines are drawn. Interest group politics will emerge as the organizations that are entering the scene begin to articulate their views in a dialogue with existing structures of power. "The project of Liberalizers" is, to quote Przeworski,

to relax social tension and to strengthen their position in the power bloc by broadening the social base of the regime: to allow some autonomous organizations of the civil society and to incorporate the new groups into the authoritarian institutions. In the light of this project, liberalization is to be continually contingent on the compatibility of its outcomes with the interests or values of the authoritarian bloc. (Przeworksi, 1991, p. 57).

It follows that liberalization as "a controlled opening of political space," while aiming to create "political stability," is an inherently unstable process (Przeworski, 1991, p. 57). In Vietnam, the most striking result so far of that process is the widening of the nonpolitical private sphere of the individual. New space is opened up, within which the individual, the family, and the enterprise can improve their material well-being and enjoy access to a wider range of information. In this new-won freedom lies a major dynamic factor that, while being indispensable for the success of *doi moi* as perceived by the leadership, also contains a built-in demand for institutionalization and further expansion of "civic space." The process of change generates its own dynamics.

## 11.5  Conclusions

Nothing works like success, and developments in Vietnam since 1989, the year of the price and exchange rate reform, must by any reasonable standards be considered a success in terms of economic growth and stabilization. The reform measures stood the test and, as a consequence, the reformists within the CPV were able to build consensus in support of further steps. A virtuous circle emerged serving national as well as party interests. As a consequence, it has been possible to define the main elements in the reforms process for the years 1994–97 in a way that has satisfied the international financial institutions and laid the foundation for structural adjustment lending. Within the framework of the Consultative Group, an implicit contract on reform and concessional financing has been entered into. It remains to be seen whether those who favor continued reform will win the support of the Eighth Party Congress, scheduled for 1996. The development process has in many ways become increasingly open-ended, as the importance of "research, probing and discovery" (i.e., practical results) rather than "voluntarism" (i.e., ideology) has been recognized, and for the moment the reformers have prevailed. Still, there are strong tendencies to enhance the role of the state and to maintain public ownership of key means of production, increasingly seen as the essence of socialism (Marr, 1994, p. 6). Four excerpts from recent Vietnamese documents illustrate this tendency:

• "The state-run economy has failed to play its leading role in production and circulation." (Communist Party of Vietnam, 1994)

• "State-run commerce" must preserve "a necessary share of retail trade." (Ibid.)

• "Capital allocated from the budget should be invested mostly in the construction of socioeconomic infrastructure, a number of key industrial enterprises and a number of processing units for agriculture, forest, and aquatic products and for export goods and services." (Ibid.)

• "According to government-approved scheme, the country within this year will strengthen some major state-owned import and export corporations that are expected to dominate the distribution of essential goods and to establish major export channels." (*Vietnam Investment Review*, 1995b, based on an interview with the minister of trade)

We have argued that Vietnam's reform process can be divided into three stages: the embryonic, rather unintended beginning in 1979; the commitment to reform at the "*doi moi* Party Congress" of 1986; and the drastic, and remarkably successful, price and monetary reform package of 1989. Is Vietnam about to take further steps on the reform path, steps that would suggest that the reform process would be entering a fourth stage? Against such a notion there is the fact that certain elements of the third phase have developed less than could have been expected. That is particularly true regarding privatization of SOEs, a process that has hardly begun, and the dimensions of the reform that are directly related to the large question of the role of the state. The latter constitutes a sphere in which different party and government statements indicate considerable ambivalence.

What speaks in favor of suggesting that a fourth stage is about to begin is the increasing importance attached to administrative reform. By pursuing this line, the CPV and the government are showing a readiness to deepen the reform and to broaden it to encompass questions of state-party relations that are of crucial importance for future possibilities to develop state capacity as well as for the possibility of institutionalizing the results reached in the liberalization process (Sorensen, 1992). Such a deepening of the reform would sustain the development toward a more open economy capable of maintaining the rates of growth required in order to catch up.

## Notes

David Dollar is chief of the Macroeconomics and Growth Division of the World Bank, and Börje Ljunggren is ambassador of Sweden to Vietnam. Views expressed are those of the authors and do not necessarily reflect the opinions of the World Bank or of the Swedish government. This paper was prepared for the Conference on Participation of Reforming Economies in the Global Trading and Financial System UNU/WIDER, Helsinki, Finland, May 26–27, 1995.

1. Table 11.1 does not include Vietnam's exports to the Soviet Union during the 1988–91 period. Those exports were minor, probably amounting to several hundred million dollars' equivalent at their peak. Excluding them from the table has the effect of modestly exaggerating the growth of Vietnam's exports. For the 1992–93 period, Vietnam's exports to Russia (now in hard currency) are included. At that time the exports amounted to U.S.$100–200 million per year. The potential bias of excluding the Soviet trade is much more serious on the import side, where Vietnam received very significant flows from its major ally. In Table 11.2 we have included Vietnam's major imports from the Soviet Union during 1988–91: refined petroleum, steel, fertilizer, and other such inputs. Because data on these were available in physical units, it was possible to value them at world market prices. Thus Table 11.2 should reflect quite accurately Vietnam's overall imports during the period in which its trade was shifting from COMECON partners to East Asian market economies.

## References

Beresford, Melanie. 1988. *Vietnam—Politics, Economics and Society*. London: Pinter.

Beresford, Melanie. 1993. "Some key Issues in the Reform of the North Vietnamese Industrial Sector." Working Paper no. 9. Canberra: Research School of Pacific Studies, Australian National University.

Communist Party of Vietnam. 1994. Political Report of the Central Committee to the Midterm Party Conference. Hanoi: CPV.

Dapice, David, ed. 1995. *In Search of the Dragon's Tail: Economic Reform in Vietnam*. Cambridge, Mass.: Harvard Institute for International Development/Harvard University Press.

Dollar, David. 1993. "Vietnam: Successes and Failures of Macroeconomic Stabilization." In Börje Ljunggren, ed., *The Challenge of Reform in Indochina*. Cambridge, Mass.: Harvard Institute for International Development/Harvard University Press.

Dollar, David. 1994. "Macroeconomic Management and the Transition to the Market in Vietnam." *Journal of Comparative Economics* 18:357–75.

Do Muoi. 1995. *Vietnam: New Challenges and New Opportunities*. Hanoi: Gioi.

Hy Van Luong. 1992. *Tradition and Revolution in a North Vietnamese Village*. Honolulu: University of Hawaii Press.

Kornai, Janos. 1992. *The Socialist System: The Political Economy of Communism*. Princeton: Princeton University Press.

Le Dang Doanh. 1994. "Vietnam Country Report." Paper prepared for an international conference in Osaka, October 30–31.

Le Dang Doanh. 1994–1995. "*Doi Moi* in Review: A Snapshot of 1994." *Vietnam Economic Times*, December/January, pp. 18–19.

Le Duan. 1977. *Selected Writings*. Hanoi: Foreign Language Publishing House.

Ljunggren, Börje, ed. 1993. *The Challenge of Reform in Indochina*. Cambridge, Mass.: Harvard Institute for International Development/Harvard University Press.

Marr, David. 1994. "The Vietnamese Communist Party and Civil Society." Paper presented at the 1994 Vietnam Update Conference: Doi Moi, the State and Civil Society. Australian National University, Canberra, November 10–11.

Przeworski, Adam. 1991. *Democracy and the Market: Political and Economic Reform in Eastern Europe and Latin America*. Cambridge: Cambridge University Press.

Riedel, James. 1992. "On the Trail of the Tigers." Working paper. Washington, D.C.: Johns Hopkins/SAIS.

Ronnås, Per. 1992. *Employment Generation Through Private Entrepreneurship in Vietnam*. Geneva: ILO.

Ronnås, Per. 1993. "Private Entrepreneurship in the Nascent Market Economy of Vietnam—Markets and Linkages." Paper prepared for the European Vietnam Studies Conference. Copenhagen, Nordic Institute of Asian Studies, August 19–21.

Socialist Republic of Vietnam. 1994. Report of the Government of the Socialist Republic of Vietnam to the Consultative Group Meeting, Paris, November 15–16. Hanoi: (SRV.)

Sorensen, Georg. 1992. *Democracy and the Developmental State*. Aarhus, Denmark: Institute of Political Science, University of Aarhus.

Swedish International Development Authority (SIDA). 1994. *State, Market & Aid—Redefined Roles*. Stockholm: SIDA.

UNDP and World Bank. 1993. "Vietnam: Policies for Transition to an Open Economy." Washington, D.C.: UNDP–World Bank Trade Expansion Program.

*Vietnam Economic Times*. 1995. "What Is to Be Done." February, pp. 30–31.

*Vietnam Investment Review*. 1995a. "WTO Membership Ahead, Says Khai." February 13–19, p. 5.

*Vietnam Investment Review*. 1995b. "Triet Calls for 25 pc Annual Export Growth." February 20–26, p. 1.

de Vylder, Stefan, and Adam Fforde. 1988 *Vietnam: An Economy in Transition*. Stockholm: Swedish International Development Authority.

de Vylder, Stefan, and Adam Fforde. 1996. *From Plan to Market: The Transition in Vietnam 1979–1994*. Boulder, Co.: Westview.

Wade, Robert. 1990. *Governing the Market: Economic Theory and the Role of Government in East Asian Industrialisation*. Princeton: Princeton University Press.

Woodside, Alexander. 1989. "Peasants and the State in the Aftermath of the Vietnamese Revolution." *Journal of Peasant Studies* 16, no. 4: 283–97.

World Bank. 1992. *Vietnam: Restructuring Public Finance and Public Enterprises*. Washington, D.C.: World Bank.

World Bank. 1993. *Vietnam: Transition to the Market*. Washington, D.C.: World Bank.

World Bank. 1994. *Vietnam: Public Sector Management and Private Sector Incentives*. Washington, D.C.: World Bank.

# 12        India

## Manmohan Agarwal

Until recently, India persisted with the import substitution industrialization development strategy it had adopted in the 1950s, in common with many other developing countries. However, the Indian import substitution strategy differed from that adopted by most developing countries in two respects. First, it stressed investment for producing basic capital and intermediate goods rather than for producing consumer goods. Second, the government, rather than the private sector, was mainly responsible for investment and production in these basic industries. Furthermore, the government influenced private-sector decisions, especially with regard to capital formation and international trade through quantity controls (Bhagwati and Desai, 1970; Bhagwati and Srinivasan, 1975). The Indian development strategy had an economic and a political motive; its design and execution were strongly influenced by the Soviet example, as discussed below.

The survival of the strategy for over three decades despite a series of periodic crises—such as those in 1957–58, 1966–68, 1973–74, 1980–81, and 1990–91—could perhaps be explained by the fact that the crises, except for the one in 1957–58, were generated by exogenous shocks.[1] The 1966–68 crisis resulted from a succession of poor harvests; the rest, from developments largely in the international oil market though, in the case of the 1990–91 crisis, the reduction of remittances from workers in Kuwait (who returned to India following the invasion of Kuwait by Iraq) was also important. These crises consisted of a balance of payments crisis sometimes, though not always, accompanied by a fiscal crisis. The response to the crises was a mixture of adjustments in the government's fiscal policies and in financing, as new sources of international finance were tapped. However, until recently there was no change in the basic import substitution strategy or the regulatory mechanism used to implement the strategy, although many policy adjustments were made to accelerate growth in the face of changing constraints. A major adjustment was the increasing share of the private sector in industrial investment as the government faced a severe resource shortage.

The chapter is organized as follows: Section 12.1 states the development strategy adopted by Indian policy makers and emphasizes the economic and political considerations that influenced the choices. Section 12.2 discusses the measures that were adopted to deal with the balance of payments crises that erupted from time to time, and the impact of these measures on the basic development strategy. Section 12.3 deals with the performance of the economy in the period before the crisis in 1990–91 that resulted in the abandonment of the earlier strategy. It concentrates on the economic factors that were most responsible for the 1990–91 crisis. Section 12.4 discusses the reforms and analyzes their effect.

## 12.1   The Development Strategy

Indian policy makers aimed at a development strategy that would meet the economic objective of rapid improvement in the living standards of the people, and the political objective of insulating the government's economic and foreign policies from external pressures and interference. The desire for policy autonomy was both an end in itself and a means to implement policies for rapid growth; this desire for policy autonomy was a result of the colonial experience, which was reinforced by incidents in the early years after independence was achieved in 1947.[2]

The strategy of import substitution in basic industries under the aegis of the public sector suited the policy makers' economic and political objectives. Its economic logic, discussed below, was that growth of a capital-shortage economy could be maximized by concentrating investment in basic industries. Rapid economic growth was essential for reduction of poverty because redistribution of the current GNP would result in only a small reduction in poverty. In any case, substantial redistribution of income or assets was not politically feasible. Development of basic industries would also provide a foundation for an independent armaments industry, which was considered essential for implementing the foreign policy of nonalignment. The Soviet experience was influential in the decision to concentrate investments in basic industries.[3] The Soviet economy had grown rapidly through concentration of investment in basic industries that were instrumental in the strong defense effort during World War II.

The decisive role of the public sector in the strategy was justified by the lack of private entrepreneurship and of capital needed for the increased investment required for an acceleration of the growth rate. The public sector, it was hoped, would also prevent concentration of wealth. Income distribution was to be made more equal over time through a more equal distribution of the additional income (rather than redistribution of existing incomes and assets) and a very progressive tax system. Public investment would also help maintain spatial balance not only between the different regions (the regional distribution of industrial activity was very skewed at the time of independence) but also between towns and villages. The policy makers believed that the market could not be trusted to maintain balance among these goals. Their negative view regarding the capability of the market to maintain an adequate level of economic activity and its growth was based on the performance of the world economy during the interwar years. On the other hand, the Soviet experience of rapid industrialization during that period reinforced their belief that a strong government role in the management of the economy was essential.

The idea of five-year plans and their design and implementation owed much to Soviet experience (Chakravarty, 1989; Desai and Bhagwati, 1975). In particular, the Indian plans were based on elaborate input-output exercises that were designed to provide an adequate physical supply of a good that would be demanded by technical conditions. The need to maintain financial balance was overlooked. In other words, not only must the output of the capital goods sector equal the required investment, but financial savings to finance this investment must be adequate. If the financial balance was not maintained, the required investment would have to be realized through forced savings brought about by inflation. When the neglect of financial balances led to the inevitable appearance of inflation arising from the imbalance between aggregate demand and supply, or from shortages of crucial products such as food, the policy makers responded by tightening price controls or by allocating scarce supplies through licenses.

Though the broad policy framework remained unchanged for four decades, adjustments were made to cope with changing constraints (see Table 12.1).

At the beginning of the 1950s, when Indian planners launched their successive five-year plans to promote growth of the economy, they identified three bottlenecks that limited the process. First was the low level of savings and investment. A massive investment program could not be initiated because of a shortage of investable resources and of entrepreneurs. Second was the unbalanced industrial structure. Manufacturing was traditionally concentrated in cotton textiles and jute, to the exclusion of machine building. In other words, capital formation via new investment was

**Table 12.1**
Constraints and the policy framework

| Period | Constraints | Policies |
|---|---|---|
| First three plans (1951–65) | 1. Low level of savings and investment | Investment financed by higher savings through accumulated foreign exchange reserves |
| | 2. Unbalanced industrial structure | Stress investment in basic industries |
| | 3. Low agricultural production per capita | Undertake land ownership and institutional reform |
| Second and third plans (1956–65) | In addition, lack of foreign exchange to finance imports of machinery for investment | Rely on foreign aid; later, introduce exports incentives, license use of foreign exchange; increase investment in basic industries |
| Annual and fourth plans (1966–73) | 1. Stagnant agricultural production | Improve profitability of agricultural production by introducing new technology; stress economic incentives |
| | 2. Declining foreign aid, which aggravated low rates of savings and investment, and balance of payments crisis | Cut back public-sector investment; raise national savings in both public and private sectors |
| Fifth and sixth plans (1974–84) | 1. Balance of payment pressure; higher price of oil | Investment in oil sector |
| | 2. Low growth of output of industry and of capacity utilization; stagnant productivity in industry | Gradual liberalization of imports of intermediate goods, then of capital goods, followed by technology imports; increased private-sector role in industrial production |

bound to require imports of machines. Third was the low agricultural production per capita. These constraints guided the design of policy during the first three plans, which lasted until the mid-1960s.

The planners' view that the inadequate savings and investment rates were the most binding constraint was shaped by defining the growth process in terms of the Harrod-Domar growth model. This model, in which the growth rate of the economy equals the savings rate divided by the capital-output ratio, underlay the First Five-Year Plan (1951–55). Accelerating the growth rate required a stepping up of the savings rate because the planners believed that the capital-output ratio was technologically given. This framework was further elaborated in the Mahalanobis model, in which the investment rate was tied to the domestic production of capital goods. It formed the basis of the Second and Third Five-Year Plans, covering the years 1956–65. The identification of investment with domestic production of capital goods, which could be true only in a closed economy, provided the basis for an investment pattern geared toward domestic production of capital goods.[4] The large-scale plants required for their production were set up in the public sector. This decision suited the other objectives of the government, such as preventing the concentration of wealth.[5]

These investments were financed by taxation and foreign funds. The latter came initially from the accumulated foreign exchange reserves, and later from foreign aid. Almost all the aid came from the industrialized Western countries and international institutions dominated by them. However, Soviet aid supported crucial investments because Western aid donors were often unwilling to back industrial investment in the public sector. Soviet assistance made possible public-sector investment in sectors such as steel, machine building, and mining industries. It was also more effective in transferring technology (Desai, 1987; Lele and Agarwal, 1991). The foreign exchange crisis of 1957–58, resulting from the stepped-up imports of capital goods and unanticipated imports by the private sector, was believed to be temporary. The planners hoped to resolve it as soon as the domestic capital goods industry started supplying the required machines. But as the foreign exchange shortage persisted, policy makers increasingly had recourse to export incentives.

The low level of grain output per capita also limited rapid capital formation. The supply of food grains had to be raised so that the industrial proletariat could be fed. Indeed, lagging grain production and the increasing dependence on imports, heightened by the droughts in the mid-1960s, resulted in a wide-ranging debate about the relative importance of two types of capital—capital in the form of machinery and capital in the form of wage goods (Bhagwati and Chakravarty, 1969; Chakravarty, 1969, 1989). The debate emphasized that the wage-goods constraint, which was effective, resulted in a higher real wage in the industrial sector, and eroded profitability and savings in the emerging industrial sector. Therefore, the imperative to increase grain production resulted in a major shift in the strategy for agricultural development. The earlier efforts to reform the land tenure system and stress community development programs were geared toward changing the socioeconomic environment. The new strategy, however, stressed improved profitability of farming through introduction of new technologies and the supply of required inputs in a balanced package. The need to supply the new inputs to agriculture resulted in a slight shift in the investment strategy as the share of investment allocated to sectors producing agricultural inputs increased.

The relative importance of the public and private sectors in total investment also shifted because farming was predominantly private.

As noted earlier, a large part of investment in the economy during the Second and Third Five-Year Plans (1956–65) was financed by foreign funds, largely from official sources. A cutback in foreign financing in the mid-1960s resulted in a decline in public-sector investment and a change in the planners' investment strategy. The government introduced policies to raise the rate of domestic savings by both the private and the public sectors. Public-sector savings were increased by higher taxes and by increasing profits in state-owned enterprises. However, the aid cutback had a chain effect: it reduced public-sector investment and created excess capacity in the capital goods industry. At the same time, measures to raise savings via taxes resulted in an industrial recession, stagnation in employment in the large-scale, industrial sector, and decline in per capita income. The government therefore had to introduce measures to alleviate economic distress. The poverty programs consisted of subsidized food, credits, or other services and increased employment in the public sector. These resulted in higher government budgetary outlays in the long run and a higher relative share of public-sector consumption and investment outlays, further aggravating the shortage of public-sector investable resources.

By the mid-1970s, the earlier constraints seemed to have been overcome: the savings rate had moved up to about 18 percent, and the current account deficit had gone down to about 1 percent of GDP; food imports were reduced; the industrial structure was much more diversified with significant production of capital goods; and there was a large and growing entrepreneurial class. Both the public and private sectors contributed to the higher savings rate. While the overall savings rate went up from about 13 percent during the third plan (1961–65) to about 18 percent, the public-sector savings rate was up from about 3 percent to over 4 percent (having fallen to about 2 percent during the period of the annual plans for 1966–68): higher savings from the government budget and increased profits of public enterprises contributed to higher public-sector savings. The increased savings supported a higher investment rate despite the decline in foreign aid.

The shift in the strategy for developing the agricultural sector, and the oil price increase that prompted the government to undertake large investments in oil exploration and production, influenced the allocation of public-sector investment. For instance, investment was switched to the energy and fertilizer sectors from steel, machine building, and transport and communications. The share of energy in total public-sector investment increased from about 15 percent in the third plan (1961–65) to 18 percent in the fourth (1969–73) and fifth (1974–78) plans. The public sector continued to incur more than half the total investment.

The low level of capacity utilization in manufacturing and the lagging industrial growth continued to be the main problems. The government acted to boost capacity utilization by allowing imports of intermediate goods. The policy makers believed that the measure would accelerate industrial growth by lowering the capital-output ratio and encouraging new investment. However, they failed to recognize that the excess capacity was a structural problem because licenses for imports of intermediates goods were usually related to capacity.

Although growth picked up in the second half of the 1970s, the overall impression at that time was that industry continued to stagnate, and that further steps were needed to accelerate industrial and overall growth. This debate proceeded against the background of the large accumulation of foreign exchange reserves and food stocks in the mid-1970s. Some participants in the dialogue saw the accumulation of large food stocks as an indicator of lagging demand in the economy. They advocated a more active government investment policy to raise demand (Chakravarty, 1979). Others argued that the earlier squeeze in public-sector investment had created infrastructural bottlenecks that required the modernization and expansion of infrastructural facilities.

## 12.2 Policy Responses to the Balance of Payments Crises

The policy responses to the balance of payments (BOP) crises broadly reflected the two-sector division of the economy that formed the policy makers' analytical framework, which was formalized in a series of growth models. The goods markets were divided into the market for consumer goods and the market for capital goods (Chakravarty, 1969). This separation reflecting an analytical abstraction was reinforced by the policy framework. Since imports of consumer goods were banned for most of the period, policies regarding the consumer goods market dealt with the output of consumer goods and its division between the home and foreign markets. The total production of consumer goods, particularly in the short run, often depended on imported intermediate goods. In addition, the exchange rate determined the allocation of this production between the domestic and foreign markets, as well as its cost of production through its impact on the price of imported intermediate goods. The demand for

consumer goods was influenced by the government's fiscal policy, the main
objectives of which were a low rate of inflation and a viable BOP position.
The effect of fiscal policy on aggregate consumer demand depended on the
size of the fiscal deficit, its financing, and the composition of government
expenditures. Therefore, the net supply of foreign exchange depended on
the government's fiscal policy and the real exchange rate, which was more
often varied through export incentives and the rate of inflation rather than
through changes in the nominal exchange rate.

The net supply of foreign exchange from the consumer goods market
had to be matched with the net demand for foreign exchange from the
capital goods market, which depended significantly on the size of the
plan. Though the size of the plan influenced the government's tax and
expenditure policies, the pricing policy for public enterprises, domestic
and foreign borrowing, and the extent of money creation, its main impact
in managing the BOP crises arose from the resulting demand for imported
capital goods. The size of the plan not only affected the imports of capital
goods directly, it also changed the composition of investment via its
impact on the import intensity of the investment program. Therefore, the
debate on the ways of responding to the BOP crises was often phrased in
terms of the size of the plan, although, as noted above, the size of the plan
influenced the basic development strategy, the role of the government,
and the policy instruments at its command. The size of the plan was
related to the availability of foreign financing and the formulation of trade
policy via the import content of investment. Therefore, foreign financing
had a pervasive influence on development strategy over the years. It was
not confined to the conditionality associated with borrowing from the
International Monetary Fund (IMF).

The specific policy responses to the BOP crises consisted of (1) the
search for new sources of financing; (2) the adjustment in the size of the
plan to match available financing, and in the composition of investment
for cutting back current and future imports; (3) import controls to manage
the composition of the import basket—the basic trade-off here was the
division between imports of intermediate and capital goods because
imports of consumer goods were banned; and (4) export promotion to
relax the foreign exchange constraint.[6]

### 12.2.1   Search for New Sources of Financing

The search for new sources of financing was evident in the very first crisis
of 1957–58, when the government approached the World Bank for assis-

tance. The establishment of the Aid India Consortium permitted substantial investments in the remaining years of the second plan (1956–60) and in the third plan (1961–65). Foreign aid financed about a sixth of all investment during these plans and an even higher proportion of public-sector investment. Similarly, the oil crisis of 1973–74 resulted in borrowing from the IMF and several oil-producer-financed facilities. In the 1980s and the 1990s, the government tapped the IMF and sought deposits from nonresident Indians.

### 12.2.2   Adjustments in the Investment Program

The government clearly adjusted the investment program after the cutoff of aid by the United States and the World Bank in the mid-1960s (Lele and Agarwal, 1991). The fourth plan, which was to cover the years 1966 to 1970, was postponed for three years; in the meantime, annual plans with a considerably lower volume of public investment were implemented. The public-sector investment program was also lowered following the foreign exchange crisis in 1957–58, which was brought about by the increased volume of capital goods imports to implement the greatly expanded public-sector investment program and imports of consumer goods by the public in anticipation of either a devaluation of the rupee or tighter import controls. The changed pattern of investment aimed at cutting back import dependence—also a feature of the overall planning effort—was evident in the decisive extension of the import substitution strategy on two fronts. First, following the massive grain harvest failures in the mid-1960s, the green revolution was implemented with a view to raising domestic food production. Second, investment in oil exploration and refining was stepped up after the oil price increase in the 1970s. Such shifts were successful in reducing the BOP pressure.

The green revolution substantially reduced the need for food imports so that, beginning with the 1970s, such imports have rarely exceeded 2 to 3 percent of imports, whereas earlier they had been much higher. Imports of food grains, financed largely with PL 480 aid, averaged three million tons during the late 1950s and early 1960s, and reached a peak of ten million tons in the drought years of the mid-1960s, when they were about 10 percent of domestic consumption (Lele and Agarwal, 1991). Similarly, the stepped-up investment in oil exploration, production, and refining reduced reliance on imported oil throughout the 1980s. The volume of petroleum imports through most of the 1980s was lower than in 1980–81; the lowest volume was in 1984–85, when it was only 60 percent of the 1980–81 volume.

Lower government savings also resulted in a scaling down of public investment in manufacturing, which was increasingly passed on to the private sector.[7] The share of manufacturing in planned investments was maintained at about 20 percent in the 1970s (only slightly lower than in earlier years); but the share dropped to 15.5 percent in the sixth plan (1980–84) and to 13.4 percent in the seventh plan (1985–89); (see Table 12.2). The government's role in the development strategy increasingly came to be centered on investment in infrastructure and on schemes for alleviating poverty via income transfers to the poor.

### 12.2.3   Import Controls and Export Promotion

In response to the BOP crises until the beginning of the 1980s, the government tightened import controls and provided greater incentives for exports through various promotion schemes. The controlled trade regime was not liberalized until the start of the 1990s.

The government's response to the 1980 crisis pointed to a shift in its policy kit. It did not intensify import controls in the BOP crisis following the second oil shock in 1979–81 or the Gulf crisis in 1990–91, except temporarily. This shift was a reflection of the recognition that import controls were counterproductive.

While the Indian policy makers' adoption of an import substitution development strategy followed a pattern common to many developing countries, the plan documents lacked an explicit discussion of the role of foreign trade in the development strategy. Evidently, the government's policies in the first and second plans (1951–60) were driven more by the structure of India's exports and the speed with which this pattern could be changed than by a pessimism about prospects for the growth of the world economy (which in turn could boost Indian exports). Thus, India's export prospects were initially considered to be poor because they consisted largely of agricultural products. These were limited not only by domestic supply problems but also, in the planners' view, by the large Indian share of world agricultural exports. The planners also thought that it would take time to develop competitiveness in exports of manufactures, particularly of new export goods. Unfortunately, the potential for textile exports was neglected. Furthermore, official analysis of the constraints facing Indian exports or of the efficacy of the various export incentive schemes was missing.

Until the 1991 liberalization, policy-making was guided by the view that the basic policy was sound, and only marginal adjustments were needed

**Table 12.2**
Plan outlays in the Indian economy (percent of total)

| | First (1951–55) | Second (1956–60) | Third (1961–65) | Annual (1966–68) | Fourth (1969–73) | Fifth (1974–78) | Sixth (1980–84) | Seventh (1985–89) |
|---|---|---|---|---|---|---|---|---|
| Agriculture | 31.3 | 21.0 | 12.7 | 16.7 | 14.7 | 16.4 | 13.9 | 14.4 |
| Irrigation | | | 7.8 | 7.1 | 8.6 | 10.6 | 10.0 | 7.6 |
| Power | 13.3 | 9.7 | 14.6 | 18.3 | 18.6 | 18.4 | 28.1 | 28.2 |
| Industry | 5.0 | 24.1 | 22.9 | 24.7 | 19.7 | 21.7 | 15.5 | 13.4 |
| Transport and communication | 26.4 | 28.0 | 24.6 | 18.5 | 19.5 | 16.8 | 16.2 | 17.4 |
| Other | 24.0 | 17.2 | 17.4 | 14.7 | 18.9 | 16.1 | 16.3 | 19.0 |

*Source:* Various issues of the *Economic Survey*, Ministry of Finance, Government of India.
*Note:* Figures for agriculture for the first and second plans include irrigation. Other sector refers to social sectors including provision for water and development of sewerage.

for removing specific constraints that prevented the economy from growing faster. For instance, encouraged by higher foreign exchange reserves in the mid-1970s, the government relaxed controls on imports of intermediate goods, components, and spare parts, resulting in fuller utilization of domestic manufacturing capacity. Similarly, in the 1980s, controls on the imports of capital goods and technology were relaxed in order to overcome the slow growth of productivity in Indian industry. But the regulatory framework for industrial investment and production, as well as for imports, continued; it was not until the 1990–91 BOP crisis that this regulatory framework was largely eliminated.

## 12.3  Economic Performance

The performance of the Indian economy from the stabilization efforts of the mid-1960s (following the aid cutback) to the economic crisis of 1990–91, and the policy changes it prompted, was mixed. The overall picture is one of relatively stable performance—moderate rates of inflation with slight acceleration in periods of higher oil prices, and slowly accelerating growth (Table 12.3). However, this acceleration was accompanied by a rising deficit in the government budget (partly because of rising consumption outlays) and in the current account BOP. While these deficits signaled underlying imbalances in the economy, the imbalances were not extraordinarily large until the mid-1980s, suggesting that they might not have required sharp crisis management measures if the Gulf War had not occurred. As a result, the policy makers were ambivalent about the

**Table 12.3**
Economic performance of the Indian economy (percent, annual average during the period)

|  | 4th Plan (1969–73) | 5th Plan (1974–78) | 6th Plan (1980–84) | 7th Plan (1985–89) | 1990–91 |
|---|---|---|---|---|---|
| Real GNP growth | 3.4 | 5.0 | 5.5 | 5.6 |  |
| Inflation, CPI | 6.5 | 6.9 | 10.5 | 7.7 | 9.0 |
| Share, in GDP, of |  |  |  |  |  |
| Budget deficit | 5.6 | 6.4 | 9.7 | 11.7 | 12.6 |
| Current account balance | −0.7 | 0.5 | −2.5 | −2.5 | −3.4 |
| exports | 3.7 | 5.4 | 4.9 | 5.0 | 6.2 |
| imports | 4.1 | 6.4 | 8.1 | 7.3 | 8.2 |
| Personal consumption | 71.9 | 69.8 | 71.7 | 69.5 | 67.0 |
| Government consumption | 8.8 | 8.6 | 9.8 | 11.3 | 11.1 |
| Fixed investment (net of stock change) | 15.1 | 17.4 | 19.8 | 21.9 | 23.1 |

need for and the type of reform. The measures that were implemented during the Gulf War were generally accepted, but a political consensus on the country's future development strategy with regard to the desired rate of growth and the required reform was missing. The policy makers justified the changes in terms of managing the crisis (generated by the events in the Persian Gulf) rather than in terms of the need to move away from the regulatory framework in order to accelerate the economy's growth rate.

### 12.3.1 Budget Deficits and Policymaking in the 1980s

The increasing budget deficits and their financing are shown in Table 12.4. Seigniorage and the inflation tax provided relatively fixed amounts of budget deficit financing during the 1980s, and the gap was largely financed by domestic borrowing. This reliance on domestic borrowing contributed to a rising ratio of domestic debt to GDP and, consequently, to a rising share of interest payments in the government's current outlays. But despite the substantial gap between the actual deficit and the deficit that would stabilize the debt/GDP ratio, the acceleration in the rate of inflation was limited and considerably lower than the rate that would stabilize the debt/GDP ratio at the prevailing level of budget deficits.

The traditional Keynesian framework (Kenen, 1985) is helpful for analyzing the effects of these budget deficits on the Indian economy because (1) trade had a small share in GDP; (2) the BOP deficits were not financed by private capital flows that in turn could influence aggregate demand via changes in private wealth (the impact of these deficits on aggregate demand depended on the manner in which the stock of public debt and its composition affected government expenditures); and (3) the government could determine the domestic interest rate independently of international considerations because free mobility of capital was absent. The national monetary system was insulated from the international system and from the consequences of the financing of the BOP deficit. When the government started attracting foreign capital through nonresident deposits, the interest rate on such deposits had to be internationally competitive, but this deposit rate was not linked to the domestic interest rate structure. Therefore, these flows were effectively segregated from the domestic capital market.

Given these arrangements with a fixed nominal exchange rate, the effect of large government expenditures was to raise incomes, prices, interest rates, and the BOP deficit in the short run. In the long run, the

**Table 12.4**
Financing of India's budget deficits

| Year | Actual deficit | Sustainable deficit | Seigniorage | Inflation tax |
|------|------|------|------|------|
| 1969–70 | 0.046 | 0.030 | 0.005 | 0.016 |
| 1970–71 | 0.053 | 0.015 | 0.006 | 0.000 |
| 1971–72 | 0.067 | 0.015 | 0.006 | 0.000 |
| 1972–73 | 0.000 | 0.015 | 0.006 | 0.000 |
| 1973–74 | 0.000 | 0.031 | 0.006 | 0.015 |
| Average | 0.030 | 0.022 | 0.006 | 0.006 |
| 1974–75 | 0.055 | 0.028 | 0.005 | 0.015 |
| 1975–76 | 0.062 | 0.028 | 0.005 | 0.015 |
| 1976–77 | 0.064 | 0.030 | 0.006 | 0.015 |
| 1977–78 | 0.063 | 0.031 | 0.006 | 0.017 |
| 1978–79 | 0.071 | 0.034 | 0.007 | 0.017 |
| Average | 0.063 | 0.030 | 0.006 | 0.016 |
| 1979–80 | 0.075 | 0.036 | 0.007 | 0.018 |
| 1980–81 | 0.090 | 0.037 | 0.007 | 0.018 |
| 1981–82 | 0.083 | 0.035 | 0.006 | 0.018 |
| 1982–83 | 0.095 | 0.037 | 0.007 | 0.020 |
| 1983–84 | 0.096 | 0.040 | 0.007 | 0.022 |
| 1984–85 | 0.112 | 0.041 | 0.008 | 0.021 |
| Average | 0.097 | 0.038 | 0.007 | 0.020 |
| 1985–86 | 0.104 | 0.042 | 0.007 | 0.023 |
| 1986–87 | 0.124 | 0.045 | 0.008 | 0.025 |
| 1987–88 | 0.117 | 0.047 | 0.008 | 0.026 |
| 1988–89 | 0.113 | 0.047 | 0.008 | 0.026 |
| 1989–90 | 0.123 | 0.049 | 0.009 | 0.027 |
| Average | 0.117 | 0.047 | 0.008 | 0.026 |
| 1990–91 | 0.126 | 0.049 | 0.008 | 0.027 |
| 1991–92 | 0.109 | 0.047 | 0.008 | 0.026 |
| 1992–93 | 0.112 | 0.047 | 0.008 | 0.026 |
| 1993–94 | 0.103 | 0.046 | 0.008 | 0.026 |

*Notes:* The sustainable deficit is calculated on the assumption of 5 percent GDP growth and 8 percent annual inflation. The inflation tax is the issue of money by the government to meet the demand for money at the current level of real GDP and higher price level, namely, the deficit that can be financed by issue of money to mainatin a particular constant rate of inflation at a constant real GDP. Seigniorage is the increase in money issue to meet demand for money when real income increases. The sustainable deficit includes the inflation tax and seigniorage. In addition, it maintains a constant proportion of real bonds to real GDP (both domestic and foreign bonds). For a discussion of the methodology, see Wijnbergen (1992)

BOP deficit would lead to a decrease of foreign exchange reserves and a lower money supply, so that the original level of income would be restored but the higher interest rate and the higher price level would lower private expenditures. Thus, the larger government expenditures would crowd out private expenditures. The Indian government's objective was to develop a policy framework that would translate the higher income levels of the short run into the longer run by offsetting the negative effect of a higher interest rate on investment and by controlling the negative effects, such as higher inflation and a larger BOP deficit.

The policy makers sought to implement this objective by maintaining a high rate of investment that would contribute to an outward shift in the supply function. The share of fixed capital formation in GDP was raised from about 15 percent in the fourth plan (1969–73) to about 17 percent in the fifth plan (1974–78), 20 percent in the sixth plan (1980–84), and 22 percent in the seventh plan (1985–89). At the same time,the share of gross public-sector capital formation in GDP increased from 6 percent in the fourth plan (1969–73) to 7 percent in the fifth (1974–78), and to about 10 percent in the sixth and seventh plans (1980–89), all contributing to filling the gaps in the infrastructure. But higher levels of government investment were limited by the government's ability to raise resources and the need to maintain several poverty programs.

Despite revenues rising from 11 percent of GDP at the beginning of the fourth plan (1969–73) to over 19 percent at the end of the seventh plan (1985–89), government outlays for consumption and investment increased even faster, from 20 percent to 39 percent, so that the government's borrowing requirements increased from about 5 percent of GDP to 13 percent. Foreign borrowing financed about 10 percent of public-sector investment, and the foreign debt remained relatively stable at about 10 percent of GDP. The main sources of financing were domestic debt from sources other than the central bank: the ratio of domestic debt to GDP increased from about 30 percent in the fourth plan (1969–73) to about 60 percent in the seventh (1985–89).[8] As a result of this borrowing, the share of interest payments increased sharply from about 1 percent of GDP at the end of the 1970s to 4.4 percent at the end of the seventh plan. Interest payments on domestic debt accounted for the lion's share of these liabilities: they were about 4 percent of GDP at the end of the seventh plan (1985–89).

The management of the likely short-run effects of the higher government deficit on the BOP and on the rate of inflation emerged as the main policy issues toward the end of the 1980s. In particular, a higher rate of growth, which could ease the burden of future debt-servicing obligations, had to be achieved. The policy makers faced the dilemma of fine-tuning interest rate management: an increase in the interest rate would choke off some private investment and nullify the growth effect, but low interest rates would discourage domestic savings. The government used two devices to resolve the dilemma. It provided greater tax incentives to the public to invest in various public-sector savings schemes. It also allowed private, large-scale industry to tap household savings through development of the capital market and provided tax incentives for investment in shares of private companies. The disinvestment of foreign enterprises in the 1970s had generated large capital gains and increased the willingness of households to hold stocks and debentures. The share of stocks and debentures in household savings rose steadily from approximately 1 percent up to the mid-1970s to 10 percent in 1991–92.

This boom was amply rewarded as the increase in stock prices accelerated from 3 percent per year in the 1970s to 8 percent in the first half of the 1980s, over 20 percent in the second half of the 1980s, and even more rapidly in the late 1980s and early 1990s. Even though the nominal interest rate was left unchanged, the real return could be raised by giving tax breaks to portfolio investors, or by encouraging investment in the capital market, where the returns were mainly in the form of capital gains, which received favorable tax treatment.

At the same time, the BOP had to be managed via an accurate forecast of the availability of foreign financing and its implications for future debt servicing. The devaluation of the rupee to limit the size of the BOP deficit posed the risk of a rapid shift of output by raising exports and reducing imports. This in turn would fuel the domestic rate of inflation, which was already beginning to rise because of increased government outlays. However, the exchange rate could be adjusted to make the current account deficit match the capital inflows in order to manage the BOP. The extent of the exchange rate depreciation was thus governed, on the one hand, by the need to minimize reduction in domestic availability of goods and, on the other hand, by the need to match the current account deficit with capital inflows. In any case, there was a substantial real devaluation of approximately 40 percent in the 1980s as a result of the nominal devaluation. The share of exports and of imports in GDP remained relatively stable in the 1980s despite this real devaluation. This implied that the real devaluation mainly neutralized the effect of the excess demand generated by the government, which would normally have resulted in a decrease in exports and an increase in imports. The main adjustment on the demand side was through reduced consumption, particularly among the higher income groups. By all accounts, the percentage of the population below the poverty line decreased substantially in the 1980s.

Thus, during the early 1990s, the policy makers aimed at maintaining a high level of government expenditure, keeping a low interest rate (to encourage private investment), reducing private consumption (by raising indirect taxes), encouraging higher savings via incentives to save, and encouraging foreign capital inflows (otherwise, higher exports would have reduced domestic availability of goods). The policy makers wanted the pace of domestic growth to pick up so that unduly high levels of debt service both internally and externally could be avoided.

The strategy was on the whole successful. Growth picked up; the rate of inflation, the government budgetary deficit, and the BOP deficit were for the most part manageable. But several factors threatened to derail the strategy, not the least of which was the political situation, which limited the government's ability to manage the substantial budgetary and BOP deficits in the late 1980s. The increasing reliance on short-term foreign borrowing had made the economy vulnerable to external shocks (Joshi and Little, 1994). Also, a relatively small fiscal adjustment, reducing the fiscal deficit by 4 to 5 percent of GDP, could have significantly reduced the macroeconomic imbalance. Its effect on the growth rate would depend on how this reduction in the budget deficit was brought about. Over time, several policy makers argued that the regulatory framework did not provide the necessary incentives for rapid productivity growth that would enable the economy eventually to compete in the world market and pay off the accumulated debt. The short-run crisis created by the Gulf War provided an opportunity to move in this direction. But framing the need for change in terms of short-term adjustment implied that the mobilization of public opinion in favor of reform for higher, long-term growth was missing.

The approach combined elimination of the regulatory framework with the necessary fiscal adjustment. Although much of the regulatory mechanism at the center has been eliminated, it awaits further streamlining, and progress at the state level has been limited. Combined with the historical differences in physical and human infrastructure, the uneven pace resulted in a skewed inflow of foreign capital. Whether this would complicate political management or force the lagging states to speed up the process of reform is uncertain at this stage.

## 12.4  Economic Reform and Its Effects

A combination of external and internal events created the crisis of 1991.
The Gulf War resulted in a steep rise in the price of petroleum. The value
of petroleum imports rose by 60 percent and accounted for over 60 percent of the total increase in the import bill of $3.5 billion in 1990–91 (the
current account BOP deteriorated by $2.8 billion). The problems created
by this massive deficit were aggravated by the withdrawal of deposits
that nonresident Indians had been maintaining with the Indian banking
system, and by the refusal of commercial banks to extend short-term credit
to the Indian government.[10] By March 1991, India's foreign exchange
reserves could finance an import bill of only three weeks.

The external crisis coincided with internal political turmoil that prevented a swift and substantial policy response from the government.
Finally, adjustment measures were adopted when a new government was
elected in July 1991. These measures aimed not only at managing the
short-run BOP crisis but also at steering the BOP on a long-term, sustainable path so as to restore confidence in the economy and stop the
capital flight. The principal measures for putting the economy on a long-
term sustainable path involved a change in the government's economic
role (Bhagwati, 1993). They implied a reduction in the growing budget
deficits, in the government's regulation of private economic activity, and
in its direct role in economic activity (initially by allowing private-sector
investment in industries that had earlier been reserved for the public sector, and later via privatization). The government agreed with the IMF on
a long-term plan for the reduction of the deficit as a precondition for
access to the IMF's standby facility. The central government deficit, which
had reached 8.4 percent of GDP in 1990–91, was to be reduced to 5.7
percent in 1992–93, and further in the years ahead, via cuts in outlays on
subsidies, defense, and capital account spending, and in transfers to states
and public enterprises.

A critical feature of the policy package involved the management of
foreign trade through the exchange rate rather than through licenses. As a
first step, the rupee was devalued from Rs.21 to the dollar in June 1991 to
a dual exchange rate that averaged approximately Rs.29 for exports and
Rs.31 for imports. The dual exchange rate was abolished in 1993 and the
exchange rate since then is determined by the market.[11] The Indian currency is at present convertible for current account transactions as defined
by article VIII of the IMF. The combination of the 1991 devaluation and
the unification of the exchange rate resulted in a nominal devaluation of

the rupee by about 50 percent. Moreover, the elimination of government control of foreign trade was aimed at enhancing the role of the market, contributing to economic efficiency and eventually leading to a viable, long-term policy framework.

Import controls, which were tightened at the start of the program, were soon eliminated for imports of intermediate and capital goods. Such imports were also freed from exchange controls and were allowed to be financed largely by purchases of foreign exchange from the market. Controls on imports of consumer goods, however, remain. The government also announced that it would gradually lower import duties, which at the start of the reform averaged over 100 percent, with the maximum reaching almost 400 percent. The maximum duty was gradually reduced to 55 percent. Under the Uruguay Round agreement, the government has agreed to an upper limit on tariffs of 35 percent.

At the same time, the government reduced its role by allowing private units to enter into production activities that were previously reserved for the public sector. The sectors available to private industry have been gradually increased: private, including foreign, firms are now allowed to enter the infrastructure sectors.[12] Also, private enterprise operations have been freed from the existing network of licenses and controls. The licenses were required for expansion of current production capacity and new capacity creation, for technology imports and their financing, for industrial location, and for choice of inputs. Government approval was also necessary for foreign investment. These licensing requirements have been largely eliminated. The entry of foreign capital has been liberalized. Foreign equity participation, earlier restricted to 40 percent of share capital, has been raised to 51 percent; the process of granting permissions has been streamlined; and foreign technology agreements have been liberalized.

The liberalization of foreign investment, however, has been hampered by the two-good framework that had underpinned earlier Indian planning. The government has failed to answer the question: should foreign investment be encouraged in all sectors or only in the core and high-technology sectors? It has given the impression that it wishes to encourage more foreign investment in infrastructure development. The long lags in planning and implementing such projects partly explain the slow inflow of foreign capital.

The BOP has turned around since the introduction of the 1991 reforms. The acceleration of export growth has resulted in a substantial accumulation of foreign exchange reserves. The volume of exports had stagnated during the sixth plan (1980–84) with an average annual growth rate of only 2.6 percent. It grew at 7.7 percent during the seventh plan (1985–89; Government of India, 1995). The export growth rate, which declined immediately after the crisis from 11 percent in fiscal 1990–91 to 7.5 percent in 1991–92 and 6.9 percent in 1992–93, increased to 22.2 percent in 1993–94 and an estimated 15 percent in 1994–95.[13] Foreign exchange reserves of almost $20 billion (as of mid-1995) are worth over eight months of imports. Economic activity also has picked up. Real GDP growth rate, which had declined to 0.9 percent in 1991–92, averaged 4.3 percent in 1992–93 and in 1993–94, and is estimated to have increased to 5.3 percent in 1994–95. This growth rate has resulted from an overall improvement in most agricultural and industrial sectors.

Developments on a number of fronts have not been so favorable. The budgetary restraint was reversed substantially after the initial correction in the two years after the crisis of the summer of 1991. The deficit of the entire government as a share of GDP had averaged 11.7 percent during the seventh plan (1985–89), rising to 12.3 percent in the last year of the plan, and to 12.6 percent in 1990–91. It declined to 10.9 percent in 1991–92 and to 10.4 percent in 1992–93, then increased to 11.9 percent in 1993–94. Government outlays, which were cut back from an average of 38.1 percent of GDP in the seventh plan to 36.5 percent in 1992–93, went up again to 37.6 percent in 1993–94. The entire increase resulted from the higher current outlays by the central government. Because the share of tax revenues in GDP declined during this period from an average of 17.1 percent during the seventh plan to 15.8 percent in 1993–94, the deficit would have increased even more were it not for the larger contributions from public-sector enterprises to finance investment on government account. These contributions increased steadily from 2.1 percent of GDP in 1990–91 to 3.9 percent in 1993–94. As a result, the rate of inflation has remained more or less constant at an annual rate of 10 percent.

The pattern of the budget deficit financing has remained relatively unchanged. The share of foreign financing has decreased slightly from an average of 7.3 percent in the seventh plan (1985–89) to 5.6 percent in 1993–94 (after increasing to 9.4 percent in 1991–92 because of exceptional BOP support); the share of money creation has decreased from 16.8 percent in the seventh plan to 12.3 percent in 1993–94; credits from the banking system financed almost 50 percent of the budget deficit in 1994–95, the same level as in 1991–92, which was higher than the average of 43 percent during the sixth plan (1980–84) and of 46 percent during the seventh plan (1985–89).

Private domestic capital and foreign capital are currently allowed into many sectors that were previously reserved for the public-sector; however, the operation of public-sector enterprises has remained in limbo. Partial divestment of state ownership that has taken place is geared more to raising resources for the budget than to improving the efficiency of public enterprises. Such divestment has left majority ownership and management control in the hands of the government; therefore, it is unlikely that operational efficiency will improve. Again, the nontransparent sale of shares of these enterprises has aroused public suspicion of socialist cronyism being replaced by private cronyism.

The growth rate of GDP has returned to the earlier performance (with the exception of the dip in 1991–92 to 0.9 percent). It might, however, prove difficult to maintain an annual growth rate of 5 percent. The share of fixed capital formation in GDP has declined from approximately 23 percent in the late 1980s and early 1990s to 21 percent. The declining share of public-sector savings in the latter part of the seventh plan (1985–89) has continued, so that its share in GDP is about 2 percent lower than the seventh plan average, despite increased savings by public-sector enterprises. The share of private-sector fixed capital formation in GDP has declined from the level achieved in the last two years of the seventh plan but is at about the same rate as the average for the seventh plan. The pattern of private savings also seems to be changing—the share of corporate savings in GDP has almost doubled from the levels at the end of the seventh plan to 4 percent in 1993–94, though the level of household savings seems to have taken a sharp dip from 20 percent of GDP to 16 percent. It is not clear if this is a permanent shift. It is also not clear whether the decline in household savings has resulted from the financial scandal in the stock market and subsequently from the changes in rules that have reduced stock market investment opportunities for small investors.

Income disparities seem to be widening, although detailed evidence in support of the phenomenon is not available. Salaries of managers and of financial and information experts in the private sector have gone up astronomically. In response, public-sector employees have asked the Pay Commission (which is set up periodically to fix wages in the public sector) for a substantial increase in their wages. Such large wage increases would worsen the budget deficit and the financial position of public-sector enterprises. Of course, higher incomes could lead to accelerated growth as the size of the market expands, providing scope for exploitation of economies of scale. But they also could sharpen the political divisions arising from the worsening personal and regional income disparities and adversely affect the investment climate, and therefore growth.

## 12.5   Conclusions

There has been a substantial change in the development policy adopted by policy makers since 1991 in comparison with the earlier strategy. Though the outcome of this strategy in terms of growth and employment is still uncertain, India has overcome the first stage of the economy's stabilization. The growth rate has recovered to levels reached before the 1991 crisis with a lower budgetary deficit and a lower BOP deficit. Though India still remains a relatively closed economy, in that the share of trade in GNP is small, the financing of the BOP deficit has only a small impact on private wealth (and through that on private-sector economic behavior), and domestic interest rates remain insulated from international rates, important steps have been taken to integrate the Indian economy into the world economy. The elimination of licensing and controls is probably irreversible. It is unlikely that Indian policy makers will be allowed to intensify trade controls either by the IMF or by the BOP Committee of the World Trade Organization. The commitment by the Indian government under the Uruguay Round agreement to reduce maximum tariffs to 35 percent will prevent a return to the protective industrial policy behind high tariff barriers. Private capital inflows are playing an important role in financing the current account BOP deficit and in modernizing Indian industries. These developments not only will promote economic growth but also will bolster India's position in the international diplomatic and power alignments. At the same time, organized domestic support for the earlier licensing and control system has eroded.

Additional reforms are needed to further integrate India into the world economy. The elimination of quantitative restrictions on imports of consumer goods, further reduction of high tariffs, and allowing Indian nationals to hold foreign assets are the next urgent items on the reform agenda.

## Notes

Thanks are due to Padma Desai and Stanislaw Wellisz for helpful comments.

1. Here and later in the text, the year refers to the financial year, which runs from April 1 to March 31 of the next year.

2. For instance, the Indian request for food aid following a poor harvest in 1950 was rejected by the U.S. Senate after India criticized U.S. actions during the Korean War. Congress also

wanted aid to be made conditional on U.S. involvement in decisions regarding Indian thorium deposits. See Lele and Agarwal (1991) for a discussion of the effect of foreign policy events on Indian economic policy.

3. See Desai and Bhagwati (1975) for an analysis of the two strands of Fabian and Marxist socialism on economic policy-making in India.

4. Investment in fixed capital would occur in a closed economy only if capital goods were produced domestically, because capital goods imports are ruled out by assumption.

5. See Bhagwati and Desai (1970) for a discussion of the objectives served by concentration of investment in the public sector.

6. See Joshi and Little (1994) for a discussion of macroeconomic adjustment policies in India, and Bhagwati and Srinivasan (1975) for a discussion of trade policies.

7. This shift in public-sector investment pattern also resulted in a shift in the nature of Soviet aid to India (Desai, 1979, 1987).

8. Government borrowing from the central bank increased from approximately 1 percent of GNP at the beginning of the fourth plan to over 3 percent by the end of the seventh plan.

9. The higher rate of growth of the economy allowed living standards of the richer half of the population to increase while the poverty ratio was declining. However, the richer classes wished their consumption standards to rise even faster, and it is the rate of growth of this consumption that was controlled by government policy.

10. The disruptions in the Soviet Union adversely affected Indian economic prospects. Soviet economic assistance was suspended, and there was a sharp reduction in Indian exports to the region, caused in part by payments uncertainties. The resolution of the bilateral ruble debt in 1993 has contributed to the recovery of Indo-Russian trade since 1993.

11. The foreign exchange market consists of foreign exchange supplied by exporters, and foreign exchange demanded by importers. The interaction of the demand and supply determines the exchange rate. The central bank intervenes to prevent disorderly conditions; it intervened in 1992–93 to prevent an appreciation of the exchange rate that might hurt exports and to build confidence in the economy by accumulating foreign exchange reserves. Export earnings have to be repatriated because the capital account is not fully liberalized.

12. The entry rules for foreign firms in the infrastructure sectors were not transparent, leading to accusations of corruption and renegotiations of projects when state governments changed. Therefore, the short-circuiting of procedures in order to expedite the inflow of foreign capital was counterproductive because it resulted in delays due to the subsequent investigation of corruption charges and renegotiation of projects.

13. Fluctuations in Indo-Russian trade contributed to this instability (Government of India, 1995).

## References

Bhagwati, J. 1993. *India in Transition: Freeing the Economy.* Oxford: Clarendon Press.

Bhagwati, J., and S. Chakravarty. 1969. "Contributions to Indian Economic Analysis: A Survey." *American Economic Review* 59, no. 4, pt. 2 (September): 1–73.

Bhagwati, J., and P. Desai. 1970. *India: Planning for Industrialization*. Oxford: Oxford University Press.

Bhagwati, J., and T. N. Srinivasan. 1975. *India*. New York: Columbia University Press.

Chakravarty S. 1969. *Capital and Development Planning*. Cambridge, Mass.: MIT Press.

Chakravarty S. 1979. "On the Question of Home Market and Prospects for Indian Growth." *Economic and Political Weekly* 14, spec. no. (August).

Chakravarty S. 1987. *Development Planning: The Indian Experience*. Oxford: Clarendon Press.

Chakravarty S. 1989. "Development Economics: Some Basic Issues." First Marshall Lecture, delivered at Cambridge University.

Chakravarty S. 1991. "Development Planning: A Reappraisal." Second Marshall Lecture. *Cambridge Journal of Economics* 15.

Desai, P. 1979. Review of Deepak Nayyar, ed., *Economic Relations Between Socialist Countries and the Thirld World. Soviet Studies* (April): 295–297.

Desai P. 1987. "The Soviet Union and Cancun." In Desai, *The Soviet Economy: Problems and Prospects*. Oxford: Basil Blackwell.

Desai, P., and J. Bhagwati. 1975. "Socialism and Indian Economic Policy." *World Development* 3, no. 4 (April): 213–221.

Government of India, Ministry of Finance. 1995. *Economic Survey, 1994–95*. New Delhi: The Ministry.

Government of India, Planning Commission. Plan Documents. New Delhi: The Planning Commission. Various issues.

Joshi V., and I. M. D. Little. 1994. *India: Macroeconomics and Political Economy: 1964–1991*. Washington, D.C.: World Bank.

Kenen, P. B. 1985. "Macroeconomic Theory and Policy: How the Closed Economy Was Opened." In P. B. Kenen and R. W. Jones, eds., *Handbook of International Economics*. Vol. 2. Amsterdam: North Holland.

Lele, U., and M. Agarwal. 1991. "Four Decades of Economic Development in India and the Role of External Assistance." In U. Lele and I. Nabi, eds., *Transitions in Development: The Role of Aid and Commercial Flows*. San Francisco: ICS Press.

Wijnbergen S. 1992. "External Debt, Fiscal Policy, and Sustainable Growth in Turkey." Baltimore: Johns Hopkins University Press.

# Index